"This is one of the most engaging books I have seen in a while."
—Terri Earnest, University of Texas at San Antonio

"It is easy to follow, has excellent content, and promotes active learning."
—Kimberly Dodson, Western Illinois University-Quad Cities

Where print meets digital and engaging content meets academic rigor

THE JUSTICE SERIES

across the CJ curriculum...

CJ2012
Fagin

Corrections
Alarid & Reichel

Policing
Worrall & Schmalleger

Criminal Investigation
Lyman

Criminal Procedure
Worrall

Juvenile Delinquency
Bartollas & Schmalleger

Coming in 2013:

CJ2013
Fagin

Criminology
Schmalleger

Transportation first became an official aspect of England's punishment system in the seventeenth century but not a major component until the eighteenth century.

The Transportation Act of 1718 allowed transportation as a substitute to execution and also made it a punishment in its own right.

Transportation sentences were typically seven years for noncapital offences or for life for those who had had their death penalties commuted.

American colonies

Prisoners became indentured servants and the British gave up all responsibility for them.

Australia

Rather than becoming indentured servants in Australia, prisoners remained the responsibility of the British government, which continued to have control over them.

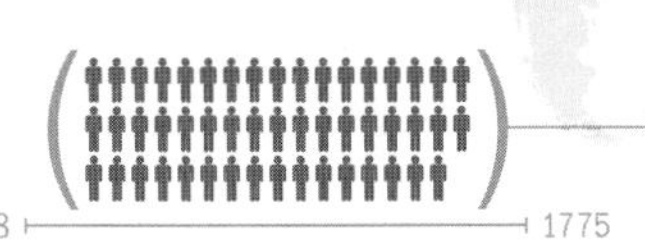

718 — 1775

Some **50,000 prisoners** were transported to the American colonies before 1775 when the American Revolution stopped transportation of British prisoners.

1788 — 1868

From 1788 to 1868, more than **160,000 convicts** were transported from England and Ireland to Australia. Transportation ends throughout Australia in 1868.

Norfolk Island, about 1,000 miles east of Sydney, became the most notable penal colony because of the unbearable discipline.

Norfolk Island jail

CJ2012

JAMES A. FAGIN
Lincoln College—Normal
Normal, Illinois

PEARSON

Boston Columbus Indianapolis New York San Francisco Upper Saddle River
Amsterdam Cape Town Dubai London Madrid Milan Munich Paris Montreal Toronto
Delhi Mexico City São Paulo Sydney Hong Kong Seoul Singapore Taipei Tokyo

Editorial Director: Vernon R. Anthony
Senior Acquisitions Editor: Eric Krassow
Assistant Editor: Megan Moffo
Editorial Assistant: Lynda Cramer
Director of Marketing: David Gesell
Marketing Manager: Cyndi Eller
Senior Marketing Coordinator: Alicia Wozniak
Marketing Assistant: Les Roberts
Senior Managing Editor: JoEllen Gohr
Senior Project Manager: Rex Davidson
Senior Operations Supervisor: Pat Tonneman
Creative Director: Andrea Nix
Art Director: Mary Siener, Design Development
Text and Cover Designer: Mary Siener
Cover image: z03/ZUMA Press/Newscom
Media Project Manager: Karen Bretz
Full-Service Project Management: Bev Kraus/ S4Carlisle Publishing Services
Composition: S4Carlisle Publishing Services
Printer/Binder: Courier/Kendallville
Cover Printer: Lehigh/Phoenix Color Hagerstown
Text Font: Minion, 9.5/12

Jared Loughner Jared Lee Loughner is accused of opening fire on U.S. Representative Gabrielle Giffords and numerous bystanders during a gathering of constituents outside an Arizona supermarket on January 8, 2011. Six people were killed, and 14 people were injured, including Giffords, who was shot in the head and left in critical condition. A federal grand jury indicted Loughner on a total of 49 counts of murder and attempted murder. On March 9, 2011, Loughner pleaded not guilty to all 49 charges. The case is currently on hold since a federal judge found him mentally incompetent to stand trial.

Library of Congress Cataloging-in-Publication Data
Fagin, James A. (James Arlie)
CJ2012 / James A. Fagin.
p. cm.
ISBN-13: 978-0-13-281835-3
ISBN-10: 0-13-281835-3
1. Criminal justice, Administration of—United States. I. Title. II. Title: CJ 2011.
III. Title: Criminal justice 2012.
HV9950.F343 2013
364.973—dc23

2011042927

10 9 8 7 6 5 4 3 2 1

ISBN 10: 0-13-281835-3
ISBN 13: 978-0-13-281835-3

BRIEF CONTENTS

$65,000

The average cost per year to provide round-the-clock health care to an elderly, ill inmate.

January 1, 1825

The New York House of Refuge juvenile reformatory admitted nine children (six boys and three girls).

CONTENTS

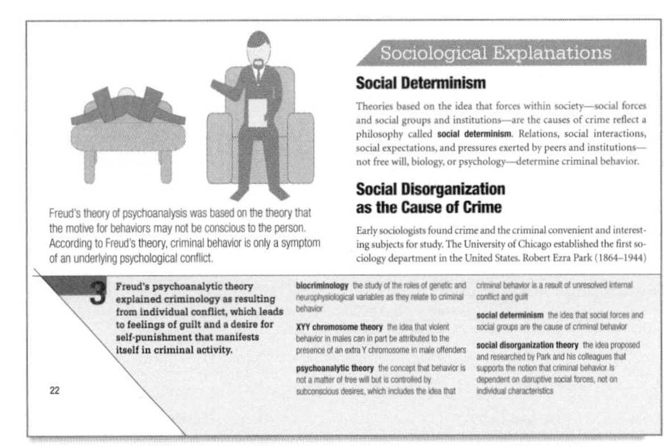

Sociological Explanations

Social Determinism

Theories based on the idea that forces within society—social forces and social groups and institutions—are the causes of crime reflect a philosophy called **social determinism**. Relations, social interactions, social expectations, and pressures exerted by peers and institutions—not free will, biology, or psychology—determine criminal behavior.

Social Disorganization as the Cause of Crime

Early sociologists found crime and the criminal convenient and interesting subjects for study. The University of Chicago established the first sociology department in the United States. Robert Ezra Park (1864–1944)

Freud's theory of psychoanalysis was based on the theory that the motive for behaviors may not be conscious to the person. According to Freud's theory, criminal behavior is only a symptom of an underlying psychological conflict.

3 **Freud's psychoanalytic theory explained criminology as resulting from individual conflict, which leads to feelings of guilt and a desire for self-punishment that manifests itself in criminal activity.**

biocriminology the study of the roles of genetic and neurophysiological variables as they relate to criminal behavior

XYY chromosome theory the idea that violent behavior in males can in part be attributed to the presence of an extra Y chromosome in male offenders

psychoanalytic theory the concept that behavior is not a matter of free will but is controlled by subconscious desires, which includes the idea that criminal behavior is a result of unresolved internal conflict and guilt

social determinism the idea that social forces and social groups are the cause of criminal behavior

social disorganization theory the idea proposed and researched by Park and his colleagues that supports the notion that criminal behavior is dependent on disruptive social forces, not on individual characteristics

22

Learning Objective **Key Terms**

Learning objectives are reinforced and summarized throughout each chapter, while key terms run along the base of the page as well.

1945 Prior to World War II, there was little attention focused on the criminal justice system. A decade of prosperity followed the war, and crime remained low.

1955 Rosa Parks refused to move to the back of the bus; her arrest initiated a boycott of public transportation and many acts of civil disobedience.

1961 Civil rights workers attempted to desegregate bus stations and waiting rooms. A bus in which they were traveling was fire-bombed and the demonstrators where beaten. NAACP leader Medgar Evers was murdered.

1964 **The Civil Rights Act** is enacted, making it illegal for businesses, hotels, restaurants, and public transportation to deny citizens service based on their race.

1965 Gallup poll reports that Americans view crime as the most serious problem in the country.

1965 President Lyndon Johnson declares **War on Crime.**

1967 The United States enters the Vietnam War. Political protests against the war generate conflict with police.

1968 **Omnibus Crime Control and Safe Streets Act is passed.**

1970 National Guard troops open fire on unarmed student demonstrators on the Kent State University campus. Four students are killed.

Timelines

Timelines highlight important dates in criminal justice history.

Search and Seizure

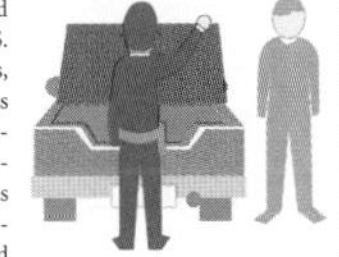

The rights of the accused are based on rights guaranteed by the U.S. Constitution, state constitutions, and legislation. Often, the Court is called on to interpret the application of these rights to specific actions of the police. Numerous changes in law, society, and technology and science have occurred since the drafting of the Constitution. Inventions such as the telephone, automobile, and the Internet emerged more than 100 years after the writing of the Constitution, so there is no specific reference in the Constitution as to how these modern technologies affect the constitutional rights envisioned by the authors of the Constitution. Thus, the Court must often interpret the intent of the Constitution as applied to modern society.

Illustrations

Simple, full-color illustrations serve as visual representations of important topics in the text.

Rehabilitation

Rehabilitation and restoration are more contemporary philosophies defining the purpose of criminal sanctions. **Rehabilitation** calls for criminal sanctions to "cure" the offender of criminality. The rehabilitation model often is referred to as the medical model in that it views criminality as a disease to be cured. Some believe that rehabilitation of offenders is impossible. Advocates of rehabilitation favor approaches involving psychology, medical treat

Rehabilitation emphasizes preparing the offender for reentry into society.

HERE'S SOMETHING TO THINK ABOUT . . .

With his own TV series, Duane Chapman, or Dog the Bounty Hunter, is not your typical bounty hunter. His dress, badge, and armament may suggest he is a law enforcement agent but he and other bail bondspeople and bounty hunters are private, for-profit individuals. The United States is one of the few countries to use private individuals to effect fugitive recovery. This practice provides a service at no cost to the courts, despite the concerns regarding the lack of licensing, training, and qualifications for bounty hunters. Should bounty hunters be government employees?

Here's Something to Think About

Current and sometimes controversial topics engage the student, encourage classroom discussion, and promote comprehensive learning.

Pros and Cons of Bail Whereas 50 percent of arrested persons are released from jail within 24 hours, approximately 28 percent are not released until 1 week after their arrest, and 10 percent remain incarcerated after 1 month of their arrest. For those who will not be prosecuted (recall that about 25 percent of those arrested will not be prosecuted), 1 to 30 days or more in prison can be a significant burden. For those who have been wrongly arrested, spending from 1 to 30 days in jail while waiting for bail can seem unfair and unnecessarily punitive. Thus, there are important reasons for an effective bail system and alternatives to traditional cash bails.

50% of persons arrested are released within 24 hours

28% are released 1 week after arrest

10% remain incarcerated after 1 month of their arrest

Compelling Stats

Engaging, pertinent, and interesting data are often buried in text or dull charts. Here we pull out and highlight compelling statistics to pique student interest and encourage critical thinking throughout the entire text.

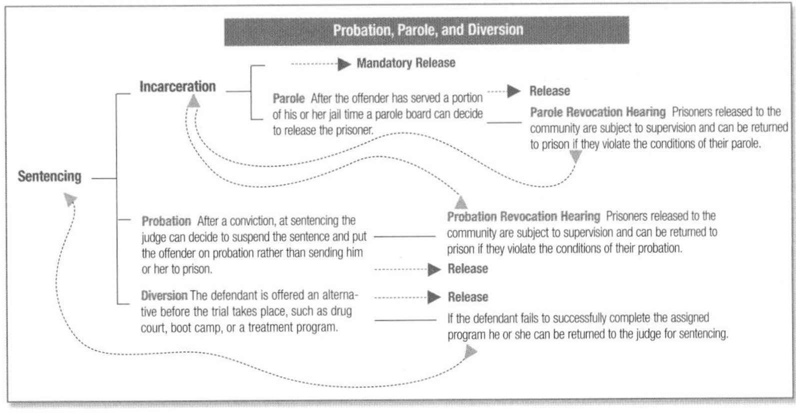

Flowchart

Complex and process-driven concepts are broken down into visual flowcharts, much like an instructor would draw in a lecture setting.

PREFACE

Introducing the Justice Series

When best-selling authors and instructional designers come together, focused on one goal—improve student performance across the CJ curriculum—you come away with a groundbreaking new series of print and digital content, namely the *Justice Series.*

Several years ago we embarked on a journey to create affordable texts that engage students without sacrificing academic rigor. We tested this new format with Fagin's *CJ 2010* and Schmalleger's *Criminology* and received overwhelming support from students and instructors.

The Justice Series expands this format and philosophy to more core CJ and criminology courses, providing affordable, engaging instructor and student resources across the CJ curriculum. As you flip through the pages, you'll notice this book doesn't rely on distracting, overly used photos to add visual appeal. Every piece of art serves a purpose—to help students learn. Our authors and instructional designers worked tirelessly to build engaging info-graphics, flowcharts, pull-out statistics, and other visual graphics that flow with the body of the text, provide context and engagement, and promote recall and understanding.

We organized our content around key learning objectives for each chapter, reinforcing throughout and tying it all together in a new objective-driven, end-of-chapter layout. Not only is the content engaging to the student, it's also easy to follow and focuses the student on the key learning objectives.

While brief, affordable, and visually engaging, you'll quickly see the Justice Series is no quick, cheap way to appeal to the lowest common denominator. It's a series of texts and support tools that are instructionally sound and student approved.

Additional Highlights to the Author's Approach

- The text is flexible and can be used for traditional 16-week classes or accelerated shorter terms. Each chapter is independent and instructors can craft a course curriculum to include those chapters that best address the class and programs goals.
- The text has the most current data and statistics available. Statistics are the latest available and case law includes the most current cases available at the time of publication.
- The *Here's Something to Think About* features highlight contemporary events that students will recognize from current media coverage and national news. Instructors will be able to use this feature to promote further discussion, research, and exploration by requiring students to identify the interrelationship between current events and the text.
- Chapter content and style reflect the more than three decades of academic and practical experience of the author in law enforcement and corrections. The clear, easy-to-read style is designed to tell a story about the criminal justice system so that students will be interested in the content, motivated to explore the topic further, and will apply course content to everyday events.

Groundbreaking Instructor and Student Support

Just as the format of the Justice Series breaks new ground in publishing, so does the instructor support that accompanies the series.

Interactive Lecture PPTs

The Interactive Lecture PowerPoints will enhance lectures like never before. Award-winning presentation designers worked with our authors to develop PowerPoints that truly engage the student. Much like the text, the PPTs are full of instructionally sound graphics, tables, charts, and photos that do what presentation software was meant to do—support and enhance your lecture. Data and difficult concepts are presented in a truly interactive way, helping students connect the dots and stay focused on the lecture. The Interactive Lecture PPTs also include in-depth lecture notes and teaching tips so you have all your lecture material in one place.

A New Standard in Testing Material

Whether you use a basic test bank document or generate questions electronically through *MyTest*, every question is linked to the text's learning objective, page number, and level of difficulty. This allows for quick reference in the text and an easy way to check the difficulty level and variety of your questions. MyTest can be accessed at **www.PearsonMyTest.com**.

MyCJLab

MyCJLab™ is a dynamic program designed to support the way students learn and instructors teach. We've integrated our groundbreaking interactive simulations and media into a new, robust course management and assessment program. With *MyCJLab*, instructors can either manage their entire course online or simply allow students to study at their own pace using personalized assessment tools. From practical gamelike simulations to media-enhanced critical thinking exercises, instructors can tailor the course to the needs of their students. In addition, our new media search tool organizes current Criminal Justice-related videos, news articles, and other media from the Internet for quick and easy access in and out of the classroom.

Whether you're an expert in digital learning or new to online enhancements, *MyCJLab* provides student engagement and instructor support for all levels of learning and teaching. Note: An access code is needed for this supplement. The access code can be packaged with the book for a discounted price, or students can purchase an access code separately from the MyCJLab site at **www.MyCJLab.com**.

Download Instructor Resources from the Instructor Resource Center

To access supplementary materials online, instructors need to request an instructor access code. Go to **www.pearsonhighered.com/irc** to register for an instructor access code. Within 48 hours of registering, you will receive a confirming e-mail including an instructor access code. Once you have received your code, locate your text in the online catalog and click on the Instructor Resources button on the left side of the catalog product page. Select a supplement, and a login page will appear. Once you have logged in, you can access instructor material for all Pearson textbooks. If you have any difficulties accessing the site or downloading a supplement, please contact Customer Service at http://247.prenhall.com.

About the Author

Jim Fagin is a pioneer in criminal justice education and has been involved in innovative criminal justice education programs worldwide for over three decades. He developed one of the earliest models of statewide delivery of criminal justice undergraduate and graduate degrees. During the developing years of criminal justice education, the Law Enforcement Assistance Administration (LEAA) developed model curriculums to promote quality education among middle and senior criminal justice administrators. Jim Fagin worked as a consultant for the LEAA to develop model curriculum in administration, management, planning, and research. These model curriculums were developed by an elite team of practitioners and educators and field tested throughout the United States.

Jim Fagin wrote some of the classical literature on computer crime, police bargaining and unions, presidential security, domestic disturbance resolution, and hostage negotiations. These works emerged from active involvement with federal, state, and local police departments.

Jim Fagin was a training officer and polygraph examiner for the Wyandotte County (Kansas) Sheriff's Department and a Commissioned Police Officer in the Kansas City (Kansas) Police Department. He has worked as a consultant with federal, state, and local law enforcement agencies and correctional facilities. He served on the Kansas Victims' Rights Commission to help establish the charter victims' rights legislation for the state. He has been a criminal justice professor, graduate dean, and college president. Presently he is a professor and Director of the Criminal Justice Program at Lincoln College – Normal (Illinois). He received his B.A. degree from the University of Nevada, Las Vegas, and his M.S. and Ph.D. from Southern Illinois University.

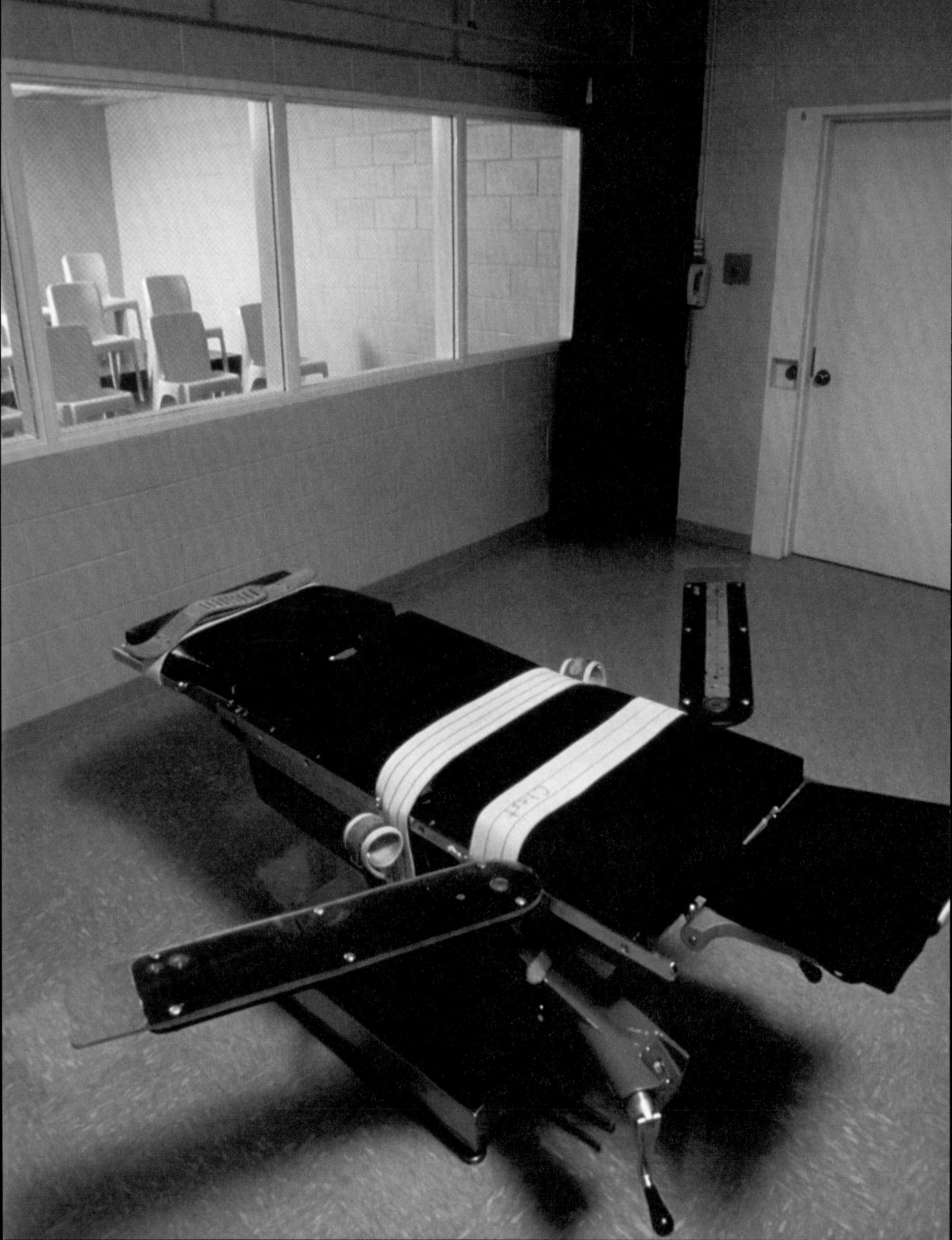

CRIMINAL JUSTICE

1

HOW DO YOU AVOID CONVICTING AN INNOCENT PERSON?

In 2011, Illinois abolished the death penalty. The controversial debate to abolish the death penalty began in 2000 when then governor George Ryan commuted the sentence of every inmate on death row because of his concern that the Illinois criminal justice system may have sentenced innocent persons to the death penalty.

The death penalty is controversial and often debated. This debate centers on important questions, such as: Does the state have the legal and moral right to put citizens to death? How do you avoid convicting an innocent person? Since the death penalty is irreversible it is vitally important that there be no error in executing a person convicted of a crime.

While the death penalty is an important aspect of the criminal justice system, each year millions of persons become involved in the system in other ways. For persons accused of a crime it is important that they receive a fair trial, that the law is fairly applied, and that it does not infringe upon their civil rights.

This chapter examines the American criminal justice system and the many ways it attempts to ensure a proper balance between public safety and individual rights. The criminal justice system is a complex process shaped by numerous influences including history, philosophy, sociology, economics, and social values. The criminal justice system can be described as an input–process–output model. The agencies and processes focus on moving people from arrest to final disposition while ensuring that due process rights are observed.

1. **What historical events influenced the development of our current criminal justice system?**
2. **How does the balance between the need to maintain order and the rights and freedoms of individual citizens impact our criminal justice system?**
3. **What are the strengths and weaknesses of the U.S. criminal justice system?**
4. **What are the steps of the criminal justice system?**

THE CRIMINAL JUSTICE SYSTEM CAN BE DESCRIBED AS AN INPUT–PROCESS–OUTPUT MODEL.

Contemporary Events That Have Shaped the Modern CJS

1955 Rosa Parks refused to move to the back of the bus; her arrest initiated a boycott of public transportation and many acts of civil disobedience.

1945 Prior to World War II, there was little attention focused on the criminal justice system. A decade of prosperity followed the war, and crime remained low.

1961 Civil rights workers attempted to desegregate bus stations and waiting rooms. A bus in which they were traveling was fire-bombed and the demonstrators where beaten. NAACP leader Medgar Evers was murdered.

1964 **The Civil Rights Act** is enacted, making it illegal for businesses, hotels, restaurants, and public transportation to deny citizens service based on their race.

1965 Gallup poll reports that Americans view crime as the most serious problem in the country.

1965 President Lyndon Johnson declares **War on Crime.**

1967 The United States enters the Vietnam War. Political protests against the war generate conflict with police.

1968 **Omnibus Crime Control and Safe Streets Act is passed.**

1970 National Guard troops open fire on unarmed student demonstrators on the Kent State University campus. Four students are killed.

1972 The **President's Commission on Law Enforcement and Administration of Justice** concludes that most people had lost confidence in the police.

1977 A blackout in New York City results in city-wide looting and disorder.

1992 The beating of Rodney King by Los Angeles police officers resulted in outrage and raised tensions between the police and the community.

1994 **Community Oriented Policing Services (COPS)** This legislation provides funds to hire more police. Police presence in urban areas, with an emphasis on foot patrol and community interaction, is increased.

1995 The number of serious, violent crimes begins a decline that continues throughout the late 1990s and into the 2000s, when the numbers begin to level off.

2001 Hijacked commercial airplanes strike the World Trade Center towers and the Pentagon. A third plane crashes in Pennsylvania.

2001 President George W. Bush declares **War on Terrorism.**
2001 USA Patriot Act is passed.

2010 2nd Amendment Incorporated

Rioting and the Fear of Crime

The mid-1940s is a good starting point for the study of the modern criminal justice system. Prior to World War II, the criminal justice system was dominated by political influences, there was little national attention focused on the criminal justice system, the federal agencies and federal government were not significant players, the crime rate was generally low, and for the most part any problems with the criminal justice system were perceived as problems concerning local administration, issues, and reforms.

Four phenomena stirred interest in the criminal justice system and led to its prominence as one of the most examined and criticized aspects of the government:

1. the Civil Rights Movement,
2. the Vietnam War,
3. the rising crime rate and the public's increased awareness of it, and
4. the terrorism attacks of September 11, 2001.

In many respects, these four influences were interrelated and cumulative in their effect on the criminal justice system.

Civil Rights and War Protests

Protests against institutional racism and U.S. involvement in the Vietnam War posed major challenges to the criminal justice system. Prior to the **Civil Rights Act of 1964,** businesses, hotels, restaurants, and public transportation could and did refuse service with impunity to Black citizens. For example, in 1956, the University of Alabama expelled its first Black student, Autherine Lucy, on the grounds that her presence was a threat to public order. In the South, Blacks were frequently the victims of lynching, violence, and denial of public and private services.

Civil rights leader Martin Luther King Jr. promoted the tactic of civil disobedience, which also challenged the criminal justice system. One of the most well-known examples of civil disobedience occurred in 1955 when Rosa Parks refused to move to the rear of the bus, as required by the law, and was arrested. Although King advocated nonviolence, there were many who rioted.

Political protests against U.S. involvement in the Vietnam War also generated acrimonious conflict in which the police often were captured on film engaged in brutality against the protesters. For example, on the Kent State University campus in 1970, National Guard troops opened fire on unarmed student demonstrators, killing four students and injuring many more.

1 **Public awareness of safety issues in the 1960s made crime a government priority and led to legislation to improve the criminal justice system.**

The Civil Rights Act of 1964 declares that it is illegal for businesses, hotels, restaurants, and public transportation to deny citizens service based on their race

President's Commission on Law Enforcement and Administration of Justice concludes that most people had lost confidence in the ability of the police to maintain law and order

War on Crime was declared by President Lyndon Johnson to counter crime and social disorder

During this period, the crime rate continued to climb to the point that, according to a 1965 Gallup poll, Americans viewed crime as the most serious problem in the country.[1] In 1968, 31 percent of Gallup survey respondents said they were afraid to walk in their own neighborhoods at night, and by the end of 1972, the number had risen to 42 percent. Many citizens thought that the police were part of the cause, not the solution, to the rising crime rate. The **President's Commission on Law Enforcement and Administration of Justice** concluded that most people had lost confidence in the ability of the police to maintain law and order.[2]

The War on Crime

The criminal justice system appeared to be failing. To counter the attack of crime and social disorder, on July 25, 1965, President Lyndon Johnson declared a **War on Crime.** He authorized a series of federal presidential commissions to study crime and justice in the United States and to recommend suggested reforms to restore public confidence.

The findings of the President's Crime Commission concluded that fear of crime had eroded the basic quality of life for many Americans. It also recognized the importance of crime prevention, as opposed to crime fighting, and the necessity of eliminating injustices in the criminal justice system.

THE PRESIDENT'S CRIME COMMISSION CONCLUDED THAT FEAR OF CRIME HAD ERODED THE BASIC QUALITY OF LIFE FOR MANY AMERICANS.

Omnibus Crime Control and Safe Streets Act of 1968

In response to recommendations of the President's Crime Commission and demands from the public, substantial resources were added to the criminal justice system. For example, to attract better-qualified personnel, the police had to increase salaries; as a result, policing costs skyrocketed in major cities.[3] To help defray these costs, local and state governments sought assistance from the federal government, whose response was to pass the Omnibus Crime Control and Safe Streets Act of 1968.

The **Omnibus Crime Control and Safe Streets Act of 1968** created the **Law Enforcement Assistance Administration (LEAA)** and the Law Enforcement Educational Program (LEEP). The LEAA acted as a conduit for the transfer of federal funds to state and local law enforcement agencies. However, these funds were not without "strings."

The LEAA appointed the **National Commission on Criminal Justice Standards and Goals,** which had the purpose of formulating specific standards and goals for police, courts, corrections, juvenile justice, and crime prevention. To receive the generous funds available from the federal government, local and state agencies had to show that they had implemented the commission's standards and goals. Many of the advances made within law enforcement agencies were a result of compliance with standards and goals necessary to qualify for federal funds.

The **Law Enforcement Educational Program (LEEP)** was a branch of the LEAA. The goal of LEEP was to promote education among criminal justice personnel.

After massive amounts of federal assistance, numerous reform efforts, and the adoption of innovative strategies by the police, courts, and corrections, public confidence in the criminal justice system was restored and the crime rate dropped. Residents of large cities reported that they felt safe using public transportation. Violent crime rates for nearly all categories dropped. Things were looking up for public confidence in the criminal justice system until September 11, 2001.

The biggest crisis in the twenty-first century was caused by a foreign attack on the United States. Just as President Johnson had declared a war on crime, President Bush declared a **War on Terrorism**.

President Bush appointed a new Cabinet position—Secretary of the Office of Homeland Security—to coordinate the antiterrorism activities among federal law enforcement and intelligence agencies. The attack on the World Trade Center towers led to a call for greater police powers, including expanded authorization for wiretaps, expanded powers of search and seizure, and expanded powers to detain foreign nationals.

Legitimate government depends on the effective operation of the criminal justice system. Citizens have granted the criminal justice system great powers, including the power of life and death. Thus, criminal justice is a much more complex endeavor than simply enforcing the law or waging a war on crime, drugs, or terrorism. When challenged with a choice between safety and liberty, people often choose safety over liberty. The War on Terrorism poses one of the most serious threats since the 1960s to the balance between safety and liberty.

Omnibus Crime Control and Safe Streets Act of 1968 creates the **Law Enforcement Assistance Administration (LEAA)** to act as a conduit for the transfer of federal funds to state and local law enforcement agencies

National Commission on Criminal Justice Standards and Goals formulates specific standards and goals for police, courts, corrections, and crime prevention

Law Enforcement Educational Program (LEEP) is created, the goal of which is to promote education among criminal justice personnel

War on Terrorism is declared by President George W. Bush in response to the attacks of September 11, 2001. The new cabinet position of Secretary of the Office of Homeland Security is created

Law and Order Versus Individual Rights

This concept of limiting freedom for the common good is very old. For example, Greek philosopher Aristotle argued that it was necessary that people be governed by law because of their inability to govern themselves

1. because of a tendency to react to fear and emotion rather than reason,[4] and
2. because people are subject to corruption.[5]

In the United States, it is argued that individual freedom is limited

1. to ensure order within society,
2. to protect citizens from one another, and
3. to promote the common welfare.

Society uses several means to achieve these goals, including informal and formal sanctions. **Informal sanctions** include social norms that are enforced through the social forces of the family, school, government, and religion. These social institutions teach people what is expected for normative behavior. In addition to teaching normative behavior, these primary social institutions also provide punishment when people violate **social norms**. In the informal system, parents punish children for disobedience, bosses reprimand employees, teachers discipline students, and religious groups call on offenders to repent for their sins.

Social order and the common welfare also are promoted through use of **formal sanctions** (such as laws) found within the criminal justice system. Frequently, the informal and formal systems of order maintenance overlap.

For the most part, people conform to the rules of society, including both formal and informal rules. However, when someone breaks the rules of society, the system responds. Formal sanctions are carried out by the criminal justice system. In the United States, the **criminal justice system** is based on the enforcement of obedience to laws by the police, the courts, and correctional institutions. When group and society norms are codified into law, government has the power to compel obedience to the rules on pain of punishment, including death.

The more homogeneous and stable the people and their belief systems, the fewer the violations of social norms. In a homogeneous, stable society with a common belief system, there is less need for reliance on a formal **system of social control** to maintain order and regulate interactions. Social control systems operate most effectively and efficiently where there is constant and unified, overt and covert, and cultural and social support from all control agencies.[6] However, contemporary U.S. society is not characterized by a homogeneous and stable group of people with a common belief system. Rather, the United States is characterized by great diversity in race, religion, ethnicity, and values.

The criminal justice system has assumed an important central role in **order maintenance.** The criminal justice system is an important part of conflict resolution, crime prevention, order maintenance, and the preservation of individual liberties.

The Balance Between Individual Rights and the Power of Government

In *Two Treatises of Government* (1690), philosopher John Locke argued that all human beings are endowed with what he called "natural rights." These rights are given to people by a power higher than government, and people cannot be deprived of them. Governments exist, according to Locke, to serve individuals. People surrender certain rights with the understanding that they will receive as much, or more, in other benefits, such as safety, order, and preservation of property rights. Locke conceded that the government must have the power of physical force to protect people and their property from the physical violations of others.[7] However, this power was to be balanced against the need to preserve individual liberty.

John Locke's philosophies had a great influence on Thomas Jefferson when he drafted the Declaration of Independence.[8] This document declares that people have unalienable rights given to them by their Creator. These rights include life, liberty, and the pursuit of happiness.

PEOPLE HAVE INALIENABLE RIGHTS GIVEN TO THEM BY THEIR CREATOR. THESE RIGHTS INCLUDE LIFE, LIBERTY, AND THE PURSUIT OF HAPPINESS.

2 **The rights of individuals in the United States are limited by the need to maintain social order, while the powers of government are limited by the principles stated in the U.S. Constitution.**

informal sanctions social norms that are enforced through the social forces of the family, school, government, and religion

social norms the expected normative behavior in a society

formal sanctions social norms enforced through the laws of the criminal justice system

criminal justice system the enforcement, by the police, the courts, and correctional institutions, of obedience to laws

system of social control a social system designed to maintain order and regulate interactions

order maintenance a system of maintaining the day-to-day life of ordinary citizens, a primary goal of the criminal justice system

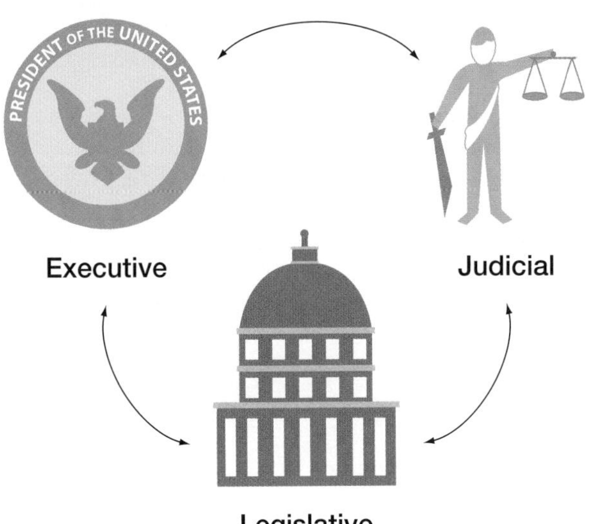

The Constitution of the United States of America reflects a distrust of a strong centralized government. The new government defined in the Constitution consists of three independent branches: the executive, the legislative, and the judicial. The Constitution divides power among these three branches of government and provides checks and balances. It set up a federal court system and gives power to the states to set up court systems as they deem appropriate. The original 10 amendments, called the Bill of Rights, were added to the Constitution in 1791. The **Bill of Rights** delineates certain guaranteed freedoms of citizens, such as trial by jury, freedom of speech, and the right to be secure in one's home from unreasonable search and seizure.

HERE'S SOMETHING TO THINK ABOUT...

The Constitution is over 200 years old. How should the Supreme Court apply the Constitution to contemporary questions of civil rights such as cyber and phone privacy, discrimination, terrorism, and other concerns absent in the eighteenth century?

THE BILL OF RIGHTS DELINEATES CERTAIN GUARANTEED FREEDOMS OF CITIZENS IMPORTANT TO THE CRIMINAL JUSTICE SYSTEM.

THE BILL OF RIGHTS

AMENDMENT I: ***FREEDOM OF SPEECH*** Congress shall make no law respecting an establishment of religion, or prohibiting the free exercise thereof; or abridging the freedom of speech, or of the press; or the right of the people peaceably to assemble, and to petition the Government for a redress of grievances.

AMENDMENT II: ***THE RIGHT TO BEAR ARMS*** A well regulated Militia, being necessary to the security of a free State, the right of the people to keep and bear Arms, shall not be infringed.

AMENDMENT III: No Soldier shall, in time of peace be quartered in any house, without the consent of the Owner, nor in time of war, but in a manner to be prescribed by law.

AMENDMENT IV: ***UNREASONABLE SEARCH AND SEIZURE*** The right of the people to be secure in their persons, houses, papers, and effects, against unreasonable searches and seizures, shall not be violated, and no Warrants shall issue, but upon probable cause, supported by Oath or affirmation, and particularly describing the place to be searched, and the persons or things to be seized.

AMENDMENT V: ***SELF INCRIMINATION*** No person shall be held to answer for a capital, or otherwise infamous crime, unless on a presentment or indictment of a Grand Jury, except in cases arising in the land or naval forces, or in the Militia, when in actual service in time of War or public danger; nor shall any person be subject for the same offence to be twice put in jeopardy of life or limb; nor shall be compelled in any criminal case to be a witness against himself, nor be deprived of life, liberty, or property, without due process of law; nor shall private property be taken for public use, without just compensation.

AMENDMENT VI: In all criminal prosecutions, the accused shall enjoy the right to a speedy and public trial, by an impartial jury of the State and district wherein the crime shall have been committed, which district shall have been previously ascertained by law, and to be informed of the nature and cause of the accusation; to be confronted with the witnesses against him; to have compulsory process for obtaining witnesses in his favor, and to have the assistance of counsel for his defense.

AMENDMENT VII: In Suits at common law, where the value in controversy shall exceed twenty dollars, the right of trial by jury shall be preserved, and no fact tried by a jury, shall be otherwise re-examined in any Court of the United States, than according to the rules of the common law.

AMENDMENT VIII: Excessive bail shall not be required, nor excessive fines imposed, nor cruel and unusual punishments inflicted.

AMENDMENT IX: The enumeration in the Constitution, of certain rights, shall not be construed to deny or disparage others retained by the people.

AMENDMENT X: The powers not delegated to the United States by the Constitution, nor prohibited by it to the States, are reserved to the States respectively, or to the people.

Bill of Rights delineates certain guaranteed freedoms of citizens, such as trial by jury and freedom of speech

Defining the Criminal Justice System

The criminal justice system is not a static model, but a dynamic model that is constantly evolving, changing, and redefining itself. This dynamic nature has always been a characteristic of the U.S. criminal justice system, and the description of it in this book is only a portrait of one place and time.

Agencies and People

The criminal justice system is divided into three categories of agencies: police, courts, and corrections. Each of the agencies in the criminal justice system is independent. There is no single agency that has oversight control of all of the criminal justice agencies. This decentralization and autonomy is an intentional characteristic of the American criminal justice system. One of the values of the early founders of the United States was a mistrust of a strong, centralized government and as a result, the U.S. government was created with numerous checks and balances. This philosophy is mirrored in the criminal justice system.

The main agencies in the criminal justice system are:

1. the police,
2. the courts,
3. the probation and parole agencies, and the jails, prisons, and other correctional agencies.

These agencies exist at the local, state, and federal levels of government. Each jurisdiction has its own distinctive criminal justice agencies that provide services to the local, state, or federal government. For example, there are local police, state police, and federal police. Likewise, there are local, state, and federal courts and correctional institutions.

One of the difficulties of capturing the dynamics of this multilevel system is understanding that the local, state, and federal political agencies, although independent, are at the same time united and interdependent.

An analogy for the criminal justice system is a picket fence. In the **picket fence model**, the horizontal boards in the fence represent the local, state, and federal governments, and the vertical boards represent the various functions within the criminal justice system, such as law enforcement, courts, and corrections. For example, local municipal courts have their own missions, personnel, and resources. However, a case can be appealed from a local municipal court to a state court, and from a state court to a federal court. Thus, each court system is separate, but each is linked by a vertical picket.

Federal Govt
State Govt
Local Govt
Police
Courts
Corrections

Process and Flow

The process and flow of the criminal justice system refers to the means by which people accused of a crime enter the criminal justice system, are found guilty or not guilty, and are punished or exit the system.

No agency or person oversees the status of an offender's process through the criminal justice system. Rather, each agency processes people through their part of the system independently, which often results in bottlenecks.

Here's Something to Think About...

Often the Supreme Court must address issues of personal liberties about which there is controversy and little guidance from the U.S. Constitution. For example, in City of Ontario v. Quon, *in 2010, the Supreme Court had to decide if SWAT officer Sergeant Jeff Quon's Fourth Amendment protection against unreasonable search was violated when his employer, the Ontario, California, Police Department, searched the text messages sent and received by Sgt. Quon off duty using his department-issued cellphone. The search turned up hundreds of sexually explicit text messages to his wife and his mistress resulting in disciplinary action against Sgt. Quon. The Court ruled unanimously that the chief's search did not violate Sgt. Quon's constitutional protection against unreasonable searches. When issuing decisions on contemporary questions, what should the Court use as guidance?*

The criminal justice system is a dynamic model of interrelated, independent agencies that operate under numerous checks and balances.

picket fence model model of the criminal justice system, with the local, state, and federal criminal justice systems depicted as three horizontal levels connected vertically by the roles, functions, and activities of the agencies that comprise them

Criminal Justice Models

The criminal justice system has more than one purpose. One of the primary purposes is to provide for the orderly interaction of citizens in a complex society. The criminal justice system also has the goal of promoting socially approved behaviors, morals, and values. Another goal is to provide an environment that promotes commerce by encouraging honesty and trust in commercial transactions. There are various means to achieve each of these goals, but there is no single best criminal justice system.

The criminal justice system of a society reflects its values as well as its desire to be safe from crime. In the United States, the criminal justice system reflects a balance between crime control and due process; both goals are esteemed, and the balance between them changes from time to time. More than other criminal justice agencies, the U.S. Supreme Court monitors the balance between individual rights and community safety. Through its power of judicial review, the Court can declare when laws violate constitutionally protected liberties and can declare certain practices of the criminal justice system unconstitutional.

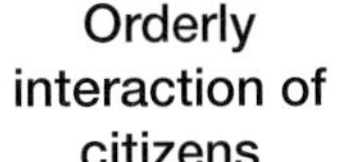
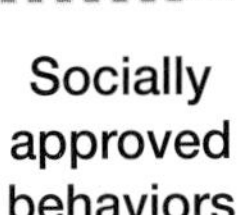

Crime Control Versus Due Process

The preservation of citizens' individual rights must be balanced against the necessity to enforce laws and maintain social order. Law without order is anarchy, but order without law is tyranny. The balance between law and order resembles a pendulum that swings back and forth between the two values. Concern for due process swung to its most liberal extent in the 1960s and then back to the right again with the "law and order" platform on which Richard Nixon based his campaign for the presidency. In that period of social unrest, many people were receptive to the promise of crime control, community safety, and swift—preferably harsh—justice for the offender. This emphasis on efficient and effective justice is known as the **crime control model.**

Crime control cannot be achieved at the expense of constitutionally protected liberties. The emphasis on ensuring that individuals are protected from arbitrary and excessive abuse of power by the government is known as **due process.** Due process means that in the quest for crime control, the government is bound to follow certain rules and procedures. Even if a person is guilty, if the government does not follow the rules and procedures in obtaining a conviction, the courts can void the conviction.

THE CENTRAL PREMISE OF THE CRIMINAL JUSTICE DUE PROCESS MODEL IS THE PRESUMPTION OF INNOCENCE.

The basic sources of due process rights are the U.S. Constitution and the Bill of Rights, both of which guarantee protections against unreasonable searches, forced and self-incriminating testimony, excessive bail and fines, and cruel or unusual punishment, as well as rights to a speedy public trial by jury.

Due process guards against abuse of power by police, prosecutors, courts, and corrections at the expense of swift and sure justice for the victim. By insisting that the government operate within certain limitations in securing the conviction of the accused, citizens are protected against the misuse of the enormous power of the government, which could be brought to bear in prosecuting the individual. It is better that a guilty person should escape the punishment of justice than an innocent person be wrongfully punished.

The central premise of the criminal justice due process model is the **presumption of innocence.** Regardless of overwhelming evidence against the accused, the court proceeds on the presumption that until the guilt of the accused is proven beyond a reasonable doubt in a court of law, the defendant will be treated as if he or she were not guilty of the charges.

HERE'S SOMETHING TO THINK ABOUT...

The power of judicial review gives courts the power to void criminal convictions and set the defendant free if the defendant was denied due process rights. In such cases the guilt of the defendant is irrelevant. The release of defendants who have committed serious violent crimes may endanger public safety. Should there be other remedies for violation of a defendant's rights?

crime control model a model of the criminal justice system in which emphasis is placed on fighting crime and protecting potential victims

due process rules and procedures for protecting individuals accused of crimes from arbitrary and excessive abuse of power by the government

presumption of innocence most important principle of the due process model, requiring that all accused persons are treated as innocent until proven guilty in a court of law

The Criminal Justice Process

As mentioned previously, the criminal justice system has three major components: police, courts, and corrections. Within these three major components are criminal justice agencies that have various roles to play in making this system work. Each of the agencies is independent, but they must work together. Each has a limited role in processing the defendant, and the system has a built-in process for moving offenders from the police to the courts to corrections. Here are the six major processes in the criminal justice system.

POLICE

1. Deciding What Is a Crime

Boundaries are set for determining who and what behaviors are subject to the criminal justice system. In the United States, these boundaries are determined by criminal laws that define illegal behaviors. Criminal laws are fluid and change over time.

2. Detecting a Crime and Arresting a Suspect

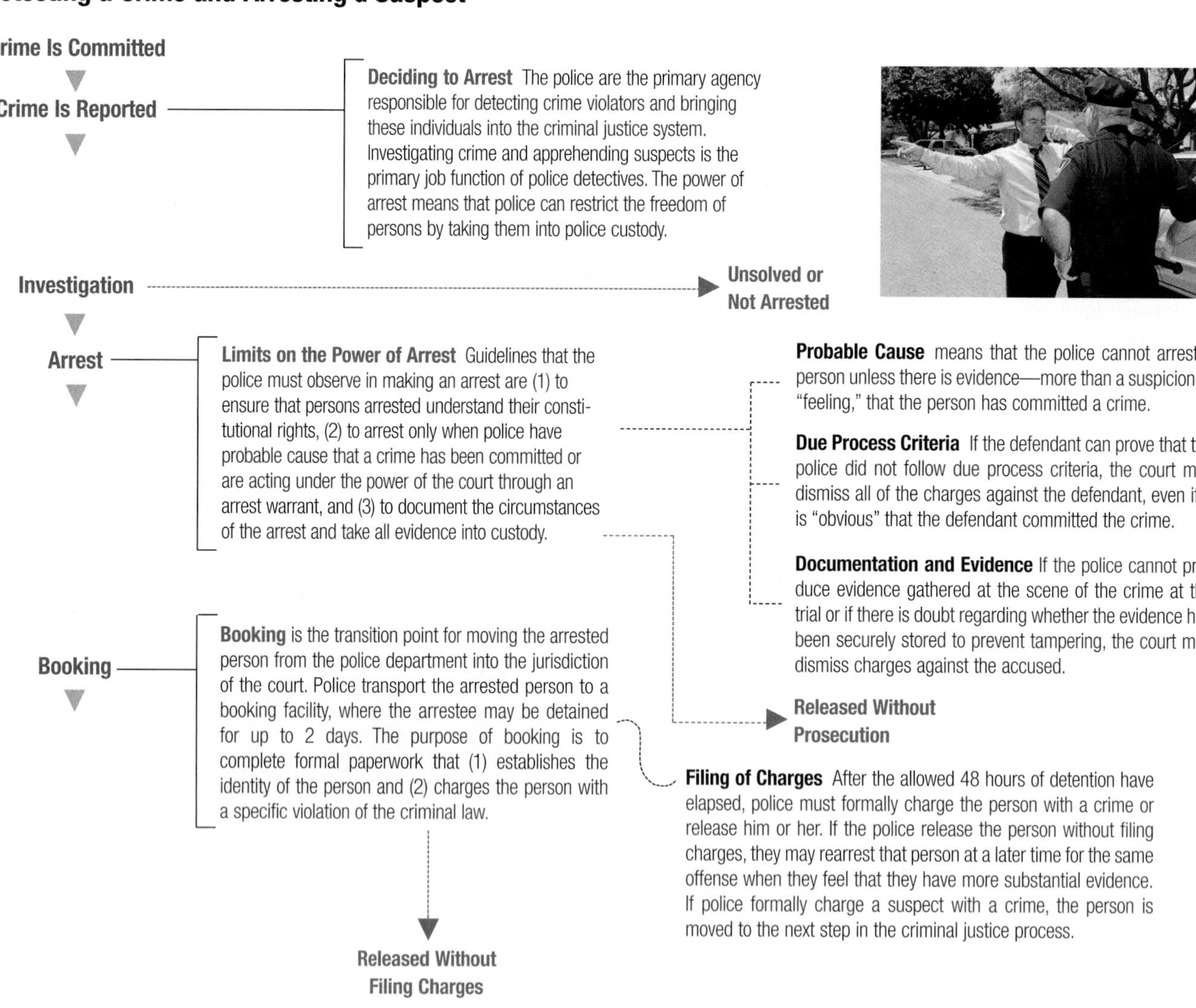

4

▶ Crime Is Committed ▶ Crime Is Reported ▶ Investigation ▶ Arrest ▶ Booking

arrest restricting the freedom of a person by taking him or her into police custody

booking police activity that establishes the identification of an arrested person and formally charges that person with a crime

3. Deciding to Prosecute (Pretrial)

In this next step of the due process model, the prosecuting attorney reviews the charges filed by the police and the supporting evidence collected. If the prosecutor accepts the case, the defendant is processed further in a preliminary hearing and arraignment, beginning with the first appearance.

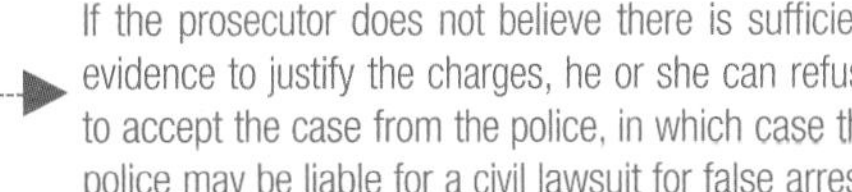

If the prosecutor does not believe there is sufficient evidence to justify the charges, he or she can refuse to accept the case from the police, in which case the police may be liable for a civil lawsuit for false arrest.

Misdemeanors | **Felonies**

The defendant can be charged with misdemeanor crimes, felony crimes, or a combination of both. The defendant's rights are protected by a review of the charges through a process including initial appearance, preliminary hearing, grand jury, and arraignment.

Initial Appearance

Initial Appearance After the paperwork is forwarded to the prosecuting attorney, the accused is brought before a magistrate judge for a first appearance. The magistrate judge reviews the charges, advises the defendant of his or her rights, and sets bail. If charges filed could result in a prison sentence of 6 months or more, then the judge will determine whether the person has funds for a lawyer, and if not, will arrange for a lawyer to represent him or her at no charge.

Bail As part of the initial appearance the magistrate decides whether the defendant should be released on bail or held in a correctional facility until trial. For minor charges, the amount of bail may be set by a schedule of established fees. The amount of bail is typically based on the fines levied if the person is found guilty. Bail can be denied for reasons of community safety or the belief that the defendant is a flight risk.

Preliminary Hearing

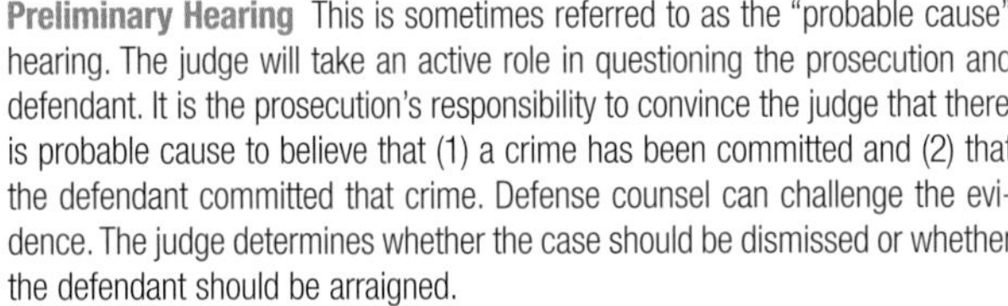

Preliminary Hearing This is sometimes referred to as the "probable cause" hearing. The judge will take an active role in questioning the prosecution and defendant. It is the prosecution's responsibility to convince the judge that there is probable cause to believe that (1) a crime has been committed and (2) that the defendant committed that crime. Defense counsel can challenge the evidence. The judge determines whether the case should be dismissed or whether the defendant should be arraigned.

Judge Dismisses Charges

If charges are dismissed, the prosecution may gather additional evidence and/or modify the charges and bring the defendant before the court again.

Diversion

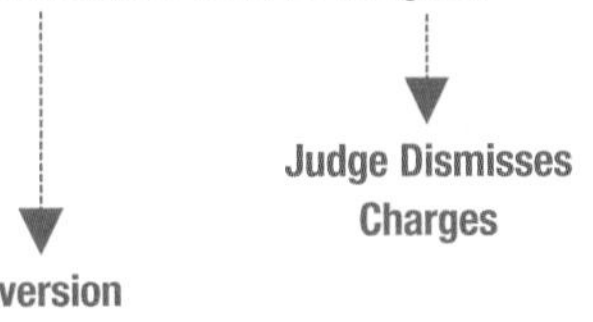

Diversion Certain types of defendants such as youthful offenders, first-time offenders, nonviolent offenders, drug dependent offenders, and domestic violence offenders may be offered an alternative to the trial and possible conviction and punishment. In return for pleading guilty, defendants are diverted into counseling, educational, or rehabilitation programs. Upon successful completion of the diversion program, the charges against a defendant may be completely dismissed.

Grand Jury

Grand Jury This is made up of a panel of citizens selected to hear evidence against an accused person. Much like a jury, there is a presiding judge and the prosecution presents evidence and witnesses to convince the jury that a crime has been committed. The major difference is that the defendant and his or her attorney are not present. If the grand jury determines that there is probable cause, a true bill is returned and an indictment is written.

Grand Jury Dismisses Charges

If the charges are dismissed, the prosecutor can still use a preliminary hearing to try to bring the defendant to trial.

Indictment This is a formal, written legal document authorizing the court to issue an arrest warrant. An indictment does not establish guilt—it only authorizes the prosecution to move to the next step.

Arraignment

Arraignment At the arraignment, the defendant appears before the court with his or her attorney to hear the formal charges from the prosecution. The charges may differ from what was filed by the police. The prosecution will have chosen the charges based on the evidence they have to prove the guilt of the defendant. If the charges are changed after the arraignment, the defendant will need to go back to the preliminary hearing and indictment step. The defendant is asked how he or she pleads. Either before or after arraignment, most often the defendant or prosecutor initiates an offer of a plea bargain. Plea bargains are agreements wherein the defendant admits guilt, usually to lesser charges or an agreement to sentence reduction, rather than taking the case to trial.

Motion The prosecution or the defense can request a formal ruling from the judge on matters such as competency of the defendant to stand trial, location of the trial, or objections to the evidence.

Plea

Not Guilty → **Setting a Trial**

Guilty

No Contest
Usually this plea is entered when the defendant anticipates that there may be civil liability for his or her actions, i.e., a civil law suit.

Sentencing
The judge sets a date for sentencing. The judge can decide not to accept the guilty plea and set a trial date instead.

Initial Appearance

initial appearance a judicial hearing before a magistrate, following booking; the magistrate judge reviews the charges, advises the defendant of his or her rights, and sets bail

Bail

bail a promise, sometimes backed by a monetary guarantee, that the accused will return for further proceedings

Preliminary Hearing

preliminary hearing a hearing before a magistrate judge in which the prosecution presents evidence to convince the judge that there is probable cause to bring the defendant to trial

Grand Jury

grand jury a panel of citizens that decides whether there is probable cause to indict a defendant on the alleged charges

Indictment

indictment the formal verdict of the grand jury that there is sufficient evidence to bring a person to trial

4. Determining Guilt

At the trial, the judge or the jury makes the decision whether the defendant committed the crime. Some states allow defendants to waive their right to a jury trial and leave the decision to a judge. This is called a bench trial.

The Trial

Jury Trial Evidence is presented by the prosecution to convince the jury that the defendant is guilty of the crime that he or she is charged with. The defendant's attorney may present evidence to counter the prosecution's evidence. The jury is instructed to use only the evidence presented at the trial. After all the evidence is presented, the jury is asked to make a verdict.

Diversion This is another means of settling a case while avoiding trial. The defendant is diverted from the correctional system through alternatives such as community service.

Not Guilty Verdict – defendant is freed

Mistrial If the jury cannot come to a unanimous verdict, the judge will declare a mistrial. The prosecution has the option of requesting a new trial.

Plea Bargain Most cases do not go to trial. Sometime during the criminal justice process, even after the trial has begun, the defendant may contact the prosecution and request that a deal be made (a plea bargain). The prosecutor may also initiate a plea bargain. In a plea bargain, the defendant agrees to plead guilty in return for concessions from the prosecution.

Guilty Verdict

5. Deciding on Punishment

If the defendant is found guilty, it is the responsibility of the judge to determine the punishment.

Sentence

Sentence To determine what sentence the defendant is to receive, the judge is guided by the law and input from the presentence investigation report. The law provides minimum and maximum guidelines for lengths of imprisonment and fines.

Presentence Investigation Report This is an investigation by a probation and parole officer. This report includes evidence that might not have been presented at the trial. This could include previous crimes that the defendant has committed and the defendant's employment status. Because the defendant has been determined to be guilty, many of the due process rights are no longer in effect.

Sentencing Hearing This is a gathering before the judge, who hears appeals in which the prosecution and the defense make arguments about the presentence report and the sentence. The judge listens to arguments of the two sides and determines the final sentence to be imposed.

Appeal

Appeal The defendant retains the right to appeal both the sentence and the conviction to a higher court. An appeal must be made on the claim that a judicial error occurred during the trial that substantially affected the outcome of the trial. The defendant cannot appeal based on the claim that he or she is innocent. An appeals court can choose to hear or reject the appeal. If the appeal is successful, the appeals court will order that the judicial error must be corrected. This is not a decision that the defendant is not guilty. If the judicial error cannot be corrected, the trial verdict will be set aside and the defendant will be granted a new trial. The final appeal court is the U.S. Supreme Court.

CORRECTIONS

6. Carrying Out the Sentence

There are three main categories of corrections agencies: (1) institutional corrections, (2) probation and parole, and (3) community corrections.

Corrections

Institutional Corrections These include jails, state prisons, and federal penitentiaries. Many of the due process rights that the defendant was entitled to are gone.

Probation and Parole In many cases a defendant does not serve time in a correctional facility, or he or she may not serve out the full sentence. Probation allows the defendant to fulfill his or her sentence through certain conditions imposed by the court. Parole allows the defendant to serve less than the maximum sentence.

Community Corrections This is often called intermediate sentencing. It is a form of punishment short of incarceration. Intermediate sanctions may include house arrest, community service, and intensive probation supervision. Counseling, drug rehabilitation, and restitution are often elements included in intermediate sanctions.

Release

4

Arraignment

arraignment a short hearing before the judge in which the charges against the defendant are announced

Jury Trial

jury trial the jury determines the guilt of the defendant

Bench Trial

bench trial a judge determines the guilt or innocence of the defendant

Sentence

sentence the punishment determined by a judge for a defendant convicted of a crime

Appeal

Corrections

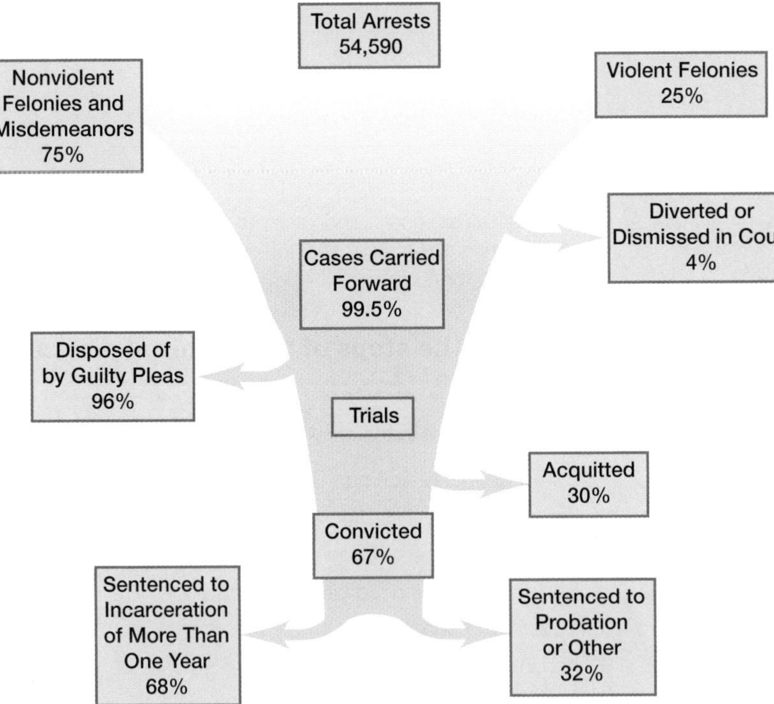

The Criminal Justice Funnel As you can see most cases never make it to a formal trial. Defendants are released at various points as the case proceeds through the criminal justice system. More than 90 percent of cases are settled by a guilty plea. Usually guilty pleas result from plea bargaining. Plea bargains may involve the dismissal of charges, the reduction of charges, the sentence for the offense, and/or the institution where the defendant will serve his or her sentence. Plea bargains may include diversion from the criminal justice system. Defendants who committed crimes due to drug abuse may be diverted to drug treatment programs in lieu of criminal trial. Many youthful and first-time offenders are offered probation in exchange for a plea agreement. As a result only selected cases actually go to trial, resulting in a relatively high conviction rate. It would overwhelm the criminal justice system if it was necessary to provide all defendants a trial. Some argue plea bargains are unfair and have many potential problems. Should plea bargaining be abolished? Why?

HERE'S SOMETHING TO THINK ABOUT...

The criminal justice system is governed by the rule of law. The supreme law of the land is the U.S. Constitution. The rights and due process requirements of those accused of crimes are embodied in the first eight amendments of the U.S. Constitution. (The first 10 amendments are known as the Bill of Rights; however, Amendments IX and X are not related to the criminal justice system.) These amendments define the fundamental liberties and the due process rights of individuals.

The rights enumerated in the first eight amendments have not always applied to the states and some of the rights still do not apply to the states today. The application of the rights required in the Bill of Rights to the states is called the incorporation of the Bill of Rights, *or* incorporation *for short. It was not until the beginning of the twentieth century that the U.S. Supreme Court began applying rights enumerated in the Bill of Rights to the states. In one of the first cases in 1925, the Court declared that states were bound to observe First Amendment free speech protections (*Gitlow v. New York, *1925).*

Most of the rights associated with the criminal justice system were not incorporated until the Warren Court of the 1960s. The Warren Court produced such notable decisions as Mapp v. Ohio, *1961;* Aguilar v. Texas, *1964;* Klopfer v. North Carolina, *1967; and* Gideon v. Wainwright, *1963.*

The most recent amendment the Supreme Court decided to incorporate was the Second Amendment right regarding firearm ownership. In McDonald v. the City of Chicago et al., *in 2010, the Supreme Court declared that the guarantee of the Second Amendment to bear arms applies to individuals.*

Some rights that have not been incorporated are the right to indictment by a grand jury (Amendment V), protections against excessive bail and excessive fines (Amendment VII), and the right for a jury trial for juveniles (Amendment VI).

Do you think all of the rights provided in the Bill of Rights should be applied to the states? Why?

probation a disposition in which a convicted defendant is offered an opportunity to avoid serving any time in prison by agreeing to fulfill conditions set forth by the court

parole early release from prison before the maximum sentence is served, based on evidence of rehabilitation and the good behavior of the inmate

CHAPTER 1
Criminal Justice

Check It!

1 WHAT historical events influenced the development of our current criminal justice system? p. 4

Four phenomena stirred interest in the criminal justice system and led to its prominence as one of the most examined and criticized aspects of the government:

1. the Civil Rights Movement,
2. the Vietnam War,
3. the rising crime rate and the public's increased awareness of it, and
4. the terrorism attacks of September 11, 2001.

In many respects, these four influences were interrelated and cumulative in their effect on the criminal justice system.

2 HOW does the balance between the need to maintain order and the rights and freedoms of individual citizens impact our criminal justice system? p. 6

The American criminal justice system has its origins in a revolt against tyranny and a strong, centralized government that usurped the rights of its citizens. A decentralized system with many checks and balances ensures maximum preservation of constitutionally guaranteed liberties and rights. Due process protects the rights of the accused without regard to guilt.

3 WHAT are the strengths and weaknesses of the U.S. criminal justice system? p. 8

The criminal justice system is a dynamic model of interrelated, independent agencies. The system is divided into three categories of agencies: police, courts, and corrections. Local, state, and federal governments are separate but are linked by common activities, goals, and interests. There is no single agency that has oversight control of all of the criminal justice agencies. This system allows for numerous checks and balances.

4 WHAT are the steps of the criminal justice system? p. 10

Six major processes in the criminal justice system are:

1. Deciding what is a crime.
2. Detecting a crime violation and making an arrest.
3. Determining if the accused is to go to trial.
4. Deciding guilt or innocence in the trial.
5. Determining punishment.
6. Administering the punishment.

The police are responsible for investigation, arrest, and booking. A magistrate judge reviews the charges to determine if they are legitimate, advises the person of his or her legal rights, and determines bail.

A case moves from the police to the prosecutor via the preliminary hearing or grand jury system.

At the arraignment, the defendant pleads not guilty, guilty, or no contest to the charges. Guilt or innocence is determined by the judge in a bench trial or by the jury in a jury trial.

The judge determines the appropriate sentence for a convicted defendant. The sentence is announced at a sentencing hearing. Appeals of a verdict are based on alleged judicial errors, not innocence.

The convicted defendant may become an inmate in a correctional facility or may be put on probation. Parole permits, under certain conditions, early release from a correctional facility.

Overall, these processes act like a funnel for moving people through the criminal justice system.

Assess Your Understanding

1. Which of the following influenced public confidence in the criminal justice system during the latter part of the twentieth century?
   a. fear of crime
   b. civil rights rioting
   c. protests over U.S. involvement in the Vietnam War
   d. all of the above
   e. none of the above

2. What is the importance of the Bill of Rights in the U.S. Constitution?
   a. The Bill of Rights defines the balance between individual rights and the power of government.
   b. The Bill of Rights provides for separation of powers among the three branches of government.
   c. The Bill of Rights outlines the roles and functions of the various criminal justice agencies.
   d. none of the above

3. Which amendment in the Bill of Rights prohibits unreasonable search and seizure?
   a. First Amendment
   b. Fourth Amendment
   c. Fifth Amendment
   d. Eighth Amendment

4. Which of the following is the central premise of the criminal justice due process model?
   a. the focus upon crime control
   b. the assumption that if arrested a person must be guilty
   c. the presumption of innocence
   d. plea bargaining

5. Which model emphasizes the necessity to enforce laws and maintain social order?
   a. the due process model
   b. the crime control model
   c. both a and b
   d. neither a nor b

6. Which process in the criminal justice system involves a panel of citizens selected to hear evidence against an accused person to determine if there is probable cause to issue an indictment?
   a. booking
   b. initial appearance
   c. arraignment
   d. grand jury

7. Who determines what sentence the convicted defendant is to serve?
   a. the jury
   b. a panel of citizens
   c. the judge
   d. the prosecutor

ESSAY

1. Describe the factors that influenced public confidence in the criminal justice system during the latter part of the twentieth century.
2. How does the check and balance system work to limit the power of each of the three branches of government?
3. What is the importance of the Bill of Rights to the criminal justice system?
4. Compare and contrast the crime control model and the due process model of criminal justice.
5. Describe the process from arrest to carrying out the sentence or dismissal from the system for a defendant who is processed through the criminal justice system.

ANSWERS: 1. d, 2. a, 3. b, 4. c, 5. b, 6. d, 7. c

Media

Go to the *Chapter 1: Criminal Justice* section in *MyCJLab* to test your understanding of this chapter, access customized study content, engage in interactive simulations, complete critical thinking and research assignments, and view related online videos.

Additional Links

To watch a YouTube video explaining the purpose of the civil grand jury, see www.youtube.com/watch?v=NvRtH5cUxY0&NR=1

You can view and download high-resolution images of the Declaration of Independence, the Constitution, and the Bill of Rights at www.archives.gov/national-archives-experience/charters/charters.html

To view a presentation on the thirty-fifth anniversary of the Kent State Vietnam protest massacre, visit the C-SPAN video library at www.c-spanvideo.org/program/186598-1

Libertarian, politician, and 2004 presidential candidate Michael Badnarik presents his views on the Bill of Rights at www.youtube.com/view_play_list?p=7AB02F069017B232

For an overview of the American criminal justice system, see the discussion at www.youtube.com/watch?v=Vad1tiiUwuU

For a short introduction to plea bargaining, see www.5min.com/Video/Legal-Advice-Plea-Bargaining-34095298

To read the slip opinion of the U. S. Supreme Court of *McDonald vs. the City of Chicago et al.,* 2010, the case which incorporated the Second Amendment, see www.supremecourtœ.gov/opinions/09pdf/08-1521.pdf

CRIME: WHY AND HOW MUCH

2

Why did 22-year-old Jared Lee Loughner shoot U.S. Representative Gabrielle Giffords at a Tucson, Arizona, public meeting and then fire randomly into the crowd shooting 10 people, six of them fatally? Should it have been possible to identify the potential danger Loughner posed prior to his deadly attack?

Loughner's mental competence has been questioned as there are reports he demonstrated antisocial behavior as early as high school. Should mental health professionals have identified his potential for violence? Also, he was expelled from Pima Community College for inappropriate behavior in class. He was rejected by the Army as "unqualified for service," and he had two previous offenses, one being for drug possession. Was there something in his background that should have alerted officials to the grave potential danger he posed to society?

Why would a person deliberately murder strangers? Are there certain traits common to mass murderers? Do criminals have characteristics or behaviors that uniquely identify them? These and other important questions about offenders and offending are those which scholars and criminal justice professionals strive to answer.

The study of offenders and offending to answer such questions is referred to as *criminology.* Criminology plays an important role in the criminal justice system as the theories produced therein are often used to implement laws, prevention programs, rehabilitation programs, and sentencing strategies. From mass murderers like Loughner to the common thief, scholars gather data and construct theories to explain why people commit crimes. The explanations as to the causes of criminality are numerous and diverse. Theories may even be contradictory. For example, some theories posit crime as a logical and free choice of the offender while other theories propose that criminal behavior is the result of heredity and biological traits.

Theories explaining criminal behavior may appear rather bizarre, such as one theory that claims a correlation exists between unpopular names and delinquency.[1] Another theory proposes that blue lights can reduce crime and suicides in public places.[2] Some authorities in the Philippines believe that the singing of Frank Sinatra's version of "My Way" in karaoke bars can trigger assaults and homicides.[3] Some theories have become more accepted by the criminal justice system than others. The theories most incorporated into laws, punishment, and treatment and prevention programs are based on the premise that the causes of criminal behavior are related to social interactions.

This chapter examines various early and modern theories proposed to explain crime. These theories focus on free-will choice and biological, psychological, and sociological explanations of crime. The chapter closes with a discussion of victimology and the strategies to get an accurate count of crime in the United States.

1 **What influence did classical and neoclassical criminological theorists have on modern criminology and the criminal justice system?**

2 **How did earlier biological theories of crime evolve into the modern explanations of biological causation of crime?**

3 **How can criminality be explained in terms of Freud's psychoanalytic theory?**

4 **What are the basic tenets of the major sociological explanations for criminal behavior?**

5 **How do the major victimology theories explain what factors influence victimization?**

6 **What agencies maintain accurate crime statistics, and how do these affect the criminal justice system?**

THE EXPLANATIONS AS TO THE CAUSES OF CRIMINALITY ARE NUMEROUS AND DIVERSE. THEORIES MAY EVEN BE CONTRADICTORY.

Criminology Theories Timeline

Early Theories: Middle Ages to Enlightenment Early nonscientific theories emphasized moral weakness and evil spirits as the cause of criminality.

1469–1527 Machiavelli argues that humans are naturally selfish, evil, and violent.

1692 Salem Witch Trials During this time, any unusual event was attributed to mystical powers and witchcraft. Citizens used the judicial process to rid the colonies of so-called satanic influences.

1764 Cesare Beccaria is the founder of **classical criminology.** His theory was based on the principle that people seek to do what brings them pleasure and avoid what causes pain. With Beccaria's studies, the concept that theories of criminology should be based on data and observations emerges.

1789 Jeremy Bentham is the founder of **neoclassical criminology.** Similarly to Beccaria, Bentham believed that individuals refrain from criminal behavior when the threat of punishment outweighs the pleasure to be derived. Unlike Beccaria, he believed in mitigating circumstances, such as the age and mental capacity of the offender.

1848 Marx and Engels lay the foundation premises for **conflict theories** of crime.

1859 Charles Darwin's *On the Origin of the Species* is used by others to promote the view that criminals had failed to evolve properly.

1875 Richard Dugdale's study of the Jukes's family tree causes him to conclude that criminality is an inherited trait.

1876 Cesare Lombroso theorizes that criminal behavior is a characteristic of humans who failed to fully develop from primitive humans' behavior.

1892 The University of Chicago is the first U.S. university to establish a Department of Sociology. **The Chicago School** psychologists focus on the application of principles of the newly formed discipline of sociology to the analysis of criminal behavior.

1901 The field of psychology is formalized with the founding of the **Psychological Association in London.**

1906 *The American Journal of Abnormal Psychology* publishes an article about **Sigmund Freud's psychoanalytic theories** and methods.

1925 Social disorganization theory is first proposed by Chicago School psychologists **Robert Park** and **Ernest Burgess.** This theory emphasizes the influence of the social and economic environment upon criminal behavior.

1939 Edwin Sutherland publishes *Principles of Criminology,* in which he proposes the **differential association theory,** which becomes the most popular explanation of criminal behavior, especially for juveniles.

Role of Theories in Criminology

Persons who explore the causes of crime are interested in both the formal systems for the control of behavior, such as the legal system, and the informal systems of control, such as the family, school, social group, and religious affiliation. They are interested in observing how these systems influence behavior and what happens when there are conflicts among these various control systems. For example, what happens when a teenager is encouraged by peers to consume alcoholic beverages when he or she is aware of the legal prohibitions against it and his or her parents have indicated their disapproval? Does the teen drink, as encouraged by peers, or abstain, as encouraged by his or her parents and the law? Which factors are most influential in determining behavior? Do all people react the same in similar circumstances, or is one's behavior also influenced by other qualities, such as self-control and personality? By studying such behaviors and gathering reliable data about individuals and their social environment, the criminologist seeks to construct theories that can be used to predict behavior.

The purpose of a theory is not to predict what a specific individual will do in a specific case. Rather, **theories** attempt to define general principles that will apply in a number of similar cases, but not necessarily in all cases. Thus, if 95 of 100 people would act a certain way under certain conditions, the claim could be made confidently that the variables correlate significantly with the behavior, despite the fact that for 5 people, the variables did not cause them to commit a crime. Theories attempt to define and explain the factors that influence or determine behavior and how these factors interrelate.

The Path from Early to Modern Theories of Crime Causation

Early nonscientific theories emphasized moral weakness and evil spirits as the cause of criminality. Early explanations of deviant and criminal behavior were derived primarily from nonscientific methodologies. Most of these nonscientific investigations searched for principles underlying human conduct and thought based on logic or beliefs assumed to be true. These principles often were based on social and religious morals instead of empirical observations and facts. It was believed that people are, or can be, inherently evil.

Modern theories of crime causation are complex because they recognize the interaction of many variables as necessary and sufficient in explaining criminal behavior. Modern theories explaining criminal behavior are based on scientific inquiry, which involves observation and isolation of variables relating to cause and effect. Modern scientific explanations of criminality have evolved from simple theories with few variables to complex theories built on extensive data and research.

Classical and neoclassical theories of crime causation bridged the transition from early nonscientific theories to modern scientific theories of crime causation.

1 **Classical and neoclassical theorists were the first to propose that crime is a matter of free choice and that criminals should have rights in the criminal justice system.**

criminology theories attempts to generalize principles that can explain factors which influence offending, victimization, and rehabilitation

In classical and neoclassical theories, the explanation for crime is based on the assumption that criminal behavior is a matter of choice. The individual has free will to choose to commit or refrain from criminal behavior. The individual's choice of behavior is influenced by a rational analysis of the gain to be achieved from committing the criminal act versus the punishment or penalty that could be suffered if sanctioned by society for the criminal behavior. Theories that share this assumption of free will and rational choice are commonly called **classical school theories** or **neoclassical school theories**.

Two theorists representing the classical and neoclassical theories are Cesare Beccaria (1738–1794) and Jeremy Bentham (1748–1832), considered the founders of classical and neoclassical criminology, respectively. Their theories were a radical departure from the contemporary thought of their time, which credited spirits and demons as the cause of "bad" behavior.

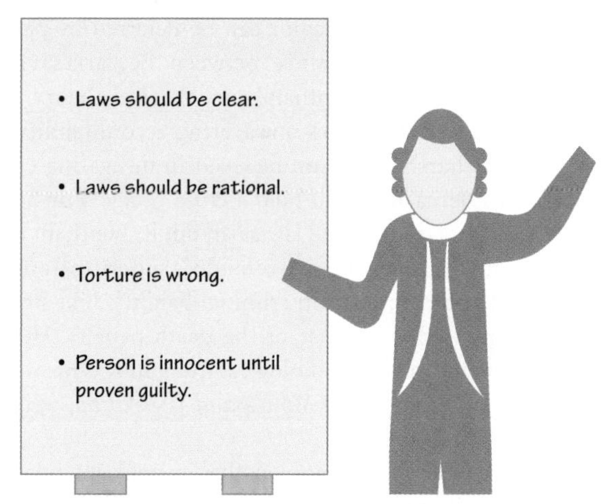

Many of Beccaria's principles are incorporated into the foundation of the American criminal justice system.

Beccaria and Classical Theory

While Cesare Beccaria's ideas actually preceded the development of criminology as an academic discipline, he is known as the founder of classical criminology because his theories about crime marked the beginning of a new approach to criminological thought that would eventually lead to modern theories. Beccaria was an Italian nobleman and jurist who was dissatisfied with the justice system of his time and attempted to bring about change. During the 1700s, the Italian criminal justice system was a barbaric system that leaned toward extreme punishments and questionable justice. Laws were unwritten, arbitrary, and unfairly applied. The situation was made worse by unschooled judges whose decisions were often arbitrary and based to a large degree on the social class of the accused. The penalties handed out by the courts consisted of corporal and capital punishments that were considered a source of public entertainment. Defendants had no rights, there was no due process, and torture was regarded as an effective interrogation method.

On Crimes and Punishment Beccaria composed a single volume addressing his concerns about the criminal justice system of Italy, *Dei delitti e Delle Pene,* published in 1764 and translated into English in 1768 under the title *Of Crimes and Punishments.*[4] In 1771, he was appointed Counselor of State and a magistrate. Beccaria probably had no idea that his short text would become the single work responsible for a revolution in the philosophy of criminal justice. Even today, Beccaria's ideas seem completely contemporary and can be clearly identified as the foundation underlying the contemporary American criminal justice system.

His essay clearly summarized the concept of the criminal justice system as a social contract based on logic, goal orientation, and humanistic principles. The concepts in his books—innocent until proven guilty, trial by a jury of one's peers, the right of appeal, the classification of crimes, equal treatment of all people before the court, and so on—reflect the principles of American jurisprudence.

The Pain–Pleasure Principle Beccaria was influenced by the Age of Enlightenment. His ideas on the cause of criminal behavior were based on the philosophical axiom that people are rational. He reasoned that people seek to do that which brings them pleasure and to avoid that which causes pain. He further assumed that members of society are responsible for their actions. There are no mitigating circumstances or excuses for one's criminal behavior. The same standard of justice and punishment should be applied to people of all ages and mental abilities. He advocated certain, swift punishment of appropriate intensity and duration for the offense committed, for the purpose of deterring people from committing crimes. According to Beccaria, the reason for the continued presence of crime in eighteenth-century Italian society was that the criminal justice system did not provide for swift, certain, and appropriate punishment.

Beccaria opposed the death penalty but argued that the uncertainty of punishment—for few judges even then were willing to send a man to the gallows for the theft of a loaf of bread—diluted the effectiveness of the threat of punishment. Basically, Beccaria argued that even minor punishments would be more effective if they were swift and certain. If one stole a loaf of bread and it was virtually certain that he or she would immediately receive a punishment appropriate to the crime, he argued, such punishment would be more effective than the threat of death, which was rarely carried out for minor theft. This concept—that criminal behavior is a matter of free will and choice and that certain, swift, and appropriate pain will deter people from criminal behavior—is the basic premise of the classical theory of criminology.

Bentham and Neoclassical Theory

English philosopher and scholar Jeremy Bentham is credited with the formation of the neoclassical school of criminology,[5] which is similar to the classical school in that the basic foundation is the concept that criminal behavior is a matter of free will and the

classical school theories the school of thought that individuals have free will to choose whether or not to commit crimes and that criminals should have rights in the criminal justice system

neoclassical school theories a school of thought that is similar to classical school theories, except for the beliefs that there are mitigating circumstances for criminal acts, such as the age or mental capacity of the offender, and that punishment should fit the crime

choice to commit criminal behavior can be deterred by pain and punishment. The major difference between Beccaria's classical theory of criminology and Bentham's neoclassical theory is that Bentham believed that Beccaria's unwavering accountability of all offenders was too harsh. Bentham believed in mitigating circumstances. Whereas Beccaria would hold a child of age 5 or 6 just as responsible for a violation of the law as an adult, Bentham argued that children under the age of 7 and offenders suffering from mental disease should be exempt from criminal liability. Like Beccaria, Bentham was opposed to the use of the death penalty. His most significant contribution to criminological thought was his work *An Introduction to the Principles of Morals and Legislation,* written in 1780 and published in 1789.

Like Beccaria, Bentham reasoned that people are calculating humans who logically evaluate the pleasure to be gained by the commission of an act versus the punishment to be suffered for it. When the pain of punishment outweighs the pleasure to be derived, individuals refrain from criminal behavior. Harsher prohibitions and punishments were both unnecessary and inefficient. If one were deterred from theft by the threat of 3 strokes of the cane, then a threat of 20 strokes or of hanging made the judicial system seem ignorant and inappropriate.

Bentham's theory regarding the balancing of pain and pleasure as a means to discourage criminal behavior is known as the *felicitic calculus*—the pain versus pleasure principle. Bentham's philosophy is called "utilitarianism," and states that a rational system of jurisprudence provides for the greatest happiness for the greatest number of people. Based on the principles that people act rationally and that the punishment should fit the crime, Bentham's neoclassical philosophy became the foundation of the English jurisprudence system, and hence the American jurisprudence system.

Belief in Free Will and Individual Choice

When Beccaria's and Bentham's ideas about criminal behavior were published, they competed primarily with irrational arguments of demon possession, class-based justice, and harshly exaggerated punishments. Today, the idea remains popular that crime is a matter of free will and a choice based on the weighing of potential pleasure and pain. The contemporary criminal justice system appears to be based ultimately on the principles of classical and neoclassical criminology. Proponents of harsh punishments, abolishment of parole, and trying juveniles as adults often phrase their arguments in logic similar to that found in classical and neoclassical thought.

The twentieth century ushered in a new era of scientific inquiry. Many of the scientific fields that emerged at the turn of the twentieth century, such as sociology, psychology, and psychiatry, offered innovative theories to explain human behavior. Scholars quickly adopted this new knowledge to explain criminal behavior, and often, the validity of these new explanations was tested through the criminal justice system.

The Positive School

The scientific method emphasizes that knowledge about criminal behavior should be gathered using tools such as observation, surveys, case studies, statistics, and experimentation. The **positive school** includes most modern theories of criminology. The positive theories can be divided into three major schools based upon the emphasis of the primary cause of crime: biology, psychology, and sociology. Theories based upon sociology and psychology have had a greater impact upon the criminal justice system than biological theories have.

Modern theories of crime are based upon the premise that, contrary to the assumption of classical theories that individuals have free will and choose to commit crime, people commit crimes because of internal or external factors that can be observed and measured. These positivist scholars and scientists were also known as determinists.

Biological Explanations

Darwin's *Origin of Species* (1859) provided an important portal for the development of new positive criminological theories. One of the dilemmas in the advancement of premodern criminological theories was the belief commonly held in Christian theologies that humankind was created by God in God's image and therefore is inherently good. This foundational belief, while consistent with the free-will school of thought, posed great difficulties for any theory asserting that some people are not created good but are bad from birth. To say that one was born "bad" seems to place the fault with God or to deny the goodness of God's creation. If people are good from birth, on the other hand, then it becomes necessary to explain how one becomes bad. The theory of evolution and adaptation of the species provided an answer to this question.

Early biological theories emphasized that a person's criminal nature was an inherited characteristic. That is to say, a person is a criminal because his or her parents were criminals. The original cause of the criminality was assumed to be the failure of this genealogical line to fully "evolve." Two studies attempting to apply a heredity model to the analysis of criminal behavior were the study by Richard Dugdale (1841–1883) of the Jukes family and the study of Martin Kallikak's family tree by Henry Goddard (1866–1957). These studies, although flawed in their conclusion, suggested that criminality is an inherited trait. Dugdale traced the family tree of Ada Jukes, showing how this single person was responsible for hundreds of criminals and imbeciles.[6] Dugdale was so impressed by the criminal lineage of Ada Jukes that he called her the "mother of criminals." Goddard compared the biological offspring from Martin Kallikak's wife, "a woman of his own quality," and his illegitimate son from a servant girl. Goddard noted a significant difference in the two lineages and concluded that criminality is a degenerative trait transmitted through biology.[7]

Needless to say, these studies were not scientific. For one thing, they failed to identify and account for all the variables that might be involved in the outcomes. Despite this and other defects in scholarship, studies like these set the stage for developments in the positive

2 **Early proponents of biological explanations for crime believed that individuals committed crimes because of inherited traits or their failure to fully develop as normal humans, whereas modern biocriminologists concede that environmental factors can influence inherited predispositions to criminality.**

positive school modern theories of crime, primarily based on sociology and psychology, that people commit crimes because of uncontrollable internal or external factors, which can be observed and measured

HERE'S SOMETHING TO THINK ABOUT . . .

What causes violent behavior? Some contemporary research has focused on violent video games, music with violent lyrics, and children who display a lack of emotions such as guilt and remorse as factors that correlate with violent behavior in juveniles and young adults. Research by Brad Bushman, psychology professor at Ohio State University, suggests action-packed, violent video games may cause an increase in aggressive behavior. Other researchers and criminal justice professionals suggest that gangsta rap contributes to violence and criminal behavior. Nathalie Fontaine at Indiana University in Bloomington studied 9,500 twins and found that children who rated high on a scale of "callous-unemotional traits" at age 7, 9, and 12 were at the highest risk for destructive, antisocial behavior. What do you think are some causes of violent behaviors in juveniles?

school of criminology. Cesare Lombroso's theory of the "criminal man" was the first important positivist theory to emerge.

Lombroso and Criminality

Cesare Lombroso (1835–1909) was an Italian medical doctor who took an interest in the causes of criminal behavior. He was particularly influenced by previous scholars whose writings suggested that criminality was inherited. He was influenced by Darwin's theory of adaptation and nonadaptation, and he assumed that criminals were throwbacks to an earlier stage of evolution.

For his theory explaining criminal behavior, Lombroso collected extensive data from Italian prisoners and Italian military personnel. Lombroso believed that criminal behavior was a characteristic of humans who had failed to fully develop from their primitive origins, such that criminals were closer to apes than to contemporary humans. Criminals could be differentiated clearly from noncriminals on the basis of distinctive physical features, such as protruding jaws, sloping foreheads, left-handedness, and red hair. Lombroso concluded that criminals were cases of atavism—reversions to primitive times.[8]

Criminals were born inferior and prehuman, according to Lombroso. Thus, little could be done to prevent such persons from becoming criminals or to rehabilitate them. Lombroso made extensive physical measurements to define what he called the "criminal man."[9] The study of the physical traits of criminals was called **atavistic stigmata**.

Lombroso's theories were further developed by Raffaele Garofalo (1852–1934) and Enrico Ferri (1856–1929). Although the theories of Garofalo and Ferri contained significant deviations from those of Lombroso, the central theme was that criminals should not be held morally responsible for crimes because they did not choose to commit the crimes. The positive school of criminology, led by Lombroso, Garofalo, and Ferri, argued that the concept of free will is a fiction. Lombroso suggested that preventive actions would have little or no impact on the prevention of criminal behavior. Ferri was more hopeful that preventive measures could overcome congenital tendencies. He favored obliging criminals to work, believing that a strong work ethic could help a criminal overcome defects of character. Garofalo focused more on psychic anomalies and the reform of the judicial system of Italy. For example, he argued that juries were ill equipped to make judgments regarding the fate of criminals because criminality was more a medical condition than a moral defect. This "medicalization" of crime had an enduring impact on the criminal justice system and is commonly associated today with drug-related crimes.

Influence of Biological Determinism

Despite the fact that Lombroso's theory was later invalidated, it was and continues to be influential in the study of criminology and upon the criminal justice system. For example, his theory influenced the way in which convicted persons were treated in prison. Emphasis on corporal punishment and moral correction through religious instruction was replaced by an emphasis on identification, isolation, and extermination. For example, castration was a common correctional treatment based on the belief that criminality is an inherited characteristic. In his opinion supporting castration as a valid treatment for criminals, U.S. Supreme Court Justice Oliver Wendell Holmes Jr. declared, "It is better for all the world, if instead of waiting to execute degenerate offspring for crime, or to let them starve for their imbecility, society can prevent those who are manifestly unfit from continuing their kind."

IT IS BETTER FOR ALL THE WORLD, IF . . . SOCIETY CAN PREVENT THOSE WHO ARE MANIFESTLY UNFIT FROM CONTINUING THEIR KIND.

Modern Biological Explanations

Lombroso proposed his theory of criminality without benefit of the knowledge provided by modern genetic science. As the contribution of genetics to various human conditions was recognized, several studies revisited Lombroso's basic axiom that criminality is inherited. Studies of identical twins performed by Karl O. Christiansen[10] and

atavistic stigmata the study of the physical traits of criminals, a method used by Lombroso

others all concluded that, for identical twins, if one twin engaged in criminal behavior, the probability that his or her identical twin would be a criminal was statistically significantly higher.

Proponents of the biological perspective on criminal behavior argue that some people are born with a biological predisposition to be antisocial—to behave in ways that run counter to social values and norms. Unlike early biological determinists, modern biocriminologists concede that environmental factors can inhibit or stimulate hereditary predispositions for criminality. **Biocriminology** focuses on research into the roles played by genetic and neurophysiological variables in criminal behavior.

Modern biology-based theories identify a diverse number of variables suspected of contributing to criminal behavior. Often, these theories have emerged after scientific discoveries have revealed new knowledge about how the brain works and the contribution of genetics to behavior. For example, as the role of chromosomes became clear in influencing certain human characteristics, the **XYY chromosome theory** of violent behavior emerged. The normal male has an X and a Y chromosome in the cells that determine the sex of a person. It was discovered that some males have an extra Y chromosome, and studies of male prisoners convicted of violent crimes have found a high correlation between conviction for a violent crime and the presence of an extra Y chromosome.

HERE'S SOMETHING TO THINK ABOUT . . .

Modern research on the links between genes, violence, and the environment continues as researchers focus on the interaction of environmental factors and certain genetic traits. Much of the research focuses on lifestyle and the MAOA gene, which helps regulate key brain chemicals like dopamine. The theory is that environmental factors such as anxiety and early development influence the epigenome system which turns genes on and off, regulating their expression. This combination is thought to have the potential to create a greater likelihood of antisocial behavior. Several defendants have invoked such a defense in court. Critics dismiss the research and suggest misapplication may raise ethical questions such as those associated with earlier theories of eugenics.[12] If violence is influenced by genes, what impact would this knowledge have on ideas of crime prevention and punishment?

Psychological Explanations

Freud and Psychoanalysis

At the end of the 1800s, Sigmund Freud introduced his new **psychoanalytic theory**. In the twentieth century, the science of psychoanalysis became universally accepted as a way of understanding previously unexplainable human behavior.[11] Freud based his theory on the underlying assumption that behavior is not a choice of free will but is controlled by subconscious desires. Furthermore, not all behavior is rational. Some behaviors are not only irrational, but also destructive. Yet, despite the self-destructive nature of some behaviors, Freud argued that, frequently, people are unable to control them. At the root of Freud's theory is the concept that human thoughts and actions are controlled by the three components of the unconscious mind: the superego, the ego, and the id.

Freud did not focus on the study of criminal behavior. However, his theory of psychoanalysis has been extensively applied to the study of criminals. Freud's theory provides a completely different perspective on criminal behavior. To simplify a fairly complex theory, it could be said that in Freudian theory, crime is a symptom of a person's unresolved psychological conflict.[13] This conflict is caused by free-floating feelings of guilt and anxiety. The person feels guilty but does not know why. To alleviate the feelings of guilt, the person commits a crime so that he or she will be punished. The punishment brings temporary relief. However, because the punishment is not truly related to the source of the feelings of guilt, the guilt returns, and it is necessary for the person to commit another crime. This dysfunctional cycle of guilt and criminal behavior continues because, in reality, the punishment received cannot alleviate the feeling of guilt.

With regard to murder, Freud's analytic theory applies more to serial murderers, who kill one victim at a time over a period of time, than to mass murderers, who kill more than one victim at a single time.

Freud's theory of psychoanalysis was based on the theory that the motive for behaviors may not be conscious to the person. According to Freud's theory, criminal behavior is only a symptom of an underlying psychological conflict.

Sociological Explanations

Social Determinism

Theories based on the idea that forces within society—social forces and social groups and institutions—are the causes of crime reflect a philosophy called **social determinism**. Relations, social interactions, social expectations, and pressures exerted by peers and institutions—not free will, biology, or psychology—determine criminal behavior.

Social Disorganization as the Cause of Crime

Early sociologists found crime and the criminal convenient and interesting subjects for study. The University of Chicago established the first sociology department in the United States. Robert Ezra Park (1864–1944)

3 Freud's psychoanalytic theory explained criminology as resulting from individual conflict, which leads to feelings of guilt and a desire for self-punishment that manifests itself in criminal activity.

biocriminology the study of the roles of genetic and neurophysiological variables as they relate to criminal behavior

XYY chromosome theory the idea that violent behavior in males can in part be attributed to the presence of an extra Y chromosome in male offenders

psychoanalytic theory the concept that behavior is not a matter of free will but is controlled by subconscious desires, which includes the idea that criminal behavior is a result of unresolved internal conflict and guilt

social determinism the idea that social forces and social groups are the cause of criminal behavior

social disorganization theory the idea proposed and researched by Park and his colleagues that supports the notion that criminal behavior is dependent on disruptive social forces, not on individual characteristics

HERE'S SOMETHING TO THINK ABOUT . . .

Research by Professor Frank R. Ascione shows clear connections between animal abuse and domestic violence and child abuse.[14] Nevada State Prison (NSP) used this theory to establish a rehabilitation program for prisoners. It was hypothesized that if prisoners can learn to care and bond with animals, it would result in positive personality changes. At NSP selected prisoners are paired with a rescue dog from the local humane shelter. The dog is housed in the same cell as the prisoner and the prisoner interacts with the dog to eliminate the behaviors that made the dog unadoptable. The program is considered a success by the inmates, prison officials, and the humane shelter. Prisoners who care for the dogs report they perceive positive personality and behavior changes in themselves. What do you think of this claim?

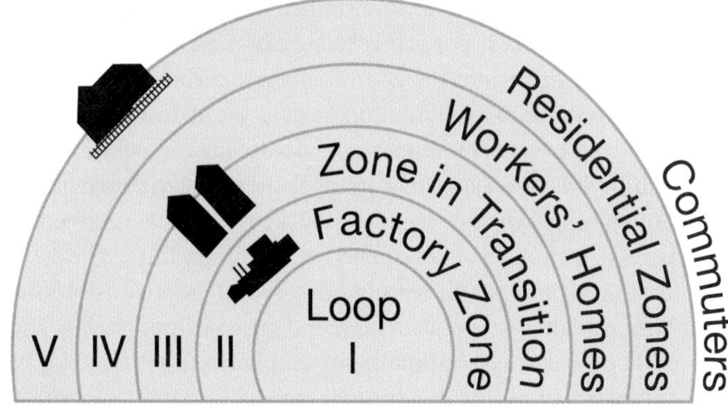

FIGURE 2.1 Zone theory provided a unique explanation of crime in that its most significant causes were the economic and physical environments. Zone theory suggested that if the physical and economic environments could be improved, the crime rate would drop even if the same people remained. According to zone theory, people committed crime because of external influences, not because they were "bad" or morally "defective." This perspective has been very influential in modern crime prevention programs.

was one of the founders of this department, and he focused on explaining and understanding social disorder. Park believed that human behavior is influenced by the environment and that an overcrowded and disordered environment leading to social isolation contributes to deviant and criminal behavior.[15] Gathering data from the surrounding Chicago area, Park and his students engaged in a comprehensive study of the relationship between urbanization and social isolation, based on Emile Durkheim's theory of anomie. Anomie is a feeling of "normlessness" and lack of belonging that people feel when they become socially isolated. According to Durkheim, people with anomie lack the ties to society that would inhibit them from committing crimes against society.

Social Disorganization Theory In the early 1900s, Chicago grew rapidly as a result of industrialization and immigration. Park's research demonstrated that criminal behavior was independent of individual characteristics and much more dependent on disruptive social forces. This is called social disorganization theory.[16] Subsequent studies by Clifford Shaw and others demonstrated that Chicago was divided into territorial patterns with distinct populations.[17] Each population had a distinct ecological niche and a life of its own that was more or less conducive to crime. This environment-based theory of criminal behavior became known as zone theory.

Zone Theory According to **zone theory**, developed by Park and Burgess, social environments based on status disadvantages—such as poverty, illiteracy, lack of schooling, unemployment, and illegitimacy—are powerful forces that influence human interactions (Figure 2.1). Studies by Shaw and McKay showed that from 1900 to 1933, the highest rates of delinquency persisted in the same neighborhoods of Chicago, even though the ethnic composition changed.[18] Thus, the basic cause of delinquency was not the ethnicity of the juveniles, but the social structures, institutions, and environmental variables in that zone. As one moved away from the industrial heart of the city, the rates of delinquency dropped.

Since the 1930s, social disorganization theory and especially zone theory have had a strong influence on crime-prevention efforts. Based on the assumption that social conditions such as unemployment, poor schools, and substandard housing are significant factors contributing to delinquency and crime, many government-sponsored programs have attempted to fight crime by improving employment opportunities, social services, schools, and housing. **Crime prevention through environmental design (CPTED)** was founded on the theory that crime prevention is related to environmental design, particularly housing design. Another crime-prevention program rooted in social disorganization theory is the "broken window theory," discussed further in Chapter 4. This crime-prevention program is based on the idea that signs of neighborhood neglect, community deterioration, and tolerance of petty crime all contribute to more crime and crime-inducing environments.[19]

Differential Association Theory

Learning theory and the concept of socialization, which are shared by both sociology and psychology, were the basis for **differential association theory**, which proposes that criminal behavior is learned entirely through group interaction. This theory, proposed by Edwin Sutherland (1883–1950), argues that criminal behavior is learned in intimate peer groups that reward or reinforce antisocial or delinquent behaviors.[20]

zone theory a concept, developed by Park and his Chicago School colleague Burgess, that juvenile delinquency is caused by zones of social environments based on status differences, including poverty, illiteracy, lack of schooling, unemployment, and illegitimacy—but not ethnicity

crime prevention through environmental design (CPTED) government-sponsored programs that are based on the theory that crime can be prevented through environmental design, especially housing design

differential association theory the concept that criminal and delinquent behaviors are learned entirely through group interactions, with peers reinforcing and rewarding these behaviors

4

Modern sociology emphasizes the power of relationships, social interactions, social conditions and expectations, and pressures exerted by peers and institutions—not free will, biology, or psychology—as the determining factors of criminal behavior.

Thus, a life of crime is culturally transmitted through peer groups. One reason that this theory is popular is because it offers an explanation of delinquency that does not depend on other sociological factors that might be involved in crime causation, such as social disorganization.

Sutherland's explanation does not refer to environmental or class factors, and it does not suggest that criminals are necessarily mentally defective, morally bankrupt, or economically deprived. Rather, Sutherland emphasizes that criminal or deviant behavior is simply learned behavior.

Because of its basis in learning theory, differential association theory can explain white-collar crime and crime by upper-class adolescents. Differential association theory emphasizes that criminal behavior is the result of learning through normal social interactions. If a "good kid" from a middle- or upper-class family has criminal friends whom he or she respects, then during the normal course of social interactions with them, the "good kid" will learn criminal behavior.

Although learning theories continue to dominate criminological thought and social programming, they have several significant shortcomings. They do not adequately explain how and why a person chooses to learn criminal behavior. For example, why is it that one police officer spends a lifetime career in close association with criminals without respecting their criminal values, while another police officer begins to accept those values and engages in criminal behavior soon after employment?

Social Control Theories

Social control theory emphasizes that social and cultural values exert control over individuals' behavior and that social institutions enforce those values. Social institutions that contribute to the formation of social values are the family, school, neighborhood, religion, and government. These institutions exert control both informally (e.g., parental disapproval or social rejection) and formally (e.g., school suspension or arrest). The influence of informal and formal systems of social control make people basically law abiding to the extent that they identify with and conform to social expectations.[21]

Social control studies focus on the reasons that people conform to norms. People of all socioeconomic backgrounds are subject to the temptation of crime and desire what they do not have. People also have impulses that they do not act on and desires that they do not fulfill. What, then, causes some people to turn to crime and others not to? Social control theories emphasize that both environmental variables and individual self-control are influential in preventing or suppressing criminal behavior.[22]

Neutralization Theory Gresham Sykes and David Matza's **neutralization theory** is based on the assumption that one cannot completely resist criminal behavior and that most people have committed some criminal or deviant act at one time or another. They have argued that deviant and criminal behavior produces a sense of guilt and that the pains of

Merton's Strain Theory

	Acceptance of Goals	Rejection of Goals
Acceptance of Means	**CONFORMITY** Accept society's goals and work to achieve them through culturally acceptable means. • focus on education • achieving career success	**RITUALISM** Person rejects society's goals, but does not turn to crime or other deviant behaviors. • acceptance of lack of means • career success is not important
Rejection of Means	**INNOVATION** Accept society's goals but have little legitimate means for achieving them. • writing bad checks • fraud • embezzlement • burglary	**RETREATISM** Rejects society's goals and the traditional means for achieving them. • "drops out" of society • drug use and addiction • vagrancy and homelessness
		REBELLION Rejects society's goals and the means to achieve them, instead they create their own goals and transformational means. • Reverend Martin Luther King Jr. • Ghandi • Mother Theresa

social control theory the focus on the social and cultural values that exert control over and reinforce the behavior of individuals

neutralization theory the concept that most people commit some type of criminal act in their lives and that many people are prevented from doing so again because of a sense of guilt, while criminals neutralize feelings of guilt through rationalization, denial, or an appeal to higher loyalties

conscience are sufficient to keep most people from engaging in extended and extensive criminality. Sykes and Matza explain that criminals learn neutralization techniques that allow them to avoid being guilt ridden.[23]

Neutralization techniques include psychological defenses, such as rationalization, denial, and appeal to higher loyalties.

Strain Theory

Sociologist Robert Merton formulated a popular theory called **strain theory**, which is based on the assumption that people are law-abiding but will resort to crime when they are frustrated in finding legitimate means to economic success.[24] His theory assumes that people are motivated to achieve the comforts and security of a middle-class lifestyle, but that some people find that they cannot achieve this goal through traditional, socially acceptable means. Unable to adapt, these individuals might then resort to illegal means to achieve this goal.

According to Merton, people attempt to adapt means to goals in five basic ways: conformity, innovation, ritualism, retreatism, and rebellion.[25]

Merton believed that social conditions, especially poverty and ethnicity, are powerful factors in determining the adaptations that individuals make to socially prescribed goals and the lifestyles that develop as a result. It was predicted that the greatest proportion of crime would be found in the lower classes because, Merton believed, lower-class people have the least opportunity to reach middle-class goals legitimately. Also, in such a diverse society as the United States, it might be presumptuous to assume that everyone shares the same value system and common goals. Nevertheless, strain theory has had a major impact on the government's response to crime. Programs such as Head Start, Job Corps, and others aimed at providing economic opportunities to the poor and disadvantaged are justified by the belief that economic opportunity deters crime.

Cultural Deviance Theories

Whereas strain theory is based on the core values of the wider society, **cultural deviance theories** are based on the idea that the values of subcultural groups within the society have even more power over individual behavior. Organized crime families, juvenile gangs, and hate groups can be described as deviant subcultures. Cultural deviance theorists focus on differences in values and norms between mainstream society and subcultural groups, including immigrant groups who entered the United States during the first half of the twentieth century.

Cultural deviance theories begin with the assumption that subgroups or subcultures within a society have different value systems. Albert Cohen defined distinct subcultures in terms of variables such as parental aspirations, child-rearing practices, and classroom standards. Cohen used the term **reaction formation** to describe how lower-class youths reject middle-class values, which they perceive that they cannot achieve and therefore create unique countercultures.[26]

Thorsten Sellin (1938) advocated that crime was not necessarily a case of bad people engaging in deliberate or negligent harm to others. Sellin argued that cultural diversity could be the cause of crime. In a homogeneous society with strong identification with the values of the group, there is little need for formal enforcement of laws, as most people will conform to the group norms and values.

Sellin believed that criminal law reflects normative values of the dominant culture or ethnic group. In a society where there is a diversity of cultural or ethnic groups, the behaviors of members of the minority culture or ethnic group may be rejected and labeled criminal. Sellin proposed that there were two types of cultural conflict: primary conflict and secondary conflict. Primary conflict occurs when the norms of two cultures clash. Secondary conflict occurs within the evolution of a single culture, as when children reject the values and conduct norms of their parents. Today's modern "global village" provides numerous examples in which cultural diversity is considered criminal. Consider the following examples of cultural diversity as the cause of crime.

In the United States, cultural conduct norms that may be contrary to the law include parents who do not believe in childhood immunizations, compulsory schooling, or certain medical treatments to save lives and preserve the health of their children. Some members of the Fundamentalist sect of the Latter Day Saints Church find themselves in violation of the law because of their beliefs regarding polygamy. For example, one fundamentalist sect believes that men must have at least three wives to reach heaven. Although polygamy is illegal, it is believed that tens of thousands of fundamentalists and others continue the practice in the United States.[27]

HERE'S SOMETHING TO THINK ABOUT . . .

Cultural conflict theories emphasize the conflicting values of subcultures in society. One prime example of such conflict is "honor killings"—killing for dishonor or disrespect for cultural or religious values. The United Nations has documented honor killings in Egypt, Iraq, Turkey, Pakistan, India, and other countries. Although rare, there are examples of honor killings in the United States. In April 2011, Faleh Hassan Almaleki was convicted in Arizona for the murder of his 20-year-old daughter. Almaleki murdered his daughter by running over her because she was "too Westernized, defying Iraqi and Muslim values." As the Muslim and other minority populations increase in the United States, it can be expected that there will be more legal conflicts with the values and mores of subcultures. To what degree should the CJS accommodate subcultural values that are contrary to the law?

strain theory the assumption that individuals resort to crime out of frustration from being unable to attain economic comfort or success

cultural deviance theories theories based on the idea that the values of deviant subcultural groups within society, such as organized-crime families, juvenile gangs, and hate groups, have great power over individuals' behavior

reaction formation a term that Cohen used to describe the rejection of middle-class values by lower-class youths, who believe that they cannot attain these values and therefore create unique countercultures

TABLE 2.1 Explanations of Criminal Behavior

Type of Explanation	School of Thought	Theory	Proponent	Cause of Crime
Moralism				Evil; sin, spirit possession
Free Will	Classical	Pain–pleasure principle	Cesare Beccaria	Rational free choice
	Neoclassical	Utilitarianism	Jeremy Bentham	Rational free will except for the young and the insane
Biological Determinism	Evolutionary	Darwinism; concept of atavism	Cesare Lombroso Richard Dugdale (Ada Jukes)	Heredity; no free will and thus no moral accountability
		Somatotype	Willliam Sheldon	Inherited predispositions revealed through body type
	Biocriminology	XYY chromosome; hormones; nutrition; MBD (minimal brain dysfunction)		Physiological disorders or chemically induced aggression
Psychological Determinism		Psychoanalytical theory	Sigmund Freud	Psychopathology; irrational, unresolved, unconscious conflict from guilt/anxiety from childhood trauma
		Criminal personality		Antisocial attitudes and lack of self-control
Social Determinism	Environmentalism	Zone theory	Robert Ezra Park	Society; dysfunctional social environments
	Interactionism	Differential association theory	Edwin Sutherland	Socialization in delinquent peer groups
		Cultural deviance	Albert Cohen	Socialization in deviant subculture or counterculture
	Social control			Breakdown of social institutions; lack of conformity
		Containment theory	Walter Reckless	Loss of self-control and social control
		Neutralization theory	Gresham Sykes/David Matza	Rationalization of antisocial acts
		Social bond theory	Travis Hirschi	Loss of sense of attachment
		Labeling theory	Howard Becker	Society's reactions to deviance
	Structuralism			Social structure; structure of opportunity
		Strain theory	Robert Merton	Frustration in achieving middle-class goals legitimately because of poverty or ethnicity
		Differential opportunity	Richard Cloward and Lloyd Ohlin	Blocked opportunities to reach goals
		Conflict theory		Social inequality; class conflict; institutional discrimination
			Richard Quinney	Criminal justice system as a weapon of the ruling class; racial discrimination
			Freda Adler	Gender inequality

Solution to Crime	Critique
Elimination of offenders from society	No scientific data underlying claims of causes of criminal behavior
Deterrence through pain of punishment over pleasure of crime	No limited liability for the young or mentally ill
Deterrence through laws fitting the punishment to the crime	Theory does not acknowledge the possible influence of biological, sociological, or psychological factors
Prevention impossible; give medical treatment (and castrate or sterilize criminals)	Theory formulated prior to emergence of knowledge concerning sociology, psychology, and biological influences
Prevention through identification	Hypotheses depend upon correlational statistics with little demonstration of causality
Medical treatment and control	Cannot isolate variables assumed to cause deviant behavior
Counseling and rehabilitation	Understanding of behavior depends upon intuitive knowledge of subconscious motives
Early childhood intervention	Describes the thinking and behaviors but does not attribute a cause
Reduce anomie through environmental design and urban renewal; reduce poverty	Most people from the same "bad" environment do not commit crimes
Diversion and re-education	More useful in explaining juvenile rather than adult behavior
Distinguish cultural diversity and dissent from deviance	Explains only a limited number of crimes
Enforcement of social values and norms	Not possible to measure strength of "bonds"
Strengthening of institutions, such as the family	Little consideration for biological and psychological influences
Strengthening of social and emotional bonds to others and to society	Does not explain why some are able to justify their behavior, others not
	Explains a limited number of crimes
	Limited applicability
Level the playing field; provide opportunity	
Eliminate frustrations and disadvantages or help people overcome them	Assumes universal aspiration for "middle-class" life
	Assumes economic motivation for crime
Social and political equality; redistribution of wealth and power in society	More philosophy than science
Equal rights; equal protection	Assumes class warfare is universal and irreversible
Equal rights; equal protection	Major premise cannot be proven

Conflict Theories

Conflict theorists focus on how a society's system of social stratification (the division of society into social classes) and social inequality influence behavior.[28] **Conflict theories** are based on the assumption that powerful ruling political and social elites—persons, groups, and institutions—exploit the less powerful and use the criminal justice system to their own advantage to maintain their power and privilege.[29] In this view, criminology is the study of crime in relation to society's haves and have-nots.

Theories of crime based on social inequality have their roots in the social criticisms of Karl Marx and Friedrich Engels in nineteenth-century Europe. Marxism assumes a division between the poor (workers) and the rich (property owners and capitalists) in which the rich control the various social, political, and economic institutions of society. The rich use their power and position to control the poor.[30] Present-day conflict theorists suggest that reducing social inequality is the only or best way to reduce criminal behavior.[31]

In the 1960s, Richard Quinney argued that the criminal justice system is a state-initiated and state-supported effort to rationalize mechanisms of social control, which are based on class structure. The state is organized to serve the interests of the dominant economic class. Quinney saw criminal law as an instrument that the state and the ruling class use to maintain and perpetuate the social and economic order.[32] Some conflict theorists went so far as to claim that there is a deliberate conspiracy to suppress the lower classes, especially the "dangerous poor."[33]

Feminist criminology assumes that the underlying cause of criminal behavior by females is the inequality of power between men and women. Advocates such as Freda Adler,[34] Meda Chesney-Lind and Kathleen Daly,[35] and Rita J. Simon[36] argue that the inequality of political, economic, and social power and wealth is the root cause of female criminal behavior.

Conflict theorists have strongly criticized mainstream criminology and the criminal justice system. Research data began to support claims that inequality of opportunity contributes to crime, and inequalities were found to exist in the operation of the criminal justice system. It was found, for example, that disproportionate numbers of

HERE'S SOMETHING TO THINK ABOUT . . .

Theories of crime causation are complicated by the fact that there is not universal agreement upon what actions are crimes or deviant behaviors. The sign located along Highway 50 in Nevada advertises the services of several houses of prostitution along with other businesses. In most states, operating such a business would be a felony. Even in Nevada, prostitution is legal in some counties and illegal in others. There are many examples in which actions that are legal in one state are illegal in another.

Conflict theories argue that the law is based on political power. For example, the feminist perspective on the law and prostitution differs significantly from conservative morality perspectives. Crimes and deviant behavior are defined in relationship to community values, but which of these values are codified into laws is influenced by many variables. Furthermore, community values are constantly changing. Sometimes when laws do not change with community values, the public pays little attention to the law and engages openly in the prohibited behavior. What are some laws that do not reflect contemporary values?

poor and minority citizens were being stopped, arrested, and incarcerated compared with other groups.[37] Radical criminologists such as William Chambliss saw the law and the system as a means of institutional discrimination rather than as a means of providing fairness in justice.[38] While efforts have been made to address these criticisms of the criminal justice system, conflict-based theories of crime causation have not had a role in crime prevention or rehabilitation programs.

The Other Side of Crime: Victimology

Understanding victimology as well as criminal behavior is an important aspect of comprehending the criminal justice system. **Victimology** is the study of victims and their patterns of victimization. From this perspective, the question is not why certain individuals (or groups) engage in criminal behavior; instead, the emphasis is on explaining why certain people (or groups) experience victimization at certain times and in certain places. Similarly, research on criminal justice has focused on how offenders are processed through the criminal justice system. Victimologists, in contrast, examine the dynamics of the administration of justice as it relates to crime victims.

The Demographics of Criminal Victimization

Like criminal offending, criminal victimization is not randomly distributed among the populace. Patterns of victimization show a high degree of consistency with respect to where and when they occur and who is victimized.

- Individuals between the ages of 12 and 24 have the greatest chance of becoming the victims of crime, especially violent crime (see Figure 2.2). Generally, from the early- to mid-20s, as one gets older, the rate of victimization decreases, with those older than age 65 having the lowest rate of victimization for all crimes across gender and race.
- Men are victimized at higher rates than women are. For every offense except sexual assault or rape and simple assault, men have higher victimization rates than women.
- Females most often are victimized by someone they know. Females report that more than three fourths (78 percent) of those who violently victimize them are known to them. Women are much more likely to be violently victimized by family members, spouses, boyfriends, or other persons known to them. This relational phenomenon is known as intimate victimization.

78%

The percent of women who were victimized by someone known to them.

- Males report that they are almost as likely to be victimized by someone known to them (51 percent) as they are by strangers (49 percent).[39]
- Violent victimization of women is more likely to be repetitive and occurring over a period of time rather than as an isolated event, a random attack by a stranger, or a secondary consequence of being a crime victim (i.e., a robbery victim who is assaulted by the assailant).
- Even when women are the offenders rather than the victims, the data suggest that more than half of incidences in which women were arrested for killing a male intimate partner were precipitated by some sort of physical attack by their victim or claims of self-defense.[40]
- Women who are victimized by nonstrangers are less likely to report their victimization. A study of 4,446 college women indicated that 95 percent of the women who were raped did not report this to the police, and 100 percent of attempts of sexual coercion were not reported to the police.[41]
- Blacks were victims of overall violence, robbery, aggravated assault, and personal theft at rates higher than those for Whites in 2003. Blacks and Whites were equally likely to experience rape or sexual assault in that same year.
- Native Americans experienced violence at a rate significantly higher than all other races. Among Native Americans age 25 to 34, the rate of violent crime victimizations was more than 2 1/2 times the rate for all persons the same age.[42] Between 1992 and 2001, Native Americans

12–24

The age of individuals who have the greatest chance of becoming victims of crime, especially violent crime.

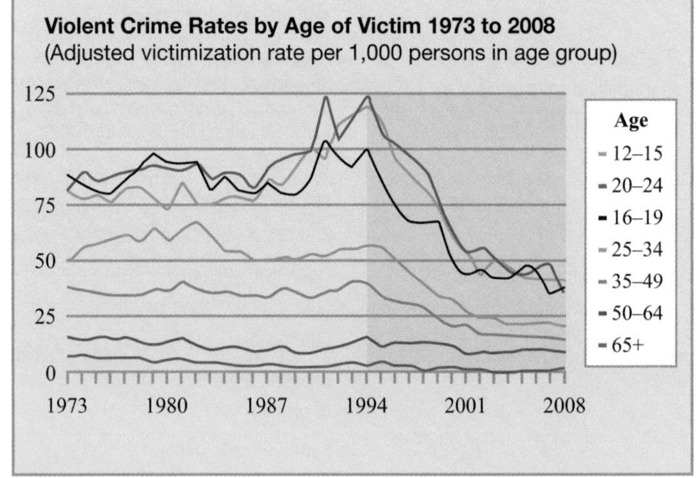

FIGURE 2.2 Victimization is not randomly distributed. One factor which influences the rate of victimization is the age of the victim. The relationship between age of the victim and rate of victimization has remained constant over the past 30 years.

Victims of crime are not randomly spread out among the general population; rather, there are highly consistent patterns of victimization regarding who will be victimized, when, and where.

conflict theories theories based on the idea that the most politically and socially powerful individuals and organizations use the legal system to exploit less-powerful individuals and to retain their power and privileges

feminist criminology the proposal that female criminal behavior is caused by the political, economic, and social inequality of men and women

victimology the study of victims and the patterns of how they are victimized

experienced violence at rates more than twice that of Blacks, 2 1/2 times the rate of Whites, and 4 1/2 times that of Asians.

- Hispanics were victims of overall violence at about the same rate as non-Hispanics. However, Hispanics were significantly more likely to be victims of aggravated assault than were non-Hispanics.
- In general, the wealthier a person is, the less chance there is that he or she will be a victim of violence. According to 2003 data, the relationship between victimization and income varies but is not consistent in all categories of victimization.

Situational Characteristics of Victimization

Just as victimization is not randomly distributed among types of persons, neither is it randomly distributed in time or place. Because U.S. society is highly segregated based on people's personal characteristics, especially race and income, it is not all that surprising to find that spatial patterns of victimization are highly correlated with the demographic distribution of persons. Victimization is more likely to occur in places where there is a high density of high-risk social groups.

Urban centers hold the bulk of those living at or below the poverty level in the United States, and the victimization rate for cities reflects this fact. In 2002, urban residents had a rate of violent victimization nearly 1.5 times that of rural residents. Suburban and rural residents were victimized at similar rates. However, some small cities are now experiencing a rise in crime rates, especially violent crimes. Some attribute the increase to "dislocation"—that is, as larger cities make it more difficult for criminals to prey on victims, criminals are leaving cities and moving their illegal activities to smaller cities.[43]

Theoretical Explanations for Victimization

National data support the observation that crime victimization is not random. If this is the case, then what are the factors that influence who is victimized and when the victimization occurs? Scholars in the field generate both descriptive data of victimization and theories to explain this phenomenon. Just as criminologists use crime data to construct theories to explain why some people commit crimes and others do not, scholars who study victimization construct theories to explain why some people are victims and others are not.

The two most prominent explanations as to the cause of victimization are victim-precipitation theories and lifestyle theories of victimization.

Victim-Precipitation Theories These theories are based on the concept that victims themselves precipitate, contribute to, provoke, or actually cause the outcome. These theories assume that some crimes, especially violent crimes, are interactions, or transactions, between victims and offenders. The victim often influences his or her own criminal victimization.

Victim precipitation means that the victim is not simply an object acted upon by a criminal. Victim precipitation is said to have three facets:[44]

HERE'S SOMETHING TO THINK ABOUT . . .

A criticism of victimology theories is that these theories place "blame on the victim." Women's rights groups argue victimology theories suggest that the victim of a sexual assault contributes to the crime by her behavior, dress, lifestyle, or provocation. They argue there is a double standard in that victims of sexual assault are held responsible for their victimization whereas victims of other violent crimes are not labeled as contributing to the crime. Do you agree with this criticism?

1. **Victim contribution** refers to a person's action or lack of action that makes their victimization more likely.
2. **Victim proneness** implies that some individuals or groups have a quality that makes them more likely to become victims of crimes. This can also refer to the fact that some victims are easy targets. For instance, illegal immigrants may be targeted because they cannot report victimization to the police for fear of being deported.
3. **Victim provocation**, the third dimension of victim-precipitation theory, suggests that the victim is the primary cause of his or her victimization. Marvin Wolfgang's 1958 study of Philadelphia homicides, taken from police records for the years 1948 to 1952, brought the concept of victim provocation into the mainstream of criminological thought. Wolfgang found that, in a significant proportion of criminal homicide incidents (26 percent), the victim had actually initiated the confrontation, either verbally or through physical force.[45]

Lifestyle Theories of Victimization These theories seek to explain why victimization can differ in quantity but remain the same in quality. Researchers examined household data taken from surveys in eight cities in 1972. In the examination of the data, researchers found that although rates of victimization fluctuated from city to city, individual and situational factors within each locale remained much the same. For example, in all eight cities, youths were at a much greater risk of victimization than older persons, and men had substantially higher rates of victimization than women.

victim-precipitation theories theories based on the concept that victims in some way contribute to or provoke crimes committed against them

victim contribution the idea that victims' actions or lack of action creates the likelihood of their being victimized

victim proneness the idea that certain victims are likely to be targeted as victims because of some individual or group quality that they have

victim provocation the idea that a victim is the main cause of his or her victimization

The researchers found that the following conditions were met:

- The victim and offender had the opportunity to come in contact with one other.
- There was some dispute between the two.
- The offender was willing to use force or stealth to achieve his or her goal.

The researchers believed that these factors were based largely on the victim's lifestyle.

Theory of Personal Victimization Lifestyle stands as the centerpiece of the **theory of personal victimization** because it is the patterned routines of a person's everyday activities that predict the chances of exposure to high-risk situations. For example, an individual's socioeconomic status places constraints on his or her place of residence, access to post-secondary education, access to jobs, and the like.

Differential association refers to the concept that people who associate regularly with others engaged in unlawful behavior are more likely to be victimized because of their increased exposure to high-risk situations and environments.

Routine Activities Theory Another theory of victimization focuses on the contexts of crime in terms of the opportunities for victimization. In 1979, Lawrence Cohen and Marcus Felson developed an approach for analyzing changes in the level of crime over time known as **routine activities theory.**[46] Like lifestyle theories, it recognizes the importance of people's everyday actions in an explanation for criminal victimization. Routine activities theorists assume that all humans are motivated by the desire to have things that give them pleasure or benefit and to avoid those things and situations that inflict pain. Most important to the explanation for criminal victimization, according to Cohen and Felson, are the differential opportunities that exist for victimization.

Differential opportunities are determined by the structure of our everyday lives: the time we leave home, the route we take to work, our mode of transportation, our favorite places for entertainment, and other routines of contemporary existence. Routine activities theory focuses on the circumstances in which crime occurs.

The routine activities approach to crime is limited to an explanation for predatory crime. Cohen and Felson define **predatory crime** as acts "involving direct physical contact between at least one offender and at least one person or object which that offender attempts to take or damage."[47] Because Cohen and Felson include objects as well as persons in their definition of predatory crime, their theory is not limited to interpersonal offenses such as assault, robbery, and rape. Property offenses such as burglary and larceny are considered predatory crimes as well.

Predatory victimization depends on the interaction of three variables in a social situation:

1. the presence of at least one likely offender;
2. the presence of at least one suitable target; and
3. the absence of capable guardians (who might prevent the crime).

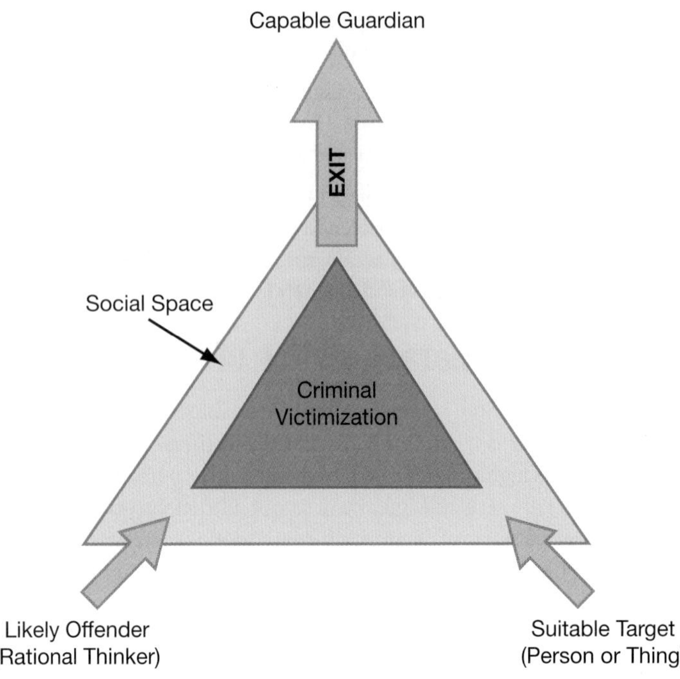

FIGURE 2.3 Cohen and Felson's routine activities theory emphasizes that crime does not occur in a vacuum. In other words, crime requires the interaction of an offender and a victim at a particular time and place. Thus, the lifestyle choices of a victim play an important role in whether or not a crime occurs. Also, the presence of a "capable guardian" may prevent a crime from occurring. In modern society many believe that video surveillance cameras can act as a "guardian" to deter crime. As a result, video surveillance of entire metropolitan areas is common.

Figure 2.3 shows the relationships among these three variables in any situation or "social space" where there is an opportunity for crime. The suitable target arrives in this space through lifestyle behaviors. The likely offender arrives through rational choices. The opportunity for crime is enhanced as the potential guardian departs or is absent from the space.

Rational Choice Theory of Crime The key assumption of routine activities theory is the idea that crime is motivated through rational choice. Rational choice theory is based on the fundamental belief that human behavior is directed toward those things that bring pleasure or benefit or that minimize painful, unpleasant experiences.

If rational choice theorists are correct, altering the balance of costs and benefits for likely offenders can reduce victimization. One way to do this is called **target hardening.** Target hardening is the foundation for many popular crime-reduction programs. Crime-prevention programs, such as Neighborhood Watch programs, programs to increase the level of lighting in streets and neighborhoods, and surveillance cameras, are based on the assumption that these changes will cause the potential criminal to reevaluate the risk of committing a

theory of personal victimization the theory that a person's lifestyle contributes to the predictability of high-risk situations

differential association the concept that those who associate with people engaged in criminal activities are at risk of being victimized

routine activities theory an analysis of changes in levels of crime over time that recognizes people's everyday actions as components of victimization

differential opportunities the chances of individuals being victimized based on the structure of their everyday lives

predatory crime crime involving direct physical contact between the offender and his or her target, which may be a person or an object, that the offender intends to damage or take

target hardening crime-prevention measures such as Neighborhood Watch groups, antitheft devices, and increased street lighting

HERE'S SOMETHING TO THINK ABOUT . . .

In 2011, federal prosecutors announced an aggressive attack on illegal Internet gambling. Although online poker is illegal in the United States, the Internet allows access to sites in other countries where it is legal. Some question whether U.S. law applies to such online gambling operations. Others question whether online gambling should even be a crime. What do you think?

crime in these target-hardened environments. Another example of target hardening is vehicles that have integrated ignition–steering wheel locking systems, antitheft alarms, built-in global tracking devices, and satellite-activated ignition cut-off systems.

Target hardening is one of the key components of defense against terrorist attacks in the United States. Particularly attractive targets of terrorism—such as commercial aviation, nuclear reactors, federal buildings, infrastructure (e.g., bridges and tunnels), and symbolic targets (e.g., famous monuments and symbols of government and business)—have been examined for their vulnerability, and additional security measures have been taken to make it more difficult to attack these targets.

The Victims' Rights Movement

Several events were key to the emergence of the **victims' rights movement**. First, the 1960s brought general concern about individual rights in many arenas, including civil rights, women's rights, inmates' rights, gay rights, and students' rights. The women's rights movement was a particularly strong supporter of victims' rights because its agenda included addressing the harms caused by the way in which the criminal justice system processed rape cases and domestic violence cases. Second, several government initiatives increased awareness and provided financial support for victim-assistance programs. Results from national surveys helped raise awareness of the harms caused by crime and documented the large number of victims who do not report their victimization to the police. The Law Enforcement Assistance Administration (LEAA) provided funds to assist in the professionalization of law enforcement. The LEAA also provided funds for the support of innovative programs to reduce crime and research to evaluate the impact of these programs. Third, the number of victims' rights organizations increased dramatically, and national coordinating bodies such as the **National Organization for Victim Assistance (NOVA)** were founded.[48]

The accomplishments of NOVA, founded in 1976, include helping to pass the 1984 Victims of Crime Act and the 1982 Victim and Witness Protection Act, both of which provide counseling, information, referrals, and direct assistance to crime victims, as well as support and training to victim advocates.[49] President Ronald Reagan adopted victims' rights as one of his priority domestic policy issues. He convened the President's Task Force on Victims of Crime in 1982. This task force made more than 60 recommendations for new legislation to be enacted to protect the rights and interests of crime victims in the criminal justice system.

The victims' rights movement has had tremendous success. Almost all the legislative initiatives proposed by the 1982 President's Task Force have been enacted. All 50 states have passed a crime victims' bill of rights, attempting to ensure that victims are treated with dignity and compassion, are informed about the decisions made regarding their cases, and are able to participate in this decision making. Some 29 states have amended their constitutions to focus on the rights of crime victims. Several federal laws have also been passed. In 1982, the federal Victim and Witness Protection Act established policies and procedures regarding how federal officials should treat crime victims and also served as a national model for state legislation.

Crime Victims' Rights Act of 2004 The 2004 federal crime victims' rights legislation was the outgrowth of an eight-year campaign led by Senators Jon Kyl (R–AZ) and Dianne Feinstein (D–CA) to provide strong assurances to crime victims that their rights would be recognized by the criminal justice system. The federal legislation was passed by Congress in early October 2004 and signed into law by President Bush on October 30, 2004.

The new law, known as the **Crime Victims' Rights Act**, is the most successful effort of the crime victims' rights movement to date. The law amends Title 18 (Part II, Chapter 25/Section 3771) of the Federal Criminal Code. Federal law now guarantees crime victims the following rights: to be reasonably protected, notified, present, and heard at various stages in the criminal justice system; to confer with the prosecutor; to receive restitution; to expect proceedings free from unreasonable delay; and to be treated with fairness and respect.

"Victimless" Crimes? Can There Be a Crime Without a Victim?

Edwin M. Schur defined victimless crimes as crimes that do not have any evident victim.[50] Victimless crimes usually include drug use, prostitution, suicide (and assisted suicide), abortion, gambling, and exhibitionism.

Victimless crimes have a certain degree of arbitrariness to them, as the behavior might be defined as criminal in one jurisdiction but not in another or a violation of the moral values of one group—even

victims' rights movement a movement that emerged from public concern about civil rights, women's rights, gay rights, students' rights, inmates' rights, and from government initiatives for increased victim awareness and financial compensation

National Organization for Victim Assistance (NOVA) an organization that helped to pass the 1984 Victims of Crime Act and the 1982 Victim and Witness Protection Act, both of which provide counseling, information, and assistance to crime victims

Crime Victims' Rights Act enacted in 2004, a law that guarantees crime victims a number of rights, including the right to be involved in various stages of the criminal justice system and the rights to protection and restitution

HERE'S SOMETHING TO THINK ABOUT . . .

Sixteen states and Washington, D.C. have passed legislation that allows for the use, cultivation, and possession of marijuana for medical purposes. However, these acts are still illegal under federal law. There is tremendous debate as to whether certain drug use should be legal, whether drug use is deviant behavior, even if drug use is harmful. How do drug laws reflect social and community values?

a minority group—but not of another. For example, prostitution is criminal behavior in Clark County, Nevada, but it is considered a legal business and occupation in neighboring Nye County, Nevada. Also, 16 states and Washington, D.C. have passed laws to allow the medical use of marijuana. However, marijuana use for any reason remains illegal in other states and under federal law.

One of the most common justifications of the criminalization of victimless crimes is that, although there might be no apparent harm to persons or property, the behavior harms society, and under the legal construct of the law, the victim is society. This justification is commonly used in defending laws against drug use, prostitution, and gambling. For instance, many policymakers express the concern that widespread gambling will lead to increased crime, drug and alcohol use, and other social or psychological problems—all of which will be a financial burden to society. "They worry that gambling and its consequences will destroy individual lives, wreck families, and weaken societal institutions" or they believe that "compulsive or pathological gamblers will turn to drug sales or other crimes to finance their habit and pay their debts."[51]

Often, those who oppose the criminalization of victimless crimes organize and attempt to pass legislation that would legalize or decriminalize the behavior. Proponents of medical use of marijuana, physician-assisted suicide, and prostitution have formed organizations to work to change society's treatment of these behaviors. For example, in a new wave of activism, many prostitutes are organizing, staging public events, and coming out publicly to demand greater acceptance and protection.[52] "Advocates of prostitute rights contend that it is a viable source of income for many women and that sexual activity between adults for money should be treated as any other form of legal labor."[53]

Opponents of legalized prostitution argue that there is a connection between those who hire prostitutes and those who sexually exploit children, and that women who engage in prostitution are "victims of sadistic and predatory violence by customers, and scores suffer from drug addiction and mental illness."[54]

Civil Remedies for Victims Because compensation and restitution have limitations, crime victims are increasingly relying on civil litigation as another way to help them recover from the harms caused by crime. Victims have used **civil remedies**—civil court processes to recover from the psychological, financial, emotional, and physical harms of crime. Civil suits are particularly empowering because crime victims are directly involved in these cases. A victim decides to pursue a civil action against the offender, a third party, or both; works directly with his or her attorney to prove liability; and chooses to accept or reject a settlement offer. The goal of such civil suits is to help victims work through the trauma caused by crimes, recover expenses from crimes, and restore confidence in their ability to control their own destinies.[55]

A good example of a civil remedy is the O.J. Simpson case. Simpson was acquitted at his criminal trial in 1995 for the murders of Nicole Brown and Ronald Goldman. However, the victims' families brought a civil action against Simpson, and he was found liable for damages. The families were awarded a $33.5 million civil judgment.[56]

Crime victims can also bring suits against third parties for contributing to their victimization. Universities, hotels, restaurants, shopping malls, and office buildings can be sued for their failure to protect victims because of negligence or failures in security. These lawsuits encourage businesses and other organizations to enhance their safety and security measures and encourage others to invest in preventive actions to avoid being sued.[57]

Despite the advantages of civil remedies, there are some disadvantages. In a civil lawsuit, the financial burden falls on the victim. The victim is responsible for obtaining and paying an attorney and all of the investigation costs in pursuing the civil case. Some attorneys might agree to take civil cases based on contingency. Contingency means that an attorney agrees to forgo payment in return for a percentage of the potential settlement.

Counting Crime

Crime statistics and measures of the criminal justice system are subject to error, and the further one goes back, the more prominent the errors appear. Today, various official agencies, such as the Federal Bureau of Investigation, the **Bureau of Justice Statistics**, and the National Criminal Justice Reference Service, gather and disseminate data about nearly every aspect of the criminal justice system.

Criminologists use the FBI's Uniform Crime Report, a database of local and state crimes that are reported; the National Incident-Based Reporting System, which provides detailed information about such crimes; and the National Victimization Crime Survey, which includes survey information from victims, many of which do not report their victimization, to identify trends in crime.

civil remedies processes in civil courts that enable victims to recover from the psychological, financial, emotional, and physical damages of crime

Bureau of Justice Statistics a federal agency that gathers and disseminates data about almost all aspects of the criminal justice system

As you read in Chapter 1, public fears about controlling crime and maintaining order arose during social upheavals dating to the 1950s, but the roots of those fears began in the 1920s, when crime was perceived mainly as a big-city problem. After World War I, more people migrated to the cities. As urban populations swelled, the public became more concerned with crime. In the 1920s, Cleveland, Ohio, and Chicago, Illinois, were among the first major cities to perform crime surveys.[58,59] These surveys were motivated by the desire to correct what were perceived as major deficiencies in the criminal justice system. The basic premise was that the absence of crime is the best measure of police effectiveness. If reforms to the criminal justice system were effective, it was believed that the results would be reflected in decreasing crime rates.[60]

The public perception that the Great Depression of the 1930s brought a crime wave heightened interest in crime statistics. The news media exaggerated the crime wave with colorful stories of organized crime figures and infamous public enemies such as John Dillinger, Charles "Pretty Boy" Floyd, George "Baby Face" Nelson, and Bonnie Parker and Clyde Barrow. Stories of bank robberies were front-page news. The public was entertained with stories of shoot-outs with the police.

The average citizen was left with the impression that crime was everywhere and no one could do much about it. Without a way to determine objectively whether crime was increasing or decreasing, the public had no idea which side—the criminal justice system or the criminals—was winning. Without crime statistics, it was not possible to determine the impact of the money spent, the resources invested, reform efforts, or new laws on the problem of crime.

Two important measures of crime statistics to emerge are the Uniform Crime Report and the National Crime Victimization Survey (see Figure 2.4).

The Uniform Crime Report

On June 11, 1930, Congress passed the first federal legislation mandating the collecting of crime data. The Federal Bureau of Investigation was charged with the responsibility of collecting crime data from police departments and disseminating the data to the nation.

The Crime Clock One of the initial data-presentation strategies used by the FBI, which is still in use today, is the **Crime Clock**, which reports how often a crime occurs. The Crime Clock is used to emphasize that crime is occurring nearly all of the time. For example, according to the Crime Clock in 2009, larceny-theft occurred every 5 seconds, burglary was committed every 14.3 seconds, and aggravated assault every 39.1 seconds. Based on the Crime Clock, it is easy for citizens to conclude that they can hardly walk outside their homes without becoming a crime statistic. These data are distorted, however. Although it might be accurate to say that a murder occurs every 34.5 minutes, this does not mean that every 34.5 minutes a murder occurs in every community. It means that every 34.5 minutes a murder occurs somewhere in the United States.

Uses of UCR Data Over the years, crime data collected by the FBI and published under the title **Uniform Crime Report (UCR)** have become useful as databases for examining crime trends. These data have numerous purposes: as a measure of crime rates, as a factor in indexes calculating the quality of life in U.S. cities, and as a factor in policy decisions. Based on UCR trend data, municipalities might decide to add more police officers to their forces. Grants aimed at crime prevention and curbing drug crime use UCR data to measure effectiveness. The release of new UCR data is often anxiously awaited by many agencies because they want to know whether recent changes such as community policing, neighborhood watches, and "get-tough" sentencing policies have had an impact on the crime rate.

UCR Data Collection The UCR had its origins at a time when there were no computers, no computerized databases, and no statistics and graphics software. Crime data were collected, stored, and transmitted manually. Collecting and reporting crime data were labor-intensive processes. Most police departments kept file cabinets filled with cards detailing each crime. The cards were arranged by case number and offense and were filed under the various crime categories (murder, rape, burglary, etc.). Anyone wanting to know the number of burglaries committed during a particular period, for example, had to go to the file cabinet, pull the cards for burglary, and count the number of cards one by one. Under the circumstances, the FBI had to adopt rules for counting crimes that were consistent with the limitations imposed by the system.

The Hierarchy Rule Each crime card contained the information for one case or incident based only on the most serious charge. However, during a single incident, several crimes might have been committed. A person might have been both robbed and assaulted, and both crimes would be noted in one police report, recorded on one card, and filed under "Robbery." This method of counting only the most serious

	UCR	NCVS
Geographic coverage	National and state estimates, local agency reports	National estimates
Collection method	Reports by law enforcement to the FBI on a monthly basis	Survey of 42,093 households and 77,852 individuals age 12 or older were interviewed
Measures	8 Part I Index crimes and 19 lesser crimes reported by law enforcement	Reported and unreported crime; details about the crimes, victims, and offenders

FIGURE 2.4 Comparison of the UCR and the NCVS
There are several important differences between the crime data reported by the FBI's Uniform Crime Report and the Bureau of Justice Statistics National Crime Victimization Survey. These differences include who collects the data, how the data are collected, and what data are collected. The differences result in different crime statistics reported.

Source: Bureau of Justice Statistics, 2010.

Crime Clock a method used by the FBI to report how often crimes occur

Uniform Crime Report (UCR) a database of information about reported crimes collected by the FBI over time

crime in incidents involving multiple crimes is called the **hierarchy rule**. Also, if more than one victim was involved in an incident (e.g., a group of people was robbed), the UCR reported only the most serious offense for the incident as a whole and not for individual victims. As one can imagine, the use of the hierarchy rule results in an undercounting of crime.

The UCR does not report data for all crimes. It provides data for only 27 criminal violations, which are divided into two categories: serious crimes and less-serious crimes.[61] The serious crimes are reported in Part I of the UCR, and the less-serious crimes are reported in Part II. The first eight crimes listed in Part I are called the Crime Index. Part I and Part II crimes are listed in Table 2.2.

Clearance Rate The **clearance rate** refers to the percentage of crimes solved versus those that are unsolved. *Solved* means that the police believe they know the perpetrator of a crime; however, it does not mean that the perpetrator has been arrested, prosecuted, convicted, or incarcerated. It merely means that the police are reasonably certain that they know who committed the crime. In most cases, a crime is "cleared" by the arrest of the suspect, but police consider a crime cleared if they believe the suspect committed the crime, regardless of whether there is a conviction. Other cases in which a crime is cleared even though the suspect is not charged or tried include the suspect's death, immunity from arrest, or flight beyond the reach of U.S. law enforcement.

Why UCR Data Are Inadequate There are several major shortcomings of UCR data that encourage the collection of crime data by other means. One shortcoming is that UCR data represent only crimes that are known to the police; unreported crimes are not included. The lack

TABLE 2.2 FBI's *Uniform Crime Report*, Part I and Part II Offenses

Part I Offenses (Crime Index)	Part II Offenses
Criminal Homicide Murder, nonnegligent manslaughter, and nonjustifiable homicide. Manslaughter by negligence is a Part I crime but is not included in the Crime Index.	**Simple Assault** No weapon or serious injury
Forcible Rape "Carnal knowledge," includes sexual assault; does not include statutory offenses	**Forgery and Counterfeiting**
Robbery "Taking" or attempting to take anything of value from a person by force, threat, or fear	**Fraud**
Aggravated Assault Attack on a person for the purpose of inflicting bodily harm, usually through use of a weapon	**Embezzlement**
Burglary Breaking or entering a structure to commit a felony or theft, including attempt	**Stolen Property** Buying, selling, and receiving
Larceny Includes theft of property that does not involve force, violence, or fraud	**Prostitution and Commercialized Vice**
Motor Vehicle Theft Does not include motorboats, construction equipment, airplanes, or farming equipment	**Sex Offenses** Statutory rape and offenses against morality
Arson Willful or malicious burning or attempt to burn any property for any reason	**Drug Abuse Violations** State or local laws against unlawful possession, sale, use, growing, or manufacturing of opium, cocaine, morphine, heroin, codeine, marijuana, and other narcotic and dangerous nonnarcotic drugs
	Gambling
	Offenses against Family and Children Nonsupport, neglect, desertion, abuse
	Driving Under the Influence Of alcohol or drugs
	Liquor Laws State or local laws
	Drunkenness
	Disorderly Conduct
	Vagrancy
	All Other Violations Of state or local laws
	Suspicion Suspect released without charge
	Curfew and Loitering Laws Persons under age 18
	Runaways Persons under age 18 in protective custody

Source: Federal Bureau of Investigation, *Uniform Crime Report,* 2009.

hierarchy rule an old police method of counting only the most serious crime in a single incident involving multiple crimes

clearance rate the percentage of crimes solved versus those that are unsolved

of this type of information is particularly significant: People often do not report crimes because they have a lack of confidence in the police, including the lack of confidence in the ability of the police to do something about the crime, the lack of confidence that the police are not corrupt, and the lack of confidence that no harm will befall innocent people if they report a crime.

In addition, the UCR (1) includes data only about local and state crimes, not federal offenses; and (2) depends on the voluntary cooperation of local and state police agencies for data collection. When the UCR began, federal law enforcement agencies did not play as prominent a role in crime fighting as they do today. Today, nearly all local and state police agencies report crime data to the FBI, but this was not always the case. In the early years, many local police departments did not report crime data because they lacked adequate record keeping or personnel to gather the facts, they feared embarrassment, or they simply did not want to report the data. To this day, there is no official sanction of local and state police for failing to report crime data to the FBI.

Finally, UCR data are about local and state crimes, but definitions of crimes are not the same from place to place. In one jurisdiction, a felony theft might be defined as the taking of property valued at $100, whereas in another jurisdiction, the limit for felony theft might be $1,000. One of the most troublesome problems with UCR data is the definition of *rape.* The UCR uses a definition that is not as inclusive as the one used by states that have adopted progressive sexual assault criminal codes. The UCR defines *forcible rape* as "the carnal knowledge of a female forcibly and against her will." In 2011, the UCR redefined "forcible rape" to bring it in line with the contemporary definition used by most states.

The National Incident-Based Reporting System

The FBI recognized the shortcomings of the old UCR crime data survey methods and instituted a plan to address many of these problems. Taking advantage of the computer technology that is now available in crime reporting, the new system, called the **National Incident-Based Reporting System (NIBRS)**, is now more than a simple frequency count of crime. Under NIBRS, additional data about crimes will be reported, including information about the place of occurrence, the weapon used, the type and value of property damaged or stolen, personal characteristics of the offender and the victim, the nature of any relationship between the two, the disposition of the complaint, and so on. The new NIBRS data will provide much more insight into the crime picture, and researchers will have greater success in correlating crime data with other factors suspected of contributing to the incidence of crime and effective crime prevention.

Other Sources of Crime Data

National Crime Victimization Survey Another major data collection effort to address the shortcomings of the UCR data is the **National Crime Victimization Survey (NCVS)**. The NCVS dates back to 1972, when it was recognized that a significant number of crimes go unreported to the police. Some of the reasons that crime victims do not report crime to the police are that they believe the police will or can do nothing about it, they fear retaliation and further victimization, they fear that they will be arrested because of their immigration status, or they believe that the police are part of the problem.

The NCVS collects victimization information from a representative sample of U.S. households.[62] Each household in the sample is interviewed twice a year, and a household is part of the national sample for 3.5 years. The NCVS was authorized in 1972, and the first survey was conducted in 1973. The goals of the victimization survey were

- to develop detailed information about the victims of crime;
- to initiate a data-collection effort detailing the consequences of crime;
- to provide systematic information about the dark figures of crime by estimating the number and types of crimes not reported to police;
- to provide uniform measures of selected types of crime; and
- to permit comparisons of crimes over time and types of areas.[63]

The NCVS gathers data about crime incidents such as the relationship between the victim and the offender, any use of drugs or alcohol, bystander behavior, suspected offender gang involvement, and self-protection measures taken by the victim. The survey gathers data from crime victims; thus, it does not gather data about homicide. The following list shows the kinds of data included in the NCVS.

Type of criminal victimization
Month in which victimization occurred
Time at which victimization occurred
Location of victimization
Victim–offender relationship
Self-protective actions taken
Self-protection outcomes
Type of property loss
Crime reporting to police
Reasons for nonreporting
Offender characteristics
Drug and alcohol use
Victim characteristics
Psychological consequences for the victim
Financial consequences for the victim

The NCVS does provide important data not gathered by the Uniform Crime Report, but it also has deficiencies. The NCVS depends on

National Incident-Based Reporting System (NIBRS) a database that includes specific data about reported crimes, including the place of occurrence, weapon used, type and value of property damaged or stolen, and personal characteristics of any relationship between the offender and the victim

National Crime Victimization Survey (NCVS) a survey that gathers detailed information about crimes from victims using a representative sample of U.S. households

self-reported data by the victim, which may be inaccurate. The survey is sent to households, so it does not reliably pinpoint the geographical location where the crimes occurred, as do the UCR data. Also, household members who have previously withheld information about victimization from family members are not likely to report their victimization in the NCVS.

The early surveys were called the National Crime Survey (NCS). After about two decades of data gathering, shortcomings of the NCS data were revealed. As a result of demands for better data on violence against women, the NCS was revised in 1993 to provide more information on the extent of victimization that occurred within families. Also, methodological adjustments were made in the NCS to help people recall victimization more accurately in order to increase reliability. As a result of these changes, there are some cautions that should be observed when comparing trends in data prior to 1993 to trends in data after 1993 (see Figure 2.5).

Comparisons between UCR data and NCVS data have consistently confirmed the belief that there was, indeed, a vast difference between reported crime data and victimization data. A comparison of the reported incidents of sexual assault by the NCVS and the UCR indicates that the UCR significantly underreports sex crimes. In 2002, the UCR reported 95,136 forcible rapes, whereas the NCVS reported 322,060 rapes. Robbery, aggravated assault, burglary, and larceny were all reported by the NCVS at rates two or three times greater than the rates given in the UCR data.

With data from two databases, researchers can compare trends in the data of reported crime to estimated total crime. Often, these data are revealing, as reported crime in the UCR might increase not because of an actual increase in the crime rate, but because of the increase in reported crime.

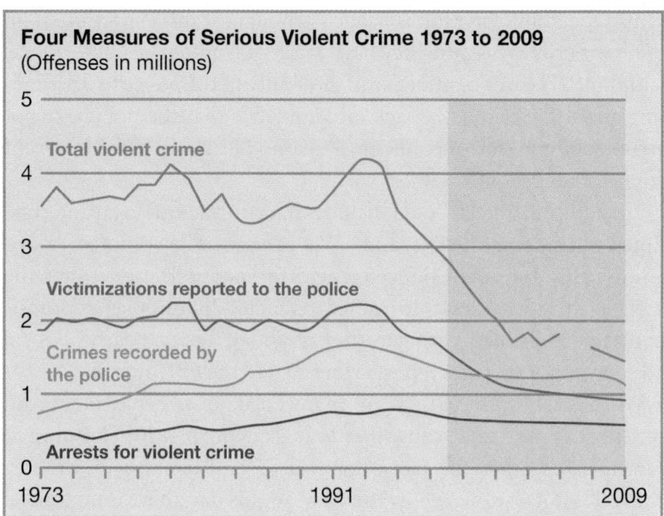

Figure 2.5 The serious violent crimes included are rape, robbery, aggravated assault, and homicide. Although each measure is different, both the NCVS and the UCR show that serious violent crime levels declined in recent years. The NCVs redesign was implemented in 1993; the area with the lighter shading is before the redesign and the darker area is after the redesign. Also, NCVS determined the data for 2006 are not comparable with other years due to changes in survey design; therefore, the data are omitted from the chart. The data before 1993 are adjusted to make them comparable with data collected since the redesign. The NCVS is a household survey of about 134,000 persons age 12 and older in 77,200 households twice each year about their victimizations from crime.

Source: Bureau of Justice Statistics, Key Facts at a Glance, http://bjs.ojp.usdoj.gov/content/glance/cv2.cfm, July 3, 2011.

HERE'S SOMETHING TO THINK ABOUT . . .

Cultural deviance theorists posit criminality is the result of different value systems and norms among dominant cultural groups and minority subcultural groups. The changing demographics of American society give new life to these theories. Studies project that Latinos will become the largest minority group in the United States. There are more than 7 million Muslims in the United States and their influence is becoming more evident upon the American culture and criminal justice system. The criminal justice system to a large extent is based upon the values of a "white, middle-class, Protestant, economically grounded" society. As the demographics shift conflicts emerge between the dominant cultural values and the values of the increasingly powerful subcultures. In what ways, if any, do you see the criminal justice system changing to reflect the values and norms of subcultural groups?

CHAPTER 2

Crime: Why and How Much

Check It!

1 WHAT influence did classical and neoclassical criminological theorists have on modern criminology and the criminal justice system? p. 18

In the 1770s, Cesare Beccaria, founder of classical criminology, first developed the concepts on which the American criminal justice system is based: innocent until proven guilty, the right to a trial by a jury of one's peers, the right of appeal, and so on. Jeremy Bentham, founder of neoclassical criminology, shared most of Beccaria's views, but he believed in mitigating circumstances and thought that punishment should fit the crime. Bentham's neoclassical theory provided the foundation of the English criminal justice system and hence the American justice system. Both Beccaria and Bentham departed from earlier views of crime in that they believed that crime was a matter of free will, rather than evil spirits or moral weakness.

2 HOW did earlier biological theories of crime evolve into the modern explanations of biological causation of crime? p. 20

Early biological theories of crime focused almost entirely on criminality as an inherited trait, whereas modern biocriminologists have come to accept that environmental factors, as well as inherited predispositions to crime, play a role in criminal behavior.

3 HOW can criminality be explained in terms of Freud's psychoanalytic theory? p. 22

Freud's psychoanalytic theory explains criminal behavior as resulting from unresolved psychological conflict caused by feelings of guilt, which lead an individual to commit crimes as a form of self-punishment.

4 WHAT are the basic tenets of the major sociological explanations for criminal behavior? p. 23

1. Social disorganization theories explain criminal behavior as resulting from disruptive social forces and from factors relating to low status, such as poverty, illiteracy, unemployment, illegitimacy, and deteriorating communities.
2. Differential association theory explains criminal behavior as being learned in peer groups that reinforce and reward such behavior.
3. Social control theories emphasize the role of social and cultural values as influencing whether or not individuals engage in criminal behavior.
4. Strain theory proposes that people resort to crime out of frustration when they cannot find legitimate means of economic success.
5. Cultural deviance theories emphasize the influence of deviant subcultures on criminal behavior.
6. Conflict theories focus on inequalities in society as the reason for criminality.

5 HOW do the major victimology theories explain what factors influence victimization? p. 28

Victimization is not random, but occurs in highly consistent patterns and demographics.

6 WHAT agencies maintain accurate statistics, and how do these affect the criminal justice system? p. 32

National databases such as the UCR, NIBRS, and NCVS collect data that centralize and identify crime rates and trends; detailed information about reported crimes, criminals, and their victims; and similar detailed information about unreported crimes, respectively. These data also provide criminologists with insight into specific crimes and trends in crimes, and the ability to correlate crime data and develop effective crime-prevention measures.

Assess Your Understanding

1. What was the difference between classical theories of crime causation and early nonscientific theories?
   a. Early nonscientific theories were based on the assumption that crime was caused by biological flaws in humans.
   b. Classical theories were based on experimental data, and nonscientific theories were not.
   c. Classical theories assumed crime was a free-will choice.
   d. Classical theories assumed crime was caused by demons, spirits, or supernatural causes.

2. Which of the following reflects the difference between Beccaria's and Bentham's theories of crime causation?
   a. Beccaria assumed crime was caused by hereditary traits, and Bentham assumed crime was caused by psychological traits.
   b. Beccaria assumed crime was caused by demons, and Bentham assumed crimes were caused by weak moral character.
   c. There is no difference between the two theories.
   d. Beccaria provided no exceptions for criminal liability, whereas Bentham believed in mitigating circumstances.

3. Who is known as "the founder of classical criminology"?
   a. Darwin
   b. Beccaria
   c. Goddard
   d. Lombroso

4. Which of the following proposed that crime was caused by hereditary traits?
   a. Dugdale and Goddard
   b. Bentham
   c. Freud
   d. Burgess

5. Which of the following posited crime was the result of subconscious motives and emotions?
   a. Lombroso
   b. Freud
   c. Christiansen
   d. Garofalo

6. Edwin Sutherland's theory of crime causation was based on which of the following fundamental principles?
   a. Crime is caused by hereditary traits.
   b. Crime is the result of subconscious motives and emotions.
   c. Crime is a free-will choice.
   d. Crime is a learned behavior.

7. Merton's strain theory classified persons who used criminal means to achieve their goals as which of the following?
   a. rebellion
   b. retreatism
   c. innovation
   d. ritualism

8. Which of the following measures of crime reported to the police are gathered and published by the Federal Bureau of Investigation?
   a. UCR
   b. NCVS
   c. CJS Crime Stat
   d. USA Crime Report

9. Which one of the following attributes crime to a loss of self-control and social control?
   a. Robert Park
   b. Albert Cohen
   c. Howard Becker
   d. Walter Reckless

10. According to the feminist perspective of criminology, what is the underlying cause of criminal behavior by females?
   a. inequality of power between men and women
   b. that females are biologically disposed to commit crimes
   c. failure of females to develop a moral code of ethics
   d. socialization with other females who commit crime

11. What is the fundamental principle underlying the study of criminal victimization?
   a. Criminal victimization is random.
   b. Criminal victimization is not randomly distributed among the populace.
   c. Nearly all victims are responsible for their own victimization due to their behavior.
   d. All persons are victimized at the same rate.

12. Which of the following is a Part I offense?
   a. sex offenses including statutory rape and offenses against morality
   b. forgery and counterfeiting
   c. arson
   d. embezzlement

ESSAY

1. What contributions did the early classical theorists of crime causation make to the understanding of crime and criminals?
2. Which theories of crime causation have been most influential upon the American criminal justice system? Why?
3. Compare and contrast the schools of criminological theories based on the underlying assumption of free will and biological, psychological, and sociological causation.
4. According to social determinism theories of crime causation, how do environmental factors influence criminal behavior?
5. What are some of the reasons why many of the programs to prevent juvenile delinquency are based on Edwin Sutherland's theory of differential association?
6. What are four ways of measuring crime? How do these measures differ from each other?
7. Why do reported crime and victimization data differ depending on the methodology used to collect the data?
8. What is the underlying assumption of victimization theories?

ANSWERS: 1. c, 2. d, 3. b, 4. a, 5. b, 6. d, 7. c, 8. a, 9. d, 10. a, 11. b, 12. c

Media

Go to the *Chapter 2: Crime: Why and How Much* section in *MyCJLab* to test your understanding of this chapter, access customized study content, engage in interactive simulations, complete critical thinking and research assignments, and view related online videos.

Additional Links

To read Cesare Beccaria's classical work *Of Crimes and Punishment*, go to www.constitution.org/cb/crim_pun.htm

One of the interesting proposals of Jeremy Bentham was the panopticon, a unique "all-seeing" prison that provided round-the-clock observations of prisoners, but prisoners could not see their observers. To see an image of the panopticon and read more information about it, see http://cartome.org/panopticon1.htm

The TruTV Web site has further information and illustrations related to Cesare Lombroso's theories of criminal man, at www.trutv.com/library/crime/criminal_mind/psychology/crime_motivation/4.html

For information about Sigmund Freud and to view his writings, view the Sigmund Freud Archives, at www.freudarchives.org/

The Victim Rights Law Center (VRLC) was established in 2003 as the first nonprofit law center in the nation solely dedicated to serving the needs of rape and sexual assault victims. To obtain information about the VRLC, go to www.victimrights.org/

See http://bjs.ojp.usdoj.gov/ to view crime and victimization statistics from the Bureau of Justice Statistics.

Some conflict theories emphasize the importance of cultural value differences between different groups. One major contemporary conflict is between the values held by certain persons of the Islamic faith and those of Western countries. This 60-minute presentation by Ayaan Hirsi Ali, a former member of the Dutch parliament, highlights her collaboration with filmmaker Theo van Gogh on the movie *Submission,* which criticized the treatment of women in Islamic societies. Mr. Van Gogh was assassinated in Amsterdam in 2004 by a Muslim man who was offended by the movie and had threatened Ms. Hirsi Ali. She also talked about the practice of Islam in Western countries and women's rights issues. To view the video, go to www.c-spanvideo.org/program/199197-1

For a video commemorating National Crime Victims' Rights Week, and highlighting the importance of victim rights legislation, visit www.youtube.com/watch?v=I3biv8e3-Ys

The 1956 film *The Bad Seed* addressed the debate between the role of nature versus nurture in the development of the criminal personality. For more information about the film and to watch a trailer, go to www.imdb.com/title/tt0048977/

For a short video on the work of Cesare Lombroso, father of criminology, go to www.youtube.com/watch?v=n29YBwBUTxM&feature=related

To download a copy of *The Jukes: A Study of Crime, Pauperism, Disease and Heredity* by Richard Dugdale, go to http://digitalarchive.gsu.edu/col_facpub/1/

In 2007, *Time* magazine listed serial killer Ted Bundy's crimes as one of the top 25 crimes of the century. To see this coverage, go to www.time.com/time/2007/crimes/14.html

To view of a presentation by Meda Chesney-Lind, feminist criminologist and editor of "Female Gangs in America," on women in gangs as part of the 2010–2011 "GANGS: Strategies to Break the Cycle of Violence" speaker series, go to www.youtube.com/watch?v=sKSgSvDgZG8. The series is produced by the UCLA Department of Social Welfare at the UCLA Luskin School of Public Affairs.

Go to www.fbi.gov/about-us/cjis/ucr/ucr to view information about the Federal Bureau of Investigation's *Uniform Crime Reports.*

CRIMINAL LAW CONTROL VERSUS LIBERTY

3

Laws represent the collective wisdom of the community as to how to best promote peaceful and fair interaction among persons. However, there is great diversity among the values of the millions of people in the nation so it is not surprising that often great conflict is generated when new laws are proposed. Thus, the process by which bills become law must protect the rights of all persons, especially minorities.

One example of the conflict that can be generated by new laws is the recent trend in a number of states to pass laws requiring voters to present identification to vote in elections. Those who support voter identification laws argue that requiring voters to present identification to vote will prevent voter fraud. Those opposed to voter identification laws argue that such laws disenfranchise voters, make it harder for some to vote, and is politically motivated to achieve these very outcomes.

The rise of voter identification bills started after the election of President Obama. Republicans claim voter identification laws are necessary to prevent voter fraud. Democrats claim the purpose of the law is to discourage the young, students, the poor, minorities, and new voters from participating in elections—voters who contributed significantly to the election of Obama as president in 2008.

When Rhode Island and South Carolina passed voter identification laws in 2011, former President Clinton lashed out against the laws claiming they were a return to post–Civil War Jim Crow segregation laws of the southern states. In response to South Carolina's law, the nation's strictest voter identification law, Jesse Jackson called for the U.S. Justice Department to overturn the South Carolina law based upon the state's past electoral discriminatory behavior. Jackson called the law a "modern poll tax" noting that the U.S. Supreme Court has declared poll taxes and literacy tests unconstitutional.

1 How are federal, state, and local criminal laws created and changed?

2 How are the limits imposed on criminal laws defined?

3 What are the elements of a crime that must be present to prosecute offenders?

4 What are the major defenses against charges of criminal conduct?

5 How are crimes categorized and defined according to the Model Penal Code?

This chapter examines the role of criminal law in defining the balance between control and liberty. It reviews the making of laws and the differences between laws of the federal, state, and local government. It discusses the limits of the law, the various criminal defenses, and the elements of some of the most common crimes.

LAWS REPRESENT THE COLLECTIVE WISDOM OF THE COMMUNITY AS TO HOW TO BEST PROMOTE PEACEFUL AND FAIR INTERACTION AMONG PERSONS.

The Rule of Law

After breaking away from England, the American colonists rejected both the Church and the king as supreme authorities and declared that the United States is founded on the superiority of the rule of law. The **rule of law** declares that the standards of behavior and privilege are established not by kings or religious leaders, but by rules and procedures that define and prohibit certain behaviors as illegal or criminal and prescribe punishments for those behaviors. All people, regardless of rank, title, position, status, or wealth, are accorded the same rights and privileges under the law. Three major categories of law are civil law, administrative law, and criminal law. This chapter focuses on an examination of criminal law.

The Making of Law

Why do governments—local, state, and federal—create criminal laws? The American Law Institute, a private, voluntary association of distinguished judges, lawyers, and law teachers, gives five reasons for the establishment of laws[1]:

1. to forbid and prevent conduct that unjustifiably and inexcusably inflicts or threatens substantial harm to individual or public interests;
2. to subject to public control persons whose conduct indicates that they are disposed to commit crimes;
3. to safeguard conduct that is without fault from condemnation as criminal;
4. to give fair warning of the nature of the conduct declared to constitute an offense; and
5. to differentiate on reasonable grounds between serious and minor offenses.

Specific laws might be passed because they prohibit actions that are thought to be harmful to society. For example, prohibitions against murder, rape, robbery, and arson are seen as serving all people in society. Such acts are prohibited because they are considered harmful in themselves, or ***mala in se.*** Other laws might be passed because some people feel that there is a need to regulate certain actions; thus, for example, there are parking regulations, minimum drinking-age limits, and various licensing regulations. Acts that violate such regulations are ***mala prohibita***—prohibited only because of the law and not because they are necessarily harmful or inherently evil.

Much debate is generated about what laws should be passed and what purposes the laws actually serve. Some laws are based on the morals and values of a community. Laws against abortion, obscenity, same-sex marriages, and drug use often are based on moral and ethical beliefs not shared by all members of society. Some laws are passed based on public fear. For example, kidnapping was made a federal crime after the 1932 kidnapping and murder of the son of Charles Lindbergh, an aviator of international fame. Megan's Law, which requires the registration of sexual offenders, was passed after a sexual offender unknown to the community abducted and murdered a young child.

Some laws are regulatory in nature (*mala prohibita*) such as parking laws and others define criminal conduct (*mala in se*) such as robbery.

Federal Criminal Laws

Federal criminal laws are found in

1. the U.S. Constitution,
2. U.S. Criminal Code,
3. judicial decisions interpreting code, and
4. executive orders.

The only crimes defined in the U.S. Constitution are treason and sedition.

Creating a Federal Criminal Law

A bill is introduced

The bill can be introduced by a senator or a member of the house of representatives

Sent to the Senate

The bill is sent to committees, it may be marked up, and if approved, it is sent to the full Senate

Sent to the House of Representatives

The bill is sent to committees, it may be marked up, and if approved, it is sent to the full House of Representatives

The merits of the bill are debated and a vote is taken, if the bill passes it is passed on to the other house of Congress for debate and vote

The merits of the bill are debated and a vote is taken, if the bill passes it is passed on to the other house of Congress for debate and vote

Members of the Senate and the House meet to resolve any differences, a single version of the bill is agreed upon

The Senate votes on the amended bill, if it passes it goes to the President

The Houses votes on the amended bill, if it passes it goes to the President

The President can sign the bill, veto it, or take no action

If the President signs the bill, it becomes law

If the President vetoes the bill Congress can pass the law by a two-thirds vote of both houses

If the President takes no action on the bill the bill may die

1 **Local, state, and federal governments create laws. Each has a distinct process for the creation and revision of laws.**

rule of law the principle that standards of behavior and privilege are established by laws and not by monarchs or religious leaders

mala in se acts that are crimes because they are inherently evil or harmful to society

mala prohibita acts that are prohibited because they are defined as crimes by law

State Criminal Laws

The sources of state criminal laws are the state constitution, state criminal codes, common law, and judicial decisions interpreting codes and the common law. Each state has the right to enact criminal laws deemed appropriate for its citizens. This autonomy leads to great variety in state laws, but most states have similar criminal laws because (1) all state criminal laws must preserve the rights guaranteed in the U.S. Constitution, (2) many states (approximately 22) have adopted portions of their criminal codes from the Model Penal Code published by the American Law Institute in 1962, (3) state criminal laws had as their common origin early English common law, and (4) if one accepts the consensus model, then laws will serve similar public benefits in each of the states.

STATE CRIMINAL CODES DIFFER SIGNIFICANTLY AMONG STATES. ANY PERSON WITHIN A STATE IS UNDER THE JURISDICTION OF THE LAWS OF THAT STATE.

State constitutions cannot negate any right guaranteed in the U.S. Constitution, but a state's constitution can add to rights not covered by the U.S. Constitution. Most state criminal codes are passed by state governments in a similar manner as the federal criminal codes. A bill must originate in one of the state legislative bodies, be passed by both bodies, and then be endorsed by the governor of the state. Like the president, state governors have veto power and the power to create rules and regulations through executive orders.

In their particulars, state criminal codes differ significantly among states. Any person within a state is under the jurisdiction of the laws of that state, regardless of the person's state of residence or citizenship. Thus, a person from a state that permits carrying a concealed weapon who travels to a state that prohibits such behavior must conform to the law of the latter and cannot carry a concealed weapon there.

One of the distinctions between federal criminal laws and state criminal laws is the area of law known as **common law**, or unwritten law. Criminal law in the United States was greatly influenced by early English common law. English criminal law was based on the assumption that the vast majority of citizens were illiterate and thus would not understand written law. Thus, written laws were stated simply, leaving it to judges to interpret and apply laws to specific situations. Federal courts and federal judges are specifically prohibited from operating under the rules of common law.

Local Criminal Laws

The sources of local criminal laws are city or county charters, municipal or county ordinances or violations, common law, and decisions of municipal judges interpreting codes and common law. Nearly all local criminal laws are misdemeanors or violations. Serious criminal conduct is called a **felony**, and less-serious criminal conduct is called a **misdemeanor**. The difference between a felony and a misdemeanor is usually defined by the amount of time in prison or jail that the offender can receive as punishment for violation of a statute. Felonies commonly are crimes for which an offender can receive a punishment of 1 year or more in a state prison, whereas misdemeanors are crimes for which an offender can receive a punishment of 1 year or less in a state prison or county jail.

Violations, a relatively new classification of prohibited behaviors, commonly regulate traffic offenses.[2] A violation is less than a misdemeanor and might carry the punishment of only a fine or suspension of privilege, such as losing one's driver's license temporarily. Many states have redefined misdemeanor traffic offenses as violations. The advantage of this is that violations free up the resources of the criminal courts for more-serious cases and allow for speedier processing of cases through the system.

Local criminal codes are the products of city councils and county governments. Similar to the president and governors, chief executive officers of cities and counties have the power to prohibit or regulate behavior through executive orders. Otherwise, there is great diversity in the ways in which municipalities and counties draft and pass local criminal codes. Local criminal codes have limited jurisdiction and are enforceable only within the city or county limits. Local criminal codes cannot deny rights guaranteed by the state constitution or the U.S. Constitution.

HERE'S SOMETHING TO THINK ABOUT . . .

There are significant differences among state laws regarding the use of deadly force and self-defense. Improper use of deadly force can result in charges of homicide being filed against the defender. Some cities have strict laws regarding gun ownership, virtually prohibiting the legal use of a firearm in self-defense, even in one's home. Some states require persons to retreat if they can do so safely while other states allow homeowners to "stand their ground." Most state laws require the defender to have fear of death or great bodily harm before deadly force can be used to defend oneself. What are the laws concerning the use of deadly force in your city/state?

common law unwritten, simply stated laws, based on traditions and common understandings in a time when most people were illiterate

felony serious criminal conduct punishable by incarceration for more than one year

misdemeanor less serious criminal conduct punishable by incarceration for less than a year

principle of legality the principle that citizens cannot be punished for conduct for which no law against it exists

***ex post facto* laws** laws providing that citizens cannot be punished for actions committed before laws against the actions were passed and that the government cannot increase the penalty for a specific crime after the crime was committed

The Limits of the Law

There are limits on criminal law to protect the rights and freedoms of the citizens.

Seven benchmarks are used to assess the legality of criminal laws.

1. Principle of Legality

The government cannot punish citizens for specific conduct if no specific laws exist forewarning them that the conduct is prohibited or required. The **principle of legality**, which has its roots in the Roman Empire, requires that laws must be made public before they can be enforced.

2. *Ex Post Facto* Laws

Ex post facto ("after the fact") laws are related to the principle of legality. The ***ex post facto* law** principle declares that persons cannot be punished for actions committed before the law prohibiting the behavior was passed.[3]

The principle of *ex post facto* law also prohibits the government from increasing the punishment for a specific crime after the crime was committed. Assume, for instance, that a person is convicted of mass murder in a state that does not have the death penalty. The public, upset by the brutality of the crime, might support a successful campaign to change the law and adopt a death penalty for mass murder. Even with the new law, however, the convicted person's sentence cannot then be changed from life in prison to death.

THE GOVERNMENT CANNOT PUNISH CITIZENS FOR SPECIFIC CONDUCT IF NO SPECIFIC LAWS EXIST FOREWARNING THEM THE CONDUCT IS PROHIBITED.

A defendant must be tried under the rules of evidence and laws that were in effect at the time the alleged crime was committed.

3. Due Process

There are two types of due process rights: substantive and procedural. Substantive **due process** limits the power of government to create crimes unless there is a compelling and substantial public interest in regulating or prohibiting a certain type of conduct.

Procedural due process requires the government to follow established procedures and to treat defendants equally. Procedural laws regulate the conduct of the police, the courts, and the criminal justice system in general. These laws, called rules of evidence, define, for example, what is fair treatment, what order of events must be followed, what types of evidence can be admitted at a trial, and the rights of defendants.

Because of procedural due process, case law precedents play a significant role in adjudication in the U.S. system of justice. Attorneys can argue that the court must allow similar evidence or testimony as was admitted in the past in similar cases. This system of case law is called ***stare decisis.***

To change the basis on which precedents are judged, a court must explain why it is changing its interpretation and what the new criteria for judgment are. A case in which such a change of opinion is declared by the court is called a landmark case. Since the 1960s, for example, the U.S. Supreme Court has issued numerous landmark decisions affecting the criminal justice system in matters such as search and seizure, confessions, and prisoners' rights.

4. Void for Vagueness

The law must say what it means and mean what it says. Laws that do not provide reasonable guidelines that define the specific prohibited behaviors are **void for vagueness.** For instance, a New Jersey statute that made it a crime to be a member of a gang was struck down because the court declared that the word *gang* was too vague.[4]

Laws must use wording that clearly specifies what behavior or act is unlawful. Vague wording subject to different interpretations, such as *immoral, indecent, too close,* and *interfere with,* does not provide the average person with sufficient information to determine whether his or her behavior is in violation of the law.

5. Right to Privacy

Laws that violate reasonable personal privacy may be declared void. The **right to privacy** is not clearly delineated in the U.S. Constitution, but it is a constructed right, inferred from the provisions of the First, Third, Fourth, and Ninth Amendments. Some state constitutions, such as those of Alaska, Florida, and Hawaii, have explicit rights to privacy.

However, the Supreme Court has upheld state statutes making it a crime to possess child pornography. Thus, privacy is not an overarching right that permits otherwise harmful or prohibited behaviors merely because they are performed in one's home.

6. Void for Overbreadth

Laws that have been declared **void for overbreadth** are laws that go too far; that is, in an attempt to prevent a specific conduct, the law not only makes that conduct illegal, but it also prohibits other behaviors that are legally protected.

A law that is void for overbreadth is not vague in what it prohibits (as in the case of a law that is void for vagueness); rather, it simply prohibits legal activities as well as illegal activities.

2 **There are limits on criminal law to protect the rights and freedoms of citizens. The rule of law is based on the principles of rationality and justice.**

due process substantive due process limits the government's power to criminalize behavior unless there is a compelling reason for the public interest to do so; procedural due process requires that the government follow standard procedures and treat all defendants equally

stare decisis the U.S. system of developing and applying case law on the basis of precedents established in previous cases

void for vagueness the principle that laws that do not use clear and specific language to define prohibited behaviors cannot be upheld

right to privacy the principle that laws violate personal privacy cannot be upheld

void for overbreadth the principle that laws go too far in that they criminalize legally protected behavior in an attempt to make some other behavior illegal cannot be upheld

7. Cruel and Unusual Punishment

To be valid, a law must specify the punishment to be applied for violation of the law. If that punishment is in violation of the Eighth Amendment, which prohibits cruel and unusual punishment, it may be declared unconstitutional. This legal philosophy appears to be based on the premise of classical criminology that punishment should be appropriate to the crime. Although the argument of cruel and unusual punishment has frequently been applied to cases involving the death sentence, the focus of the prohibition is on applying the principle of proportionality for the appropriate punishment for a crime.[5]

Sentencing a person to prison for drug addiction is cruel and unusual, as drug addiction is deemed an illness rather than a criminal behavior. However, sentencing a person for possessing or using drugs is not cruel and unusual.[6]

The Supreme Court has ruled that the use of corporal punishment in prison is cruel and unusual and has prohibited such punishment.

Elements of a Crime

Punishments specified by law are based on the principle of proportionality. Less-serious harms, such as misdemeanors, carry lesser punishments than do more-serious harms, which are felonies. However, even for felonies, there are various degrees of punishment. Determining what punishment should be attached to a crime depends on the conduct and the intention of the actor or perpetrator. The actions and intentions of a person who commits a crime are called the **elements of a crime.** Each crime is defined by these elements. Two important elements are ***actus reus*** and ***mens rea***.

actus reus

The actions of the person American law is firmly rooted in the classical criminological principle that persons are punished for their actions. Thus, one of the first elements of a crime is that the law must define the actions that constitute the crime. The action must be voluntary in the sense that criminal law does not prosecute persons for accidents or unintentional actions that are not negligent or reckless. However, the law does provide that, in two cases, *actus reus* can be other than direct criminal behaviors. These are failure to act and possession.

- **failure to act or crimes of omission** The criminal intent of a crime may be failure to act when there is a legal duty to act.
  - In crimes of omission, hospitals, caregivers, and even bystanders can come under the requirement of a legal duty to help another. The state of Alaska requires that a motorist render assistance to stranded motorists. A number of states have passed "Good Samaritan" laws that extend legal protection to a person who helps someone in distress. Parents are considered to have a legal duty to aid and assist their children.
- **possession** The possession of an illegal or prohibited item can constitue *actus reus.*
  - ***constructive possession***: when a person knows that an item is contraband and he or she doesn't have actual possession, but the person is in control of the item; the mailing of contraband is an example
  - ***knowing possession***: when a person has actual possession and is aware that what he or she possesses is contraband
  - ***mere possession***: when a person has actual possession but is not aware that what he or she possesses is contraband

mens rea

The intent of the person The person must have criminal intent or "a guilty mind." The action must intend harm. Harms that result from accidental actions may have civil liability but are not criminal. The only direct evidence of *mens rea* is the defendant's confession. Otherwise, in criminal law, *mens rea* is determined primarily by circumstantial or indirect evidence. There are four types of criminal intent.

- ***general intent***: This refers to the commonsense understanding that an action may cause harm. The law infers what commonsense suggests, even if the defendant denies the intent. The law assumes it is logical to assume that a person who shoots and kills another, but claims that he or she did not intend to shoot the person but only to "scare" the person, had general intent to cause harm.
- ***specific intent***: This refers to the actions taken to knowingly commit a crime; for instance, larceny requires taking property with the intent to permanently deprive the owner of that property.
- ***transferred intent***: This covers incidences in which a person injures another but did not intend to harm that person. This includes a case in which a person is intending to hurt someone, but misses and an innocent third party is injured.
- ***constructive intent***: This refers to a situation in which a person does not intend to harm anyone but should have known that his or her actions created a risk. Shooting a gun into the air on New Year's Eve is an example of this.

The Model Penal Code distinguishes four types of intent: ***purposely, knowingly, recklessly,*** and ***negligently.*** Each has a lesser degree of criminal intent, and will have a lesser punishment assigned. For instance, a person who purposely causes the death of another is guilty of murder, whereas someone who causes the death recklessly is guilty of manslaughter.

elements of a crime the illegal actions (*actus reus*) and criminal intentions (*mens rea*) of the actor along with the circumstances that link the two, especially causation

actus reus an element of crime in which people are punished for their actions; thus, the law does not prosecute persons for actions that are not voluntary or that are accidental and do not involve recklessness or negligence

mens rea an element of crime in which a person must have criminal intent, or a "guilty mind," for his or her actions to be criminal

failure to act an exception to *actus reus* in which a person fails to act when there is a legal duty to act

possession an exception to *actus reus* in which a person is in possession of an illegal item

general intent criminal intent in which a person has commonsense understanding that the results of his or her actions might cause harm

Strict Liability Some actions are considered criminal without the necessity of any criminal intent. These actions are called **strict liability crimes**. Parking violations are an example of strict liability laws. The registered owner of an illegally parked vehicle is held liable for the fine regardless of whether he or she parked the car, was operating the car, or even had knowledge of the parking violation. Strict liability crimes tend to be either minor offenses such as traffic offenses or serious offenses that society has deemed to deserve additional protection. In most states, sex with a minor is a strict liability crime in that the law places an affirmative burden on the defendant to affirm the legal age of the minor. In some states, even if the minor lies about his or her age, the defendant is assumed to have criminal intent.

IN MOST STATES, SEX WITH A MINOR IS A STRICT LIABILITY CRIME IN THAT THE LAW PLACES AN AFFIRMATIVE BURDEN ON THE DEFENDANT TO AFFIRM THE LEGAL AGE OF THE MINOR.

Incomplete Crimes, or Inchoate Offenses

One cannot be convicted of a crime for thinking about murder, rape, robbery, larceny, burglary, or any other crime. The law punishes people only for what they do, not what they think. Crimes that go beyond mere thought but do not result in completed crimes are called incomplete crimes, or **inchoate offenses**. The three common inchoate offenses are described in the following paragraphs.

Solicitation **Solicitation** is the urging, requesting, or commanding of another to commit a crime. The other person does not have to have *mens rea* or any intent whatsoever of complying with the solicitation to commit the crime. Solicitation is a criminal charge against the person making the offer, command, or encouragement, not against the person to whom the offer is made. The crime of solicitation requires specific criminal intent. A person who makes a remark such as, "We should steal that car and take it for a ride," to a general group of people has not satisfied the specific intent required for solicitation.

Conspiracy Conspiracy requires no *actus reus* other than communication. A plot to commit a bank robbery is not a conspiracy if it is not shared or if no steps are taken in preparation for the planned robbery. **Conspiracy** by definition requires two or more people to plan a crime. Actions that require two people, such as fornication, bigamy, bribery, and gambling, are not considered examples of conspiracy. Thus, if a correctional officer accepts money to help an inmate escape, the two could not be charged with conspiracy. The appropriate criminal charge would be bribery, which requires at least two persons—one to make the offer and the other to accept the offer.

Conspiracy requires that two or more people take steps in preparation for the commission of a crime. Any step or steps taken may constitute conspiracy. In the case of a bank robbery that is anticipated to take months to plan and hundreds of steps to execute, the first meeting of the parties involved to discuss how to proceed constitutes a conspiracy. Furthermore, the parties to a conspiracy do not have to meet face-to-face. They may satisfy the requirements of conspiracy by any form of collaboration, including verbal, written, or electronic. As another example, if two or more persons plan to commit forgery and take steps to obtain a certain type of paper required to commit forgery, this is sufficient *actus reus* to constitute conspiracy. The supplier of the items needed for the commission of a crime is not guilty of conspiracy unless the supplier is aware of the illegal use planned for the materials.[7]

Attempt What happens when things do not go as the criminal planned and he or she is not able to complete the intended criminal activity? Has a crime been committed? Yes, he or she has committed the crime of **attempt**. For most crimes that can be committed, there is a corresponding crime of attempt—that is, attempted murder, attempted kidnapping, attempted rape, attempted burglary, and so forth. Attempt is the closest act to the completion of the crime and therefore carries a greater punishment than conspiracy or solicitation but a lesser punishment than if the crime had been completed.

Renunciation of Criminal Intent It is possible that a person might have criminal intent and might take steps toward completing a crime but then change his or her mind before the crime is fully executed. Does renunciation of criminal intent absolve one of punishment? No, it does not.[8] If a person approaches a bank with a mask, a gun, and a note demanding money from the teller and then changes his or her mind and goes home, the person nevertheless has satisfied the criminal intent requirement to be charged with attempted bank robbery. If a person intends to commit burglary but is frightened away by a noise after committing trespass, the person has satisfied the criminal intent requirement to be charged with attempted burglary. A person who demands sex under threat of force but

HERE'S SOMETHING TO THINK ABOUT . . .

Law Library Sign made with license plates at Nevada State Prison

This sign made of license plates at the Nevada State Prison identifies the prison law library for inmates. Every prison must maintain a law library for inmates. Inmates must be given the opportunity to research the law regarding their conviction and to file appeals (at no cost) to the court. An inmate may be assisted by another inmate, sometimes called "a jailhouse lawyer," in the legal research and filing of the appeal. The law grants a unique status to inmates in that normally only a licensed attorney may perform this work. Why do you think the law allows "jail house lawyers" to perform these services?

The actions and intent of the criminal, as well as the seriousness of the crime, all carry weight in determining punishment.

specific intent criminal intent in which a person knowingly takes action to commit a crime

transferred intent criminal intent in which a person intends to harm a person but instead harms a different person

constructive intent criminal intent in which a person does not intend to harm anyone but should have known that his or her actions created the risk of harm

constructive possession a person being in control of contraband but not having actual possession of it

knowing possession a person actually being in possession of an item and knowing that it is contraband

mere possession a person actually being in possession of an item but not knowing that it is contraband

strict liability crimes actions that are considered criminal without the need for criminal intent

is "talked out of it" by the victim has satisfied the criminal intent requirement to be charged with attempted rape.[9] The law does not take the view that a stroke of luck or a retreat from criminal activity based on fear of getting caught makes one immune from criminal prosecution.

Criminal Defenses

The fact that a person has committed an act that, by law, constitutes a crime does not mean that the person will be held criminally liable for that crime in a court of law. There are numerous **defenses** that a person can offer at trial as justification. Two types of defenses to criminal charges are a perfect defense, in which the person is excused from all criminal liability and punishment, and an imperfect defense, in which the person's liability or punishment is reduced. The most common defenses are described in the following paragraphs.

- **Alibi** The use of an alibi as a defense requires that the defendant present witnesses who will give testimony in court or other evidence establishing the fact that the defendant could not have committed the offense. The most common alibi strategy is for defendants to claim that they could not have been at the scene of the crime at the time the crime was committed and to offer witnesses who will testify to that fact. The jury is the ultimate judge of an alibi. The jury may choose to believe or not to believe the testimony of alibi witnesses or the evidence presented.
- **Consent or Condoning by the Victim** The defense that the victim gave permission for the act, or condoned the act, is not a valid defense for criminal actions.[10] For example, consent is not a valid defense in mercy killing or assisted suicide. Dr. Jack Kevorkian constructed a "suicide machine" to help terminally ill patients end their lives. Despite the consent—even pleas—of the victims for his assistance in committing suicide, the Michigan court that heard the case did not recognize the defense of consent. Likewise, consent is not a defense in murder–suicide pacts, and in those cases, any surviving member can be charged with murder.

  Consent or condoning by the victim is a valid defense for a number of actions in which injury is a foreseeable risk and the behavior is socially and legally acceptable. Consent is a legitimate defense for certain physical violence in sporting events, even violence resulting in death. For example, if a professional boxer in a sanctioned boxing match causes the death of his or her opponent, consent is a defense against homicide. Consent is a defense for violence in some sports, such as hockey, but not in others, such as basketball, where violence is not common. Even in sports such as hockey, excessive violence such as strikes to the head with a hockey stick may be criminal.
- **Entrapment or Outrageous Government Conduct** Entrapment or outrageous government conduct are related to the principle that a defendant's criminal actions must be voluntary. If agents of the government provided both the *mens rea* and the means to commit the crime, the courts have ruled that the defendant may be defended on the grounds of entrapment or outrageous government conduct. Entrapment is an affirmative defense, which means that the defendant must admit that he or she committed the crime as alleged. The person is not innocent but claims that if it had not been for the actions of government agents, he or she would not have committed the crime.

  Entrapment is different from encouragement, in which law enforcement officers might pretend that they are victims or co-conspirators in crime, promise the suspect benefits from committing the crime, or offer to supply materials or help the suspect obtain contraband.
- **Immunity or Privilege** In the defense of immunity, the accused has special protection against being prosecuted. Four forms of this defense are diplomatic immunity, legislative immunity, witness immunity, and privilege. **Diplomatic immunity** grants foreign diplomats complete immunity from any criminal prosecution, including murder and traffic violations. In return for extending immunity to foreign diplomats, U.S. diplomats in foreign countries receive the same protection. If a foreign diplomat commits a serious felony crime in the United States, the only recourse for

There are several types of defenses that can be offered at a trial.

HERE'S SOMETHING TO THINK ABOUT . . .

Justice, 1875 Virginia City, Nevada Courthouse

Private organizations may make rules similar to laws, in that they prohibit or regulate behavior. However, the rules cannot infringe upon the constitutionally protected rights of citizens. When private rules infringe upon rights of citizens often it is necessary for the injured party to file a civil lawsuit to seek relief. For example, Raed Jarrar successfully sued JetBlue Airways for $240,000 for violation of his First Amendment rights when the airline refused to allow him to board while wearing a t-shirt with Arabic writing which read "We Will Not Be Silent." The ACLU called the case "a victory for free speech and a blow to the discriminatory practice of racial profiling." What are some obstacles to obtaining a judgment by use of a civil lawsuit?

inchoate offense an action that goes beyond mere thought but does not result in a completed crime

solicitation the requesting or commanding of another to commit a crime

conspiracy the planning by two or more people to commit a crime

attempt an incomplete criminal act; the closest act to the completion of a crime

defenses justifications or excuses defined by law by which a defendant may be released from prosecution or punishment for a crime

diplomatic immunity the granting of immunity, or protection from any kind of criminal prosecution, to foreign diplomats

4 Several defenses, defined by law, can be used in court to excuse an accused offender or to lessen his or her criminal liability.

the U.S. government is to ask for the diplomat's recall to his or her country or to request that the country voluntarily waive the diplomat's immunity.

A lesser form of immunity extended to lawmakers in the United States is **legislative immunity**. Dating back to the English rule of the American colonies, most representatives and senators receive limited immunity from arrest while the legislature is in session. Unlike diplomatic immunity, legislative immunity only postpones the time that the legislator can be arrested until after the legislative session is adjourned. Also, legislative immunity does not protect the legislator from arrest for felonies and treason.

In **witness immunity**, the defendant admits to the criminal acts as charged but, in exchange for his or her cooperation with a government investigation, is granted immunity from further prosecution based on the offered testimony. Witness immunity is commonly used in organized crime, drug trafficking, and corporate crime cases.

The defense of **privilege** is the claim that the defendant violated the law but is immune from punishment because of his or her official office or duty. For example, the courts have recognized as a privilege the right of operators of emergency vehicles to violate traffic regulations when responding to a call. Law enforcement officers and correctional officers have the defense of privilege in certain cases involving the use of deadly force. For example, correctional officers can use deadly force to prevent an inmate from escaping even if there is no fear of death or great bodily harm to the officer—or to anyone else—in certain cases.

- **Involuntary Actions and Duress** Involuntary actions and duress are similar defenses. A defense of involuntary action is a claim by the person that the action or behavior was not voluntary. The person's behavior might not have been voluntary in that it was an accident or that he or she could not control the behavior through no fault of his or her own. Accidents can even include actions resulting in injury or death to another. In February 2006, former Vice President Dick Cheney, for example, accidentally shot and seriously wounded his friend Harry Whittington in a hunting accident. Because the wounding was an accident, there were no criminal charges filed. However, the defense of involuntary action cannot be used to defend against criminal liability for behaviors committed as a result of alcohol consumption or drug use if the person voluntarily consumed the alcohol or drugs.

  Similar to the involuntary defense is the **defense of duress**, in which the person claims that he or she did not commit the actions of his or her own free will. However, unlike the involuntary defense, in the defense of duress, the person claims that his or her behavior was compelled by the use or threat of force by another. A simple example of this defense is when a bank teller gives the bank's money to a robber. It could be argued that the bank teller does not have the authority to give away the bank's money, but the teller has not committed a crime because the actions are not voluntary. The teller is operating under duress.

  However, the defense of duress cannot be used as a defense in homicide. The law does not allow the taking of one life even to save that of another.

- **Mistake or Ignorance of Fact or Law** Laws are published as a matter of public record, partly so that offenders cannot claim ignorance of the law as an excuse for their behavior. Most citizens know very little of the many volumes of law that govern their lives, but the law usually does not recognize ignorance of the law as a valid defense. Ignorance of the law may be considered a defense if the law in question is so unusual or obscure that the court finds that a reasonable person would not have knowledge of it. However, simple ignorance of the law is not a defense against prosecution or punishment for crimes.

  Mistake or ignorance of fact, on the other hand, is a valid defense. If, at the end of class, you pick up a backpack that you think is yours and walk out of the class, have you stolen the backpack if it in fact belongs to another student? If a person has a reasonable belief that the action he or she is doing is legal, mistake of fact may be a valid defense. **Mistake or ignorance of fact** is a defense that claims to negate the requirement of *mens rea,* or criminal intent. Thus, there is a great difference between the standard used to distinguish ignorance of the law and mistake of fact.

- **Necessity** The defense of **necessity** is sometimes known as the defense of the "lesser of two evils." Necessity is an affirmative defense in which the defendant must admit that he or she committed the act but claims that it was done because of necessity or need and not because of *mens rea.* This defense is commonly used against charges of property crime, such as trespass, theft, and burglary.[11] In the classic case in which this defense is successful, the defendant is faced with a life-threatening situation and chooses to commit an illegal act to save his or her life. For example, a cross-country skier caught in an unexpected blizzard might break into a mountain home, start a fire, and consume food found there. Under normal circumstances, these actions constitute the crime of burglary, but because of the threat of death from exposure to the elements, the court may recognize the defense of necessity as a perfect defense.

- **Self-Defense** The claim of **self-defense** is a complex defense usually associated with murder and physical assault. Again, this is an affirmative defense: The defendant admits to the murder or assault but claims that he or she lacked criminal intent. The lack of criminal intent is based on the claim that the defendant was protecting himself or herself from deadly attack or serious bodily injury.[12] The courts have also recognized self-defense when applied to (1) protecting another from deadly attack or serious bodily injury and (2) defending one's home from invasion. The act of self-defense used by the defendant must be appropriate and proportional to the force used by the attacker. Before deadly force is justified as self-defense, the attacker must create a situation in which the defendant fears death or great bodily harm. Timing is

legislative immunity the protection of senators and representatives of Congress from arrest only while the legislature is in session, except for felonies and treason

witness immunity a situation in which a defendant admits to committing a crime but is granted immunity from prosecution in exchange for cooperation with a government investigation

privilege a type of defense in which the defendant claims immunity from punishment for an admitted violation of the law because it was related to his or her official duties

defense of duress a legal claim by a defendant that he or she acted involuntarily under the threat of immediate and serious harm by another

mistake or ignorance of fact an affirmative legal defense in which the defendant made a mistake that does not meet the requirement for *mens rea*

necessity an affirmative legal defense claiming that the defendant committed an act out of need, and not *mens rea* a controversial issue in capital cases involving the claim of self-defense. For example, is a routinely abused spouse or child justified in killing an attacker when not under immediate threat of deadly attack or serious bodily injury?[13]

The use of self-defense in protecting one's home against invasion varies significantly among states. Some states require that, when reasonable, the occupant of the house must first attempt to flee from the home to escape attack. Other states do not have such a requirement but follow the "castle doctrine," which means that occupants have the unqualified right to protect their home against trespass.[14] Most states do not permit the claim of self-defense in resisting arrest—whether lawful or unlawful—by a police officer.[15]

- **Youth** A 14-year-old boy steals a car, refuses to stop when pursued by the police, and ends up destroying the vehicle in a high-speed crash. Is he just a kid and therefore held to a different standard of culpability from that of an adult? Since 1899, the answer for the U.S. criminal justice system has been yes. Prior to 1899, age was a defense based on the British principle that children under 7 years of age, and possibly even under 14 years of age, could not form *mens rea.*

  In 1899, Cook County (Chicago) adopted the use of juvenile court. This separate court system operated under significantly different rules and standards of proof to adjudicate the crimes of youthful offenders under the age of 18 separately from adult offenders. The use of juvenile court quickly caught on and is now practiced in all 50 states.[16]

- **Insanity** The **insanity** defense has an interesting connection to Sir Robert Peel, the father of modern policing. In 1843, Daniel M'Naghten suffered the paranoid delusion that Sir Robert Peel, then Prime Minister of England, intended to kill him. Based on this belief, M'Naghten undertook to kill Peel first in what M'Naghten perceived as a form of self-defense. He obtained a pistol and lay in wait for Peel to pass by. Fortunately for Peel but unfortunately for his secretary, Edward Drummond, M'Naghten shot, missed Peel, and struck and killed Drummond.[17]

  M'Naghten was tried for murder but was acquitted based on his successful insanity defense.[18] Alarmed at the verdict, the English law regarding insanity was changed to make it more difficult for a successful insanity defense. Under the new standard a defendant could be considered insane only if he or she met two conditions: (1) He or she suffered from a disease or defect of the mind, and (2) the disease or defect must have caused the defendant either not to know the nature and quality of the criminal act or not to know that the act was wrong. This standard for insanity became known as the M'Naghten standard. This standard became the primary requirement for a successful insanity defense in Great Britain and the United States.

Defenses to crimes can be divided into two major categories: an alibi defense and an affirmative defense. In an alibi defense, the defendant denies that he or she committed the crime and offers proof that he or she could not have done so. Usually this proof involves an alibi—that is, evidence that at the time of the crime, the defendant was not at or near the scene of the crime. Affirmative defenses can be divided into justifications, excuses, and exemptions. In each, the defendant admits to some of the elements of the crime but denies that all of the elements were present. Usually, in these defenses, the defendant admits to the *actus reus* but denies criminal intent.

Crimes by Law

The State	Persons	Habitation	Property	Public Order	Public Morals
SEDITION					
Treason Sedition	Murder Rape Sexual Assault Kidnapping Robbery Assault	Burglary Arson	Theft Larceny Embezzlement Fraud Receiving Stolen Property Forgery	Disturbing the Peace Inciting to Riot	Prostitution Gambling

self-defense an affirmative legal defense in which a defendant claims that he or she acted to protect himself or herself or another person against a deadly attack or invasion of his or her home

insanity a legal claim by a defendant that he or she was suffering from a disease or mental defect and that the defect caused the defendant not to understand the difference between right and wrong

5 The Model Penal Code classifies crimes into categories by victims as well as defines specific offenses of crimes.

Crimes are defined by laws, and the laws governing society are numerous, complex, and diverse. The federal, state, and local governments have specific, different, and overlapping criminal codes. It would not be possible to specifically address the particulars of each of these different laws in a discussion of the different crimes. Thus, law texts and criminal justice texts do not use actual federal and state laws when discussing the various crimes but instead use the laws and definitions of the Model Penal Code. The **Model Penal Code** is not the law of the federal government or any state government, but is a set of guidelines, developed in 1962 by the American Law Institute, for what are considered the best practices or legal codes. Most textbooks on criminal law discuss the laws as presented by the Model Penal Code rather than actual federal or state laws.

THE CRIME OF RAPE SHOWS HOW CRIMINAL CODES REFLECT CHANGING SOCIAL VALUES. RAPE IS ALSO ONE OF THE FEW BEHAVIORS IN WHICH CRIMINAL LIABILITY IS DETERMINED BY THE INTENT RATHER THAN THE ACT, BECAUSE CONSENSUAL SEX IS NOT A CRIME.

The Model Penal Code classifies crime according to the victim of the crime. Crimes are classified in the following ways:

- **Crimes Against the State**
- **Crimes Against Persons** In the Model Penal Code, crimes against persons include homicide, rape, sexual assault, kidnapping, robbery, and assault and battery. These specific offenses are discussed to illustrate important points about criminal law: the elements required for an offense, the grading of the offense, and how the offense and the punishment reflect social values.

Homicide The definition of **homicide**—the killing of one human being by another—takes into account the harm done to the victim and the different degrees of criminal intent. Based on the degree of harm intended, homicides are divided into murder and manslaughter. **Murder** is divided into first-degree murder—the premeditated and deliberate killing of another—and second-degree murder. Second-degree murder includes the killing of another without premeditation, with the intent to inflict serious bodily injury but not death, as the result of extreme recklessness, and during the commission of a felony in which there was no intent to kill or injure another. **Manslaughter** is the killing of another without malice—that is, without the specific intent to kill. The Model Penal Code divides manslaughter into three categories: voluntary, involuntary, and vehicular.

Rape or Sexual Assault The crime of rape, or the more contemporary term *sexual assault,* shows how criminal codes reflect changing social values. Rape is also one of the few behaviors in which criminal liability is determined by the intent rather than the act, because consensual sex, unlike nonconsensual sex, is not a crime. The lack of consent makes **rape** a crime. Since the 1950s, states no longer have required proof of resistance. Starting in the 1970s, numerous other changes have been made to the elements necessary to prove rape. Many states have changed the classification from rape to sexual assault to more clearly identify the crime as an assault as opposed to a sexual act. Sexual assault has been defined to include all sexual penetration with the penis or any other object. States also have enacted statutes recognizing that men also can be raped, by women or by men. The marital rape exception has been eliminated in many states. Finally, some states have enacted rape shield laws that prohibit the defense from questioning the victim about past sexual experiences.

Kidnapping Kidnapping is the taking away by force of a person against his or her will and holding that person in false imprisonment. In defining kidnapping, the taking of a person against his or her will is commonly called asportation. Thus, one of the elements of kidnapping is that it must be proved that the defendant moved the victim against his or her will from one place to another. If a perpetrator does not move his or her victim, the lesser crime of false imprisonment or unlawful restraint may be applicable.

Robbery **Robbery** is the taking and carrying away of property from a person by force or threat of immediate use of force. Houses are burgled, but only people can be robbed. Robbery actually involves the elements of two crimes: theft from crimes against property, and assault from crimes against persons.

Assault and Battery **Assault** is defined as inflicting injury on another, whereas battery is the unlawful striking of another. The actual state codes governing assault and battery vary significantly. Some states use the terms interchangeably or have defined the crime as *assault and battery* instead of one crime called *assault* and another crime called *battery.* Mayhem is an offense similar to battery, but the elements of mayhem require unlawfully and violently depriving the victim of full use of any part of the body, such as a hand, foot, or eye. If a firearm or other dangerous weapon is used in the crime, it becomes the more serious offense of aggravated assault or battery.

- **Crimes Against Habitation** Burglary and arson are crimes committed against places where people live. Both offenses require specific criminal intent. Burglary requires the person to commit the crime of trespass with the specific intent to commit a crime thereafter. Arson requires the specific intent to commit a malicious burning.

Model Penal Code guidelines for U.S. criminal codes published in 1962 by the American Law Institute that classify and define crimes into categories

homicide the killing of one human being by another

murder all intentional killings and deaths that occur in the course of aggravated felonies

manslaughter the killing of another without the specific intent to kill

rape (sexual assault) nonconsensual sexual acts

robbery the taking away of property from a person by force or the immediate threat of force

assault the crime of willfully inflicting injury on another

HERE'S SOMETHING TO THINK ABOUT . . .

The following U.S. Supreme Court decisions are landmark cases in criminal justice. The name of each landmark case is followed by a brief description.

Weeks v. United States, *1914—established the exclusionary rule disallowing evidence obtained in violation of constitutional rights*

Mapp v. Ohio, *1963—incorporated Fourth Amendment search rights to state courts*

Gideon v. Wainwright, *1963—guaranteed defendants the right to an attorney at trial*

Miranda v. Arizona, *1966—established a defendant's right to counsel, right against self-incrimination, and that the defendant understands these rights*

Klopfer v. North Carolina, *1967—guaranteed defendants a speedy trial*

Terry v. Ohio, *1968—allowed police to "pat down" a person for personal safety reasons*

Witherspoon v. Illinois, *1968—prohibited the exclusion of those opposed to capital punishment from capital crime juries*

Furman v. Georgia, *1972—declared the death penalty was applied in an arbitrary and capricious manner*

Gagnon v. Scarpelli, *1973—declared a probationer's sentence can only be revoked after preliminary and final revocation hearings*

Roper v. Simmons, *2005—abolished capital punishment for juveniles*

District of Columbia v. Heller, *2008—ruled the Second Amendment protected an individual's right to own a firearm*

McDonald v. City of Chicago et al., *2010—incorporated the Second Amendment right to bear arms*

Burglary The modern offense of **burglary** combines two less-serious crimes—trespass and intent to commit a crime—into a serious felony crime. The Model Penal Code and most state codes define several degrees of burglary and expand burglary to include property other than homes, such as cars, campers, airplanes, tents, and vacation cabins. Burglary does not require breaking and entering or the intent to steal.[19] A person who remains in a habitation when not authorized to do so satisfies the criminal intent of burglary. For example, someone who enters a public building during authorized hours and hides until after-hours is considered to have committed the specific intent of trespass required of burglary. The modern offense of burglary does not require the burglar to actually "break" anything, and entering a marked, restricted space is burglary even if there is no door, lock, or obstacle to open or cross.

It is common to think of burglary as a crime involving the intent to steal something. Modern burglary statutes require only that once a person commits trespass, he or she intends to commit another crime, whether it be a felony, such as theft, or a misdemeanor, such as vandalism. A person who commits only trespass with no specific intent to commit another crime has not satisfied the specific criminal intent required for the crime of burglary. Modern burglary statutes also cover a multitude of structures where people live and sleep, in addition to abandoned homes and partly constructed houses.

Arson **Arson** is the willful and malicious burning or attempted burning of any structure, including one's own. Because of the many motivations a person might have for burning a structure and the serious harm that can come to innocent parties, nearly all malicious burnings constitute arson.[20]

Modern arson codes also include destroying a structure by the use of explosives. Arson includes the burning of homes, factories, personal property, and vehicles. If the structure is occupied, even if the arsonist is unaware of this fact, the crime is the more serious crime of aggravated arson. The crime of arson may also be considered aggravated arson if a firefighter or law enforcement officer is injured or killed while responding to the fire. Accidental burnings, or burnings without malice, are not criminal. However, a person who burns his or her private property in a way that endangers the public may be charged with arson. For example, a person motivated to burn his or her automobile, which is parked on a public street, may be charged with arson even if the person owns the automobile and there is no lien or insurance claim on it.

- **Crimes Against Property** Numerous statutes define offenses against property, including theft, larceny, embezzlement, receiving stolen property, false pretenses, forgery, and uttering. Modern criminal codes concerning crimes against property make it illegal to take stocks, bonds, checks, negotiable paper, services and labor, minerals, crops, utilities, and even trees. Virtually all property falls within the scope of modern larceny statutes.

Larceny Larceny is the most commonly committed crime in the United States. The Model Penal Code defines **larceny** as the wrongfully taking and carrying away of another's property with the intent to permanently deprive the property's owner of its possession.

burglary a combination of trespass and the intent to commit a crime

arson the malicious burning of a structure

larceny the wrongful taking of another's property with the intent to permanently deprive its owner of its possession

CHAPTER 3

Criminal Law: Control vs. Liberty

Check It!

1 HOW are federal, state, and local criminal laws created and changed? p. 42

Federal criminal laws must be initiated as bills in the Senate or House of Representatives and are enacted or amended by a majority vote of both, unless the president takes no action or vetoes them, in which case a two-thirds majority vote of both the House and Senate is required. The process for state criminal laws is similar, except the governor plays the role of the president. Local criminal laws—nearly all of which are misdemeanors or violations—are produced in diverse ways by city councils and county governments.

2 HOW are the limits imposed on criminal laws defined? p. 44

Seven benchmarks define the legality of criminal laws:

1. principles of legality
2. *ex posto facto* law
3. due process
4. void for vagueness
5. right to privacy
6. void for overbreadth
7. cruel and unusual punishment

3 WHAT are the elements of a crime that must be present to prosecute offenders? p. 46

The elements of a crime that must be present for prosecution are *actus reus,* in which a person voluntarily committed a criminal act, and *mens rea,* in which a person committed a crime with the intention to do so.

4 WHAT are the major defenses against charges of criminal conduct? p. 47

The major defenses against criminal charges are the following:

1. alibi
2. consent or condoning by the victim
3. entrapment or outrageous government conduct
4. immunity or privilege
5. involuntary actions
6. mistake or ignorance of fact or law
7. necessity
8. self-defense
9. youth
10. insanity

5 HOW are crimes categorized and defined according to the Model Penal Code? p. 49

1. Crimes against the state include treason and sedition.
2. Crimes against persons include murder, rape, sexual assault, kidnapping, robbery, and assault.
3. Crimes against habitation include burglary and arson.
4. Crimes against property include theft, larceny, embezzlement, fraud, receiving stolen property, and forgery.
5. Crimes against public order include disturbing the peace and inciting to riot.
6. Crimes against public morals include prostitution and gambling.

Assess Your Understanding

1. What is the assumption regarding laws considered *mala in se*?
   a. The law is regulatory in nature.
   b. The offense is a victimless crime.
   c. The law prohibits acts considered by most people as harmful to society or persons.
   d. The punishment for the offense is a maximum of one year in jail or prison.

2. What is one of the basic assumptions of the rule of law?
   a. The president of the United States is exempt from most laws.
   b. Laws are applied differently to certain classes of persons based on wealth or social status.
   c. Laws are based on moral and religious principles which promote order and harmony in society.
   d. Standards of behavior established by law apply to all people equally.

3. Which of the following punishments is most appropriate for a defendant found guilty of a felony offense?
   a. a sentence of 18 months in a state prison
   b. a sentence of 10 days in a county jail
   c. suspension of the person's driver's license for one year
   d. a fine of $300 and 40 hours of community service

4. The philosophy that the court must allow similar evidence as that admitted in the past is known as which of the following?
   a. principle of legality
   b. *stare decisis*
   c. inchoate offenses
   d. privilege

5. If a defendant claims self-defense to the charges of shooting and killing another, generally what is required for a successful defense?
   a. The defendant must have believed he or she was in danger of great bodily harm or death.
   b. The person killed must have been armed with a firearm.
   c. The person killed trespassed upon the defendant's property at night.
   d. The person killed was attempting to steal the defendant's property.

6. The element of *mens rea* refers to which of the following?
   a. the actions of the defendant
   b. the criminal intent of the defendant
   c. the defendant's knowledge that his or her behavior was illegal
   d. whether the crime is a felony or a misdemeanor

7. Actions that are considered criminal without the necessity of any criminal intent are which of the following?
   a. *ex post facto* crimes
   b. inchoate crimes
   c. crimes against the state
   d. strict liability crimes

8. Which of the following statements is true?
   a. The defense of mistake and ignorance of the law are the same defense.
   b. If one did not know that what he did was against the law, then this is always a valid defense.
   c. Mistake may be a valid defense but ignorance of the law is seldom a valid defense.
   d. The defenses of mistake and ignorance of the law are known as "the lesser of two evils."

9. Which of the following is necessary for the crime of conspiracy?
   a. The parties to the conspiracy must meet face to face.
   b. Two or more persons must take steps in preparation for the commission of a crime.
   c. The parties to the conspiracy must complete all but the last step of the crime.
   d. Anyone who assists in the crime in any way is part of the conspiracy.

10. According to the Model Penal Code, burglary is a crime against which of the following?
   a. habitation
   b. property
   c. persons
   d. public order

ESSAY

1. How are criminal laws created and changed?
2. How does the right of due process regulate the conduct of the police, the courts, and the criminal justice system?
3. What are the elements of a crime that must be proved to demonstrate a person has committed a criminal offense?
4. Describe the four types of incomplete crimes.
5. Describe how crimes are classified by the Model Penal Code.
6. What is the difference between a perfect defense and an imperfect defense to charges of criminal conduct?

ANSWERS: 1. c, 2. d, 3. a, 4. b, 5. a, 6. b, 7. d, 8. c, 9. b, 10. a

Media

Go to the *Chapter 3: Criminal Law Control Versus Liberty* section in *MyCJLab* to test your understanding of this chapter, access customized study content, engage in interactive simulations, complete critical thinking and research assignments, and view related online videos.

Additional Links

For more information about the Model Penal Code, see http://en.wikipedia.org/wiki/Model_Penal_Code

Further information about the U.S. Federal Code can be found at www.gpoaccess.gov/uscode/index.html

To view the Uniform Code of Military Justice (the laws and procedures for military personnel), go to www.au.af.mil/au/awc/awcgate/ucmj.htm

To obtain more information about the history of the insanity defense and the various alternative pleas which have emerged for defendants claiming diminished capacity, go to http://topics.law.cornell.edu/wex/insanity_defense

To view the criminal codes of your state, go to www.legallawhelp.com/legal_law_channels/criminal_law/codes_by_state.html and follow the links to your state or the state of your choice.

To view the controversial arguments of David Freidman, American economist, author, and libertarian theorist, on why criminal laws should be abolished, go to http://vimeo.com/2268972

To view a short video of the basics of criminal go to www.youtube.com/watch?v=GDxloQRiuDQ

To view an interview with an attorney who made the change from civil law to criminal law, see "Why Make a Career Change to Criminal Law?" at www.5min.com/Video/Why-Make-a-Career-Change-to-Criminal-Law-245935418

There are several short videos explaining how a bill becomes a law. The School House Rock video is a classic aimed at explaining the process to a younger audience. See www.youtube.com/watch?v=mEJL2Uuv-oQ

To view other videos explaining how a bill becomes a law, visit one of the following: www.youtube.com/watch?v=vp_je95-r7E

www.britannica.com/EBchecked/media/68316/Mark-Andrews-and-Thomas-Eagleton-talk-about-how-Congress-passes

While the process of making laws is similar to the federal government, each state has its own unique procedure. To view a video on how laws are made in the state of Louisiana, go to www.youtube.com/watch?v=OU4c4n2-rc8

STATE TROOPER

ROLES AND FUNCTIONS OF THE POLICE

4

In 2011, the shoreline between Manhattan and Jones Beach State Park was a very large crime scene. Law enforcement officials discovered that the stretch of isolated beaches had become a dumping ground for as many as 10 bodies. The bones included both those of adult humans and a toddler. Some of the bodies had been there for years.

Over 100 local, state, and federal investigators from different jurisdictions converged on the vast crime scene to comb for evidence. Evidence collection experts, behavior science investigators, and criminal profilers assisted in the investigation. The investigators will employ state-of-the-art investigation tools in the search for the killer. Already investigators have determined that some of the victims were sex workers who advertised on Craigslist and concluded these victims were killed by a serial killer. The investigation may take years to complete and cost hundreds of thousands of dollars.

The ability to assemble such a group of professional crime fighters is a relatively new phenomenon. A governmental agency composed of professionally trained, full-time personnel whose responsibility is to maintain law and order in society is a relatively new approach to crime fighting. The first such agency was started in London in 1829. Full-time professional police departments did not emerge in the United States until just before the twentieth century. However, in this short time the public has come to view the police as the primary agency for fighting crime, maintaining order, and performing many other functions in modern society.

Policing in the United States both historically and today is influenced by many factors as the civilian police reflect the values, resources, and priorities of the community and nation. Policing has been influenced by the philosophy of the founding fathers reflected in the U.S. Constitution, the vast geography of the country, and the public expectations of professionalism and roles of the police. The various law enforcement agencies in the United States have been implemented and have evolved over time.

1 **How did American policing develop, and what is its connection to the London Metropolitan Police of 1829?**

2 **How is jurisdiction related to the organization of the contemporary U.S. system of policing?**

3 **What are the major federal law enforcement agencies, and what are their duties?**

4 **What are the major types of state law enforcement agencies, and what are their jurisdictions?**

5 **What are the unique aspects of a sheriff's department's administrative structure and law enforcement duties?**

6 **What are the jurisdictions of city police, and what services do they provide?**

7 **What are the hiring and training procedures for police officers?**

8 **How do social values and other factors influence policing strategies?**

This chapter reviews the history and development of policing in America and discusses the personnel and agencies that comprise American policing.

POLICING IN THE UNITED STATES IS INFLUENCED BY MANY FACTORS AS THE CIVILIAN POLICE REFLECT THE VALUES, RESOURCES, AND PRIORITIES OF THE COMMUNITY AND NATION.

Development of Policing

The British Police System

1653 Oliver Cromwell tries a military solution to the problem of maintaining law and order in British cities. This strategy of military policing reduces personal freedoms and sharply contrasts with rising expectations of democratic values. English citizens find this solution worse than the problem.

1774 The Westminster Watch Act is established to deal with the problem of public law enforcement. Using a system of night watchmen, bailiffs, and gate guards, Westminster attempts to control sex, swearing, drinking, and brawling.[1]

1828 Sir Robert Peel is appointed Home Secretary of England. He is expected to deal with the growing problem of street crime in London.

1829 The British Parliament passes the London Metropolitan Police Act. Under Sir Robert Peel's leadership, a full-time, paid, uniformed police agency is established to promote public safety, enforce criminal codes, and bring criminals to justice.

The U.S. Police System

1776–1850 Gradually, various municipalities abandon the use of part-time personnel and volunteers and adopt London-style policing in an effort to promote public safety.

1789 The U.S. Marshals Service and the U.S. Postal Inspection Service are established.

1850 Private security agencies such as Brinks, Pinkerton, and Wells Fargo provide investigative services and protection of private property. They fill the void created by limitations of local police to cover wide jurisdictions.

1862 Congress creates the Office of Internal Revenue and authorizes it to investigate tax evasion.

1865 The U.S. Secret Service is founded.

1877 Congress passed an act prohibiting the counterfeiting of any coin, or gold or silver bar.

1894 The Secret Service began informal part-time protection of President Cleveland.

1896 ***Plessy v. Ferguson*** This federal court case establishes the doctrine of "separate but equal" treatment of minorities, specifically African Americans. Employment of black police officers, both in the South and in northern cities, is suspended.

Contemporary Policing

One of the most distinctive characteristics of policing in the U.S. criminal justice system is that it is performed by nearly 18,000 fragmented, semiautonomous law enforcement agencies. Each police agency has its own chief administrator, headquarters, rules and regulations, jurisdiction, and training standards.

No single agency has oversight responsibility for all of these different police agencies. There is no central authority, person, or agency to coordinate police activities, to enforce compliance with rules, to investigate charges of police abuse of power, or even to see to it that the police are doing a good job.

In trying to understand the country's system of policing, a good starting point is to examine the jurisdiction of the various agencies. Each law enforcement agency's powers, responsibilities, and accountability are determined by its jurisdiction. **Jurisdiction** refers to the geographical limits such as the municipality, county, or state in which officers of the agency are empowered to perform their duties. Jurisdiction also refers to the legitimate duties that the department can perform. Some agencies have a relatively small geographical jurisdiction but a large number of legitimate duties. Other agencies have an expansive geographical jurisdiction but limited legitimate duties. For example, the geographical jurisdiction of a municipal police officer ends at the city limits, but Federal Bureau of Investigation (FBI) agencies have geographical jurisdiction in all 50 states, the District of Columbia, U.S. territories, and certain federal reservations. However, the legal jurisdiction of the FBI is limited to federal laws mandated by Congress.

There are three major divisions of the political jurisdiction of law enforcement agencies: federal, state, and local. These political jurisdictions are determined by which government body (federal, state, or local) exercises authority over the agency.

Federal Law Enforcement

Federal law enforcement agencies, each with a different jurisdiction and administrative leadership, have been developed to handle the enforcement of federal laws. These agencies are under the administrative control of the executive branch of the federal government. The president, with the approval of the Senate, appoints the chief executive officers of the various federal law enforcement agencies.

While federal, state, and local agencies might have similar responsibilities, there are distinct differences among the agencies. Federal agencies enforce only federal laws. There are different court systems for federal crimes, state crimes, and local crimes, as well as different rules of evidence in each court level. When there are overlapping responsibilities, most of the time, the various agencies work cooperatively. However, there are times when agencies have conflicts.

1 **American policing was initially based on Sir Robert Peel's London system, which, in 1829, was the first to establish a full-time, paid, uniformed police agency; over time, the U.S. system evolved to adapt to changes in society and beliefs about law enforcement.**

jurisdiction the geographical limits of responsibility and legitimate duties of law enforcement officers

federal law enforcement agencies agencies that enforce only federal laws and are under the control of the executive branch of the federal government

Organization of U.S. Police Agencies

- Federal Police
  - Military Police
  - Tribal Police
  - Federal Civilian Law Enforcement
    - U.S. Marshals Service
    - U.S. Postal Service
    - Secret Service
    - FBI
    - Bureau of Alcohol, Tobacco, and Firearms
    - Drug Enforcement Agency
- State Police
- County Police
- City Police

Often federal law enforcement agencies work together due to overlapping jurisdictions and expertise.

Source: U.S. Immigration and Customs. www.ice.gov/news/galleries Public domain

Federal Jurisdiction and Police Powers

Most federal agencies have jurisdiction in all 50 states, the District of Columbia, and U.S. territories. The legal jurisdiction of each agency is determined by legislation and executive orders. Federal agencies are often charged with the same responsibilities as are state and local law enforcement agencies. For example, both the FBI and state and local law enforcement agencies have jurisdiction over bank robberies, kidnappings, and drug crimes.

There are three distinctively different types of federal agencies: military police, Native American tribal police, and civilian police.

Military Police

Military police perform law enforcement duties on military bases, on certain federal lands, and in certain cases involving military personnel. Each of the four branches of military service (Army, Navy, Marines, and Air Force) has adopted its own unique strategy for providing police services, conducting criminal investigations, and maintaining order. For example, the Army utilizes military personnel to perform these activities. The Army's Military Police (MP) provides services similar to local police in traffic enforcement and the maintenance of order. Major crimes are handled by the United States Army Criminal Investigation Division Command (USACIDC). On the other hand, the Navy has a predominately civilian-employee-based agency to investigate major crimes, the Naval Criminal Investigation Service (NCIS).

Each branch of the military service also has its own criminal justice system, including court and correctional institutions, which are separate from the civilian criminal justice system. Military law enforcement and military justice are based upon the Uniform Code of Military Justice (UCMJ) rather than on state or federal laws.

Tribal Police

Native American reservations are considered sovereign territories, where local and state police have no jurisdiction. Federal police and the military have limited jurisdiction on these reservations. Each Native American reservation has the legal authority to establish its own **tribal police** to provide police services. In addition to tribal police departments, police services on tribal lands are provided by the FBI and the Bureau of Indian Affairs. The jurisdiction of each agency is not easily defined and, in the past, has been the subject of conflict, particularly between tribal police and the FBI.

Research suggests that public safety on Native American reservations has been neglected by the U.S. criminal justice system, resulting in a public safety crisis on the reservations. The rate of violent victimizations per 1,000 Native Americans age 12 or older for 2009 was more than twice the rate for the nation as a whole (50 per 1,000 persons).[2]

The federal government has recognized this problem, and since 1999, federal grants totaling \$89 million have been awarded to reservation police departments nationwide to increase the ranks of uniformed officers, enhance community policing efforts, and sustain trial courts.[3] In 1995, the attorney general established the Office of Tribal Justice to coordinate tribal issues for the Department of Justice (DOJ). Intended to increase the responsiveness of the DOJ to Native American tribes and citizens, the purpose of the Office of Tribal Justice is to ensure better communication by serving as a permanent point of contact between the DOJ and federally recognized tribes.

Despite these efforts, crime rates on reservations continues at record high rates. In 2009, the economic stimulus package included \$248 million for criminal justice infrastructure projects on Native American lands with the goal of reducing these crime rates. The main targets are domestic assaults and drug crimes. Also targeted for reduction

military police police who are members of the military and provide law enforcement services on military bases, on certain federal lands, and in cases involving military personnel

tribal police police that provide law enforcement services on Native American reservations, where local and state police have no jurisdiction, and federal police have only limited jurisdiction

2 **The U.S. criminal justice system has no central authority to oversee police activities, but instead, there are numerous federal, state, and local agencies with responsibilities for specific geographic and legal areas.**

Development of Policing

1901 In response to the assassination of President William McKinley, the duties of the Secret Service are expanded to include the protection of the president.

1905–1932 **August Vollmer,** Chief of Police in Berkeley, California, emphasizes education, professionalism, and administrative reform, and is known as the father of modern American policing. Vollmer's contributions include scientific crime-detection practices, training for police officers, selection of police officers based on performance testing, and a vision of an expanded role of police officers in the community beyond that of "thief catchers."

1908 President Theodore Roosevelt creates the Bureau of Investigation, the forerunner of the FBI, to provide detective services to the executive branch of the federal government.

1913 A typical Boston police officer is recruited from the working class and makes $1,400 per year after 6 years of service. He works 75 hours a week with 1 day off in 15. He receives little or no training and is hired on the basis of his obedience to authority, physical strength, and size.

1919 The emergence of the United States as the world's industrial leader after World War I brings significant changes to policing. Increased population density in New York, Boston, Philadelphia, Detroit, and Chicago, along with increased ethnic diversity, produce social disorder. Most people consider the primary threats to public order to be street violence, gangs, and vices such as gambling, drinking, and prostitution.

1934 The National Firearms Act is passed, and the Treasury Department is charged with the duty of collecting federal taxes on firearms.

1939 After World War I, Franklin D. Roosevelt charges the FBI with the responsibility for domestic intelligence matters relating to espionage and subversive activities.

1952 The Office of Internal Revenue is reorganized to include the newly created Alcohol and Tobacco Tax Division.

1968 The Gun Control Act is passed and the Alcohol, Tobacco, and Firearms Division (ATF) is created.

1970 The Organized Crime Control Act increases ATF responsibilities to include explosives.

1972 The Civil Rights Act of 1964 is amended to prohibit discrimination by local, state, and federal criminal justice agencies.

1973 All duties related to alcohol, tobacco, firearms, and explosives are transferred from the Internal Revenue Service to the ATF.

1973 The Drug Enforcement Administration (DEA) is formed.

1982 The Anti-Arson Act makes arson a federal crime and gives the ATF responsibility for investigations.

1995 The Office of Tribal Justice is established to coordinate Native American tribal issues for the Department of Justice.

2003 The formation of the Department of Homeland Security combines 22 existing agencies under a single command.

is the unique crime of pillaging artifacts from tribal lands in the Southwest. Attorney General Eric Holder has proposed a number of changes in both federal responsibilities and the organizational structure of the DOJ to help combat the public safety crisis on Native American lands.[4]

Federal Civilian Law Enforcement

There are approximately 50 federal civilian law enforcement agencies. Some are small, with limited duties, while others are major agencies with international jurisdiction. The formation of the Department of Homeland Security (DHS) on March 1, 2003, had a major influence on the organizational structure and responsibilities of federal civilian law enforcement agencies. The new organization placed 22 previously independent agencies under the command and control of the DHS. The goal of this reorganization was to provide unity of command for the various semiautonomous federal agencies in an effort to enhance national security. The newly formed DHS is not a law enforcement agency, but rather a cabinet-level agency.

The largest and most visible of the federal civilian law enforcement agencies are the U.S. Marshals Service, the U.S. Postal Inspection Service, the U.S. Secret Service, the Federal Bureau of Investigation, the Bureau of Alcohol, Tobacco, Firearms, and Explosives, and the Drug Enforcement Administration.

U.S. Marshals Service The U.S. Marshals Service was one of the first two federal law enforcement agencies established by the Judiciary Act of 1789. The federal Marshals Service was the first federal agency with general law enforcement powers, with responsibilities for providing security for federal courts, serving papers of the federal courts, and enforcing federal laws.

During the late 1800s, federal marshals were responsible for maintaining law and order in the Western territories, but they often lacked the necessary manpower and resources to carry out such responsibilities. To supplement their manpower, federal marshals were authorized to enlist the service of civilians and the military to help them perform their duties. This power to "deputize" civilians and military troops for law enforcement purposes is known as *posse comitatus.*

Today, the law enforcement jurisdiction of the U.S. Marshals Service still includes federal court security and serving papers of the federal courts, but its law enforcement duties tend to be limited compared to other federal agencies such as the FBI and the DEA. However, the **U.S. Marshals Service** performs other specialized services such as the movement and custody of federal prisoners, the capture of inmates who escape from federal penitentiaries, and the protection of witnesses.

The U.S. Marshals Service often works with other law enforcement agencies to assist city, county, and state police with their fugitive cases, and it is the primary U.S. agency responsible for returning fugitives wanted in the United States from foreign countries.

U.S. Postal Inspection Service The **U.S. Postal Inspection Service,** established in the same year as the U.S. Marshals Service, is a specialized law enforcement agency responsible for the security of the United States mail and mail carriers, and for investigation of mail fraud. Its law enforcement agents are called postal inspectors and are employed by

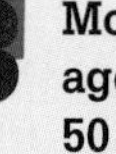

3 **Most federal law enforcement agencies have jurisdiction in all 50 states, the District of Columbia, and U.S. territories and have distinct duties that are similar to those of state and local police.**

U.S. Marshals Service the federal agency that provides security for federal courts, is responsible for the movement, custody, and capture of federal prisoners, and provides protection of witnesses in federal cases

U.S. Postal Inspection Service the federal agency responsible for the security of U.S. mail and mail carriers and for investigation of mail fraud

DEA drug busts may result in the seizure of millions of dollars in cash or drugs.

Source: Drug Enforcement Agency. www.justice.gov/dea/images_major_operations.html#2010

the United States Postal Service. The Postal Inspection Service has both armed and unarmed inspectors. Postal inspection agents have the powers of arrest, search and seizure, and the authority to carry firearms. Their geographical jurisdiction extends to wherever there is U.S. mail service; however, their primary law enforcement responsibilities are limited to crime related to protecting the integrity of mail services. The Postal Inspection Service has always had a low-key profile, despite the fact that it is one of the larger-staffed federal law enforcement agencies and has an impressive record of effectiveness. Often, the positions of postal inspectors are filled from the ranks of mail carriers.

U.S. Secret Service Another early federal law enforcement agency was the U.S. Secret Service, founded in 1865. Initially, this agency was under the control of the Department of the Treasury, as its primary duties related to investigating the widespread counterfeiting and currency violations that immediately followed the Civil War, when there were numerous legal currencies in circulation. Counterfeiting was widespread in part because it was legal for large companies, banks, and states to print and mint legal tender, or money. Also, the technology for printing money used by the federal government was relatively primitive, and the forgery of acceptable-quality counterfeit money was not difficult.

Starting in 1894, the Secret Service provided informal part-time protection of President Cleveland. However, no agency was charged specifically with the full-time responsibility and resources for protecting the president from assassination or harm. The president, like any other citizen, went about his duties and life without the protection of federal bodyguards. Motivated by the assassination of President William McKinley at Buffalo, New York, in 1901, the duties of the Secret Service were expanded to include the protection of the president.

Over time, the protective duties of the Secret Service were expanded. Today, the **U.S. Secret Service** protects not only the president but also the president's family, the vice president and designated members of his family, former presidents and their minor children, and widows of former presidents. With the assassination of presidential candidate Robert Kennedy in 1968, Congress again expanded the protection responsibilities of the Secret Service to include major presidential and vice presidential candidates. The U.S. Secret Service also protects visiting heads of foreign governments.

Federal Bureau of Investigation The Federal Bureau of Investigation (FBI) was not created until the twentieth century; however, it is perhaps the most famous of the federal police agencies. The forerunner of the FBI, the Bureau of Investigation, whose agents were unarmed, was created by executive order in 1908 by President Theodore Roosevelt. The primary purpose of the bureau was to provide detective services to the executive branch of the government. The Bureau of Investigation at first focused on finding Communist agents in the United States.

The FBI became a prominent federal police agency during the 1930s under the leadership of J. Edgar Hoover. During this time, agents of the FBI waged a war on crime that resulted in the FBI killing John Dillinger, "Pretty Boy" Floyd, "Baby Face" Nelson, "Ma" Barker, Alvin "Creepy" Karpis, and other gangsters. Unlike the negative publicity and critical review that results today when police agents use deadly force, the social context of the time was such that the killing of gangsters by the FBI was widely accepted as a great contribution to public safety.[5]

Since 1930, the responsibilities of the **Federal Bureau of Investigation** have grown steadily. In 1939, in response to the needs caused by World War I, the FBI was charged by President Franklin D. Roosevelt with the responsibility for domestic intelligence matters relating to espionage, sabotage, and subversive activities.[6]

Through legislation such as the Mann Act in 1910, the Lindbergh Law in 1932, the Fugitive Felon Act in 1934, and the National Firearms Act in 1934, the FBI has been able to assume additional criminal responsibilities. However, the FBI is not a national police force. It does not have control or jurisdiction over state and local police agencies.

In addition to criminal investigation and domestic intelligence responsibilities, the FBI also maintains and operates a sophisticated crime lab and makes the technical expertise of its crime lab available upon request to other police agencies free of charge.

The FBI operates the largest training academy in the United States for law enforcement agencies. The prestigious FBI training academy provides

The FBI provides assistance and resources to state and local police. When departments lack crime scene investigation resources, the FBI will assist them.

Source: FBI – public domain

U.S. Secret Service the federal agency that protects the president, the vice president, members of their families, major candidates for president and vice president, and visiting heads of foreign governments

Federal Bureau of Investigation (FBI) the federal agency responsible for protecting the U.S. from terrorist attacks, foreign intelligence and espionage, cyber-based attacks, and high-technology crimes, and for combating public corruption at all levels

instruction in investigation, management, computer crime, homeland security, and other important subjects to local and state law enforcement personnel. As with the crime lab services provided by the FBI, there is no tuition charged for those who attend the training academy.

The FBI also maintains the National Crime Information Center (NCIC), the nation's largest database of computerized criminal information on wanted felons, persons on parole, criminal history, and stolen items such as automobiles, boats, guns, and securities. Nearly every police agency participates in the NCIC, and it has been an invaluable tool in law enforcement in this highly mobile, contemporary society.

Following the September 11, 2001, attacks, however, public and congressional scrutiny resulted in a significant reorganization of the FBI.

To combat future terrorism, FBI Director Robert Mueller asked for hundreds of new agents, better computer resources, and a redirected mission and priorities that will force the FBI to change its organizational culture and shed its traditional case-oriented focus on criminal activity.[7] Mueller hopes to build "a Federal Bureau of Prevention whose central mission is to collect, analyze and act on information that will help prevent attacks." Mueller told Congress, "The FBI must become better at shaping its workforce, collaborating with its partners, applying technology to support investigations, operations and analyses, protecting our information and developing core competencies."

The new FBI priorities are as follows:

- Protect the United States from terrorist attack.
- Protect the United States against foreign intelligence operations and espionage.
- Protect the United States against cyber-based attacks and high-technology crimes.
- Combat public corruption at all levels.
- Protect civil rights.
- Combat transnational and national criminal organizations and enterprises.
- Combat major white-collar crime.
- Combat significant violent crime.
- Support federal, state, local, and international partners.
- Upgrade technology to successfully perform the FBI's mission.

The FBI also reorganized its Counterterrorism Division, established the Office of Intelligence, and placed more emphasis on coordination with other agencies and using intelligence information more effectively. As a result of all these changes, the FBI is focusing its recruitment on candidates who possess skills beyond those associated with traditional criminal investigation. The critical skills that the FBI is now seeking in new agents include computer science, other information technology specialties, engineering, physical sciences (physics, chemistry, biology), foreign language proficiency (Arabic, Farsi, Pashtu, Urdu, Chinese, Japanese, Korean, Russian, Spanish, and Vietnamese), foreign counterintelligence, counterterrorism, military intelligence experience, and fixed-wing pilots.

Bureau of Alcohol, Tobacco, Firearms, and Explosives The origins of the Bureau of Alcohol, Tobacco, Firearms, and Explosives (ATF) were related to the need of the Treasury Department to enforce tax laws on alcohol and tobacco. Responsibilities for firearms and explosives were added later. Initially, the agency's activities were focused on tax evaders. Early in U.S. history, the taxing of alcoholic beverages became a significant source of income for the federal government, and there was a need to collect taxes from those who evaded those taxes. In 1862, Congress created the Office of Internal Revenue within the Treasury Department and authorized the agency to investigate criminal evasion of taxes. The Office of Internal Revenue was to eventually become the ATF.

New duties were added to the Treasury Department with the passage of the National Firearms Act in 1934, as the department was charged with the duty of collecting federal taxes on certain types of firearms. In 1952, the Internal Revenue division of the Treasury Department was reorganized, and the Alcohol and Tobacco Tax Division was created. In 1968, the Gun Control Act was passed. In addition to regulatory responsibilities for firearms, the department also assumed responsibility for explosives. To fulfill these responsibilities, the Treasury Department created the Alcohol, Tobacco, and Firearms Division. In 1970, the Organized Crime Control Act increased the ATF's responsibilities for explosives. In 1972, the functions, powers, and duties related to alcohol, tobacco, firearms, and explosives were transferred from the Internal Revenue Service to ATF. In 1982, the Anti-Arson Act made arson a federal crime and gave the ATF responsibility for investigating commercial arson nationwide.

The mission of ATF is to conduct criminal investigations, regulate the firearms and explosives industries, and assist other law enforcement agencies.

Source: Bureau of Alcohol, Tobacco, Firearms, and Explosives (ATF). www.atf.gov/field/losangeles/gallery.html

HERE'S SOMETHING TO THINK ABOUT . . .

Source: Charlotte Mecklenburg, NC Police Department. http://charmeck.org/CITY/CHARLOTTE/CMPD/ORGANIZATION/SUPPORT/Pages/Citizens%20On%20Patrol.aspx

As budget cuts continue due to the economic downturn, many departments have to find a way to provide services with reduced personnel. Many have turned to citizen volunteers. Nationwide nearly 2,200 police departments utilize over 244,000 citizen volunteers, who perform diverse duties including traffic control, criminal investigation, and auxiliary policing. What concerns may arise regarding the use of citizen volunteers in law enforcement?

In 2003, the Bureau of Alcohol, Tobacco, and Firearms was transferred under the Homeland Security bill to the Department of Justice. The law enforcement functions of the ATF under the Department of Treasury were transferred to the Department of Justice. The tax and trade functions of the ATF remained with the Treasury Department with the new Alcohol and Tobacco Tax and Trade Bureau. The agency's name was changed to the **Bureau of Alcohol, Tobacco, Firearms, and Explosives** to reflect its new mission. However, the initials ATF used to identify the agency continue in common use.

Drug Enforcement Administration Another high-profile federal law enforcement agency is the **Drug Enforcement Administration (DEA)**. The DEA, founded in 1973, is one of the newest federal law enforcement agencies. The mission of the DEA is to enforce controlled-substances laws and regulations of the United States and bring to criminal and civil justice systems of the United States, or any other competent jurisdiction, those organizations and principal members of organizations involved in the growing, manufacture, or distribution of controlled substances appearing in or destined for illicit traffic in the United States; and to recommend and support nonenforcement programs aimed at reducing the availability of illicit controlled substances on the domestic and international market.[8]

This mission gives the DEA virtually worldwide jurisdiction, but at the same time, it makes it one of the most focused of the federal law enforcement agencies. Despite its worldwide jurisdiction, unlike other federal law enforcement agencies, its mission focuses primarily on violations and education related to controlled substances.

The War on Drugs and the new emphasis on the perceived dangers of criminal drug marketing and use have made the DEA a major law enforcement agency. There are over 5,000 DEA agents, and the DEA is the lead agency in countering the use of illicit drugs in the United States.

The worldwide jurisdiction of the DEA is attributed in part to the rise of the international drug cartels in the 1980s, particularly the Medellín Cartel of Columbia. Worldwide drug cartels have created the phenomenon of "narcoterrorism," whereby drug lords in some countries operate virtually unchecked by law enforcement. Also, the linkage of international drug trafficking as a fund-raising activity for terrorism has emphasized the role and importance of drug enforcement.

Other Federal Law Enforcement Agencies

Other federal agencies with law enforcement powers include the Internal Revenue Service (IRS), the National Park Service, the National Forest Service, the U.S. Fish and Wildlife Service, the U.S. Air Marshals, and a number of small agencies with limited jurisdiction.

The Central Intelligence Agency (CIA) and the National Security Agency (NSA) are two very important federal agencies. Both of these large government agencies have responsibilities related to national security, but their focus is on threats posed by foreign governments and powers. In fact, the CIA is prohibited by law from conducting any operations on American soil other than those that are administrative. Law enforcement operations related to domestic national security are handled by the FBI.

The State Police

The geographical jurisdiction of the state police is limited by state boundaries, and their legal jurisdiction is determined by legislation. State law enforcement agencies can be divided into three major types: traffic enforcement, general criminal investigations, and special investigations. Some states, such as Kentucky, have a single state police agency that is responsible for both general criminal investigations and traffic enforcement. Other states have created distinct agencies for each function. The state of Hawaii has neither a state highway patrol nor a statewide general criminal investigation agency. The state legislature of each state has the authority and discretion to establish the state police agencies that they deem most appropriate for the needs of their state.

The oldest state law enforcement agency is the Texas Ranger Division of the Texas Department of Public Safety. Stephen F. Austin is credited with the formation of the unit that became the origins of the Texas Rangers in 1823. While today, the Texas Rangers are a relatively small law enforcement agency of fewer than 150 commissioned members, the history and reputation of the Texas Rangers as a law enforcement agency in the Old West is legendary and has been the subject of many books and movies. The feelings of Texans toward the Texas Rangers is reflected by the fact that they may have the distinction of being the only law enforcement agency that is protected from disbandment by Texas state legislation.

Highway Patrol

State police agencies that focus on traffic enforcement are commonly called the **highway patrol**. The legal jurisdictions for these agencies are limited to enforcing the traffic laws and promoting safety on the interstate highways and primary and secondary roads of the state. Generally, state traffic enforcement officers do not provide general preventive patrol services to neighborhoods, as do municipal police, or engage in the investigation of crimes. State highway patrol officers enforce the

One of the oldest state police agencies is the Texas Rangers, pictured in an anonymous 1845 drawing.

Source: The Culver Pictures Collection. A group of Texas Rangers (anonymous drawing, c. 1845).

Bureau of Alcohol, Tobacco, Firearms, and Explosives (ATF) the federal agency responsible for regulating alcohol, tobacco, firearms, explosives, and arson

Drug Enforcement Administration (DEA) the federal agency that enforces U.S. laws and regulations regarding controlled substances and that supports nonenforcement programs intended to reduce the availability of illicit controlled substances domestically and internationally

highway patrol state law enforcement agencies that focus on traffic enforcement

4

The major types of law enforcement agencies are traffic enforcement, general criminal investigation, investigations of allegations of political corruption, and investigation of statewide crime networks. The geographical jurisdiction is within state boundaries and their legal jurisdiction is determined by state legislation.

various traffic laws of the state, render assistance to motorists, and promote highway safety. Highway patrol officers have the powers of arrest and search and seizure, and are authorized to carry firearms. State highway patrol officers are commonly called "troopers."

Criminal Investigation State police agencies have law enforcement powers similar to municipal police in that they are authorized to conduct criminal investigations, perform routine patrol, and provide police services. So as not to duplicate the law enforcement services provided by municipal and county police, state police focus on the investigation of statewide crimes, such as those involving drugs and narcotics, or crimes that occur in more than one jurisdiction, such as a mobile crime ring, organized crime, or serial murders. In counties in which the sheriff's department cannot provide police services to unincorporated areas in the county, the state police may provide services to these areas. Sometimes, small towns or villages will contract with the state police to provide police services for a fee rather than attempt to have their own police department.

State police can also have jurisdiction for investigation of crimes when the municipal or county police may appear to be biased. In cases in which there are charges of political corruption of local officers, voter fraud, or bribery of state officials, it might make sense to give jurisdiction for these investigations to the state police.

County Law Enforcement Agencies

The sheriff's office is the oldest local policing authority in the United States. A sheriff is elected by popular vote of county residents. In contrast, police chiefs and directors of state and federal law enforcement agencies obtain their positions through political appointment.

Most modern sheriffs are elected to 4-year terms. In many county elections, sheriffs are expected to affiliate with a political party and to raise funds to campaign for the position. Qualifications to run for sheriff are minimal. The most common requirements are a minimum age and no felony convictions. A successful campaign, political affiliation, and public appeal are more important in obtaining the office of sheriff than are job experience, education, or law enforcement abilities. It is not uncommon for some sheriffs to have no previous background in law enforcement prior to being elected.

Often seen in the news for his "tent city" jail or his stand against illegal immigration, Sheriff Joe Arpaio of Maricopa County (AZ) is probably the best known sheriff in the United States.

Source: Maricopa County Sheriff's Office. www.mcso.org/Media/Gallery.aspx

Because a sheriff has countywide jurisdiction, whereas local police departments have only municipal jurisdiction, the sheriff is generally designated as the **chief law enforcement officer** of the county. The chief law enforcement officer of the state is the attorney general, and the chief law enforcement officer of the United States is the U.S. attorney general.

Administrative Structure of the Sheriff's Department The sheriff is empowered to appoint officers to help him or her carry out the duties of the office. These officers are called deputy sheriff officers. The second in command of the sheriff's office sometimes retains the old English title of undersheriff. Deputy sheriffs wear different uniforms from those of local police within their county to distinguish the two departments. The star-shaped badge worn by deputy sheriffs is a carryover from the old English office of the sheriff, whereas officers in most police departments wear shields.

This system of selecting deputy sheriffs was based on the belief that an elected sheriff should be able to appoint employees on the basis of loyalty. If a sheriff failed to win reelection, the incoming sheriff had the authority to dismiss the deputy sheriffs and award the jobs as political patronage to those who had helped him or her win office.

Until the latter half of the twentieth century, sheriffs selected their deputies based on the same criteria on which they had obtained their own offices—politics. Deputy sheriffs served at the pleasure of the sheriff, and those who did not campaign or contribute to the sheriff's election effort could be fired. Deputies could be fired for supporting the sheriff's opponent or even for being perceived as a liability. Likewise, deputies could be hired as a reward for supporting the sheriff in his or her campaign or because they were friends or relatives.

Today, there are state-mandated minimum training requirements for law enforcement officers. As a result of court rulings prohibiting the dismissal of deputy sheriffs for failing to campaign for the sheriff (or in some cases, campaigning for the sheriff's opponent), most sheriff's departments use a civil service selection process for the appointment of sworn officers. Deputy sheriffs are selected based on competitive examinations that test job knowledge, skills, and abilities, and can be dismissed from their jobs only for legitimate reasons.

Law Enforcement Duties of the Sheriff The sheriff's department can have three major responsibilities: law enforcement duties, serving as **officers of the court**, and operating the county jail. The Office of the Sheriff was the first and only local law enforcement agency in the late eighteenth and early nineteenth centuries. The sheriff and his deputies were empowered to enforce the laws of the county and state, to make arrests, to engage in preventive patrol, and to carry firearms. With the rise of municipal policing in the latter half of the twentieth century, the role of the sheriff in providing law enforcement services diminished. Today, in practice, it is often the municipal police who assume major responsibility for law enforcement and the sheriff's department that provides police services for citizens who live in unincorporated or rural areas of the county. However,

5 **A sheriff campaigns and is elected as the chief law enforcement officer of a county and need not have any law enforcement experience; he or she can appoint deputy sheriffs to help carry out the office of the sheriff's duties of enforcing laws, serving as officers of the court, and operating the county jail.**

chief law enforcement officer the highest-ranking law enforcement official within a system; the sheriff is the chief law enforcement officer of a county; the attorney general is the chief law enforcement officer of a state; and the U.S. attorney general is the chief law enforcement officer of the United States

officer of the court a law enforcement officer who serves the court by serving papers, providing courtroom security, and transporting incarcerated defendants

in some major metropolitan areas, very little of the county is unincorporated, and the law enforcement services of the sheriff overlap those of municipal police.

The Office of Sheriff is the oldest local law enforcement agency in the United States with roots that extend back to the Middle Ages and the English Office of Sheriff appointed by the King of England. As such, in the United States, the sheriff was initially the only person responsible for detecting crime and bringing criminals to justice. However, in the twentieth century, the local police quickly assumed responsibility for criminal investigations. As the unincorporated portion of counties diminished, the sheriff's responsibility for criminal investigation also diminished. Today, the criminal investigation responsibilities of a sheriff's office varies greatly from county to county. Some sheriff's offices have significant criminal investigation responsibilities, and others have none at all. In some counties where the sheriff has responsibility for criminal investigations, some small cities in the county will contract with the sheriff's office for traffic and criminal investigation services. Sheriff's offices that have law enforcement units have different standards for hiring, training, and pay for what are called "road" officers versus those deputies who work in the jail.

ALTHOUGH THE GEOGRAPHICAL JURISDICTION OF MUNICIPAL POLICE OFFICERS IS LIMITED COMPARED TO COUNTY, STATE, AND FEDERAL AGENTS, THEIR LEGAL JURISDICTION IS THE MOST COMPREHENSIVE OF ALL THE POLICE AGENCIES.

There is the potential for conflict between sheriff departments and city police regarding geographical jurisdiction concerning crimes and routine patrol, as in some counties there are overlapping jurisdictional claims. Unlike state police agencies that may offer specialized criminal investigation services to a community, the sheriff's department and the city police provide similar services, which may duplicate each other.

The City Police: "The Cops"

When most people refer to "the police" they mean the municipal police. Many town and city residents appear not to appreciate or notice the difference among deputy sheriffs, state police, and municipal police officers. Commonly referred to simply as "the cops," municipal police officers far outnumber all other types of law enforcement officers combined.

Often local police are involved in youth activities, drug education programs, and community activities.

Each incorporated town or city in the United States has the power to establish its own police department and laws. Thus, there are over 12,000 municipal police departments. Typically, the size of a municipal police department increases as the population of the city increases, and the largest police departments are found in the largest cities.

Large cities can employ thousands of police officers, but most municipal departments are much smaller. Over 90 percent of the municipal police departments employ fewer than 50 officers and serve populations of less than 25,000.[9] The police department is one of the major expenses of any city. The budget for a small police department averages about \$1.7 million per year, and large departments might have budgets that exceed \$300 million.[10] New responsibilities related to the War on Terrorism have strained the budgets of many police departments.

\$300 million
Budgets of large police departments can exceed this amount

90%
Number of municipal police departments employing fewer than 50 officers

Jurisdiction of Local Police

The geographical jurisdiction of a municipal police officer is limited to the city limits. Once outside his or her municipal jurisdiction, a local police officer's powers to arrest, search, or even carry a firearm may not be recognized.

Although the geographical jurisdiction of municipal police officers is limited compared to county, state, and federal agents, their legal jurisdiction is the most comprehensive of all of the police agencies. Municipal police officers have the authority to enforce both city and state laws, and often their authority is based on common law rather than statutory law. Common law authority gives the officers broad discretion in determining what behaviors are illegal.

As cities have merged into large metropolitan areas, police departments have responded by expanding the geographical jurisdiction of municipal police officers through intercity agreements. In large metropolitan areas such as Dade County (Florida) and Las Vegas, intercity and county agreements have established the **metro police**. These agreements provide for greater geographical jurisdiction to avoid the problems that would develop if the police did not have any powers outside of their city limits.

metro police local police agency that serves several geographic locations, such as a large city or county

6 **The city police, or "cops," are limited by the geographical limits of the city but have the greatest legal jurisdiction of all police enforcement agencies, with authority for traffic enforcement, accident investigation, patrol and first response to incidents, and property crime, violent crime, and murder investigations.**

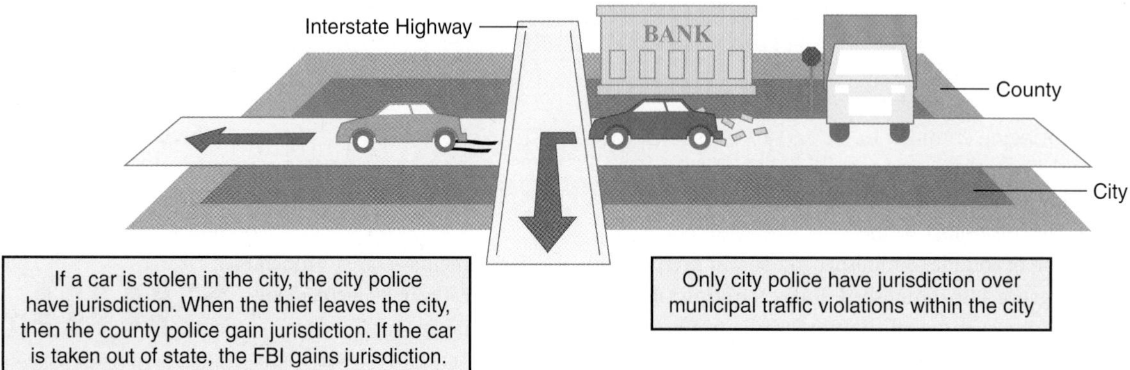

Police Patrol, Crime Prevention, and Other Services

Municipal police are responsible for a wide variety of services. The most commonly demanded services of the municipal police include traffic enforcement, accident investigation, patrol and first response to incidents, property crime investigation, violent crime investigation, and murder investigation. Municipal police departments also end up assuming *de facto* responsibility for many things that are not their job, because they are one of the very few government agencies available 24 hours a day, 7 days a week, and they will dispatch an officer to the scene. Thus, it is common to find that municipal police agencies also have responsibilities for animal control, search and rescue, emergency medical services, civil defense, communication and technical support services, jail operations, **order maintenance,** and even firefighting in some cities.

In an effort to save money, some smaller cities have combined the police department and the fire department. Commonly called the Department of Public Safety, the officers of these departments receive training in both law enforcement and firefighting.

Serving Shifts and Districts

The organizational structure of police departments is also based on geography. Departments divide the geographical area for which they are responsible into small units called districts, beats, or precincts. Each geographical unit is given a name or number relating to its location, its natural boundaries, or its place in the local economy, such as business district, warehouse district, waterfront, or downtown. The size of a unit and the number of officers assigned to it are based on population density and demand for police services in the area.[11]

The need to deliver round-the-clock services means that police departments have to have multiple time-based shifts. Most small police departments have three shifts. Medium-sized and large police departments may have multiple and even overlapping shifts. Overlapping shifts provide for additional coverage during times of high demand for police services. Thus, the organizational structure must provide for supervision, officers, and support for the various districts and time-shifts.

Special Police

Special police include airport police, park police, transit police, public school police, college and university police, public housing police, game wardens, alcoholic beverage control agency police, and special investigative units. The largest single employer of special police is the New York City Transit Police, with over 4,000 full-time officers.

Special police have limited jurisdiction both in geographic and police powers. They are hired, trained, and equipped separately from municipal police officers, sheriff's deputies, and state officers. Many state colleges and universities have police departments rather than security departments.[12] The employees of these campus police departments have general police powers on the state campus, have the right to make arrests and conduct searches, and have the authority to carry and use firearms. They are police departments, but they provide services only for specific campuses. Although special police agencies perform essential services, are the source of a substantial number of jobs, and contribute significantly to the public safety of citizens, they have had little impact or influence on the development of the criminal justice system.[13]

order maintenance noncrime-fighting services performed by police, such as mediation, providing for the welfare of vulnerable persons, and crime control

special police police with limited jurisdiction. Special police have very narrowly defined duties and sometimes extremely limited geographical jurisdiction

Administrative Structure of the Municipal Police

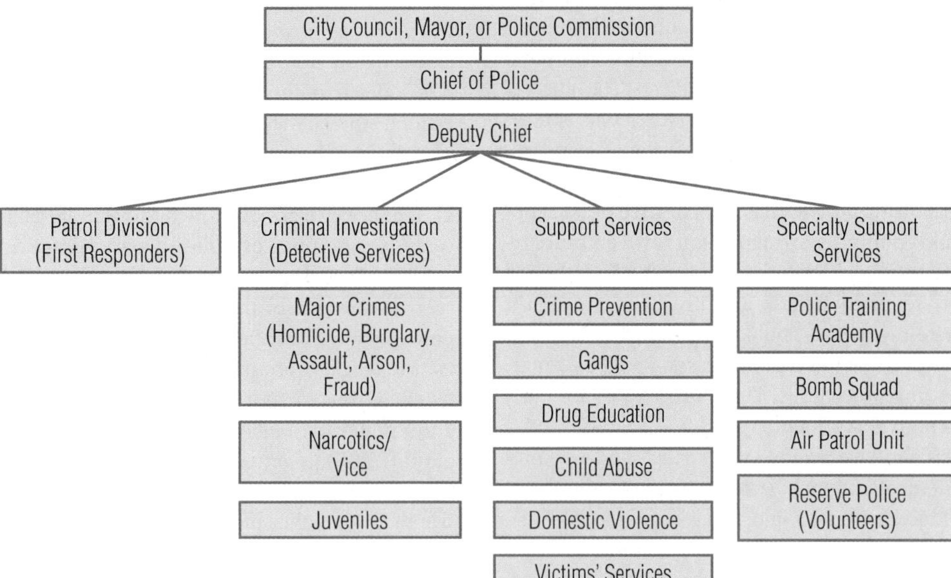

Administrative Structure of the Municipal Police

The chief administrative officer of the police department is usually called the **chief of police**. The chief obtains his or her position by appointment. In smaller cities, the chief may be directly appointed by the mayor or city council. In larger cities, the chief may be appointed by a police commission appointed by the city council. Unlike the sheriff, who is elected for a specified number of years, the chief may have no guarantee of the term of his or her appointment. For this reason, chiefs are said to "serve at the pleasure of the mayor or the city council." This political relationship between the chief and city administrators has influenced local policing.

The second-in-command of the police department is usually called the **deputy chief** or assistant chief. This person is selected by the chief from among the higher-ranking police administrators. Promotions among other ranks and the hiring of new police officers for the department are usually accomplished through competitive civil service exams based on job-related skills, abilities, and knowledge. These officers are called "sworn" personnel because they must take an oath to uphold the laws of the city, state, and county and to execute faithfully the responsibilities of their offices.

"Nonsworn" personnel of the police department, such as secretaries, office workers, and technicians, are referred to as civilian employees. Civilian employees do not have the powers granted to sworn police personnel of arrest, search and seizure, and the right to carry a firearm. Sworn personnel normally enjoy what is referred to as "civil service protection," which means that after completing their probation period of employment, they cannot be dismissed from their jobs without cause and due process.[14]

Police departments have a system of military-style ranks in a hierarchical pyramid, with a chain of command from officer to chief.[15] This is termed a *command-and-control structure*, as in the organizational chart. Although also organized in terms of a command-and-control structure, federal law enforcement agencies do not use military titles; instead, they use titles such as "field agent," "supervisor," "agent-in-charge," and "director."

The police organizational chart differentiates among the various functions that the department performs. The most common divisions are patrol, detective services, and support services. The patrol division is the largest organizational unit. Detective services include the investigation of crimes such as fraud, burglary, arson, and homicide. Larger departments allow for specialization among detectives, including juvenile officers, vice squad officers (gambling and prostitution), and other divisions based on types of crime. Support services might include special units for community crime prevention, drug education in schools, juvenile delinquency, child abuse, missing children, drunk drivers, gangs, domestic violence, repeat offenders, hate crimes, victims' services, and more.[16] Specialty support units include the police training academy, the air patrol unit, the bomb squad, and the reserve or auxiliary police (volunteers who assist in police duties).

Selection of Police Officers

Every police department is faced with the challenge of recruiting and retaining highly qualified men and women to fill the ranks of the police department. Large cities, such as New York and Chicago, have to recruit thousands of police officers each year. Most smaller cities recruit only one or two officers per year.

chief of police the chief administrative officer of a municipal police agency

deputy chief the second in command below the chief of police. In a large police department, there may be several deputy chiefs each commanding a large unit within the police department.

7 **Candidates must take written and oral tests, physical and psychological tests, drug-screening tests, and pass background checks; selected candidates complete training at a police academy followed by field training under the supervision of an experienced officer.**

The process of becoming a police officer is unlike applying for an entry-level position in private industry. The hiring process takes months to complete, and the initial training can take up to 6 months. During this time, applicants will be screened, examined, tested, observed, stressed, and evaluated in many different ways. They will be tested for their physical, psychological, and intellectual fitness as police officers. The object of this extensive screening and training process is to produce police officers who can perform their duties to the high professional standards demanded by the department, the community, and the law.

There is no universal hiring process that must be used by local police agencies. Each city and county department sets its own entrance requirements, salary levels, testing procedures, and timetable. Although there are no universally required criteria and procedures, over the years—as a result of state regulations, public expectations, Supreme Court decisions, and civil and criminal liability cases—police agencies have adopted a set of hiring procedures. These procedures are fairly uniform from department to department.

Supreme Court decisions have required that hiring standards must reflect job-related requirements, cannot be arbitrary, and cannot discriminate on the basis of race, national origin, religion, or sex.[17] The major impact of these decisions has been to eliminate minimum height requirements, which were once as high as 6 feet for some police departments; to eliminate nonjob-related physical tests such as climbing 10-foot walls; and to eliminate discrimination based on race, color, and gender.

The usual process for hiring includes a written test, an oral interview, a physical examination, fitness testing, psychological testing, a background check, a drug-screening test, and, in some departments, a polygraph examination.[18]

A prominent change in minimum job qualifications for police officers has been an increased emphasis on recruiting from a more educated pool of applicants.[19] The requirement of a minimum of a high school education was not universal in the 1960s. College-educated officers were rare. Even college-educated police executives were rare, as it is estimated that less than 1 percent of local police chiefs had a bachelor's degree in the 1960s. Today, nearly all local police departments require a minimum of a high school diploma or general equivalency degree (GED) to apply for employment.[20, 21]

A 1967 presidential commission recommended that a 4-year college degree should be the minimum requirement for employment as a local police officer.[22] Although this standard has not been adopted universally, a number of police departments require some college or a 4-year college degree to apply for the position of police officer.[23]

A major factor that promoted the emphasis on college-educated police officers was the federal Law Enforcement Assistance Administration (LEAA) program. From the late 1960s to the early 1980s, the federal government administered an educational loan and grant program under the LEAA, called the Law Enforcement Educational Program (LEEP), to encourage criminal justice personnel and applicants to attend college. Under LEEP, college students who indicated their desire to join a police department after graduation, as well as employed police officers, could obtain student loans to attend the colleges of their choice. In return for remaining in the criminal justice system after graduation from college, their educational loans were forgiven. Nearly 100,000 students took advantage of this government program.[24]

The LEEP program was discontinued in the early 1980s, but the number of college-educated police officers has continued to grow. Other factors, such as the adoption of new communication and computer technologies by the police, continue to increase the demand for college-educated police officers. For example, computer literacy is becoming a common job requirement for police officers, as all police departments serving more than 50,000 people use computers, and nearly 25 percent of larger departments (100,000–1,000,000) use laptop computers.[25]

Today, most new police officers must receive between 400 and 1,100 hours of training before they are allowed to exercise their powers as a police officer.[26] In addition, many states have required that every police officer must complete a minimum number of hours of training each year to retain his or her police powers.

After candidates are interviewed, tested, and screened, a number of selected candidates are given notices to report to a **police academy** and undertake up to 1,100 hours of training. The academy emphasizes academic learning, physical fitness, and development of the recruits' aptitude for police work. In the academy, the recruit learns the specific laws of the state, county, and/or city of his or her jurisdiction.[27]

Most departments use some form of in-service training or **field-training program** to further evaluate the suitability of the candidate for police work after graduation from the training academy.[28] During this period of time, the academy graduate works directly under the supervision of an experienced officer. The experienced officer evaluates the "street-sense" and attitude of the new officer and assesses his or her ability to be a good cop.[29]

The field-training program may last only several weeks, but most departments keep a newly hired officer on a probationary status for up to a year. During this time, the department reserves the right to dismiss the officer without having to show cause.

HERE'S SOMETHING TO THINK ABOUT . . .

Source: Federal Bureau of Investigaton. www.fbi.gov/news/photos/image/people/ert.jpg

To solve crimes, police agencies use sophisticated and sometimes controversial tools. The photo shows members of an FBI response team digging up buried "bodies" at the "body farm" to observe the characteristics of decay over time. The Austin (TX) Police Department and a few other departments use drone technology for urban monitoring. By 2013, it is expected that drone surveillance will be much more pervasive. Also, the Internet, various social networks, and cell phones have become common tools for crime investigators. One concern related to many of these new investigative tools is the loss of privacy. How should the right to privacy be balanced with the need to gather information?

8 Modern policing reflects the values of the communities through several strategies and theories.

police academy a facility or program for the education and training of police officers

field-training program a probationary period during which police academy graduates train in the community under the direct supervision of experienced officers

Policing Strategies

One of the more powerful influences on police professionalism and community satisfaction with police services is how the police go about their job of providing services and what services the police think are most important to provide.[30] Police scholar James Q. Wilson proposed that rather than viewing police behavior as random and independent of community values, the style of policing and hence the behavior of the police officer should be viewed as closely related to the type of city government and community expectations.

An important point to emerge from the studies of Wilson is the premise that there is a link between police behavior and community values. The police do not act randomly, nor do they develop values in a vacuum. Police strategies reflect a department's values, which reflect community values.

Community Policing

During the 1960s and 1970s, the crime rate began to climb. Cities burned. Drugs, gangs, and crime became pandemic. The image of police omnipresence proved to be a myth as cities were consumed with disorder and riots that the police could neither prevent nor control. Fear of crime, increasing violence, mistrust of the police, and serious doubts about the professionalism of the police resulted in widespread dissatisfaction with police services—especially with the municipal police.[31] It is not surprising that since the late 1980s, new policing strategies have been adopted by many police departments as a reflection of the public's dissatisfaction with traditional policing. One of these new policing strategies came to be known as "community policing."[32]

Community policing developed during the 1960s and 1970s as citizen disenchantment with police services and criticisms of police professionalism led to experimentation with different policing strategies.[33] One of the early strategies used during this period was team policing.[34] **Team policing** attempted to establish small units of police personnel who would assume responsibility for public order and crime control within a geographical area. It was thought that this decentralization would encourage more police–community involvement. Unfortunately, because of the incompatibility of the decentralized decision-making strategy of team policing and the highly centralized command-and-control administrative model of policing, team policing was strategically incompatible.

DESPITE ITS POPULARITY AND WIDESPREAD USE, THERE IS NO UNIVERSALLY ACCEPTED DEFINITION OF COMMUNITY POLICING. AS A RESULT, MANY POLICE DEPARTMENTS HAVE DECLARED THAT THEY HAVE ADOPTED COMMUNITY POLICING; HOWEVER, EACH COMMUNITY POLICING PROGRAM IS DIFFERENT.

What Is Community Policing? Despite its popularity and widespread use, there is no universally accepted definition of community policing. As a result, many police departments have declared that they have adopted community policing; however, each community policing program is different.[35] The common characteristics of **community policing** are these:

- focus on decentralized strategies that promote crime prevention rather than rapid response, crime investigation, and apprehension of the criminal[36]

HERE'S SOMETHING TO THINK ABOUT . . .

Source: Federal Bureau of Investigation. http://www.fbi.gov/contact-us/legat

A number of U.S. law enforcement agencies have an international presence as shown by the map of worldwide FBI offices. The Drug Enforcement Agency conducts operations in Mexico, Afghanistan, and other countries where drug production and export affect the United States. Even the New York Police Department has officers stationed overseas. What are some problems U.S. law enforcement agencies may have operating in foreign countries?

team policing a decentralizing development during the 1960s and 1970s in which small units of police personnel took responsibility for a particular geographical area

community policing decentralized policing programs that focus on crime prevention, quality of life in a community, public order, and alternatives to arrest

- focus on promoting the quality of life of the community and public order rather than law enforcement[37]
- use of alternatives other than arrest and force to solve the cause of the problem rather than responding to the symptoms of the problem[38]

Broken Windows and Zero Tolerance Although each police department has approached community policing differently, an underlying theme of community policing is a partnership between the police and the community. In this partnership, the police become problem identifiers, dispute resolvers, and managers of relations rather than crime fighters, law enforcers, and the "thin blue line."[39]

Underlying this strategy of public order is the **broken window theory.**[40] In an interesting experiment, an automobile was parked in a neighborhood and left. It was discovered that the automobile was more quickly vandalized if a window on the parked automobile was broken than if the automobile was left undamaged. The message sent by the broken window was, "Nobody cares—other acts of vandalism are okay."

When applied to a neighborhood, the broken window theory means that if vacant buildings are left untended, if graffiti is tolerated, and if public order violations such as public drinking, disruptive behavior by youths, and vandalism are permitted, these will be signals to people that nobody cares about the community, leading to more serious disorder and crime.[41]

One of the strategies associated with the broken window philosophy is strict enforcement for minor violations of the law, such as public drinking, after-hours use of parks, loitering, and even jaywalking. This strict enforcement is called the **zero-tolerance strategy,** and the assumption behind this strategy is that it will send the message to more serious lawbreakers that if even such minor offenses are noticed by the police, then more serious offenses also will bring prompt police action. According to the broken window theory, tolerance by the police and the community for people breaking "small laws" demonstrates the community's apathy and leads to more serious crime.

Police Partnership and Public Order Studies conducted in the 1970s indicated that much police work actually involved order maintenance as opposed to crime fighting.[42] In fact, in only about 5 percent of all dispatched calls in most cities does the officer have a chance to intervene or make an arrest. Despite the emphasis of the police on rapid response time, these studies suggested that rapid response time was, in general, an ineffective crime-fighting strategy. The philosophy of community policing holds that order maintenance, not law enforcement, is the root of crime fighting. If a community has a high degree of public order, more serious crime is less likely to develop.[43]

Frequently, when police seek to enter into a partnership with the residents of a neighborhood to promote public order and to fight crime, both sides must learn to trust each other and to communicate. Neither the police nor the community are accustomed to working with each other. The old division between "us and them" or "police and civilians" had worked effectively to separate the community and the police. In working in partnership with the community, sometimes community expectations were quite surprising to the police. In one attempt to establish community policing in a public housing project, police officers thought that initially the residents would want to see the police direct their resources toward fighting drug dealing, violence, or youth gangs. To their surprise, the major complaint of the residents was illegally parked cars and abandoned vehicles.

Problem-Oriented Policing Community policing emphasizes attacking the root problem that causes crime instead of responding to the symptoms of the problem by arresting offenders and taking victimization reports. This approach to crime fighting is sometimes called problem-solving policing or **problem-oriented policing.** Problem-oriented policing emphasizes three main themes:[44]

- increased effectiveness by attacking underlying problems that give rise to incidents that consume patrol and detective time;
- reliance on the expertise and creativity of line officers to study problems carefully and develop innovative solutions; and
- closer involvement with the public to make sure that the police are addressing the needs of citizens.

Rather than being reactive, problem-solving policing emphasizes the role of the police as proactive—acting before crimes are committed. Seldom, or never, are they expected to take steps to find out what was the cause of the crime or conflict and what would prevent it from recurring.[45] Problem-oriented policing focuses on resolution of the problem.

Scanning, Analysis, Response, and Assessment (SARA) One commonly used technique in problem-solving policing is scanning, analysis, response, and assessment (SARA).[46]

Scanning is the process of gathering data about an incident that would allow an officer to define the problem.

Analysis is the search for information that would let an officer understand the underlying nature of the problem and its causes and consider a variety of options for its resolution.

Response requires an officer to work with citizens, businesses, and public and private agencies to implement a solution that would impact the cause of the problem.

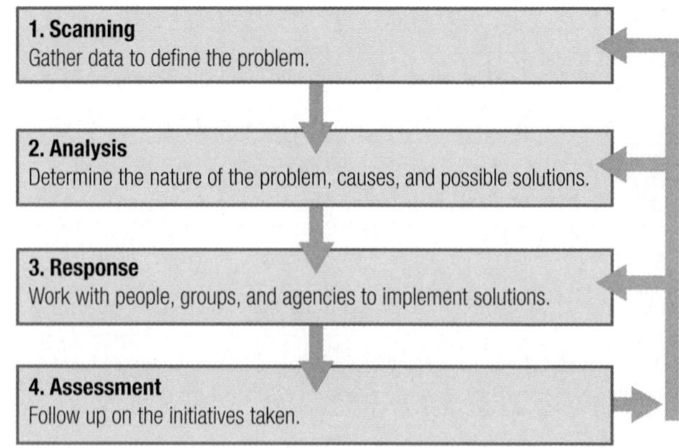

broken window theory the belief that ignoring public order violations and disruptive behavior leads to community neglect, which fosters further disorder and crime

zero-tolerance strategy strict enforcement of the laws, even for minor violations

problem-oriented policing a proactive type of community policing that focuses on solving the underlying problems of delinquency and crime

HERE'S SOMETHING TO THINK ABOUT . . .

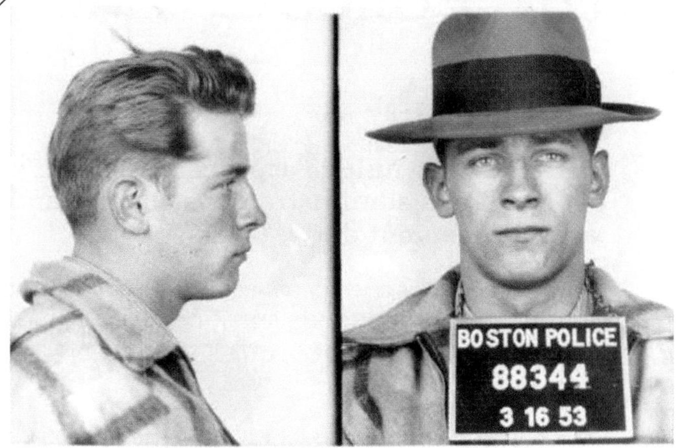

Policing has been characterized by incompetency, misconduct, and corruption. While advances have been made these continue to be a concern. For example, when Mafia figure James (Whitey) Bulger was arrested in 1953, many feared he would reveal the names of officials who helped him elude capture. Bulger claimed during his criminal career he made payoffs to both Boston police officers and FBI agents. A 2011 Justice Department investigation of the New Orleans Police Department concluded, "The department is severely dysfunctional on every level: one that regularly uses excessive force on civilians, frequently fails to investigate serious crimes and has a deeply inadequate, in many cases nonexistent, system of accountability." The trial of Captain Jon Burge, of the Chicago Police Department, revealed systematic police torture and violation of civil rights. Rural departments are not exempt. In southern Illinois, Gallatin County Sheriff Raymond Martin was sentenced to life in prison for 15 felony drug counts and a foiled plot to have potential witnesses killed. Some police misconduct may be motivated by racial discrimination, as in the Dallas (TX) Police Department, in which officers were citing immigrants for being "non-English-speaking drivers" when there was no such law. What can be done to help improve policing?

Assessment requires the officer to follow up on the initiative taken to see if it has had the desired effect.

Challenges of Community Policing If community policing is so great, why isn't everyone doing it? Critics argue that community policing will not last because, like team policing, it requires that decision-making be decentralized in the police administrative structure. Problems are solved through decisions made by the lowest-ranking persons in the organization.

Decentralization of Decision-Making The decentralization of decision-making runs counter to the traditional paramilitary command-and-control organizational culture of the police. Some argue that "despite scholarly opinions, the street cops tend to prefer the quasi-military style."[47] This argument is based on the assumption that the traditional law enforcement strategy gives the police officer a better sense of control, structure, and direction in an otherwise chaotic environment.

Need for Retraining Community policing requires more-educated officers and officers with creative problem-solving abilities.[48] Police officers must view members of the public as a potential resource in crime fighting rather than as potential criminals. Some argue that the police officer's separation or isolation from the community makes it possible for him or her to engage in grisly interactions such as assaults, accident victims, and shootings, day after day as duty demands, without becoming impaired by emotional overload.

Crime Displacement Versus Elimination Many believe that the dislocation of crime is a major problem with community policing. Although community policing and problem-solving strategies may reduce robberies, burglaries, prostitution, and car thefts in one neighborhood, they may not eliminate the crimes but merely drive them to another part of the community or to another community.

Minority Communities Some people have expressed serious concern over the ability of community policing strategies to work in minority neighborhoods.[49] Supporters of community policing dispute this claim, and it is not clear what effect the minority race or ethnicity of an officer has on community policing efforts in minority neighborhoods.

Tyranny of Neighborhoods A final concern over community policing strategies is the "potential tyranny of neighborhoods." In an effort to promote quality of life and to fight crime, neighborhoods may mistake diversity and tolerance for crime and disorder. Neighborhoods can be places of congeniality, sociability, and safety, but they can also be places of smallness, meanness, and tyranny. The minority youth walking in a white neighborhood may find that he becomes a target of the police and the community because he is different, not because he is criminal.

The Future of Community Policing The jury is still out on the benefits of community policing strategies, although they are popular with the public. It is too early to tell if community policing strategies will be universally adopted. As more police departments document their efforts at community policing strategies, data will accumulate. It may be that community policing strategies might have little impact on crime rates, but instead, a much greater impact on the community's fear of crime.

Traditional police strategies have emphasized crime fighting and investigation and have paid little if any attention to citizens' fear of crime. Police have assumed that fear is caused by criminal victimization. They reasoned that if criminal victimization is reduced, fear of crime would naturally diminish. However, research has shown that the causes of fear of crime do not stem so much from criminal victimization as other interactions and environmental cues.[50] The level of fear of crime does not necessarily go down as the crime rate drops. Community policing may be an effective strategy for reducing citizens' fear of crime, because one of the positive effects of the adoption of community policing strategies seems to be that it promotes the belief by citizens that the community has been empowered. Citizens feel less helpless in the face of rising crime rates. Even in communities where crime rates do not decrease with the adoption of community policing strategies, the self-confidence of the community seems to improve and the fear of crime decreases.

CHAPTER 4

Roles and Functions of the Police

Check It!

1 HOW did American policing develop, and what is its connection to the London Metropolitan Police of 1829? p. 56

The American system of policing was based on the London system developed by Sir Robert Peel in 1829 and evolved over time to adapt to changes in American society and its beliefs about law enforcement.

2 HOW is jurisdiction related to the organization of the contemporary U.S. system of policing? p. 57

The U.S. has no centralized authority for police activities, but instead, it has many federal, state, and local police agencies with responsibilities within geographical and legal jurisdictions.

3 WHAT are the major federal law enforcement agencies, and what are their duties? p. 58

Most federal law enforcement agencies have jurisdiction in all 50 states, the District of Columbia, and U.S. territories.

1. Marshals Service: responsible for security for federal courts, custody of federal prisoners, and protection of witnesses
2. Postal Inspection Service: responsible for the security of U.S. mail and mail carriers and investigation of mail fraud
3. Secret Service: protects the president, vice president, members of their families, major candidates for president and vice president, and visiting heads of foreign governments
4. FBI: responsible for protecting the U.S. from terrorist attacks, foreign intelligence and espionage, cyber-based attacks, and high-tech crimes, and for combating public corruption at all levels
5. ATF: responsible for regulating alcohol, tobacco, firearms, explosives, and arson
6. DEA: enforces U.S. laws and regulations regarding controlled substances domestically and internationally

4 WHAT are the major types of state law enforcement agencies, and what are their jurisdictions? p. 61

The major state law enforcement agencies are traffic enforcement, general criminal investigations, and special investigations; their geographical jurisdiction is within state boundaries.

5 WHAT are the unique aspects of a sheriff's department's administrative structure and law enforcement duties? p. 62

Sheriffs are elected as chief law enforcement officers of a county, need not have law enforcement experience, and can appoint deputy sheriffs to enforce laws, serve the court, and run the county jail.

6 WHAT are the jurisdictions of city police, and what services do they provide? p. 63

The jurisdiction of city police is within city limits; their duties include traffic enforcement, accident investigation, patrol and first response to incidents, and property crime, violent crime, and murder investigations.

7 WHAT are the hiring and training procedures for police officers? p. 65

Candidates must take written and oral tests, physical and psychological tests, drug-screening tests, and pass background checks. Selected candidates complete training at a police academy followed by field training under the supervision of an experienced officer.

8 HOW do social values and other factors influence policing strategies? p. 66

Modern policing reflects the values of the communities through several strategies and theories:

1. community policing
2. broken window theory and zero tolerance
3. police partnership and public order
4. problem-oriented policing
5. scanning, analysis, response, and assessment (SARA)

Assess Your Understanding

1. Which of the following law enforcement agencies has the largest geographical jurisdiction?
   a. municipal police
   b. county sheriff
   c. state police
   d. U.S. Marshals Service

2. Which branch of the military service uses a predominately civilian employee–based staff to investigate major crimes?
   a. U.S. Navy
   b. U.S. Army
   c. U.S. Air Force
   d. U.S. Marines

3. Which of the following is a federal civilian law enforcement agency?
   a. tribal police
   b. Naval Criminal Investigation Service
   c. U.S. Secret Service
   d. Department of Homeland Security

4. Which of the following agencies is known as "officers of the court" and assists the courts by providing courtroom security and serving the official papers of the court?
   a. municipal police
   b. county sheriff
   c. state police
   d. all of the above

5. How do most county sheriffs obtain their position?
   a. appointment by the governor
   b. competitive civil service hiring process
   c. election
   d. appointment by a commission or committee

6. Which agency provides courtroom security for federal courts?
   a. U.S. Marshals Service
   b. private security guards
   c. FBI
   d. county sheriff or local police where the federal courthouse is located

7. Which agency is responsible for protecting the president and vice president of the United States?
   a. FBI
   b. U.S. Secret Service
   c. Special Presidential Security Office of the Department of Homeland Security
   d. none of the above

8. How does the typical chief of police obtain his or her position?
   a. appointment by a police commission, city council, or mayor
   b. popular election
   c. competitive civil service hiring process
   d. appointment by the governor

9. Which of the following may be used by police departments in selecting new police recruits?
   a. written examination
   b. physical fitness testing
   c. background check
   d. all of the above

10. Which of the following is characteristic of sworn police personnel?
    a. Sworn police personnel are mostly support and staff personnel.
    b. Only middle- and upper-level police administrators are sworn police personnel.
    c. Only detectives are sworn police personnel.
    d. Sworn police personnel have the power of arrest, search, and seizure, and to carry a firearm.

11. Which of the following is a characteristic of community policing?
    a. emphasis upon rapid response to crime and apprehension of criminals
    b. emphasis upon crime prevention and community involvement
    c. use of scientific crime fighting techniques and strategies
    d. setting of policing goals by community action groups

ESSAY

1. How is jurisdiction related to the organization of the contemporary U.S. system of policing?
2. Compare and contrast the three types of federal law enforcement agencies.
3. Describe the major types of state law enforcement agencies and their responsibilities.
4. What are the responsibilities of the office of the sheriff?
5. Describe the hiring and training procedures for police recruits.

ANSWERS: 1. d, 2. a, 3. c, 4. b, 5. c, 6. a, 7. b, 8. a, 9. d, 10. d, 11. b

Media

Go to the *Chapter 4: Roles and Functions of the Police* section in *MyCJLab* to test your understanding of this chapter, access customized study content, engage in interactive simulations, complete critical thinking and research assignments, and view related online videos.

Additional Links

Go to www.met.police.uk/history/archives.htm to see a detailed history including historic photographs of the London Metropolitan police.

All of the major law enforcement agencies have excellent Web sites that provide information about many aspects of the agencies, including employment opportunities. Many law enforcement agencies have Facebook sites. Visit some of the Web sites of major law enforcement agencies such as the following to review the information available about these agencies: www.fbi.gov, dea.gov, usmarshals.gov, nyc.gov/html/nypd/html/home/home.shtml, chicagopolice.org, lapdonline.org

Go to www.fbijobs.gov to see employment information for the Federal Bureau of Investigation including the physical fitness requirements and background disqualifiers.

Go to www.ncis.navy.mil/ to view the Web site of the Naval Criminal Investigation Service. The site provides information about the NCIS and a link to employment opportunities with NCIS.

To view a number of videos published by the Drug Enforcement Agency, go to www.justice.gov/dea/multimedia.html

To view a number of videos published by the Federal Bureau of Investigation, go to www.fbi.gov/news/videos/view

To download a number of documents published by the U.S. Secret Service including information on employment with the U.S. Secret Service, protection, investigations, and data, go to www.secretservice.gov/downloads.shtml

To watch a short video promoting a career with the San Diego Sheriff's Department, go to www.youtube.com/watch?v=nX1Os9dR-5E

To watch a 2011 Fox News story on investigations of police misconduct by the U.S. Department of Justice, go to www.youtube.com/watch?v=AUiZO24bQaY

See the Web site of the National Sheriffs' Association, at www.sheriffs.org/, for more information about the Office of Sheriff.

The first state police created after the forerunner of the Texas Rangers was the Pennsylvania State Police Department. For more information about the Pennsylvania State Police, go to www.psp.state.pa.us/portal/server.pt/community/psp/4451

Tribal Justice and Safety at the Department of Justice is a new agency focusing on justice and safety on traditional Native America lands. To obtain more information, see their Web site at www.tribaljusticeandsafety.gov/

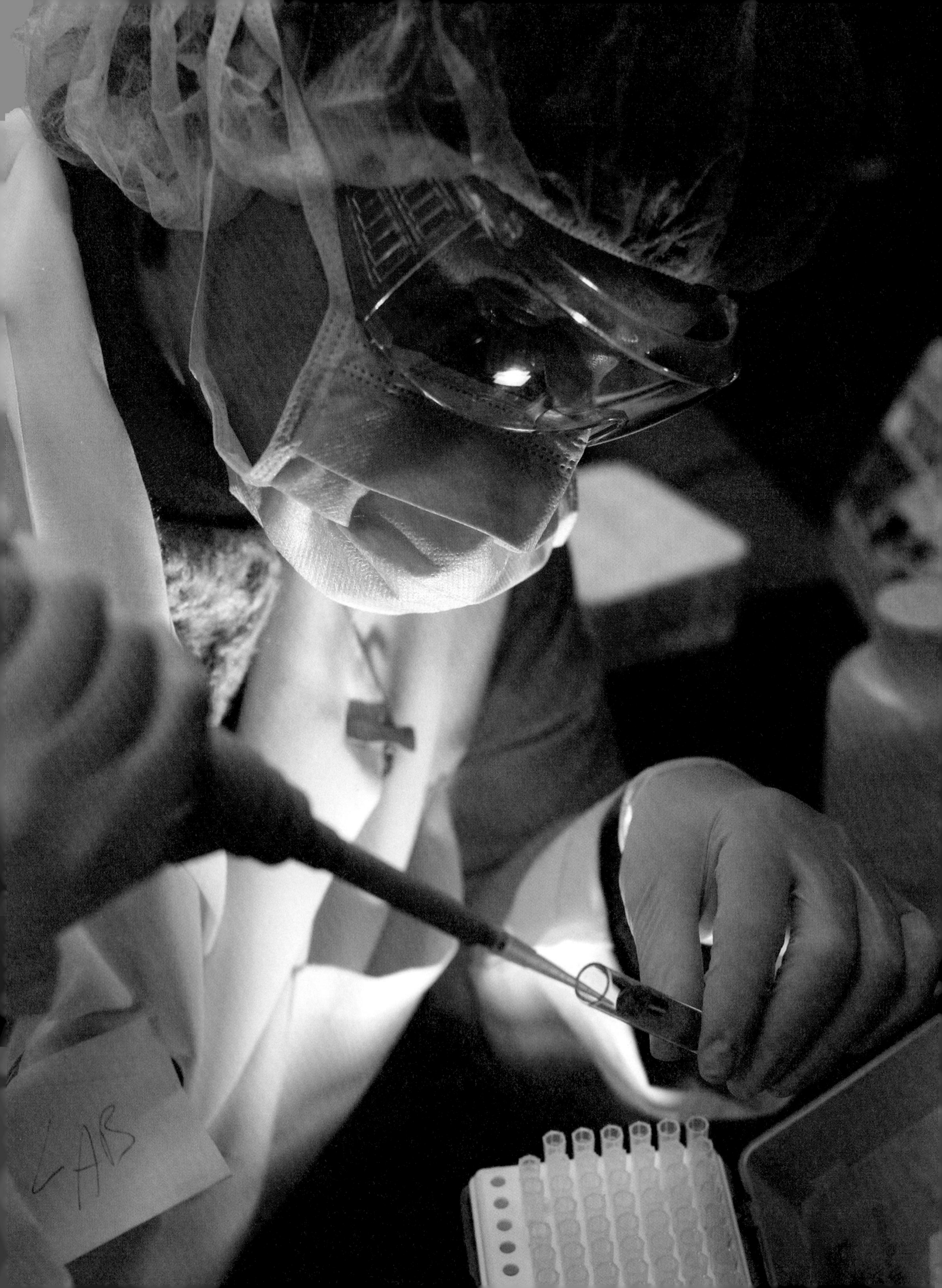
LAB

POLICE OFFICERS AND THE LAW

5

The U.S. Constitution guarantees certain due process rights to those accused of crimes. However, the Constitution lacks specificity regarding the interpretation of these rights in the twenty-first century. The decisions of the U.S. Supreme Court define today's due process rights. This process continues to evolve and the interpretations of rights change as social values, technology, and scientific knowledge change. An examination of one aspect of the Sixth Amendment right of a defendant to confront the witnesses against him or her provides a glimpse into this complicated and often lengthy process.

It took the U.S. Supreme Court two decades to define one particular aspect of Sixth Amendment rights. Prior to 1993, forensic evidence such as alcohol blood content, fingerprint identification, drug identification, and other forensics tests were introduced as reports without requirement that the person who performed the test appear in court to testify or to submit to cross-examination by the defense.

A series of critical reports, mostly by the National Academy of Sciences, revealed major flaws in forensic laboratories which were mostly within law enforcement institutions. As these reports emerged, the Court issued a series of decisions changing the standards for forensic evidence. The change started with *Daubert v. Merrell Dow Pharmaceuticals* (1993), in which the Court ruled that scientific testimony had to meet an objective standard. In *Crawford v. Washington* (2004) and *Melendez-Diaz v. Massachusetts* (2009), the Court upheld the right of defendants to cross-examine the person who performed the forensic test. A final ruling in *Briscoe v. Virginia* (2011) declared "certificates of analysis" or testimony from someone other than the person who performed the actual procedure violated the defendant's Sixth Amendment rights. Thus, after two decades a new standard has emerged regarding Sixth Amendment rights.

This chapter discusses the balance between crime fighting and due process rights and the various U.S. Supreme Court decisions that have helped shape and interpret the protections provided by the U.S. Constitution.

1. **What are procedural laws, and how do they affect the actions of the police?**
2. **What are the rules of evidence for police actions regarding the collection of evidence, and what landmark cases were involved in establishing the exclusionary rule?**
3. **What guidelines must police follow in conducting searches that do not violate citizens' constitutional rights?**
4. **What exceptions allow search and seizure by police without a warrant?**
5. **What rights are citizens guaranteed while in police custody regarding interrogations and confessions?**
6. **Under what circumstances may police legally make an arrest or hold a person in custody?**

THE CONSTITUTION GUARANTEES DUE PROCESS RIGHTS TO THOSE ACCUSED OF CRIMES. HOWEVER, THE CONSTITUTION LACKS SPECIFICITY REGARDING THE INTERPRETATION OF THESE RIGHTS IN THE TWENTY-FIRST CENTURY.

Procedural Law and Oversight of the Police

Even for serious felonies such as murder, rape, and child sex offenses, failure to provide the accused the rights guaranteed to them or to follow required procedural law can result in their release from the criminal justice system. The police are responsible for the detection and investigation of crimes and for the arrest of the alleged offender. However, as they perform these responsibilities they are required to do so without violating the rights of the accused.

Procedural law is a body of laws for how things should be done at each stage of the criminal justice process. These laws are developed through legislative and judicial oversight. Police practices are affected by city and county councils, state legislatures, and the federal Congress. These legislative bodies can pass laws that limit or expand police jurisdiction, create standards, and provide remedies for police practices not acceptable to the community. For example, some states, such as the Commonwealth of Pennsylvania, have in recent years passed legislation restricting the use of radar speed traps by municipal police in response to allegations of abuse.

According to the separation of powers, police officers have the power to arrest people, but not the power to prosecute people for the charges on which they have been arrested. The power to file a criminal complaint against a defendant—even to decide who will be brought to court to face charges and who will not—rests with the judicial branch of government in the hands of an independent prosecutor's office.

Rules of Evidence

The police have the primary responsibility for detecting and investigating crime, gathering evidence to present in court, and arresting suspects. However, they do not have unrestricted powers in fulfilling these responsibilities and must perform these duties within prescribed limits set by legislation, judicial oversight, and the Constitution. One of the most influential criminal justice agencies regulating police behavior is the U.S. Supreme Court. The Supreme Court has the power to review cases to determine whether the constitutional rights of the accused have been preserved. It also has the power to establish the rules by which courts operate. Rules that relate to the presentation of evidence in a trial are called the rules of evidence.

Rules of evidence stipulate the requirements for introducing evidence and define the qualifications of an expert witness and the nature of the testimony he or she may give. According to the rules of evidence, for example, the prosecutor must show the defense the evidence he or she has gathered against the defendant. Rules define when evidence is relevant to the case and to particular issues in the case.

Rules of evidence affect police officers' conduct because collecting evidence is part of their job. If evidence is not collected properly, it can be declared inadmissible, in which case it cannot be used against a defendant. For example, if a defendant is on trial for the illegal possession

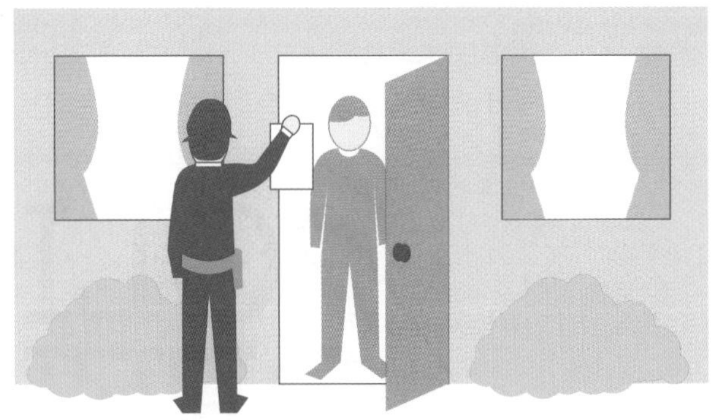

of drugs and the drugs that he or she is accused of possessing are declared inadmissible as evidence, the prosecutor cannot present this evidence to the jury. Thus, the prosecutor has no case.

The Exclusionary Rule

Evidence can be declared inadmissible under the **exclusionary rule**, which prohibits the use of evidence or testimony obtained in violation of civil liberties and rights protected by the U.S. Constitution. The exclusionary rule originated with the 1914 Supreme Court case *Weeks v. United States*.[1] In the *Weeks* case, the U.S. Supreme Court ruled that evidence against Weeks that had been obtained without a warrant was in violation of his protections under the Fourth Amendment.

Evolution of the Exclusionary Rule

1914 ***Weeks v. United States*** establishes the exclusionary rule, which prohibits the admission in federal courts of evidence obtained in violation of Fourth Amendment rights

1918 ***Silverthorne Lumber Co. v. United States*** establishes the fruit of the poisoned tree doctrine, which prohibits the admission in federal courts of indirect as well as direct evidence obtained illegally

1949 ***Wolf v. Colorado*** incorporates the exclusionary rule as a state right

1961 ***Mapp v. Ohio*** requires that all states adhere to the exclusionary rule

2006 ***Hudson v. Michigan*** allows the exception to the exclusionary rule that evidence collected in violation of the "knock-and-announce rule" does not require the suppression of that evidence

2009 ***Herring v. United States*** allows the exception to the exclusionary rule that if police conduct involves only isolated carelessness, evidence obtained by them is admissible

2010 ***Berghuis v. Thompkins*** ruled persons have a duty to assert their right to remain silent

1 **By law, the police must follow strict procedures while gathering evidence, performing searches and seizures, interrogating suspects and witnesses, and arresting suspects so as not to violate their constitutional rights.**

procedural law the body of laws governing how things should be done at each stage of the criminal justice process

rules of evidence requirements for introducing evidence and testimony in court

exclusionary rule a rule that prohibits the use of evidence or testimony obtained in violation of the Fourth and Fifth Amendments of the U.S. Constitution, established in *Weeks v. United States* (1914) and extended to all state courts in *Mapp v. Ohio* (1961)

The Fourth Amendment

The right of the people to be secure in their persons, houses, papers, and effects, against unreasonable searches and seizures, shall not be violated, and no Warrants shall issue, but upon probable cause, supported by Oath of affirmation, and particularly describing the place to be searched, and the persons or things to be seized.

Initially, the exclusionary rule applied only to federal courts. The rights guaranteed by the First Amendment (freedom of speech and freedom of association), the Fourth Amendment (privacy and search and seizure), the Fifth Amendment (self-incrimination and double jeopardy), and the Sixth Amendment (the right to confront witnesses) did not apply to the actions of local police or state courts. Until 1949, state courts were free to write their own rules of evidence.[2]

Fruit of the Poisoned Tree Doctrine

At first, the exclusionary rule established in the *Weeks* case applied only to primary (directly obtained) evidence, but not to secondary evidence. For example, if federal agents obtained the business books of a company by unconstitutional means, those books could not be used as evidence to incriminate the defendant, but a copy of the information could. Also, inadmissible evidence could lead to other evidence, which then could be introduced in court. Thus, if an unconstitutional search produced a map indicating where a defendant had buried the body of the person he or she was accused of murdering, the map could not be introduced as evidence. However, using the knowledge obtained from the map, police officers could find the body and introduce it as evidence.

Four years after the *Weeks* decision, the Supreme Court reconsidered the exclusionary rule and added another rule of evidence, known as the **fruit of the poisoned tree doctrine.** The name of the doctrine comes from the analogy that if the tree is "poisoned," then the "fruit" of the tree also will be poisoned. In *Silverthorne Lumber Co. v. United States* (1918), the Supreme Court declared that the rules of evidence applied not only to evidence directly obtained by illegal means but also to any other evidence obtained indirectly.[3] Under this rule, the copy of the business books and the body found through the aid of the map are not admissible as evidence.

The U.S. Supreme Court required the federal courts to follow this rule but still did not interfere in the procedures of state courts. Only 17 states chose to adopt similar rules of evidence. However, in *Wolf v. Colorado* (1949), the U.S. Supreme Court declared that state courts had to enact procedures to protect the rights of citizens against police abuses of search and seizure.[4] *Wolf v. Colorado* gave the states wide latitude in developing rules of evidence such as the exclusionary rule and the fruit of the poisoned tree doctrine to discourage such abuses. Twelve years later, in 1961, the Court decided that the states had failed to act to protect the constitutional rights of the defendant.

Application to State Courts: *Mapp v. Ohio*

Historically, the Supreme Court did not interfere with state courts, but with the incorporation of the exclusionary rule, this practice started to change. Without any "punishment" for gathering evidence and obtaining confessions contrary to constitutional protections, local and state law enforcement officers paid little attention to the federal constitutional rights of citizens. They knew that any evidence they obtained would be admissible at trial in state court. It was common practice for police to search without a warrant or probable cause, obtain confessions by the use of force, and in general ignore the constitutional rights of suspects. Then, in 1961, in *Mapp v. Ohio*, the U.S. Supreme Court reversed itself and required state courts to use the exclusionary rule.[5]

WITHOUT ANY "PUNISHMENT" FOR GATHERING EVIDENCE AND OBTAINING CONFESSIONS CONTRARY TO CONSTITUTIONAL PROTECTIONS, LOCAL AND STATE LAW ENFORCEMENT OFFICERS PAID LITTLE ATTENTION TO THE FEDERAL CONSTITUTIONAL RIGHTS OF CITIZENS.

The facts of *Mapp v. Ohio* are that Cleveland, Ohio, police officers received a tip from an informant that a bombing suspect was at the home of Dolree Mapp and that there was evidence at her house to connect her to the numbers racket. When police officers went to Mapp's home and asked permission to search her house, she refused. The police officers returned and announced that they had obtained a search warrant. When she asked to see the search warrant, they showed her a piece of paper, which she grabbed and stuffed into her dress. The police officers forcibly retrieved their "search warrant," which actually was a blank piece of paper.

The police proceeded to search Mapp's house without a search warrant, probable cause, or consent. They did not find the bombing suspect or the numbers evidence, but they did find a bag of obscene books and arrested her for possession of obscene materials. Mapp was convicted in state court for possession of obscene materials. Mapp felt that her Fourth Amendment rights had been violated, but when she appealed, the Ohio Supreme Court upheld the conviction. Mapp appealed to the U.S. Supreme Court, which ruled that local police officers were accountable to the same standard as in *Weeks v. United States.* Therefore, the evidence obtained illegally was inadmissible. Mapp's conviction was reversed.

fruit of the poisoned tree doctrine a rule of evidence that extends the exclusionary rule to secondary evidence obtained indirectly in an unconstitutional search, established in *Silverthorne Lumber Co. v. United States* (1918) and in *Wolf v. Colorado* (1949)

2 **The exclusionary rule prohibits police from collecting direct or indirect evidence without a search warrant, consent, or probable cause.**

Mapp v. Ohio was the first case in which the U.S. Supreme Court applied the exclusionary rule to state courts. All state courts were then required to adopt rules of evidence, which declared that evidence would be inadmissible in criminal court if it was gathered without a warrant, probable cause, or consent. The exclusionary rule has been considered one of the most important doctrines in deterring police misconduct. It was not created by legislation and is not found in the Constitution. The Supreme Court created the rule as a means to respond to violations of constitutional rights by the police.

Exceptions to the Exclusionary Rule

The 1961 landmark case *Mapp v. Ohio* has been the standard for police conduct. Other decisions affecting the admissibility of evidence in state courts followed quickly and had sweeping effects on state criminal court procedures. However, recent decisions have cast doubt on the commitment of the Supreme Court to the usefulness of automatic suppression of evidence resulting from minor police misconduct.

Hudson v. Michigan In this case, the Court in 2006 ruled that the failure of the Detroit police to knock and announce themselves before entering the home of Booker T. Hudson was not sufficient error to justify suppressing the drugs they found under the exclusionary rule.

Herring v. United States This case involved a more significant deviation from the exclusionary rule. Bennie Dean Herring had been arrested in 2004 based on erroneous computer records showing an outstanding warrant for his arrest. As permitted by law when making a lawful arrest, the arresting officer immediately made a search of Herring and his vehicle. The search resulted in the discovery of a pistol and methamphetamine. The pistol was illegal because Herring was a convicted felon. Within 15 minutes of the automobile stop, arrest, and search, the arresting officer was notified that the outstanding warrant was void and that the police computer was in error. Herring was convicted and appealed based on the exclusionary rule that the search was unconstitutional, because without a valid warrant for arrest, there was no probable cause for the search. The facts of the case were undisputed. It was predicted that Herring's conviction would be dismissed based on Herring's arguments. However, in 2009, the Roberts Court ruled that the error by the police was minor and should be balanced against the seriousness of the crime. Writing for the majority, Justice Roberts said, "The exclusion of evidence should be a last resort and judges should use a sliding scale in deciding whether particular misconduct by the police warranted suppressing the evidence they had found. . . . To trigger the exclusionary rule police conduct must be sufficiently deliberate that exclusion can meaningfully deter it, and sufficiently culpable that such deterrence is worth the price paid by the justice system." Although the "sliding scale" is a common practice in other countries, it has been rejected in the United States since the 1914 *Weeks* decision. In *Berghuis v. Thompkins* (2010) the U.S. Supreme Court issued a significant reversal of the rights granted by *Miranda.* The Court required that the suspect must clearly tell police that he does not want to talk. Previously under *Miranda* the police had the burden of showing that a Miranda warning was given and that it was understood by the accused. The Court's decision ruled a written waiver was not necessary and if a Miranda warning was given, an uncoerced statement by the accused "establishes an implied waiver of the right to remain silent."

HERE'S SOMETHING TO THINK ABOUT. . .

The plain-view doctrine allows police to make an arrest without a search warrant. Several states are considering modification of this doctrine to grant immunity in cases of 911 calls for drug overdose victims and the person who calls for medical assistance. Hundreds of persons die from lack of treatment due to the fear that the police may arrest persons present at the scene. Without immunity often drug overdose victims are abandoned by those who could help. What would be some considerations in granting legal immunity to overdose victims and those who call for assistance?

Search and Seizure

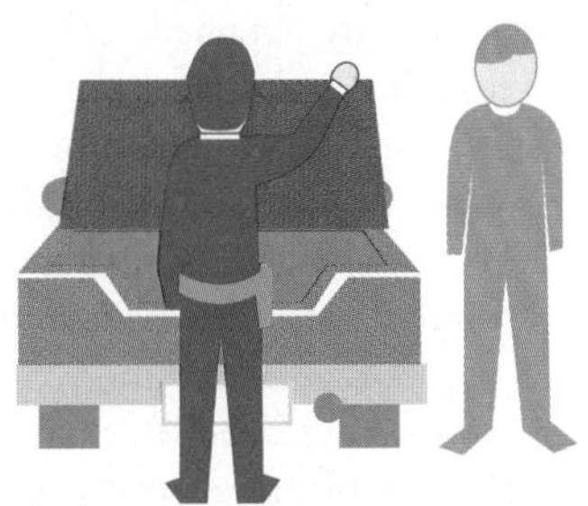

The rights of the accused are based on rights guaranteed by the U.S. Constitution, state constitutions, and legislation. Often, the Court is called on to interpret the application of these rights to specific actions of the police. Numerous changes in law, society, and technology and science have occurred since the drafting of the Constitution. Inventions such as the telephone, automobile, and the Internet emerged more than 100 years after the writing of the Constitution, so there is no specific reference in the Constitution as to how these modern technologies affect the constitutional rights envisioned by the authors of the Constitution. Thus, the Court must often interpret the intent of the Constitution as applied to modern society.

The Fourth Amendment and the Right to Privacy

The courts establish guidelines to the police through case law that provides rulings on what actions violate constitutional rights. Evidence gathered in a manner that violates the constitutional rights of the accused cannot be used in court to prove the guilt of the defendant.

The police can legally search and seize evidence when they have a valid search warrant or probable cause, when evidence is in plain view, and when a person with the authority to do so consents; police may also search a person who has been arrested, pat down a person whom they believe to be armed, and search an automobile when they have probable cause to stop the driver.

The Fourth Amendment does not guarantee absolute privacy in one's person, house, papers, and effects. Actually, the "right to privacy" is not guaranteed in the Constitution but is a right that is "inferred" from other rights guaranteed by the various amendments. As such, the right to privacy is not clearly defined. In some cases the government can access what some may consider private information and in other cases they cannot.

Medical Records When Keith Emerich of Pennsylvania reported to his doctors, who were treating him for an irregular heartbeat, that he regularly drank more than a six-pack of beer a day, his doctors reported this information to the Pennsylvania Department of Transportation as required by a state law. The law required doctors to report any physical or mental impairments that could compromise a patient's ability to drive safely. Emerich had no traffic convictions for over 20 years, but based on the information provided by his doctors, his driver's license was suspended. Emerich objected that the information he provided his medical doctor was private and confidential and should not have been reported to the commonwealth. However, the Court, after considering the balance of medical privacy versus public safety, ruled that in this case, as in other similar cases, the concern for public safety outweighed the individual's right to privacy.

However, in 2004, when the Justice Department wanted Northwestern Memorial Hospital in Chicago to disclose records on abortions performed at the hospital, a federal appeals court rejected the demand. The Justice Department claimed that the abortion records were needed in an upcoming lawsuit to test the claims of doctors who maintained that the Partial-Birth Abortion Ban Act would prevent them from performing medically necessary procedures. The federal appeals court rejected the Justice Department's claim, saying that access to such records would violate the privacy rights of women.

Reasonable Expectation of Privacy In some cases, the courts are required to decide what is a reasonable expectation of privacy. For example, when Lonnie Maurice Hill was arrested in 2003 for drug charges, he challenged the constitutionality of his arrest. Hill and a woman entered a convenience store's one-person unisex restroom. The store clerk called the police and reported this activity as suspicious behavior. When the police arrived, Hill and the woman refused to respond to the officer's request for them to open the bathroom door. When police opened the door they found marijuana and cocaine inside the restroom and arrested Hill on drug-related charges. Hill appealed that he had an expectation of privacy in the restroom. At his defense, his lawyer raised the question of whether a married couple, a parent and child, or a disabled person and an assistant occupying a single-person bathroom would be suspicious behavior. Despite these arguments, the Eighth U.S. Circuit Court of Appeals rejected Hill's claim that his expectation of privacy in the public restroom made the drugs seized by the officer inadmissible as evidence.

Electronic Monitoring At times, the Court must decide how new technology affects constitutionally protected rights, as in the case concerning event data recorders (EDRs). These devices are electronic monitoring systems in cars and trucks that track and record data, such as whether airbags deployed, whether passengers wore seatbelts, and the speed of the vehicle. EDRs are installed in 65 to 90 percent of 2004 and later model vehicles.

Typically, EDRs store the last 5 seconds of data. However, they can easily be programmed to store up to months of data. The data can be retrieved—much like the "black box" of an airplane—in the event of a crash. Also, the data are transmitted to such services as On-Star. Many drivers are not aware that their car is recording such data. Most states have no laws requiring that drivers be advised of this device. Data from EDRs have been used by law enforcement to obtain a number of convictions for vehicular homicide because police can prove the speed of a vehicle and whether the vehicle was accelerating or braking at the time of an accident. Concerned that the collection of such data violates the privacy rights of drivers, North Dakota has proposed legislation that would require that drivers be informed if their vehicles have EDRs installed and that would restrict access of police, insurance companies, and car manufacturers to such data. No doubt the courts will have to decide whether such technology violates the privacy of motorists and whether evidence gathered by EDRs can be used in obtaining criminal convictions.

Search Incident to Lawful Arrest

The Fourth Amendment requires that evidence must be obtained by police with the use of a valid **search warrant** issued by a judge or by a search based on probable cause. **Probable cause** is the likelihood that there is a direct link between a suspect and a crime. Despite this seemingly limited authority to gather evidence by searches outlined in the Constitution, the courts have authorized a number of other circumstances under which the police can gather evidence without a warrant or probable cause.

The Supreme Court has granted that when police make a lawful arrest, they are entitled to make a search of the person arrested without a search warrant. This is called **search incident to lawful arrest.** The question has arisen as to how extensive a search police can make under this justification. They cannot extend their search to rooms not occupied by the person arrested and to areas beyond the person's reach, because a search incident to lawful arrest is limited to the area within the immediate control of the person.[6] Otherwise, evidence obtained is not admissible in criminal court. Evidence obtained from a search incident to lawful arrest can include containers found within the reach of the arrestee, firearms within reaching distance, and evidence under the car seat or couch cushion on which the person is sitting.

In 2004, the U.S. Supreme Court expanded the authority of police to make searches incident to lawful arrest when they ruled that police do not need a warrant to search a car when the person they have arrested was recently in the car. The Supreme Court's ruling permits warrantless searches whenever the arrestee was a recent occupant and still in the vicinity of the car. The ruling will most likely result in further appeals, because it did not define "how recent is recent, or how close is close." Thus, it will be left up to future cases to determine the limits authorized by this decision.

search warrant legal permission, signed by a judge, for police to conduct a search

probable cause the likelihood that there is a direct link between a suspect and a crime

search incident to lawful arrest the right of police to search a person who has been arrested without a warrant

Fourth Amendment Rights Regarding Search and Seizure

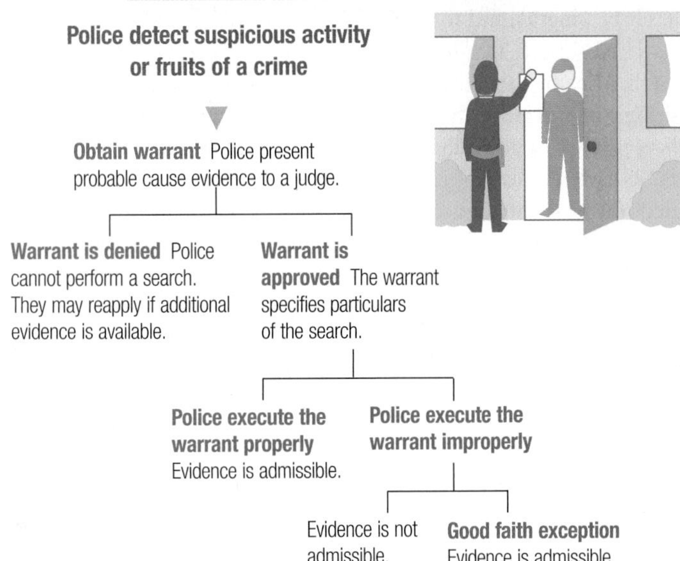

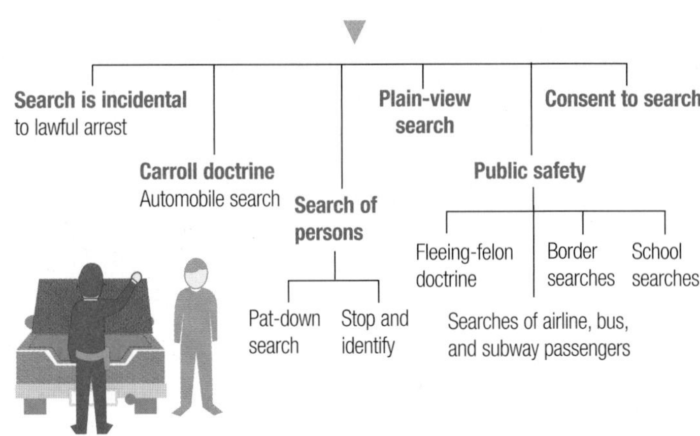

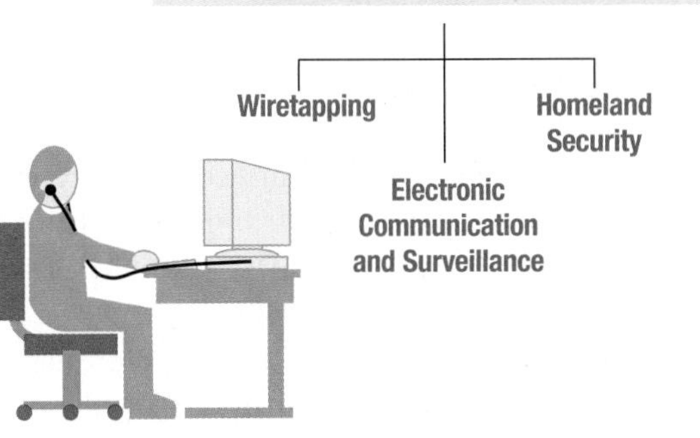

Plain-View Searches

Evidence in the plain view of police officers is admissible in criminal court (*Harris v. United States*).[7] This assumes that a police officer had the legal right to be where he or she was. If a police officer is invited into someone's home and that person was thoughtless enough to leave on the table a pile of marijuana that he or she was in the process of cleaning and sorting, the Supreme Court has ruled that such evidence obtained in a **plain-view search** is admissible. However, a police officer cannot move objects to get a view of the evidence.[8] For example, if the marijuana on the table had been completely covered with a cloth, the police officer could not remove the cloth (without permission, a search warrant, or probable cause) to see what was there. Likewise, if a police officer were to enter a room and move electronic equipment to see the serial numbers to check against a list of stolen merchandise and find a match, such evidence would be inadmissible without permission, a search warrant, or probable cause.[9] However, the police are not required to be heedless or inattentive to their environment. In the language of the Court, "inadvertence is not necessary."[10] A police officer who sees a cloth covering something on a table and smells marijuana may have probable cause to look under the cloth.

Whether evidence from a plain-view search is admissible can depend on even minor variations. For example, if a 6-foot-tall police officer is walking by a 5-foot-high fence and sees a marijuana plant growing on the other side on private property, the evidence is in plain view. If a 5′8″ police officer is walking by a 6-foot-high fence and then stands on a ladder and sees a marijuana plant growing on the other side, the evidence is not in plain view. Similarly, the Supreme Court has ruled that a police officer using a flashlight to look into an automobile at night does not violate the plain-view doctrine. However, a police officer using binoculars to view evidence might violate the plain-view doctrine.

Consent to Search

If a person gives permission for a search, any evidence discovered is admissible (*Florida v. Jimeno*, 1973).[11] The person who gives permission must have the authority to do so. For example, a landlord cannot give valid permission to search an apartment currently occupied by a tenant but can give permission once the tenant vacates the apartment. A motel owner cannot give permission to search a motel room rented to a guest but can give permission to search the room after the guest checks out. A parent can give permission to search the room of a legal dependent living in the same house but cannot give permission to search the room of a boarder living in a room rented in the house. The complexity of society has resulted in numerous rulings by the courts defining who has the authority to grant permission to search.

plain-view search the right of the police to gather without a warrant evidence that is clearly visible

Search of Automobiles

The Carroll Doctrine As early as 1925, the Supreme Court addressed the question of the constitutionality of searches of automobiles without a search warrant. Recognizing that the mobility of automobiles adds a new dimension to searches, the Court established the Carroll doctrine, based on *Carroll v. United States* (1925).[12] According to the **Carroll doctrine,** evidence obtained in the search of an automobile without a warrant is admissible in criminal court if:

1. a police officer has probable cause to believe that a crime has occurred; and
2. the circumstances are such that delay in searching the automobile would result in loss of the evidence.

This rule requires that an officer must have probable cause to stop the car in the first place.[13] If an officer does not have the authority to stop the car, any evidence obtained in a search is not admissible.

Trained Dog Sniffing In *Illinois v. Caballes* (2005, No. 03923), the Supreme Court extended the power of the police to search vehicles by permitting a trained dog to sniff a car for drugs without the need for any particular reason to suspect the driver of a narcotics violation. Justice Stevens, arguing for the majority opinion of the Court, said, "A dog sniff conducted during a concededly lawful traffic stop that reveals no information other than the location of a substance that no individual has any right to possess does not violate the Fourth Amendment." As long as the "search" by the dog does not unreasonably prolong the traffic stop and the police had the legal right to stop the vehicle, the police do not need "specific and articulable facts" suggesting drug activity to justify the use of the dog.

Impounded Vehicles Any evidence obtained during an inventory of the contents of a lawfully impounded vehicle is admissible in criminal court.[14] For example, if the police arrest a driver for driving while under the influence of alcohol and impound the vehicle, they can perform a thorough search of the vehicle, including any locked glove compartments or trunks. They also can remove any boxes, suitcases, or other items and search those items. The police may even force locks for the purpose of inventorying the contents of an automobile. The philosophy is that the police assume liability for the loss of anything of value in the vehicle when they impound it and therefore are authorized to inventory the entire vehicle and its contents to establish the presence and value of any contents. Also, locked containers in a vehicle might hide things that pose a danger to police or the public, such as a bomb hidden in a suitcase in the vehicle, in which case the police have a right and duty to determine such danger.

Search of Persons

Pat-Down Search The U.S. Supreme Court has appreciated the fact that the police operate in an environment that can be life threatening. Thus, the police are allowed to take certain reasonable precautions in dealing with the public. In the course of taking reasonable precautions, such as frisking or patting down a detainee suspected of carrying a weapon, if the police find incriminating evidence, such evidence is admissible in criminal court. The doctrine governing the search of persons without probable cause but with reasonable suspicion is called the **pat-down doctrine** and has its origins in *Terry v. Ohio.*[15]

Concealed Weapons Police officers frequently approach or are approached by citizens to interact. At close range, a citizen's possession of a weapon could be deadly to an officer. In some contexts, the police may be able to determine by simple visual inspection whether a citizen is carrying a concealed weapon, but outer clothing often makes it impossible to tell. In such cases, officers are authorized to conduct a limited pat-down search of outer clothing when they have a reasonable concern that the citizen is armed. Probable cause is not required under these circumstances.

A pat-down search may be conducted solely to ensure the safety of the officer.[16] If in the course of a pat-down, the police officer feels an object that might be a weapon, the officer legally can reach into the pocket or clothing to further explore the nature of the object. If the officer still believes that the object might be a weapon, he or she may remove the object and examine it. If it is a weapon, and the person is not authorized to carry it, the weapon is admissible as evidence. However, if the officer feels an object that clearly is not a weapon but might be illegal, such as a bag of narcotics, the officer may not reach into the pocket to explore the nature of the object or remove it for inspection. An object acquired in an illegal pat-down search is not admissible as evidence in a court of law, unless it is immediately apparent by touching the object that it is contraband.

Stop and Identify In 2004, the Supreme Court significantly altered the scope of searches that police may conduct justified by the 1968 *Terry v. Ohio* case. The Supreme Court upheld the conviction of Larry D. Hiibel of Nevada[17] for refusing to give a deputy sheriff his name. Although the offense was a misdemeanor, the court's ruling upheld the concept that in a routine stop of a citizen, the police have the authority to demand that the citizen answer their questions. Previously, it was understood that the police had the power to stop citizens under the authority of *Terry v. Ohio* but that citizens were under no obligation to answer a police officer's questions. The Court ruled that there was no violation of the Fifth Amendment for a citizen to be required to disclose his or her name and that such information does not incriminate a citizen in violation of the Fifth Amendment. The ruling might have been influenced by the concern that if the Supreme Court did not uphold this authority, a ruling the other way would have protected terrorists and encouraged people to refuse to cooperate with police.

Drug smuggling and other drug laws have resulted in the interesting situation in which people swallow drugs wrapped in some type of protective covering or conceal drugs in personal body cavities in an effort to prevent their detection by the police. Even if the police have probable cause to believe that someone has swallowed illegal drugs in an effort to conceal them, the Court has been fairly consistent in requiring a search warrant to retrieve drugs by medical procedures such as pumping the stomach or conducting invasive searches of the body.[18]

Carroll doctrine terms allowing admissibility of evidence obtained by police in a warrantless search of an automobile when the police have probable cause that a crime has occurred and delaying a search could result in losing evidence

pat-down doctrine the right of the police to search a person for a concealed weapon on the basis of reasonable suspicion, established in *Terry v. Ohio* (1968)

4 **The police may conduct searches without a warrant when there is a serious threat to public safety and when they act in good faith that they have a valid warrant; they may also use deadly force against a fleeing suspect when his or her escape poses clear and present danger to the public.**

Other Exceptions to the Warrant Requirement

Since the 1960s, the U.S. Supreme Court has restricted the situations in which the police may conduct a search without a warrant. However, the Court has continued to recognize that there are certain circumstances that may justify a warrantless search. The two most common exceptions to the requirements for a search warrant are public safety and good faith.

Public Safety Exceptions

Certain situations require immediate action by the police. If the police are chasing a person who has just committed a crime using a firearm and catch the person but fail to find the firearm on him or her, the Court has ruled that the police have the right to perform a search without a warrant in places where the person may have discarded the firearm. The justification for this is the **public safety exception**, the argument that if the search is not performed immediately, the presence of the weapon in the community may pose a serious threat to public safety.[19] For example, if a person committed armed robbery and fled from the police into a mall but did not have a firearm when caught, the police would be justified in immediately searching the stores in the mall for the weapon. There is the danger that a citizen, especially a juvenile, might find the weapon and accidentally harm someone by discharging it. The firearm, if found by police in a warrantless search, would be admissible as evidence.

Searches of Airline and Bus Passengers Another example of the public safety exception is the acceptance of searches of airline passengers without probable cause or warrant requirement for the public good. The justification for this kind of search is that it is necessary for public safety and that passengers implicitly consent to be searched in exchange for the right to board an airplane. Law enforcement officers extended this philosophy to bus passengers. In an effort to detect drug smugglers who use public transportation to move illegal drugs from Florida to the Northeast, law enforcement officers obtained permission from bus companies to search the possessions and baggage of bus passengers. Arguing that they had the permission of the operating companies, similar to permission given by the airline industry to search air passengers, officers began routine searches of bus passengers, a practice known as "working the buses." Evidence seized in these searches could legally justify an arrest and be used as evidence in court.[20]

Searches of Subway Passengers In 2005, the police extended the public safety exception to justify random searches of subway passengers for explosives in response to perceived terrorist threats against U.S. mass transit systems following terrorist attacks on London's bus and subway system. The American Civil Liberties Union (ACLU) protested the random searches as a violation of the Fourth Amendment. The ACLU expressed concern that if random searches of subway passengers was permitted under the public safety exception, police could extend the scope of the searches to include virtually any public space. The court did not uphold the ACLU's protests.

U.S. Customs officials also have been granted greater leeway by the Supreme Court under the public safety exception to conduct warrantless searches.

Border Searches Searches of persons and property at border checkpoints and entry ports do not require probable cause, reasonable suspicion, or a search warrant. Federal border officers may search persons and property virtually at will. Property may be destroyed in the search, and searches of persons may be intrusive. This power is granted to border security personnel by both legislation and case law. Consent of the person to search is not necessary because persons do not have the right to refuse to be searched. Evidence found of illegal activity or contraband such as drugs is admissible in criminal court.[21]

School Searches Although not police officers, school administrators have been granted broad discretionary power to search students, students' property such as backpacks and purses, and students' school lockers. Evidence obtained in these searches can be used both for disciplinary action and for criminal charges. The Court has recognized the power of school administrators to perform searches of students both on school property and "near" school property. The Court has held that students do not have an expectation of privacy concerning property in "student" lockers because the lockers are under the ownership and control of the school. However, a 2009 case concerning the strip search of a middle school student set a limit on school administrators' power to search. The Supreme Court ruled that school strip searches are not reasonable.[22]

THE COURT HAS RECOGNIZED THE POWER OF SCHOOL ADMINISTRATORS TO PERFORM SEARCHES OF STUDENTS BOTH ON SCHOOL PROPERTY AND "NEAR" SCHOOL PROPERTY.

The Good Faith Exception

Another common exception to the requirement of having a warrant or probable cause to conduct a legal search is when the police act in good faith. In most cases, the **good faith exception** applies when there is some type of clerical error resulting in the police executing what they think is a valid search warrant but in reality it is not. A common example would be when the police have probable cause to obtain a valid search warrant but there is clerical error and the address of the premises to be searched is entered incorrectly in the search warrant document. Acting in good faith that they have a valid warrant, the police search the location described in the search warrant. What happens, if in the course of this

public safety exception the right of the police to search without probable cause when not to do so could pose a threat of harm to the public

good faith exception an exception to the requirement that police must have a valid search warrant or probable cause when they act in good faith on the belief that the search was legal

mistaken search the police find evidence of criminal activity such as illegal drugs? Because the search was not authorized by the warrant and the police had no probable cause to perform the search of the "innocent" party, is the evidence discovered at the wrong premise admissible in criminal court? Initially, the Court did not support the good faith exception, taking the position that good faith by the police does not override the violation of the valid search warrant requirement.[23] However, the Court later reversed itself and allowed evidence obtained in good faith but without a valid search warrant to be admitted in evidence.[24] This principle may be expressed as the exclusionary rule applying only in cases in which there is police misconduct involved.

Issues of Privacy

Wiretapping Another area affected by the Fourth Amendment in which the Supreme Court has reversed itself is the issue of obtaining evidence by **wiretapping**, a form of search and seizure of evidence involving telephone communications. At the time the U.S. Constitution was drafted and the rights of citizens were enumerated in the Bill of Rights, there obviously was no mention of the right of privacy of one's telephone communications or messages sent by computer or e-mail. A hundred years after the drafting of the Constitution, the telephone was invented and law enforcement officers began listening in on private telephone conversations between bootleggers. Using the information obtained by listening to these conversations, the police were able to make arrests and win convictions. In one case, the bootleggers appealed their conviction, and in 1928, the Supreme Court heard its first case in the area of electronic communications (*Olmstead v. United States*, 1928).[25]

Initially, the Court ruled that the telephone lines and public telephone booths were not an extension of the defendant's home and were therefore not protected by the constitutional guarantee of privacy. Thirty-nine years later, the ruling in *Olmstead* was reversed, and it was declared that electronic communication was indeed private communication and protected as a constitutional right (*Katz v. United States*, 1967).[26] Violating this privacy without consent, probable cause, or a warrant constitutes illegal search and seizure.

Electronic Communications The issue of privacy in relation to electronic communications has gone beyond court-mandated rules of evidence, requiring new legislation. Major pieces of legislation addressing electronic communications privacy are the Electronic Communications Privacy Act of 1986, the Communications Assistance for Law Enforcement Act of 1994, the Telecommunications Act of 1996, and the USA Patriot Act. These laws provide specific details governing the collection of evidence by wiretaps and other means and the definition of what electronically transmitted information is protected by the expectation of privacy.

Except in cases of suspected terrorism, law enforcement officers generally must satisfy stringent requirements before they can obtain information transmitted electronically or stored in computer databanks, such as stored e-mail messages. If law enforcement officers fail to follow the provision of the law, not only is the evidence not admissible in court, but for some violations, the officer may be subject to fines or incarceration.

HERE'S SOMETHING TO THINK ABOUT...

A device called a data extraction device (DED) when connected to a cellphone can override user lock codes and retrieve all data from a cellphone. The ACLU of Michigan claims the Michigan State Police (MSP) have used this device in violation of Fourth Amendment rights and state law. The MSP deny any wrongdoing and say they use the DED only in high-level cases that require digital forensics methods such as child pornography cases. In 2011, the ACLU filed a Freedom of Information Act request for records on the use of the DED. The MSP responded it would cost the ACLU $544,000 to produce the information. Should police be required to fully cooperate without cost when accused of misconduct?

Homeland Security The USA Patriot Act, President Executive Orders, and other legislation have significantly altered the limits of the power of law enforcement to perform searches. In cases of Homeland Security, searches can be performed without a warrant, whereas in a criminal case the search would be unconstitutional. The impact of new legislation on the power of law enforcement agencies is discussed in Chapter 13.

Incarceration Once incarcerated in a correctional institution, the inmate loses all expectation of privacy and can be searched, including invasive searches, without a warrant or probable cause. Visitors to correctional institutions are considered to have consented to search by their presence in the institution. The Court has distinguished between inmates and persons who are held temporarily by police in "holding cells." Persons arrested are subject to search. However, the Court has ruled that strip searches may be unreasonable for persons who have been arrested for minor offenses such as traffic offenses.

Deadly Force and Fleeing-Felon Doctrine

Public safety is at the crux of rulings on deadly force used at the discretion of police. Prior to 1985, shooting at fleeing suspects who refused to stop as commanded was a common and legal police practice involving the use of **deadly force.**

Many police departments had standard operating procedures detailing the circumstances under which an officer was justified in firing warning shots or using deadly force. Some departments allowed officers to use deadly force against fleeing people who were only "suspected" of committing crimes, and some jurisdictions did not differentiate between misdemeanors or felonies when using deadly force against a fleeing suspect. This practice was known as the fleeing suspect or **fleeing-felon doctrine**. The police justified this practice on the basis of public safety. They argued that a suspect allowed to escape could be a potential danger to the community. If the person were suspected of having committed murder, they reasoned, a failure to apprehend might create an undue risk for the public—a justification for use of deadly force.

wiretapping a form of search and seizure of evidence involving communication by telephone

deadly force the power of police to incapacitate or kill in the line of duty

fleeing-felon doctrine the police practice of using deadly force against a fleeing suspect, made illegal in *Tennessee v. Garner* (1985), except when there is clear and present danger to the public

Prohibition Against Deadly Force In *Tennessee v. Garner* (1985), the Supreme Court disagreed with that reasoning.[27] Attorneys representing Garner, who had been slain by a police officer in pursuit when Garner refused to stop, made the argument that the officer's use of deadly force was a form of search and seizure for which the officer lacked probable cause or a warrant. The Court accepted the validity of the argument and ruled that the search and seizure by deadly force against a fleeing suspect was a violation of the person's constitutional rights. The ruling in *Tennessee v. Garner* immediately superseded the rules of all police departments and the laws of the states that had permitted the practice. All law enforcement officers (local, state, and federal) were immediately prohibited from using deadly force as a means to stop a fleeing suspect. If the ruling was ignored, the officer and department could be held liable in a lawsuit for violation of the person's constitutional rights.

This ruling caused great confusion for a period of time as law enforcement officials and state legislators tried to determine the limits of the prohibition.[28] For example, if a person committed murders in the presence of a police officer and then threw down his or her weapon and fled from the scene, and if there were no other way to stop the person from escaping, could the officer use deadly force? The argument for the use of deadly force is based on the potential threat that an escaped murderer poses to a community. The argument against the use of deadly force is based on the fact that after the person threw down his or her weapon, that person was no longer an immediate threat to the officer or the public, such that the use of deadly force was an unreasonable violation of his or her constitutional rights. If deadly force were used and the person died, he or she would be deprived the right to a trial by jury for the alleged criminal conduct.

Clear and Present Danger Although there are legitimate arguments to support both the prohibition and sanction of the use of deadly force in this case, the present legal position is that when there is a **clear and present danger** to the public posed by the escape of the person, deadly force may be justifiable.[29] In the lack of a clear and present danger, the use of deadly force to apprehend a fleeing suspect or criminal is a violation of the person's constitutional rights.

High-Speed Vehicular Pursuits Such pusuits of fleeing persons have posed a difficult question as to the right of police to engage in these pursuits. A number of such high-speed pursuits have resulted in death or bodily harm to the person being pursued and to innocent parties. Lawsuits have been filed asking the courts to prohibit or at least restrict high-speed vehicle pursuits by the police, but in general the courts have upheld the right of the police to pursue fleeing persons even when there is no reasonable suspicion or probable cause that the person has committed a crime other than a traffic violation. However, police departments have adopted rules and guidelines aimed at reducing deaths and injuries caused by such pursuits by regulating when officers can engage in such pursuits and when high-speed pursuits should be discontinued.

HERE'S SOMETHING TO THINK ABOUT...

The limits of warrantless searches often are based on previous court decisions. For example, a Florida court ruled it was permissible for DEA agents to press the suitcases of two drug suspects with their hands in order for drug dogs to sniff any drug-laced air being emitted. Citing this as a precedent, the Illinois Supreme Court ruled it was permissible for an officer to ask a motorist to roll up her windows and turn on the interior blower fan while a drug dog sniffed for the presence of drugs inside. Do you agree the cases are similar?

Interrogations and Confessions

The Fifth and Sixth Amendments govern the admissibility of testimony obtained through interrogations and confessions. The confession is an effective method of convincing a jury that the defendant has committed the crime of which he or she has been accused. In fact, nearly a quarter of all convictions overturned in recent years based on DNA and other evidence have involved false confessions.[30] For example, in the infamous 1989 Central Park jogger case, five young defendants provided elaborate and detailed confessions as to how they committed the crime and were found guilty by a jury. As unexplainable as it seems, the confessions were false. After serving 13 years for a crime they did not commit but to which they confessed, the real offender, Matias Reyes, confessed to the crime. His confession was confirmed by DNA and other evidence and the five defendants were released.

Police must read suspects their Miranda rights before interrogation; they may not obtain confessions from a suspect by use of force, by around-the-clock interrogations, or by lying beyond the limits of professional conduct; they also may not delay a suspect's court appearance, conduct unfair line-ups, or refuse a suspect's request for an attorney to be present during interrogation.

clear and present danger a condition relating to public safety that may justify police use of deadly force against a fleeing suspect

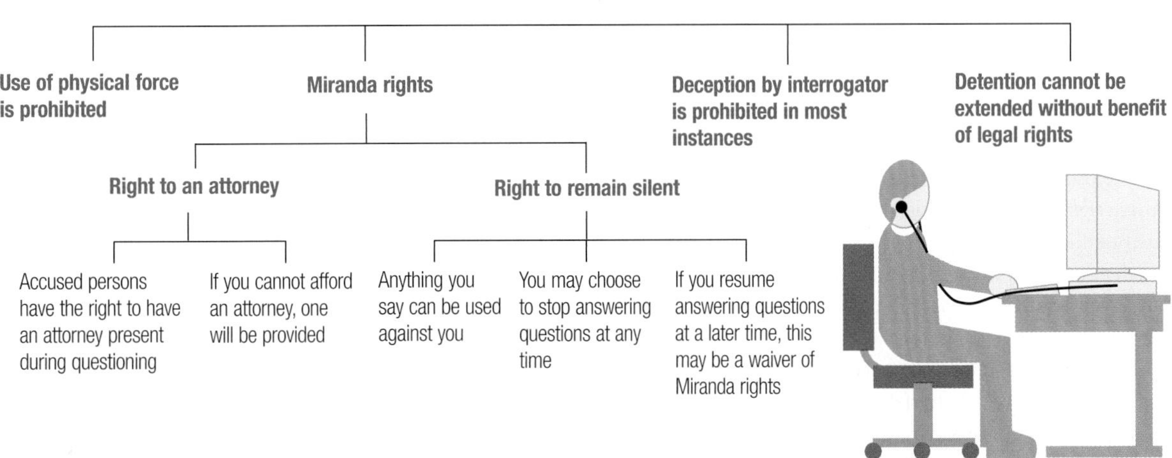

The Fifth Amendment

No person shall be held to answer for a capital, or otherwise infamous crime, unless on a presentment or indictment of a Grand Jury, except in cases arising in the land or naval forces, or in the Militia, when in actual service in time of War or public danger; nor shall any person be subject for the same offence to be twice put in jeopardy of life or limb; nor shall be compelled in any criminal case to be a witness against himself, nor be deprived of life, liberty, or property, without due process of law; nor shall private property be taken for public use, without just compensation.

The Sixth Amendment

In all criminal prosecutions, the accused shall enjoy the right to a speedy and public trial, by an impartial jury of the State and district wherein the crime shall have been committed, which district shall have been previously ascertained by law, and to be informed of the nature and cause of the accusation; to be confronted with the witnesses against him; to have compulsory process for obtaining witnesses in his favor; and to have the Assistance of Counsel for his defense.

Waiver of Rights

In some cases, the accused provides a confession to the police. However, confessions must be obtained within court-imposed criteria. Even if the police are successful in obtaining a confession, it may be inadmissible in court if it was not obtained properly. To be admissible, a confession must be given knowingly and voluntarily, it cannot be obtained as a result of threat or pain, and the suspect must be informed of his or her rights.

Standards for an Admissible Confession

- The confession must be given knowingly and not as a consequence of lies or deception.
- The suspect must be informed of his or her rights.
- The confession must be voluntary.
- Confessions may not be obtained through threats, such as threatening to turn an illegal foreign alien over to Immigration authorities for deportation, threatening to report a mother to child protective services for child abuse to have her children taken away from her, or threatening to report suspects to a welfare agency for the purpose of having their welfare benefits suspended.
- Confessions may not be obtained through use of pain or through constructive force, such as beating up one suspect in front of another and telling the second suspect that he or she is next if a confession is not forthcoming.

Use of Physical Punishment and Pain

Law enforcement practices traditionally have not been conducive to protecting citizens' Fifth Amendment rights. The U.S. Supreme Court has addressed the admissibility of confessions obtained by the use of force in several landmark cases:

- *Brown v. Mississippi* (1936): The court ruled that confessions obtained by force were tainted.
- *Ashcraft v. Tennessee* (1944): The court ruled that confessions obtained by the use of around-the-clock interrogation were not voluntary and were therefore inadmissible.

Fifth Amendment provides several important due process rights regarding the rights of the defendant

Sixth Amendment provides the defendant constitutionally protected rights related to the trial, witnesses, and right to counsel

The Right to an Attorney

Because of concern that the rights of the suspect are protected against **self-incrimination**, the court has required that a suspect is entitled to have an attorney present when he or she is interrogated by the police, as well as in court.

Right to an Attorney in Court The right to have the benefit of an attorney when accused of criminal charges was established in the landmark case of *Gideon v. Wainwright* (1963).[31] The details of the case are striking, because they illustrate the influence that a single case concerning a relatively obscure defendant can have on the entire criminal justice system.

Gideon was convicted of burglary and sentenced to an extended prison term under the habitual offender act. He did not have the funds to hire an attorney to represent him in court, and the state refused to grant him one free of charge. Left to defend himself, Gideon apparently did not do very well against the trained and experienced state prosecutors, and he was convicted of the crime. While in prison, Gideon sent a handwritten letter to the Supreme Count in which he protested the unfairness of his conviction. He argued that it was unfair for him to have to defend himself, without the benefit of counsel, in a court of law against the resources of the state.

After due consideration, the Court agreed with Gideon's position and issued an opinion that he was entitled to a new trial and that at this trial he was entitled to be represented by an attorney. If he could not afford an attorney, the state would have to provide him one free of charge. Gideon was found not guilty in his retrial. Gideon's case established the practice of **indigent defense**. If a person cannot afford an attorney, it is the duty of the state to provide legal counsel.

Extensions of the Right to an Attorney Once this right was established, it was extended beyond the courtroom. In *Argersinger v. Hamlin* (1972), the right to an attorney was extended to include anyone facing a potential sentence of imprisonment, not just felony.[32] It was extended to juveniles accused of crimes in *In re Gault* (1967).[33] In *Escobedo v. Illinois* (1964), the right to an attorney was extended to include the right to have an attorney present during police interrogation.[34]

Limitation on the Right to an Attorney The Court has made several changes regarding the right to an attorney when questioning suspects. In *Michigan v. Jackson* (1986) once a person requests an attorney, the police must cease questioning the person. In *Maryland v. Shatzer* (2010) the Court ruled if the suspect requests an attorney and refuses to answer questions, police may reinitiate questioning without counsel 14 days after release from custody.

Delayed Court Appearance

A 1968 law known as the McNabb-Mallory rule placed a 6-hour time limit between the time of interrogating a suspect and his or her first court appearance. The purpose of the law was to limit abuses made possible by extended detention and interrogations without the benefit of legal rights. The Supreme Court acknowledged that confessions obtained after lengthy detention and interrogation called into question the credibility of the confessions obtained.

Limits on Deception

Court rulings have not clearly prohibited police from obtaining a confession by lying to the suspect.[35] For example, confessions have been admitted even when obtained by police falsely telling one suspect that his partner in crime had confessed and named him as the "trigger man." Also, confessions have been admitted when obtained by placing a police officer dressed in prisoner clothing in the same cell as the suspect. Confessions have been prohibited when obtained through the use of other types of deception. In *Leyra v. Denno* in 1954, the police used a psychiatrist to obtain a confession from the suspect, who thought he was receiving treatment for a medical condition. The psychiatrist persuaded the suspect that he would feel better if he confessed to his crime. The court ruled that such deception was beyond the acceptable limits of professional police conduct and that the confession obtained was inadmissible.[36]

Miranda Rights

In the famous case of *Miranda v. Arizona* (1966), the court issued an opinion in which it summarized all of the rights of a citizen during police arrest and interrogation.[37] Initially, the court was very strict in requiring that these rights, known as the **Miranda rights,** were read word-for-word to all suspects during arrests and interrogations. Gradually, however, the Miranda protections have been weakened by exceptions. Courts have decided that it is not necessary unequivocally to advise persons of all Miranda rights and that they do not have to be advised of their rights at the beginning of questioning. Controversies surrounding

Miranda

- You have the right to remain silent.
- Anything you say can be used against you in a court of law.
- You have the right to talk to a lawyer and to have a lawyer present when you are being questioned.
- If you want a lawyer before or during questioning but cannot afford to hire a lawyer, one will be appointed to represent you at no cost before any questioning.
- If you answer questions now without a lawyer here, you still have the right to stop answering questions at any time.

Do you understand each of these rights I have explained to you?

Having these rights in mind, do you now wish to answer questions?

Do you now wish to answer questions without a lawyer present?

self-incrimination statements made by a person that might lead to criminal prosecution

indigent defense the right to have an attorney provided free of charge by the state if a defendant cannot afford one, established in *Gideon v. Wainwright* (1963)

Miranda rights rights that provide protection from self-incrimination and confer the right to an attorney, of which citizens must be informed before police arrest and interrogation, established in *Miranda v. Arizona* (1966)

Miranda have included concerns of law enforcement that the requirement to advise people of their rights impedes efficient police work.

Interrogating Outside Miranda This is an interrogation tactic used by law enforcement. In this practice the officer first questions the suspect without advising the suspect of his or her rights. If a confession is obtained, the suspect is advised of his or her rights and a second interrogation is performed. The assumption is that it is easier to obtain a confession without advising the suspect of his or her Miranda rights. The first confession is discarded; and the second confession, the one in which the suspect was advised of his or her rights, is used in court. The Court ruled that this tactic was a police strategy "adapted to undermine the Miranda warnings."

THE STANDARDS FOR INTERROGATION OF JUVENILES DIFFER FROM THOSE FOR ADULTS. BASICALLY, JUVENILES ARE NOT CONSIDERED CAPABLE OF WAIVING THEIR RIGHT TO REMAIN SILENT.

Exceptions to Miranda However, not all confessions require that the suspect be advised of his or her Miranda rights. Confessions given freely prior to an opportunity for police to advise a suspect of his or her rights are admissible, and confessions given to third parties are admissible. An example of the former is a spontaneous confession given by a suspect immediately after the arrival of the police, such as the case in which a husband who murdered his wife exclaimed, "I murdered her!" to the police when they arrived. Another example is when a Southern California couple bragged on the "Dr. Phil" show about engaging in a large-scale shoplifting scheme, police used the information in their investigation. The information was not obtained through interrogation by the police. Therefore, the information could be used even though the couple was not advised of their Miranda rights.

Right to Remain Silent

Miranda rights are based on the rights against self-incrimination guaranteed in the Fifth Amendment. Thus, defendants have the well-known "right to remain silent" or "Fifth Amendment" right during their trials and cannot be compelled to provide testimony that may incriminate them. Furthermore, the law provides that the prosecution cannot tell or imply to the jury that a defendant's silence implies guilt.

Police Lineups

The Fifth Amendment also protects the rights of suspects in participating in a **police lineup.** In a police lineup a victim or witness is given an opportunity to identify a suspected perpetrator from among a number of suspects. What are a suspect's rights in a lineup? Landmark cases have addressed the following questions:

- Can the police compel a suspect to appear in a lineup?
- Can the police compel a suspect to submit handwriting samples or voice samples?
- What constitutes a "fair" lineup?
- At the scene of a crime, can the police drive a witness by a suspect to see if the witness can identify the person as someone who participated in the crime?
- Does the suspect have the right to have his or her attorney present during a lineup?

Rulings have suggested that suspects' guarantees against self-incrimination apply in police lineups, but not to the degree that they apply in police interrogations. Law enforcement officers need to perform certain investigative tasks essential to gathering information about a crime. So long as the police act in a professional and fair manner, they have greater latitude than in interrogations.[38] For example, police officers can drive a witness by a suspect to see if the witness can identify the person as someone who participated in the crime, and this can be done without informing the suspect or obtaining the suspect's consent. Suspects can be required to participate in a lineup without their consent and can be required to give a handwriting or voice sample.[39]

Lineups must be fair, however, and must meet the following requirements:

1. Suspects have the right to have an attorney present.
2. A lineup must contain suspects who are similar and match the description given by the witness.
3. A lineup must contain actual suspects and not police personnel masquerading as suspects.[40]
4. A lineup must contain persons who are known to the police not to be capable of being the offender. The inclusion of such persons acts as a check on the witnesses' credibility.

One of the abuses of lineup standards that gained nationwide publicity was the Duke lacrosse rape case. In the case lacrosse players from Duke University were accused of sexually assaulting a female dancer at a party. The prosecuting attorney had the victim select those who had assaulted her from a photo lineup. However, the prosecutor included only pictures of Duke lacrosse players who were at the party. Thus, no matter whom the victim selected, he was a possible offender.

DNA evidence has exposed a number of cases in which a witness mistakenly identified a person as the offender only to be exonerated at a later time by DNA evidence. Although eyewitness identification is persuasive in convincing jurors of the guilt of the defendant, some research questions the accuracy of lineup identification.

Juveniles

The standards for the interrogation of juveniles differ from those for adults. Juvenile rights are discussed further in Chapter 12. Basically, juveniles are not considered capable of waiving their right to remain

police lineup an opportunity for victims to identify a criminal from among a number of suspects

silent. The consent of a guardian or the juvenile's attorney is normally necessary prior to police interrogation.

Interrogations and the War on Terrorism

Recent concerns over alleged abuse of terrorist suspects to obtain confessions have been raised in U.S. courts. A common situation arises when accused terrorists being tried in U.S. courts claim that their confession was obtained by the use of torture when they were captured or transported outside the United States for interrogation. For example, Ahmed Omar Abu Ali was tried in a Virginia federal court in 2005 on charges that he was a member of al Qaeda and was plotting to assassinate President Bush. Abu Ali's lawyers wanted their client's confession ruled inadmissible, because Abu Ali claimed that the confession was obtained by the use of torture. He claimed that he was arrested in Medina, Saudi Arabia, in June 2003 and gave a false confession to stop the torture. Also, he later gave a confession to the FBI, but that confession was ruled invalid because the FBI disregarded Abu Ali's request for an attorney. Therefore, when he was tried in a U.S. federal court, the prosecution relied on the confession he gave in Medina. The judge ruled that there was insufficient evidence to establish that the confession was obtained through torture and allowed it as evidence. It is likely that there will be more allegations similar to this as more persons are tried for terrorism under similar circumstances. Courts will have to give consideration to what evidence is necessary to establish that a confession was obtained by the use of torture and whether such a confession is admissible.

HERE'S SOMETHING TO THINK ABOUT. . .

Police often are called upon to make on-the-spot decisions about the lawfulness of people's behavior. For example, when a few transgendered women removed their tops and revealed their surgically enhanced breasts on Rehoboth Beach, Delaware, lifeguards asked them to put their tops back on as the law prohibited this behavior. They initially refused but did so before police arrived. No one was arrested as Police Chief Keith Banks explained they had done nothing illegal despite the law against being topless in public. Chief Banks explained that since they have male genitalia, they cannot be charged with indecent exposure for showing their breasts. Can you think of other situations in which police must make immediate decisions regarding the law in cases which may not be clear-cut?

Arrest

The court has the authority to issue arrest warrants. To obtain an arrest warrant from a court, the police must present probable cause evidence that a crime has been committed by the person identified in the warrant. Arrest warrants can also be obtained as the result of a grand jury issuing a "true bill."

Limitations on police powers of arrest stem from abuses by the English government during the colonial period in the American colonies and in England. As a result of historical suspicion against the government's power to incarcerate citizens on questionable charges or without due process, the powers of the police to make an arrest are limited. Law enforcement officers can initiate an **arrest** only under the following conditions:

1. with an arrest warrant issued by the court;
2. when they observe a violation of the law;
3. under exigent circumstances, that is, circumstances in which unless immediate action is taken by the police the evidence may be destroyed or the suspect escape; and
4. when they have probable cause to believe that someone has committed a crime.

In many states, the police are limited to arresting people justified by probable cause that someone has committed a crime only when the crime is a felony.

Entrapment and Police Intelligence Activities

The U.S. Supreme Court has required that arrest cannot be contingent on **entrapment**, in which the police provide the motivation and means for committing the crime (*Jacobsen v. United States*, 1992).[41] Entrapment is a defense against criminal charges in court.

Police intelligence activities in the past have sometimes involved entrapment. During the 1950s, 1960s, and early 1970s, many police departments, especially large departments, engaged in active intelligence gathering. Intelligence gathering occurs when the police gather information about people who are not currently under suspicion or investigation for a specific crime. The primary targets for police intelligence units during these decades were

1. suspected members of the Communist Party, defined as a danger to the United States;
2. people engaged in or suspected of engaging in protests against U.S. involvement in the Vietnam War; and
3. people engaged in civil rights protests.

6 **Police cannot legally arrest a person based on entrapment or police activities that infringe on rights to privacy; many people believe that as a result of the War on Terrorism, the Justice Department is denying suspects—sometimes without any reasonable suspicion—of many guaranteed rights.**

arrest the restriction of the freedom of a person by taking him or her into police custody

entrapment the illegal arrest of a person based on criminal behavior for which the police provided both the motivation and the means, tested in *Jacobsen v. United States* (1992)

The federal law enforcement agency most actively engaged in the gathering of intelligence information was the FBI under the directorship of J. Edgar Hoover.

The justification for intelligence gathering was that if a crime occurred, law enforcement already would have sufficient information about citizens to quickly identify suspects and make arrests, thereby protecting the public from subversives and terrorists. However, abuses by the FBI and state and municipal police departments led to public concern, legislative initiatives prohibiting intelligence-gathering activities, and Supreme Court cases condemning the targeting of citizens for intelligence operations who were not under suspicion of committing a crime. The full extent of FBI abuses finally became known through the Freedom of Information Act, and police intelligence activities came to be seen as an unjustifiable intrusion on the constitutionally protected privacy of citizens. However, attitudes toward police intelligence changed again dramatically on September 11, 2001. Horrifying terrorist attacks on the World Trade Center in New York City and the Pentagon in Washington, DC, changed the balance between privacy and security, with far-reaching consequences.[42] New legislation has enhanced the intelligence-gathering capacity of the FBI.

Enemy Combatants

Critics accuse the Justice Department of denying due process to many persons accused of or suspected of terrorism in the War on Terrorism. For example, a report by the Human Rights Watch accuses the federal government of indiscriminate and arbitrary arrests of males from predominately Muslim countries without sufficient probable cause or even reasonable suspicion.[43]

Also, the Human Rights Watch and the ACLU accuse the Justice Department of abusing the material witness law to detain terror suspects. The **material witness law,** enacted in 1984, allows federal authorities to hold a person indefinitely without charging him or her with a crime if they suspect that the person has information about a crime and might flee or be unwilling to cooperate with law enforcement officials.[44] The Human Rights Watch and the ACLU charge that the Justice Department has used the material witness law to detain 70 persons, about one third of them U.S. citizens, on suspicion of terrorism although questionable evidence exists for these detentions. The Justice Department has apologized to at least 13 persons for wrongly detaining them under the material witness law.[45] One of the more publicized abuses of the material witness law was the detention of Portland, Oregon, lawyer Brandon Mayfield, whom the FBI wrongly accused of being connected to the Madrid train bombings of 2004.

Of great concern to those who fear that the War on Terrorism is eroding due process rights is the Justice Department's denial of access to the civilian courts for those accused or suspected of terrorism. The use of the Enemy Combatant Executive Order to detain alleged terrorists and al Qaeda members has seriously alarmed proponents of constitutional rights. The use of this executive order, combined with the use of military tribunals instead of civilian court trials, denies accused enemy combatants access to civilian courts. This process of determining guilt denies them the due process rights to an attorney, to confront the witnesses against them, to know of the evidence the government has against them, and the right to a public trial by their peers.

HERE'S SOMETHING TO THINK ABOUT. . .

When a police officer violates the constitutional rights of a citizen, he or she is disciplined by the police department. Also, a civil lawsuit can be filed by the offended party against the officer and the department. However, what happens when an entire police department demonstrates a pattern of disregard for the constitutional rights of community members?

Since the Violent Crime Control and Law Enforcement Act of 1994, the U.S. Justice Department has the power to sue state and local governments over patterns or practices of policing that violate the Constitution or laws of the United States. The Justice Department can seek a consent decree that provides for an independent external federal monitor or auditor to oversee compliance with the decree. The monitors measure police performance and assist in the development of more effective police management. According to the Vera Institute of Justice, the first successful consent decree obtained by the Justice Department was the Pittsburgh Police Department in 1997. Since then, successful consent decrees have been obtained against many of the major police departments in the United States, including the Los Angeles Police Department; the state of New Jersey; Riverside, California; Montgomery County, Maryland; the Philadelphia Police Department; the Washington, D.C., Police Department; and the Cincinnati Police Department.

The latest police force targeted for Justice Department monitoring is the New Orleans Police Department. A 2011 Justice Department investigative report concluded, "While other departments generally have problems in specific areas, like the use of excessive force, New Orleans has every issue that has existed in our practice to date, and a few that we hadn't encountered before." In addition to the Justice Department investigation, there are nine other federal criminal investigations into the department for criminal misconduct—including murder.

Some argue local communities rather than the federal government should be responsible for policing misconduct. Do you agree? Why?

material witness law a law that allows for the detention of a person who has not committed a crime but is suspected of having information about a crime and might flee or refuse to cooperate with law enforcement officials

CHAPTER 5

Police Officers and the Law

Check It!

1 WHAT are procedural laws, and how do they affect the actions of the police? p. 76

By law, the police must follow strict procedures while gathering evidence, performing searches and seizures, interrogating suspects and witnesses, and arresting suspects so as not to violate their constitutional rights.

2 HOW do the rules of evidence influence police actions? p. 77

The rules of evidence define what evidence will be admitted at a trial. Evidence gathered contrary to these rules cannot be used in trial to convict the defendant. The rules of evidence define the procedural due process rights by declaring what police procedures violate constitutional rights. Landmark cases mark a change in the due process rights.

3 WHAT are the major due process rights that police must follow in conducting searches? p. 78

The exclusionary rule guides police actions in conducting searches. Evidence gained from searches that violate constitutional rights is inadmissible. The major guidelines that police must follow in conducting searches are that searches must be justified by use of a search warrant, probable cause, consent, or exigent circumstances.

4 WHAT exceptions allow search and seizure by police without a warrant? p. 81

Police may search and seize evidence that is in plain view, when they have voluntary and informed consent to search, when a lawful arrest is made, and where there are exigent circumstances in which the public would be in danger or evidence destroyed without an immediate search.

5 WHAT rights are citizens guaranteed regarding interrogations? p. 84

With the exception of providing one's identity, citizens do not have to answer questions that may incriminate them, they have the right to have an attorney present during questioning, the police must inform citizens of their constitutional rights prior to questioning them, and citizens who are tried do not have to testify in court.

6 WHAT are the due process rights of arrest? p. 88

Police can exercise their authority to arrest citizens if they have an arrest warrant, if they have probable cause that a crime has been committed or they observe a violation of the law, or under exigent circumstances.

Assess Your Understanding

1. How does the exclusionary rule affect police searches and seizures?
   a. The exclusionary rule prohibits the use of evidence in court which has been obtained in violation of the defendant's constitutional rights.
   b. The exclusionary rule provides a time limit as to how long the officer has to collect evidence.
   c. The exclusionary rule prohibits defendants from excluding evidence from being used in a trial if the officer obtained the evidence in good faith.
   d. The exclusionary rule applies only to federal courts.

2. Which of the following required state courts to follow federal court procedural law regarding evidence obtained in violation of the defendant's constitutional rights?
   a. *Weeks v. United States*
   b. *Mapp v. Ohio*
   c. *Terry v. Ohio*
   d. *Tennessee v. Garner*

3. The right to be secure in one's person, house, papers, and effects against unreasonable search and seizure is guaranteed by which amendment?
   a. First Amendment
   b. Second Amendment
   c. Fourth Amendment
   d. Sixth Amendment

4. Which type of search does the Carroll doctrine address?
   a. search of airline passengers
   b. pat-down searches
   c. warrantless searches of automobiles
   d. lineup identification searches

5. Which of the following authorized police officers to perform warrantless pat-down search without probable cause or reasonable suspicion for the safety of the officer?
   a. *Mapp v. Ohio*
   b. *Harris v. United States*
   c. *Weeks v. United States*
   d. *Terry v. Ohio*

6. Which of the following is a true statement?
   a. Subway passengers and bus passengers may only be searched if there is reasonable suspicion, probable cause, or a warrant.
   b. School officials cannot search a student unless they have a search warrant or a police officer is present.
   c. Searches at border checkpoints and entry ports do not require probable cause, reasonable suspicion, or a search warrant.
   d. Wiretaps are exempt from search and seizure regulations as they are not considered a constitutional right to privacy.

7. The Sixth Amendment provides for which of the following constitutional rights?
   a. the right against self-incrimination
   b. the right to be secure in one's home, papers, and effects
   c. the right against unusual punishment
   d. the right to a speedy and public trial

8. The right to have the benefit of an attorney when accused of criminal charges was provided by which of the following cases?
   a. *Gideon v. Wainwright*
   b. *Brown v. Mississippi*
   c. *Mapp v. Ohio*
   d. *Terry vs. Ohio*

9. Which amendments govern the admissibility of testimony obtained through interrogations and confessions?
   a. First and Second Amendments
   b. Third and Fourth Amendments
   c. Fifth and Sixth Amendments
   d. Seventh and Eighth Amendments

10. Which due process rights does the U.S. Justice Department acknowledge are afforded to enemy combatants accused of terrorist acts against the United States?
   a. the right to an attorney
   b. the right to a speedy and public trial
   c. the right to confront the witnesses against them
   d. none of the above

ESSAY

1. How does the court oversee and enforce that the police do not violate the constitutional rights of persons?
2. What was the effect of *Mapp v. Ohio* upon state court criminal trials?
3. What exceptions allow search and seizure by police without a warrant?
4. What rights are persons guaranteed while in police custody regarding interrogations and confessions?
5. Under what circumstances may police legally make an arrest or hold a person in custody?
6. What is the fruit of the poisoned tree doctrine and how does it affect police searches for evidence?
7. What guidelines has the Court established for police search and seizure regarding the Fourth Amendment and the right of privacy?
8. How did *Tennessee v. Garner* (1985) change the fleeing-felon doctrine adopted by most police departments in the United States?

ANSWERS: 1. a, 2. b, 3. c, 4. c, 5. a, 6. c, 7. d, 8. a, 9. c, 10. d

Media

Go to the *Chapter 5: Police Officers and the Law* section in *MyCJLab* to test your understanding of this chapter, access customized study content, engage in interactive simulations, complete critical thinking and research assignments, and view related online videos.

Additional Links

In each session of the U.S. Supreme Court new opinions are issued that can affect due process and police procedures. To view the most recent opinions of the U.S. Supreme Court, go to www.supremecourtus.gov and click on "recent decisions" to see a list of the latest rulings. Browse through the cases and select a case of interest to view in greater detail.

Go to www.archives.gov/exhibits/charters/constitution.html to view the U.S. Constitution and the various Amendments.

The National Association for Civilian Oversight of Law Enforcement maintains a roster of state resources for civilian oversight of the police at www.nacole.org

Go to www.fbi.gov and in the search box enter "interrogations." The resulting search will provide links to numerous articles, publications, and press releases related to interrogation policy and practices including the newly formed interrogation unit for "high-value" terrorists.

To watch a short video to the reaction of the LAPD and the community to the end of the consent decree, go to http://abclocal.go.com/kabc/video?id=6924748

To watch a short video regarding your rights when questioned by a police officer, go to www.5min.com/Video/Legal-Advice-Talk-to-Cops-34095281

You can review the U.S. Supreme Court opinion issued in *Berghuis v. Thompkins*, one of the most significant cases defining Miranda rights in the past decade, at www.supremecourt.gov/opinions/09pdf/08-1470.pdf

THE COURT SYSTEM

6

The U.S. court system is complex, reflecting hundreds of years of history side-by-side with contemporary values and technology. The process of convicting a defendant requires the prosecution to obtain a guilty verdict within a prescribed manner following due process procedures. This task may be a labyrinth, taking years or decades to work through, and the outcome is never certain.

This complex system of arresting, trying, and convicting a defendant is a process. Movies and television shows compress criminal trials into short time lines and give the illusion that the path through the courts is simple, direct, and quick. This illusion is far from the truth.

The U.S. has a dual court system consisting of the federal courts and the state courts reflecting the division of power between the federal government and the state governments. The balance of power between the two is addressed in Article I of the Constitution and the Tenth Amendment. The dividing line between federal and state authority is defined by the courts which interpret these documents in individual cases, thus affecting individual defendants. One such case is *Bond v. United States* (2011), in which Carol A. Bond challenged her conviction for violation of the Chemical Weapons Convention of 1993 in the U.S. Supreme Court.

When Ms. Bond, a microbiologist, learned that her husband was the father of her best friend's child she retaliated against her former friend by placing harmful chemicals on her friend's car, mailbox, and doorknob. Rather than the local police charging her with a crime, the federal government charged her with using unconventional weapons in violation of the Chemical Weapons Convention of 1993. Ms. Bond used a chemical slightly more harmful than vinegar which she obtained online and the friend suffered only a minor injury. Ms. Bond argued that the crime should have been prosecuted under state law and Congress did not have the constitutional power to use a chemical weapons treaty to prosecute her.

The Court heard the appeal and the justices argued about the applicability of Article I and the Tenth Amendment. The appeals court had ruled that Ms. Bond did not have standing to raise a Tenth Amendment defense as only states can invoke the amendment. Chief Justice John Roberts questioned that ruling and Justice Kagan argued the case could be reviewed based only upon the claim that Congress exceeded its authority under Article I. The justices' decision is important not only to Ms. Bond but also to those who support the Obama health care law as challenges to the law are based upon similar arguments.

This chapter examines the organization of the federal and state U.S. court system and the role of the criminal courts within this system.

1 What are the historical foundations and dual structure of the U.S. court system?

2 What are the differences between criminal law and civil law?

3 How is the federal court system organized, and what are the responsibilities of each level of the federal courts?

4 How is the state court system organized, and what are the responsibilities of each level of the state courts?

MOVIES AND TELEVISION SHOWS COMPRESS CRIMINAL TRIALS INTO SHORT TIME LINES AND GIVE THE ILLUSION THAT THE PATH THROUGH THE COURTS IS SIMPLE, DIRECT, AND QUICK. THIS ILLUSION IS FAR FROM THE TRUTH.

Foundation and Structure of the Judicial System

Over the centuries, society's ways of dealing with harms against others have changed. At one time, people felt that if another person harmed their reputation, they could challenge the offending party to a duel to the death. In the western frontier of the late nineteenth century, disputes sometimes were settled by gunfights. Today, however, people are prohibited from seeking private revenge and personal justice through the use of violence. The government requires that all wrongs—whether accidental, negligent, or criminal—be handled by the criminal justice or civil justice system.

The concept of a "court" vested with the power to arbitrate disputes can be traced back to the earliest times. One of the earliest references to court refers to the power of kings, rulers, and nobility to resolve disputes. Disputes were brought before the king or ruler, and the parties to the dispute argued their case. The opinion of the monarch frequently was unchallengeable and based primarily on his or her personal power, values, and interpretation of the dispute. As society became more sophisticated, it became necessary to develop a system of **jurisprudence**—a philosophy of law—to settle disputes. In such a system, there is a body of written law to regulate interactions. These laws or codes provide people with guidelines that regulate behavior.

The jurisprudence system of the United States was influenced primarily by the Justinian Code, the Napoleonic Code, and the common law of Great Britain. The Justinian Code, developed under the Roman emperor Justinian I, was influential in shaping the civil law of Europe and that of the Spanish colonies in Mexico and Latin America. The Napoleonic Code, designed by Napoleon Bonaparte to unify the laws of his empire, became the basis of the legal system of the State of Louisiana, a French colony. English common law was the main foundation on which the American jurisprudence system was built.

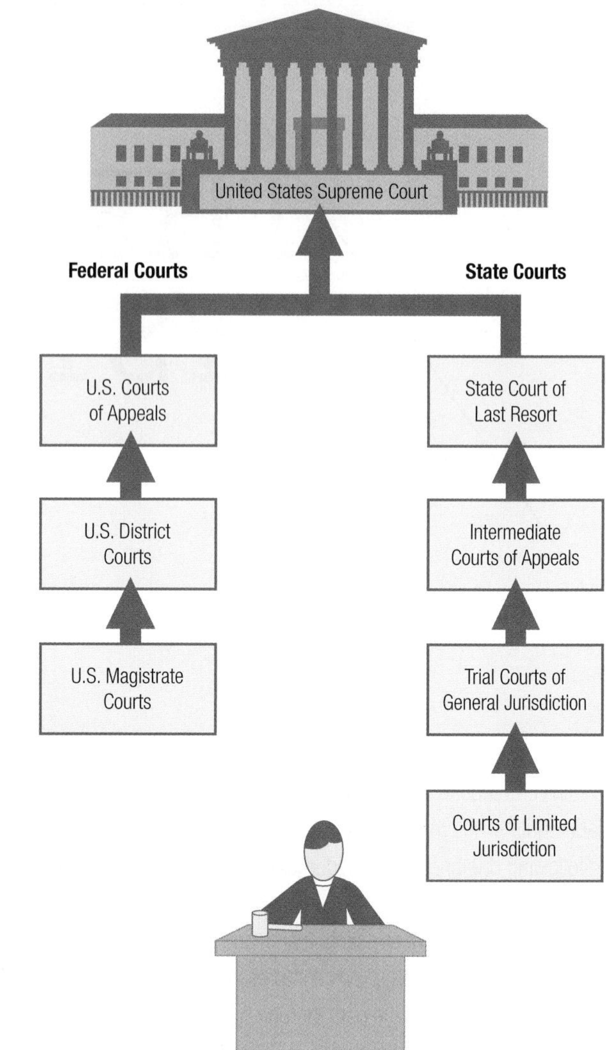

FIGURE 6.1 Hierarchy in the Judiciary
The majority of cases in both the state and federal court system are disposed in the lower courts.

Dual Court System

In the **dual court system**, the court systems of the various states are sovereign governmental jurisdictions, each equal in importance and with separate political jurisdictions. The term *dual* means that there are two systems of courts. The federal courts are distinct from the state courts but do have limited jurisdiction over the state courts. Thus, within both the federal and state systems, there are many further distinctions and divisions of the jurisdiction of the courts. The jurisdiction of the federal courts is defined in **Article 3, Section 2** of the U.S. Constitution.

> The judicial power shall extend to all cases, in law and equity, arising under this Constitution, the laws of the United States, and treaties made or which shall be made, under their authority; to all cases affecting ambassadors, other public ministers and consuls; to all cases of admiralty and maritime jurisdiction; to controversies in which the United States shall be a part; to controversies between two or more states; between citizens of the same state claiming lands under grants of different states; and between a state or the citizens thereof, and foreign states, citizens, or subjects.

The **Eleventh Amendment,** ratified in 1795, restricted the jurisdiction of the federal courts by declaring that a private citizen from one state cannot sue the government of another state in federal court. The **Tenth Amendment** provided that powers not specifically delegated to the federal government were reserved to the states. Under this authority, each state has the responsibility and power to establish its own court system. Modern American jurisprudence, both federal and state, includes codes of civil, criminal, and public law as well as codes of civil and criminal procedures.

Unlike the thousands of police departments that operate independently of each other, the courts are organized in a hierarchy of authority whereby the decisions of each lower court can be reviewed and reversed by a higher court (see Figure 6.1). Also, unlike the police,

1 The United States has a dual system of politically separate courts, federal and state, which adjudicate criminal and civil cases.

jurisprudence a philosophy or body of written law used to settle disputes

dual court system the political division of jurisdiction into two separate systems of courts: federal and state; in this system, federal courts have limited jurisdiction over state courts

Article 3, Section 2 the part of the U.S. Constitution that defines the jurisdiction of the federal courts

Eleventh Amendment a provision that prohibits a citizen from one state from suing the government of another state in federal court

Tenth Amendment a provision that powers not specifically delegated to the federal government are reserved for the states

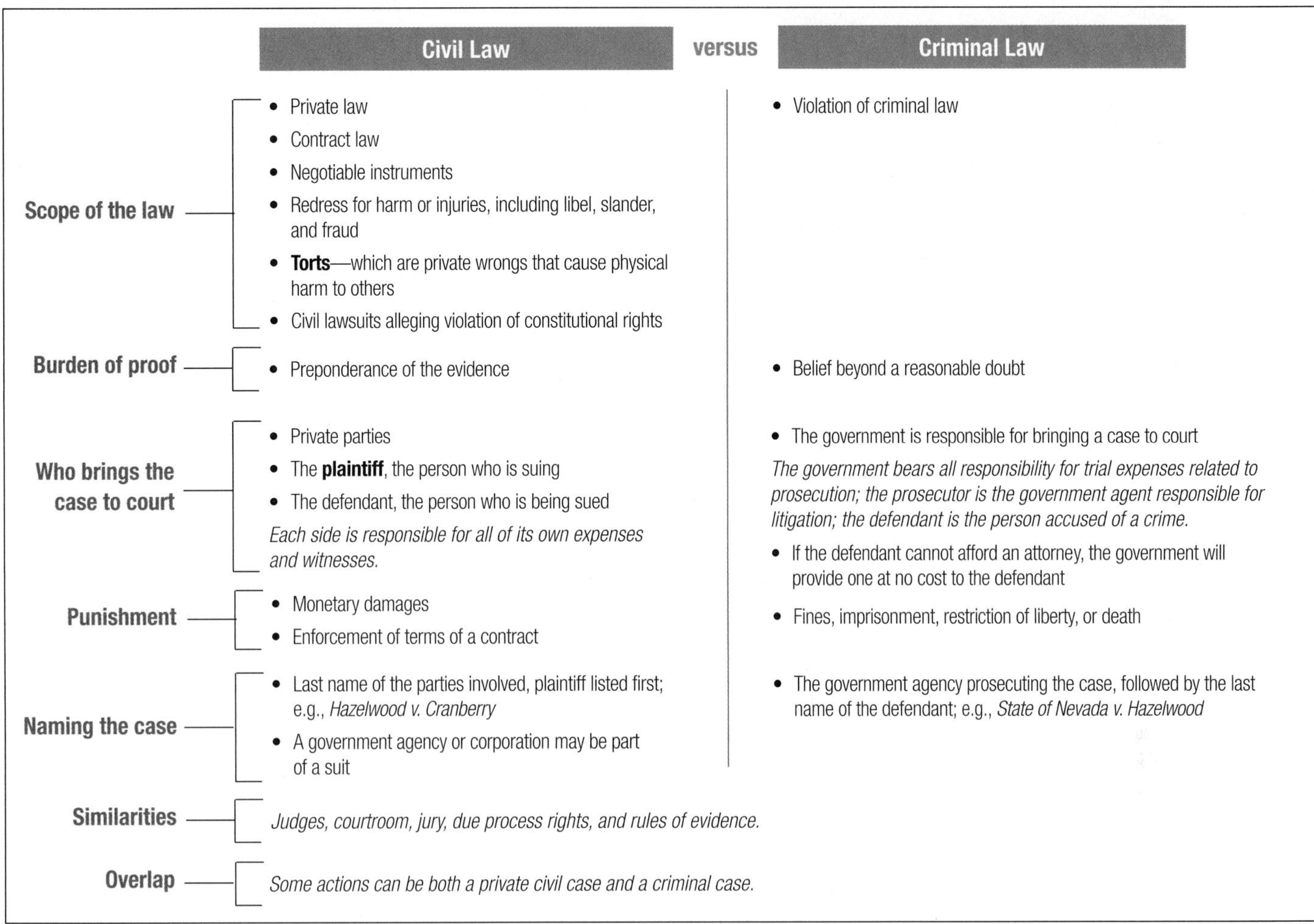

	Civil Law	versus	Criminal Law
Scope of the law	• Private law • Contract law • Negotiable instruments • Redress for harm or injuries, including libel, slander, and fraud • **Torts**—which are private wrongs that cause physical harm to others • Civil lawsuits alleging violation of constitutional rights		• Violation of criminal law
Burden of proof	• Preponderance of the evidence		• Belief beyond a reasonable doubt
Who brings the case to court	• Private parties • The **plaintiff**, the person who is suing • The defendant, the person who is being sued *Each side is responsible for all of its own expenses and witnesses.*		• The government is responsible for bringing a case to court *The government bears all responsibility for trial expenses related to prosecution; the prosecutor is the government agent responsible for litigation; the defendant is the person accused of a crime.* • If the defendant cannot afford an attorney, the government will provide one at no cost to the defendant
Punishment	• Monetary damages • Enforcement of terms of a contract		• Fines, imprisonment, restriction of liberty, or death
Naming the case	• Last name of the parties involved, plaintiff listed first; e.g., *Hazelwood v. Cranberry* • A government agency or corporation may be part of a suit		• The government agency prosecuting the case, followed by the last name of the defendant; e.g., *State of Nevada v. Hazelwood*
Similarities	*Judges, courtroom, jury, due process rights, and rules of evidence.*		
Overlap	*Some actions can be both a private civil case and a criminal case.*		

wherein federal agencies have no authority over state and local agencies, federal courts do have some authority over state courts. Each state has a final court of appeals, but it is possible to appeal a state decision to the U.S. Supreme Court, which may or may not choose to hear the case. Decisions of lower federal courts also can be appealed to the next higher court and ultimately to the U.S. Supreme Court. When the U.S. Supreme Court makes a ruling regarding the constitutionality of a law, due process right, or rule of evidence, that decision is binding on all federal and state courts.

Civil Versus Criminal Law

Individuals are responsible for seeking redress in a civil court when they are harmed by a violation of a civil law. **Civil law** is referred to as private law because it addresses the definition, regulation, and enforcement of rights in cases in which both the person who has the right and the person who has the obligation are private individuals. There are significant differences between the civil justice system and the criminal justice system.

The burden of proof in a civil court is a "preponderance of the evidence," whereas the burden of proof in a criminal court is "beyond a reasonable doubt." The O. J. Simpson case for the alleged murder of his ex-wife, Nicole Brown Simpson, and Ron Goldman is an example in which the government was unsuccessful in proving the criminal charges against the defendant, but the victims' families were able to obtain a monetary judgment for damages in civil court.

Private Parties Must Initiate Civil Cases Redress for civil wrongs, contract violations, and torts must be initiated by the individual and fall within the jurisdiction of the civil court. Civil cases far outnumber criminal cases, and the jurisprudence system is driven primarily by the court's role as mediator in civil cases.

The criminal justice system is responsible for detecting, prosecuting, and punishing people who violate criminal laws that have been created by political bodies such as the city, county, state, or federal government. After a criminal law is passed, it is the responsibility of the police to detect law violators. The responsibility of the court is to determine whether a person violated the law. Finally, the responsibility of corrections is to punish offenders for violation of the law.

tort a private wrong that causes physical harm to another

plaintiff the party who files a civil lawsuit against the party who is alleged to have done harm (the defendant)

civil law also called private law, the body of law concerned with the definition, regulation, and enforcement of rights in noncriminal cases in which both the person who has the right and the person who has the obligation are private individuals

2 The criminal justice system is responsible for detecting, prosecuting, and punishing those who violate criminal laws enacted by the government; civil law enforces rights between private individuals.

The Federal Court System

The authority for establishing a federal court system is in Article 3 of the U.S. Constitution. Congress created the lesser courts referred to in Article 3 on September 24, 1789. Congress passed the federal Judiciary Act that established 13 courts, one for each of the original states. Initially, the federal courts had few cases, because there were few federal laws. The Supreme Court originally consisted of six justices, but today there are nine justices—one chief justice and eight associate justices—on the Supreme Court. The number of justices is not determined by the U.S. Constitution.

Overview of the Federal Court System

Marbury v. Madison For the first three years of its existence, the Supreme Court had virtually nothing to do and did not review any judicial decisions. The landmark decision that established the power and role of the Supreme Court and, by inclusion, its lesser courts was *Marbury v. Madison* (1803). In *Marbury v. Madison,* under the leadership of Chief Justice John Marshall, the Supreme Court claimed the power to review acts of Congress and pronounce whether congressional acts were constitutional. This claim gave the Supreme Court the power to nullify acts of Congress. It also asserted that the Court has the power to review congressional acts without having to wait for a case to be brought before the Supreme Court. This power to declare congressional acts unconstitutional—the power of **judicial review**—has been the most important power that the Supreme Court exercises. The Supreme Court sees its primary mission as the guardian of the Constitution and accomplishes that goal by exercising its power of judicial review.

The federal court system has undergone significant revisions during its history. Today, instead of 13 courts, the federal judiciary has a unified, four-tier structure of over 100 courts covering the United States and its territories. The federal judiciary is divided into 13 federal judicial circuits that are much larger than those of the state courts and cover various geographical jurisdictions, as shown in Figure 6.2.

100
federal courts covering the United States and its territories

13
federal judicial circuits

The federal court system is responsible for the enforcement of all federal codes in all 50 states, U.S. territories, and the District of Columbia. This includes responsibility for civil, criminal, and administrative trials. The federal court system is also responsible for the trials involving local codes and ordinances in the territories of Guam, the Virgin Islands, and the Northern Mariana Islands. If a person violates a federal law, he or she can be tried at any federal district court within the circuit. Thus, a person accused of mail fraud in Oklahoma could be tried in Oklahoma, Arizona, Colorado, Kansas, New Mexico, Utah, or Wyoming.

The federal court system is responsible for both civil and criminal cases, but there are many more federal district court civil trials than there are criminal trials. Criminal trials, especially trials for violent crimes, are only a small part of the workload of the federal court.

United States District Courts

- Trial courts of original jurisdictions—those that decide whether the defendant is guilty and, if so, the punishment
- Special courts

Hear civil and criminal cases—the majority of the cases are civil
95 district courts in the United States

United States Magistrate Courts

- Organized by the Federal Magistrates Act of 1968
- Prisoner litigation, such as habeas corpus, and civil rights appeals
- Bail review
- Detention hearings
- Arraignments
- Preliminary examinations
- Initial appearance hearings
- Issues search warrants and arrest warrants
- Assists district courts
- Tries Class A misdemeanors and petty offenses

As shown in Figure 6.3, the federal court is divided into four tiers of responsibility: the U.S. magistrate courts, the trial courts, the appeals courts, and the U.S. Supreme Court. **U.S. magistrate courts** are federal lower courts whose powers are limited to trying lesser misdemeanors, setting bail, and assisting district courts with various legal matters. **U.S. district courts** are the federal system's trial courts of original jurisdiction, meaning that these are the first courts to hear charges against defendants and to render verdicts regarding these charges.

United States Courts of Appeals

Appeals are guaranteed by congressional act. Rather than have the Supreme Court handle all appeals, the federal judiciary uses **U.S. courts of appeals** to hear appeals from U.S. district courts. The right of appeal applies to both civil and criminal cases, but the focus of this discussion is on criminal appeals. Criminal appeals to the U.S. Court of Appeals must be based on the claim that the defendant was denied a fair trial or that the law that the defendant was convicted of violating was unconstitutional. Defendants cannot appeal on the grounds that they are innocent. The question of guilt is a question of **original jurisdiction** and is addressed in the U.S. District Court: The judge or the jury heard the facts of the case and rendered a decision regarding the criminality of the defendant's behavior. Thus, the U.S. appeals court will not conduct another trial to determine the guilt of the defendant.

3 **The federal court system has a hierarchical structure, including magistrate courts, district courts, courts of appeals, and the Supreme Court, all of which are responsible for enforcing all federal codes in the 50 states, the District of Columbia, and U.S. territories.**

judicial review the power of the U.S. Supreme Court to review legislation for the purpose of deciding the constitutionality of the law

U.S. magistrate courts federal lower courts with powers limited to trying lesser misdemeanors, setting bail, and assisting district courts in various legal matters

U.S. district courts trial courts of the federal system

U.S. courts of appeals the third tier of the federal court system where decisions of lower courts can be appealed for review for significant judicial error which may have affected the verdict

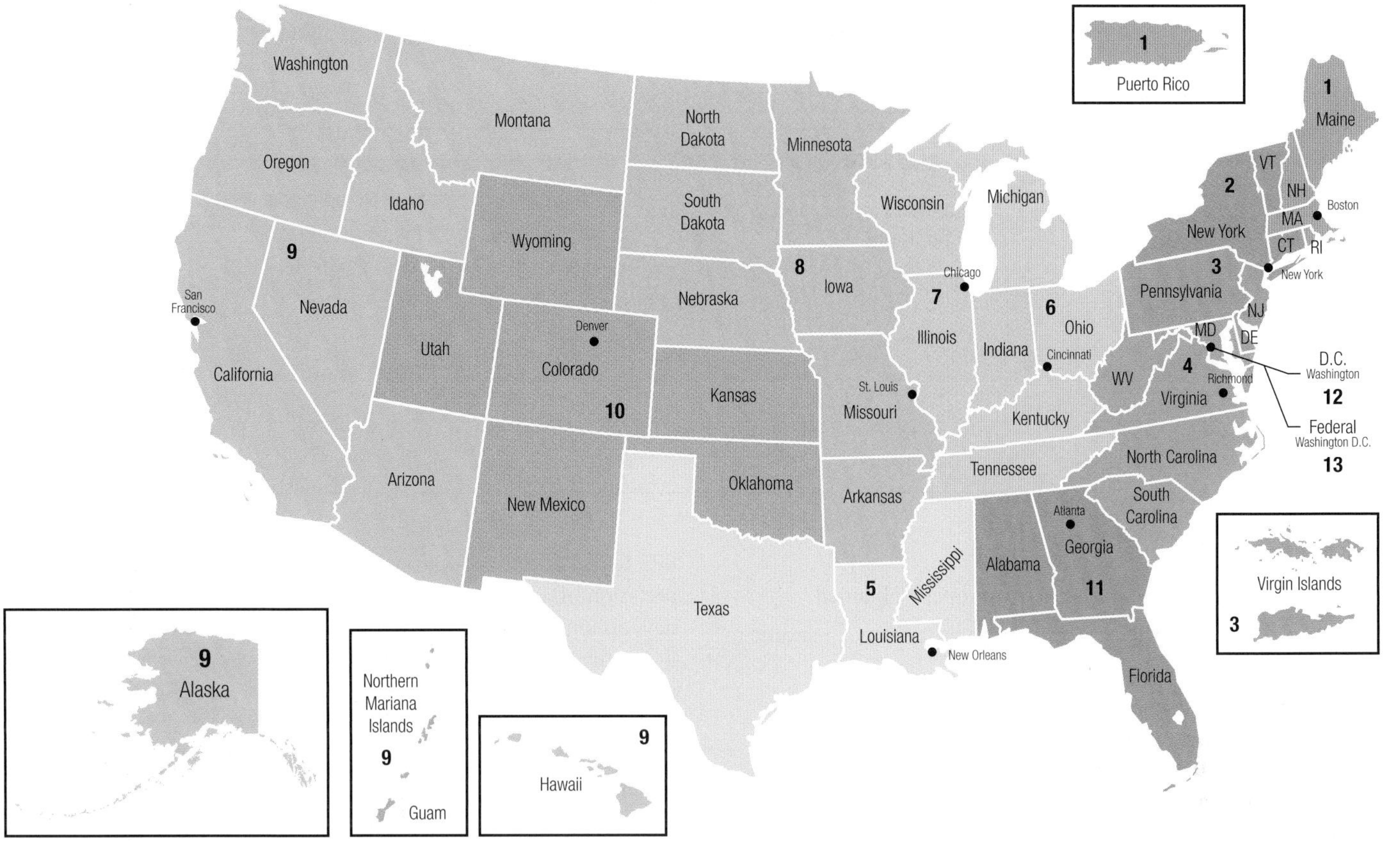

FIGURE 6.2 The 13 Federal Judicial Circuits

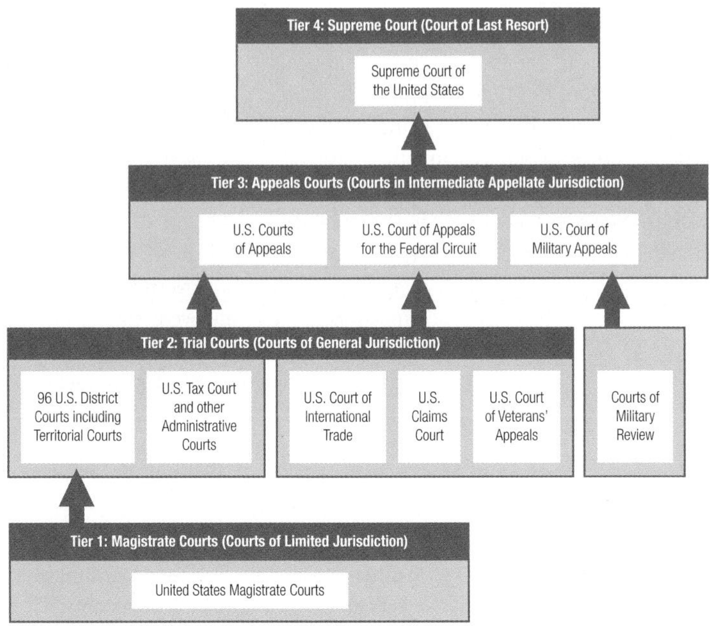

FIGURE 6.3 The Federal Judiciary

A fair trial does not mean that the defendant's trial was without error, but it does mean that there was no substantial judicial error that could have affected the outcome of the court's decision. During the defendant's trial in district court, it is the responsibility of the defendant's attorney to object to any procedure or court ruling that is thought to be unfair or unconstitutional. The district judge makes a ruling on the objection raised by the attorney, and the trial proceeds based on the judge's ruling. The objection of the defense counsel is entered into the transcript of the trial. After the trial, if the defense counsel believes that the ruling of the district judge was not correct, the judge's ruling can be appealed. If at the time of the trial the defense attorney fails to object to an unfair practice, the absence of such an objection can be considered a reason to deny the appeal.

In the U.S. courts of appeals a panel of federal judges hears appeals from the U.S. district courts. Appeals are based upon the defendant's claim that he or she did not receive a fair trial. This claim is based upon the claim that a substantial judicial error occurred which could have significantly affected the verdict. Also, the appeal can be based upon the claim that the law that the defendant was convicted of violating was unconstitutional.

original jurisdiction the first court to hear and render a verdict regarding charges against a defendant

The process of the U.S. Court of Appeals

The defendant is found guilty in the court of original jurisdiction, i.e., a U.S. magistrate court or U.S. district court. ▶ The defendant appeals, claiming that a judicial error occurred during the trial that substantially affected the outcome of the trial, i.e., a guilty verdict or the law that the defendant was convicted of is unconstitutional. ▶ A panel of judges, usually three, reviews the case. The appeals court can review the case by:

1. A review of the appeal and case documents
2. A review of the written briefs of the two sides
3. A hearing in which the two sides submit written briefs and the court hears oral arguments.

▶ Finding 

Examples of Judicial Errors

- Admitting evidence that has been improperly obtained
- Allowing prosecutorial evidence and witnesses not relevant to the trial
- Disallowing defense evidence and witnesses
- Improper trial conduct
- Misbehavior by the jury
- Instructions by the judge prohibiting the jury from considering a lesser offense
- Improper instructions by the judge to the jury

One must remember that there is a difference between judicial error and not guilty. The defendant may indeed have committed a criminal act and is, without question, guilty in the eyes of the public. There may be videotape or eyewitnesses that document the defendant's commission of the crime, and the public may be outraged when a conviction is reversed on appeal. However, to convict the defendant in a court of law, rules must be followed and the rights of the defendant must be protected.

U.S. courts of appeals are required to hear the cases brought to them on appeal from the federal trial courts within their circuit. The U.S. Court of Appeals does not conduct a jury trial. Rather, a panel of federal appeals judges, usually three, reviews the case. A review does not mean that the defendant appears before the appeals court. The appeals court may decide to review only the written briefs submitted by the attorneys and to make a decision based on the information contained in the briefs. If the appeals court decides to hear oral arguments, the attorneys come before the court and present their reasoning. Often, there are legitimate differences of opinion among legal professionals regarding an interpretation of a law, constitutional right, or court decision. The attorneys attempt to persuade the panel of judges that their interpretation is the correct one. The appeal focuses on a rule of law and not the guilt of the defendant, so no witnesses or evidence are presented during the appeals hearing. If the U.S. Court of Appeals decides that a substantial judicial error has been made, the court reviews the case and determines the appropriate action to be taken to correct the error. The decision of the appeals court may mean that the defendant receives another trial in which the judicial error is corrected, or the sentence of the defendant may be modified.

ONE MUST REMEMBER THAT THERE IS A DIFFERENCE BETWEEN JUDICIAL ERROR AND NOT GUILTY. THE DEFENDANT MAY INDEED HAVE COMMITTED A CRIMINAL ACT AND IS, WITHOUT QUESTION, GUILTY IN THE EYES OF THE PUBLIC.

13
U.S. circuit courts of appeals

4
are west of the Mississippi River

There are 13 U.S. circuit courts of appeals and about 180 federal courts of appeals judges. Each of the 13 federal judicial circuits has one location that is the principal seat of federal courts of appeal, and there are two courts of appeals located in Washington, DC. (One of the Washington, DC, courts of appeals handles civil cases related to patents, copyrights, tax disputes, and claims against the federal government.) Appeals court circuits were first established in the original 13 colonies and spread westward as the United States expanded. The geographical jurisdiction of the courts of appeals is called a **circuit court** because, originally, federal appeals judges literally traveled a circuit from one federal district court to another to hear appeals. This geographical origin of the various federal appeals circuits resulted in a disproportionate division of circuit courts east and west of

circuit court the geographical jurisdiction of a federal appeals court

A substantial judicial error affecting the outcome of the verdict was committed.	The case is returned to the lower court with orders to fix the error. The lower court may: 1. Retry the defendant 2. Correct the sentence 3. If the error cannot be corrected and still leave sufficient evidence to convict, the prosecutors may decide to drop the case.	New trial New sentence Charges dismissed
The law is unconstitutional	The verdict is voided	
No judicial error There was judicial error but it did not substantially influence a verdict of guilty. The law is constitutional	The verdict of the court of original jurisdiction is upheld	The defendant can appeal to the U.S. Supreme Court

the Mississippi River. There are only four U.S. circuit courts of appeals west of the Mississippi River.

As a result of the shift of the population centers from the East Coast to the West Coast, western U.S. circuit courts of appeals have more cases to review and also greater diversity in the values and cultures of the people within a circuit. The Ninth U.S. Circuit Court of Appeals, for instance, includes the western states, Alaska, Hawaii, and the U.S. territories of Guam and the Northern Mariana Islands. When there is widespread diversity, judges of the U.S. courts of appeals do not always have the same interpretation of the Constitution, the law, or criminal procedures. Nevertheless, the federal court system requires that decisions of the U.S. Circuit Court of Appeals are binding on all U.S. district courts within that circuit. For example, an opinion regarding the constitutionality of a search without a warrant in the Ninth U.S. Circuit Court of Appeals would be binding on all U.S. district courts in the Ninth Circuit, although not binding on the district courts in the other circuits. Although not binding, decisions from other jurisdictions can be cited as guidelines.

The United States Supreme Court

The **U.S. Supreme Court** is the highest court in the American judicial system. This means that there is no higher authority to which the defendant can appeal a decision of the Supreme Court. A decision by the Supreme Court is final and cannot be overruled by Congress. The only way to affect Supreme Court decisions is for Congress to pass a statute or constitutional amendment altering the wording of a law that the Supreme Court has declared unconstitutional. For example, in 1919, Congress passed the Eighteenth Amendment, which prohibited the manufacture, sale, or transportation of intoxicating liquors, and in 1933, repealed the prohibition with the Twenty-First Amendment. As another example, when the Supreme Court ruled that laws to collect federal personal income tax were unconstitutional (because they violated Article 1, Section 9 of the Constitution), Congress passed the Sixteenth Amendment, authorizing the federal government to lay and collect taxes on personal incomes.

In addition to its role in the criminal justice system, the Supreme Court exercises other important judicial powers. The Supreme Court is the legal mediator for lawsuits between states and between the United States and foreign countries. The Supreme Court also is the final authority for legal opinions binding on the federal government. For instance, when controversy arose over the legality of ballots cast in the State of Florida in the 2000 presidential election, the Supreme Court provided the final judgment regarding the vote count.

U.S. Supreme Court cases that determine how the Constitution is to be interpreted are called **landmark cases.** A landmark case is important because once the U.S. Supreme Court makes a ruling, the lower courts

HERE'S SOMETHING TO THINK ABOUT. . .

One reason for litigation, confusion, and appeals in the court is disagreement as to what the law actually means. Laws and regulations are often written in language that is confusing, vague, and officious. Most people do not use language like "heretofore" and "promulgated" in their writings but these are common phrases in law and regulations. In May 2011, the U.S. joined a number of nations including Britain, Portugal, Sweden, and others that require the government to use "plain language." The Plain Writing Act signed by President Obama effective October 2011 requires federal agencies to start writing plainly in all new or substantially revised documents produced for the public. A White House spokesperson endorsed the new law saying, "It is import to emphasize that agencies should communicate with the public in a way that is clear, simple, meaningful and jargon-free."

Some suspect the law will make little difference. The law lacks teeth in that there is no punishment for failure to comply with the requirements of the Plain Writing Act. Also, laws and regulations, perhaps the greatest source of confusion, are exempt from the act. Should the government be required to write laws and regulations in plain language so the average person can clearly understand the law?

U.S. Supreme Court the highest court in the U.S. judiciary system, whose rulings on the constitutionality of laws, due process rights, and rules of evidence are binding on all federal and state courts

landmark cases U.S. Supreme Court cases that mark significant changes in the interpretation of the Constitution

have to fall in line with that ruling. Landmark cases end diversity in practices and rulings among the various circuit courts of appeals. U.S. Supreme Court rulings on constitutionality also are applicable to the state courts. Landmark cases are important in determining the constitutional rights of the defendant.

Reviewing Cases Unlike the U.S. circuit courts of appeals, the U.S. Supreme Court does not have to hear a criminal case on appeal. The Supreme Court chooses cases that the justices believe address important constitutional issues. Technically, the Court must review cases when:

1. A federal court has held an act of Congress to be unconstitutional.
2. A U.S. Court of Appeals has found a state statute to be unconstitutional.
3. A state's highest court of appeals has ruled a federal law to be unconstitutional.
4. An individual's challenge to a state statute on federal constitutional grounds is upheld by a state's highest court of appeals.

In all other cases, the Court can decline to review a case. In reality, if a majority of justices does not want to review a case, the Court simply affirms the lower court's decision. If the Court decides not to review a case, there is no further appeal to the Court's decision.

In its role of judicial review of a case, the Supreme Court does not conduct jury trials and does not determine whether the defendant is guilty. The purpose of the Supreme Court's review is to determine whether a significant judicial error has been made and, if so, determine the appropriate remedy. The Supreme Court has the power to review civil lawsuits, criminal cases, and juvenile hearings. The Court is very selective in deciding what cases to review and will not hear a case until all other appeals have been exhausted. For a state case, that means that the case must have been reviewed by the state's highest court before the Supreme Court will consider it for review. Furthermore, the case must involve a substantial federal or constitutional question.

The process by which the Supreme Court chooses which cases to review begins with a clerk for a Supreme Court justice—an attorney who performs legal research for the justice. Clerks review the numerous cases that petition to the Supreme Court, select those that may merit consideration, and forward them to the Supreme Court judges. Each judge reviews the cases and decides whether a case has the potential to raise a significant federal or constitutional question. If four or more members of the Supreme Court feel that a case meets this criterion, it is selected for review. For cases selected for review, the Court issues a writ of certiorari. This authority to select cases for review is known as **certiorari power.** A **writ of certiorari** is an order to the lower court, state or federal, to forward the record of the case to the Supreme Court.

HERE'S SOMETHING TO THINK ABOUT...

The Fifth Amendment guarantees the defendant three rights regarding double jeopardy: The defendant cannot be tried twice for the same offense, cannot be retried (unless the conviction is reversed), and cannot be punished multiple times for the same offense. However, there are circumstances under which the defendant can be tried multiple times. Civil trials and criminal trials are not the same, so a defendant who is found not guilty in a criminal trial can be found at fault in a civil trial. Also, a defendant can be tried in a state court and a federal court or two different state courts for the same offense under certain circumstances.

Retrials due to a "hung jury" do not violate the Fifth Amendment. In 2011 there were two high-profile hung jury cases—former Illinois governor Rod Blagojevich and baseball homerun hit holder Barry Bonds. In the Blagojevich case prosecutors immediately retried the case and obtained convictions on 17 of 20 federal felony counts. The Bonds case was the product of a seven-year investigation. Prosecutors obtained a guilty verdict for obstruction but a hung jury on the three more serious charges. Prosecutors said they would decide whether to retry Bonds on the other counts. There is no limit on the number of times a defendant can be retried due to a hung jury. Should there be a limit?

When the Supreme Court selects a case for review, this does not mean that the defendant is not guilty, is freed, or is immediately entitled to a new trial. The Court has several options in reviewing a case. The Court can do the following:

1. examine the trial record and facts of the case and determine that no further review is necessary;
2. ask the attorneys representing the appellant to submit a written statement, called a **brief**, stating the substantial federal or constitutional issue they think needs to be decided (The attorney from the other side submits a rebuttal brief, and the Court decides on the basis of information in the briefs.); or
3. decide that the case deserves a hearing.

At a hearing, the two sides are invited to present oral arguments before the full Supreme Court. This hearing is to determine whether

certiorari power the authority of the Supreme Court, based on agreement by four of its members that a case might raise significant constitutional or federal issues, to select a case for review

writ of certiorari an order to a lower court to forward the record of a case to the U.S. Supreme Court for review

brief a written statement submitted by an appellant's attorneys that states the substantial constitutional or federal issue that they believe the court should address

the case involves a substantial federal or constitutional issue, and the attorneys must confine their arguments to this issue. The parties to the case may be given only one hour to argue their case. The Supreme Court justices will ask questions of the attorneys, but few cases are decided by this method.

After reviewing a case, the Court declares its decision and can issue a written opinion explaining the reasons for its decision. A case that is disposed of by the Court without a full written opinion is said to be a **per curiam opinion.** The Court can affirm the case or reverse the lower court's decision. In affirming a case, the Supreme Court finds that there was no substantial judicial or constitutional error and the original opinion of the lower court stands. In a criminal case, this means that whatever sentence was imposed on the defendant may be carried out or continued. If the Court is hearing an appeal by the government, which lost the case in lower court, then an "affirm" might mean that the lower court's decision stands.

Remedies for Judicial Error Reversing the case means the Court found that a judicial error or unconstitutional issue was central to the lower court's decision. Most cases are not reversed. The Court has reversed about 25 percent of all of the cases decided on merit.[1] In a criminal case, reversal does not mean that the defendant is freed, not guilty, or receives a reduced sentence. It means that the Supreme Court found the conviction of the defendant to be flawed and that conviction is "vacated." After the case is reversed, it is remanded. **Remanded** means that the case is returned to the court of original jurisdiction—the court that first convicted the defendant—with the instructions to correct the judicial error, called a "remedy."

If the judicial error involved the introduction of inadmissible evidence, such as an illegal confession or search and seizure or inappropriate testimony, then the remedy requires a new trial in which the inadmissible evidence cannot be used. If a conviction cannot be obtained without this evidence, the prosecution may decide not to ask for a new trial. In that case, the charges are dismissed and the defendant is set free. If the prosecution decides to retry the case, the defendant may or may not be convicted at the new trial.

Not all judicial errors require a new trial. Judicial errors also can involve an incorrect sentence being assessed against a defendant, and the court of original jurisdiction may be instructed to recalculate the sentence. A common criminal appeal for a reduction of sentence is the appeal for a reduction of a death sentence to the lesser sentence of life in prison.

When a long-incarcerated individual appeals on a writ of habeas corpus, an appeal to the Supreme Court can take decades. Although long delays are unusual, in some cases defendants have served the length of their sentence by the time the Supreme Court hears their case. Delays often are due to the large caseload of the Supreme Court and its limited ability to review and decide on appeals. Some critics of the judicial system have argued that such a delay in justice is the same as justice denied. There appears to be no immediate solution to this problem, as new issues involving substantial questions of constitutional rights, due process, human rights, and civil liberties come before each session of the U.S. Supreme Court.

Characteristics of the State Court System

State courts are authorized and organized autonomously by each state. If there is a legal dispute between states, the federal courts have jurisdiction. The purpose of state courts is to try defendants charged with violations of state laws or the state constitution. A state also contains smaller political jurisdictions, such as cities and counties, and each of these has its own legal codes. Therefore, states must establish court systems that provide for a defendant to be tried for allegedly violating a city or county ordinance. Like the federal court system, the state court system has a number of specialized courts dealing with noncriminal cases. As in the federal courts, criminal trials compose only a small percentage of the state court's activities.

State court systems uniquely reflect the history of each state. For example, Pennsylvania's judiciary system began as a disparate collection of courts, some inherited from the reign of the Duke of York and some established by William Penn. They were mostly local, mostly part time, and mostly under control of the governor. All of the state courts were run by nonlawyers, and final appeals had to be taken to England. The Judiciary Act of 1722 was the colony's first judicial bill. It established the Pennsylvania Supreme Court and the Court of Common Pleas. The court system changed again with the Pennsylvania Constitution of 1776 and the Constitution of the United States. After that, the most sweeping changes in Pennsylvania's judiciary came in 1968. The Constitution of 1968 created the Unified Judicial System, consisting of the supreme court, superior courts, and commonwealth courts; common pleas courts; the Philadelphia municipal court; the Pittsburgh magistrate court; Philadelphia traffic court; and district justice courts. Pennsylvania's judicial system is illustrated in Figure 6.4.

Like Pennsylvania, most states designed their state court system when they were admitted into the Union. Thus, the states consisting of the original thirteen colonies have the oldest state courts, and Alaska and Hawaii have the newest. Over time, the philosophy, mission, and values of the citizens of the states change, and many states have found it necessary to redesign their state court system. Most of those states have chosen models that resemble the four-tier federal court system. The four-tier system consists of the following:

1. courts of limited jurisdiction,
2. courts of general jurisdiction,
3. courts of intermediate appellate jurisdiction, and
4. courts of last resort.

per curiam opinion a case that is disposed of by the U.S. Supreme Court without a full written opinion

remanded after the U.S. Supreme Court's reversal of a decision of a lower court, the return of the case to the court of original jurisdiction with instructions to correct the judicial error

4 **Each state organizes its own court system to settle legal disputes and criminal matters that violate the state constitution or state or local ordinances. Most states have a four-tier system, which includes courts of limited jurisdiction, courts of general jurisdiction, courts of intermediate appellate jurisdiction, and courts of last resort.**

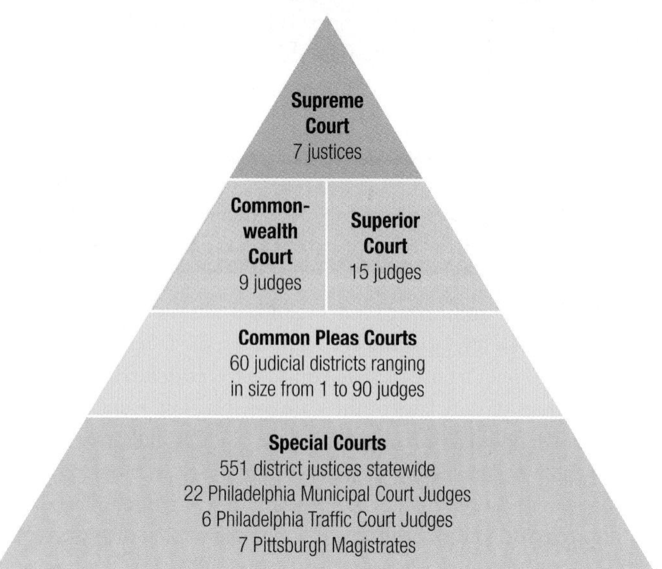

Figure 6.4 The four-tier structure of the Commonwealth of Pennsylvania court system is similar to the federal court system.

Each state has unique names for the various courts within its system. Each state has granted different jurisdiction to the various courts within its system based on geography, subject matter, and hierarchy. Each state has a hierarchy of appeals from the lowest court to the court of last resort.

Courts of Limited Jurisdiction

State courts with original jurisdiction—the power to determine if the defendant is guilty—are divided into courts of limited jurisdiction and general trial courts. **Courts of limited jurisdiction** are known as justice of the peace courts, municipal courts, and magistrate's courts.

Courts of limited jurisdiction frequently are not **courts of record**—courts in which the trial proceedings are recorded. For example, traffic courts, municipal courts, and county courts frequently are not courts of records because no written record is made of the trial in these courts. Thus, a case that is appealed to a higher court from a limited jurisdiction court must have a trial de novo, or new trial. A new trial is required because there is no written record of the lower court's proceedings to determine whether a judicial error occurred.

Justice of the peace courts and municipal courts perform similar functions, hearing minor criminal cases involving municipal and traffic laws, issuing search and arrest warrants, setting bail, and arraigning defendants. Traditionally, justice of the peace courts are associated with rural geographical jurisdictions, whereas municipal courts are associated with urban geographical jurisdictions. Another court of limited jurisdiction is the county court, where counties can try defendants for violations of county laws. Most courts of limited jurisdiction also perform noncriminal functions, such as processing civil suits, accepting passport applications, and performing marriages. Some courts of limited jurisdiction try civil cases with limited dollar amounts. These courts are commonly referred to as "small claims courts."

Courts of General Jurisdiction

The general trial courts of the state judicial system are the workhorses of the criminal justice system. State **general trial courts** handle all kinds of criminal cases—from traffic violations to murder. General trial courts are courts of record. A full transcription (i.e., a word-for-word recording of the proceeding) is made for every trial in a general trial court. Nearly all appeals for criminal cases originate from state general trial courts. General trial courts are called circuit courts, superior courts, district courts, courts of common pleas, and courts of first instance.

Appellate Courts

Most states have an intermediate appellate court that acts in a similar capacity as the U.S. Court of Appeals. Some common names for these are Court of Criminal Appeals, Court of Appeals, Appellate Court, Court of Special Appeals, Appellate Division of Superior Court, Superior Court, and Commonwealth Court. These **appellate courts** do not have original jurisdiction and review cases for judicial error and other significant issues concerning due process, civil rights, and federal and state constitutional questions.

Courts of Last Resort

Each state has a court of final appeals. The names given to these various courts of last resort are Supreme Court, Supreme Judicial Court, Court of Appeals, and High Court. Oklahoma and Texas have two separate courts of last resort: The Supreme Court of Criminal Appeals handles criminal cases, and the State Supreme Court handles all other cases. Each state determines the number of judges who sit on the court of last resort, typically five to nine justices.

The state **court of last resort** has appellant jurisdiction and acts much like the U.S. Supreme Court. Its primary purpose in criminal cases is to review a selected number of cases that may have a significant state or federal question. After reviewing the case, the state's court of last resort can decide to affirm the case or to reverse and remand the case. After a criminal defendant has exhausted all appeals in the state court system, he or she can appeal the case to the U.S. Supreme Court.

courts of limited jurisdiction state courts of original jurisdiction that are not courts of record (e.g., traffic courts, municipal courts, or county courts)

courts of record courts in which trial proceedings are transcribed

general trial courts state courts of original jurisdiction that hear all kinds of criminal cases

appellate courts state courts that have the authority to review the proceedings and verdicts of general trial courts for judicial errors and other significant issues

court of last resort a state court of final appeals that reviews lower court decisions and whose decisions can be appealed to the U.S. Supreme Court

HERE'S SOMETHING TO THINK ABOUT...

The role of appellate courts is to review for significant errors affecting whether the defendant received a fair trial. Trial judges and defense attorneys also have a responsibility to screen for errors during the trial. Usually the defense indicates evidence or testimony is unfair by objecting to the testimony. If the judge agrees, he or she can order the jury to disregard the testimony. In a few cases the error can be so significant that a more severe remedy is required. For example, in July 2011, after the second day of testimony in the trial of former seven times Cy Young Award winner major league baseball pitcher Roger Clemens for obstruction of Congress and perjury, Washington, D.C., federal judge Reggie Walton stopped the trial and declared a mistrial.

The case had taken more than three years to come to court, had involved congressional hearings into the so-called baseball steroid scandal, and cost millions of dollars. During congressional hearings Clemens denied that he had ever injected steroids or human growth hormone. The trial was the result of a three-year investigation that concluded Clemens lied to Congress regarding the use of steroids.

Judge Walton stopped the trial because prosecutors had shown a video of congressional testimony to the jury in which Laura Pettitte testified that her husband Andy Pettitte, the star government witness in Clemens's trial, had told her that Roger Clemens admitted to him using human growth hormones. In pretrial motions the judge had advised prosecutors they could not use the video as it was hearsay evidence and attempted to bolster the credibility of the government's star witness with inadmissible evidence. When prosecutors played the video the judge stopped the trial and after conferring with the defense ruled the testimony would make it "difficult if not impossible" for Clemens to be judged fairly after the prosecutor's error. Judge Walton ruled the error was so serious that a special hearing would be held to determine if the government would be allowed to retry the case.

Justice in the courtroom is complicated and, unlike entertainment media, real trials are not smooth and error-free events. An important role of the court, especially the appellate courts, is to sort out the errors and determine which ones significantly affected the verdict and to provide a remedy when an error has occurred. Do you think most criminal trials provide the defendant a fair trial? Do you think appellate courts effectively catch and correct unfair verdicts?

CHAPTER 6

The Court System

Check It!

1 WHAT are the the historical foundations and dual structure of the U.S. court system? p. 94

The justice system of the United States is based on the Justinian Code, the Napoleonic Code, and English common law. The dual court system forms a unified judicial system in which a case from the lowest state court could ultimately be reviewed by the U.S. Supreme Court, whose decisions are binding on all federal and state courts.

2 WHAT are the differences between criminal law and civil law? p. 95

Criminal law is concerned with actions that are prohibited by the government because they are harmful to society. Civil law addresses the definition, regulation, and enforcement of rights between private individuals.

3 HOW is the federal court system organized, and what are the responsibilities of each level of the federal courts? p. 96

The federal court system is a four-tier, unified judicial system composed of the following:

1. Magistrate courts, which are federal courts with limited jurisdiction; they handle prisoner litigation, try lesser misdemeanors, set bail, conduct preliminary examinations and arraignments, issue search and arrest warrants, and assist district courts.
2. District courts, which are the courts of original jurisdiction for all federal trials in the United States.
3. Courts of appeals, which hear appeals from federal district courts to determine whether substantial judicial error could have affected the outcomes of cases.
4. The Supreme Court, which is the highest court in the United States and the absolute court of last resort; its rulings, such as on issues of constitutionality, due process, and rules of evidence, are binding on all federal and state courts.

4 HOW is the state court system organized, and what are the responsibilities of each level of the state courts? p. 101

Each state has the power to organize its own judicial system. Most states have four-tier organizational structures with responsibilities that parallel those of the federal judiciary system.

Assess Your Understanding

1. Which of the following are required by the U.S. Constitution?
   a. local police agencies
   b. state police agencies
   c. correctional facilities
   d. federal court system

2. What is the burden of proof to convict a defendant in a criminal trial?
   a. preponderance of the evidence
   b. proof beyond a reasonable doubt
   c. probable cause
   d. a majority vote of the jury

3. Which of the following is characteristic of a civil trial?
   a. The burden of proof is belief beyond a reasonable doubt.
   b. The sanctions may include fines or imprisonment.
   c. The plaintiff is responsible for own expenses and witnesses.
   d. none of the above

4. What principle was established by *Marbury v. Madison*?
   a. the power of judicial review
   b. the division of the federal courts into 13 circuits
   c. the separation of civil and criminal cases in the federal courts
   d. the reorganization of the federal court system

5. Appeals to state and federal appeals courts must be based upon which of the following claims?
   a. The defendant was wrongfully convicted.
   b. A significant error occurred during the trial which may have affected the outcome of the verdict.
   c. The government has discovered new evidence and wants to retry the case in which the defendant was found not guilty.
   d. all of the above

6. If the U.S. Supreme Court accepts a criminal case upon appeal, which of the following is true?
   a. The defendant is immediately released from prison pending the outcome of the Court's ruling.
   b. The defendant must be granted a new trial.
   c. The Court may dispose of the appeal without issuing an opinion regarding the decision.
   d. If the Court finds that a significant error occurred during the trial, the defendant must be released from prison immediately.

7. If a state supreme court makes a ruling regarding a criminal case that has been appealed to state's supreme court, which of the following is true?
   a. The defendant cannot appeal the case to any other court.
   b. The defendant can appeal the case to the U.S. Court of Appeals.
   c. The defendant can ask the state court to reconsider its decision.
   d. The defendant can appeal the case to the U.S. Supreme Court.

8. What is a writ of certiorari?
   a. a ruling by an appeals court or supreme court to a lower court to forward the record of a case to the court for review
   b. a ruling that a significant error occurred during a trial which may have affected the outcome of the verdict
   c. a ruling that a defendant was wrongfully convicted
   d. a per curiam opinion

9. In which of the following courts usually is no transcription of the trial made?
   a. supreme court
   b. appellate court
   c. court of original jurisdiction
   d. court of limited jurisdiction

10. Which court determines if a defendant is guilty of the charges filed against him or her by a bench or jury trial?
    a. court of original jurisdiction
    b. appeals court
    c. both A and B
    d. none of the above

ESSAY

1. Describe the U.S. dual court system.
2. Compare and contrast criminal cases and civil cases.
3. How is the federal court system organized, and what are the responsibilities of each level of the federal courts?
4. Describe the relationship between the federal court system and the state court system.
5. What are the grounds in which a conviction by a court of original jurisdiction can be appealed to a higher court?
6. Describe the organization of the state court system.
7. What are the remedies available to an appeals court if the court finds a significant error occurred which may have affected the verdict?
8. Describe the options the U.S. Supreme Court has if it decides to review a case on appeal.

ANSWERS: 1. d, 2. b, 3. c, 4. a, 5. b, 6. c, 7. d, 8. a, 9. d, 10. a

Media

Go to the *Chapter 6: The Court System* section in *MyCJLab* to test your understanding of this chapter, access customized study content, engage in interactive simulations, complete critical thinking and research assignments, and view related online videos.

Additional Links

Go to www.cnn.com/JUSTICE/ for information on current criminal and civil trials.

See www.uscourts.gov for a wealth of information on the various U.S. federal courts, as well as useful links and employment opportunities.

To review the facts of some of the most famous trials throughout history, such as the trials of Socrates, Galileo, the Salem Witchcraft Trials, Charles Manson, O.J. Simpson, and President Clinton, go to www.law.umkc.edu/faculty/projects/ftrials/ftrials.htm

Current statistics regarding the U.S. courts can be viewed at http://bjs.ojp.usdoj.gov/

Each of the state courts maintains a Web site which provides information about the organizational structure of its courts and other information about the state's court.

To find your state court Web site, go to www.google.com and type in "state courts." Find the state you are interested in and follow the links to the state's court Web site.

Go to www.findlaw.com to look up landmark U.S. Supreme Court cases.

For a short review of the stages in a criminal case from arrest to trial, go to http://link.brightcove.com/services/player/bcpid1569843954?bctid=1578615932

In this 75-minute C-Span interview, U.S. Supreme Court Associate Justice John Paul Stevens moderated a discussion on the crucial 1803 case of *Marbury v. Madison* that established a judicial right to review whether legislation is constitutional. www.c-spanvideo.org/program/284332-1

A shorter video on *Marbury v. Madison* can be found at www.youtube.com/watch?v=uLRO5iCWpps

For a rare look inside the U.S. Supreme Court building, watch this CNN video at www.youtube.com/watch?v=Unyswl36q8w&feature=related

In this 47-minute C-SPAN interview, chief justice John Roberts speaks about the workings of the Supreme Court, his role as chief justice, federal court budgets, and cameras in the courtroom. He also responds to questions from the audience. www.c-spanvideo.org/program/FourthCi

COURTROOM PARTICIPANTS AND THE TRIAL

7

After missing for 31 days Cindy Anthony reported the disappearance of her 2-year-old granddaughter, Caylee Anthony, on July 15, 2008. On October 14, Orlando, Florida, authorities indicted Caylee's mother, Casey Anthony, for first degree murder and sought the death penalty. On July 5, 2011, when the verdict of the trial was read in an Orlando courtroom, 91 percent of the television viewing audience was watching along with 142 million listeners on radio.

Except for the trials of the "rich and famous" most criminal trials are little noticed by the public. Casey Anthony was neither rich nor famous. In fact, her indigent defense was handled by Jose Baez, a relatively unknown attorney. For what ever reason, the Casey Anthony trial became the social media trial of the century.

EXCEPT FOR THE TRIALS OF THE "RICH AND FAMOUS" MOST CRIMINAL TRIALS ARE LITTLE NOTICED BY THE PUBLIC.

The jury pool had to be drawn from the neighboring Tampa Bay area, as it was impossible to find unbiased jurors in the Orlando area. During the six-week trial, the jury was sequestered due to the intense media coverage. The prosecution's case was based upon circumstantial evidence and the defense emphasized the prosecutor's burden of proof.

On July 5, 2011, when the jury delivered its verdict after less than 11 hours of deliberation, the public was stunned. The jury found Casey Anthony not guilty of the felony charges related to Caylee's death. Death threats were made against the jurors, the defense lawyers, and Casey Anthony. Jurors were berated on the media for "letting Casey get away with murder." Fearing for her life Casey Anthony went into hiding.

1 What is the basic legal philosophy of a trial in the U.S. legal system?

2 What are the guidelines for determining which court has jurisdiction over a crime?

3 What are the major pretrial proceedings?

4 How do the Sixth Amendment and the Speedy Trial Act of 1974 affect a trial?

5 What are the roles of the various people involved in a criminal trial?

Legal experts defending the criminal justice system emphasized a not guilty verdict did not mean that the jurors did not "believe" Casey was not responsible for the death of Caylee. In his closing arguments Jose Baez told the jurors his biggest fear was that jurors would base their verdict "on emotions, not evidence."

Following the trial civil lawsuits were filed, the media emphasized the millions of dollars Casey could make, and new bills, called Caylee's law, were proposed. Caylee's law would impose strict requirements for parents to report the death or disappearance of a child. Jose Baez denounced the death penalty citing the trial as an example of why "we all need to stop and look and think twice about a country that decides to kill its own citizens." Critics complained the coverage of the trial blurred the lines between news and entertainment.

The Casey Anthony trial definitely is not your typical criminal trial. However, it demonstrates how each trial is unique and influenced by the personalities of the criminal trial participants. It shows how public opinion and legal verdicts are vastly different from each other. Also, it shows how criminal trials are related to numerous outcomes—some intentional and some unintentional.

This chapter discusses what normally happens in the criminal trial and roles of the criminal trial participants.

The Adjudication Process

A criminal trial is a complex event involving many participants. Many of these participants do their work behind the scenes. Most trials attract little media attention, but sensational trials can command nationwide media coverage. The public's perception of a criminal trial is strongly influenced by the media, because few people outside of the criminal justice system have reliable knowledge of the adjudication process. Many people, however, have watched criminal trials portrayed by the media. Some media presentations of trials are essentially complete fiction. The guilty party rarely, if ever, bursts forth from the public seating and confesses to the crime in the middle of the trial. Despite the importance and complexity of trials, most trials last only a couple of days. TruTV and other public broadcasts of actual criminal trials provide the public with an accurate view of a criminal trial, but few viewers have the interest and patience to observe a criminal trial from start to finish, because trials can be boring events to watch.

The concept that a trial is a "battle" between the state and a legal "champion" who represents the defendant is the basic legal philosophy of the American criminal justice system. Trials seek to establish the guilt of the defendant and, if guilty, to determine appropriate punitive sanctions. Trials are complex because many criminal justice agencies and personnel—police, prosecutors, judges, jurors, victims, offenders, and many more—must interact in the pursuit of justice. Often the parties in a trial are in conflict with each other, so there is no guarantee that the process will go smoothly. Police officers seek to have the most serious charges possible filed against defendants, whereas prosecutors seek to have charges for which they can get a guilty plea or verdict. Prosecutors seek to convict defendants, whereas defendants hope for a verdict of not guilty. Victim and defendant may offer different accounts of events.

This chapter provides a description of the adjudication phase—in other words, the criminal trial. It examines the people involved in this process, the decisions that have to be made to bring a defendant to trial, and the opposing ideologies that play out in the adjudication process. These opposing ideologies are the pursuit of punishment for the guilty and the desire to provide the accused with constitutional rights to protect him or her from abuse by the criminal justice system.

Jurisdiction

Civilian criminal trials occur in federal court if the offense is a violation of federal law, or in state or local courts if the offense is a violation of state or local law. If the offense is a federal felony, the trial occurs in a district court with jurisdiction over the offense. Usually, jurisdiction means that some part of the crime was committed within the geographical jurisdiction of the district court. If the offense is a misdemeanor, the trial occurs in a federal magistrate court. Defendants accused of violating state statutes are tried in a state court of limited jurisdiction for misdemeanor crimes and in a state court of original jurisdiction for felony crimes.

Trials in Courts of Limited Jurisdiction

Trials in courts of limited jurisdiction usually concern crimes such as simple assault, disorderly conduct, trespass, and larceny. In a typical case, the defendant is arrested by a local police officer and appears before the court for a trial within a few weeks. Usually, the defendant is not guaranteed the right to an attorney because the punishment does not exceed the threshold at which the government must provide defendants with an attorney if they cannot afford legal counsel. Most trials consist of the police officer telling the judge what law the defendant is alleged to have violated and the evidence supporting his or her assertion, followed by the defendant's rebuttal. For the most part, these trials are fairly simple affairs. Few witnesses are called to testify, and only a minimum of evidence is introduced. The entire trial may last only minutes.

Courts of limited jurisdiction are not courts of record, so no transcript is made of the proceedings. Scheduling of trials is simple in that many defendants are given the same trial date and time. The court starts the day with the first case and proceeds through the others as time permits. These are not jury trials, and the judge renders an immediate decision following the conclusion of the arguments. The defendant has the right to appeal the decision to a court of general trial jurisdiction.

Each local or municipal court has its own distinctive procedures, depending on factors such as the legal training of the judge, the judicial resources of the municipality or county, and the number of cases that the court hears. In rural areas, the justice of the peace court may be held only once a week, whereas in large urban cities, the municipal court may hear cases daily. Because of the diverse and variable nature of trials in courts of limited jurisdiction, the focus of this chapter is on trials in state courts of general jurisdiction and federal district courts.

Trials in Courts of General Jurisdiction and Federal District Courts

Most felony criminal trials occur in state courts of general jurisdiction or U.S. district courts. Because there are more felony crimes committed in violation of state laws than federal laws, the number of state felony criminal trials is much higher than the number of federal

1 **The concept that a trial is a "battle" between the state and a legal champion who represents the defendant is the basic legal philosophy of the American criminal justice system.**

Following the arrest and booking

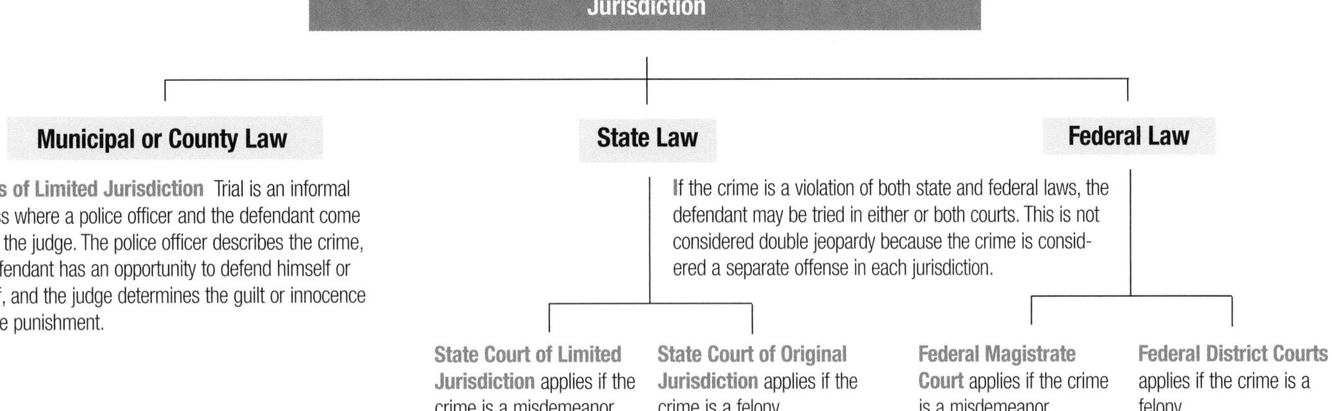

felony trials. Trial procedures for state and federal courts of general jurisdiction are similar. This chapter discusses the general procedures that apply to both state and federal courts and highlights when there is a difference between the two.

One of the first decisions that must be made when a person is arrested for a felony crime is which court has jurisdiction. The general guidelines for determining jurisdiction have to do with which laws were violated and the geographical location of the crime. If the crime was a violation of both federal and state laws, the defendant may be tried in either or both courts. Violations of federal and state laws are considered different offenses and do not constitute trying the person twice for the same offense, which is prohibited by the Fifth Amendment of the Constitution. Thus, if the crime is in violation of both federal and state laws, it is not considered **double jeopardy** to try the defendant in both federal court and state court.

As a practical matter, however, most defendants are not tried in both federal and state courts. Usually, the federal or state prosecutor with the strongest case takes the lead in bringing the case to trial. Bank robbery, both a federal crime and a state felony, is one crime in which this question frequently arises. Federal and state prosecutors could both choose to try the defendant for bank robbery, but usually only one prosecutor files charges. Often, the arresting agency is a factor in determining who files charges. If the bank robber is arrested by the Federal Bureau of Investigation, federal charges are filed, and if the defendant is arrested by the state or local police, state charges are filed.

Federal courts claim jurisdiction for crimes committed in the United States; its territories; maritime jurisdictional limits; federal, Native American, and military reservations; and U.S. registered ships at sea. For a state court to have jurisdiction of a case, all or part of the crime must have been committed within the state. If part of the crime is committed in a state, the state may claim jurisdiction over other parts of the crime, even crimes committed in another state. It is not considered double jeopardy to try a defendant in two or more states for what would appear to a layperson to be the same crime. States are sovereign political entities; thus, violation of the laws of several states is not considered the "same crime," and each state retains jurisdiction.

For example, if a person is abducted in one state and transported across the state line, where he or she is murdered, both states can claim jurisdiction over the crime. Both states could try the defendant for kidnapping and murder, even though the kidnapping happened in one state and the murder happened in another. If two (or more) states claim jurisdiction over a crime, the state officials must negotiate to determine who will first prosecute the defendant. The states also will have to negotiate whether the defendant will be tried in both states if he or she is convicted by the first state. If the defendant is convicted and is to be tried in the second state, the states must negotiate whether the trial will occur before or after the convicted defendant has served his or her sentence for the crime. If the crime is first-degree murder and one state has the death penalty but the other state does not, the decision concerning in which state to try the defendant becomes even more important.

double jeopardy the rule that a defendant can be charged only once and punished only once for a crime; if tried and found innocent, the defendant cannot be retried even if new evidence of his or her guilt is discovered.

2 **State misdemeanor crimes are tried in state courts of limited jurisdiction; state felony crimes are tried in state courts of general jurisdiction; and federal felony crimes are tried in U.S. district courts.**

Pretrial Proceedings

When the police arrest a suspect, the prosecutor has a very short time to decide if the charges are appropriate and if the evidence, even though incomplete at this stage, is sufficient to bring the case to trial. In some cases, the police and the prosecutor may have worked together to investigate and compile the necessary evidence prior to the arrest of the suspect.

Due Process The government must present evidence to an impartial judicial body that a crime has been committed and that there is reasonable belief that the person accused committed the crime.

Prosecutorial Discretion The prosecuting attorney decides if he or she wants to proceed with the case or drop it. The prosecutor may decide to:

- Drop the charges
- Add additional charges
- Reduce the charges

Initial Appearance

Initial Appearance After the paperwork is forwarded to the prosecuting attorney, the accused is brought before a magistrate judge for a first appearance. The magistrate judge reviews the charges, advises the defendant of his or her rights, and sets bail. If charges filed could result in a prison sentence of 6 months or more, then the judge will determine whether the person has funds for a lawyer and, if not, will arrange for a lawyer to represent him or her at no charge.

Preliminary Hearing

Preliminary Hearing This is sometimes referred to as the "probable cause" hearing. The judge will take an active role in questioning the prosecution and defendant. It is the prosecution's responsibility to convince the judge that there is probable cause to believe that (1) a crime has been committed and (2) that the defendant committed that crime. Defense counsel can challenge the evidence. The judge determines whether the case should be dismissed or whether the defendant should be arraigned.

Grand Jury

Grand Jury Some states and the federal government make use of grand juries to determine if a case should go forward. The grand jury is made up of a panel of citizens selected to hear evidence against an accused person. Much like a jury, there is a presiding judge and the prosecution presents evidence and witnesses to convince the jury that a crime has been committed. The major difference is that the defendant and his or her attorney are not present. If the grand jury determines that there is probable cause, then an indictment is written. This is called a true bill.

Arraignment

The defendant is formally charged with the crime or crimes they are alleged to have committed and are asked to enter a plea. If the defendant pleads not guilty a trial date is set. If the defendant pleads guilty there is no trial and a sentencing hearing is set.

Pretrial Motions

motion for discovery a pretrial motion filed by the defense counsel, requesting that the prosecutor turn over all relevant evidence, including the list of witnesses, that the prosecution might use at the trial

motion for suppression a pretrial motion made by the defense to exclude certain evidence from being introduced in the trial

motion for change of venue a pretrial request, made either by the prosecutor or the defense, to move the trial to another courtroom in the same jurisdiction

motion for continuance a pretrial request made either by the prosecutor or the defense to delay the start of the trial

motion for dismissal a pretrial defense motion requesting that the charges against the defendant be dismissed

motion for a bill of particulars a pretrial motion that allows the defense to receive more details as to exactly what items the prosecution considers illegal if a defendant is charged with possession of burglary tools, illegal weapons, drug paraphernalia, or illegal gambling paraphernalia

motion for severance of charges or defendants a pretrial request that the defendant be tried for each of multiple charges separately or that multiple defendants charged with the same crime be tried separately

The police and prosecutor work together to determine the charges to be brought against the defendant. After the arrest but before the trial, decisions also must be made about setting bail, determining the defendant's competency to stand trial, and plea bargaining.

pretrial motions are requests by the prosecutor or defense made in advance of the trial

initial appearance the Court determines the charges against the defendant are legitimate, advises the defendant of his or her rights, sets bail, and assesses the need for legal representation for the defendant

preliminary hearing or probable cause hearing the Court determines if there is sufficient evidence to charge the defendant with a crime

grand jury an alternative method, which is confidential, to determine if there is sufficient evidence to charge the defendant with a crime

due process court rules which define the standards for a "fair" trial

Charges and Proceedings Before Trial

The Constitution requires that citizens must be informed of the charges against them before being tried in a court of law. The first step toward bringing a person to trial is the arrest and booking of the person, which formally charges him or her with having committed a crime. The process of bringing a person to trial involves the joint activity of the police and the prosecutor. One of the first questions to answer is whether the defendant will be arraigned before a state court or in the U.S. magistrate court. The defendant must be arraigned before the court, federal or state, that will exercise jurisdiction over the case. Usually, federal agents take the accused to a U.S. magistrate court for arraignment, whereas local and state law enforcement officers take the accused before the appropriate state court. Because both courts may have jurisdiction in the case, a defendant who is first arraigned before one court may later be arraigned before another.

Determining the Charges: The Police and the Prosecutor

When the accused is first arrested, the law enforcement officer files a report charging the person with a crime. After the person is booked, a magistrate reviews the charges filed against the accused and determines that the police have filed constitutional charges against the person and have provided the person with his or her constitutionally protected rights. The police and the prosecutor then work together to bring the case to trial and secure a conviction without violating due process.

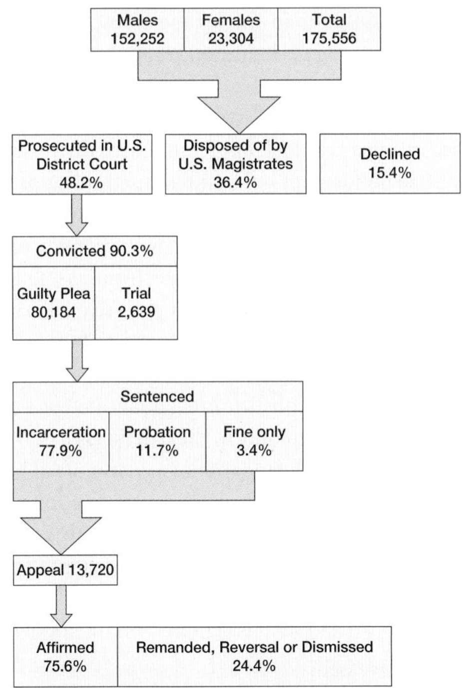

FIGURE 7.1 Disposition of Federal Suspects Arrested in 2008 October 1, 2007–September 30, 2008

Source: Bureau of Justice Statistics, Federal Justice Statistics 2008 (2011) http://bjs.ojp.usdoj.gov/index.cfm?ty=pbdetail&iid=1745

Due Process The framers of the U. S. Constitution included the provision that due process must be used in bringing a person to trial for a criminal offense. Recall that due process has been interpreted to mean that the government must present evidence to an impartial judicial body that a crime has been committed and that there is reasonable belief that the person accused committed the crime. The prosecutor, not the arresting officer, is responsible for presenting this evidence.

Prosecutorial Discretion After reviewing the police reports and in some cases talking to the arresting officers, the prosecuting attorney must decide if he or she wants to proceed with the case or drop it. The fact that the police have arrested and booked a suspect is no guarantee that the prosecutor will see the same merit in the case that the police did. The prosecutor may decide that the police do not have sufficient evidence to prove the charges beyond a reasonable doubt and may refuse to move the case forward. Figure 7.1 summarizes the disposition of federal suspects arrested in 2008. About 17 percent of cases presented to federal prosecutors are not accepted for further action.

It is also very common for the prosecutor to modify the charges alleged by the police before moving the case forward. The prosecutor has the following options:

- dropping charges;
- adding additional charges; or
- reducing the charges.

The police may have arrested a person for first-degree murder, but the prosecutor may believe that the evidence warrants only charges of second-degree murder. This power of prosecuting attorneys is called **prosecutorial discretion.** The prosecutor also exercises power in the preliminary hearing, information, indictment, and arraignment.

Relationship Between Prosecutor and Law Enforcement Law enforcement and the prosecution are each autonomous criminal justice agencies, but without cooperation between them, it is difficult to achieve a successful prosecution. When the police arrest a suspect, the prosecutor has a very short time to decide if the charges are appropriate and if the evidence, even though incomplete at this stage, is sufficient to bring the case to trial. The relationship between the prosecutor and the arresting officer(s) is an important factor in this decision. Serious felony crime is most likely to be handled by veteran detectives who have an ongoing relationship with the prosecutor. The prosecutor depends on the detectives' professionalism and competence in making the decision to take the case.

In some major cases, the police and the prosecutor work together prior to the arrest of the suspect. In important cases, taking months or years to investigate and compile the necessary evidence, the prosecutor may be an active partner with the police. Some prosecutors even have their own investigative staff that can gather additional evidence to help support the charges. In major felony cases in which the prosecutor and

prosecutorial discretion the power of a prosecutor to decide whether or not to charge a defendant and what the charge(s) will be, as well as to gather the evidence necessary to prosecute the defendant in a court of law

Three other important decisions before the trial

Bail

Bail As part of the initial appearance, the magistrate decides whether the defendant should be released on bail or held in a correctional facility until trial. For minor charges, the amount of bail may be set by a schedule of established fees. The amount of bail is typically based on the fines levied if the person is found guilty. Bail can be denied for reasons of community safety or the belief that the defendant is a flight risk.

Alternative to bail

- **Bail Bondsagent** is an agent of a private commercial business that contracts with the court to guarantee the defendant's return to court. The accused pays a fee to the bondsagent that is usually 10 percent of the bond.
- **Release on Recognizance (ROR)** The accused's release is based on the promise that he or she will return for trial.
- **Conditional Release** The accused is released with conditions, such as drug or alcohol treatment programs.
- **Unsecured Bond** The defendant signs a promissory note to pay the court if he or she does not return.
- **Signature Bond** is used for minor offienses, like traffic violations. The accused is released immediately after signing a promise to appear in court.

Competency to Stand Trial

Competent to stand trial means that the defendants can comprehend the charge and are able to assist their attorneys in their defense. It usually is determined by the ruling of a federal magistrate court judge or similar-level state judge.

Plea Bargaining

Plea Bargain is the opportunity offered by the prosecutor to plead guilty to lesser charges. Plea bargaining can be initiated by the prosecuting or the defending attorney at many different points in the process up until the jury renders a verdict.

law enforcement officers work together, the prosecutor may want to use the grand jury to obtain an arrest warrant rather than have the police arrest the suspect on probable cause.

Arraignment Checks and balances against police and prosecutorial power are provided by the initial screening of the first appearance and preliminary hearing. In addition, the prosecutor must present evidence to the court at the arraignment that the defendant should be tried for the offense. At the **arraignment** hearing, the prosecutor has the dilemma of how much evidence he or she should present to convince the court. The arraignment is the final stage before the trial, and the charges filed at this time are the charges on which the defendant will be tried. The prosecutor needs to present enough evidence to convince the court that the defendant should be held over for trial. However, the more evidence that the prosecutor presents, the more information the defense has to prepare for the trial. Thus, the prosecutor wants to present enough evidence to secure a trial date but not so much that the defense will be able to determine the entire prosecution strategy.

Three other important decisions that are made before the trial are:

1. setting bail,
2. determining the competency of the defendant to stand trial, and
3. plea bargaining.

Bail

One of the hallmarks of the American criminal justice system is the assumption that defendants will be treated as if they are innocent until they are proven guilty. Essential to the fulfillment of that principle is the premise that a defendant will not be incarcerated prior to conviction unless absolutely necessary for public safety. The mechanism to provide for the pretrial release of the defendant is bail.

Bail has its roots in English history and has been used since before the Norman Conquest in 1066. In an era before prisons were used to detain people prior to trial, the English magistrate would place prisoners with private parties who would guarantee that they would be delivered to the court when it was time for trial. To ensure that these custodians would perform their duties properly, they were required to sign a bond, known as a private surety, promising that if they failed to produce the prisoners on the trial date, they would forfeit a specified sum of money or property. The new American government adopted a variation of this pretrial procedure. Rather than entrust the accused to a custodian, the Eighth Amendment of the Constitution recognized the concept of bail and also specified that excessive bail should not be required of the accused. In the U.S. criminal justice system, **bail** is a system of pretrial release of the accused in a criminal proceeding based on a guarantee by the accused—or a bail bondsagent—that the accused will appear in court as required. The most common method of guaranteeing the appearance of the defendant is to require a cash bond or some property of value.[1]

The Eighth Amendment does not specifically state that a defendant is guaranteed bail. It states only that excessive bail should not be required. The U.S. Supreme Court has interpreted the wording of the Eighth Amendment to mean that the defendant does indeed have a right to bail.[2] Initially, the constitutional guarantee of bail was not a state requirement but applied only to the federal courts.[3] However, the question of whether a state defendant has a guarantee of bail has never been a significant constitutional issue, because state constitutions and judiciary practices have provided defendants with this right. Both federal and state courts have recognized that the right to bail is not an unrestricted right.

The controversy over bail has centered on the following factors:

1. What is excessive bail?
2. When can bail be denied?
3. Does the bail system discriminate against the poor?

Excessive Bail The Supreme Court has declared that **excessive bail** must be based on standards relevant to guaranteeing that the defendant will

arraignment the defendant is formally charged with a crime and is asked to enter a plea

bail release of the defendant prior to trial

excessive bail Eighth Amendment prohibits bail which is excessive but there is no uniform standard as what "excessive" is

HERE'S SOMETHING TO THINK ABOUT . . .

With his own TV series, Duane Chapman, or Dog the Bounty Hunter, is not your typical bounty hunter. His dress, badge, and armament may suggest he is a law enforcement agent but he and other bail bondspeople and bounty hunters are private, for-profit individuals. The United States is one of the few countries to use private individuals to effect fugitive recovery. This practice provides a service at no cost to the courts, despite the concerns regarding the lack of licensing, training, and qualifications for bounty hunters. Should bounty hunters be government employees?

not take advantage of his or her freedom and flee prior to the trial.[4] Thus, there are no standard limits of excessive bail that apply to all cases. The court has the power to consider each case individually, based on the totality of the circumstances. The court can consider factors such as the seriousness of the crime, the defendant's prior criminal record, the strength of the state's case, and the defendant's financial status. In some cases, the court has set bail at millions of dollars, and this has not been considered excessive.

IF BAIL DISCRIMINATES AGAINST THE POOR, THE POOR MAY NOT RECEIVE THE SAME QUALITY OF JUSTICE AS THE RICH.

Denial of Bail Bail is not an absolute guarantee, and defendants, under some circumstances, can be denied bail (*United States v. Salerno*).[5] Initially, the Supreme Court narrowly defined the purpose of bail as ensuring that the defendant would appear for trial. Both the federal judiciary and the state judiciaries recognized cases in which the defendant's pretrial release could pose a potential danger to society and bail should be denied. Starting in the 1970s, state judiciaries enacted danger laws that allowed the court to deny bail for certain offenses in which public safety could be a concern. The most common use of this denial of bail was for allegations of murder and drug offenses. The 1984 federal Bail Reform Act provided the same authority to federal judges.[6] The 1984 Bail Reform Act allowed the court to make the assumption that the defendant may pose a danger to others or to the community. Once the court makes this determination, it is the burden of the defendant to demonstrate that he or she is not a flight risk and is not a danger to persons or the community.[7]

For most misdemeanor offenses, bail is set based on a set fee schedule; that is, for most common offenses, a predetermined bail is set by the judge in advance, committed to written record, and used by booking to know what bail to set without a judge's instructions. Bail is an integral part of the initial appearance. For more serious felony cases, there is a bail hearing in which the prosecutor and the defense argue before the judge the merits of pretrial release. In the federal judiciary, bail hearings are held before magistrate judges. In most state courts, bail hearings are handled by courts of limited jurisdiction. Bail hearings are not decided by a jury, and following short oral arguments, the judge has wide discretionary powers as to granting bail and setting the amount.

Discrimination Against the Poor If bail requires the posting of a cash bond, it seems obvious that low-income defendants are not going to have access to the right of bail because of their lack of available money. Without the ability to post a cash bond, the poor are likely to remain incarcerated until their trials. Given the fact that even simple felony cases may take months before they come to trial, it is possible that the poor may spend more time in jail awaiting their trials than the length of sentences they may receive at the end of their trials. (When this does happen, defendants are credited with time already served and are released.) Accused persons who are not incarcerated have greater opportunities to assist in their defense. Thus, if bail discriminates against the poor, the poor may not receive the same quality of justice as the rich. Recognizing that a cash bail system may discriminate against the poor, the judiciary has established alternatives.

The Bail Bondsagent A **bail bondsagent** is an agent of a private commercial business that has contracted with the court to act as a guarantor of the defendant's return to court. A bail bondsagent is not a state or federal employee but rather a private party operating a for-profit business. Other than the Philippines, the United States is the only country to use a commercial for-profit business independent of the judicial system to secure bail for a defendant. In fact, in England and Canada, it is a crime for another to agree to pay a defendant's bond for profit. Even in the United States, four states (Illinois, Kentucky, Oregon, and Wisconsin) have abolished commercial bail bonds. In these states bail is a responsibility of the courts.

A bail bondsagent acts as an intermediary and posts the bond for the accused. If the defendant shows up for all scheduled court appearances, the court returns the amount of bail posted by the defendant and the defendant pays the bail bond company a nonrefundable fee for its service. This fee is usually 10 percent of the bond but may be higher, because there is no set limit on the bail bond company's fee. At a 10 percent fee, a person whose bail is set at $1,000 would have to pay the bail bond company $100 for its services. A person whose bond is set at $50,000, a more realistic figure for a

bail bondsagent an agent of a private commercial business that has contracted with the court to act as a guarantor of a defendant's return to court

serious felony crime, would have to pay $5,000. Bail bond companies can refuse to underwrite the bail of a defendant if they do not believe that the defendant is a good risk.

Bond Jumpers and Bounty Hunters A person who fails to appear for a court appearance is said to have "jumped bond." When a person jumps bond, the court will allow the bail bondsagent a certain amount of time to return the defendant to the custody of the court before revoking the posted bond. Bail bond businesses are not criminal justice agencies, but when they post bail for a defendant they are considered to be agents of the court. This power allows the bail bondsagent to require the defendant to sign a legally binding contract, waiving the right of extradition. This means the agent can track down and bring back the bond jumper.

As an agent of the court, the bail bondsagent, who is not a law enforcement officer, does not have to observe the restrictions placed on the police in seeking the return of the person who fails to appear for his or her court appearance. Essentially, the bondsagent may use any means necessary to return the person to the jurisdiction of the court. The bondsagent may be authorized to carry firearms, can use the threat of force to compel the defendant to return, and can kidnap the defendant and forcibly return him or her to the court against his or her will. The bondsagent does not have to have an arrest warrant to enter a private residence where the defendant has sought refuge and can trespass anywhere the defendant is hiding. The bondsagent is allowed to pay a third party to search for and return a bond jumper. There are no minimum requirements or mandated training for people who track down and return defendants. Commonly called "bounty hunters," bondsagents have greater powers than police officers do in the pursuit of bond jumpers.

Alternatives to Cash Bond Despite the widespread use of the bail bonds system, there are criticisms of it and of the conduct of bail bondsagents in returning bond jumpers. One of the primary criticisms is that even with fees at 10 percent of the total bond, the bail bonds system still discriminates against the poor, and a disproportionate number of the poor who are accused of crimes and have bail set are persons of color. Charges of institutionalized racial discrimination have led both federal and state courts to implement a number of alternatives to the cash bond system.

Release on recognizance (ROR) provides for the pretrial release of the accused, based merely on the defendant's unsecured promise that he or she will return for trial. The success of the program has caused many states to adopt the use of ROR. The provision is most appropriate for nonviolent offenses when the defendant has ties to the community and is not a flight risk.

Unsecured bond and signature bond are pretrial release systems that allow the defendant to be released on his or her promise to return for trial. An **unsecured bond** releases the defendant, who signs a promissory note to pay to the court a predetermined amount similar to a cash bail bond if he or she does not fulfill this promise.

A **signature bond** is commonly used for minor offenses, such as traffic law violations. It is similar to ROR but much simpler. There are no prequalifications for a signature bond, and no one makes an assessment of the defendant's flight risk or danger to the community. A signature bond allows the police officers, acting as agents of the court, to release the accused immediately after he or she is charged with the offense if he or she signs a promise to appear in court. When a police officer asks a motorist to sign a traffic citation, the motorist's signature is not a confession of guilt but a promise to appear in court. If the motorist does not sign the citation, he or she forfeits the right to a signature bond and the police officer has the authority to take the motorist into custody. After booking, the motorist will be required to post bond.

Conditional release and third-party custody are interesting alternatives to cash bail. Conditional release and a closely related type of bail, called supervision release, require the defendant to agree to a number of court-ordered terms and restrictions. Common terms of conditional release include participation in drug or alcohol treatment programs, attendance at anger-management classes, compliance with a restraining order, and regular employment. Supervision release has the additional stipulation that the defendant, similar to someone on parole or probation, must report to an officer of the court at regular intervals. Third-party custody allows the court to release a pretrial defendant to the custody of an individual or agency that promises to be responsible for the defendant's behavior and to guarantee his or her participation in the legal process. The two most common conditions are placing a defendant with his or her family or with attorneys who assume responsibility for their clients. Youthful offenders are the most likely candidates to be placed with their families. An adult member of the family assumes responsibility for a defendant's day-to-day behavior and appearances at scheduled court appointments.

Pros and Cons of Bail Whereas 50 percent of arrested persons are released from jail within 24 hours, approximately 28 percent are not released until 1 week after their arrest, and 10 percent remain incarcerated after 1 month of their arrest. For those who will not be prosecuted (recall that about 25 percent of those arrested will not be prosecuted), 1 to 30 days or more in prison can be a significant burden. For those who have been wrongly arrested, spending from 1 to 30 days in jail while waiting for bail can seem unfair and unnecessarily punitive. Thus, there are important reasons for an effective bail system and alternatives to traditional cash bails.

50%
of persons arrested are released within 24 hours

28%
are released 1 week after arrest

10%
remain incarcerated after 1 month of their arrest

Competency to Stand Trial and the Insanity Defense

Prior to the trial, it is the responsibility of the court to determine that the defendant is competent to stand trial. **Competent to stand trial** means that defendants comprehend the charges against them and are able to assist their attorneys in their defense. Competency to stand trial

release on recognizance (ROR) provides for the pretrial release of the accused, based merely on the defendant's unsecured promise to appear at trial

unsecured bond releases the defendant based on his or her signing a promissory note agreeing to pay the court an amount similar to a cash bail bond if he or she fails to fulfill the promise to appear at trial

signature bond the release of a defendant based on his or her signature on a promise to appear in court, usually for minor offenses such as traffic violations

conditional release a bail alternative in which the defendant is released from custody if he or she agrees to court-ordered terms and restrictions

competent to stand trial the concept that a defendant comprehends the charges against him or her and is able to assist his or her attorney with the defense usually is determined by the ruling of a federal magistrate court judge or similar-level state judge. Health is one of the most common reasons a pretrial defendant may not be competent to stand trial. A defendant who has a serious disease and is undergoing treatment can experience serious side effects that affect his or her judgment. A defendant who is wounded by the police may not be competent to stand trial because of the need for medical treatment. A defendant with a medical condition affecting intellectual capacity may be considered incapable of understanding the charges against him or her. Declaring a pretrial defendant not competent to stand trial is a temporary ruling. When the defendant becomes competent to stand trial, the court will order that the trial proceedings resume or begin.

The claim that a defendant is not guilty by reason of insanity is an affirmative defense that must be made prior to the trial. After the insanity defense is declared, the court orders a series of psychiatric examinations to assess the defendant's mental state. The results of examinations are admissible as evidence during the defendant's trial. A finding of not guilty by reason of insanity is not determined by the medical professionals who examine the defendant, however, but by the jury.

Plea Bargaining

Another pretrial activity is **plea bargaining**, and a great majority of cases are disposed of by this method without ever going to trial. Both the police and the victim often object to the practice of plea bargaining, but the prosecutor must make the best use of the resources of his or her office. The police and the victim object to plea bargaining on the grounds that the offender typically is not punished to the fullest extent of the law. After working to gather the necessary evidence and witnesses to help convict the defendant, law enforcement officers would like to see the defendant prosecuted on the most serious charges. Victims often want the same thing, but often for revenge or retribution or satisfaction that justice has been provided. Yet prosecutors often decide to offer defendants the opportunity to plead guilty to lesser charges. Why?

Time and Cost One reason is that preparation for trial is a time-consuming and costly endeavor. The prosecutor's office has the actual responsibility for trial preparation and bears the majority of the costs associated with gathering evidence, interviewing witnesses, and other preparations. Most prosecutors have only a limited staff and budget and cannot possibly take every case to trial. Furthermore, the court has only so much time to hear cases. Thus, the prosecutor's office must select which defendants to take to trial and which to offer plea bargains. Many offenses are settled by plea bargains, whereas a small percentage of defendants are convicted by trial. With few exceptions, plea bargaining is an integral part of the path in a criminal trial because it keeps the costs of justice affordable.

Community Interest In deciding to offer or to accept a plea to a lesser charge, the prosecutor must make an important professional judgment as to how to best serve community interests with the limited department resources. A plea bargain guarantees a guilty verdict. The prosecutor wins a conviction in approximately 80 percent of the cases that are taken to trial, but without plea bargaining, the prosecutor would not be able to devote the personnel and resources necessary to prepare for trial in these cases. Thus, plea bargaining helps free up time for the more difficult cases. Also, without plea bargaining, the prosecutor risks a substantial investment in time and resources, only to have the defendant found not guilty and escape all punishment. A guilty plea obtained by a plea bargain ensures that the defendant will have a criminal record and will receive some punishment or treatment.

The irony is that career criminals seem to benefit more from this practice than do minor criminals or the innocent. Obviously, the innocent can only be harmed by the practice of plea bargaining. A defendant accused of a serious crime such as capital murder who is not guilty may be tempted to accept or offer a plea bargain for a lesser crime that does not carry the threat of the death penalty for fear of being wrongfully convicted and executed. Plea bargaining most benefits major criminals such as the burglar who has committed 300 burglaries, the serial rapist who has committed numerous sexual assaults, and the drug dealer who has constantly engaged in drug trafficking.

CAREER CRIMINALS SEEM TO BENEFIT MORE FROM PLEA BARGAINING THAN DO MINOR CRIMINALS OR THE INNOCENT.

Clearing Cases The prosecutor might not have sufficient evidence to convict a career burglar for all of the burglaries that he or she has

HERE'S SOMETHING TO THINK ABOUT . . .

In 2011, state and federal government continued to face serious economic challenges including threats of debt default and closing government offices. The ongoing financial crisis has taken a toll on the criminal justice system, including the courts. For example, California courts have been described as "collapsing" by Presiding Judge Katherine Feinstein. In July 2011, according to the Associated Press, the San Francisco Superior Court announced that it was laying off more than 40 percent of its staff and shuttering 25 courtrooms because of budget cuts and a $13.75 million budget deficit. When courtrooms close, justice comes to a stop. What harms occur when courtrooms close?

plea bargaining the negotiation between defendant and prosecutor for a plea of guilty for which in return the defendant will receive some benefit such as reduction of charges or dismissal of some charges

committed and might not even know of all of the crimes the defendant has committed. If the prosecutor agrees to charge the defendant with only a single burglary in return for a confession to 300 burglaries, what does the prosecutor gain? First, the prosecutor and the police are able to "clear" the 299 burglaries, even though the defendant is not prosecuted for them. By accepting this offer, the police and the prosecutor can report a higher clearance rate to the public. Second, the prosecutor knows that even if a defendant is convicted of multiple offenses, he or she may end up serving the prison sentences concurrently instead of consecutively. Thus, the extra time and effort required to obtain the multiple convictions may make little difference in the actual outcome.

Questionable Confidence in the Case Finally, the prosecutor might not be completely confident of the evidence or witnesses. Perhaps the prosecutor believes that at the last moment a victim may refuse to testify. Witnesses to crimes committed by gang members or organized crime figures may become concerned about their safety or the safety of their families, for instance, and may refuse to testify or may give weak and inconclusive evidence. A young witness, especially a child, may pose special difficulties for the prosecutor. In other instances, the prosecutor might believe that the reputation of the arresting police officer or reliability of evidence gathered by the police might not stand up to cross-examination. Any of these reasons may make the prosecutor reluctant to take the case to trial.

Initiation of Plea Bargaining Plea bargaining can be initiated by the prosecuting or the defending attorney at many different points in the criminal justice process up until the jury renders a verdict. Plea bargaining can center on the charges or the sentence. At arrest the police and prosecutor typically charge the defendant with as many crimes as possible, beginning with the most serious crime. In return for dropping the more serious charges, the defendant offers his or her guilty plea. Plea bargaining can involve the police, the prosecutor, the judge, and defense counsel, but seldom involves the victim. In some cases, the victim is not even informed of the decision to accept a plea bargain. The defendant may provide the police with information regarding other criminals or crimes in return for their help in convincing the prosecutor to accept the defendant's plea bargain. The defendant may not have been the principal offender and may offer to testify against other defendants in exchange for a plea bargain. Plea bargains for testimony against fellow partners in crime is risky, however, because the information often is unconvincing to a jury.

Sentence Bargaining In **sentence bargaining**, the defendant seeks leniency. Sentences can range from probation to life imprisonment. The defendant may offer to plead guilty to the charges in return for the prosecutor's recommendation to the judge for a minimum sentence. A sentence of probation, even a long period of probation, is preferable to hard time in prison. Some defendants want to negotiate about where they will serve their time, the type of facility, or its security level. Because they control the charges to be filed against the defendant, prosecutors can bargain for reduction of the charges directly. However, the judge has control over the sentence, so sentence bargaining frequently involves pretrial negotiation among the prosecutor, defense counsel, and judge. Although the prosecutor and the defense may propose plea bargains, the judge must approve of any negotiated guilty plea to ensure that the rights of the defendant are protected. Thus, it is contrary to the ethics of the court for judges to initiate plea bargains or to encourage a defendant to agree to a plea bargain. The American Bar Association standards recommend that the "trial judge should not participate in plea discussions."[8] The Federal Rules of Criminal Procedure also state that the court should not participate in negotiating guilty pleas.[9] Some states have similar prohibitions. Despite these prohibitions, judge participation in plea bargaining is a characteristic of the criminal justice system.

Preparation for the Criminal Trial

After arraignment—assuming that the defendant is competent to stand trial, no alternative diversion is offered, and no plea bargain is struck—the case proceeds forward in the criminal justice process. It becomes one of the few arrests that actually results in a criminal trial. For a case to come to trial, it must be placed on the **court docket,** or calendar. Attorneys, defendants, and courtroom personnel must know when the case is scheduled for trial and how long the trial is expected to last, because the demand for judges and courtrooms exceeds the limited resources of the criminal justice system. Defendants released on bail, especially when guilty, may want to postpone their day in court.

Once a case is on the docket, the actual time that a defendant must wait for his or her day in court is not left to the defendant or to the government. The Sixth Amendment of the Constitution guarantees that defendants will receive a speedy trial, but the Constitution does not define what constitutes speedy. The right to a speedy trial is not the same as the statute of limitations. The **statute of limitations** is the length of time between the discovery of the crime and the arrest of the defendant. Various crimes have different acceptable lengths of time between the crime and the arrest. Usually, less serious crimes have a shorter period for prosecuting the defendant, and more serious crimes have longer periods. Customarily, there is no statute of limitations for the crime of murder.

THERE IS NO STATUTE OF LIMITATIONS FOR THE CRIME OF MURDER.

sentence bargaining the defendant negotiates with the prosecutor for a reduction in length of sentence, reduction from capital murder to imprisonment, probation rather than incarceration, or institution where the sentence is to be served in return for a guilty plea

court docket the calendar on which court cases are scheduled for trial

statute of limitations legal limits regarding the length of time between the discovery of a crime and the arrest of the defendant

The Sixth Amendment Right to a Speedy Trial

Like other amendments in the Bill of Rights, the Sixth Amendment right to a speedy trial originally extended only to federal crimes in federal courts. It was not until 1967 that the Supreme Court made the Sixth Amendment applicable to state courts as well. Before then, states did not have to provide a speedy trial unless guaranteed by the state constitution.[10] The definition of speedy trial differed substantially among states. Some states required that the trial take place in less than 2 months' time, and others allowed a case to come to trial years after the defendant was arrested. Initially, the Supreme Court did not provide specific guidelines to help determine what constitutes a speedy trial. The Court took the view that a speedy trial is a relative matter and may vary in length of time from arrest to trial because of the circumstances of the case.[11]

Klopfer v. North Carolina The judicial interpretation of the right to a speedy trial changed dramatically in the late 1960s and early 1970s, beginning with the 1967 case of *Klopfer v. North Carolina.*[12] Peter Klopfer, a professor at Duke University, was arrested for trespassing while engaged in a sit-in at a segregated motel and restaurant. Klopfer initially was tried for trespassing, which resulted in a hung jury. In such cases, the state has the right to retry the defendant. The prosecutor decided not to bring the case to trial, but at the same time refused to dismiss the charges against Klopfer. The laws of North Carolina allowed the prosecutor to postpone a trial indefinitely, even over the defendant's demand for a speedy trial. At the time, the state of North Carolina did not guarantee defendants the right to a speedy trial.

Thus, Klopfer was left in a state of legal limbo. At any time the prosecutor could decide to reactivate the criminal charges against the defendant, and the defendant had no recourse for lack of a speedy trial. Klopfer's case was appealed to the U.S. Supreme Court on the grounds that North Carolina denied him his constitutional rights. On appeal, the Supreme Court agreed and declared the North Carolina law unconstitutional. The right to a speedy trial was extended to state courts and, spurred by the *Klopfer* case, many states adopted speedy trial legislation. The Sixth Amendment right applies even if a defendant, for whatever reason, does not object to a delay. In 1972, in ***Barker v. Wingo,*** the Supreme Court issued a ruling that a defendant's failure to demand a speedy trial does not amount to a waiver of the Sixth Amendment right.[13]

Although guaranteeing the right to a speedy trial, the Sixth Amendment does not specify the remedy if this right is denied. If a defendant is denied a speedy trial, what should the court do? After the *Klopfer v. North Carolina* ruling that extended this right to state courts, the Supreme

HERE'S SOMETHING TO THINK ABOUT . . .

On May 14, 2011, Nafissatou Diallo, a maid at the Sofitel New York Hotel accused Dominique Strauss-Kahn of sexual assault. At the time Strauss-Kahn was head of the International Monetary Fund and considered to be a leading candidate for the 2012 French presidency. Manhattan District Attorney Cyrus Vance quickly filed charges against Strauss-Kahn and asked the court to deny bail on the grounds he was a flight risk. Strauss-Kahn claimed the accusations were a setup by his political opponents in France. The case attracted international media attention and sparked a crisis in diplomatic relations with France.

Some argued the district attorney moved too quickly to indict Strauss-Kahn. Criticism from within the district attorney's office suggested Vance was perhaps motivated by the recent loss of two high-profile cases and was too focused on media coverage. After the indictment, information concerning the background of the alleged victim emerged which cast serious doubt on her credibility. Investigations revealed Ms. Diallo had connections with criminal elements and had given inconsistent testimony as to what happened. When Ms. Diallo gave media interviews—a very unusual behavior for an alleged rape victim—the case began to fall apart. Stauss-Kahn was released from house arrest, his hearing was postponed, and in the end all criminal charges were dropped against Strauss-Kahn.

The Manhattan District Attorney's Office handles 110,000 cases per year. As district attorney, Vance is responsible for determining which of those cases will be prosecuted and on what charges. As an elected official his judgment will affect his chances of reelection in 2013.

Do you think the fact that the district attorney is an elected official influences his or her decisions in prosecuting cases?

Barker v. Wingo the court ruled that the defendant's failure to request a speedy trial does not negate the defendant's right to a speedy trial

clearing cases refers to the status of a criminal offense. When the police or prosecutor assert that the perpetrator of the crime is known, the case is "cleared"

4

In 1967 *Klopfer v. North Carolina* upheld a defendant's Sixth Amendment right to a speedy trial by requiring that charges be dismissed by the state if such right is not respected. The Speedy Trial Act of 1974 requires that, in most federal cases, a defendant must be brought to trial within 100 days of arrest.

Court found it necessary to review cases in which some state defendants failed to receive a speedy trial. In 1973, the Supreme Court decided that the remedy to be applied when a defendant does not receive a speedy trial is that the charges against the defendant will be permanently dismissed, and the prosecutor subsequently will not be allowed to bring these charges against the defendant. However, the Court also ruled that delays caused by the defendant's actions, such as requests for postponement, claims related to competency to stand trial, and other requests for delays, cannot be considered a denial of the right to a speedy trial.

The Speedy Trial Act of 1974

These Supreme Court rulings caused both federal and state courts to change the way they did business. Previously, prosecutors could select some cases for prosecution and leave others to a later time without any concern for the delay in bringing a case to trial. After the Supreme Court ruling, prosecutors had to be mindful of bringing all cases to trial in a timely manner or risk losing the ability to prosecute. The Speedy Trial Act of 1974 turned this concern into a crisis. The Speedy Trial Act of 1974 required a specific deadline between arrest and trial in federal courts. Fully implemented in 1980, the act required that, except in a few well-defined situations and barring delays created by the defendant, the defendant would be brought to trial within 100 days of his or her arrest or the charges could be dismissed and could not be reinstated. When a federal defendant is charged with a crime, the clock starts, and the prosecutor has 30 days to seek an indictment or formally charge the defendant with a violation of the law. If the defendant is indicted, the prosecutor has 70 days after the indictment or information to start the trial.[14] The clock is stopped for delays attributable to the defendant, such as postponements or escape to avoid prosecution. The clock may not stop when the delay is attributable to the prosecutor, however, even if the delays are beyond the prosecutor's control.

Rules of Evidence

Each court is governed by certain rules of evidence. **Rules of evidence** are laws that shape law enforcement and court practices, defining how the trial will be conducted, how evidence will be introduced, how the parties to the trial will act, and the order of the proceedings. Deviation from rules of evidence constitutes a judicial error, which leads to appeals. If a rule of evidence is violated, the prosecution or the defense can appeal the case. If an appeals court finds that the violation is a serious breach of the rules, the defendant has not received a fair trial.

Each state court and the federal courts have different rules. To represent clients in a particular court, attorneys are required to demonstrate that they have competent knowledge of the rules of evidence for the court hearing the case. To represent a client in a court of appeals or the state or federal Supreme Court, attorneys may need to pass an examination on the rules of evidence.

Usually, attorneys qualify for practice in state trial courts of limited and general jurisdiction by virtue of their good standing in the state bar association. The federal trial courts have different rules of evidence, requiring that the lawyer demonstrate competency in the federal rules of evidence before he or she can present a case in federal court.

The rules of evidence regulate nearly every aspect of the trial. Rules of evidence can be mundane, such as the rule that only the original of a document can be introduced as evidence. In addition, rules of evidence determine what evidence is relevant, what evidence is permissible, what evidence cannot be introduced, what evidence an expert witness may present to the jury, what questions can be asked of witnesses, and what is required before an item of physical evidence can be introduced into the trial.

If during the trial the prosecutor or defense counsel believes that a rule of evidence has been violated, it is his or her duty to raise objections to the judge. To do this, the attorney says, "I object on the grounds that. . . ." For example, if the prosecution asks a witness a question that the defense feels the witness is not competent to answer, the defense attorney objects on the grounds that the question calls for the witness to make a conclusion that he or she is not competent to make. Objections include questions that are not relevant to the present case or that call for the witness to comment about the mental state of the defendant (e.g., whether the defendant was angry). If the judge agrees, he or she declares that the objection is sustained, and the witness is instructed not to answer the question or the evidence will not be presented to the jury. If the judge does not agree, he or she overrules the objection. After the trial, the case can be appealed if the prosecution or defense believes the judge made a judicial error.

Participants in the Criminal Trial

Many people are involved in making a criminal trial possible. Those present at the trial can be divided into four groups:

1. government employees responsible for the business of the court;
2. the defendant and his or her legal counsel;
3. the jury; and
4. witnesses (including the victim). Note that the only role the victim has in the trial is that of a witness.

Duties and Rights of Participants

Power of the Judge The power of the judge lies in his or her absolute and immediate ability to fine or imprison people for contempt of court. If the judge believes that an attorney, either defense or prosecution, has violated a professional standard of conduct during the trial, he or she can impose a fine or term of imprisonment for **contempt of court.** Unprofessional conduct can include being late for court, continuing to argue with the judge when told to stop, or more serious violations regarding witness and evidence integrity. It is difficult to appeal a contempt of court decree. Contempt of court is not a crime and, thus, the person does not have the

continued on page 122

rules of evidence administrative court rules governing the admissibility of evidence in a trial

contempt of court a charge against any violator of the judge's courtroom rules, authorizing the judge to impose a fine or term of imprisonment

People Necessary for a Criminal Trial

The Judge

The Judge is a central figure in the trial and is a neutral party. His or her role is similar to that of a referee at a sports game. The judge determines what evidence can be presented at the trial, which witnesses can testify and about what, and when there will be courtroom breaks. The judge has authority over courtroom personnel, attorneys, the jury, members of the media, and the public in the courtroom.

Witnesses

Witnesses There are two types of witnesses: lay and expert. Lay witnesses can testify to what they saw, heard, felt, smelled, or otherwise directly experienced. Lay witnesses cannot provide testimony as to the motivation of the defendant. Expert witnesses can testify as to conclusions or hypothetical questions based on scientific certainty, the cause of death, or the identity of an unknown substance that was tested.

The Jury

The Jury decides if the evidence and witnesses prove beyond a reasonable doubt the guilt of the defendant. This is an awesome responsibility, and it is given to 12 laypersons. The jury hears evidence from the prosecution and the defense and decides which is most credible. If the defendant pleads not guilty by reason of insanity, the jury decides whether the defendant was insane.

The Clerk of Court

The Clerk of Court works directly with the trial judge and is responsible for court records and paperwork both before and after the trial. Usually, each judge has his or her own clerk of court. The clerk of court issues summonses and subpoenas for witnesses, receives pleas and motions and forwards them to the judge for consideration, and prepares all case files that a judge will need for the day. During the trial, the clerk of court records and marks physical evidence introduced in the trial and swears in the witnesses.

The Court Reporter

The Court Reporter, also called the court recorder, transcribes every word spoken by the judge, attorneys, and witnesses during the trial. He or she is responsible for making a permanent written record of the court's proceedings.

The Bailiff

The Bailiff is usually a county deputy sheriff or a U.S. deputy marshal. The county sheriff is responsible for providing bailiffs for court security for state courts, and a U.S. marshal is responsible for providing court security for federal courts. The bailiff is an armed law enforcement officer who has the power of arrest and the power to use deadly force if necessary. For most bailiffs, courtroom security consists of escorting the jury in and out of the courtroom and maintaining order in the court at the direction of the judge.

The Prosecutor

The Prosecutor is not an employee of the court but does represent the government. The prosecutor brings charges against the defendant, gathers evidence necessary to prosecute the defendant, and presents evidence at trial. The prosecutor's primary goal is not to convict the defendant but to see that the person who committed the crime is brought to justice and to demonstrate to the court that the evidence supports a conviction beyond a reasonable doubt.

The Defense

The Defendant is the person accused of committing a crime in a criminal case. The defendant may choose to assist in his or her defense or may choose to remain passive and let the defense attorney handle the case.

The Defense Attorney In any criminal trial in which the maximum punishment exceeds 6 months in prison, the defendant is entitled to a jury trial and the right to be represented by an attorney. There are two types of defense attorneys: public defenders and private defense attorneys. The defendant may hire any defense attorney registered to practice law before the court and as many private defense attorneys as he or she can afford. If the defendant cannot afford to hire a private defense attorney, the court will appoint and pay for an attorney to represent the defendant. In rare cases, the defendant may choose not to have a defense attorney but to represent himself or herself.

clerk of court a government employee who works directly with the trial judge and is responsible for court paperwork and records before and during a trial

court reporter (court recorder) a stenographer who transcribes every word spoken by the judge, attorneys, and witnesses during a trial

bailiff a county deputy sheriff or U.S. deputy marshal responsible for providing security and maintaining order in a courtroom

defense attorney the defendant will have an attorney appointed by the court or a private attorney paid for by the defendant to represent him or her in the trial

5 Many participants are essential to a trial, including the judge, the clerk of courts, the prosecutor, the court reporter, the defendant, the defense attorney, the bailiff, the jurors, and witnesses.

The Criminal Trial

Civilian Criminal Trial

The prosecutor has 30 days to seek an indictment or information. If the defendant is indicted, the trial is placed on the docket and the prosecutor has 70 days to start the trial.

Trial is placed on the docket

Pretrial Motions

Motion Prior to the trial the prosecutor and defense attorney may make pretrial motions regarding various procedural matters and evidence. Motions are formal written requests requesting that the judge make a ruling regarding some aspect of the trial. Some of the more common motions include a motion for discovery, a motion for suppression of evidence, a motion for change of venue, or a motion for continuance.

Jury Selection

Jury Selection is the process of selecting impartial citizens for the jury, a process known as ***voir dire.*** The seating of the jury signals the official start of the trial. Once the jury is seated (selected), the trial is considered officially started. At this point if the prosecutor does not proceed with the trial, it is not possible to start the trial over again or have a new trial as the second trial would be considered double jeopardy or trying the defendant twice for the same offense.

Opening Statements

Prosecution Statements The trial starts with the prosecutor's opening statement. The opening statement explains to the jury the specific charges against the defendant and may include the prosecutor's theory concerning how and why the crime was committed and outline the evidence that the prosecutor will introduce during the trial.

Defense Statement After the prosecutor's opening statement, the defense may make an opening statement. Sometimes the defense waives this presentation and instead chooses to see what the prosecutor's case is before committing to a defense.

There are two types of witnesses

- **Lay witnesses** can testify only to what they heard, saw, felt, smelled, or otherwise directly experienced. Laypersons usually cannot give secondhand or **hearsay evidence**—information about events they heard only from others.
- **Expert witnesses,** on the other hand, make inferences beyond the facts and give testimony based on their expert knowledge.

Prosecution Witnesses and Evidence After the opening statements, the prosecution presents witnesses and evidence to convince the jury of the defendant's guilt.

There are two types of evidence

- **Real evidence** physical evidence, such as a gun, a fingerprint, a photograph, or DNA matching
- **Testimonial evidence,** the testimony of a witness

- **Direct evidence** is any evidence that connects the defendant to the crime.
- **Circumstantial evidence** suggests that the defendant has performed an act but there are other possible interpretations.

Legal standards of evidence require that evidence must be competent, material, and relevant. Competent means that the evidence must be reliable or trustworthy. Material means that it has legitimate bearing on the decision of the case. For example, testimony of a person's good citizenship is not material to charges of sexual assault. Relevant evidence, similar to material evidence, means the evidence is applicable to the issue in question.

The Prosecution rests When the prosecution has presented all of the evidence and witnesses, the prosecution rests. There may be a short recess between the end of the prosecution's case and the defense.

Defense Witnesses and Evidence Usually the defense begins with a motion for dismissal of the charges based on the claim that the prosecution did not prove a prima facie case establishing the guilt of the defendant beyond a reasonable doubt. However, it is very rare for the judge to accept this motion. After this, the defense presents witnesses and evidence to rebut the claims of guilt presented by the prosecutor and to establish the innocence of the defendant. When the defense has presented all of the evidence and witnesses, the defense rests.

Prosecution Rebuttal The prosecutor has the option of rebutting evidence introduced by the defense witnesses. However, it is not common for the prosecutor to present rebuttal evidence.

voir dire the process through which a jury is selected from the members of the jury pool who have been determined to be eligible for service

real evidence physical evidence, such as a gun, a fingerprint, a photograph, or DNA matching

testimonial evidence the testimony of a witness

hearsay evidence information about a crime obtained secondhand from another rather than directly observed

lay witness a citizen who testifies only to what he or she heard, saw, felt, smelled, or otherwise directly experienced

Closing Arguments

When the two sides are finished with presenting evidence, each side is given the opportunity to summarize its case and evidence to the jury in what are called closing arguments. The closing argument is a persuasive speech to the jury in which each side tries to convince them of the guilt or innocence of the defendant. The prosecution argues that the evidence proves the defendant guilty beyond a reasonable doubt, and the defense argues that the prosecution has failed to demonstrate this standard of proof.

Note that it is not necessary for the defense to establish that the defendant is innocent, only that the prosecution has not proven the defendant guilty beyond a reasonable doubt.

Charge to the Jury

Charge to the Jury The judge declares a short recess and drafts the charge to the jury. The charge to the jury summarizes the legal principles relevant to the case, the standard of evidence required for conviction, and the weight that the jury can give to evidence.

Jury Deliberates

Jury Deliberation The jury retires to the jury deliberation room to discuss the evidence and come to a verdict. During the deliberations only the bailiff of the court can communicate with the jurors.

The Verdict

The Verdict The judge calls the trial to order and asks the jury if they have reached a verdict. After the foreperson announces the verdict, the members of the jury are polled individually to publicly affirm that he or she agrees with the verdict.

Not Guilty

If the defendant is not guilty, he or she is released from custody.

Guilty

If the defendant is guilty, the judge sets a date for the sentencing. After sentencing the defendant is transferred to the custody of the state or federal correctional authorities.

Hung Jury

If the jury cannot reach a verdict the jury is said to be a hung jury. The judge may encourage the jury to continue to deliberate after announcing that they are unable to come to a unanimous verdict. The consequence of a hung jury is that the trial must be completely redone.

Appeals The defendant may appeal a guilty verdict. The appeal must claim that a significant error occurred during the trial that substantially affected the jury's verdict. In some cases the appeal may be based on new evidence that was not available at the time of the trial (e.g., DNA evidence). In some cases the defense may claim that the judge has provided faulty instruction on the law or the evidence during the charge to the jury. The defendant cannot appeal based on a claim that he or she has been wrongfully convicted.

Sentencing Hearing

Sentencing In capital cases there is a sentencing hearing to determine if the defendant is eligible for the death penalty.

The sentence can be challenged.

Transfer to Corrections

expert witness gives testimony based on his or her expert knowledge and can make inferences beyond the facts

direct evidence evidence that connects the defendant with the crime

circumstantial evidence evidence that implies that the defendant is connected to the crime but does not prove it

legal standards of evidence standards requiring that evidence and the testimony of witnesses must be competent, material, and relevant

charge to the jury written instructions about the application of the law to a case that the judge gives to the jury to help them reach a verdict

HERE'S SOMETHING TO THINK ABOUT . . .

Judges, prosecutors, and defense attorneys are lawyers. They practice what is known as "public law" and they comprise a minority of lawyers. The path to become a lawyer is similar for both public and private attorneys. After the bachelor's degree one must obtain admission to a law school. Admission is very competitive and based in part on one's undergraduate grade point average and score on the Law School Admissions Test (LSAT). Law school requires two to three years of graduate studies. The curriculum for law students is similar for both those who want to be public attorneys and those who will go into private practice. Graduates receive the Juris Doctor (JD) degree. In addition to calling themselves lawyers, both men and women may also use the title "esquire." After law school the graduate must pass the state bar examination to become a licensed attorney.

There are many civil service positions but those who want to become prosecutors or judges frequently must obtain their office by political election. Defense attorneys are either public defenders employed by the government or private defense attorneys. Those who practice public law, including judges, often make less money than those who go into private practice. Public defenders make the least with a national average of $40,976 to $78,987.

same rights as a defendant accused of a crime. Contempt of court can bring substantial penalties. For example, witnesses who will not testify may be held in prison for up to 2 years for contempt of court.[15]

The public, the jury, and the members of the media may be fined or imprisoned for contempt of court. If people in the courtroom are unruly, the judge can impose a fine or hold them in jail for contempt of court. The power of the judge even extends to appropriate dress of persons in the courtroom. Jury members can be fined or imprisoned for violating the orders of the judge not to discuss the case. The media most often run afoul of the judge's authority by violating a **gag order**—an order that the evidence or proceedings of the court may not be published or discussed publicly. If disclosure of evidence or testimony may jeopardize the defendant's receiving a fair trial, the judge has the authority to order all parties to refrain from discussing or publishing this information. Members of the media who violate this order can be held in contempt of court.

4 million
indigent defenses a year

at a cost of:

$1,000,000,000

Bench Trial The judge's role can be complicated in a bench trial when the judge, rather than a jury, determines whether the defendant is guilty. In a **bench trial**, the judge must act as impartial mediator during the trial and, at the conclusion of the trial, must make a determination of guilt. Bench trials often are prohibited in cases involving serious felonies.

Courtroom Security The parties before the court are often emotionally charged, and judges and court personnel often express concerns that security may not be adequate to ensure their safety. Although security checkpoints and metal detectors enhance the security of the court, there is still the ever-present threat to court personnel. Several high-profile security incidents in 2005 emphasized the serious security threats that bailiffs face. In Atlanta, Georgia, on March 11, 2005, Brian Nichols, age 34, on trial for rape and kidnapping, grabbed a gun from a sheriff's deputy during his trial and began shooting in the courtroom. He killed Superior Court Judge Rowland Barnes and his court reporter. He managed to escape from the courthouse and in the process killed another deputy who confronted him as well as a federal customs agent. The incident sparked concern for improved court security and more security personnel.

The Defendant The defendant does not have to testify during the trial, nor can the prosecutor indicate that the defendant's choice not to testify might indicate that he or she is guilty. The defendant may actively assist his or her attorney or may remain passive during the trial. In some cases, the defendant may be his or her own attorney. If the court deems the defendant competent, even if the defendant has no formal legal training or license, in some cases the defendant may represent himself or herself. In some states, even if a defendant represents himself or herself, an attorney is appointed to assist the defendant in his or her defense.

Indigent Defendants A defendant who cannot afford a private attorney is known as an indigent defendant. When a defendant is charged with a crime, a judge inquires as to the defendant's ability to afford an attorney. Defendants indicating they cannot afford an attorney are required to complete a financial statement and submit it to the court. The court examines the defendant's finances and decides on the matter. About half of all criminal defendants accused of a felony crime cannot afford an attorney, and for larger counties this number increases to 80 percent.[16] **Indigent defense** services represent a substantial expense in the criminal justice system. For example, the largest 100 counties handle over 4 million indigent defenses a year at a cost of over one billion dollars.[17]

Jury Service Jurors are citizens required by law to perform jury duty. The court wants jurors who are fair, competent, and able to serve. Selecting a fair and competent jury and deciding legitimate excuses for jury duty have been major challenges for the court.

Jury of One's Peers The Constitution requires that people be tried by a jury of their peers. The Supreme Court has not interpreted this literally, however. A white, middle-class man does not get a trial by a jury of white, middle-class men. Rather, the jury pool is selected from a broad base of citizens who are representatives of the community. Many

gag order a judge's order to participants and observers at a trial that the evidence and proceedings of the court may not be published, broadcasted, or discussed publicly

bench trial a trial in which the judge rather than a jury makes the determination of guilty

indigent defense defense counsel provided for a defendant who cannot afford a private attorney

HERE'S SOMETHING TO THINK ABOUT . . .

During the mid-1900s the average salary for criminal justice personnel was so low as to fail to attract the best, and sometimes even qualified, candidates. Below average salary for police and correctional officers was a barrier to professionalization and was blamed in part for corruption and misconduct. During the last 20 years the compensation and benefits for police and corrections officers has steadily increased. Today the median salary for the typical police officer is $49,875, and $39,373 for correctional officers.

The salary for judges during the mid-1900s was significantly higher than other criminal justice personnel and comparable to private industry. In the 1960s federal judges earned more than law school deans or law professors. However, unlike salaries for police and corrections personnel, the salary for judges has declined since 1970. Since 1970 judges' pay has declined by 23.9 percent when adjusted for inflation. Today, federal judges make less than law school deans or professors.

Starting in 1970 with Chief Justice Warren Burger, upon each new year, the chief justice of the Supreme Court has asked Congress to increase the salary of federal judges warning of the consequences if Congress did not raise it. Today, the salaries of attorneys in private practice are higher than those who practice public law. The median salary for state judges is $142,616. Before accepting the position of chief justice of the U.S. Supreme Court, John Roberts earned $1 million in private practice. As chief justice he earns $223,500. In 2010, Chief Justice Roberts abandoned the New Year's tradition of asking Congress for an increase in federal judges' salary. Roberts cited the overall downturn in the economy and said Congress was probably getting tired of hearing the same request as his justification.

New York is one of the hardest hit states. New York judges have not had a raise in 12 years. In the 1970s judges in New York were the best paid nationally. Today their salaries are ranked 46th in the country. As a result, one in ten judges is leaving the bench. Many are going into private practice where they can earn 10 times the salary. For example, in 2011, Judge James McGuire resigned as state judge to accept a partnership in a law firm for a salary of $1.4 million.

What is a fair salary for a judge? Is there a relationship between the quality of justice and the salary of the judge?

jurisdictions have used voter registration lists as the pool from which to select jurors. Studies have clearly demonstrated, however, that this pool of candidates is biased, because voter registration lists underrepresent minorities and people with lower income.[18] The current practice in many courts is to select jurors from more representative sources, such as licensed drivers or people listed in the telephone book.

Exemptions from Jury Duty Citizens are paid for jury duty by the government, but the rate of pay is very low, ranging from only a few dollars to $40 per day. Most jurors serve for only short periods but may be asked to serve for extended periods; for some jurors, even a few days may impose a severe hardship. Also, some citizens may not be competent to serve as jurors. For these and other reasons, the court may excuse citizens from jury duty. Each jurisdiction determines the rules for excusing citizens from jury service, but the rules must not discriminate against a person because of race, gender, or other characteristics that are considered in violation of the law. For example, until 1975, many states automatically excluded women, especially women with children at home, from jury duty. In ***Taylor v. Louisiana*** (1975), the Supreme Court decided that the exclusion of women from jury duty created an imbalance in the jury pool and was not justified.[19] Legitimate reasons for excuse from jury duty include illness, conviction of a felony crime, or not being able to comprehend English. Members of certain professional groups, such as physicians, may be excluded from jury duty, based on the reasoning that jury service would be detrimental to community safety. Other members of professional groups, such as attorneys, police officers, and legislators, may be excluded from jury duty, based on the reasoning that they may not be able to be neutral and make decisions based only on the evidence presented in court. Most jurisdictions require jury service only once a year.

UNTIL 1975 MANY STATES AUTOMATICALLY EXCLUDED WOMEN WITH CHILDREN AT HOME FROM JURY DUTY. THE SUPREME COURT DECIDED THAT THE EXCLUSION OF WOMEN FROM JURY DUTY CREATED AN IMBALANCE IN THE JURY POOL AND WAS NOT JUSTIFIED.

Jury Requirements Although essential to ensuring a fair and public trial by one's peers, jury duty is disdained by some. Thus, it is necessary for the court to ensure that, despite the reluctance by some citizens to respond to a summons for jury duty, those called do indeed respond. As a result, there are penalties,

Taylor v. Louisiana ruled the exclusion of women from jury duty created an imbalance in the jury pool

including fines and jail time, for those who unlawfully avoid jury duty and for anyone, such as employers, who interfere with, intimidate, or threaten citizens to prevent them from fulfilling their civic duties.

The Constitution does not require a jury of 12 persons. This number is a tradition but is not a legal requirement, and obtaining 12 people to serve on a jury can be a challenge. All states require 12 jurors for capital cases, and all but six states require 12 jurors for felony trials. Fourteen states allow misdemeanor trials with only six jurors. Other states allow criminal trials with a jury of seven or eight jurors.[20]

Justice Is the Goal

Police charges against a defendant are merely suggestions to the prosecutor. The prosecutor's charges at arraignment are but a hope. The decision of guilt is decided at a trial. Despite a constitutional guarantee of a trial by jury, over 90 percent of those charged with felony crimes choose to forego this procedure and plead guilty. A great number of professionals come together to make a trial possible. In the American judicial system, the trial is a conflict situation between the prosecutor and the defense. At the trial, the playing field is not level, but is tipped in favor of the defendant. The U.S. judicial system recognizes the incredible power of the state compared to the limited resources of the accused and, therefore, provides a number of opportunities to balance the power between the state and the defendant. Thus, even if the defendant is convicted, he or she has the right to appeal, a right denied to prosecutors if they lose the case. The procedure and rules of the trial are well defined, but the strategy and risk that go into the decision making and presentation of evidence are left to the professional judgment of the participants in the trial. Despite the differences among the various courts, all work toward a common objective—justice.

CHAPTER 7

Courtroom Participants and the Trial

Check It!

1 WHAT is the basic legal philosophy of a trial in the U.S. legal system? p. 108

A trial is a battle between the state and the defendant's lawyer.

2 WHAT are the guidelines for determining which court has jurisdiction over a crime? p. 109

1. state misdemeanor crimes: tried in state courts of limited jurisdiction
2. state felony crimes: tried in state courts of general jurisdiction
3. federal felony crimes: tried in U.S. district courts

3 WHAT are the major pretrial proceedings? p. 110

1. The police and prosecutor determine the charges to be brought against the defendant.
2. Bail is set or denied.
3. The defendant's competency to stand trial is established.
4. Plea bargaining may occur, in which a prosecutor allows a defendant to plead guilty to lesser charges to avoid a trial.

4 HOW do the Sixth Amendment and the Speedy Trial Act of 1974 affect a trial? p. 117

1. *Klopfer v. North Carolina* of 1967 upheld a defendant's right under the Sixth Amendment to a speedy trial.
2. In 1973, the Supreme Court ruled the denial of a defendant's right to a speedy trial requires charges against him or her to be dismissed.
3. The Speedy Trial Act of 1974 requires that in most federal cases a defendant must be brought to trial within 100 days of arrest.

5 WHAT are the roles of the various people involved in a criminal trial? p. 119

- The judge has absolute authority over all matters in a trial.
- The clerk of courts is responsible for maintaining all court records and marking evidence.
- The defendant is the person accused of committing a crime.
- The defense attorney represents the defendant.
- The prosecutor represents the government in the role of seeing that the person who committed the crime is brought to justice.
- The court reporter transcribes every word spoken by all participants in a trial.
- The bailiff is a law enforcement officer who maintains security and order.
- The jurors are citizens who are the ultimate judges of whether evidence and witnesses prove the guilt of the defendant beyond a reasonable doubt.
- Witnesses are either laypersons who testify to what facts that they directly experienced or experts who testify based on their expert knowledge and thus can make inferences beyond the facts.

Assess Your Understanding

1. What is usually required for a court to have jurisdiction over a crime?
   a. The person must be arrested in the jurisdiction of the court.
   b. The person must be booked in the jurisdiction of the court.
   c. Some part of the crime must have been committed within the jurisdiction of the court.
   d. The court must be within the state of resident of the defendant.
2. Which of the following is not a state court of record?
   a. courts of limited jurisdiction
   b. district courts
   c. appellate courts
   d. supreme courts
3. Most federal criminal trials occur in which of the following courts?
   a. magistrate court
   b. district court
   c. appeals court
   d. supreme court
4. Which of the following occurs during arraignment?
   a. The grand jury determines if the case should go forward for prosecution.
   b. The defendant is charged with the crime(s) he or she is alleged to have committed and is asked to enter a plea.
   c. The prosecutor presents evidence to a judge who determines whether the case should go forward or be dismissed.
   d. none of the above
5. Which of the following determines what charges, if any, will be filed with the court against a defendant?
   a. the police
   b. the judge
   c. the prosecutor
   d. either a or b
6. Which of the following is a true statement?
   a. All defendants must be granted bail but the amount of the bail is not limited so some defendants may not be able to afford bail.
   b. All forms of bail require the defendant to guarantee they will appear in court by depositing a certain amount of cash or other monetary value with the court.
   c. Bail bondspersons are employees of the court.
   d. The Eighth Amendment states that excessive bail should not be required of a defendant.
7. What happens if a defendant is found to be incompetent to stand trial?
   a. Charges against the defendant are dismissed.
   b. The defendant is declared insane and is committed to a civil mental hospital for treatment.
   c. The trial is postponed until the defendant can comprehend the charges against him or her and is able to assist in the defense.
   d. The trial proceeds if the defense attorney agrees that he or she will be able to provide an adequate defense for the defendant.
8. Which of the following is subject to plea bargaining?
   a. the charges against the defendant
   b. the sentence the defendant will receive
   c. the institution where the defendant will serve his or her time
   d. all of the above
9. What is the primary goal of the prosecutor?
   a. to convict the defendant
   b. to demonstrate to the court that the evidence supports a conviction beyond a reasonable doubt
   c. to discover what really happened during the alleged crime
   d. none of the above
10. The current practice of many courts is to select jurors from which of the following?
    a. licensed drivers, voter registration list, telephone book, and persons with state identification cards
    b. voter's registration list only
    c. licensed drivers only
    d. the state census

ESSAY

1. What is the basic legal philosophy of a trial in the U.S. legal system?
2. What are the guidelines for determining which court has jurisdiction over a crime?
3. Name three common pretrial motions and describe what the motion requests of the court.
4. What rights are guaranteed by the Sixth Amendment?
5. What is the difference between the preliminary hearing and the arraignment?
6. How is a grand jury different from a preliminary hearing?
7. Explain prosecutorial discretion.
8. Explain the various types of bail and how they work.
9. Discuss the differences between the role of the judge and the role of the prosecutor in a criminal trial.
10. Describe the major steps in a criminal trial.

ANSWERS: 1. c, 2. a, 3. b, 4. b, 5. c, 6. d, 7. c, 8. d, 9. b, 10. a

Media

Go to the *Chapter 7: Courtroom Participants and the Trial* section in *MyCJLab* to test your understanding of this chapter, access customized study content, engage in interactive simulations, complete critical thinking and research assignments, and view related online videos.

Additional Links

Go to www.uscourts.gov/districtcourts.html, the official Web site of the federal judiciary, for information about district courts, including many links to other resources.

Go to www.bailacademy.org to view training programs for bail enforcement agents.

To view a history of the judges of the U.S. Supreme Court, go to http://judgepedia.org/index.php/Supreme_Court_of_the_United_States

For information about the Law School Admission's Test and other information concerning application for law school, go to the homepage of the Law School Admission Council, at www.lsac.org/

A directory of law schools in the United States can be found at www.hg.org/schools.html

The Court Officers and Deputies Association of the National Sheriffs Association Web site provides information about best practices for court room security at www.sheriffs.org/coda/index.asp

Go to www.state.il.us/court/ for extensive information about the history and personnel of the state of Illinois court system. Each of the state courts will have a similar Web site that you can visit for information about the court system. For example, the Web site for California courts is www.courts.efsca.gov/courts.htm

Visit the Web site www.law.umkc.edu/faculty/projects/ftrials/hinckley/hinckleyinsanity.htm for information concerning the insanity defense.

To watch a CBS *60 Minutes* interview with retired U.S. Supreme Court Justice John Paul Stevens, leader of the Court's liberal wing, go to www.youtube.com/watch?v=BLT04r7n4dE

For a short explaination of pretrial motions, go to www.viddler.com/explore/everspark/videos/58/

To watch a video regarding some concerns about plea bargaining, go to www.klfy.com/story/15155796/lets-make-a-deal?clienttype=printable

To hear why an attorney chose a career as a criminal defense attorney, go to www.5min.com/Video/Being-a-Criminal-Defense-Attorney-303377560

POLITI
POLITI

SENTENCING 8

Anders Behring Breivik admitted to killing nearly 80 people in a cold-blooded attack he prepared for months in advance in Oslo, Norway. In the United States, Breivik would be eligible for the death penalty in most states and in the federal court or at least life in prison without parole. In Norway, the maximum sentence he can receive is 21 years imprisonment. Few persons convicted of crime in Norway ever serve more than 14 years in prison. However, under a frequently used sentence option he may be imprisoned for up to 5 additional years after his sentence if he is still considered dangerous to society. He could serve life in prison 5 years at a time.

Each country determines its own criminal sanctions, and the range of sentences is diverse. Nations practicing Sharia law have sentences of corporal punishment that include whippings, caning, and amputations. The United States has abolished corporal punishment as a criminal sentence. Most European countries have eliminated the death penalty, but the United States remains one of the few Western countries to impose the death penalty as a criminal sanction.

What is the purpose of criminal sanctions? Is it to punish the offender, to obtain revenge, to provide an example to deter others, to rehabilitate the offender, or to protect society from further harm? In the United States, there is no one answer to this question. The courts, both state and federal, have adopted diverse sentencing options. Sentencing options have frequently been adopted based on fear, loss of confidence in the criminal justice system, or belief that offenders cannot be rehabilitated. Retaliation and retribution are often the bases for sentencing in the United States There is no evidence-based research regarding sentencing, public safety, and rehabilitation of offenders.

While sentencing models are diverse and each state and the federal government have autonomy in sentencing, the U.S. Supreme Court has oversight responsibility to determine that sentences do not violate constitutional rights under the Eighth Amendment which provides that punishments should not be cruel and unusual. The Court has required major reforms in capital cases. At one time the Court halted all death sentences until states could demonstrate that the death penalty was not applied capriciously and arbitrarily. In *Presley v. Georgia* (2010), the Court ruled that "judicial proceedings conducted for the purpose of deciding whether a defendant shall be put to death must be conducted with dignity and respect."

1 **What are the purposes of sentencing?**

2 **How does the criminal justice system sentence the offender with mental illness?**

3 **What factors influence whether a defendant receives a fair sentence?**

4 **What is the process of a presentence investigation and sentence hearing?**

5 **How do various sentencing models influence a sentence?**

6 **How have U.S. Supreme Court rulings affected the death penalty sentence, and how has the Court responded to civil rights challenges to the death penalty?**

SENTENCING OPTIONS HAVE FREQUENTLY BEEN ADOPTED BASED ON FEAR, LOSS OF CONFIDENCE IN THE CJ SYSTEM, OR BELIEF THAT OFFENDERS CANNOT BE REHABILITATED. RETALIATION AND RETRIBUTION ARE OFTEN THE BASES FOR SENTENCING.

Convictions and sentencing must be fair and respectful of constitutional rights. When sentences are considered unfair often there is public outcry for justice. Some examples include the movement to change the 100:1 sentencing disparity for crack versus powder cocaine, the movement to abolish the death penalty, and the demand for options for convicted persons to appeal their conviction based on a claim of factual innocence.

This chapter discusses the purposes and types of sentences, sentencing models, and the death penalty.

Purpose of Criminal Sanctions

Imposing a sentence is a complex interaction of people and philosophies. This chapter discusses the various reasons given to justify criminal sanctions, the process by which judges determine appropriate sentences, and the growing public concern regarding the insanity defense and the death penalty.

With over 1 million sentences handed down by judges each year, there is a great variety in the sentencing of defendants. Some sentences can be quite unusual. For example, an Olathe, Kansas, high school student convicted of battery for vomiting on his Spanish teacher was sentenced to spend 4 months cleaning up after people who throw up in police cars.[1] Also, a North Dakota man was sentenced to 2 days in jail for failing to license his cat.[2] In another case, Family Court Judge Marilyn O'Connor of Rochester, New York, sentenced a dysfunctional, drug-addicted couple not to procreate again until their children are being raised by a natural parent, or are no longer being cared for at the expense of the public.[3] Sentences can be influenced by a number of factors. For instance, convicted rapist Stephen Terry Bolden was sentenced for multiple crimes, including first-degree rape, by Arizona Circuit Judge George Greene to 99 years plus two consecutive life sentences. When Bolden told Judge Greene that he (Greene) was "real rude during the sentencing hearing," Greene added an additional 5 days in prison to the sentence.[4]

Some cases attract national attention, such as the sentence given to Joseph Pannell. In 2008, 58-year-old Joseph Pannell pleaded guilty to the 1969 shooting of a Chicago police officer, Terrence Knox. Knox was not killed but his right arm was permanently damaged by the shooting. After the shooting, while he was released on bail, Pannell fled to Canada, where he married a Canadian and worked as a library research assistant. He was arrested in 2004 but was not extradited to the United States until 2008. He was charged with aggravated battery, attempted murder, and bail-jumping, for which he could have been sentenced up to 23 years in prison. According to the Bureau of Justice Statistics, the average sentence for a violent felon offense is 92 months in prison. Pannell received a sentence of 30 days in jail, 2 years' probation, and a $250,000 fine to be paid to a foundation that helps the families of injured Chicago police officers.[5] Such a sentence is rare, especially one involving a large donation to a foundation. Mr. Pannell said of the sentence, "We must seek to move away from adversarial confrontation and towards peaceful reconciliation and conflict resolution."[6]

How do judges determine the appropriate punishment for a crime? Judges are guided by the law, as the law must provide the type and range of punishments that may be imposed after conviction. However, these laws are passed by legislators based on public sentiment as to the purpose and effect of various punishments.

The history of punishment in the United States is rooted in economic sanctions, corporal punishment, and death. However, the concept of serving time in a prison or jail as punishment for a crime is a fairly new philosophy of the criminal justice system. Historically, punishments in England and in the American colonies consisted primarily of fines, ordeals, and torture. Criminals who could not afford to pay the fines imposed on them could be sold into economic servitude, a form of slavery, to pay the fines. **Corporal punishment** included whipping, branding, dunking, confinement to the stocks or pillories, and other pain-inflicting rituals.

Five contemporary philosophies regarding the purpose of punishment are as follows (see Table 8.1 for summary of philosophies):

1. deterrence
2. incapacitation
3. retribution
4. rehabilitation
5. restorative justice

These are simple categories for classifying punishment, but often the law and circumstances are not so simple. Criminal sanctions may have more than one purpose and may have unstated or contradictory purposes.

Deterrence

Deterrence is based on the principle that punishment should prevent the criminal from reoffending. The problem is to identify what punishment or threat of punishment effectively prevents people from committing crimes or criminals from reoffending. Punishments based on deterrence include economic sanctions, corporal punishment, and threat of bodily harm, all of which are based on the premise that people seek pleasure and avoid pain. For example, as a means to stop Hartford, Connecticut, high school students from cursing, a joint effort by school and police officials gave citations to students who swear while defying teachers and administrators. Students who swear are fined $103. If the student cannot pay the fine, the student's parents are required to pay the fine. The theory underlying the use of fines is that the painful experience of the fines will discourage students from continuing to swear. In this case the practice seems to support the theory: Although there are critics of the actions of the police and school officials, officials report that the incidents of swearing have dropped to "almost nothing."[7]

Corporal Punishment Some people profess that corporal punishment is an effective deterrent to misconduct in raising properly behaved children and ensuring proper conduct in schools. As a result of this deeply rooted belief, attempts to pass laws prohibiting the use of corporal punishment against children and students by parents and teachers have been unpopular and met with limited success.[8]

Although corporal punishment has been abandoned as an official punishment in the United States, many foreign countries continue

1 **The purposes of sentencing a criminal are to deter others from committing crimes, to incapacitate a criminal so that he or she cannot commit other crimes, to serve as retribution for the harm done by the offender, to rehabilitate the offender, and to restore peace and justice in the community.**

corporal punishment the administration of bodily pain as punishment for a crime

deterrence the philosophy and practices that emphasize making criminal behavior less appealing

TABLE 8.1 Philosophies of Punishment

Types of Punishment	Purpose of Punishment	Examples	Pros and Cons
Deterrence			
General Deterrence	Prevent nonoffenders from committing crimes	Expose nonoffenders to punishment received by offenders	Little cost, simple to administer Assumes free-will model of criminal behavior
Specific Deterrence	Prevent offenders from reoffending	Infliction of pain and punishment to make crime less attractive than the rewards.	Little cost, simple to administer Assumes free-will model of criminal behavior
Incapacitation	Prevent offender from having the opportunity to reoffend	Banishment, transportation, warehousing, "lock and feed" Confiscation of cars of DUI and profits of criminals	Effective if the offender is removed from the community Long-term incarceration is expensive; provides no provisions for reentry or rehabilitation
Retribution	To "repay" the offender with like punishment; to satisfy the desire of the victim for revenge	Infliction of similar injuries as the victim received Physical punishments during incarceration Death penalty for murder	Provides emotional satisfaction to victims and survivors Little or no emphasis on rehabilitation; courts have prohibited inflicting intentional pain on prisoners; death penalty very expensive
Rehabilitation	"Cure" the offender	Medical model; drug treatment, counseling, education, job skills training	Emphasizes reentry and rehabilitation Offender seems to receive benefits while the victim is ignored
Restorative Justice	"Heal" the community and conflict resolution	"Truth commissions," "healing ceremonies," restoration mediation and victim-offender mediation	Goal is to promote public safety and restore offenders to community Often involves difficult and long-term process Better results in small, close-knit community

to use some form of corporal punishment as official sentences. In 2000, Nigeria introduced Islamic law, which sanctions the use of corporal punishment. Despite this, Nigeria received international criticism in January 2001 for flogging a 17-year-old Muslim girl 100 times for having premarital sexual relations, and later, in August, for sentencing a 20-year-old woman to 100 lashes with a cane for having an extramarital affair.[9] Also in 2001, in just 4 days, Iran sentenced 20 people to be lashed. Their crime was drinking alcohol, an offense against Islamic law. Each offender received 80 lashes.[10]

Some people still advocate that the return of corporal punishment would benefit crime control. For example, in 2005, Las Vegas Mayor Oscar Goodman suggested that whippings or canings should be brought back for children who get into trouble. Goodman said, "I also believe in a little bit of corporal punishment going back to the days of yore. I'm dead serious. Some of these [children] don't learn. You have got to teach them a lesson. They would get a trial first."[11] Despite such vocal advocates for the return of corporal punishment, or the adoption of the practice of caning, a common practice for a number of other nations, to the American criminal justice system, there appears to be little support for this movement.

Specific and General Deterrence **Specific deterrence** is when an individual who has committed a crime is deterred from committing that

HERE'S SOMETHING TO THINK ABOUT . . .

In Louisiana in 1946, when electric shock failed to kill Willie Francis, the Court agreed that a second attempt was permissible. In 2009, Ohio was unable to find a suitable vein in the attempted execution of Romell Broom and had to reschedule the execution. In 2011, when Andrew Urdiales's Illinois death sentence was commuted, California requested his extradition to try him for five murders in California. If an execution fails, is it fair to do it again?

specific deterrence a concept based on the premise that a person is best deterred from committing future crimes by the specific nature of the punishment

crime in the future by the nature of the punishment. Punishment with the power of specific deterrence would cause offenders not to drink alcohol again, for example, or not to harass women again, because of the unpleasant experience they suffered for their last offense.

General deterrence is the ability to prevent nonoffenders from committing crimes. General deterrence is based on the logic that people who witness the pain suffered by those who commit crimes will desire to avoid that pain and hence will refrain from criminal activity. Based on this belief, corporal punishment is often carried out in public so that others may witness the event. For example, in the Iranian floggings for drinking alcohol, over 1,000 people gathered in Vali-e-Asr Square in Teheran to watch the lashings. In England and the United States, hangings were once public events, and parents brought their children to witness what happened when one broke the law. Some advocates of general deterrence today propose that the death penalty would be a greater deterrent to crime if executions were broadcast live on television.

Sterilization and Deterrence The dark side of deterrence is the historical belief, first made popular by Cèsare Lombroso, that crime is hereditary and that criminals should be sterilized to prevent future crime. Sterilization of criminals was practiced in the United States during the early twentieth century. In the United States today, a chemical version of castration is legal, but the few cases in which it has been used have drawn criticism and protest. Supreme Court Justice Oliver Wendell Holmes argued for sterilization as an effective means to prevent crime. One criminologist has even argued that the drop in crime in the 1980s and 1990s was a result of the increase in abortion in the general population. Other countries have used sterilization to reduce the births of "socially undesirable" persons. Between 1935 and 1975, Sweden sterilized more than 63,000 citizens to improve Sweden's genetic stock. It is alleged that between 1944 and 1963, approximately 4,500 Swedish citizens were lobotomized, often against their will, as a form of treatment for homosexuality.[12] Until 1996, Japanese law allowed the forced sterilization of people with a broad range of mental or physical handicaps, hereditary diseases, and leprosy. Japanese Health Ministry statistics indicate that nearly 850,000 people were sterilized between 1949 and 1996.[13] The law was changed in 1996 as a result of a change in public sentiment.

Incapacitation

Another view of punishment is that if criminals cannot be deterred from committing further crimes, they should be prevented from having the opportunity to commit other crimes, a condition referred to as **incapacitation**. The theory of incapacitation assumes that offenders cannot be rehabilitated and it will never be safe to release them back into society. The death penalty is an extreme form of incapacitation in that those offenders executed are guaranteed not to be capable of reoffending. In the absence of the death penalty, incarceration in a correctional institution is the alternative to incapacitate the offender.

Two of the oldest forms of incapacitation are banishment and transportation. Banishment as a criminal sanction may have begun in prehistoric times. **Banishment** removed offenders from society, often under the stipulation that if they returned, they would be put to death. This removal could be for a period of time or forever. In societies in which the protection and support of the group were essential to survival, banishment was considered a punishment nearly equal to death. **Transportation** removed offenders from society by literally moving them to another place. England made extensive use of transportation as a criminal sanction. Until the American Revolutionary War, prisoners were transported to the American colonies. After the American Revolution, English convicts were transported to Australia until the mid-nineteenth century.[14]

Some states still practice limited forms of banishment or legal exile whereby offenders are prohibited from residing within the state. Modern society has made transportation of offenders to penal colonies impractical. However, the federal government in a sense uses a form of transportation in regard to enemy combatants imprisoned at Guantanamo Bay, Cuba. The federal government has removed prisoners from captivity by sending them to countries that agree to take them.

Modern means of incapacitation include confiscating the cars of accused drunk drivers and the property and valuables of drug dealers and members of organized crime. The argument of those in favor of the law is that without a car, it would be impossible to drive while intoxicated, and without wealth, it would be impossible to engage in illegal businesses such as drug dealing. The most common form of incapacitation, however, is imprisonment. The public belief underlying this practice is that, behind bars, a criminal is effectively prevented from having the opportunity to commit more crimes. This belief underlies proposals for long prison sentences, especially for repeat offenders. Such a philosophy is sometimes referred to as "warehousing" or "lock and feed."

HERE'S SOMETHING TO THINK ABOUT . . .

Execution of Rainey Bethea, the last public execution in the United States, 1936

Until the 1800s it was commonplace for executions, mostly hangings, to be a public event. The last public execution in the United States was in 1936 in Owensboro, Kentucky. An estimated 20,000 people attended the event. The adoption of the gas chamber and the electric chair was the downfall of the public execution as these could not be conducted outdoors. Today the technology exists to allow in-prison executions to be recorded and broadcasted to the public. Videos of executions carried out in other countries are readily available on the Internet. Do you favor public broadcasting of executions? Why?

general deterrence the concept based on the logic that people who witness the pain suffered by those who commit crimes will desire to avoid that pain and will refrain from criminal activity

incapacitation deterrence based on the premise that the only way to prevent criminals from reoffending is to remove them from society

banishment the removal of an offender from the community

transportation the eighteenth-century practice by Great Britain of sending offenders to the American colonies and, later, to Australia

These terms emphasize that the primary purpose of sentencing is to separate the offender from the public for as long as possible.

Those opposed to incapacitation as the primary purpose of sentencing point out that most prisoners are released back into society. They also state that although incarceration may appear to protect the public from the offenders' crimes, it does little to protect fellow inmates and correctional officers from victimization.

Retribution

Retribution, or "just-desserts," is the argument that criminals should be punished because they deserve it. Retribution is associated with "get-tough" sentencing and the philosophy of an eye for an eye, which advocates that those who do wrong should pay for their crimes in equal measure. Traditionally, retribution was the victim's revenge. The victim was entitled to inflict punishment or to see that punishment was inflicted on the offender. Many who favor the death penalty argue that it is the most appropriate punishment for convicted murderers.

In cases of murder, society and family members often want retribution by the death of the offender.

Retribution relates to people's emotional response to a crime. For example, Kim Davis, 34, stole a car in Independence, Missouri. When he discovered that a 6-year-old child had been left in the vehicle, he tried to shove the boy outside. The boy became tangled in the seat belt, but Davis refused to stop. Horrified motorists who witnessed the awful scene pursued him for 5 miles before he was stopped. The boy did not survive the ordeal. Davis was charged with second-degree murder, robbery, child abuse, and kidnapping. A witness to the crime suggested that Davis should be "dragged himself, just like he dragged that kid."[15] In retribution, the criminal suffers—perhaps in a like manner—for the crime.

Those who believe that the purpose of sentencing is retribution are often disappointed that the offender does not suffer enough as a result of the sentence imposed. Because the U.S. criminal justice system does not allow relatives to carry out the execution of offenders or the offender to be brutalized by corporal punishment, often, retribution emphasizes long prison terms. The belief in retribution is reflected in the statement of Malissa Wilkins. Wilkins's two young children were killed when Jennifer Porter, a former elementary school dance teacher, hit the children with her car and killed them. Porter fled the accident. After Porter's arrest and conviction, Florida Circuit Judge Emmett Battles could have sentenced Porter to 15 years in prison. However, the judge took into account Porter's clean past record and other factors, and sentenced her to 3 years of probation and 500 hours of community service. At the sentencing, Wilkins sobbed and urged the judge to sentence Porter to prison. Wilkins said, "I want her to be punished. I want her to go to prison. I want her to see what it's like to lose someone."[16] Wilkins's sentiments reflect the underlying philosophy of retribution.

During the nineteenth and twentieth centuries, many prison officials and the public favored the idea that punishment was retribution. As a result, prison conditions often were deliberately harsh and cruel, and physical punishment was administered liberally to inmates. The public expected that prisoners would be punished while incarcerated.

Rehabilitation

Rehabilitation and restoration are more contemporary philosophies defining the purpose of criminal sanctions. **Rehabilitation** calls for criminal sanctions to "cure" the offender of criminality. The rehabilitation model often is referred to as the medical model in that it views criminality as a disease to be cured. Some believe that rehabilitation of offenders is impossible. Advocates of rehabilitation favor approaches involving psychology, medical treatment, drug treatment, self-esteem counseling, education, and programs aimed at developing ethical values and work skills. Most rehabilitation efforts focus on juvenile delinquents and youthful offenders. The juvenile justice system is based on the principle that its primary purpose is to rehabilitate. The criminal justice system and the public may accept that the purpose of criminal sanctions is to rehabilitate children and first-time offenders but often totally reject this premise for repeat and career offenders. Thus, the public may be willing to give the 14-year-old burglar the chance to turn his or her life around, but they would just as soon see the 45-year-old sexual offender spend the rest of his or her life in prison rather than give the system a chance to rehabilitate him or her.

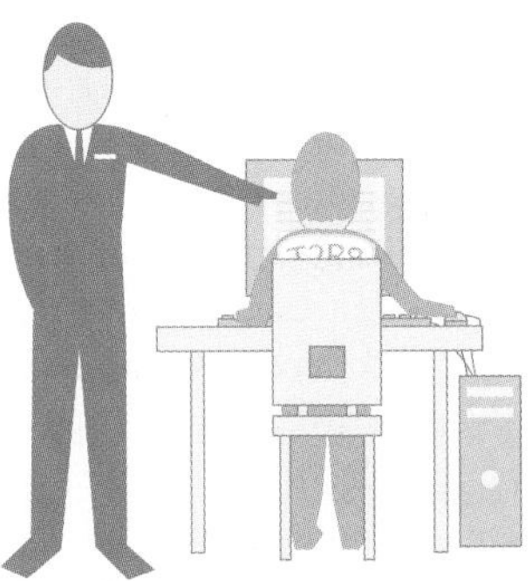

Rehabilitation emphasizes preparing the offender for reentry into society.

Restorative Justice

Restorative justice focuses on rehabilitating the victims rather than the offenders. Rehabilitation often is criticized for forgetting the victim. The focus in rehabilitation is on the offender and what needs to be done to make him or her a productive, normal member of society. The restorative

Restorative justice strives to heal the broken bond between the offender, victim, and society.

retribution deterrence based on the premise that criminals should be punished because they deserve it

rehabilitation deterrence based on the premise that criminals can be "cured" of their problems and criminality and can be returned to society

restorative justice a model of deterrence that uses restitution programs, community work programs, victim-offender mediation, and other strategies to not only rehabilitate the offender but also to address the damage done to the community and the victim

justice model does not argue against the rehabilitation of the offender, but it does advocate that the needs of the victim also must be central. Crime has a harmful effect on the victim and society, and justice requires that this harm be removed as much as possible. Restorative justice programs use restitution, community work programs, victim–offender mediation, and other strategies both to rehabilitate the offender and to address the damage done to the community and the victim. South Africa used this model to help heal the division between blacks and whites. South Africa's Truth and Reconciliation Commission allows those who committed hate crimes during apartheid, who confessed and repented of their crimes, to escape criminal sanctions.

One of the characteristics of restorative justice is the concept that the offender should be made to provide some contribution to the community. In the American criminal justice system this concept is translated into practice by sentencing the offender to additional penalties other than or in addition to incarceration. The most common penalties related to restorative justice include sentences requiring restitution to the victim and community service. This sanction is most often used in property offenses and least used in drug and weapon offenses. Community service is included as a penalty in about 5 percent of all offenses. Community service is based on the philosophy that the offender should provide services that help the community as a way to make up for the harm he or she did to the community.

The Special Case of Offenders with Mental Illness

On July 28, 2009, San Antonio police responded to a crime scene to find a 3½-week-old boy dismembered. At the scene, his hysterical mother, Otty Sanchez, had a self-inflicted wound to her chest and her throat partially slashed. She screamed to police, "I killed my baby! I killed my baby! The devil made me do it."[17] In 2001, Andrea Yates drowned her five children in her Houston-area home. She said that she did so because the devil made her do it. These women obviously have mental illness. At the trial, Yates was found not guilty by reason of insanity. Most likely, Sanchez will also be found not guilty by reason of insanity. Why should these women "escape" punishment when the criminal justice system is based on the fundamental principle that an offender must have committed the criminal act of his or her own free will?

The insanity defense is based on the legal principle that defendants lack the necessary *mens rea* to be held criminally liable for their actions. Criminal law provides a similar defense for young children and for people with diminished intellectual capacity or mental retardation. Because the insanity defense is based on the claim of mental illness, people often mistake insanity as a mental health term. However, insanity is only a legal term, not a mental health term.[18] Only a jury, and not mental health professionals, can pronounce that a defendant is insane.

Defining Insanity

Federal courts and state courts have different standards for defining insanity, but all federal courts use the same standard. When John Hinckley attempted to assassinate former President Ronald Reagan, he was acquitted in federal court based on a plea of insanity. The federal test of insanity in the early 1980s was whether defendants lacked the capacity to appreciate the wrongfulness of their conduct or to conform their conduct to the requirements of the law. Because of the public outrage over the laxity of the federal insanity standard, however, this standard was made more conservative, making it more difficult to prove claims of insanity.[19] The U.S. Congress passed the Insanity Defense Reform Act of 1984, under which the federal courts adopted a new standard of insanity. A defendant must prove insanity at the time of the crime by clear and convincing evidence. Mental disease or defect is no longer considered sufficient to avoid punishment. "Psychiatric evidence which negates *mens rea* . . . negates an element of the offense rather than constituting a justification or excuse."[20]

When the defendant pleads not guilty by reason of insanity, the court arranges for the defendant to be examined by mental health professionals prior to the trial. The court, the defendant, and the prosecutor have input as to who is selected to examine the defendant. At the trial, these mental health professionals are called as expert witnesses to give their opinion as to the defendant's state of mind at the time of the crime. The defense must prove that the defendant could not understand that his or her actions were criminal due to mental illness. The prosecution must present evidence that the defendant was capable of forming the necessary *mens rea* to be held accountable for his or her criminal actions. It is not unusual at a trial to have mental health professionals give very different assessments of the defendant's mental health. The jury must digest the evidence and decide whether the defendant's mental health meets the legal standard of insanity. If it does, the defendant is **not guilty by reason of insanity.** If it does not, the defendant is guilty as charged.

HERE'S SOMETHING TO THINK ABOUT . . .

Punishment for criminal actions is based on the classical criminological principle that the offender committed the offense of his or her own free will. The law refers to this as mens rea *or "guilty mind." The insane defendant is not guilty of a criminal act and cannot be punished because he or she did not know the action was criminal. Concerned that the insanity plea may result in a dangerous person being set free to harm the community, some states have adopted more conservative legal definitions of insanity or provided for sentencing alternatives such as "guilty but insane" which provide for mandatory custody. What is a good balance between treatment and punishment for the mentally ill?*

A defendant found not guilty by reason of insanity must undergo a civil commitment examination to determine whether the defendant should be released or confined to an institution for persons with mental illness until the medical staff determines that he or she is no longer a danger.

not guilty by reason of insanity a verdict by which the jury finds that a defendant committed the crime but was insane

The Insanity Defense Reform Act of 1984

The Insanity Defense Reform Act of 1984 requires that, in federal courts, the defendant found not guilty by reason of insanity must undergo a **civil commitment examination** within 40 days of the verdict. The civil commitment process determines whether the defendant should be released or confined to an institution for persons with mental illness. The purpose is to determine whether defendants are a danger to themselves or to the public. If found to be a danger to the public or themselves, defendants may be involuntarily confined to a civil mental health institution until the medical staff determines that they are no longer a danger. In addition, defendants may be forced to undergo medical and drug treatment and may be denied their liberty for the rest of their lives. Because a successful insanity defense usually leads to a sentence that differs little from life imprisonment, the insanity defense is not used for misdemeanors or lesser felonies but almost exclusively in first-degree homicide cases.

State Courts and the Insanity Plea

State courts have adopted diverse standards for a successful insanity defense. Some still use the awareness-of-right-and-wrong test, others have adopted the Model Penal Code substantial capacity test, and a few have adopted standards combining elements of both. A number of states have adopted a new verdict: **guilty but mentally ill.** Michigan was the first state to adopt this verdict in 1975. The verdict provides the jury the option of finding that the defendant, indeed, has mental illness, perhaps suffering from a serious mental illness, but was "sufficiently in possession of his faculties to be morally blameworthy for his acts."[21]

In states that have adopted it, the guilty but mentally ill verdict is an alternative to the not guilty by reason of insanity verdict. Thus, the jury has the option of finding defendants mentally ill but morally responsible for their acts, or insane and lacking the *mens rea* to be held criminally liable. In the latter case, the defendant is involuntarily confined to a civil mental health facility, but if found guilty but mentally ill, the defendant is sentenced to incarceration in a state prison following psychiatric treatment. During confinement at a mental institution, if doctors determine that the defendant is no longer suffering from mental illness, he or she is not released but is transferred to the state prison to serve his or her sentence. The time that the offender spent in the mental institution counts toward the sentence to be served. Once returned to the regular prison population, offenders may still be considered to have mental illness to some degree, but their medical and psychiatric problems will not excuse them from incarceration for their crimes.

Public Fear of the Insanity Plea

The public fear that the successful use of the insanity defense poses a grave danger because it allows defendants to escape incarceration does not appear to be justified. A very small number of defendants choose to plead not guilty by reason of insanity.[22] Offenders found to be not guilty by reason of insanity rarely obtain their freedom following the verdict.[23] Media coverage has sensationalized unusual cases, such as that of Lorena Bobbitt, who successfully pleaded insanity to a charge of cutting off her husband's penis and was freed completely within 2 months of the verdict, and John Hinckley, who escaped possible lifetime incarceration by use of the insanity plea. However, these cases are

TABLE 8.2 Factors That Can Prevent a Fair Sentence

Courtroom Participant	Possible Misconduct	Negative Impact on the Criminal Justice System
Legislation	Unfair, unconstitutional, or discriminatory legislation	Loss of respect for the law, civil and violent protest against the law
Judge	Selection of incompetent or biased judges, criminal misconduct regarding judicial decisions, abuse of powers, biased decisions	Wrongful convictions, verdicts based on bribery and influence, distrust of the courts
Prosecutor	Prosecutorial misconduct	Wrongful prosecution of defendants, guilty defendants escape justice, public sees the criminal justice system as biased and unfair
Defense Attorney	Overburdened public defenders are unable to provide adequate representation	Innocent defendants may fail to receive a fair trial, wrongful convictions resulting from inadequate representation, delays in trials resulting in innocent defendants spending unnecessary pretrial time in jail
Jury	Biased	Unfair decisions based on emotion or prejudice rather than facts
Presentence Investigator	Inaccurate presentence investigation report	Sentencing recommendations based on inaccurate information resulting in recommendations for sentence lengths that are either excessive or insufficient. Because the presentence investigation is based on the assumption that the defendant is guilty, the protests of a wrongfully convicted defendant will be held against the defendant as uncooperative and failure to take responsibility for his or her actions

civil commitment examination a determination of whether the defendant should be released or confined to an institution for persons with mental illness

guilty but mentally ill a new type of verdict in which the jury finds a defendant mentally ill but sufficiently aware to be morally responsible for his or her criminal acts

not typical of defendants found guilty by reason of insanity.

What happens in sentencing when a defendant is not successful in his or her insanity plea? The judge may require that after conviction, the offender undergo another mental competency examination. If the offender is found mentally unfit for incarceration in the state or federal prison, he or she is placed in a maximum-security mental health facility that can provide appropriate psychiatric treatment. Some states have special correctional facilities for such patients. Medical authorities determine if or when the offender can be returned to the prison population. The time spent in the medical institution counts toward the sentence to be served.

THE GREATEST FEAR IS ELECTION CAMPAIGN DONATIONS WILL PREJUDICE JUDGES. THE COST OF JUDICIAL CAMPAIGNS HAS GREATLY INCREASED, AND SOME JUDICIAL CAMPAIGNS SPEND MILLIONS OF DOLLARS TO GET ELECTED.

A Fair Sentence

Sentencing recommendations based on inaccurate information result in recommendations for sentence lengths that are either excessive or insufficient. Because the presentence investigation is based on the assumption that the defendant is guilty, the protests of a wrongfully convicted defendant will be held against the defendant as uncooperative and failure to take responsibility for his or her actions.

The public and the ethics of the criminal justice system demand a sentence that is fair and unbiased. (See Table 8.2 for factors that can affect a fair sentence.) There are six major factors which have significant impact on the impartiality of a sentence:

1. the law,
2. the judge,
3. the prosecutor,
4. the defense attorney,
5. the jury, and
6. the presentence investigator.

Laws Laws are enacted by legislation and must specify the punishment for an offense. If the law is unjust or discriminatory, it fails to provide justice. Laws that are inequitable and discriminate by race, gender, religion, or other constitutionally protected groups are the most often targeted for change. Over time, many laws have been considered racially inequitable. Perhaps the most egregious were the "Jim Crow" laws that provided for inequality in treatment of Blacks and access to the criminal justice system. Although legislation has been passed in an attempt to eliminate such laws, there are still debates as to the equality of contemporary laws and punishments. One of the most controversial laws directly related to a fair sentence was the 100:1 ratio in sentencing for crack cocaine versus powder cocaine. The sentence for 50 grams of crack cocaine was a minimum of 10 years. The amount required to trigger a 10-year sentence for powder cocaine was 5,000 grams. The difference is significant in that 80 percent of criminals sentenced for crack-related offenses are Black. Attorney General Eric Holder called the disparity egregious.[24] The Fair Sentencing Act of 2010 narrowed the sentence disparity to 18:1. but some still disagreed. Also, the new law created cries of protest as to whether the law applied retroactively to reduce previous sentences.

Judges A fair and impartial judge is the cornerstone of justice. One of the important considerations in securing fair and impartial judges is the selection process. Federal judges are nominated by the president and approved by the Senate. Once selected, federal judges can be removed only by impeachment, a process that has rarely been used or successful. The founding fathers selected this method with the hopes that it would shield federal judges from political influences in their judicial duties and decisions.

Concerns About the Election of State Judges However, the states took a different approach to selecting judges. Most of the states adopted a selection process that depends in one way or another on popular elections. According to the National Center for State Courts, 87 percent of all state court judges face elections. The use of popular elections to select judges is unique to the United States because only two other nations use popular elections in the selection of judges (Switzerland and Japan). Furthermore, in those two countries, the use of popular elections applies only in certain cases and is not generally used.

The concern is that election pressures can influence a judge's judicial decisions. For example, one study found that all judges increase their sentences as reelection nears.[25] Perhaps of greater concern is the fear that election campaign donations will prejudice judges. The cost of judicial campaigns has greatly increased, and some judicial campaigns spend

HERE'S SOMETHING TO THINK ABOUT . . .

Some choose to take sentencing into their own hands. Chicagoan Ashley Steele, 21, allegedly shot Derrick Gray, 40, three times accusing him of giving her herpes. When Florida pastor Terry Jones held a mock trial ending with the burning of the Koran, Muslim protestors in Afghanistan killed over 20 persons and injured 81 in protest. Reverend Jones reports he has received 300 death threats and had been advised by the FBI that there was a $2.4 million contract on his life. In modern society the government assumes all power to punish persons for wrongdoing. Should there be exceptions for grievous wrongs? Why?

Equitable laws, an unbiased judge, a fair and unbiased prosecutor, a capable defense attorney, an unbiased jury that does not engage in misconduct, and a fair presentence investigator are factors necessary for a fair sentence.

millions of dollars in a bid to get elected. There are two concerns. First, the cost of a judicial election is so great that highly qualified candidates may be eliminated by candidates who have fewer qualifications but more money. Secondly, there is concern that large donors may "buy" special consideration. One West Virginia case concerning the possible judicial bias that could occur as a result of large campaign contributors is *Caperton v. A.T. Massey Coal Co.* (2009). Caperton, the owner of a small coal company, successfully argued in court that the much larger A.T. Massey Coal Company forced him into bankruptcy because of unfair business practices and received a $50 million jury award. Massey appealed the $50 million award. In the West Virginia judicial elections, Massey had contributed $3 million to the campaign of Brent Benjamin for state Supreme Court justice. The newly elected Judge Benjamin was party to the panel of five appellate judges hearing the appeal, and he refused to recuse himself. The vote was 3 to 2, with Benjamin casting the deciding vote. Caperton appealed to the U.S. Supreme Court that Benjamin was biased by the large campaign donation from Massey.

Despite calls for reform, the U.S. Supreme Court has refused to intervene in the selection process for judges used by states. In 2008, a case before the U.S. Supreme Court challenged the method used by New York state to choose its trial judges. The case claimed that the New York state system of choosing candidates for judges by convention rather than primary elections is a patronage-tainted system that favors party cronies and minimizes voters' input because they have no voice in the selection of the candidates on the ballot. The U.S. Supreme Court ruled that states are free to use the method of their choice to select judges even if that system has obvious flaws.

Prosecutors The assumption that a prosecutor is fair and unbiased is an essential element of a fair trial and sentence. Prosecutors are supposed to use the immense powers of the government to discover who committed a crime, gather evidence to prosecute the defendant, and present the best possible case against the defendant. It is unethical for the prosecutor to demonstrate bias in selecting which crimes to prosecute or to charge defendants without regard for the evidence regarding their possible innocence. The criminal justice system is not perfect, and there are incidences wherein prosecutors have not acted professionally and within ethical standards. Two notorious examples include the following:

1. The allegations that the hiring and firing of Justice Department attorneys were based on political ideology and loyalty to the Republican Party rather than professional credentials during the Bush Administration.
2. The unethical behavior of former Durham, North Carolina, prosecutor Michael B. Nifong in 2007. As prosecutor, Nifong charged students of the Duke University lacrosse team with sexual assault and other crimes even though evidence that he possessed demonstrated the defendants were not guilty. Nifong's behavior was not only considered unethical, but he also was found to have committed criminal actions, resulting in a 1-day jail sentence as well as disbarment. As a result of his prosecutorial misconduct, the former defendants filed a multimillion-dollar lawsuit against the city.

Defense Attorneys The quality of the accused's defense attorney can have an influence on the fairness of the verdict and sentence. The extensive use of public defenders in the criminal justice system to represent the indigent raises concerns that those who cannot afford a private attorney may receive less competent representation, resulting in conviction and longer sentences. The public defender system is in crisis in many states.

500 the average number of felony cases per year handled by a Florida public defender

2,225 the average number of misdemeanor cases per year handled by a Florida lawyer

Public defenders have taken to rejecting new cases arguing that it would be unethical to overburden themselves to the point that they are unable to provide each defendant with adequate representation.

Juries The criminal justice system attempts to provide juries that are unbiased. In a high-profile case, the *voir dire* process can be lengthy and expensive. However, there are possible faults with the jury process wherein jury members may be biased, resulting in both wrongful convictions and guilty defendants being freed. During the 1960s there were a number of high-profile civil rights cases where juries failed to convict persons accused of civil rights violations because of their personal prejudices. At other times jurors engage in wrongful actions such as conducting their own investigations, discussing the case with other persons, or disregarding the judge's instructions. One example of blatant misconduct occurred in the trial of former Orange County sheriff Michael S. Carona on federal corruption charges. Radio "shock jocks" John Kobylt and Ken Chiampou of KFI-AM in Los Angeles urged citizens who were prospective jurors to lie to the court during *voir dire* with the purpose of getting on the jury and voting guilty based on pretrial public information suggesting that the former sheriff was guilty.[26]

Presentence Investigators Finally, the presentence investigation reports play a very important role in arriving at a fair sentence for a convicted defendant. They, too, should be unbiased and accurate to ensure that sentencing is fair.

Presentence Investigation Report

A presentence investigation involves gathering information about the convicted offender to help determine the best sentence. Following conviction, either by plea or trial, the defendant is returned to jail and the judge begins the process of determining the appropriate sentence. Federal and state judges of general trial jurisdiction are assisted in this process by a staff of people who conduct a presentence investigation.

Unlike the impression of trials and sentencing given by television and the movies, in which arrest, trial, and sentencing follow in rapid

4 **Before sentencing, a presentence investigator investigates the background of the convicted offender and the circumstances surrounding the offense, interviews him or her, and makes a recommendation at the sentencing hearing, during which victim impact statements may be heard.**

succession, the process from arrest to sentencing is rather lengthy. One-half of all persons arrested for a felony are sentenced in 184 days. Generally, the more serious the crime, the longer the time from arrest to sentencing.[27] Thus, the median time from arrest to sentencing for larceny is only 99 days, but the median time from arrest to sentencing for murder is 412 days.

The Offender's Background and Attitude

The **presentence investigator** is a person who works for the court and has the responsibility of investigating the background of the convicted offender and the circumstances surrounding the offense. Federal courts use federal probation and parole personnel to serve as presentence investigators. Each state court has its own method for staffing presentence investigators. Some states use state probation and parole officers, whereas in other states presentence investigators are employees of the court. The presentence investigator has the responsibility of investigating the life led by the offender, any previous crimes and punishments received, the offender's attitude toward his or her crime, and the impact of the crime on the community and victims. After conviction, a defendant is expected to cooperate with presentence investigators and does not have the right to remain silent. All previous crimes committed by the offender may be considered in the sentencing process. The defendant's employment history, family relationships, and reputation in the community may all be considered. Other factors that influence the recommendation include prior convictions and the seriousness of the current offense, including the extent of harm to others as a result of the crime.

The offender may be required to complete interviews and life history forms as part of the presentence investigation. Defendants who refuse to provide information may be classified as uncooperative, which can be a factor in sentencing. Convicted defendants who do not accept responsibility for their guilt or do not express remorse for their crime may receive a more severe sentence.

HERE'S SOMETHING TO THINK ABOUT . . .

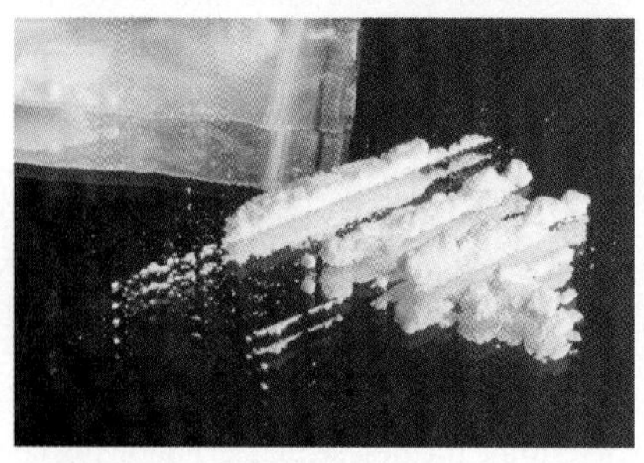

Sentences should be fair. Many believed the 100:1 sentencing disparity between powder and crack cocaine discriminated against minorities. In 2011, the Fair Sentencing Act of 2010 reduced the sentence disparity to 18:1. However, the new law did not specify if the sentencing reform applied to offenses committed before the law went into effect in August 2011. The U.S. Sentencing Commission voted unanimously to retroactively apply the amended guidelines but this could be overruled by Congress in November 2011. If applied retroactively, about 12,000 people would be eligible for a sentence reduction of about 3 years. What is the fair thing to do?

The Presentencing Recommendation The presentence investigation report contains a recommendation for specific criminal sanctions, including a recommendation for prison time, probation, fines, community service, or other sanctions. If an offender is assessed a fine and is unable to pay the fine, he or she cannot be imprisoned in lieu of the fine. Thus, the presentence investigator will review the convicted offender's financial resources to determine what he or she can pay in fines or restitution. When the report is completed, the presentence investigator will forward it to the judge for his or her review. The judge will forward a copy of the report to the prosecutor and the defense attorney. The investigator's role is important. In over 90 percent of cases, the judge accepts the recommended sanctions outlined in the presentence investigation report. Both the prosecution and defense will have an opportunity to rebut the presentence investigation recommendation.

Sentencing Hearing and Victim Impact Statements

The judge sets a date for a sentencing hearing, at which the prosecution and the defense have the opportunity to critique the recommended criminal sanctions. The presentence investigator may be called to testify as to how he or she compiled the data for the report and what influenced him or her in making a specific recommendation for criminal sanctions.

The judge also may allow **victim impact statements** at the presentence hearing, in which victims of the crime have a chance to influence sentencing. Victim impact statements are controversial. Technically, defendants are punished for what they did, regardless of who the victims were. Sentencing is not supposed to be based on whether the victim was a homeless person or a beloved member of the community. Because of the emotional nature of the victims' testimony, some civil rights advocates consider victim impact statements prejudicial and biased.[28] Defenders of victim impact statements argue that the harm and suffering caused to others is an appropriate factor in determining the offender's sentence. Both the defense and the prosecutor can appeal the sentence.

Sentencing Models

Juries (except in bench trials) determine the guilt of defendants, but judges are responsible for determining the sentence that defendants receive. In sentencing, judges evaluate the circumstances of the cases of everyone who pleads guilty or is convicted of an offense. A judge must also evaluate the possible sentences allowed by law and then select the sentence that best fits the case. All criminal laws passed by the state legislature or the U.S. Congress must specify the punishment or range of punishments that a judge can impose if a defendant is found guilty of violating that law. The only constitutional guideline for sentencing is the Eighth Amendment prohibition against cruel and unusual punishment. The U.S. Supreme Court has allowed a broad interpretation of this amendment and, thus, few punishments have been found to be cruel and unusual.

An indeterminate sentencing model gives the judge broad discretion in determining a sentence, whereas structured sentencing models require fixed sentences, mandatory sentences, or sentencing guidelines; presumptive sentencing is a balance between sentencing guidelines and mandatory sentencing.

presentence investigator a person who works for the court and has the responsibility of investigating the background of the convicted offender and the circumstances surrounding the offense

victim impact statements testimony by victims at a convicted offender's sentencing hearing

TABLE 8.3	Sentencing Models	
Sentencing Model	**How Sentencing Works**	**Advantages/Disadvantages**
Indeterminate Sentencing	Legislation provides a very broad range for crimes (e.g., 1 to 20 years) and the judge decides the sentence based on individual circumstances.	Allows for discretion to adjust the length of the sentence to fit the individual circumstances. Can result in intentional or unintentional discrimination. Sentences from judge to judge may vary so much as to appear to be unfair.
Structured Sentencing Determinate	Legislation mandates a range of incarceration, usually in months, for crimes, and the judge decides a sentence within these ranges (e.g., 18 to 24 months). The sentence is reduced for factors such as first offense, youthful offender, and cooperating with the police, but increased for aggravating factors.	Strives to ensure that all offenders receive an equal sentence for the same crime. Still allows the judge leeway for individual circumstances. Often the range of the sentence is not based on any research regarding the effectiveness and appropriateness of the sentence range.
Structured Sentencing Mandatory	Legislation provides a fixed sentence for offenders found guilty. The judge has no discretion in sentencing. Usually used for certain crimes such as those involving firearms and drugs.	Guarantees that defendants will not receive a light sentence at the judge's discretion. Provides no discretion for individual circumstances. Offenders who may have benefited from diversion, counseling, or probation will be sentenced to imprisonment.
Structured Sentencing Mandatory – Habitual Offender	Similar to mandatory sentencing in that legislation specifies a specific period of incarceration on a finding of guilt with no discretion given to the judge to alter the sentence. However, it is applied only to repeat offenders.	Provides the public with a sense of public safety that dangerous offenders will receive long prison sentences. Can be triggered by minor offenses, and when applied to youthful offenders, can result in long sentences, which can be very expensive with little impact on rehabilitation or release of the offender.
Structured Sentencing Presumptive	1984 federal legislation and sentencing guidelines issued by the U.S. Sentencing Commission provided extremely specific sentence guidelines based on the "primary" offense and then increased or decreased by the presence of mitigating or aggravating factors.	The goal of presumptive sentencing is to provide fair and unbiased sentences. The judge has little discretion based on individual circumstances. U.S. Supreme Court rulings declared the use of the Federal Sentencing Guidelines unconstitutional. Sentencing guidelines are only constitutional when considered advisory for the judge.

Sentencing Models

The traditional criminal sanctions that a judge may impose are fines, imprisonment, probation, or some combination of these. Federal judges in U.S. District Courts, military judges, and state judges in courts of general trial jurisdiction in states with the death penalty also may sentence a defendant to death. Judges are guided by the law as to the minimum and maximum sentence that a convicted defendant can receive. However, especially for state judges, the difference between the minimum and maximum punishment may vary greatly. Thus, each sentence requires the judge to give careful consideration to the individual circumstances of the case. Seldom is sentencing an automatic or routine function in which the outcome is always predictable.

AT ONE TIME, STATE AND FEDERAL JUDGES HAD NEARLY COMPLETE DISCRETION IN SENTENCING AN OFFENDER, BECAUSE MOST STATES AND THE FEDERAL COURTS USED THE INDETERMINATE MODEL OF SENTENCING.

At one time, state and federal judges had nearly complete discretion in sentencing an offender, because most states and the federal courts used the indeterminate model of sentencing. The **indeterminate sentencing** model gives the judge the most power and flexibility in setting the sentence of the offender. In the late nineteenth century, as incarceration became a

indeterminate sentencing a model of sentencing in which judges have nearly complete discretion in sentencing an offender

common punishment for serious crimes, the predominant correctional philosophy was that offenders should demonstrate that they had changed their criminal attitudes and lifestyles as a condition of release. Thus, judges were given wide latitude in the sentences they could impose for crimes. Because no one could predict exactly when offenders would demonstrate that they were rehabilitated, offenders were given sentences of indeterminate length. For example, an offender might receive a sentence of a minimum of 1 year and a maximum of 20 years in prison. The exact number of years to be served would be determined by the prisoner's behavior and progress toward rehabilitation.

Indeterminate sentencing came under criticism in the late twentieth century. In addition to giving the judge wide latitude in sentencing, indeterminate sentencing also gave extensive power to prison authorities. In reality, it was prison authorities, not the judge, who determined the term of the sentence to be served. Prison officials could arbitrarily exercise this power with little or no oversight. To cure the ills of indeterminate sentencing, state and federal legislation adopted **structured sentencing** models, including the following:

1. determinate sentencing
2. mandatory sentencing and habitual offender laws
3. sentencing guidelines
4. presumptive sentencing

HERE'S SOMETHING TO THINK ABOUT . . .

Virginia Senator Jim Webb (D)

Source: http://webb.senate.gov/photos/images/official1.jpg

In the 1960s and 1970s presidential commissions conducted comprehensive reviews of the criminal justice system and recommended significant reforms. U.S. Senator Jim Webb (D-VA) thinks it is about time to create a commission to conduct a thorough evaluation of the nation's criminal justice system again. Webb has proposed the National Criminal Justice Commission Act. Despite several failed attempts to pass the legislation, Webb was hopeful by progress in the House and Senate in 2011. Webb says the bill would create "a blue-ribbon commission to look at every aspect of our criminal justice system with an eye toward reshaping the criminal justice system from top to bottom. . . It is time to examine its interlocking parts, to learn what works and what does not, and make recommendations for reform." Is there a need for a major review of the criminal justice system? Why?

Determinate Versus Indeterminate Sentencing

In **determinate sentencing**, the offender is sentenced to a fixed term of incarceration. This term may be reduced by parole or good behavior, but other than that, the inmate knows when he or she is scheduled for release from prison. Determinate sentences are also known as flat sentences or fixed sentences. Determinate sentencing was a sentencing reform that emerged in the 1970s to provide more equity and proportionality in sentencing. Proponents claimed that it would eliminate racial discrimination.[29]

Determinate sentencing reform did not become popular, however. Only Arizona adopted a determinate sentencing model. A few other states (California, Illinois, Indiana, and Maine) adopted sentencing models based on determinate sentencing but still provided for discretion in sentencing.[30]

Mandatory Sentencing and Habitual Offender Laws

A controversial sentencing model is **mandatory sentencing**—the strict application of full sentences, adopted because of public perception that offenders were "getting off too light." Concerned that judges were too lenient in sentencing, many states adopted legislation mandating that offenders convicted of crimes serve the sentence for that crime as specified by law. Thus, sentencing was not left to the discretion of the judge. Mandatory sentences have been applied mostly to crimes involving drugs or the use of firearms. For crimes with mandatory sentences, if the defendant is convicted, the sentence for the crime is specified by the law, and the judge has no authority to change the sentence based on mitigating circumstances. For example, if the law states that the prison term for committing a crime with a firearm is 2 years, then the judge must sentence the defendant to 2 years. Critics of mandatory sentencing argue that there may be unique circumstances in a case that make mandatory sentences inappropriate. Judges are critical of mandatory sentences, because they greatly reduce the authority of the judge in determining the sentence. Concerned that the criminal justice system was ignoring domestic violence or not taking domestic violence cases seriously, several states adopted mandatory sentencing for conviction of domestic violence. Sometimes, these sentences are for short periods, such as 48 hours, or involve only probation. Nevertheless, the convicted offender finds that he or she can no longer escape punishment for domestic violence.[31]

Mandatory sentencing also has been applied to repeat offenders through **habitual offender laws.** California has received much press concerning its **three-strikes law,** in which repeat offenders receive longer mandatory sentences. Proponents argue that "getting tough on crime" reduces crime by taking repeat

83%
amount of increase in number of felons serving life sentences since 1992

$1,000,000.00
Cost to keep the average inmate locked up for life

structured sentencing a sentencing model (including determinate sentencing, sentencing guidelines, and presumptive sentencing) that defines punishments rather than allowing indeterminate sentencing

determinate sentencing a model of sentencing in which the offender is sentenced to a fixed term of incarceration

mandatory sentencing the strict application of full sentences in the determinate sentencing model

habitual offender laws tough sentencing laws to punish repeat offenders more harshly

three-strikes law the application of mandatory sentencing to give repeat offenders longer prison terms

Federal Sentencing Classifications – Section 3559, Title 18
Felony
Class A – Felony Maximum sentence of life imprisonment or, if authorized, death
Class B – Felony Maximum sentence of 25 years imprisonment to life imprisonment; the death penalty is not permitted
Class C – Felony Maximum sentence of 25 years but no less than 10 years' imprisonment
Class D – Felony Maximum sentence of 10 years but no less than 5 years' imprisonment
Class E– Felony A maximum sentence of 5 years but more than 1 year of imprisonment
Misdemeanor
Class A – Misdemeanor Maximum sentence of 1 year of imprisonment but no less than 1 month imprisonment
Class B – Misdemeanor Maximum sentence of 6 months' imprisonment but no less than 30 days
Class C – Misdemeanor Maximum sentence of 30 days' imprisonment but no less than 5 days

offenders off the streets. Opponents argue that the three-strikes law creates situations in which offenders are receiving disproportionately long prison terms for minor crimes, such as possession of drugs.

As a result of the "get-tough" sentencing policies, especially the three-strikes sentencing policy, the number of convicted felons serving some kind of life sentence has increased 83 percent since 1992.[32] Supporters of these new sentencing policies defend long sentences by citing the significant decline in crime since their adoption, but opponents criticize the long sentences, pointing out that it will cost about $1 million to keep an inmate locked up for life. With over 125,000 inmates sentenced to life terms, the costs, which fall primarily on state taxpayers, of getting tough on criminals are extremely high. As a result of these costs and claims that factors other than long prison terms may account for the significant drop in crime, many states are reconsidering mandatory sentencing and three-strikes laws.[33] The American Bar Association (ABA) has recommended an end to mandatory minimum sentences and overly harsh prison terms for nonviolent offenders.[34]

A 2004 report by the American Bar Association said that long prison terms should be reserved for criminals who pose the greatest danger to society and who commit the most serious crimes. Ennis Archer, ABA president in 2004, critiques overly harsh and mandatory sentences, saying, "For more than 20 years, we have gotten tougher on crime. Now we need to get smarter."[35] Even Supreme Court Justice Anthony M. Kennedy has criticized overly harsh prison terms for nonviolent drug offenders, saying, "Our resources are misspent, our punishments too severe, our sentences too long."[36]

Sentencing Guidelines

Sentencing guidelines have been adopted by most states. In **sentencing guidelines,** crimes are classified according to seriousness, and a range of time is mandated for crimes within each category. Each state has its own classification for the seriousness of a crime and the corresponding length of sentence that can be imposed for that crime. Federal crimes are defined by Section 3559, U.S. Code, Title 18 into felonies and misdemeanors and are representative of the scheme used by most states in setting sentencing guidelines. The federal court distinguishes five classifications for felony crimes and three classifications for misdemeanors.

Presumptive Sentencing

Presumptive sentencing is a structured sentencing model that attempts to balance indeterminate sentencing with determinate sentencing. Presumptive sentencing gives discretionary powers to the judge within certain limits. The best-known presumptive sentencing model is used by the federal court according to the Sentencing Reform Act of 1984. The Sentencing Reform Act of 1984 set minimum and maximum terms of imprisonment for the various federal offenses. It then provided an adjustment for the offender's criminal history and for aggravating or mitigating circumstances. After conviction, the judge must sentence the offender using the Federal Sentencing Guidelines Manual.[37] Based on the offense and the offender's history, a base sentence is determined in months (e.g., 135–180 months). The offender's sentence can be increased by adding months for aggravating factors such as the use of a firearm, failing to cooperate with arresting authorities, lack of remorse, failure to recover stolen property, and so forth. The offender's sentence also can be shortened by months for mitigating factors, such as cooperating with arresting authorities, making restitution, providing information to authorities leading to the arrest of others involved in the crime, and so forth. The judge literally calculates a sentence using the base sentence in months listed in the Federal Sentencing Guidelines Manual and the addition and subtraction of months to this base sentence based on aggravating and mitigating factors. If the judge departs significantly from the federal sentencing guidelines, he or she must provide written reasons for this deviation at the sentencing hearing. The prosecution or defense can appeal the sentence.

Federal judges protested the imposition of the federal sentencing guidelines, arguing that they violated the separation of powers clause. The argument was that the legislative branch of the government did not have the authority to dictate sentencing guidelines to the judicial branch of the government. Ironically, the U.S. Supreme Court was the final arbiter of the dispute and ruled that Congress is within its powers to legislate sentencing guidelines.[38]

Restrictions on Plea Bargaining The Sentencing Reform Act of 1984 restricted, but did not abolish, plea bargaining. First, sentence-reduction plea bargaining cannot permit the offender to receive less than the minimum mandatory sentence for the offense.[39] Second, if plea bargaining results in reduced charges, the court record and plea bargaining agreement

sentencing guidelines a sentencing model in which crimes are classified according to their seriousness and a range of time to be served is mandatory for crimes within each category

presumptive sentencing a structured sentencing model that attempts to balance sentencing guidelines with mandatory sentencing and at the same time provide discretion to the judge

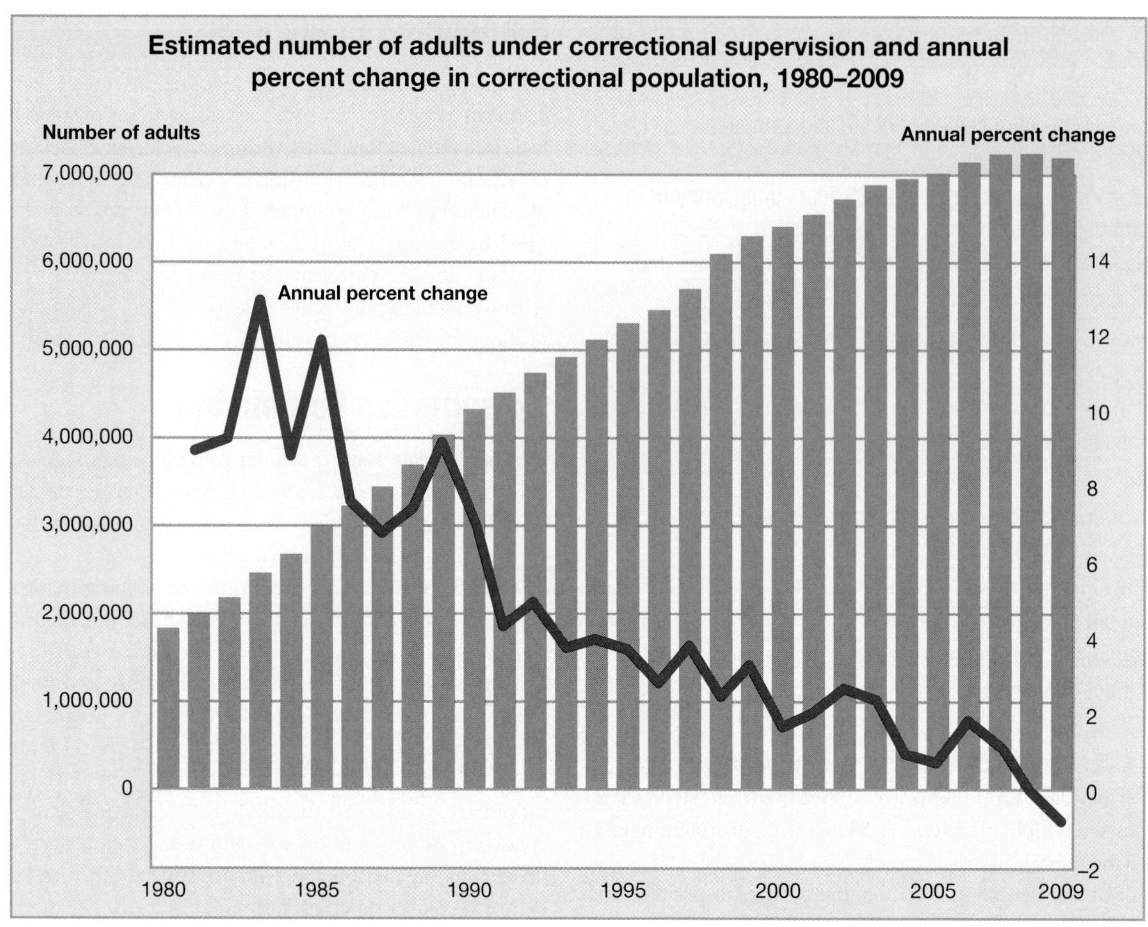

The emphasis on "get tough" sentencing starting in the 1970s resulted in a steady increase of adults under correctional supervision. *Source:* Lauren Glaze, *Correctional Populations In the United States, 2009* (Bureau of Justice Statistics, Washington, DC, 2010).

must fully disclose the details of the actual crime. Thus, if the crime of sexual assault is reduced to burglary, the court record will still contain the details of the crime of sexual assault. This record is public information. Thus, offenders cannot hide their crimes from the public and the media by plea bargaining to a lesser included crime.

Abolishment of Parole One consideration in the use of presumptive sentencing is that it abolishes parole, or early release from prison. This is a stumbling block for states that want to adopt a presumptive sentencing model similar to the federal court model. Parole provides for the possibility that an offender sentenced to serve 9 years in prison may only serve one third of that time. Many states depend on parole to move offenders through the correctional system, because there are not enough prison beds to accommodate the number of sentenced offenders. Thus, before these states could adopt a presumptive sentencing model, they would have to build more prisons. The federal correctional system has the ability to move inmates throughout the United States, which allows the federal government to manage prison overcrowding by moving prisoners to less-crowded facilities. State corrections do not have this option.

MANY STATES DEPEND ON PAROLE TO MOVE OFFENDERS THROUGH THE CORRECTIONAL SYSTEM, BECAUSE THERE ARE NOT ENOUGH PRISON BEDS.

Unconstitutionality Presumptive sentencing, specifically the federal sentencing guidelines, was struck down as unconstitutional by the U.S. Supreme Court in January 2005. The Court first ruled in June 2004 that Washington state's sentencing law, which was modeled on the federal sentencing guidelines, was unconstitutional because it violated the right to a trial by jury. The reasoning was that under the state's sentencing guidelines, similar to the federal guidelines, judges could take into account actions and circumstances related to the case not introduced during the trial in determining the sentence of the offender. The review of state sentencing guidelines was sparked by the review of the financial fraud case of Jamie Olis, who was sentenced to 24 years in prison. In the Washington state sentencing guidelines, there were many factors that allowed a judge to increase or decrease the length of a prison term, one of which was the financial losses of the fraud. The U.S. Supreme Court ruled that any factor that increases a criminal's sentence, except for prior convictions, must be proved to a jury beyond a reasonable doubt before it could be considered as a factor to increase sentence length.

The Washington state decision affected other states with similar sentencing guidelines. In January 2005, the U.S. Supreme Court ruled that the same reasoning made federal sentencing guidelines invalid (*United States v. Booker,* No. 04-104, and *United States v. Fanfan,* No. 04-105). The Court ruled that the federal sentencing guidelines violated defendants' rights to trial by jury by giving the judges the power to make factual findings that increased sentences beyond the maximum that the jury's finding alone would support. For example, in 2002, Mohamad Hammoud was convicted of smuggling cigarettes to raise money for the Lebanese terrorist group Hezbollah. He faced a 57-month sentence for that crime, but because of the terrorism connection and other findings by the judge, he was sentenced to 155 years.[40] The Court ruled that such increases are not constitutional.

The U.S. Supreme Court ruled that federal sentencing guidelines are "merely advisory." Justice Breyer, writing for the majority decision, said, "Judges must consult the guidelines and take them into account in imposing sentences. But at the end of the day the guidelines will be advisory only, with sentences to be reviewed on appeal for reasonableness."[41]

As a result of the Court's rulings in the Washington state case, in *United States v. Booker,* and in *United States v. Fanfan,* state and federal courts have to review those cases in which defendants were sentenced under state or federal sentencing guidelines. Also, the Supreme Court's ruling has renewed the struggle between Congress and the judiciary for control over setting criminal punishment.[42] In June 2005, then-Attorney General Albert Gonzales cited the "drift toward lesser sentences" in federal criminal cases and urged Congress to enact a new sentencing system that would incorporate a new system of mandatory minimum sentencing rules. However, the U.S. Supreme Court continued to affirm that to be constitutional, sentencing guidelines published by the United States Sentencing Commission must be advisory, not mandatory.

Truth in Sentencing

Because they cannot eliminate parole, some states have taken another approach, called truth in sentencing. **Truth in sentencing** legislation requires the court to disclose the actual prison time that the offender is likely to serve. Some states (Arizona, California, and Illinois) have gone one step further and adopted what is known as the 85 percent requirement rule, which states that the offender must serve at least 85 percent of his or her sentence before becoming eligible for release. Thus, an offender sentenced to 10 years in prison would have to serve 8.5 years before being eligible for early release. Because offenders in many states routinely serve only one-third to one-half of their sentences, the 85 percent requirement significantly increases the actual time in prison.

HERE'S SOMETHING TO THINK ABOUT . . .

Raquel Nelson, a Black 30-year-old mother, was convicted of vehicular homicide in Marietta, Georgia, by an all-white jury when her 4-year-old son was struck and killed by a driver who had been drinking, taking pain killers, was mostly blind in one eye and had a prior conviction for a hit-and-run accident. She and her son crossed the street in the middle of the block and the prosecutor accused her of causing her son's death. The driver received a 6-month prison sentence and Nelson received 12 months probation. Was the sentence fair?

Sentencing and the Death Penalty

Capital punishment—the death penalty—can be traced back to the earliest records of human history. In English common law, the roots of the American system of justice, even minor thefts could be punished by death, and the prisoner could be tortured in the process. The American colonists did not shun the use of the death penalty. The criminal codes of 1642 and 1650 of the New Haven colony mandated the use of the death penalty not only for crimes of murder and treason, but also for crimes such as denying the true God and His attributes, bestiality, theft, horse theft, and children above the age of 16 striking their natural father or mother.[43]

Many Western countries, including England, France, Germany, and Italy, have banned the death penalty. Some nations have retained the death penalty in forms that are alien to U.S. values, such as execution by Sharia law, law based on Islamic religious values. For example, in March 2000, Judge Allah Baksh Ranja of Pakistan sentenced to death a man convicted of strangling and dismembering 100 children. The judge ordered Javed Iqbal, age 42, executed in a Lahore park in front of his victims' parents. He told the prisoner, "You will be strangled in front of the parents whose children you killed. Your body will then be cut into a hundred pieces and put in acid, the same way you killed the children."[44]

In the United States, lethal injection is the predominant method of execution (36 of the 37 states with a death penalty). Nine states authorize electrocution; 4 states, lethal gas; 3 states, hanging; and 3 states, a firing squad. Seventeen states authorize more than one method—lethal injection and an alternative method—usually decided by the condemned prisoner. The federal government uses lethal injection for

truth in sentencing in the application of presumptive sentencing in states that cannot eliminate parole, the legal requirement that courts disclose the actual prison time that the offender is likely to serve

capital punishment the sentence of death

6

The Supreme Court has consistently held that the death penalty is not a violation of the Eighth Amendment right not to be subjected to cruel and unusual punishment, but it has ordered that it be applied by states fairly, without discrimination, and only to crimes of murder.

offenses prosecuted under 28 Code of Federal Regulations, Part 26. Federal cases prosecuted under the Violent Crime Control Act of 1994 (18 United States Code 3596) call for the method used in the state in which the conviction took place.[45]

The Death Penalty and Abolitionists

On December 1, 2005, Kenneth Lee Boyd was executed by the State of North Carolina. He was the 1,000th person to be executed by the United States since the Supreme Court upheld states' rights to order the death penalty in 1976. Although there were protests against the execution of Boyd, public opinion supports the use of the death penalty. However, polls show that public support of the death penalty is dropping. In 2009, approximately 60 percent of Americans supported use of the death penalty, but that is down from a high of 80 percent in 1994.[46] Some people are opposed to the death penalty in specific cases for specific reasons, such as their belief that the person is innocent, the person did not receive a fair trial, or there is reasonable doubt that justifies an alternative sentence other than death. However, some people oppose the death penalty under all circumstances and for all reasons. They do not believe that the government has the right to execute citizens. Those universally opposed to the use of capital punishment are called **abolitionists.**

The debate between abolitionists and those who favor capital punishment is very old. One of the earliest debates about the death penalty was recorded by Greek philosopher Plato regarding Socrates, who was convicted by the Athenians of corrupting the morals of the youth and was sentenced to death. A friend tried to convince Socrates that he should escape because he was wrongfully convicted and said that other cities would welcome him as a citizen because they would recognize that the sentence was unjust. Socrates refused, however, arguing, "But whether in battle or in a court of law, or in any other place, he must do what his city and his country order him; or he must change their view of what is just. . . . He who has experience of the manner in which we order justice and administer the State, and still remains, has entered into an implied contract that he will do as we command him."[47] This argument—that there is an implicit contract between the individual and the state—is the crux of one of the most controversial debates in sentencing—the role of capital punishment.

One of the primary justifications for the use of the death penalty is that it is an effective deterrent to crime. The question of whether the death penalty deters crime is disputed by research data. Beccaria, the father of classical criminology, argued that the death penalty was not an effective deterrent. He argued that life in prison was a much greater punishment and much more dreaded by the offender than death. Some research studies claim that 3 to 18 murders are prevented for every inmate put to death. Other research studies claim that there is an inverse relationship between the use of the death penalty and the crime rate—crime goes down as the use of the death penalty goes up. Most experts believe that the research is inconclusive and unreliable. There are many factors that influence the crime rate, and the number of persons executed is so small compared to the number of offenses that experts do not think that the deterrent effect of the death penalty can be accurately gauged. When there are only 30 to 50 executions per year and these occur years and even decades after the crime was committed, researchers argue that correlations and data regarding the impact of the death penalty are unreliable.

Abolitionists claim that capital punishment is ineffective in preventing crime, is unfairly administered, and is sometimes administered in error, but the central premise of their arguments is that government does not have the right to take a person's life.[48] For example, the Southern Center for Human Rights argues against the death penalty, quoting freed slave Frederick Douglass, who became a champion of civil rights: "Life is the great primary and most precious and comprehensive of all human rights . . . whether it be coupled with virtue, honor, and happiness, or with sin, disgrace, and misery, the continued possession of it is rightfully not a matter of volition; . . . [It is not] to be deliberately or voluntarily destroyed, either by individuals separately, or combined in what is called Government."[49] Both abolitionists and proponents of the death penalty also argue for their views on the basis of religious values. Until 1968, abolitionists could be excluded from capital murder juries simply because they opposed the death penalty. Abolitionists opposed being barred from capital murder juries and appealed to the U.S. Supreme Court.

In *Witherspoon v. Illinois* (1968),[50] the U.S. Supreme Court declared unconstitutional the common practice of prosecutors of excluding abolitionists from capital murder juries. After the *Witherspoon* decision, the composition of juries in capital murder cases changed in that persons opposed in principle to the death penalty could not be excluded from the jury. Obviously, the inclusion of abolitionists on capital murder cases makes it harder, or even impossible, for prosecutors to obtain a unanimous verdict for the death penalty.

HERE'S SOMETHING TO THINK ABOUT . . .

In 2011, Illinois became the sixteenth state to abolish the death penalty. As with recent states to abolish the death penalty, two factors influenced the Illinois decision: the flaws in the criminal justice system that could permit the execution of an innocent person and the high cost of the death penalty. A death penalty case may cost $3 million to prosecute and $90,000 per year to house an inmate on death row. Are these legitimate reasons for abolishing the death penalty?

abolitionists people opposed to the death penalty

A 2008 study by the Urban Institute found that in cases in which prosecutors sought the death penalty, in only about one third of the cases did the jury return a death verdict, and most of those death sentences were overturned on appeal.

The Death Penalty and Civil Rights

In the United States, the death penalty sentence can be imposed by the state, the federal courts, military courts, and military tribunals. The use of the death penalty by federal courts, military courts, and military tribunals is governed by federal laws, executive orders, and the U.S. Supreme Court. Each state has the option of adopting the death penalty as a legal punishment for crime, and 37 states have done so. States that use the death penalty as a sanction must preserve the civil rights of the condemned prisoner as defined by the state and federal constitutions. Appeal to the U.S. Supreme Court has been a common strategy of abolitionists. Most appeals are based primarily on the Eighth Amendment, prohibiting cruel and unusual punishment, and the Fourteenth Amendment, providing for equality in justice.

The Issue of Cruel and Unusual Punishment An early appeal to the U.S. Supreme Court based on the Eighth Amendment was *Wilkerson v. Utah* (1878).[51] Wilkerson appealed to the U.S. Supreme Court that his sentence of death by firing squad was cruel and unusual, but the Court upheld the constitutionality of the sentence.

The first execution by electrocution took place at Auburn Prison (New York) on August 6, 1890. William Kemmler was sentenced to be executed for murder by use of the newly invented electric chair. Kemmler appealed to the Court that electrocution was cruel and unusual punishment. The Court disagreed, however, and execution by electrocution was added as another method of carrying out the death sentence.[52] In 1947, the Court was asked to take up another gruesome debate concerning electrocution: What if the person survives the first attempt at electrocution? Willie Francis, a 15-year-old black male, was convicted of killing Andrew Thomas by shooting him five times. The apparent motive was robbery; Francis took the victim's watch and $4. When the State of Louisiana attempted to execute Francis, the electric chair failed to provide a fatal surge of electricity and Francis survived. He appealed a second attempt as cruel and unusual punishment, but the Court disagreed and he was electrocuted in the second attempt.[53]

August 6, 1890

The first execution by electrocution took place at Auburn Prison in New York state.

The most recent Eighth Amendment challenge to the death penalty involved two Kentucky inmates under sentence of death who appealed their sentence on the grounds that the three-cocktail drug mixture used in lethal injection could result in unnecessary suffering and pain.[54] The challenge brought to a halt executions in most states because lethal injection and the drug mixture used by Kentucky was the most common method of execution. In April 2008, the U.S. Supreme Court denied the inmates' appeal and ruled that the method of execution was not a violation of the Eighth Amendment.

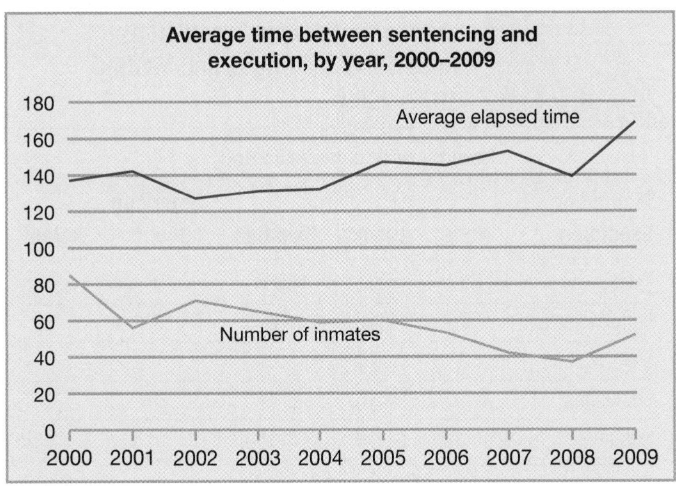

Average Time Between Sentencing and Execution, by Year

Source: Tracy L. Snell, *Capital Punishment*, 2007–Statistical Tables (Bureau of Justice Statistics, Washington, DC, 2010).

Other Civil Rights Issues The U.S. Supreme Court has also addressed other civil rights issues and the death penalty. For example, the Supreme Court has ruled that persons cannot be excluded from capital murder case juries because of their race. This situation most often arose when the defendant was Black and the prosecutor excluded Blacks from the jury by use of peremptory challenges. The Court ruled that exclusion of Blacks from the jury when the defendant was Black was racial discrimination. In 2002, the Supreme Court ruled that only juries, not judges, could decide sentences in capital cases. This ruling overturned state sentencing policies wherein the jury decided the guilt of the defendant but the judge decided whether the defendant would receive life in prison or the death penalty. The Court ruled that only the jury had the right to decide if the defendant should be eligible to be executed. Also, in 2002, the Supreme Court barred the execution of persons with mental retardation, and in 2005, barred the execution of juveniles.

Challenges to the Death Penalty

Furman v. Georgia In 1972, the U.S. Supreme Court effectively banned the use of the death penalty. In *Furman v. Georgia* (1972),[55] the Court issued its most significant ruling regarding the death penalty. Rather than focus on the physical and emotional pain of the prisoner as the grounds for regarding capital punishment as cruel and unusual, Furman's defense argued that the death penalty, as applied, was arbitrary and capricious. This argument presented evidence that a person convicted of a capital offense may or may not be executed, because the law and the state courts did not systematically apply the death penalty. Who was executed and

TABLE 8.4 **Number of Persons Executed by Race, Hispanic Origin, and Method, 1977–2009**

	Number of persons executed				
Method of Execution	White*	Black*	Hispanic	American Indian*	Asian*
Total	672	411	91	8	6
Lethal injection	576	338	89	7	6
Electrocution	83	70	2	1	0
Lethal gas	8	3	0	0	0
Hanging	3	0	0	0	0
Firing squad	2	0	0	0	0

*Excludes persons of Hispanic/Latino origin.

Source: Bureau of Justice Statistics, National Prisoner Statistics Program (NPS-8) http://bjs.ojp.usdoj.gov/content/pub/html/cp/2007/tables/cp07st16.cfm

who was not appeared to be determined randomly. The only common element in executions was not the crime but the socioeconomic and racial characteristics of the offenders—poor and Black (see Table 8.4).

The Supreme Court agreed and declared that all death penalty sentences were suspended until the state could prove that the death penalty was applied fairly. Despite this temporary ban and the Supreme Court's examination of the death penalty laws and practices

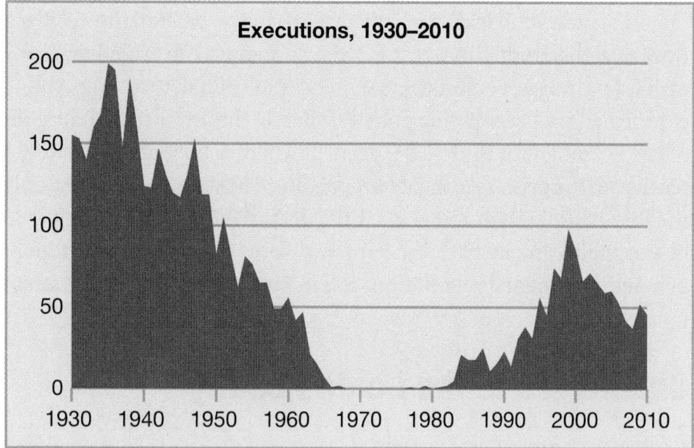

Executions declined from a all-time high in the mid-1930s to zero in 1972 when the Supreme Court banned the use of the death penalty in *Furman v. Georgia*. When executions resumed a decade later the number of executions peaked in the late-1990 and has declined since then.

Source: Tracy L. Snell, *Capital Punishment*, 2007–Statistical Tables (Bureau of Justice Statistics, Washington, DC, 2010).

of each state before the state could reinstate the death penalty, emphasis on eliminating racial bias and providing uniformity to death penalty sentences continues to be a challenge. Also, most prisoners who were under sentence of death had a less-than-average education, with the median education being 11th grade. In 2004, over 52 percent of prisoners sentenced to death did not graduate from high school nor have a graduate equivalency degree (GED).

There are two important points to note about the *Furman v. Georgia* decision. First, it did not declare that the death penalty was unconstitutional, only that the manner in which it was applied was unconstitutional. Second, all states were required to submit proof to the U.S. Supreme Court that their use of the death sentence was fair, equitable, and proportional to the crime. In effect, this ruling voided all existing death penalties and death penalty laws. Every prisoner in every state under the sentence of death was given a reprieve. However, rather than require new trials for all prisoners sentenced to death, the Court required only that the death sentence be reexamined. As a result of this ruling, each state that wanted to keep the death penalty as a sanction had to submit legislation to the Court for approval prior to resuming the use of the death penalty.

Criteria for the Death Penalty Some states attempted to satisfy the criteria by adopting mandatory death penalties for first-degree murder. The Court refused to allow this strategy, however, and required states to be more specific in defining the criteria to be used in applying the death penalty.[56] The Court further defined its criteria for proportionate punishment when it struck down Georgia's statute authorizing the death penalty for rape.[57] The Court ruled that the death penalty was grossly disproportionate to the crime. In 2008, the U.S. Supreme Court again considered whether the sentence of death was appropriate for crimes other than homicide. A number of states wanted to enact legislation that would provide for the death penalty for the rape of a child. In June 2008, the Supreme Court upheld its previous position that the death penalty was limited to the crime of murder. As a result, nearly all death penalties are for the crime of first-degree murder with aggravating circumstances.

Gregg v. Georgia In 1976, the U.S. Supreme Court issued another landmark decision in *Gregg v. Georgia* (1976),[58] which required a **bifurcated trial** structure in which trials for capital offenses had to be conducted in two separate parts. In the first part of the trial, the jury determines the guilt of the defendant. In the second part of the trial, after the defendant has been convicted, additional evidence can be introduced relevant to the punishment appropriate for the crime. Prior to 2002, although it was common to allow the jury to exclude the death penalty as an appropriate sanction for the crime, in some states the judge determined whether the defendant was sentenced to the death penalty.[59] In *Ring v. Arizona* (2002), the Supreme Court ruled that a jury, rather than a judge, must make a finding of "aggravating factors" when those factors underlie a judge's choice to impose the death penalty rather than a lesser punishment.[60]

bifurcated trial a two-part trial structure in which the jury first determines guilt or innocence and then considers new evidence relating to the appropriate punishment

Reconsideration of the Death Penalty

When more death row inmates were exonerated than executed in 2003, then governor George Ryan commuted the sentence of all inmates on death row to life in prison and called for an investigation into the use of the death penalty.[61] Illinois abolished the death penalty in 2011. The ABA called for a national moratorium on capital punishment, and 16 other states decided to examine their death penalty laws in 2000.[62] After years of debate, Florida ended the use of the electric chair in 2001.[63] In response to much criticism, Texas joined 15 other states and the federal government in passing a ban on executing murderers with mental retardation.[64] In December 2001, the Kansas Supreme Court ruled that the way the state's death penalty was handed down was unfair and must be changed, saying, "The provisions of the death penalty violated the federal constitutional provisions against cruel and unusual punishment and the guarantee of due process." This opinion voided the use of the death penalty until the state could rewrite the sentencing language.[65]

AN APOLOGY FOR THE WRONGFUL EXECUTION OF A PRISONER IS INSUFFICIENT AND DOES NOT RESTORE THE INJUSTICE DONE NOR HEAL THE HARM TO INNOCENT PERSONS.

In 2007, New Jersey adopted legislation that abolished the death penalty. In 2008, the state Supreme Court of Nebraska ruled that the electric chair is cruel and unusual punishment. This ruling effectively abolished the death penalty in Nebraska because it was the only state that still relied solely on electrocution. Although the death penalty remains in Nebraska, there is no means to carry out the sentence. Unless the state adopts new legislation authorizing the use of lethal injection, there will be no executions in Nebraska.

The Innocent Convicted Perhaps the most significant argument behind the reexamination of the death penalty is the alarming number of persons who have been wrongfully prosecuted and convicted.

439	number of inmates that Texas has executed between 1976 and September 1, 2009
35	number of wrongly convicted inmates that Texas has cleared in the same period
130	number of death row inmates who have been exonerated nationwide
242	number of wrongfully convicted persons who The Innocence Project claims have been exonerated using DNA evidence

The death penalty is final and cannot be reversed or corrected. An apology by the criminal justice system for the wrongful execution of a prisoner is insufficient and does not restore the injustice done nor heal the harm to innocent persons. For example, 60 years after Lena Baker, the only woman ever put to death in Georgia's electric chair, was executed, the State of Georgia announced that it would posthumously pardon her. Baker, a 40-year-old Black woman, was put to death in 1945 for killing her employer, a White man named E.B. Knight. At her trial, she contended that he held her as a kind of sex slave and she shot him in self-defense as he was attacking her with a crowbar. An all-male, all-White jury convicted her of capital murder in a 1-day trial, and she was executed in Georgia's electric chair less than a year later.[66] However, the Georgia Board of Pardons and Parole made it clear that the board did not find that Baker was not guilty of the crime, but it did find that the decision to deny her clemency in 1945 "was a grievous error, as this case called out for mercy."[67]

The wrongful conviction and execution of prisoners means that the guilty parties escape the justice that is due them. One study suggests that as many as 23 innocent defendants were executed between 1900 and 1988.[68] The criminal justice system is approaching a near-crisis of credibility regarding the wrongful deaths of persons accused of crime. Partly as a result of DNA evidence, many convicted prisoners are being freed from prison and death row. The impact of DNA evidence combined with recent revelations of official misconduct and corruption by police and prosecutors and with allegations of racial discrimination has led many people to question the continued use of the death penalty as a fair and just punishment.

Official Misconduct and Error A study considering 125 cases published in the North Carolina Law Review found that the leading causes of wrongful convictions for murder were false confessions and perjury by codefendants, informants, police officers, or forensic scientists.[69] The three groups of people most likely to provide false confessions are those with mental retardation, those with mental illness, and juveniles.

Malcolm Rent Johnson was convicted of rape and murder in 1982. Johnson claimed he was innocent, but forensic evidence disputed his protests of innocence. Johnson was executed on January 6, 2000. An investigation a year later into the accuracy of the forensic chemist's testimony, which was instrumental in convicting Johnson, strongly suggests that she gave false testimony about the evidence. Also, the evidence suggests that there may be at least two other cases in which the results stated in the lab report and confirmed by the state's forensic chemist contradict independent expert reexamination of the actual physical evidence.[70]

Some prisoners appear to have been wrongfully convicted because they were framed by police and/or prosecutors. Ronald Jones, who said police had beaten a confession out of him, was exonerated of charges of rape and murder.[71] After Rolando Cruz was convicted of murder and sentenced to death, a reexamination of his case resulted in his release. In addition, charges of conspiracy to obstruct justice and to commit official misconduct were filed against the police and district attorney

HERE'S SOMETHING TO THINK ABOUT . . .

Nevada State Prison exercise yard

Georgia Judge James Bodiford sentenced Brian Nichols to four sentences of life without parole, seven life sentences with parole, and 485 years for his crimes. Rapist Marvin Martin will have to serve 360 years in prison before he can be considered for parole. In 2010, at least 1 of every 11 individuals in prison is serving a life sentence, of which 29 percent will never be eligible for parole. Increasing use of life sentences is attributed to fear that due to prison overcrowding or liberal philosophy violent offenders will be released before their time and to a loss of confidence in personal redemption. However, long prison sentences have extraordinary costs associated with them. Do you favor the increasing use of long prison sentences? Why?

lawyers who prosecuted Cruz.[72] The investigation into the Los Angeles Police Department Ramparts scandal uncovered evidence that police framed numerous innocent citizens and obtained convictions on the basis of false evidence given by police officers.[73] Walter McMillian was released in 1993 after 6 years on death row, but the sheriff he claims framed him for the murder that put him there has not been prosecuted.[74] McMillian is one of 30 persons freed from death row who gathered in Chicago in 1998 for the first National Conference on Wrongful Convictions and the Death Penalty.

"THE DEATH PENALTY IS MOST FREQUENTLY IMPOSED AND CARRIED OUT ON THE POOR, THE NEGRO, AND THE MEMBERS OF UNPOPULAR GROUPS."

Ineffective Counsel Some prisoners have ended up on death row because of inadequate legal representation at trial. Gary Wayne Drinkard was convicted and spent 5 years on Alabama's death row. Drinkard was released after it was determined that his defense failed to introduce critical evidence and witnesses that would have proven his innocence. As an example of the need for death penalty reform, Southern Center for Human Rights director Stephen B. Bright presented Gary Drinkard as a witness at hearings on the Innocence Protection Act of 2001. Bright told the committee, "We have been very fortunate that the innocence of some of those condemned to die in our courts has been discovered by sheer happenstance and good luck. . . . The major reason that innocent people are being sentenced to death is because the representation provided to the poor in capital cases is often a scandal." The committee heard testimony that defendants were given lawyers fresh from law school or who had never before tried a death penalty case.[75]

In December 2001, a judge overturned the murder conviction of a man imprisoned for 27 years for murder. The judge ruled that the trial "was plagued by multiple problems which, cumulatively, present the inescapable conclusion that he was denied a fair trial." Even the widow of the murdered victim concurred, saying, "There's so much evidence that it wasn't him, and it doesn't look like there was any that says it was him."[76] Other prisoners who were wrongfully convicted have been released after 13 years,[77] 17 years,[78] and 24 years[79] of wrongful incarceration.

Racial Bias A report by the Leadership Conference on Civil Rights, a coalition of 180 civil rights groups, released in May 2000, concluded that Blacks and Hispanics are treated more harshly than Whites at every level of the criminal justice system, from investigation to sentencing.[80] A racially biased criminal justice system is deep-rooted in American history. In Virginia during the 1830s, there were only 5 capital crimes for Whites but at least 70 for Blacks.[81] Furthermore, there was a difference in severity of sentencing in which Blacks could receive the death penalty for any offense for which a White would receive 3 or more years' imprisonment.[82] In 1967, the President's Commission on Law Enforcement and Administration of Justice concluded, "The death penalty is most frequently imposed and carried out on the poor, the Negro, and the members of unpopular groups."[83] A 1973 study of offenders convicted of rape and sentenced to death shows that 13 percent of Blacks convicted of rape were sentenced to death, but only 2 percent of Whites convicted of rape were sentenced to death.[84] Blacks convicted of raping White women were more likely to be sentenced to death than Blacks convicted of raping Black women or White men convicted of raping either White women or Black women.

Furman v. Georgia (1972) explicitly recognized the application of the death penalty as potentially arbitrary and capricious and sought to put an end to sentencing abuses once and for all. The effectiveness of ending racial discrimination in the use of the death penalty is debatable, however. A 1996 Kentucky study of death sentences between 1976 and 1991 found that Blacks still had a higher probability of being sentenced to death than did homicide offenders of other races.[85]

The racial bias of the death penalty continues to be controversial. In December 2001, a federal judge overturned the death sentence of Mamia Abu-Jamal. Abu-Jamal had been convicted for the first-degree murder of Philadelphia police officer Daniel Faulkner in 1981. Abu-Jamal claimed he was a political prisoner and victim of racial discrimination.[86] In another case, a federal judge asked prosecutors to explain why they were seeking the death penalty against three alleged Latino drug gang members but not against mob boss Joseph Merlino and three other codefendants. Lawyers for the defense argued, "No distinction other than the race of the defendants . . . satisfactorily (or rationally) explains the filing of a death notice in the case at hand . . . and the decision

HERE'S SOMETHING TO THINK ABOUT . . .

U.S. laws are based primarily on Western European and Judeo-Christian values. Some countries base their laws on Islamic or Sharia law. There is great variety in the interpretation and implementation of Sharia law in Muslim societies but all claim their law is based on the Koran. While there are many similarities between U.S. and Sharia law there are striking differences and some incompatibility with a democratic state.

In 2010, Oklahoma passed a state constitutional amendment on the ballot that forbid state judges from considering international or Islamic law in deciding cases. Muneer Awad, executive director of the local Council on American-Islamic Relations, filed a lawsuit arguing the amendment violated the freedom of religion clause of the Constitution. Federal District Judge Vicki Miles-LaGrange granted a permanent injunction blocking certification of the amendment. Should courts be banned from deciding cases using Islamic law? Why?

not to return it in the Merlino matter."[87] Despite the decades of statistical data indicating that the death penalty is not color-blind, the U.S. Supreme Court has refused to admit statistical evidence of racial discrimination as a justification for reversing death sanctions against Blacks. In *McCleskey v. Kemp* (1987), the Court said that statistical data alone do not provide the level of proof necessary to claim that a specific death penalty violates the Eighth or Fourteenth Amendment.[88] A convicted person can obtain relief from the death penalty under the claim of racial discrimination only in the following circumstances:

1. if the decision makers in the case acted with discriminatory intent, and
2. if the legislature enacted or maintained the death penalty statute because of an anticipated racially discriminatory effect.[89]

The report of the Leadership Conference on Civil Rights does not blame overt racial bias for the disparities in the criminal justice system. The report, written by lawyers, says that "a self-fulfilling set of assumptions about the criminality of Blacks and Hispanics influences the decisions of police, prosecutors and judges in a way that accounts for the gap."[90] The report argues that these assumptions about the criminality of Blacks and Hispanics are far-reaching and are a primary cause for such police abuses as false arrest reports, lying under oath, and planting evidence against minority persons.[91]

What is the evidence for racial discrimination in American criminal justice? Should this be accepted as a self-fulfilling prophecy? Would statistics about racial discrimination in sentencing influence a jury to give a lighter sentence? Would a defense attorney use this argument to appeal a death sentence or try to win a stay of execution?

DNA Evidence The advent of DNA testing in the late 1980s has had a tremendous impact on the criminal justice system. By 1997, the FBI crime lab's DNA analysis unit had exonerated about 3,000 suspects. Nearly one in four of the suspects were exonerated but had already been charged with a crime before lab results were returned.[92] There are continuous reports of inmates freed from wrongful incarceration as a result of DNA evidence demonstrating that they could not have been the offenders.[93]

Collection of DNA from persons continues to expand to create vast DNA databases. In April 2009, the FBI and 15 states collected DNA samples from persons awaiting trial and from detained immigrants. In 2009, the FBI DNA database had 6.7 million profiles. The FBI projects that by 2014 it will add 1.2 million DNA profiles per year. In 35 states, minors are required to provide DNA samples upon conviction. Sixteen states take DNA from persons who have been convicted of misdemeanor crimes.

6.7 million
The number of DNA profiles that the FBI database contains as of 2009

1.2 million
Estimated number of additional profiles per year that the FBI will add to the database per year by 2014

16
Number of states that collect DNA samples from persons convicted of misdemeanors

Difficulties in Introducing DNA After Conviction The reliability of DNA evidence and the release of wrongfully convicted prisoners, often after serving years on death row, prove the fallibility of the criminal justice system. Often, the inmates who were released had to fight to get the courts to reconsider their cases. Courts have adopted rules limiting the amount of time that may pass before new evidence will be considered[94] or have refused to allow DNA testing of prisoners who have already been executed.[95] In many cases, the criminal justice system has refused to reopen cases for which DNA testing could provide new evidence.[96]

A comprehensive study of 328 criminal cases over the last 15 years in which the convicted person was exonerated suggests that there are thousands of innocent people in prison today.[97] The study identified 199 murder exonerations, 73 of them in capital cases. Yet, only two states, Illinois and New York, give inmates the right to use the latest DNA testing. Appeals procedures make it difficult to introduce DNA evidence after a conviction. Convicted defendants are not entitled to appeal the court's decision of guilt based on a claim of innocence. Most courts allow appeals only based on trial errors that could have had a significant effect on the verdict or on new evidence that was not available at the time of the trial. Appeals based on DNA evidence commonly claim the latter. However, new evidence alone is not sufficient for a successful appeal. For a case appealed based on new evidence, the court requires the defendant to demonstrate that there is a reasonable possibility that the new evidence would prove his or her innocence. If the court determines that the evidence presented at the original trial provides substantial proof of the inmate's guilt, the court will reject appeals for DNA testing. Thus, if there is physical evidence such as fingerprints, bloody clothing, the murder weapon, and reliable eyewitness testimony, the court will deny an inmate's appeal for DNA testing. The U.S. Supreme Court has upheld the denial of requests for DNA testing. In *District Attorney's Office for the Third Judicial District v. Osborne* (2009), the Court ruled that prisoners do not have a constitutional right to DNA testing after their conviction.

In some cases involving prisoners who have demonstrated through post-trial DNA testing that the trial evidence does not support their guilt, prosecutors still have refused to accept that the convicted defendant may be innocent.[98] The law does not protect the right of convicted inmates to appeal based on DNA evidence, and some states routinely destroy rape kits and other evidence that could be used to establish prisoners' innocence.[99] A study by Brandon L. Garrett at the University of Virginia School of Law found that prosecutors opposed DNA testing in about 20 percent of cases. However, in about 43 percent of DNA testing cases, the DNA test identified the perpetrator.[100]

The Debate Continues What is the purpose of sentencing? Is it to punish the offender, to rehabilitate the offender, or to protect the community? The National Institute of Justice sponsored research that examined the crime-control effects of sentences over a 20-year period, based on 962 felony offenders sentenced in 1976 or 1977 in Essex County, New Jersey.[101] The purpose of this longitudinal study was to examine the effects of the different sanctions on the offenders' subsequent criminal careers. The study concluded that the main sentencing choices available to the judges had little effect on crime-control aims. Specifically, the study concluded the following:[102]

- Except for the effect of incapacitation, whether or not the offender was sentenced to confinement made no difference in the rate of reoffending.
- Where the offender was confined made little difference—except for the unfavorable effect of placement in a youth facility.
- The length of the maximum sentence made no difference.
- The length of time actually confined made a slight difference.
- When jail was imposed along with probation, it made no difference.
- Fines or restitution made no difference.

The overall conclusion of the study was that empirical data suggested that sentences made little difference in crime control perspective.[103] Such data do not provide a happy ending to the discussion on sentencing. New and innovative sentencing strategies are constantly being tried. Laws defining the punishment for crimes and sentencing guidelines are being revised. People are examining the effect of sentencing and the fallibility of the criminal justice system and are making new recommendations to improve the criminal justice system.

Sentencing is an important crossroad in the criminal justice system. It is harmful to convict the innocent and to impose sentences that do not deter criminality. It is also harmful that there are so many possibilities for error in the use of the death penalty. Sentencing and sentencing reform will continue to be subjects of study and debate.

HERE'S SOMETHING TO THINK ABOUT . . .

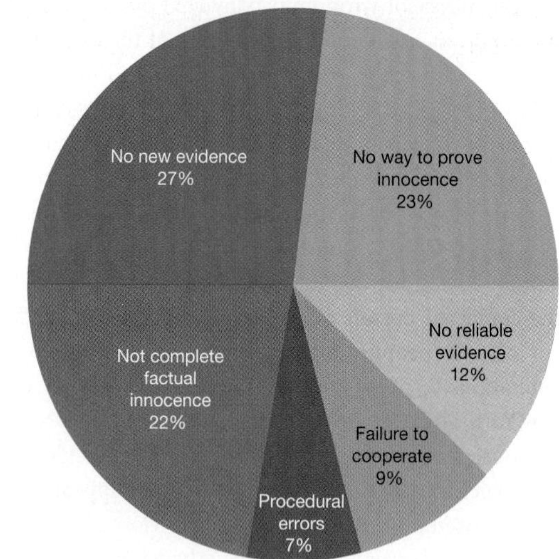

Reasons the North Carolina Innocence Inquiry Commission rejected the appeals of 897 cases. (Some cases were rejected for multiple reasons.)

Source: North Carolina Innocence Inquiry Commission, www.innocencecommission-nc.gov/stats.html, November, 2011

Sentenced to serve 75 years for rape, Michael Green, an 18-year-old Black man, proclaimed his innocence but no one listened. Green's victim picked him out of a lineup and she was certain of her identification. In 2001, a new Texas law granted inmates the right to request DNA evidence. In 2005 Green submitted a motion he typed himself for review but nothing happened for 3 years because of the backlog of requests. In 2008, Patricia Lykos was elected Harris County (TX) district attorney. She formed a unit to review the over 250 claims of innocence. After a year and a half DNA evidence identified two other men, not Green, as the assailants. Green was released after spending 27 years in prison for a crime he did not commit. The state of Texas offered Green a settlement of $2.2 million compensation payment.

Green's story is not unique. What is unique is that he was offered a compensation payment, as many exonerated persons receive no such offer. More than three-quarters of the 258 people exonerated by DNA tests in the last decade were convicted on the strength of eyewitness identifications, according to the Innocence Project.

Most state criminal justice systems do not allow an appeal based on a claim of innocence. The Harris County District Attorney's Office review of claims of innocence is unusual. Only North Carolina allows inmates to appeal their sentence based on a claim of factual innocence. The North Carolina Innocence Inquiry Commission, established in 2006, has received nearly 1,000 petitions. In only one case has the inmate been exonerated. Should all states have a means for a convicted person to appeal based on a claim of innocence?

CHAPTER 8

Sentencing

Check It!

1 WHAT are the purposes of sentencing? p. 130

The main purposes for sanctioning criminals are:

1. deterrence
2. incapacitation
3. retribution
4. rehabilitation
5. restorative justice

2 HOW does the criminal justice system sentence the offender with mental illness? p. 134

In an insanity defense, it is up to the jury to determine whether the defense has proved clearly and convincingly that the offender lacked the capacity to understand the wrongfulness of his or her conduct at the time the crime was committed. An alternative to the verdict of not guilty by reason of insanity is guilty but mentally ill, in which the defendant was sufficiently aware of his or her actions to be held morally responsible for the crime.

3 WHAT factors influence whether a defendant receives a fair sentence? p. 136

For a defendant to receive a fair sentence, the following factors are necessary:

1. equitable laws
2. a fair and unbiased judge
3. a fair and unbiased prosecutor
4. a capable defense attorney
5. an unbiased jury
6. a fair and accurate presentencing investigation

4 WHAT is the process of a presentence investigation and sentence hearing? p. 137

A presentencing investigator examines the convicted offender's background, the circumstances surrounding the crime, and the offender's attitude, or remorse. The investigator presents his or her report at the sentencing hearing, at which victim impact statements may be heard before the judge pronounces the sentence.

5 HOW do various sentencing models influence a sentence? p. 138

1. A judge has broad discretion in an indeterminate sentencing model.
2. Structured sentencing models allow the judge less discretion:
   - determinate sentencing: the offender is sentenced to a fixed term
   - mandatory sentencing: the offender is sentenced to the full sentence
   - habitual offender sentencing: the repeat offender is punished more harshly
   - sentencing guidelines: the offender is sentenced within a specified range of time
   - presumptive sentencing: sentencing guidelines are balanced with mandatory guidelines

6 HOW have U.S. Supreme Court rulings affected the death penalty sentence, and how has the Court responded to civil rights challenges to the death penalty? p. 143

The Supreme Court has consistently held that the death penalty is not cruel and unusual punishment, but it has ordered that it be applied by states fairly, without discrimination, and only to crimes of murder.

Assess Your Understanding

1. Which model of sentencing is based on the assumption that punishment should be used to prevent people from committing crimes or reoffending?
   a. rehabilitation
   b. retribution
   c. incapacitation
   d. deterrence

2. Which sentencing model focuses on punishments that prevent the offender from having the opportunity to reoffend in the community?
   a. rehabilitation
   b. retribution
   c. incapacitation
   d. deterrence

3. Why does the criminal justice system provide a different standard of punishment for offenders with mental illness?
   a. The law assumes the defendant lacks the necessary *mens rea* to be held criminally liable for his or her actions.
   b. It has always been the tradition.
   c. It would create a security problem if the mentally ill were held in the same prisons as other inmates.
   d. It would be too expensive to imprison the mentally ill as the government would be responsible for their health care.

4. Why is there concern over the selection of judges by popular election?
   a. Popular election of judges provides the political parties with little influence over the quality of justice.
   b. Federal judges are not selected by popular election and there is public concern that federal judges are out of touch with the values of the community.
   c. The cost of elections and the need to win elections may influence the fairness and impartiality of judges.
   d. none of the above

5. Which of the following data are normally gathered in a presentence investigation of a convicted defendant?
   a. the defendant's past criminal record
   b. the defendant's life history
   c. whether the defendant accepts responsibility for his or her guilt
   d. all of the above

6. How do habitual offender laws or "three-strike" laws influence the sentence a defendant receives?
   a. Only youthful offenders who commit more than three offenses are eligible for probation.
   b. Only youthful offenders who commit more than three offenses are eligible for parole.
   c. The sentence of imprisonment for convicted habitual offenders is longer than other offenders would receive for the same offense.
   d. both a and b

7. Which sentencing model requires the court to disclose the actual prison time that the offender is likely to serve as opposed to the time sentenced?
   a. presumptive sentencing
   b. sentencing guidelines
   c. mandatory sentencing
   d. truth in sentencing

8. What was the effect of *Witherspoon v. Illinois* (1968) on capital murder cases?
   a. It required a fair and impartial jury by race.
   b. It prohibited the exclusion of persons opposed to the death penalty in juries for capital murder cases.
   c. It required an equal number of men and women jurors in capital murder cases.
   d. It prohibited the sentence of death for any crime other than murder.

9. What was the effect of *Furman v. Georgia* (1972) on the use of the death penalty?
   a. It required a fair and impartial jury by race.
   b. It suspended the use of the death penalty until states could prove that the penalty was applied fairly.
   c. It provided for a bifurcated trial in capital murder cases.
   d. none of the above

10. What was the effect of *Gregg v. Georgia* (1976) on the death penalty?
    a. It required a bifurcated trial in capital murder cases.
    b. It suspended the use of the death penalty until states could prove that the death penalty was applied fairly.
    c. It prohibited the exclusion of persons opposed to the death penalty in juries for capital murder cases.
    d. It required a fair and impartial jury by race.

ESSAY

1. Describe the various models of sentencing and the stated purpose of each.
2. Why does the criminal justice system have a different standard for sentencing offenders with mental illness? What is the public concern regarding this difference?
3. What factors influence whether a defendant receives a fair sentence?
4. What is the purpose of a presentence investigation and what data does it gather?
5. How do the various sentencing models affect criminal justice sentencing practices?
6. What are the arguments for and against the death penalty?

ANSWERS: 1. d, 2. c, 3. a, 4. c, 5. d, 6. c, 7. d, 8. b, 9. b, 10. a

Media

Go to the *Chapter 8: Sentencing* section in *MyCJLab* to test your understanding of this chapter, access customized study content, engage in interactive simulations, complete critical thinking and research assignments, and view related online videos.

Additional Links

See www.curenational.org, the Web site of Citizens United for Rehabilitation of Errants (CURE). CURE is a nonprofit national organization dedicated to reducing crime through rehabilitation programs and reforms of the criminal justice system.

Go to www.derechos.org to access Derechos Human Rights, an Internet-based human rights organization that offers links to a number of other Web sites with information about the death penalty.

Go to www.innocenceproject.org to visit the Web site of The Innocence Project. The Innocence Project is a national litigation and public policy organization dedicated to exonerating wrongfully convicted people through DNA testing and reforming the criminal justice system to prevent future injustice.

To visit Web sites for and against the death penalty, see www.deathpenalty.org to view the Web site of an organization that argues against the death penalty, and www.prodeathpenalty.com to view the Web site of an organization that argues for the death penalty.

For information about the history of the death penalty and state-by-state information on executions, see the Web site of the Death Penalty Information Center at www.deathpenaltyinfo.org

To watch a short MSNBC news report on concerns about the community's fear of the release of defendants into the community who have been found not guilty by reason of insanity, go to www.bing.com/videos/watch/video/not-guilty-by-reason-of-insanity/6kx1wrz

To watch a detailed explanation of the criminal trial procedures produced for judges, go to www.youtube.com/watch?v=f9FkvCjfRBI

To see a graphic video of a caning in a Singapore prison, go to www.liveleak.com/view?i=3c9_1304013159 Warning: This video contains violence and may not be suitable for all audiences.

To watch Archbishop Desmond Tutu talk about restorative justice, go to www.youtube.com/watch?v=MCEboJ1k5Ek

To watch a short video on the presentence investigation report, go to www.youtube.com/watch?v=i7u-SMz5oHs

To watch a video on the California repeat offender enhanced sentencing (three-strikes law), go to www.youtube.com/watch?v=FyzCHZZg5P8

For more information on the Raquel Nelson case (page 143) watch one of the following videos:
www.youtube.com/watch?v=vf-kUxmkymo
www.youtube.com/watch?v=iHbk_jFyZoc
www.cbsnews.com/video/watch/?id=7374699n

To watch an Amnesty USA video on advocating the abolishment of the death penalty, go to www.youtube.com/watch?v=Er2lPq4M2f4

EAST
GATE

9 JAILS AND PRISONS

Kensley Hawkins, 60, is serving 60 years in an Illinois state prison. His projected parole date is 2028 and Hawkins has been diligent about saving money from the $75 a month he earns as a furniture assembler. Over the past 21 years he has saved $11,000 from his prison job; however, Hawkins is in danger of losing his life's savings. State law allows the Illinois Department of Corrections (IDOC) to seize inmates' assets greater than $10,000 to pay for their imprisonment. The IDOC claims Hawkins owes the state $456,000 for his incarceration to date. In addition, the IDOC is authorized to collect 3 percent of Hawkins's prison income, about $751. In 2009, the IDOC sued Hawkins for the $456,000 and the $751. The trial court awarded the state a judgment against Hawkins but denied the request to access his savings from prison income to pay for the $455,000. In June 2011, the Illinois Court of Appeals reversed the decision prohibiting the state from seizing his prison savings. Hawkins appealed the case to the Illinois Supreme Court and waits to see if the state supreme court will overturn the judgment against him and leave him with his nest egg. Why is the state of Illinois seeking his savings? They need the money.

1. **What was the philosophy in colonial times that established American jails?**
2. **How did early American jails and prison systems progress from their earliest times to the present state of prison systems?**
3. **What is the purpose of jails, and what types of jails are there?**
4. **What is the purpose of state prisons, what are their classification systems and special populations, and how do they reflect racism?**
5. **How is the federal prison system organized?**
6. **What is privatization, and what are its advantages and disadvantages?**
7. **What are some of the major challenges resulting from the record high use of incarceration?**

In the late 1700s John Howard focused Europe's attention on the horrific state of prisons and the need for reform. In the early 1800s the United States led the world in new correctional philosophies, prison design, and prison administration. In the mid-1900s the decisions of the Marshall court defined a new humanitarian era for prisoner rights. In the twenty-first century the focus of corrections is on curtailing expenses and getting by with much, much less. Illinois and nearly every other state in the nation are facing a fiscal crisis. Illinois is one of the worst-hit states. States have raided their correctional budgets as a source of funding for other state programs and services in peril.

Starting in the 1970s the correctional population began a dramatic increase requiring more and more state and federal funding to staff and run prisons. For some states the cost of jails and prisons outstripped the government's resources as prison populations hit record highs. Discussion of corrections no longer centered on the effectiveness of programs, rehabilitation of incarcerated offenders, or reentry programs but on cost containment. The upside of this crisis is that after decades of emphasis on "get tough sentencing," states are beginning to examine the wisdom of long prison terms and mass incarceration. People are beginning to ask, "Is there a better and cheaper way to handle convicted offenders?" The financial crisis has sparked new thinking as to best practices in corrections.

THE FINANCIAL CRISIS HAS SPARKED NEW THINKING AS TO BEST PRACTICES IN CORRECTIONS.

This chapter reviews the history and role of jails and prisons in the United States. It discusses the diversity of persons confined in jails, state prisons, and federal facilities. It examines the classification system and the challenges associated with special prison populations. It closes by discussing important issues associated with institutional incarceration such as prison life, the financial crisis, and the increasing use of private prisons.

Development of American Jails and Prisons

The first institutions for **incarceration** of prisoners in colonial America and the United States were local jails, which served primarily for detention prior to trial or execution rather than for punishment or rehabilitation of the criminal.[1] In 1681, for example, the community of West Jersey required that condemned persons be kept in safe confinement until the next General Assembly after the governor had reviewed their cases.[2] Prisoners were confined until their punishments could be determined. Prisoners incarcerated in local jails were expected to work for their daily keep or to pay for it. They were not housed at the expense of the community.[3] In colonial America, jails for the most part were operated by private parties, and after the Revolutionary War, they were operated by the sheriff. Early jails were more like secure houses than the fortified structures of today. Apparently, early jails were not all that secure, however, because prisoners often escaped from them. The colony of New Jersey reported 1,830 escapes from jails between 1751 and 1777, an average rate of 67 per year.[4]

THE FIRST INSTITUTIONS FOR INCARCERATION OF PRISONERS IN COLONIAL AMERICA AND THE UNITED STATES WERE LOCAL JAILS.

Early Jail Conditions

16
number of prisoners that were housed in one
12x12
foot cell in a 1767 Boston jail

Conditions in early jails were deplorable, and descriptions of them are difficult to imagine. As jails increasingly were used to incarcerate those with mental illness and the poor, overcrowding became a serious problem. One 1767 description of an early jail in Charlestown (Boston) reported that 16 debtors were housed in a single 12-by-12-foot room. The cell was so crowded that one of the prisoners died of suffocation but could not be removed until all of the other prisoners were first made to lie down to make room to retrieve the dead prisoner.[5]

In early jails, it was the prisoners' responsibility to provide for their basic necessities of life with their own funds or with the help of outside benefactors. Prisoners with the financial resources to provide for themselves could do so, but the state had no obligation to provide food or medical treatment for indigents. The more wealthy prisoners could buy additional cell space, food, and privileges, and even liquor was commonly made available to those who could afford it.[6] Prisoners who could not afford to pay for their accommodations were required to toil on public works projects in exchange for their keep. Those who could not work were allowed to beg passersby for food or money. Records indicate that some prisoners who were unable to provide for their daily needs were allowed to die of starvation.[7]

The portrait of American local jails at the birth of the nation is unpleasant to say the least. The jails were filled with all sorts of people—criminals as well as victims of misfortune. Men, women, and children were confined in the same cell, and no attempt was made to protect women and children from aggressive male prisoners. Sick prisoners were not separated from the healthy, so contagious diseases quickly and easily spread in the crowded and unsanitary conditions. Jails were not heated, did not have plumbing, and did not provide adequate per-person sleeping and living space. A primary factor in keeping the local jail population down was the death of many prisoners.[8] In 1777, English reformer John Howard traveled extensively in Europe, visiting jails and prisons. As a result, he wrote *State of Prisons*, a critical review of the brutality and inhumane conditions of Europe's penal systems. Howard's book was very influential and contributed to efforts at prison reform on both sides of the Atlantic.

Reform at Last: The Walnut Street Jail

In America, the prison reform movement had its origins with a group of Quakers called the Philadelphia Society to Alleviate the Miseries of Public Prisons.[9] In 1787, Benjamin Rush argued for prison reform at a meeting of the Society for Promoting Political Inquiries at the home of Benjamin Franklin. The Philadelphia Society to Alleviate the Miseries of Public Prisons was formed as a result, and this group lobbied the Pennsylvania legislature for humane treatment of prisoners. The group was successful, and in 1790, the Pennsylvania legislature passed a law calling for the renovation of the Walnut Street Jail in Philadelphia.[10] In addition to a humane physical facility and adequate food and water supplied at public expense,[11] the reform effort was successful in abolishing the practice of placing men, women, and children in the same cell and allowing prisoners to buy better treatment; prohibiting the consumption of alcohol by the prisoners; and separating the debtors and those with mental illness from the criminal population. Children, many confined only because they were orphans, were removed from the jail and housed in a separate building.[12]

Prisoners in the Walnut Street Jail were required to work but were paid for their labor and could earn early release for good behavior. The new jail was a great improvement over previous conditions of imprisonment, and leaders came from other states to investigate the possibility of adopting the Walnut Street Jail model for their states.[13] However, the Walnut Street Jail ultimately failed because of overcrowding, which

1 **The invention of prisons in colonial times was based on the philosophy that prisons should be terrifying places and include corporal punishment so as to rehabilitate offenders who had committed moral lapses.**

incarceration the bodily confinement of a person in a jail or prison

destroyed its ability to accomplish its mission. As a result of receiving state funding for renovation, the Walnut Street Jail became a temporary state prison, allowing prisoners from other cities in Pennsylvania to be housed there. The jail quickly filled beyond capacity.[14] Conditions deteriorated, and the cost of operating the jail became prohibitive. The goal of making prisons places for rehabilitation was crushed.

Bigger Is Better: Eastern State Penitentiary

$500,000.00
Cost to build the Eastern State Penitentiary

250 Number of prisoners that could be housed in the new building

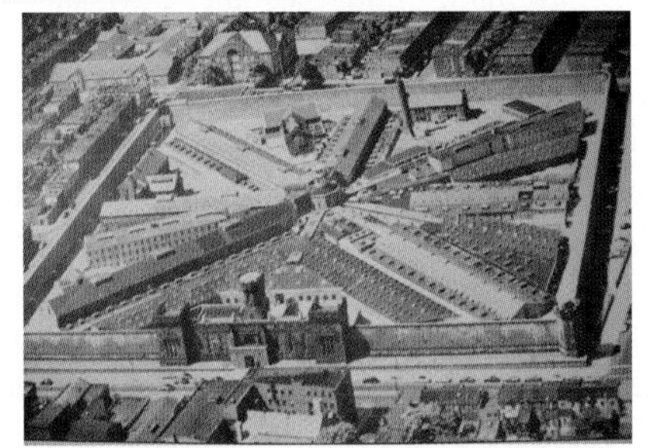

Built in 1829, Eastern State Penitentiary was the first public building built with flush toilets and hot-air heating

By 1820, the hopes that Walnut Street Jail would be the model for prison reform were dashed, and overcrowding of the state's only prison required that a new institution be built. Pennsylvania's Eastern State Penitentiary, built in 1829, was an enormous investment of state resources and was based on a new philosophy of rehabilitation. Built at a cost of $500,000 to house 250 prisoners, it was the most expensive public building in the New World and the first in the country to have flush toilets and hot-air heating.[15]

Penitence Eastern State Penitentiary was not designed as a jail or a prison but as a penitentiary. In a **penitentiary**, it was expected that inmates would reflect on their lives of crime and change their ways. To encourage this transformation, Eastern State Penitentiary had an individual cell for each prisoner. Prisoners were required to become proficient at a skill that would support them after their release, such as woodworking or leatherworking. When not working or exercising, prisoners were expected to read the Bible, the only literature allowed in their cells. Prisoners were kept in isolation from one another to avoid corrupting influences, and a "silent system" was enforced. The **silent system** required that prisoners communicate only with guards or prison officials; communication with other prisoners was forbidden. The goal of incarceration was to evoke penitence in the prisoner, with the idea that guilt and remorse or repentance would lead to rehabilitation, and prisoners could be released to lead normal, productive lives. This philosophy was compatible with the classical criminology theories and religious values of the period, emphasizing that crime was a rational choice made by the offender.

EASTERN STATE PENITENTIARY WAS NOT DESIGNED AS A JAIL OR A PRISON BUT AS A PENITENTIARY.

Self-Contained Cells Eastern State Penitentiary was a maximum-security, walled, self-contained institution. It had seven wings like the spokes of a wheel that extended from a hublike center. Inmate cells were located on either side of the wings with outside windows. In the middle of the wing was a central passageway for use by guards and prison officials. Following the model of solitary confinement, the cells were designed so that inmates could not see any part of the prison other than what was directly in front of the cell. Cells were 12 feet long by 7.5 feet wide and had a window. Some inmates had a small outside exercise yard but seldom had a chance to leave their cells. The institution's design called for all activities—working, exercise, eating, and sleeping—to be performed within the individual prisoner's cell.

As with the Walnut Street Jail, many people came to view Eastern State Penitentiary to see if it could be a solution to their penal problems. The single-cell model reduced problems with inmate discipline. Inmates rarely had the chance to violate any rules, because they seldom left their cells or interacted with other inmates. As a result, corporal punishment was practically eliminated. Inmates were motivated to be productive and abide by the rules in exchange for the chance of early release and financial reward for their work.

The Auburn System

During the early history of American prisons, the Pennsylvania model of individual cells competed for popularity against the Auburn, New York, prison model of the congregate work system as new prisons were constructed. The single-cell plan was expensive, and as prison populations increased, many states found that the cost of single-cell construction was prohibitive and turned to New York's Auburn system as the model for constructing new prisons. Built in 1816, Auburn Prison was a walled, maximum-security prison with inmate cells located in the center of a secure building. The cells in Auburn were smaller (7 feet long, 4 feet wide, and 7 feet high), with back-to-back cells stacked five tiers high. This arrangement made it possible to house many more prisoners more cheaply and with much less space. Unlike the design of Eastern State Penitentiary, Auburn's design housed inmates in the center of the building without an outside window or exercise area. The cells were poorly lit and lacked access to fresh air. The cells stacked one on top of another created a unique prison architecture, called an **inside cell block**. This architectural model for housing prison inmates became a distinctive feature of the American penal system.

penitentiary a correctional institution based on the concept that inmates could change their criminality through reflection and penitence

silent system the correctional practice of prohibiting inmates from talking to other inmates

inside cell block prison construction in which individual cells are stacked back to back in tiers in the center of a secure building

HERE'S SOMETHING TO THINK ABOUT...

The imprisonment of Native Americans raises many issues. First, although subject to U.S. laws, Native Americans living on reservations have their own separate criminal justice system. Second, Native Americans are disproportionately made victims and incarcerated. Finally, although prisons provide inmates with certain First Amendment rights to perform Native American spiritual rituals, such as using sweat lodges, these often present a challenge to prison administrators. The Court has ruled that prisons must allow Native Americans to practice their religious beliefs while incarcerated. Prison administrators classify Native American worship as an "outside" religion and provide appropriate accommodations for their rituals. In fact, prisons must provide reasonable accommodations for all religions including Satanism, Worshipers of Thor, nature worshipers, and almost any obscure sect you can imagine. Should prisons be required to accommodate unusual religious practices of inmates?

Work and Punishment Auburn's cells were too small to be the inmate's "home," as in the Eastern State Penitentiary. Auburn's cells were only for sleeping; during the day, inmates were moved to other areas to work and eat. This pattern is known as the **congregate work system**. Because inmates were moved from place to place within the prison, Auburn required a different type of administration. To minimize the opportunity for plotting escapes or uprisings, inmates were not permitted to talk to one another. However, unlike in the Eastern State Penitentiary, the silent system was more difficult to enforce, because inmates worked and ate together and met as they moved from place to place in the prison. To enforce silence, Auburn adopted a system of corporal punishment for violations of the rule. Flogging was administered as punishment, not for the crime but for violating prison rules. The floggings were designed to be painful but not to maim the inmate or require medical attention.[16]

FOLLOWING THE CIVIL WAR, APPROXIMATELY 90 PERCENT OF THOSE INCARCERATED IN THE SOUTH WERE FREE BLACKS.

Prisoners being moved from one location to another were required to march in a lockstep formation—marching in unison with one hand on the shoulder of the man ahead and all heads turned in the direction of the guard. When the inmates arrived at their destination, they continued to mark time until commanded to stop. Also, all prisoners had a similar short haircut and were required to wear distinctive clothing with stripes to clearly identify their status as prison inmates. Thus, the prisoners' schedule, movements, and appearance were strictly regulated.[17]

Solitary Confinement In 1821, the New York legislature passed a law requiring that the "worst inmates" held at Auburn be placed in **solitary confinement**.[18] These inmates were cut off from all contact with other people, including visitors, and were confined to their cells with only a Bible to read. Unlike inmates at Eastern State Penitentiary, however, Auburn inmates in solitary confinement had no work to do, no exercise yard, and a very small cell. Lacking knowledge of the harmful effects of long-term solitary confinement (the sciences of sociology and psychology did not emerge until the 1900s), the legislature had created a prison environment antithetical to rehabilitation. Inmates in solitary confinement had mental breakdowns and committed suicide. The alarming debility and death rates forced the state to abandon this practice.[19]

Economic Self-Sufficiency Because inmates worked together in the Auburn system, the prison could combine their labor in larger and more profitable industries and construction projects. The sale of prison-made goods was so successful, the prison was virtually economically self-sufficient and required few resources from the state budget.[20] Whereas the Eastern State Penitentiary model required more and more state resources to operate as the prison population rose, only 13 years after Auburn opened, the warden announced that he no longer needed state funds to run the prison.[21] The Auburn system became the prototype of the American prison. The economic advantages appealed to other states, and between 1825 and 1969, 29 state prisons were built using the Auburn model. Many of these institutions, such as New York's Sing Sing, are still in use today.[22]

Southern Penal Systems

Convict Lease System Many northern states used the Auburn system as a prison model. Southern states, however, developed their own unique prison system, based on different historical circumstances. The South retained an agrarian economy rather than an industry-based, factory economy. Southern prisons practiced the **convict lease system** to supply the farm labor once provided by slaves. Rather than build large maximum-security prisons to produce prison-labor-made goods, southern states leased prisoners to private contractors. Inmate labor was used for agricultural work, some factory work, and construction work. The private contractor assumed all responsibility for the care and support of inmates and paid the state a fee for the inmates' labor. This prisoner lease system permitted southern states to deal with great increases in the prison population following the Civil War, without requiring the states to finance the construction of prisons. For some states, a significant amount of the state's income was derived from the sale of convict labor.[23]

Chain Gangs Following the Civil War, approximately 90 percent of those incarcerated in the South were free Blacks. Work and living conditions

congregate work system the practice of moving inmates from sleeping cells to other areas of the prison for work and meals

solitary confinement the practice of confining an inmate such that there is no contact with other people

convict lease system a practice of some Southern penal systems of leasing prisoners to private contractors as laborers

for inmates were wretched, and convicts worked 12 to 15 hours a day. States did not set minimum standards for living conditions and did not inspect the sites where inmates were housed. Inmates who performed agricultural work often were housed in temporary, portable cages near the work site. Thus, prisoners were no better off than during slavery, and discipline was brutal.[24] To prevent escapes when the prisoners worked in open areas, they were shackled together in what came to be known as the **chain gang**. The prisoner death rate in this system was over twice as high in southern prisons as in northern prisons.[25]

Prison Farms The prisoner lease system was used until the 1930s, when it was replaced by the **prison farm system**, or plantation system. Rather than lease prison labor to private contractors, the state used inmate labor to maintain large prison farm complexes. These prison farms were expected to be self-sufficient and profit-making. Some states expanded the concept and used prison labor to operate other profit-making industries. To reduce the costs of operating prison farms and prison industries, states often used inmates as guards and supervisors of other inmates.

Changing social consciousness in the southern states eventually ended for-profit prisons and use of inmate "trusties" to maintain security. Arkansas, however, continued to use the prison farm system, with its many abuses, until the 1960s.[26] A series of U.S. Supreme Court cases then ruled the penal practices in Arkansas unconstitutional.[27] The Court also decided that whipping for disciplinary purposes and the use of electric shock were cruel and unusual punishments. In its decision, the Court declared, "For the ordinary convict a sentence to the Arkansas Penitentiary today amounts to a banishment from civilized society to a dark and evil world completely alien to the free world culture."[28] The State of Texas also practiced the plantation farm system and came under public criticism and the scrutiny of the Court. As in the case of Arkansas, a series of U.S. Supreme Court rulings forced Texas to reform its prison system.

Contemporary Jails and Prisons

Highest Incarceration Rate in the World At the turn of the nineteenth century, American prisons were considered at the cutting edge of correctional philosophy. American prisons attracted visitors from both other states and foreign countries to study the innovations there. Many of these visitors returned home, encouraging the adoption of these new correctional philosophies and architecture. However, by the beginning of the twenty-first century, American prisons had become known worldwide not for their innovations but for their high incarceration rate of Americans. With less than 5 percent of the world's population and a quarter of the world's prisoners, the United States has the highest incarceration rate of any country in the world. This record includes not only the number of persons incarcerated but also the length of incarceration and the crimes for which offenders are incarcerated. Bureau of Justice statistics indicate that about 2.3 million persons were incarcerated in jails and prisons in 2009. According to the Pew Center on the States, the United States is the first nation ever to reach a 1 to 100 ratio for incarceration, with an incarceration rate of 1,000 people for every 100,000 in the population, whereas England's rate is 151 and Germany's is 88. Japan incarcerates only 63 people per 100,000 of the population. The U.S. incarceration rate is six times the median of 125 for all nations.

5% of the world's population

25% of the world's prisoners

2.3 million people incarcerated in the United States in 2009

1 to 100 the United States is the first nation ever to reach this ratio for incarceration

1,000 for every 100,000 people are incarcerated in jails and prisons in the United States

Nonviolent Offenders Less than half of those incarcerated are behind bars for violent offenses. The United States incarcerates persons for nonviolent crimes such as writing bad checks and drug use and possession, which rarely produce prison sentences in other countries.[29] For example, about 20 percent of inmates are incarcerated for drug offenses. Furthermore, the United States incarcerates persons for longer sentences than do other countries. For example, the average sentence for burglary in the United States is 16 months compared with 7 months in England and 5 months in Canada.[30]

Causes of High Incarceration Rates How did the United States come to have the highest incarceration rate in the world? The U.S. response to the rising concern for public safety during the 1970s and 1980s was a "lock and feed" philosophy of incarceration that emphasized incapacitation rather than rehabilitation. The reliance on incarceration as a major response to crime resulted in legislative changes in sentencing such as emphasis on mandatory sentencing, long prison terms, reduced discretion of judges to adjust sentences downward for individual circumstances, and enhanced sentences for repeat offenders—sometimes life sentences. As these sentencing changes were engaged the correctional population rapidly grew from a rate of about 130 per 100,000 (a number similar to the world's median today) in 1980 to 1 in 100 in 2009. According to the Bureau of Justice Statistics at year end in 2007, over 7.3 million people in the United States were on probation, in jail or prison, or on parole, which is about 3.2 percent of

chain gang in the Southern penal system, a group of convicts chained together during outside labor

prison farm system in the Southern penal systems, the use of inmate labor to maintain large, profit-making prison farms or plantations

2 **American jails evolved from a series of inhumane systems that had deplorable conditions and that harshly punished and exploited inmates to the current system that protects inmates' rights.**

1 in 32 adults

The number of people on probation, on parole, in jail, or in prison

all U.S. adult residents, or 1 in every 32 adults.

The fact that the United States incarcerates offenders at a much greater rate than any other country is in and of itself not necessarily an indictment that the American criminal justice system is seriously flawed. If the United States has more crime and more criminals than other countries and incarceration provides the greatest enhancement of public safety, then the use of incarceration may be justified. The opposing sides argue strongly that their worldview reflects the reality of the use of incarceration. Proponents of the use of incarceration such as Tom Riley, spokesman for the Office of National Drug Policy Initiatives, argue the record use of incarceration has lowered the crime rate and enhanced public safety. Riley defends the use of incarceration saying, "It's true, we have way too many people in prison. But it's not because the laws are unjust, but because there are too many people who are causing havoc and misery in the community."[31] On the other hand, James Q. Whitman, a specialist in comparative law at Yale, claims the American criminal justice system is "viewed with horror" by the rest of the world.[32] The Pew Center on the States argues that the United States incarcerates too many nonviolent offenders and too many people for minor crimes and violations of probation or parole.

Statistics support both sides of the argument. For example, as the use of incarceration rose in the 1980s, the crime rate did indeed drop. However, when one examines specific states, the results are not consistent with the overall drop in crime and rise in the use of incarceration. Florida has almost doubled its prison population over the past 15 years but has experienced a smaller drop in crime than New York, which has reduced its number of inmates to below that of 15 years ago.[33]

The Rising Cost of Incarceration

States often spent no money to house state prisoners in early prisons. In fact, some states even expected that prisons would produce a profit for the state. Today's prisons are significantly different from the model of self-sufficient, no-cost-to-the-state prisons of the nineteenth century. Today, incarceration is a significant cost to local, state, and federal governments. Three changes had a significant influence on the rising cost of incarceration. Figure 9.1 highlights those factors that have contributed to the rising cost of imprisonment.

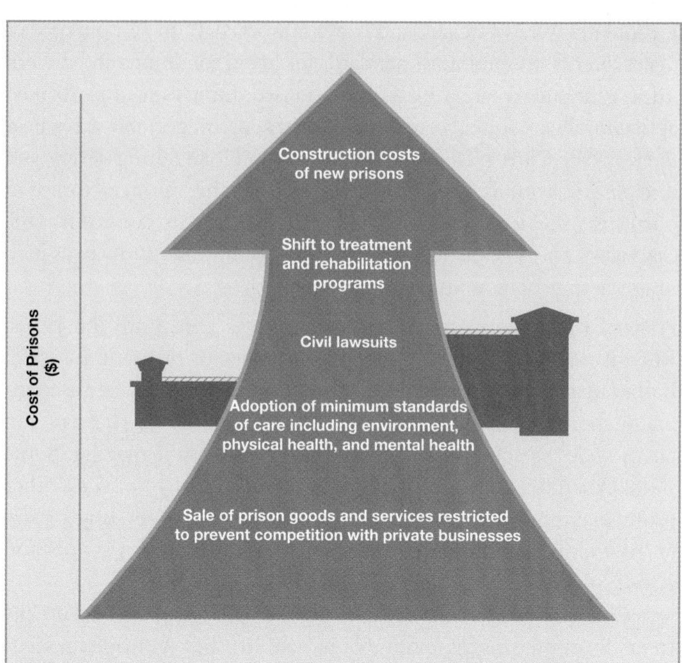

FIGURE 9.1 Factors Contributing to the Rising Cost of Imprisonment

Education and Rehabilitation Programs The first change was the abandonment of **Lombroso-based correctional philosophies** that criminality is an inherited trait. This philosophy assumes that criminals are biologically distinct from and inferior to noncriminals. Furthermore, Lombroso's philosophy assumes that because criminality is a biological trait and that the biological nature of the criminal cannot be changed, there is little or no need for rehabilitation programs—only incarceration and isolation from the community are necessary.

Lombroso's theory was very influential on correctional practices in the late 1800s and early 1900s. Lombroso's theory replaced the classical theory that criminals were weak-willed sinners who chose of their own free will to commit crime. Because criminals were thought to be predisposed to crime rather than choosing crime, rehabilitation was not a reasonable goal of the criminal justice system. Earnest Hooton (1887–1954), typical of those who believed in the inherited nature of the criminal man theory, argued that prisoners should be placed on self-contained, self-governing reservations completely isolated from society. Hooton favored the permanent incarceration of what he called "hopeless constitutional inferiors who on no account should be allowed to breed."[34]

This was the pervasive philosophy of correctional institutions in the United States throughout the early 1900s. Prisons were places of

HERE'S SOMETHING TO THINK ABOUT...

One of the challenges facing prison staff is keeping contraband out of prisons. Contraband consists of not only obvious items such as weapons and drugs but also items that may be legal outside prison. Cellphones, especially smartphones, are one such item. Inmates use cellphones to coordinate criminal activities, to communicate among gang members, and for other unauthorized communication and Internet access. What do you think are some ways inmates may obtain cellphones in prison?

Lombroso-based correctional philosophies divided persons into two distinct types: criminal and noncriminal. Noncriminals were biologically determined and therefore not amenable to rehabilitation or reform.

confinement with few or no rehabilitation programs, few comforts, strict discipline, and severe physical punishment for violation of the rules. Without the financial burden of education and rehabilitation programs, the cost of incarceration was appreciably less expensive than modern prisons. As the philosophy of the criminal man was replaced by correctional philosophies founded on sociological theories, educational and rehabilitation programs were introduced as a primary mission of prisons. These programs greatly added to the cost of prisons.

Restrictions on Prison-Made Goods and Services Secondly, the cost of incarceration was significantly impacted by legislation passed during the Great Depression (c. 1929–1940). During the Great Depression, the federal government and many states passed laws prohibiting the sale of convict-made products and services, which competed with local businesses on the open market. The operating capital that prisons had been able to generate through prison-industry-made goods and services dried up. Prison-industry goods and services were limited to supplying products to the government, a much smaller market with limited needs for goods and services.[35] It is during this era that state prisons became the exclusive manufacturers of license plates for state governments.

Recognition of Constitutional Rights of Prisoners Finally, the abandonment of the philosophy of **civil death** for incarcerated inmates resulted in significant increases in the cost of incarceration. Civil death is rooted in the law of medieval Europe and the concept of outlawry. The laws of medieval Europe provided that any person who committed a felony was outside the protection of the law. That is, he could receive no benefit of the court for any reason nor appeal any cause to the court. He was an outlaw—outside the law. Such a person was at the mercy of others because he had no redress for any harm done to him nor could he appeal to the law for protection. This concept was adapted by the United States in regard to incarcerated persons. It was the established law of the land in the United States up until the 1960s that incarcerated inmates had no right to bring any civil suit for any reason related to their imprisonment to the courts.[36] It was not until the **Warren Court** (1953–1969) that the U.S. Supreme Court ruled that constitutional protections extended to prisoners and prisoners were given the right to file civil lawsuits concerning the conditions of their incarceration. The earlier decision of *Cooper v. Aaron* (1958) ruled that states were bound by Court decisions and could not ignore them. Thus, when the Warren Court voided the doctrine of "civil death," lawsuits challenging conditions of imprisonment and denial of civil rights flooded the courts. As prisons were held accountable for providing minimum standards of living, food, and protection of civil rights, the cost of incarceration increased. Also, prisons violating minimum standards of incarceration and civil rights were subject to punitive damages.

INCARCERATED INMATES HAD NO RIGHT TO BRING ANY CIVIL SUIT FOR ANY REASON RELATED TO THEIR IMPRISONMENT TO THE COURTS.

Number of Prisons The end result of these and other influences is that contemporary prisons are expensive. One of the obvious reasons for the rising cost of corrections is that the record incarceration rate has resulted in a record number of prisons. The cost of prisons is expensive in that as the incarceration rate rises to record levels, the number of prisons required to house the inmates increases. In 1923, there were 61 prisons in the United States. It was not uncommon for states to have a single prison to house all of its inmates. The number of prisons grew to 592 in 1974 and has expanded to over 1,000 today. Prison construction is one of the most expensive construction projects because of the security and sophistication of technology required.

61
The number of prisons in the United States in 1923.

1,000
The number of prisons in the United States today.

Cost of Correctionals Prison costs are one of the fastest rising costs to state governments. State spending on corrections has increased 127 percent in the last 20 years. Five states (Connecticut, Delaware, Michigan, Oregon, and Vermont) now spend more on corrections than on higher education. One out of nine state employees works in corrections. At a cost of about $29,000 per inmate, states are spending an average of 7 percent of their budget on corrections. Prisons cost state governments about $50 billion a year and the federal government $5 billion more. The cost of imprisonment is forcing states to examine alternatives because state deficits are at record highs. Some states are forced to slash prison budgets, lay off staff, and release prisoners early because there are insufficient funds to continue to pay for the high cost of incarceration. The challenge is to reduce the costs of corrections without sacrificing public safety. Some of the programs to reduce the costs of corrections are discussed in Chapter 11 on community corrections.

HERE'S SOMETHING TO THINK ABOUT...

Large prisons are like a city and require all of the services necessary to run a city. They have schools, hospitals, post offices, restaurants, and factories. While inmates perform most of the jobs related to these services, civilian employees oversee and administer the services. Distinct from correctional officers responsible for inmate security and movement, these professionals have administrative responsibilities similar to their civilian counterparts. They include teachers, food service professionals, prison industry managers, and others. Have you considered professional employment opportunities in corrections?

civil death the legal philosophy that barred any prison inmate from bringing a lawsuit in a civil court related to his/her treatment while incarcerated or conditions of incarceration

Warren Court the U.S. Supreme Court years (1953–1969) during which Chief Justice Earl Warren issued many landmark decisions greatly expanding the constitutional rights of inmates and defendants

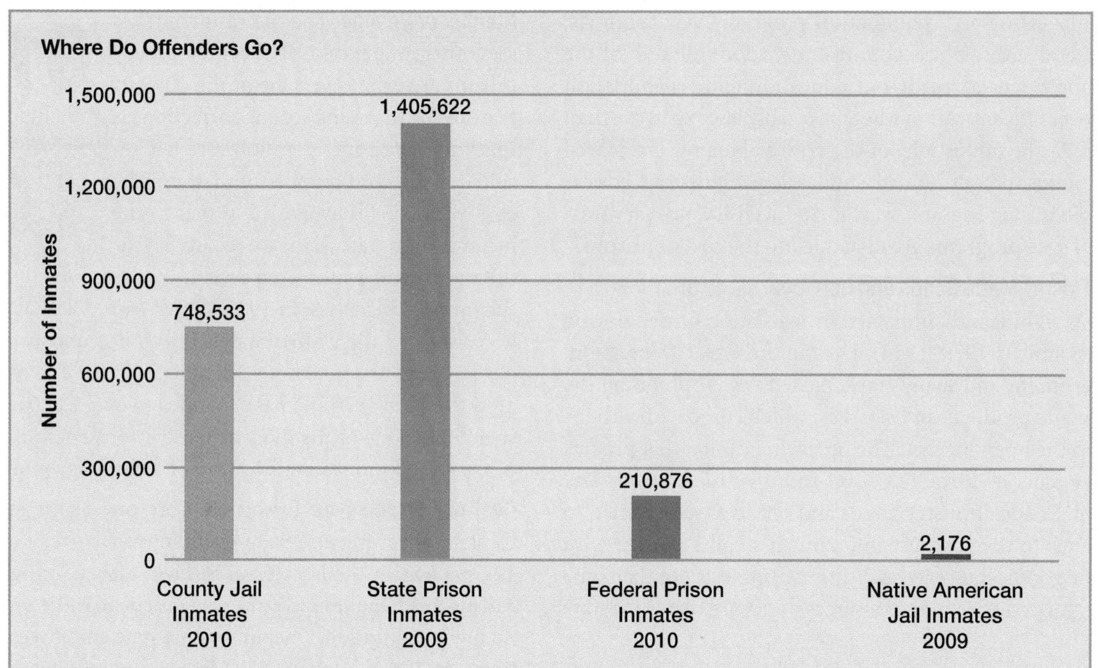

Most of the nation's prisoners are incarcerated in state prisons followed by county jails and federal prisons. The small number of Native American inmates does not reflect Native Americans incarcerated in jails and state and federal prisons. However, numbers alone do not reflect the entire story. One must remember that county jails incarcerated a wide diversity of persons from those being held prior to trial to serious felons, whereas state and federal prisons have a more homogeneous population.

Source: Todd D. Minton, "Jail Inmates at Midyear 2010 Statistical Tables" (Washington, D.C.: Bureau of Justice Statistics, April 2011); Heather West and William J. Sabol, "Prisoners in 2009" (Washington D.C.: Bureau of Justice Statistics, December 2010); Todd D. Minton, "Jails in Indian Country, 2009" (Washington D.C.: Bureau of Justice Statistics, February 2011).

Jails

The major institutions of modern civilian institutional corrections are jails, state prisons, and federal penitentiaries. In addition to these facilities, special categories of inmates are held by Native American Nations, Immigration and Customs Enforcement, military prisons, and U.S. Territories and Commonwealths. These institutions differ significantly from civilian correctional institutions and contain only a small percent of the corrections population. Of the four institutions, Immigration and Customs Enforcement (ICE) incarcerates the largest number of persons, about 27,000 in 2007 according to the Bureau of Justice Statistics. The small number of inmates reflects the fact that the total population for each of these groups is also small compared to the adult population.

JAILS ARE UNIQUE, SHORT-TERM FACILITIES USED FOR MORE PURPOSES THAN ANY OTHER TYPE OF CORRECTIONAL INSTITUTION.

Short-Term Facilities **Jails** are unique, short-term facilities that are used for more purposes than any other type of correctional institution. Jails hold defendants awaiting trial, defendants convicted of misdemeanor crimes, state and federal prisoners, persons with mental illness pending their movement to appropriate health facilities, adults of both genders, and juveniles. Jails hold local, state, federal, and military prisoners; convicted prisoners; absconders; and witnesses. However, the majority of inmates in local jails have not been convicted of a crime. They are waiting to be charged, tried, or transported to another institution. Jails hold everyone from accused murderers to persons detained for littering.

In addition to the fact that they are multipurpose, jails are unique as a gateway into the criminal justice system and corrections in particular. When a person is detained or arrested for any crime, misdemeanor, or felony, he or she first is confined in a jail. Only convicted offenders can be confined in state and federal prisons. Thus, all prisoners and most defendants enter the criminal justice system through jails. There are three types of jails: Native American country jails, federal civilian jails, and local civilian jails.

Native American Country Jails

Native American country jails incarcerate only Native Americans living in Native American country who have been sentenced by a Native American court for an offense committed there. Although Native

3 **Jails, including Native American jails, federal jails, and city and county jails, are temporary holding facilities for a variety of persons, most often those waiting to be charged, tried, or transported to another facility.**

Jails short-term, multipurpose holding facilities that serve as the gateway into the criminal justice system

tribes are regarded with a certain degree of autonomy by the federal government, they are restricted as to the crimes and punishments over which they have control. Basically, serious crimes (felonies) are the authority of the Federal Bureau of Investigation and offenders are tried in federal courts and serve time in federal civilian institutions. Thus, although the number of inmates in Native American country jails is small, about 2,220 in 2007, four times that many Native American inmates (8,600) are confined outside of Native American country.

The maximum sentence for persons confined in Native American country jails is 1 year. Therefore, most inmates are confined for misdemeanors. Native American country jails are not part of the United States civilian correctional system, are not under local or state authority, and operate independent of the Federal Bureau of Prisons. About one third of the Native American country jails are located in Arizona. These jails suffer from many of the same problems as their civilian counterparts with overcrowding being the primary problem. According to the Bureau of Justice statistics in 2007, most **Native American country jails** operate near full capacity and a number operate at more than 50 percent over rated capacity. The second challenge of Native American country jails is providing treatment and counseling programs to address the many behavioral and addiction problems of inmates in an effective way given the cultural context in which the inmates live.

Federal Jails

Federal jails are similar to local jails in that they house inmates incarcerated for misdemeanor offenses (sentences less than 1 year). However, there are more differences than similarities between the two. Federal jails do not house the diverse population of prisoners that is characteristic of local jails. The primary purpose of federal jails is to hold federal jail inmates convicted of misdemeanor crimes and federal jail inmates awaiting adjudication or transfer. Often, federal inmates awaiting trial (including felony trials) are incarcerated in local jails for a fee. Also, federal jail inmates may be transferred to one of the 11 federal jails if the jail population becomes too large or if an inmate is a disciplinary problem. Local civilian jails do not have these options.

City and County Jails

Local civilian jails face some of the most difficult challenges of the various correctional institutions. There are over 3,300 local or county jails, and they vary significantly in size. About 47 percent of these jails have a capacity of fewer than 50 inmates. Less than 3 percent of the jails have a capacity of more than 1,000 inmates.[37] A few jails have very large populations. Three of the largest jails are Rikers Island, the Los Angeles County Jail, and the Maricopa County (Arizona) Jail. Riker's Island is the city jail for New York City and is one of the largest jails in the United States both in size and population. Riker's Island is a 415-acre detention facility located on an island in the river. It has an $860 million budget and is staffed by 10,000 officers and 1,500 civilians. The inmate population of Riker's Island varies between 15,000 and 20,000 inmates. The Los Angeles County Jail and the Maricopa County Jail house over 7,000 inmates each.

415

size in acres of Riker's Island Jail in New York City

15,000-20,000

number of prisoners held at Riker's Island Jail

$860 million

yearly budget for Riker's Island

10,000

number of officers on staff at Riker's Island

Varying Jail Conditions Local governments must support and staff their jails. Thus, jail facilities vary with the economic prosperity of the city or county. In cities and counties with expanding jail prisoner populations, it can be difficult for the city or county to provide quality care and facilities for inmates. Thus, prison life in jails can range from good to bad. When cities and counties are economically challenged and do not have the resources to finance jail operations, conditions in jails can result in lawsuits by inmates and takeover by the courts. For example, in July 2004, Fulton County Jail (Georgia) was sued by inmates, censured by the Southern Center for Human Rights, and the Court threatened to appoint a receiver to oversee the jail. The jail opened in the mid-1980s. While it was under construction, it was determined to be too small, and the number of bunks was doubled, even though the number of showers, toilets, and other utilities remained the same.[38] After it opened, a third bunk was added to many cells to accommodate the increasing population. When that was insufficient, some inmates slept on mattresses in the common area. Court papers described the jail as having "windowless, steamy rooms, where the air-conditioning is broken; 59 inmates in one cellblock sharing two showers with backed-up sewage; inmates without clean underwear and uniforms due to broken laundry service; faulty record keeping that left inmates locked up although they had served their time; attacks; beatings; escapes. Blocks designed to have 14 guards have only 2."[39]

Jail Operation All states except Connecticut, Delaware, Hawaii, Rhode Island, and Vermont operate local jails, but these five states do have a combined jail–prison system operated by the state. Initially, local jails were operated by the county sheriff, and there was only one jail per county. In many states, this is still true. About 78 percent of sheriffs' offices operate a jail.[40] Jail operation is still a major responsibility of sheriffs' offices. Fully one third of all sheriffs' office sworn personnel work in jail-related positions, and 56 percent of civilian personnel work in jail-related positions.[41] Jails not operated by a sheriff's office are managed by a county department of corrections employing only civilian

Native American country jails are short-term incarceration facilities on Native American land under the sovereign control of the Native American tribe

Characteristic	2008	2009	2010
Sex			
Male	87.3%	87.8%	87.7%
Female	12.7	12.2	12.3
Adults	99.0%	99.1%	99%
Male	86.4	86.9	86.7
Female	12.6	12.1	12.3
Juveniles[a]	1.0%	0.9%	1.0%
Held as adults[b]	0.8	0.8	0.8
Held as juveniles	0.2	0.2	0.3
Race/Hispanic origin[c]			
White[d]	42.5%	42.5%	44.3%
Black/African American[d]	39.2	39.2	37.8
Hispanic/Latino	16.4	16.2	15.8
Other[d,e]	1.8	1.9	1.3
Two or more races[d]	0.2	0.2	0.6
Conviction status[b]			
Convicted	37.1%	37.8%	38.9%
Male	32.3	33.0	—
Female	4.8	4.8	—
Unconvicted	62.9	62.2	61.1
Male	55.2	54.8	—
Female	7.8	7.4	—

Note: Detail may not sum to total due to rounding.
[a]Persons under age 18 at midyear.
[b]Includes juveniles who were tried or awaiting trial as adults.
[c]Estimates based on reported data and adjusted for nonresponse.
[d]Excludes persons of Hispanic or Latino origin.
[e]Includes American Indians, Alaska Natives, Asians, Native Hawaiians, and other Pacific Islanders.

FIGURE 9.2 Jail Population by Characteristics, 2008–2010
Percent of Inmates in Local Jails, by Characteristics, Midyear 2010.

personnel. Sheriffs' departments and **county departments of corrections** otherwise perform the same jail functions (see Figure 9.2).

Functions of Locally Operated Jails The following numerous functions performed by local jails make it difficult to operate the jail and manage the inmates. Inmates range from persons waiting to post bail to murderers. Many inmates are in jail for only a brief time. Some inmates are held only until they can be transferred to another institution.

- Receive individuals pending arraignment and hold them awaiting trial, conviction, or sentencing.
- Readmit probation, parole, and bail-bond violators and absconders.
- Temporarily detain juveniles pending transfer to juvenile authorities.
- Hold persons with mental illness pending their movement to appropriate health facilities.
- Hold individuals for the military, for protective custody, for contempt, and for the courts as witnesses.
- Release convicted inmates to the community on completion of sentence.
- Transfer inmates to federal, state, and other authorities.
- House inmates for federal, state, or other authorities because of crowding of their facilities.
- Relinquish custody of temporary detainees to juvenile and medical authorities.
- Operate community-based programs with day reporting, home detention, electronic monitoring, or other types of supervision.
- Hold inmates sentenced to short terms (generally under 1 year).

Jail Population The jail population has doubled since 1983, and the rate of increase continues to climb. Figure 9.3 illustrates this increase in jail population. According to the Bureau of Justice Statistics (BJS), in 2008, 785,556 inmates were held in the nation's local jails, an increase of about 5,300 inmates from 2007. In 2008, 9 out of 10 jail inmates were adult males. Blacks were three times more likely than Hispanics and five times more likely than Whites to be in jail. Nearly half of jail inmates have not been convicted of an offense.

During the 1980s and 1990s the jail population rose rapidly in part because of the rise in state prison populations. Because jails are the gateways for felony inmates as the number of felony inmates rise, there is a corresponding increase in the number of jail inmates. To keep pace with the influx of new jail inmates, counties were constructing new jail facilities at the rate of about 500 new beds each week.[42] Some counties experienced such a rate of growth in the jail population that there was not enough new bed space, and prisoners were

500
Number of new jail beds being constructed each week

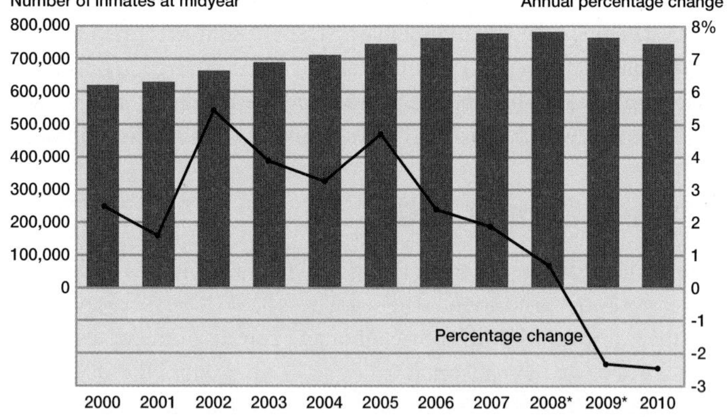

FIGURE 9.3 Number of Persons Held in Jail, 2000 –2010
From 1980 to 2006 the population of jails rose rapidly. Since 2005 the increase in jail population has slowed. What do you think are some of the reasons for this decrease in jail population?

Source: Minton, T.D. (2011). *Jail Inmates at Midyear 2010—Statistical Tables* (Washington, D.C.: Bureau of Justice Statistics, p. 1).

county department of corrections is when the sheriff does not supervise the county jail, it is administered by an independent county department

housed in corridors, outdoor tents, or trailers. Overcrowding and the use of makeshift facilities can present serious problems for local jails. For example, in May 2009, the director of Arizona state prisons suspended the use of unshaded outdoor holding cells after an inmate died when left in an unshaded enclosure for nearly 4 hours in 100 degree temperatures.[43] Despite the new building efforts, local jails operate at about 95 percent capacity and many operate beyond capacity.

Municipal Jails

Historically, local jails also included local prison facilities maintained by municipal police departments. In some counties, the sheriff maintained the county jail, and the police department maintained a separate municipal jail. These counties had both a municipal court and a county court, with each court housing its prisoners in the appropriate facility. Most municipalities have abandoned the use of the municipal or police jail. Recent state and federal regulations and standards regarding the housing of inmates have made it difficult for cities and towns to support local jails.

Municipal jails should not be confused with police holding cells, booking cells, or lock up facilities. Nearly all police departments have secure detention facilities that may look like jail cells. The primary purpose of these holding cells is the temporary housing of arrestees until they can be booked and moved to another facility or pay their bail, or until detectives can determine whether they are to be charged with a crime. These are not correctional institutions, and prisoners are not sent to these facilities to serve time as their punishment for a crime. Prisoners typically are confined in holding cells only for a period of 48 hours or less.

STATE PRISONS ARE CORRECTIONAL INSTITUTIONS CONTAINING ONLY CONVICTED OFFENDERS, USUALLY FELONY INMATES SENTENCED TO PRISON AS PUNISHMENT FOR A CRIME.

State Prisons

Unlike jails, **state prisons** are correctional institutions containing only convicted offenders, usually felony inmates sentenced to prison as punishment for a crime. Each state operates its own correctional system, and these systems differ significantly from state to state. States also vary in the number of inmates in the correctional system. Inmates in state prisons usually have been sentenced to serve a prison term of a year or more. Thus, different services, procedures, and policies are needed for prisoners than are provided in local jails.

Overall, the number of inmates in state prisons has continued to climb to record incarceration rates. However, the growth in state prison populations varies significantly by state (see Figure 9.4). Some states are experiencing double-digit growth, whereas other states are actually experiencing a decline in state prisoner population. Overall, state prisons are between 1 percent below capacity and 15 percent above capacity.[44] According to the Bureau of Justice Statistics, the state prison population has increased from 1,176,269 in 2000 to 1,319,426 in 2009. Only about 8 percent of the inmates in state prisons are female. Just over half (53 percent) of state inmates are incarcerated for violent offenses.[45]

8% of state prison inmates are female

53% of state prison inmates are incarcerated for violent offenses

In the early nineteenth century, most states built one large prison to house all state inmates. It was thought that this economy of scale would provide the best solution to the problem of housing prisoners. There was little effort to separate prisoners on the basis of age, type of offense, length of term, or criminal history. From the beginning, however, early state prisons, unlike early jails, separated prisoners by sex, maintaining separate facilities for female prisoners. Until the late twentieth century, women comprised a very small percentage of felony offenders. Thus, while early prisons for male offenders were built to house thousands of inmates, institutions for female prisoners usually were one tenth the size. Furthermore, prison architecture reflected the assumption that male prisoners were more aggressive and dangerous, and that female prisoners were more docile and less violent.[46] Based on this assumption, correctional institutions for women often lacked the fortresslike architecture and brutal discipline of prisons for men. Today, states have numerous prisons within their jurisdiction and distribute inmates among them according to a system of prisoner classification.

Prisoner Classification

States have diverse prisons, and inmates can be placed in any prison throughout the state. Each prison is distinguished by its security level and the programs available to inmates at the institution. Before incarceration in a state prison, an inmate undergoes an extensive examination and assessment to determine an assignment to a particular facility. Because inmates

STATES HAVE DIVERSE PRISONS, AND INMATES CAN BE PLACED IN ANY PRISON. EACH PRISON IS DISTINGUISHED BY ITS SECURITY LEVEL AND THE PROGRAMS AVAILABLE TO INMATES.

municipal jail city administered jails for the incarceration of offenders who are convicted of violating city ordinance in a municipal court

state prisons correctional facilities for prisoners convicted of state crimes

4 **State prisons are correctional facilities with different security levels and prisoner classifications, including special populations of inmates.**

Classification and Assignment to Initial Correctional Institution

Newly Admitted Inmates ▶

Reception and Diagnosis Center

- Search for contraband
- Prison clothes
- Prison I.D.
- Mental health evaluation
- Physical health evaluation
- Classification to determine most appropriate correctional institution—decision influenced by:
  - –mental and physical health
  - –suicide risk
  - –seriousness of offense
  - –sentence length
  - –criminal record
  - –age
  - –educational attainment
  - –gang affiliation
  - –sexual orientation
  - –communicable disease
  - –race*

**Race alone cannot be a criterion for classification. Usually race is relevant because it is often associated with gang membership.*

Dispersed to Correctional Institutions ▶

Maximum Security Minimum emphasis on programs and rehabilitation and maximum emphasis on security. Inmate movement highly restricted, and prison facility is walled with armed guard towers. Mostly cell-type housing.

Medium Security Strong security measures but a variety of education, counseling, and rehabilitation programs. Cell-type and dormitory housing.

Minimum Security Fencing or no perimeter security. Inmates may work unsupervised outside of confinement, i.e., prison farm, or to engage in community-based education or vocational programs.

Mental Health Institutions Medical hospitals for mentally ill inmates. Strong physical security measures but the institution resembles a hospital more than a walled prison. May be combined with a medical facility.

Medical Facility A medical hospital for inmates. Medium and maximum security institutions may have a small medical facility within the walls of the prison. Large medical facilities usually treat chronically and terminally ill prisoners. May be combined with a mental health facility.

Private Prison Some prisoners are selected to be sent to private prisons, which usually accept minimum and medium security inmates. May be located out of state. Primary purpose is to reduce overcrowding of state prisons.

Transfer to Another Jurisdiction In rare cases state prisons may "trade" inmates. Exceptional high-security risk inmates, i.e., state witnesses for organized crime inmates, may be transferred to another jurisdiction. In turn the state agrees to accept a similar inmate from the other jurisdiction.

remain in state custody for a relatively long time, the system attempts to determine the needs of the inmate and any characteristics that might influence placement. The correctional system also evaluates the security risks, staffing impacts, and institutional needs when deciding where inmates go. Jails use a modified form of classification. However, because of the short length of incarceration of the inmates, the lack of counseling and treatment programs, and the diversity of the inmate population, classification in jails often only sorts prisoners by a few characteristics, such as gender, juvenile or adult, security risks, and special populations. It is not uncommon in jails for persons awaiting trial on serious felony charges to be in the same environment as inmates serving time for misdemeanors.

This process of **prisoner classification**, performed in a specially designated facility, is commonly known as reception and diagnosis. At the state's reception and diagnosis facility, the classification process includes identification of the inmate, examination of the inmate's criminal record, evaluation of the inmate's mental capacity and psychological stability, and the assessment of other factors that may influence his or her assignment, such as gang membership, age, and educational achievement.

White-Collar Prisoners The incarceration of white-collar offenders and prominent political persons such as mayors, senators, governors, and so on has given rise to the increased use of private prison consultants to help such persons secure as favorable a classification as possible. High-profile, wealthy offenders often hire prison consultants to lobby for good prison placement, to mitigate sentence length, and to offer crash courses in prison culture. Martha Stewart, Michael Vick, former Pennsylvania state senator Vincent Fumo, and Bernie Madoff all used the services of a prison consultant prior to their incarceration. **Prison consultants** are private for-profit advisors who have familiarity with the prison culture and classification process. Sometimes prison consultants have obtained their expertise by serving time.

Prison officials deny that prison consultants are effective in receiving preferential treatment for their clients. However, prison consultants often are able to provide advice to their clients on the

prisoner classification the reception and diagnosis of an inmate to decide the appropriate security level in which to place the prisoner and the services of placement

prison consultants private persons who provide convicted defendants advice and counsel on how best to present themselves during classification and how to behave in prison

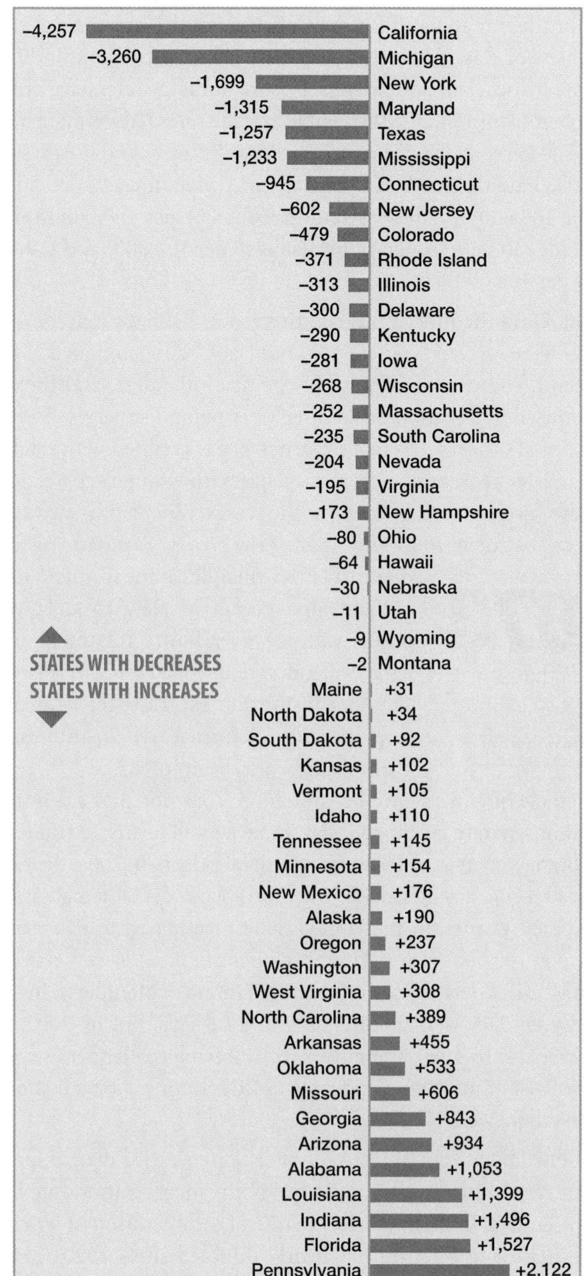

FIGURE 9.4 Change in Imprisonment Rates, 2009–2010

In 2009, the prison total population dropped after nearly 40 years of record-high increases. Future data will be examined to determine whether this is the start of a period of decline or only a temporary reduction. Prison count dropped in 26 states but the federal prison population has continued to grow due to tougher sentencing laws.

Source: Pew Center on the States, Public Safety Performance Project, 2010, p. 5.

classification process, such as how to negotiate for assignment to the best prison and how to present themselves during the classification process so as to receive the lowest possible risk evaluation. In addition to helping with the classification process, prison consultants offer their clients advice on how to behave in prison to minimize risk. Tim Miller of the San Diego-based Dr. Prison consultant service says, "It's like going to a foreign country that you've never been to before–different language, people's mannerism."[47] White-collar offenders often were once persons of wealth and power and are ill prepared to enter the prison culture. Larry Levine of the Los Angeles–based Wall Street Prison Consultants offers his clients a primer called "Fed Time 101" to help them prepare for incarceration.

Induction into the Prison At the classification facility, the inmate is inducted into the state's prison system. Prisoners exchange their clothing for prison clothing, undergo extensive and intrusive searches for weapons or contraband, are photographed and fingerprinted, and are assigned an identification number or prisoner I.D. This process is similar to the booking process that occurs when a person is first arrested for a crime, but it must be repeated, because it is possible that the inmate reporting for prison is not the person who was convicted of the crime. Such a case was discovered in October 2000, when a federal prisoner walked away from a minimum-custody federal correctional facility. When police found and returned the escapee, prison officials found that he was an impostor.[48] The convicted offender had arranged for another person to report to prison and serve time in his place. Officials had failed to detect this switch before the impostor had actually served 18 months of the other man's sentence.[49]

Inmate Placement One of the important decisions made in the classification process is where to place the new inmate. **Initial placement** includes such decisions as to which correctional facility the inmate should be assigned, the inmate's security risk level, and the living environment of the inmate. The inmate's length of sentence, seriousness of the offense, and past criminal record are important factors in deciding in which facility the inmate will initially be placed. Inmates with long prison sentences, serious offenses, and past criminal histories will be assigned to high security facilities. Nonviolent offenders with shorter sentences and no criminal record may be assigned to minimum or medium security institutions. Inmates with mental illness may be assigned to medical facilities, where they will receive treatment.

Living Environment The living environment refers to whether the inmate will be housed in a single cell, a multiple-inmate cell, or dormitory style housing. This decision can be a life and death decision, because improper assignment could result in injury or death to an inmate. For example, injury or death could result if prison authorities assign a White inmate who belonged to a White supremacist group to share a cell with a minority inmate. A mistake in classification can have serious consequences. For example, a wrongful death lawsuit was filed against Illinois correctional officials for assigning first-time

initial placement the first institution and security level of the convicted defendant

inmate Joshua Daczewitz as cell mate to Corey Fox, a murderer and mentally ill inmate who had previously threatened to kill any cell mate assigned to him. After correctional officials placed Daczewitz as cell mate to Corey Fox, Fox strangled Daczewitz.[50]

Special Prison Populations

Some prisoners may not be suited to transfer to the **general prison population.** Because of age, mental illness, depression, other health status, or other characteristic, it may be necessary to keep an inmate out of the general population.

Mental Stability During the classification process, the inmate is administered psychological tests to determine his or her mental stability. Incarceration can trigger intense depression, and as a result, some prisoners are high suicide risks. Prison officials attempt to identify such prisoners, provide assistance, and place them under constant observation in what is known as suicide watch. Some inmates require psychiatric treatment and would be a danger to others or themselves if placed in the general population. During classification, these inmates are identified and often transferred to appropriate mental health care facilities.

Lifestyle During the classification process, prison officials also try to determine whether the inmate's lifestyle or special needs should influence placement. Specific assignments may be based on the inmate's age, sexual orientation, gang affiliation, or physical health. Inmates with significant health problems, such as AIDS or tuberculosis, require extensive health care in prison. Prison officials are responsible for providing appropriate health care and protecting other inmates and staff from infectious diseases.

Age Young prisoners, usually under 25 or 26 years old, may need to be separated from older, more hardened offenders. Elderly prisoners, an increasing challenge to correctional institutions, also may need to be protected from the general prison population. The "graying of inmates" is becoming more of a problem for prisons because of longer prison sentences and demographic factors such as aging baby boomers in the prison population.

Gang Affiliation Gang affiliation also is an important consideration in determining where to house a prisoner and can be a real dilemma. Gang members placed together may post a security risk because they will conspire together. However, an inmate placed in a housing unit with rival gang members may be assaulted. In some cases, groups of gang rivals forced to live together may engage in gang warfare.

Change in Classification A prisoner's classification may be changed based on behavior, a change in status, or other consideration. For instance, a prisoner assigned to maximum security may be reassigned to medium security based on good behavior and time served. A prisoner assigned to minimum security who tries to escape, on the other hand, may be reassigned to a higher security prison.

A primary reason for classifying and assigning prisoners to various security levels is to enhance the safety of the prison environment both for the inmates and for the staff. One of the measures of the effectiveness of classification and security is the suicide rate and homicide rate in local jails and prisons. Prison homicide rates have dropped 93 percent from 1980 to 2002. Jail homicide rates have remained constant. The jail suicide rate has dropped significantly, and prison suicide rates also have declined. Jails tend to have three times the suicide rate (47 per 100,000 inmates) as state prisons (14 per 100,000 inmates). Homicide rates are similar in local jails (3 per 100,000) and state prisons (4 per 100,000).

Women Until the nineteenth century, it was believed that female offenders were "fallen" women and could not be rehabilitated.[51] In the nineteenth century, there were few female offenders, and those few were housed in a section of the men's prison and supervised by male correctional officers. Elizabeth Gurney Fry is credited with establishing the early theoretical and practical bases for women's corrections at Newgate Prison in London in the early nineteenth century. In America, between 1844 and 1848, Eliza W. B. Farnham instituted many of Fry's principles at the women's section of Sing Sing prison in New York. However, public outrage over "soft" treatment of the female offenders resulted in Farnham's dismissal. The first institution expressly for women was the Indiana Reformatory Institution for Women and Girls, built in 1873.

1873
The first prison exclusively for women is built.

Female offenders have become more common and are routinely housed in separate facilities. Today, men are still nearly 15 times more likely than women to be in a state or federal prison. In 2004, the rate for inmates serving a sentence of 1 or more years was 64 female inmates per 100,000 women in the United States, compared to 920 male inmates per 100,000 men.[52] However, these figures do not reflect the growing crisis related to incarcerated female offenders. In 1983, there were 15,652 female offenders in local jails, but by 2002, there were 273,224. In 1980, there were 13,400 female offenders serving a sentence of 1 or more years in a state or federal correctional institution; by 2009, there were 113,462.

Drug Convictions The shift to tougher sentences for drug offenses is a major reason for this dramatic rise in the incarceration rate for female offenders. In many states, the rate of incarceration of female offenders for drug offenses has nearly doubled since 1990.[53] Female offenders accounted for over 15 percent of defendants charged with a drug offense in U.S. district courts in 1999.[54] The number of boys charged with drug offenses in juvenile court from 1989 to 1998 dropped by 2 percent, but the number of girls charged with drug crimes rose by 2 percent.[55] Female offenders comprise 16 percent of the drug cases in juvenile court. In state prisons, 65 to 73 percent of female offenders admitted to regular drug use before incarceration.[56] Furthermore, it is estimated that many female offenders serving time

general prison population is the nonrestricted population of prison inmates who have access to prison services, programs and recreations

for property and sex crimes were motivated to commit these crimes by the need to obtain money for drugs.

The skyrocketing increase of female offenders has created major problems for the correctional system. Female institutions are becoming overcrowded, and female offenders have less access to vocational, educational, medical, and rehabilitation programs. For example, the percentage of female offenders receiving drug treatment while in prison is declining significantly, despite the high rate of drug use among female offenders. Today, only 15 percent of state prison inmates and 10 percent of federal prison inmates obtain drug treatment while in prison, whereas in 1991, 29 percent of state and 19 percent of federal female offenders reported participation in drug treatment programs.[57]

FEMALE OFFENDERS ARE MORE LIKELY TO SUFFER FROM HIV INFECTION AND MENTAL ILLNESS THAN ARE MALE INMATES.

80% of female inmates have dependent children

1,400 babies were born to women in prisons in 1998

1.5 million children in the United States have parents in prison

Health Issues Although female offenders suffer many of the same physical and mental health problems in prison as do male prisoners, statistics indicate that the female offenders are more likely to suffer from HIV infection and mental illness than are male inmates. At year end in 2002, about 2.9 percent of female inmates in state prisons were infected with HIV, compared with about 1.9 percent of male inmates. About 24 percent of female inmates in state and federal prisons reported suffering from mental illnesses, compared with 16 percent of male inmates.[58]

Victimization Some see female offenders as victims of men.[59] This is the view of feminist criminological theories, which argue that female offenders are victimized by a social and criminal justice system that is biased toward male dominance. Evidence of female offenders as victims of men is seen in the high rate of sexual and physical abuse reported by female offenders. About 57 percent of state female inmates and 40 percent of federal female inmates report that they were sexually or physically abused before admission, whereas only 16 percent of state male inmates and 7 percent of federal male inmates report that they were abused, and the proportions are similar for jail inmates.[60] Abuse of female offenders continues after incarceration, because there are frequent scandals involving correctional officers demanding sex from female inmates. Many former female inmates allege that during their incarceration, sex with male correctional officers in exchange for favors was commonplace. "Sexual favors are part of a hidden **prison economy,** in exchange for avoiding retribution, getting drugs, or obtaining extra privileges, such as staying up after hours."[61]

Dependent Children and Broken Families More than 1.5 million children in the United States have parents in prison.[62] The burden of incarceration falls heavier on female offenders than on male offenders. Families are more likely to be broken by a woman's confinement in the criminal justice system than by a man's.[63] On average, about 80 percent of female inmates have dependent children.[64] In 1998, 1,400 babies were delivered in prisons, only to be removed from their mothers shortly after birth.

Most mothers plan to return to their families after their release but frequently are poorly prepared for this task. Female offenders have fewer visits with family during their incarceration than do male offenders. One reason for this is that as a result of few female prisons, female offenders often are incarcerated farther from home than are male offenders. Another reason is that when male offenders are incarcerated, custody of children typically remains with the mother, whereas when females are imprisoned, grandparents frequently become the caregivers of the children. Most data suggest that incarcerated women do not see their children at all.[65] Some innovative programs try to help keep female offenders united with their families. A promising program that is effective, inexpensive, and easy to administer is Girl Scouts Beyond Bars, which provides for regular mother–daughter contact through Girl Scout programs conducted in prisons.[66]

On their return to the community, female offenders are likely to face significant problems, including parental poverty, unemployment, substance abuse, low self-esteem, and ill health. Often, the problems of the parent are visited on the children, because child abuse and neglect are common outcomes. Children of incarcerated parents are five times more likely to offend than are children whose parents have not been incarcerated. This starts a vicious cycle of crime that is difficult to break.

Although it is rare for female offenders to be executed, since 1973 the death penalty has been imposed upon 166 female offenders. This is about 2% of the total death sentences imposed. Of this number of female offenders only 12 female offenders have actually been executed since 1984. The execution of Teresa Lewis in 2010 generated controversy due to her alleged low IQ. Also, her crime was typical in that most female offenders are accused of murdering spouse or family.

FAMILIES ARE MORE LIKELY TO BE BROKEN BY A WOMAN'S CONFINEMENT IN THE CRIMINAL JUSTICE SYSTEM THAN A MAN'S.

prison economy refers to the exchange of goods, services and contraband by prisoners in the place of money

TABLE 9.1 Inmates in Custody in State or Federal Prisons, or in Local Jails, December 31, 2000, 2008–2009

Inmates in custody	Number of inmates 2000	2008	2009	Average annual change, 2000–08	Percent change, 2008–2009
Total	1,937,482	2,308,390	2,292,133	2.2%	−0.7%
Federal prisoners[a]	140,064	198,414	205,087	4.4%	3.4%
Prisons	133,921	189,770	196,318	4.5	3.5
Federal facilities	124,540	165,252	171,000	3.6	3.5
Privately operated facilities	9,381	24,518	25,318	12.8	3.3
Community Corrections Centers[b]	6,143	8,644	8,769	4.4	1.4
State prisoners[c]	1,176,269	1,324,420	1,319,426	1.5%	−0.4%
Local jails[d]	621,149	785,556	767,620	3.0%	−2.3%
Incarceration rate[e]	684	756	743	1.3%	−1.6%

Note: Total includes all inmates held in state or federal prison facilities or in local jails. It does not include inmates held in U.S. territories, military facilities, U.S. Immigration and Customs Enforcement facilities, jails in Indian country, and juvenile facilities. See the text box on page 1 of this report for a discussion about the differences between the custody and jurisdiction prison populations. See *Methodology* for sources of incarcerated data.

[a]After 2001, responsibility for sentenced prisoners from the District of Columbia was transferred to the Federal Bureau of Prisons.

[b]Non-secure, privately operated community corrections centers.

[c]Includes prisoners held in privately operated facilities under state authority. There were 71,815 state prisoners held in privately operated facilities in 2000, 96,320 in 2008, and 95,249 in 2009.

[d]Estimated number of adults and juveniles held in local jails on June 30.

[e]The total number in custody per 100,000 U.S. residents. Resident population estimates were as of January 1 of the following year.

Source: Lauren Glaze, *Correctional Populations in the United States, 2009* (Washington, D.C.: Bureau of Justice Statistics, 2010 p. 7).

Institutional Racism and Incarceration

An indicator of the criminal justice system's discrimination against minorities is the ratio of minorities to Whites in prison. Many other indicators may not show clearly that minorities are treated differently by the system, but incarceration rates clearly demonstrate that there is a **disproportionate confinement** rate for minorities. If recent incarceration rates remain unchanged, an estimated 1 of every 20 persons (5.1 percent) will serve time in a prison during his or her lifetime.[69] However, the likelihood of going to state or federal prison is disproportionate when one examines the likelihood of going to prison by race. When the numbers are adjusted for percentage of the general population, the differences by race are enormous. A White male has a 1 in 23 chance of serving time in prison; a Hispanic male has a 1 in 6 chance; and a Black male has a greater than 1 in 4 chance.[70]

Some argue that the criminal justice system does not incarcerate innocent people; thus, all the Black males in prison have committed a crime and deserve to be incarcerated. Others argue that the criminal justice system discriminates against minorities from the beginning, especially Black males, because they are more likely to be stopped, arrested, charged, convicted, and sentenced to prison than are White males.

Deprivation of the Right to Vote One of the effects of the 28.5 percent likelihood of incarceration for Black males is their disenfranchisement from the political system. The District of Columbia and 46 states deprive felons of the right to vote while they are in prison. In addition, 32 states bar offenders from voting while they are on probation, and 29 bar voting while on parole. In 14 of these states, felons are barred from voting for life.[71] It is estimated that 13 percent of the nation's Black male population cannot vote because they have been convicted of a felony.[72] In some states, such as Alabama and Florida, which have a higher percentage of black male inmates, it is estimated that one in three Black men is denied voting rights because of felony convictions.[73]

HERE'S SOMETHING TO THINK ABOUT...

Prison labor such as making license plates and furniture for the government is commonplace. Facing increasing financial pressures states are turning to other uses of prison labor. States are turning from private contractors to prison labor to do jobs such as paint government vehicles, clean courthouses, clean up campsites, pick up roadkill, and repair leaky public water tanks.

There are two concerns. First, inmate labor will displace private jobs and actually harm the state budget. Second, inmates who work in contact with the public may be a threat to public safety. Martin F. Horn, a professor at John Jay College of Criminal Justice, estimates that only 20 percent of inmates present a low enough security threat to work in public. Do you endorse the use of inmate labor?

disproportionate confinement refers to the nonrandom distribution of persons by race in correctional institutions. If the prison population reflected the same demographics as the general population confinement would not reflect racial bias

Federal Prisons

1895
The first federal prison was built in Leavenworth, Kansas.

For over 100 years after the founding of the United States, there were no federal prisons. Federal prisoners were housed in state prisons for a fee. It was not until 1895 that the first federal prison for men was constructed at Leavenworth, Kansas. Using the labor of military prisoners at the nearby United States Disciplinary Barracks at Fort Leavenworth, the first federal prison was built in the architectural style of the times. Leavenworth Prison was a walled, maximum-security prison based on the Auburn concept of inside cell blocks and congregate work. As in state prisons and local jails, the number of federal female offenders was only about one-tenth that of male offenders. The first federal prison for women was constructed in 1927. Like state prisons, oversight of federal prisons is balanced among the legislative, executive, and judicial branches of the federal government. The U.S. Congress funds federal prisons, which are under the executive control of the Office of the President. The U.S. Supreme Court has the power of judicial review and can declare that prison conditions are unconstitutional or that inmate rights have been violated.

The Federal Bureau of Prisons

Prohibition created many new federal offenses for trafficking in illegal alcoholic beverages, spurring the growth of federal prisons. In 1930, the federal government unified its prisons under the administrative control of the newly formed Federal Bureau of Prisons. After repeal of prohibition, the number of federal prisoners continued to increase as a result of federal drug prosecutions, firearms violations, and, recently, mandatory sentencing. As the federal prison population exploded, overcrowding became a serious problem, and it was necessary to construct new federal prisons. Because of the nationwide jurisdiction of the federal prison system, new prisons could be built anywhere in the United States. Federal inmates could be housed in any federal prison in the country and could be transferred among the prisons at will. This authority to transfer federal inmates anywhere in the United States has been a great advantage of the federal prison system.[74] The ability to transfer inmates from one prison to another, often separated by hundreds or thousands of miles, allows the Federal Bureau of Prisons to move troublemakers and instigators from one prison to another. It also allows inmates in overpopulated prisons to be transferred to less populated prisons. Because the Bureau of Prisons was 40 percent over capacity in 2004, this ability to transfer inmates to relieve overcrowding is important.

Alcatraz In 1934, using this power, the newly formed Federal Bureau of Prisons built one of the most infamous prisons in U.S. history—the United States Penitentiary at Alcatraz, California, in San Francisco Bay. The most violent and highest security risk inmates were then transferred from the various federal prisons to Alcatraz, a maximum-security prison without any rehabilitation, educational, or treatment programs. Its primary goal was the incarceration of high-risk inmates, and it gave little, if any, attention to rehabilitation goals, vocational programs, or educational programs. Alcatraz, which at one time housed Al Capone, prided itself on being escape proof. In 1946, Alcatraz erupted in violence as two **correctional officers** and three inmates were killed during an escape attempt. Public perception of federal prisons was shaped by this event and by movies about notorious Alcatraz inmates. The prison was closed permanently in 1963 and today remains a popular tourist destination.

1934
Alcatraz prison is built in San Francisco Bay by the newly formed Federal Bureau of Prisons.

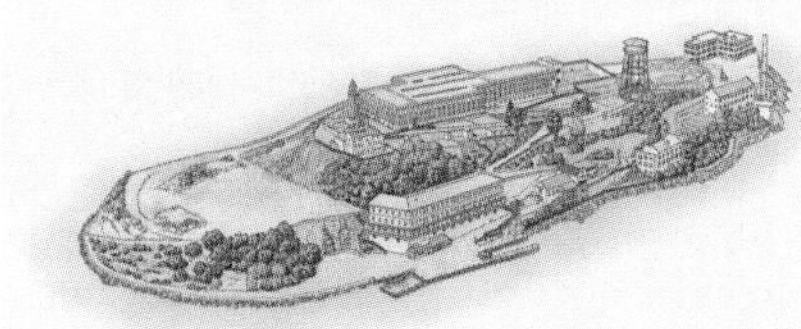

HERE'S SOMETHING TO THINK ABOUT...

In 2011 the U.S. Supreme Court affirmed in Brown v. Plata *a lower court's decision that conditions in California's prisons violate the Eighth Amendment. Justice Anthony Kennedy described California prisons as creating "needless suffering and death." The findings of the lower court concluded that "an inmate in one of California's prisons needlessly dies every six or seven days due to constitutional deficiencies." The Court gave California 2 years to reduce its prison population by more than 30,000 inmates.*

The Court's ruling is in contrast to its previous philosophy of "civil death" when it denied inmates the right to sue for conditions related to imprisonment. Writing for the minority opinion, Justices Antonin Scalia and Samuel Alito called the decision the "most radical injunction issued by a court in our nations' history." They argue the Court overstepped its constitutional authority and institutional expertise in issuing "structural injunctions" and "institutional-reform litigation." Furthermore, the minority opinion argued there would be an inevitable impact on public safety with the early release of 30,000 to 46,000 inmates. Should the courts force early releases of inmates if there is a credible threat to public safety?

correctional officer a uniformed jail or prison employee whose primary job is the security and movement of inmates

Federal prisons are a unified system of correction facilities for persons convicted of various classifications of federal crimes; the system has the advantage of being able to transport inmates to any of the federal prisons.

TABLE 9.2 Federal Prison Security Classification

Security Designation	Security Level	Characteristics	Example of Facility/Population
FPC–Federal Prison Camps	Minimum Security or Federal Prison Camps	Relatively low staff-to-inmate ratio, dormitory housing, limited or no perimeter fencing or guard towers. Work- and program-oriented, frequently adjacent to larger institutions, where inmates help serve the labor needs of the larger institution. Inmates may be allowed limited unsupervised travel and community access.	FPC Alderson, Alderson, WV. Female
FCI–Federal Correctional Institutions	Low Security	Double-fenced perimeters. mostly dormitory or cubicle housing, strong work and program components (education programs or vocational training). Higher staff-to-inmate ratio than FPCs. Inmates may be allowed community access for work and education programs.	FCI Safford, Safford, AZ. Male
FCI and USP–United States Penitentiaries	Medium Security	Medium security institutions include both FCI and USP institutions. Strengthened perimeters (double fences and electronic detection systems), higher staff-to-inmate ratio than FCI Low Security, internal movement of prisoners more restricted, mostly cell-type housing. May include wide variety of work and treatment programs. Very restricted community access.	Includes both FCI and USP institutions
USP–United States Penitentiaries	High Security	Highly secured perimeters (high walls extending underground, reinforced fences, armed guard towers), multiple- and single-occupant cell housing, highest staff-to-inmate ratio, close control of inmate movement. Inmates not permitted to have access to work or education programs in the community.	USP Leavenworth, Leavenworth, KS. Male
FCC–Correctional Complexes	Different security level institutions located in close proximity	Mission and security levels differ by institution. Interaction of the institutions, i.e., FPC may provide services or products to USP such as agricultural products.	FCC Florence, Florence, CO. Includes Medium, High, and Administrative Max and adjacent Minimum Camp. Male
Administrative–MCC, MDC, FDC, FMC, FTC, MCFP, and ADX	Multiple security levels depending on the mission of the institution. Missions include detention of pretrial offenders, medical treatment of inmates, or housing extremely dangerous, violent, or escape-prone inmates.	MCC–Metropolitan Correctional Centers MDC–Metropolitan Detention Centers FDC–Federal Detention Centers FMC–Federal Medical Centers FTC–Federal Transfer Centers MCFP–Medical Center for Federal Prisoners ADX–"Administrative-Maximum supermax" security prison	ADX Maximum security, Florence, Florence, CO
Satellite Campus	Minimum security camp	Located adjacent to the main facility to provide inmate labor and off-site work programs.	FCI Memphis, Memphis, TN
Satellite Low Security	Small, low-security satellite facility adjacent to the main institution	Located adjacent to the main facility to provide inmate labor and off-site work programs.	FCI Elkton, Elkton, Ohio

Federal Correctional Facilities

Today, the Federal Bureau of Prisons operates over 100 federal correctional facilities throughout the United States. The Federal Bureau of Prisons' central office in Washington, DC, has six regional offices to oversee the operation of federal prison facilities. Federal prisons range from the **administrative-maximum prison** in Florence, Colorado, to minimum-security federal prison farms. The federal government even operates "coed" minimum-security correctional facilities, the largest of which is in Lexington, Kentucky. Some federal prison facilities serve primarily as medical centers for federal prisoners, and others as detention centers and prison camps.

As in state prisons, the chief executive officer at a federal prison facility is the warden, who has various associates and assistants to help run the administrative units, including correctional officers, who are responsible for maintaining order and overseeing inmates. Employees of the Federal Bureau of Prisons are federal employees, who generally receive better pay and benefits than do state prison or local jail employees. Generally, however, the hiring standards are higher. Federal Bureau of Prisons employees may transfer from one federal facility to another, so opportunities for advancement are greater than in state prisons or local jails. As in state prisons, staffing in federal prisons is divided between employees who primarily perform security duties and those who provide administration and treatment services.

Privatization

A trend in corrections has been the **privatization** of jails and prisons. In 2007, states and the federal system reported over 126,000 prisoners held in privately operated facilities. Since 2000, about 6.5 percent of state and federal inmates have been in privately operated facilities. The Bureau of Justice Statistics reported that in 2008, private facilities held about 8 percent of all state prisoners and 11.7 percent of federal prisoners. Among states, Texas and Oklahoma reported the largest populations in private facilities. Six states had at least 25 percent of their prison population housed in private prisons.

129,336

Number of prisoners held in private prisons in 2009

Cost-Reduction Benefits The primary reason for housing prisoners in private facilities is to reduce costs. The cost of new prison facilities is extremely expensive. Private prisons allow local jails and state and federal prisons to house prisoners in private facilities and pay a per diem rate per prisoner rather than build new prisons to accommodate the increasing demand for bed space.

Private prisons look very similar to government prisons. The difference is that private prisons are for-profit businesses that take prisoners from local, state, and federal government and house them for a fee. Charges for housing an inmate in a private facility vary, ranging from about $25 a day per inmate to $100 a day. Thus, in a private prison there might be prisoners from several different counties and states. Also, there may be prisoners from local as well as state and federal prisons. Some prisoners are sent from long distances to be housed in private prisons. For example, Hawaii sends prisoners to private prisons in Texas. These transfers can separate inmates from family, friends, support services, and even their lawyers.

A private prison must pay for all expenses from its revenue to build and operate the prison and still be able to show a profit. Thus, controlling the cost of building and operating a private prison is important to the corporation that wishes to make a profit from its venture. There are several ways that private prisons keep costs down. Companies often receive tax breaks for building private prisons and grants for training employees. Often, private prisons are built in rural areas where land and construction costs are low and wages are below the national average.[75]

Criticisms of Privatization Critics of the privatization of corrections argue that given the emphasis on containing costs, private companies provide less training and salary to prison personnel and have higher inmate-to-correctional officer ratios than do government prisons.[76] Critics also express concern that for-profit prisons do not provide the same quality of care and supervision or the same educational, recreational, and rehabilitative services as public prisons do.

Proponents of private prisons focus almost entirely on the cost savings. Often, local, state, and federal prisons are under great pressures, including lawsuits, to reduce prison overcrowding. Unable to afford the high cost of constructing new prisons, governments turn to the use of private prisons.

AS IN STATE PRISONS, STAFFING IN FEDERAL PRISONS IS DIVIDED BETWEEN EMPLOYEES WHO PRIMARILY PERFORM SECURITY DUTIES AND THOSE WHO PROVIDE ADMINISTRATION AND TREATMENT SERVICES.

TABLE 9.3 Number of Prisoners in Privately Operated Facilities

	Number of Prisoners			Percent of
	Total	Federal	State	all Prisoners
2005	107,940	27,046	80,894	7.1
2006	113,697	27,726	85,971	7.2
2007	123,942	31,310	92,632	7.8
2008	128,524	33,162	95,362	8.0%
2009	129,336	34,087	95,249	6.8%

Source: Sourcebook of Criminal Justice Statistics, http://www.albany.edu/sourcebook/pdf/t6322009.pdf.

administrative-maximum prison is the highest security level of prison operated by the U.S. Bureau of Prisons. Supermax prisons are considered "escape-proof" regardless of the resources of the inmate

privatization a trend toward jails and prisons being run by for-profit, private companies

6 **Privitization is a trend in corrections, resulting from the need to cut costs, whereby private, for-profit businesses house state and federal prisoners for a fee; however, there are problems with privatization, especially regarding prisoners' rights and the state and federal system's retention of liability for the prisoners.**

HERE'S SOMETHING TO THINK ABOUT...

As the nation's financial crisis continues to erode the fiscal health of the states, many states are turning to private prisons to squeeze every last dollar out of the budget. However, for the past 3 years the increase in prison population has slowed and states are turning to alternatives other than incarceration. These changes have shrunk the pool of potential inmates for private prisons. Despite this change the number of inmates in private prisons continues to rise. Financially challenged states such as Arizona, Florida, and Ohio still plan to transfer thousands of state inmates to private prisons. The primary force behind this movement is the belief that private prisons save the states money. A new study by the Arizona Department of Corrections challenges this assumption.

A 2011 study by the Arizona Department of Corrections suggests that the cost difference between housing inmates in private prisons versus state prisons may be as little as 3 cents per day. Furthermore, when other factors are taken into account private prisons may actually cost more per inmate than state prisons.

A factor often not included in comparing the costs of private versus state prisons is the fact that the contracts of private prisons limit the type of inmates they will accept. Private prisons are typically medium-security prisons and their contract excludes inmates with limited physical capacity, severe physical illness, chronic conditions, and high-need mental health conditions. Basically, the private prisons take those inmates who are the least expensive to house leaving the state with the high-cost inmates. As a result, the Arizona study concludes that when these factors are taken into account and comparing the costs of imprisonment not only may there be little difference between the costs of private prisons and state prisons, but state prisons also may be less expensive.

There are few other studies with which to compare the findings of the Arizona study. Advocates for private prisons argue even if these data are accurate private prisons save the state millions of dollars in upfront construction costs and provide the ability to handle temporary increases in the prison population without the state having to commit to permanent personnel and facility costs.

Opponents argue that beyond the question of cost comparisons there are inherent flaws in the use of private prisons, including state liability and alleged substandard staff, treatment programs, rehabilitation programs, job training, and educational programs offered by private prisons. The 2010 escape of three inmates from a private prison in Kingman, Arizona, and their murderous assault upon the community suggests to some that private prisons fail to provide for adequate public safety regardless of the costs.

Do you think more research should be done to examine the costs, quality, and public safety issues associated with private prisons?

Detriments to the Surrounding Community Although private prisons help relieve the burden on overcrowded state and federal prisons, they often are criticized as detrimental to low-income communities, where most private prisons are located. Private companies market their services to the state on promises of providing jobs in low-income communities and providing inmate labor for community projects.[77] With some outstanding exceptions, pay and benefits, however, as well as prison conditions, often are below state standards.[78]

State Liability Another concern of critics is the issue of state liability for violation of inmates' constitutional rights and the abuse of inmates while housed in a private prison. Because it placed the inmate in the prison, the state retains liability but little control. Employees of private prisons are not government employees, and they and the companies that operate the prisons do not have immunity from certain lawsuits by inmates that government prisons enjoy.[79] Nevertheless, thousands of lawsuits are filed against state prisons as well as private prisons for violations of inmate rights and substandard prison conditions.[80] For example, in April 2009, a Texas jury awarded $42.5 million to the family of an inmate who was beaten to death in 2001 at a private Texas prison facility in Willacy County. The award against the GEO Group Inc., formerly named Wackenhut, is among the largest punitive damages ordered against a private prison company.[81]

Escaped Prisoners A unique problem for private prisons is the jurisdiction of law enforcement over escaped prisoners. Not all states have enacted legislation that recognizes the potential status of inmates in private prisons as escapees. Thus, a prisoner who escapes from a private prison may not have broken a state law! Also, an assault by an inmate on a correctional officer at a private facility is an assault on a private citizen (a tort), whereas an assault on a state or federal correctional officer is defined as a more serious crime.

WHEN THE GOVERNMENT INCARCERATES A PERSON IT BECOMES LEGALLY RESPONSIBLE FOR THE HEALTH AND WELL-BEING OF THOSE INCARCERATED.

Prison Life

Life in prison poses special problems for inmates, correctional authorities, and the community. When the government incarcerates a person it becomes legally responsible for the health and well-being of those incarcerated. Although the mission of correctional institutions is to protect the community by keeping prisoners securely incarcerated, there are other threats to the community. In securing inmates and protecting the community from harm, correctional institutions must do so without violating the constitutional rights of inmates. Some of the major challenges for correctional authorities are reducing/eliminating sexual violence in prison; reducing the risks caused by prison gangs; providing for the health, both physical and mental, and well-being of inmates; and reducing overall violence.

Sexual Violence in Prisons

Sexual violence in prison has become a national concern. Anecdotal stories, incomplete statistics, and testimonies before legislative bodies and public forums suggest that

7 **Some of the major challenges affecting prisons as they try to balance security with prisoners' rights are trying to reduce sexual violence and violence in general, including violence and other risks associated with gangs, and providing for the physical and mental care of the inmates.**

nonconsensual sexual violence is a serious problem. Inmate lawsuits claim that prison officials turn a blind eye to sexual violence in prison.[82] Some inmates who claim they have been raped in prison state that they were considered the "property" of prison gangs and would be bartered for money or favors.[83] Human Rights Watch issued a report concluding that "rape, by prisoners' accounts, was no aberrational occurrence; instead it was a deeply-rooted, systemic problem. It was also a problem that prison authorities were doing little to address."[84] Spurred by public demands for more accurate information on sexual violence in prisons, President George W. Bush signed into law the **Prison Rape Elimination Act of 2003** (P.L. 108-79). The legislation requires the Bureau of Justice Statistics to develop new national data collections on the incidence and prevalence of sexual violence within correctional facilities.

2004 Data on Sexual Violence In 2004, the Bureau of Justice Statistics issued its first report. The bureau surveyed 2,700 correctional facilities and found that there were 8,210 allegations of sexual violence reported and that correctional authorities substantiated nearly 2,100 incidents of sexual violence.[85] The most serious forms of sexual violence reported were inmate-on-inmate nonconsensual sexual acts and staff sexual misconduct. Nearly 42 percent of the reported allegations of sexual violence involved staff sexual misconduct, 37 percent involved inmate-on-inmate nonconsensual sexual acts, 11 percent pertained to staff sexual harassment, and 10 percent applied to inmate-on-inmate abusive sexual contact. Juvenile facilities reported the highest rates of alleged sexual violence. The survey data indicated that most allegations of sexual violence could not be substantiated due to a lack of evidence. Males comprised 90 percent of victims and perpetrators of nonconsensual sexual acts in prison and jail.

Sanctions for Sexual Violence The study further reported that jail and prison authorities had several sanctions for inmates who were found to have committed sexual violence. The most common sanctions included moving the perpetrator to solitary confinement, changing the inmate to a higher custody level, transferring the inmate to another facility, loss of good time credit, loss of privileges, and confining the inmate to his or her cell or quarters. Staff members found to have committed sexual violence were discharged, disciplined, or referred for prosecution. Juvenile systems reported the largest numbers of staff referred for prosecution (41 percent).

2007 Data on Sexual Violence Since the inception of the Prison Rape Elimination Act, the Bureau of Justice Statistics continues to issue annual reports of sexual victimization in jails and prisons. The 2007 data reported that over 12,000 (1.6 percent) jail inmates reported sexual violence involving another inmate and over 15,000 (2 percent) reported an incident involving staff. In 2007, a total of 24,700 incidences of sexual victimization were reported by jail inmates. The numbers were higher for state and federal prison inmates.[86] About 4.5 percent (60,500 inmates) of state and federal prison inmates reported sexual victimization. As with jail inmates, state and federal inmates reported a higher rate of sexual victimization by staff than by other inmates.[87]

The 2007 report of the Rape Elimination Act still notes that preventing and responding to sexual victimization of inmates does not appear to be a priority of prison administration. U.S. District Judge Reggie B. Walton, Commission Chairman of the report, recommends a zero-tolerance policy on prison sexual victimization. Other suggestions to combat the sexual victimization of inmates include background checks for staff and training of staff to help victims of sexual assault secure emergency medical and mental health treatment.[88]

1.6% of jail inmates reported sexual victimization in jails and prisons

2% of jail inmates reported an incident involving a staff member

Prison Gangs

Gang activity, a major factor in many prisons, has implications for in-prison and post-prison behavior.[89] The first prison gangs appeared in 1950. Prior to that time, strict control of prisoner movement, limited contact with the outside, absence of work release programs, and a harsh disciplinary code prevented the formation of gangs. Today, prison gangs, known as special threat or **security-risk groups,** are a serious problem. For example, Rikers Island in New York has identified 44 security-risk groups that operate within the prison.[90] Among the more common gangs operating in prison are the Aryan Brotherhood, the Black Guerilla Family, the Bloods, the Crips, La Nuestra Familia, the Latin Kings, the Mexican Mafia, Mexikanemi, Neta, and the Texas Syndicate. Most prison gangs are organized along lines of racial and ethnic identity.

Special Security Risks Prison gangs pose special security risks and create a higher risk of violence because of the following:

1. Gang codes of conduct discourage obedience to prison rules.
2. Gangs frequently are involved in trafficking of prison contraband and protection.

Gang codes require absolute loyalty to the gang. Often, to show one's commitment to the gang, new members must pass initiation tests, rituals that require the new member to make a "hit" on a rival gang member or correctional staff member. The hit usually requires only that the gang member attack the person and draw blood.[91]

HERE'S SOMETHING TO THINK ABOUT...

Michelle Alexander, author of The New Jim Crow: Mass Incarceration in the Age of Colorblindness, *criticizes "mass incarceration" as a racially based system of control that exists to serve the perceived interests of White elites. She claims the move away from "get tough" sentencing policies reflects the desire of the White middle class to avoid raising taxes, not a newfound interest in social justice. She calls for the dismantling of mass incarceration while acknowledging the economic engine generated by imprisonment. Do you agree with this claim? Why?*

Prison Rape Elimination Act of 2003 required the Bureau of Justice Statistics to survey jails and prisons to determine the prevalance of sexual violence within correctional facilities

security-risk groups groups that raise special threats, such as prison gangs

Trafficking in Contraband Gang membership extends outside the prison. Prison gangs use this characteristic to have fellow gang members smuggle contraband inside the prison during visitations, through staff members who have been bribed, or when the prisoner is outside the prison wall on work details or other forms of release. Prison gangs then use trafficking in **contraband**—such as drugs, cigarettes, money, pornography, and so on—to buy favors, recruit members, pay prison debts, and make a profit. Prisoners who compete with the prison gang business, who inform prison officials about gang activities, or who are unable to pay for gang contraband may become targets of gang violence.

Inmate Protection Many inmates join a gang for protection, so an unintended consequence of longer prison terms has been an increase in gang affiliation. Because prisoners have to stay in prison longer, they feel a greater need to be affiliated with a prison gang to provide them with protection from other gangs, from individual inmates, and from correctional staff members. Gang affiliation guarantees retaliation for any harm caused to a member by others. In extreme cases, such retaliation can lead to a vicious cycle of gang wars, as each gang continues to retaliate for the last attack. Because fear of gang retaliation may be much stronger than fear of official prison sanctions, whenever prison rules and gang codes conflict, gang members will obey their gang code.

Physical Health in Prisons

Daniel Tote, age 47, missed his release date from prison. In fact, he remained in prison 10 months beyond the expiration of his sentence. Tote was not released because he was in a persistent vegetative state as a result of head trauma that he suffered in an attack while in prison. When his sentence expired, there was no place to send him. Nursing homes would not take him because, as a prisoner, he was not eligible for Medicaid. He had no insurance and no family to care for him. Thus, he remained in the prison infirmary despite the fact that he was a free man. Eventually, the state found a nursing home in which to place him, at a cost to the state of about $40,000 a year.[92] Daniel Tote is an extreme example of a serious problem in the criminal justice system: The physical and mental health of offenders, both incarcerated and released, has become a costly and sometimes deadly public health problem with no end in sight.

Prisoners have significant physical and mental health problems. The health of an average 50-year-old prisoner approximates that of an average 60-year-old person in the free community.[93] In a survey by the Office of Justice Programs, about 40 percent of state inmates and 48 percent of federal inmates age 45 or older said they had had a medical problem since admission to prison.[94] While they are in prison, their health care is the responsibility of the state. When they are released from prison, as most are, these problems do not go away when they reenter the community. Often, the released inmate enters the community with significant physical and mental health problems that can have a serious—even deadly—impact on the public.

Long-Term Health Care The trend toward incarceration of offenders has created an unintended consequence: the creation of long-term health care obligations. As more prisoners are incarcerated and with longer sentences, the cost of prisoners' health care increases dramatically.[95] The impact of this problem can be seen in the fact that the most common **Section 1983 lawsuits** against jails and prisons involved claims of substandard medical treatment.[96] The leading causes of death in state prisons are heart diseases and cancer, which account for half of the deaths in state prisons. Most of these inmates were age 45 or older, and most of the deaths in prison (68 percent) for medical reasons were the result of preexisting conditions that the inmates had prior to admission. Many prison facilities now contain geriatric wings to house the high number of elderly inmates. These facilities provide long-term care units staffed by nurses instead of correctional officers. Older, ill inmates receive round-the-clock care that costs the state about $65,000 per year.[97]

AS MORE PRISONERS ARE INCARCERATED AND WITH LONGER SENTENCES, THE COST OF PRISONERS' HEALTH CARE INCREASES DRAMATICALLY.

The Burden of Health Care Costs For some states, the cost of health care, especially for the chronically or terminally ill, is so burdensome on the state that state legislators and parole boards have provided for early release of these prisoners to reduce the cost to the state. Other states, such as California, Illinois, and Texas, are turning to cost-cutting strategies such as telemedicine. Telemedicine provides video consultations, avoiding the cost of transporting the prisoner outside the prison to medical facilities and making it easier and cheaper to secure the services of medical doctors and specialists.

$65,000

The average cost per year to provide round-the-clock health care to an elderly, ill inmate.

The standard of health care provided by cash-starved California fell below acceptable standards of care, and a court-appointed receiver was charged with improving the health system of California state prisons. The court mandated that the state significantly reduce its prison population or build more facilities. California appealed the decision to the U.S. Supreme Court and in 2011 the Supreme Court affirmed the lower court's order. California was ordered to reduce its prison population to a maximum of 110,000 by 2013 or build more facilities. Given California's financial crisis and limited budget it is certain the state will be unable to build additional facilities so it appears the state will have to offer early release to 30,000 to 40,000 inmates.

Studies indicate that, statistically, the risk of recidivism drops significantly with age. However, prisons, especially federal prisons and prisons in states that have abolished parole, often cannot release these inmates. In other cases,

30,000

The number of inmates that California Corrections has been ordered to release by 2013. The prisoners are being released to address a predicted budget shortfall.

contraband smuggled goods, such as drugs, cigarettes, money, and pornography

Section 1983 lawsuits are civil lawsuits filed in federal court alleging that the government has violated a constitutional right of the inmate

elderly offenders cannot be released because they are serving mandatory terms or because there are no community-care facilities to release them to, as in the case of Daniel Tote. As a result, the care of geriatric inmates has become an expensive burden on the criminal justice system. In a system that is constantly competing for public funding of other needs—for example, drug treatment programs, juvenile rehabilitation programs, community policing, and even public schools and highways—it is difficult to justify spending $65,000 a year on care for each elderly prisoner. But can prisoners be released just because they are old and it is expensive to take care of them? About 45 percent of inmates age 50 and older had only recently been arrested. Older felons tend to be locked up for more serious crimes, such as rape, murder, and child molestation.[98] These offenders need to be incarcerated for the protection of the public.

OLDER FELONS TEND TO BE LOCKED UP FOR MORE SERIOUS CRIMES, SUCH AS RAPE, MURDER, AND CHILD MOLESTATION. THEY NEED TO BE INCARCERATED FOR THE PROTECTION OF THE PUBLIC.

Drug Treatment Programs Drug treatment programs for addicted inmates are another significant challenge for prison officials. Over 50 percent of prisoners can be classified as drug dependent. An estimated 21 percent of state and 55 percent of federal inmates were incarcerated in 2004 for drug law violations. About 17 percent of state prisoners reported that they committed their crimes to obtain money for drugs. Given these high numbers of drug-dependent prisoners it is important for prisons to be able to offer drug treatment programs to inmates. However, only about 39 percent of drug users were able to participate in a prison drug abuse program in 2004.

Feeding Inmates Providing for the health and well-being of inmates can be as simple as feeding them. Complaints about food have been one of the reasons given by inmates for protests and riots. Perhaps one of the most extreme examples of failing to feed inmates properly was the case of the Morgan County jail in Alabama in 2009. Morgan County provided the sheriff with a budget for the feeding of inmates. Historically, the pay for sheriffs was low and one of the strategies was to allow the sheriff to keep any unused funds for the feeding of inmates for his or her personal income. Under this system, the wives of many sheriffs provided meals for the inmates to secure a little more income. Morgan County continued the use of this scheme to supplement the sheriff's salary. However, Sheriff Greg Barlett appeared to go to the extreme. The state food allowance was $1.75 per prisoner per day, yet on this meager allowance Sheriff Barlett was able to pocket $212,000 over 3 years in unused food money.[99] Shocked at the failure to provide a minimum standard of care for inmates, U.S. District Judge U. W. Clemon issued an arrest warrant for Sheriff Barlett for contempt for failing to adequately feed inmates and incarcerated him in his own jail.

HIV/AIDS and STDs Sexually transmitted diseases (STDs), including **HIV/AIDS** and other communicable diseases, pose serious challenges to administrators of both adult and juvenile justice systems.[100] In 2002, the overall rate of confirmed AIDS cases among the nation's prison population was 3.5 times the rate of the U.S. general population. Official statistics indicate that about 2 percent of state prison inmates and 1 percent of federal prison inmates are known to be infected with HIV.[101] However, the rate of HIV/AIDS infection is not uniform throughout the criminal justice system. New York, for example, has an HIV-positive prison population of nearly 8 percent, and California has a rate of less than 1 percent.[102] The percentage of HIV-positive inmates has declined since 1998.[103] The problem affects both male and female inmates, but a greater percentage of women (2.9 percent) than men (1.9 percent) are HIV-positive as reported in 2002.[104]

AIDS-related deaths in prison have dropped dramatically, from over 1,000 in 1995 to 176 in 2005.[105] The drop in the death rate is attributed primarily to advances in medical treatments available for HIV-positive patients and better identification and management of HIV-infected inmates by prison administrators.

FEDERAL LAWS REGARDING INMATES' RIGHTS OF PRIVACY OFTEN PROHIBIT PRISON ADMINISTRATORS FROM MAKING IT GENERALLY KNOWN WHICH INMATES ARE HIV-POSITIVE.

Testing for and Treating HIV/AIDS Prisons are a critical setting for detecting and treating STDs. The testing of inmates for HIV/AIDS varies from state to state. About 19 states test all inmates at admission, whereas other states test inmates only on request or if the inmate belongs to a specific high-risk group. Most HIV-positive inmates were positive when admitted and thus did not become HIV-positive after admission to prison. Inmates contract HIV/AIDS from high-risk behavior, such as intravenous drug use or unprotected sex with partners who are infected. Many female inmates contract HIV/AIDS from prostitution. Because most inmates will be released back into the community, the identification of those with HIV/AIDS is important, because they constitute a significant percentage of the total number of Americans with HIV/AIDS.[106] Unfortunately, only 10 percent of state and federal prisons and 5 percent of city and county jails offer comprehensive HIV-prevention programs for inmates.[107]

Risks to Others in the Prison Inmates who are HIV-positive pose special problems for correctional employees. Those inmates cannot be completely isolated from the general prison population. In fact, federal laws regarding inmates' rights of privacy often prohibit prison administrators from making it generally known which inmates are HIV-positive. Thus, prison staff and other inmates may not be aware of which inmates are affected. This lack of knowledge creates concern among the prison staff, because they do not know if they are at risk of HIV infection when they handle inmates. Lacking this knowledge, the prison staff must treat all inmates as if they are potential infection

HIV/AIDS Acquired Immune Deficiency Syndrome (AIDS) is caused by a virus called Human Immunodeficiency Virus (HIV). The disease is a deficiency of the body's immune system. A person can be HIV positive but not have AIDS

risks. HIV-infected inmates may deliberately attempt to infect prison officials by biting them or by other means.

Risks to the Community on Inmates' Release When inmates who are HIV-positive are released back into the community, they may create a public health hazard without proper care or education. While in prison, inmates receive free medication and treatment, but after release, they may be responsible for their own medical expenses and treatment. Released inmates may pose a serious health hazard if they engage in unprotected sex or share needles from intravenous drug use. Female offenders pose a community health risk, because many return to prostitution to obtain the cash they need.

Tuberculosis and Other Communicable Diseases Prisons and jails also present optimal conditions of the spread of diseases such as hepatitis C, staph infections, swine flu (H1N1 flu), and **tuberculosis (TB)**.[108] Tuberculosis can be more difficult to control than HIV because it is more easily spread by contact with active cases. TB-infected inmates released back into the community have the potential to spread the disease further, because TB can remain infectious for a long time. One study reported that in 31 state prison systems, 14 percent of inmates had positive tuberculin skin test results at intake.[109]

Inmates who receive only partial treatment for TB increase the threat of epidemic in the general population, because incomplete treatment raises the risk that the disease will become resistant to medications used to treat it and will not respond to subsequent treatment. Drug-resistant forms of TB could be transmitted to others, and the result could be a widespread public health disaster. Treatment of TB is complicated. A primary TB control measure is the complete isolation of infectious cases to prevent spreading the disease to other inmates. This type of isolation requires negative-pressure isolation rooms with ventilation that does not flow into the general ventilation system. Another complication of TB is that often inmates may be coinfected with both TB and HIV. Because TB can be spread through the ventilation system, prison administrators have to take precautions to keep general prison populations from being exposed. Failure to do so may result in a lawsuit.

Deinstitutionalization In the 1960s, legislation was passed that made it difficult to commit mentally ill people who had not committed a crime to civil mental health facilities against their will. As a result, public mental hospitals were forced to release persons committed against their will unless the state could prove that the person was a danger to himself or herself or to the public. The intention of the legislation was that mentally ill people would receive community-based care instead of long-term hospitalization that differed little from incarceration. It was thought that with proper medication, community-based care would be a more humane alternative to long-term hospitalization.[113] Despite the good intentions of legislators, **deinstitutionalization** did not work as planned. There were too few community-based facilities, those with mental illness did not take their medications, and jails and prisons became the dumping ground for such individuals.[114] Persons with mental illness end up in jails and prisons for bizarre public behavior; petty crimes such as loitering, public intoxication, and panhandling; as well as serious violent crimes such as murder, sexual assault, and property crime. About half of inmates with mental illness are in prison for a violent offense.[115]

Behavioral Problems Mentally ill inmates frequently are unable to abide by prison rules and discipline. This in part is because of their mental illness and in part because of the overcrowded conditions and stresses of the correctional institution. Also, because they are unable to have "normal" interpersonal relations—a difficult challenge even for the mentally stable in prison—they are more likely to engage in fights and other violent behaviors. Unable to conform to the rules or to restrain their violent behavior, the mentally ill spend many hours in solitary confinement or segregated housing. Unfortunately, this punishment greatly increases the likelihood of depression and heightened anxiety in the mentally ill inmate.[116] The experience of being incarcerated typically exacerbates inmates' mental illness.[117] As a result, incarcerated, emotionally disturbed inmates in state prisons spend an average of 15 months longer behind bars than other prisoners. In many cases, the difference is attributed to their delusions, hallucinations, or paranoia, which make them more likely to get into fights or receive disciplinary reports.[118]

Mental Health in Prisons

Mental illness is pervasive in jails and prisons. According to the Bureau of Justice Statistics, in 2005, 64 percent of local jail inmates, 56 percent of state prisoners, and 45 percent of federal inmates had a mental health problem.[110] A comprehensive Justice Department study of the rapidly growing number of incarcerated, emotionally disturbed people concluded that jails and prisons have become the nation's new mental health care facilities.[111] According to the report, "Jails have become the poor person's mental hospitals."[112]

JAILS AND PRISONS HAVE BECOME THE NATION'S NEW MENTAL HEALTH CARE FACILITIES.

64% of inmates in local jails had a mental health problem (2005),

56% of inmates in state prisons, as well as

45% of inmates in federal prisons

Prisons as Contributing Factors of Mental Illness Prison environments contribute to mental health problems. Prisons are **total institutions**, a term sociologist Erving Goffman coined in his study of prisons and mental hospitals.[119] In prison, the inmate has little responsibility, does not have to make decisions, does not have to engage in problem solving, and does not have to plan for tomorrow. The institution meets all the inmate's basic needs. The institution dictates the inmate's schedule. Institutional rules are made without any input from the inmate. The environment is rigid, and inmates are expected to conform to the values and expectations of the institution. Individuality is discouraged, dissent is punished, and

tuberculosis (TB) a contagious infectious disease caused by a bacterial infection that primarily affects the lungs

deinstitutionalization the movement of mentally ill offenders from long-term hospitalization to community-based care

total institutions institutions that meet all of the inmate's basic needs, discourage individuality, punish dissent, and segregate those who do not follow the rules

failure to follow the rules can result in segregation from the prison population. As a consequence, the prison environment

1. does not promote effective treatment of mentally ill offenders—even people without mental health problems become depressed and mentally ill when exposed to this environment; and
2. encourages the development of **prisonization**—socialization into a distinct prison subculture with its own values, mores, norms, and sanctions.

Prisonization results in a subculture for inmates in which the rules of conduct are distinctly different from the official rules of the institution and from society in general. Prisoners learn to adapt to this prison code and conduct their life in prison by it. However, the prisoner with mental illness, who has difficulty adapting to society in general, often is unable to relate to fellow prisoners and conform to the **prison code** while at the same time maintaining the appearance of obedience to the institutional rules and norms. Often, the result of this failure to adapt to the prison code is dangerous ostracism by both inmates and administrators.

Problems for the Community All prisoners are affected by prisonization, which is why most prisoners demonstrate maladaptive behaviors when they are returned to the community. Accustomed to being told what to do, when to do it, and how to do it, released inmates often demonstrate few of the job skills desired by employers. Prisoners who have been incarcerated for long terms may have lost the ability to plan for the future, to take responsibility for their actions, and exhibit proactive behaviors. They have become passive, dependent, and fixated on the rules.

When released back into the community, the offender with mental illness is seldom cured as a result of the treatment received while incarcerated. Even if treatment and medication in prison had made a significant impact on their behavior, it is doubtful that released offenders with mental illness would continue treatment or medication. For example, a Bureau of Justice Statistics survey reported that although an estimated 13 percent of probationers were required to seek mental health treatment as a condition of their sentence, fewer than half fulfilled this requirement.[120]

Neither police nor correctional institutions have been able to make a significant impact on the problem of the offender with mental illness. Providing medications in prison is a temporary approach to a much more serious community problem. In addition to the public-order crimes they commit, offenders with mental illness commit serious offenses. For example, about 13 percent of inmates with mental illness in prisons were convicted of murder, and about 12 percent were convicted of sexual assault. Andrea Yates, for example, was mentally ill when she murdered her five young children by drowning them one by one in the bathtub of her home.

ALL PRISONERS ARE AFFECTED BY PRISONIZATION, WHICH IS WHY MOST PRISONERS DEMONSTRATE MALADAPTIVE BEHAVIORS WHEN THEY ARE RETURNED TO THE COMMUNITY.

HERE'S SOMETHING TO THINK ABOUT...

How do prisoners protest their conditions of imprisonment other than through lawsuits? One means of protest is the hunger strike. Spearheaded by inmates in the Pelican Bay State Prison security housing unit, 1,700 California inmates stopped eating July 1, 2011, to protest conditions at Pelican Bay State Prison where inmates are kept in isolation 22 hours per day. Psychiatrist and Harvard professor, Stuart Grassian, describes the conditions as "strikingly toxic" and "far more egregious than the death penalty." Some prisoners say they are committed to "taking this all the way to the death if necessary." Do you think hunger strikes can be an influence for positive change?

Mental health professionals posit that a significant percentage of youths involved in the juvenile justice system have unmet needs for mental health and substance abuse services.[121]

Prison Violence

Prisons are violent environments. Prison violence includes inmate-on-inmate violence and excessive use of force by staff. Experiments simulating prisoner–staff environments have demonstrated that the prison environment and the guard–inmate relationship have great potential to trigger violence by staff against inmates. Many times, staff violence appears to be related to hiring practices in which staff are not qualified or have backgrounds that should have disqualified them for employment. For example, in 2008, investigations revealed that more than a dozen corrections officers at the Prince George's County Jail had criminal backgrounds, including charges of theft, assault, domestic violence, DUI, and sexual assault.[122]

Prison violence is also associated with practices by prison officials that permit the use of inmates to supervise other inmates. In some cases, such as the Texas prison system in the 1960s, the use of inmates to supervise other inmates was the formal policy of these institutions. As a result of lawsuits, this practice has disappeared as the formal policy of the prison and has been replaced by a clandestine informal policy. For example, investigations by the Civil Rights Division of the United States Department of Justice and the Office of the United States Attorney into the conditions at Cook County Jail (Chicago) in 2008 alleged systematic and widespread use of violence against inmates by staff and poor supervision of inmates, resulting in unchecked inmate-on-inmate violence. A 2009 wrongful death lawsuit against correctional officials at Rikers Island Jail (New York City) accused the jail of "letting inmates run Rikers

prisonization socialization into a distinct prison subculture with its own values, mores, norms, and sanctions

prison code is the informal rules and expected behavior established by inmates. Often the prison code is contrary to the official rules and policies of the prison. Violation of the prison code can be punished by use of violence or even death

Island jail." The lawsuit claimed that prison officials did not just turn a blind eye to violence, "They authorized and directed it."[123]

Prisons—The Human Cage

Jails and prisons are designed to hold humans in a secure environment to prevent their escape. Frequently, the concern of the public is not the conditions of the jails or prisons but the perceived risk of escape and fear of harm caused by escaping prisoners. Most citizens strongly object to a jail or prison being built in their neighborhood.[124] Some citizens appear to have little sympathy for incarcerated inmates. For example, in response to a report on four suicides in a municipal jail, one editorial dismissed concerns about the deaths, arguing, "These suspects had been arrested for murder, kidnapping, burglary, drug dealing, assault and drunken driving. I do not consider these deaths as tragic losses. Rather, these four saved the overburdened taxpayers a great deal of money by taking their fates into their own hands."[125]

Jails and prisons represent a substantial financial burden and directly compete with other needed services. Often, people see every dollar that goes into jails and prisons as one less dollar to go to other services, such as schools, hospitals, medical care, public safety, and transportation. For example, when a Pennsylvania jail warden turned in a request for $500,000 for new computers for an educational program for Pittsburgh jail inmates, the county refused to process the invoice.[126] The computers were to be purchased from profits from the jail's commissary, where inmates buy candy, snacks, and toiletries, but the county government argued that the money should be returned to the taxpayers. As one official expressed, "We have taxpayers who can't even afford (computers). Before we give that type of convenience to prisoners, we should balance the budget. It's not our responsibility to educate and entertain the inmates."[127]

Recidivism rates show that jails and prisons have not proved as effective as desired. They have not protected the public from criminal activity in the long run. They have not deterred people from committing crimes through the threat or pain of incarceration, nor have they rehabilitated inmates, whether through penitence, educational training, or harsh discipline. Some have argued that prisons are nothing but warehouses in which inmates are placed because society cannot think of more effective solutions to an age-old problem. The public has become frustrated with the cost and lack of effectiveness of locking criminals in cages and waiting. Chapter 11 discusses some of the community corrections strategies that have been adopted to reduce incarceration and promote rehabilitation rather than mere incapacitation.

HERE'S SOMETHING TO THINK ABOUT…

Members of the Armed Services who are convicted of offenses under the Uniform Code of Military Justice and sentenced to imprisonment are incarcerated in military, not civilian, facilities. Each branch of the service (Army, Navy, Marines, and Air Force) operates confinement facilities. Military correctional facilities are known as military prisons, disciplinary barracks, brigs, detention facilities, or confinement facilities. Military facilities that function similar to civilian jails are known as guardhouses, stockades, or brigs.

Military prisons are staffed by military personnel and house only military personnel convicted of offenses or being held for trial. Civilians may be employed for noncustodial staff positions such as secretaries, teachers, and other support positions.

One of the oldest military prisons is the United States Disciplinary Barracks (USDB) located in Fort Leavenworth, Kansas. The USDB, known as the Castle, is the U.S. military's only maximum-security facility. Only enlisted prisoners with sentences over 5 years, commissioned officers, and prisoners convicted of offenses related to national security are confined to the USDB. The Castle was built by prison labor starting in 1875. The prisoners of the USDB also were used to build the United States Penitentiary, in Leavenworth, from 1895 to 1903. The Leavenworth Penitentiary was one of the first maximum-security federal prisons. The USDB was built using the architectural model of Eastern State Penitentiary.

Other military prisons are located throughout the United States and the world. Overseas military prisons are necessary due to the large number of military personnel stationed outside the continental United States. In addition, the military has confinement facilities, or brigs, aboard a number of U.S. naval ships such as the USS Enterprise, Nimitz, *and* Dwight D. Eisenhower.

The appearance and operation of modern military facilities closely resembles that of civilian prisons. One of the most visible differences is that correctional personnel are uniformed military personnel and inmates wear military-style uniforms. Since military prisons employ only members of the Armed Services, if one desired to work in a military prison it would be necessary to join a branch of the military. Military personnel who work in military prisons receive specialized training from the military.

Military detainment facilities for enemy combatants are distinctly different from military prisons. Perhaps the two most well-known facilities for enemy combatants are the Guantánamo Bay detainment facility located at Guantánamo Bay Naval Base in Cuba and Abu Ghraib Prison in Iraq. Military detainment facilities for enemy combatants are operated under different rules and assumptions and those confined have different rights.

What are some advantages and disadvantages of military prisons versus incarcerating military personnel in federal civilian prisons?

CHAPTER 9
Jails and Prisons

Check It!

1 WHAT was the philosophy in colonial times that established American jails? p. 156

The early philosophy was that people committed crimes as a result of moral fault and harsh treatment would result in rehabilitation.

2 HOW did early American jails and prison systems progress from their earliest times to their present state of prison systems? p. 159

Colonial jails had severe overcrowding, grouping men, women, and children, as well as serious criminals and victims of misfortune, together, and required prisoners to pay or work for their own keep.

- The Walnut Street Jail in Philadelphia was the first effort at reform, with a humane facility and treatment of inmates, as well as an early classification system.
- The Eastern State Penitentiary was a large facility with solitary cells intended for inmates to repent their crimes and rehabilitate themselves.
- The Auburn system was a model of a large, maximum security prison with tiers of single, small cells intended only for inmates to sleep, as they ate and worked in other areas.
- The Southern penal system leased convicts as laborers to private contractors.
- Contemporary prisons are very expensive because they offer educational and rehabilitation programs, are restricted in producing prisoner-made goods and services, and must recognize the constitutional rights of prisoners.

3 WHAT is the purpose of jails, and what types of jails are there? p. 162

Jails, including Native American, federal, and city and county jails, are short-term holding facilities for all types of people, usually those waiting to be charged with a crime, tried, or sent to another facility.

4 WHAT is the purpose of state prisons, what are their classification systems and special populations, and how do they reflect racism? p. 165

State prisons are long-term correctional facilities, usually for those who have committed felonies. They are classified as one of the following:

- maximum security facility
- medium security facility
- minimum security facility
- mental health facility
- medical facility
- private prison

Special populations in state prisons include

- persons with mental illness
- the elderly
- gang members
- women

The chances of Black and Hispanic males serving time in prison are much higher than that of Whites, resulting in their disenfranchisement from the political system.

5 HOW is the federal prison system organized? p. 171

The federal prison system is unified; federal prisons can be built anywhere in the United States, and federal inmates can be transported to any of the federal prisons.

6 WHAT is privatization, and what are its advantages and disadvantages? p. 173

Privatization is the trend toward prisoners being housed in privately operated facilities. The purpose and advantage of these facilities is to cut costs to the government. The disadvantages are that they may not provide the same educational and rehabilitative programs that state and federal prisons do, they are a detriment to the surrounding community, and the state or federal government still retains liability for them but little control.

7 WHAT are some of the major challenges resulting from the record high use of incarceration? p. 174

Some of the challenges facing prisons include the following:

- trying to reduce or eliminate sexual violence
- trying to reduce the risks of gang activity
- caring for the inmates with long-term physical health problems
- caring for inmates with mental health problems
- reducing inmate-on-inmate and staff-on-inmate violence

Assess Your Understanding

1. The America prison reform movement in the late 1700s was spearheaded by which of the following?
   a. the rising cost of incarceration
   b. the Philadelphia Society to Alleviate the Miseries of Public Prisons
   c. Sir Robert Peel
   d. the Bureau of Prisons

2. Why did the Auburn system of incarceration become more popular than the Pennsylvania system?
   a. The Auburn system was more cost efficient.
   b. The Auburn system proved to provide better rehabilitation of inmates when released.
   c. The Pennsylvania system did not provide for inmate work programs and training.
   d. all of the above

3. The use of chain gangs was characteristic of which of the following prison systems?
   a. the Auburn system
   b. the Pennsylvania Eastern Penitentiary
   c. the convict lease system
   d. both a and b

4. What was the philosophy of civil death as applied to inmates?
   a. Felony inmates could not file any civil lawsuits regarding their conditions of imprisonment.
   b. Inmates who died in prison received a civil burial only if someone other than the government paid for the expenses.
   c. Inmates sentenced to life in prison loss their right to vote in civil elections.
   d. Correctional officers guarding inmates were not required to be hired using competitive civil service examinations.

5. Who may be confined in a county jail?
   a. persons charged with a crime but not convicted of the crime
   b. witnesses
   c. juveniles
   d. all of the above

6. Which of the following agencies is responsible for the operation of the county jail?
   a. the county sheriff
   b. the county department of corrections
   c. the state
   d. either a or b

7. What is the purpose of prisoner classification?
   a. to determine the needs of the inmate and any characteristics that might influence placement
   b. to review the trial of the inmate to determine if the inmate may have been wrongfully convicted
   c. to determine whether the inmate will serve the time incarcerated in a jail, state prison, or federal correctional institution
   d. to determine when the inmate will be eligible for his or her first parole hearing

8. Which agency or personnel administers the federal prisons?
   a. wardens appointed by the governor of the state in which the federal prison is located
   b. the Federal Bureau of Prisons
   c. the U.S. Department of Justice
   d. the U.S Sentencing Commission

9. What is primary attraction of states to use private jails and prisons?
   a. Private prisons offer better rehabilitation and training programs than government prisons.
   b. The correctional staff of private prisons is more professional resulting in fewer lawsuits than government correctional staff.
   c. Private prisons allow governments to contain costs.
   d. Private prisons have better medical facilities for housing inmates with serious mental or physical needs.

10. Which of the following is true for mentally ill inmates in prison?
    a. Mentally ill inmates find the routine and security of prison life makes it easier for them to cope with their mental illness.
    b. Mentally ill inmates frequently are unable to abide by prison rules and discipline.
    c. Mentally ill inmates are always confined to special units separated from the general population.
    d. Inmates identified as mentally ill are transferred to civil mental health facilities or hospitals so as to be able to obtain professional treatment rather than incarcerated in prison.

ESSAY

1. What advantages led to the adoption of the Auburn system over the Eastern State Penitentiary model of incarceration?
2. What is unique about the "inside cell block" design in prison architecture?
3. What types of inmates are confined in county jails and what agency is responsible for running county jails?
4. What types of inmates are confined in state prisons and what agency is responsible for running state prisons?
5. What types of inmates are confined in federal correctional institutions and what agency is responsible for running the federal prison system?
6. How are private jails and prisons different from government-administrated jails and prisons?
7. Describe special prison populations and the problems they pose for prison administrators.

ANSWERS: 1. b, 2. a, 3. c, 4. a, 5. d, 6. d, 7. a, 8. b, 9. c, 10. b

Media

Go to the *Chapter 9: Jails and Prisons* section in *MyCJLab* to test your understanding of this chapter, access customized study content, engage in interactive simulations, complete critical thinking and research assignments, and view related online videos.

Additional Links

Go to www.gangsorus.com to view the Web site "Gangs or Us," which provides information on street and prison gangs.

Visit the Federal Bureau of Prisons at www.bop.gov

Visit the City of New York Department of Corrections Web site at www.nyc.gov/html/doc/html/home/home.shtml

Visit the Web site of Los Angeles County's Twin Towers Correctional Facility at www.lasd.org/divisions/custody/twintowers/index.html

Visit the Web site of the Southern Center for Human Rights at www.schr.org

Eastern State Penitentiary is now a tourist attraction. You can visit the Web site of Eastern State Penitentiary at www.easternstate.org

To view a BBC report on the growing problem of Muslim prison gangs in Britain, go to http://news.bbc.co.uk/2/hi/uk_news/8565408.stm

To view a video on the problems posed by the Nuestra Familia prison gangs, go to www.youtube.com/watch?v=vRMq0umehWk

To view a PBS report on the problems raised by private prisons, go to www.youtube.com/watch?v=QWqs_igPIBI

To view a Phoenix Fox News report regarding public concerns about the safety of private prisons after the escape of three murderers from the Kingman, Arizona, private prison, go to www.myfoxphoenix.com/dpp/money/private-prisons-concerns-8-9-2010

To view a 2009 C-SPAN video on the national Prison Rape Commission's final Report and proposed Standards, go to www.c-spanvideo.org/program/287355-5

To view an interview with Michelle Alexander, author of *The New Jim Crow: Mass Incarceration in the Age of Colorblindness,* go to www.youtube.com/watch?v=IgM5NAq6cGI

PROBATION AND PAROLE

10

The Associated Press reported that as Jamie and Gladys Scott left the Central Mississippi Correctional Facility in Pearl, Mississippi, they waved to reporters and yelled, "We're free!" They were free after serving 16 years on a life sentence for armed robbery. They were not eligible for parole until 2014 but Mississippi Governor Haley Barbour released them in January 2011. Their release was in part the result of the efforts of a number of advocacy groups including the National Association for the Advancement of Colored People.

GOVERNOR BARBOUR EXPLAINED THAT THE RELEASE WAS CONDITIONAL UPON GLADYS SCOTT DONATING ONE OF HER KIDNEYS TO HER SISTER WITHIN 1 YEAR.

The Scott sisters and three other accomplices were accused of robbing two men of between $11 and $200. The male accomplices aged 14 to 18 served two years in prison. The Scott sisters both claim that they are innocent and that the life sentences were excessive. The sisters carried their protest to the public with the support of several advocacy groups. In the end, public opinion appears to have convinced Governor Barbour that the sisters deserved early release.

However, some claim their release was motivated by money and not concern for justice. While incarcerated, Jamie Scott suffered kidney failure in January 2010 and had been receiving dialysis in prison. Announcing their release Governor Barbour said, "The Mississippi Department of Corrections believes the sisters no longer pose a threat to society. Their incarceration is no longer necessary for public safety or rehabilitation, and Jamie Scott's medical condition creates a substantial cost to the state of Mississippi." He further explained that the release was conditional upon Gladys Scott donating one of her kidneys to her sister within 1 year but the state would not be responsible for the cost of the kidney transplant operation.

1 Why does the criminal justice system provide for early release of inmates or no prison time for convicted offenders?

2 What are the differences among diversion, probation, and parole, and among mandatory release, good-time release, and pardon or commutation of sentence?

3 What are the origins, reasons for, processes, and advantages of probation?

4 What are the origins, the pros and cons of parole, the process of granting parole, and the conditions of parole?

5 How are probation and parole supervised?

Critics accused the state of engaging in the trading of an organ for their freedom. Also, critics complained that their release glosses over the questions of their wrongful conviction or excessive sentence. They claim the real reason for the sister's release was to avoid the cost of medical care for Jamie Scott.

This unusual early release has raised many questions. Does the release violate federal laws or ethical standards? Can and should early release be dependent upon the exchange of a human organ? What if medical conditions are such that the transplant cannot occur within the year? Does that mean the sisters must return to prison? While the Scott sisters present an unusual case, in this time of financial crisis many states are releasing more and more inmates earlier and earlier. These early releases are spurring discussion regarding the pros and cons of early release.

This chapter discusses the history of early release from prison, the arguments for and against early release, and the various types of early release that can be granted to an inmate.

States Turn to Diversion, Probation, and Parole

Prisons are expensive, and many states are forced to evaluate whether they can afford to continue locking up criminals for long periods. Since the 1970s, the number of state prisoners has increased 500 percent, making prisons the fastest-growing item in state budgets. Many states are finding that prison spending competes with other needs. Taxpayers are reluctant to keep spending money on corrections if that means there is less money to spend on schools. As a result, many states are seeking ways to reduce prison costs. States have closed prisons and cut prison budgets but that has not been enough. Studies suggest that although imprisonment is necessary for some offenders to provide for public safety, not all offenders need to be or should be incarcerated. About half of all convicted offenders are nonviolent, nonsexual offenders. Studies suggest that long-term incarceration may not be the best use of public resources for these offenders. Thus, states are turning to greater use of probation and parole as a means to curtail corrections costs.

Before discussing probation and parole in greater detail it is important to define and distinguish what is meant by diversion, probation, and parole. Some offenders do not serve any of their prison time, whereas others are sentenced to prison but released prior to the end of their term of punishment. Offenders may not serve time because they are diverted from the criminal justice system or because their sentences are suspended.

Diversion and Probation In **diversion**, the defendant is offered an alternative to a criminal trial, possible conviction, and prison sentence, such as drug court, boot camp, or a treatment program. When a defendant is convicted in a criminal court and sentenced to prison but the prison term is suspended, the defendant does not have to serve time in prison and is said to be on **suspended sentence**, or probation. Probation, a sentencing option of the trial judge, diverts the offender after conviction but prior to serving prison time.

Parole In **parole**, the offender has been sentenced to prison, serves a portion of his or her time, and is released before the maximum term of the sentence. The decision to parole a prisoner is made by a parole board. Prisoners released under probation or parole are subject to continued supervision in the community and can be returned to prison if they violate the terms of their release. Other means by which a prisoner can be released from prison other than probation and parole include mandatory release, good-time release, pardon, and commutation of sentence.

Mandatory and Good-Time Release

Mandatory Release When prisoners serve the entire length of their maximum sentence, it is required by law that they be released. This is called **mandatory release**. An inmate cannot be held in prison beyond the length of his or her sentence. Even if the prisoner obviously is not rehabilitated or prepared for reentry into society, he or she must be released after serving the time. These prisoners are released without any supervision, without any restrictions on their behavior, and frequently without any support or rehabilitation plan. Mandatory release requires that prison officials release a prisoner who has served the maximum sentence regardless of the danger that the prisoner may pose to the community. Some states have tried to protect the community from

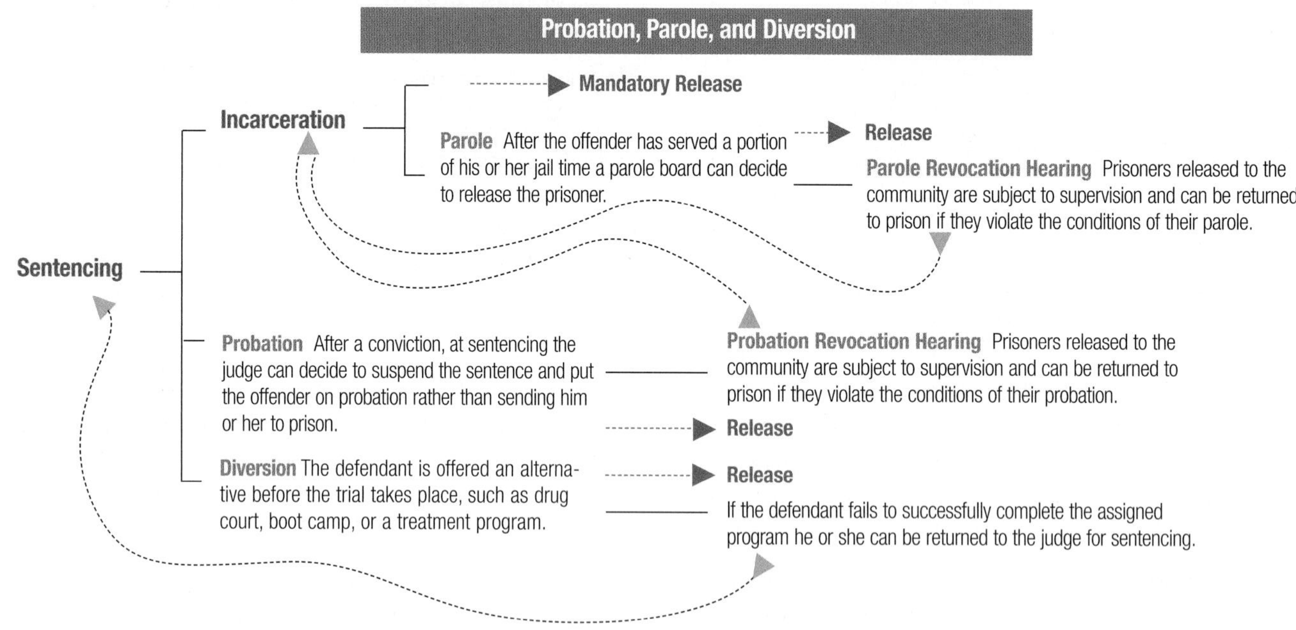

1 **To better use limited financial and correctional resources, many states are providing for alternatives to incarceration for nonviolent and nonsexual offenders.**

diversion a defendant is offered an alternative to criminal trial and a prison sentence, such as drug courts, boot camps, and treatment programs

suspended sentence another term for *probation*, based on the fact that convicted offenders must serve their full sentence if they violate the terms of release

parole the release of an inmate before his or her maximum sentence has been served

mandatory release the release of prisoners required by law after they have served the entire length of their maximum sentence

offenders who have been identified as sexual predators by prohibiting such mandatory releases until the sexual predator has been declared not a danger to the community upon release. Hence, one of the arguments for early release through probation or parole is that such release, unlike mandatory release, lets probationers and parolees reenter the community with supervision; provides behavioral restrictions; and offers social, mental health, and drug counseling services to the released inmate.

THERE ARE NO LIMITATIONS ON THE NUMBER OF PARDONS GOVERNORS AND PRESIDENTS MAY GRANT, AND THERE ARE NO GUIDELINES OR LAWS REGULATING WHO THEY MAY PARDON.

Good-Time Credit Another form of mandatory release is when prisoners have served less than their full sentences but have earned good-time credit that entitles them to an early release. **Good-time credit** toward early release is a strategy to encourage the prisoner to obey institutional rules, refrain from violence and drug use, and participate in rehabilitation and vocational programs. In place of punishment for disobedience, good-time release gives inmates an incentive to comply with prison authority and rules. When the inmate is processed into the system, a percentage of the inmate's sentence is converted into good-time behavior. For many states, this is 15 percent or more of the time to be served. For example, an inmate with a 10-year sentence could receive a credit of 15 percent of the sentence or 1.5 years as good-time behavior. Good-time computation in the federal system is much less generous than in state prison systems. The Comprehensive Crime Control Act of 1984, which includes the Sentencing Reform Act of 1984, reformed the federal good-time provisions such that federal prisoners earn a maximum of 54 days annually after completion of the first year of a sentence.

Good-Time Credit

Sentenced by the judge to 2 years for burglary, how long will the inmate serve?

When an inmate is processed into the system, a percentage of his or her sentence is converted into good-time credit. The percentage varies by state, here we assume a 20% credit.

24 months x 20% = 4.8 months

-4.8

19.2 months

If there are no infractions to deduct from the inmate's good-time credit, his or her mandatory parole date is in 19.2 months.

Good-time credit will be reduced for violations of the rules.

The inmate's sentence cannot be extended beyond the maximum sentence.

The primary purpose of good-time credit is to motivate inmates to obey prison rules.

Prison authorities use the deduction of good-time days to regulate nearly every aspect of the inmate's behavior. Loss of good time can be used as a punishment for both minor and major offenses. An inmate can lose days for not lining up when told to do so, for reporting late to work, for being in a restricted area, for insubordination, for engaging in arguments, for attacks on other inmates or correctional officers, or for possession of contraband. However, prison authorities cannot add to prison time beyond that sentenced originally by the court without a conviction for new crimes. With more serious violations, such as attempted escape or felony crime, the inmate is returned to court for trial and, if convicted, is sentenced to additional time.

Pardon and Commutation of Sentence

Executive Pardons Prisoners may not have to serve the entire length of their sentences because they are pardoned or have their sentences commuted. Pardon and commutation are forms of executive forgiveness and are not forms of probation or parole. Pardons are sometimes referred to as clemency. Pardon and commutation of sentence can be performed only by the governor of the state for state prisoners or by the president of the United States for federal and military prisoners. Pardons and commutations of sentence are acts of mercy and do not indicate that an inmate is not guilty or was wrongfully sentenced.

There are no limitations on the number of pardons that governors and presidents may grant, and there are no guidelines or laws regulating who they may pardon and under what conditions. No one has the authority to revoke a pardon or to overrule the governor or president. They may seek advice in issuing a pardon, but the absolute authority to issue pardons rests entirely within the executive authority. Also, there is no time limit for issuing a pardon. A governor or president can issue a pardon for a crime committed decades ago for which the person has already served the entire length of sentence or can issue a pardon while an inmate is still serving time. Requests for pardons usually come directly from the inmate or the inmate's supporters.

Commutation of Sentence Closely related to **executive pardon** is executive commutation of a prisoner's sentence. In **commutation of sentence**, the governor or president reduces the severity of an inmate's sentence. The most common use of executive commutation is to reduce a prisoner's sentence from death to life in prison and from life without parole to life with parole.

Also, commutation of sentence can be used to reduce the time to be served by a convicted offender without acknowledging the offender was wrongfully convicted. For example, in August 2009, Virginia

good-time credit a strategy of crediting inmates with extra days served toward early release in an effort to encourage them to obey rules and participate in programs

executive pardon an act by a governor or the president that forgives a prisoner and rescinds his or her sentence

commutation of sentence a reduction in the severity or length of an inmate's sentence issued by a state governor or the president of the United States

2 **Diversion and probation keep offenders out of prison. Parole, good-time credit, and pardon reduce the time an offender serves in prison. Mandatory release occurs when an offender serves his or her maximum time.**

HERE'S SOMETHING TO THINK ABOUT...

Many oppose early release because of their fear that offenders will pose a threat to public safety. Jimmie Terrell Smith illustrates that this fear is not unfounded. In September 2005, Illinois placed Smith on a 3-year probation. During his parole he was arrested six times and convicted twice of beating a woman and of marijuana possession. He was briefly sent back to prison on a parole violation of battery. He did not complete court-mandated mental health and anger management programs. In 2011, Smith is in Cook County Jail awaiting his trial for allegedly violently raping five females and attempted murder. He is also a person of interest in the 2008 disappearance of 15-year-old Yasmin Acree.

Those opposed to early release claim that if Smith had been retained in prison this assault on public safety could have been avoided. At least six women would have been spared death or sexual assault. Do you support early release? Why?

governor Tim Kaine commuted the sentence of three sailors who were convicted in a 1997 murder and rape case that had become a national cause célèbre as an example of wrongful convictions based on coerced confessions.[1] Governor Kaine reduced their life sentences to time served, which resulted in their release. In issuing the commutation rather than a full pardon the governor said, "The petitioners have not conclusively established their innocence, and therefore an absolute pardon is not appropriate. However, I conclude that the petitioners have raised substantial doubts about their convictions and the propriety of their continued detention."[2] Perhaps one of the most well-known commutations was that of Illinois governor George Ryan. Governor Ryan was indicted on federal criminal corruption charges and ultimately was incarcerated. However, in 2003, 2 days before he left office, Governor Ryan commuted the sentences of 167 inmates on death row and pardoned 4 others. Governor Ryan said that he was motivated by concerns that the inmates had been sentenced to death unfairly, so he commuted the sentences of every Illinois inmate on death row to life in prison even though the inmates had not even filed a clemency petition to the Governor's Office. Critics were concerned about the questionable circumstances surrounding the clemency decision of the governor given the fact that he was under federal indictment and his actions were highly unorthodox in providing clemency to a record 167 inmates who had not even asked for it. Critics challenged the governor's actions in court. However, the Illinois Supreme Court upheld his right to commute the sentences of prisoners, saying, "The governor may grant reprieves, pardons, and commutations on his own terms, and the decisions are unreviewable."[3]

The powers of pardon and commutation give the executive branch checks and balances on the powers of the courts and legislature. By releasing prisoners, chief executives can intervene to correct or erase perceived abuses or errors in sentencing or corrections. However, there are no checks and balances on the executives' power to issue pardons, creating a potential for abuse. For example, President Clinton was accused by critics of granting presidential pardons in his final days of office to those who had made large political contributions.

Probation

Probation This option is a relatively new experiment in American corrections. The roots of probation can be traced to the efforts of John Augustus (1785–1859), a wealthy Boston shoemaker who devoted himself to bringing reform to the eighteenth-century criminal justice system. He intervened in Boston's municipal court to divert a number of defendants who were sentenced to serve time in the Boston House of Corrections. Augustus was not an officer of the court nor was he connected to the criminal justice system. As a private citizen, he used his personal finances to guarantee bail for defendants selected for diversion from jail. He was critical of the conditions of the jails and prisons of his time and believed that, for many offenders, prison would lead to further harm rather than rehabilitation.

THE ROOTS OF PROBATION CAN BE TRACED TO THE EFFORTS OF JOHN AUGUSTUS.

4.2 million
number of adults on probation in 2009

819,308
number on parole

In 1841, Augustus initiated what came to be known as **probation.** He was in Boston's municipal court when a defendant was convicted of being a common drunk. Augustus asked the judge not to sentence the man to jail but to release him to his custody instead. Augustus assumed responsibility for the man's behavior and provided for his rehabilitation. After 3 weeks, he brought the man back to the court for evaluation. Augustus reported that "the judge expressed himself much pleased with the account we gave of the man, and instead of the usual penalty of imprisonment in the House of Corrections—he fined him one cent and costs, amounting in all to $3.76, which was immediately paid." From that time on, John Augustus monitored court trials and rescued more than 2,000 defendants from incarceration.[4]

Other volunteers continued Augustus's work after his death until Massachusetts passed the first probation statute in 1878. By 1900, four other states had passed similar legislation. By 1920, every state permitted juvenile probation, and 33 states had adopted a system of adult probation. Today, more people are on probation and parole than are sentenced

3 **In 1841, Boston shoemaker John Augustus initiated the concept of probation. Probation allows the offender who does not pose a risk to the community to be released with supervision. The advantages are that probationers are not a cost burden to the community and that it promotes rehabilitation.**

probation the conditional release of a convicted offender prior to his or her serving any prison time

to prison. In 2007, over 4.3 million adults under federal, state, or local jurisdiction were on probation, and about 824,365 were on parole.[5]

Probation Services

Local Courts When determining whether to grant probation, local and county court judges typically have little information on which to base that decision. Because most criminals in these courts of limited jurisdiction are convicted of misdemeanors or violations, there is less risk to the community in the event that the judge grants probation. Thus, most local and county courts do not have access to probation services that will provide them with presentence investigation reports. Also, because of the short sentences provided for the offenses (the average sentence is about 4 to 5 months) handled by these courts, probation plans requiring the probationer to participate in long-term treatment, rehabilitation, drug counseling, or anger management are not practical.

Judges in state courts of general trial jurisdiction and federal courts have much more access to probation personnel to provide presentence investigations. Also, because of the length of sentences for felons tried in these courts, probation plans can specify that the probationer participate in long-term programs. Federal probation services are provided to the court by the Office of Probation and Pretrial Services. As the name suggests, this office provides assistance to the court both in presentence investigation and in probation services.

State Probation Offices State probation offices are organized in different ways and under different authorities. Five common organizational structures for state probation are

1. within the state executive branch,
2. within local (county or municipal) executive departments,
3. under the state judiciary,
4. under local courts, and
5. under various combinations of the first four.

However, probation is not under the authority of law enforcement, the prosecutor, or corrections. In many states, like the federal government, probation and parole services are provided by the same agency. In these agencies officers may handle probation, parole, and pretrial services.

Probation Officers The status of **probation officers** as law enforcement officers varies state by state. Federal probation officers may be authorized to carry concealed weapons on and off duty. Some states grant probation officers the right to carry concealed weapons and some do not. Likewise, states grant juvenile probation officers different privileges with regard to carrying of firearms. Probation officers (both adult and juvenile) do not have the same arrest powers as police officers. The arrest powers of probation officers tends to be limited to probationers. However, with regard to the power of arrest and search and seizure of probationers, probation officers have more extensive authority, because they do not need search warrants to search a probationer, his or her residence, or his or her automobile. Furthermore, probation officers do not have to advise probationers of their Miranda rights when questioning them and probationers do not have the right to remain silent when questioned by probation officers.

Decision to Grant Probation

Probation is a sentencing option of judges. Probation or suspended sentence for both juveniles and adults can be used as a sentence for both minor and serious crimes. In fact, about half of those on probation committed misdemeanors and the other half committed felonies. See Table 10.1 for other characteristics of adults on probation and parole. An important factor in determining whether the defendant receives a suspended sentence is information about potential risks to the community if the offender is released. Judges must decide if the criminal's release poses a serious threat to the community. In many states with indeterminate sentencing, judges have great discretion in the use of probation and can suspend the sentences of those convicted of murder, burglary, theft, or traffic violations. The federal courts and some state courts have limited the judges' discretion through legislation requiring minimum sentences, mandatory sentencing, or structured sentencing. In these jurisdictions, judges may be prohibited from using probation for certain crimes.

When sentencing offenders to probation or suspended sentences judges assume:

- A sentence of prison time is an inappropriate punishment.
- The public would not be at serious risk if the offender is released into the community.
- The offender would not benefit from any prison-based rehabilitation/vocation program.
- The offender would be self-supporting if released into the community.
- The offender should not be confined due to serious mental illness.
- The offender will not commit other crimes.

The judge relies to a great extent on the presentence investigation report to make a judgment about the appropriateness of probation. The decision to grant probation as a sentence depends on the quality of information that the judge has about the defendant and his or her past record, social and family interaction, psychological profile, and employment status.

The Office of Probation and Pretrial Services provides federal judges with presentence reports to assist the judge in deciding if probation is appropriate.

Presentence investigation reports contain information about the following:

- a narrative of the circumstances of the offense;
- the defendant's entire criminal history;
- a description of the defendant's lifestyle, including employment and financial responsibility, support to family, and contribution to the community;

probation officer a state or federal professional employee who reports to the courts and supervises defendants released on probation

- available sentencing options for the crime(s); and
- factors that would support a decision for probation; that is, potential for rehabilitation, lack of risk to the community, restitution to the victim, costs to the criminal justice system, etc.

State probation officers provide similar services and reports to state judges.

Active Supervision and Treatment Most persons under sentence of probation are required to report to their probation officer on a regular basis. About 71 percent of probationers are under active supervision, which requires them to report regularly to a probation authority in person, by mail, or by telephone.[6] Probation is almost always combined with the requirement for supervision and treatment. Supervision demands that defendants report regularly to their probation officers on a daily, weekly, or monthly basis, depending on a number of factors. In addition, probationers may be required to seek professional treatment or counseling, and one justification for probation is that it allows the court to mandate treatment programs. Often, probationers must pay for treatment programs on their own. About 29 percent of probationers are drug offenders, and the conditions of their release require that they complete drug treatment programs and submit to regular and frequent drug testing. Probationers must submit to drug tests whenever probation officers so order. Frequent mandatory drug testing has proved to be an effective strategy in drug rehabilitation.

TABLE 10.1 Comparison Characteristics of Adults on Probation/Parole, 2009

	Probation	Parole
Gender		
Male	76%	88%
Female	24%	12%
Race		
White	55%	41%
Black	30%	39%
Hispanic or Latino	13%	18%
American Indian/Alaska Native/Pacific Islander, 2 or more races	2%	2%
Type of Offense		
Felony	51%	95%
Misdemeanor	47%	5%
Other	2%	
Most Serious Offense		
Drug	26%	36%
Property	26%	23%
Violent	19%	27%
Public Order	18%	—
Other	11%	11%
Weapon	—	3%

Source: Glaze, Lauren E., and Thomas P. Bonczar, Probation and Parole in the United States, 2009 (Washington, DC: Bureau of Justice Statistics 2010), pp. 26, 36, 43.

Advantages of Probation

$1,000

the yearly per person cost for probation

THE CONCERNS ASSOCIATED WITH PROBATION ARE FEAR OF FURTHER CRIMINAL ACTIVITY AND THE LACK OF PUNISHMENT FOR THE CRIME.

Cost The concerns associated with probation are fear of further criminal activity by the defendant and the lack of punishment for the crime committed. However, at a cost of about $1,000 per person per year, probation is much cheaper than prison.[7] If the probationer commits new crimes, however, the cost of the property loss or damage and the intangible costs of pain and suffering of the victims present a different picture. On the other hand, probation promotes rehabilitation through employment, opportunities for normal social relations, and access to community services and resources. Probationers are usually required to be employed or to attend school or vocational training. Employment enables offenders to support themselves and, if married, their families, and to pay taxes. The probationer is, therefore, not a burden to the taxpayer.

Attachment to the Community Probationers live in a "normal" environment. By remaining in the community, the probationer avoids the detrimental effects of the prison environment and retains relationships with family and other support groups and services. As you will recall from Chapter 2, a number of criminological theories of crime causation suggest that positive attachments to the community are a powerful factor in preventing criminal behavior.

Conditions of probation provide for supervision of the probationer's behavior and lifestyle. Standard conditions require that the probationer maintain employment, have a place to live, refrain from drug and alcohol use, and avoid socializing with known criminals. The probationer is monitored to ensure that he or she abides by these conditions. Additional conditions may include successful completion of a drug or alcohol rehabilitation program. While on probation, the probationer remains under supervision and must comply with all the terms and conditions of probation. Proponents of probation argue that long-term oversight of offenders at low cost to the community is superior to unsupervised release of prisoners.

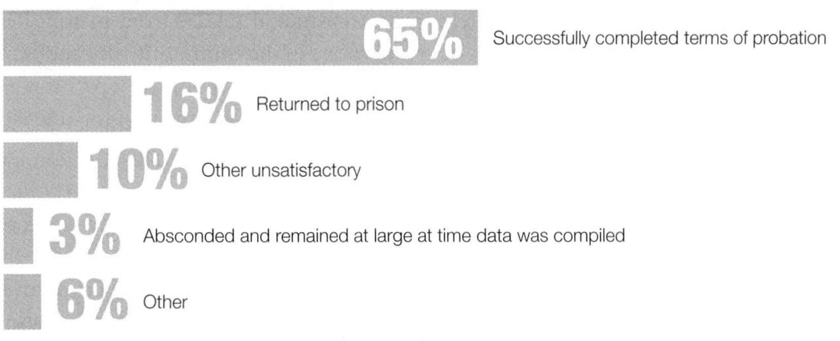

FIGURE 10.1 Adults Leaving Probation, by Type of Exit, 2009

Source: Glaze, L.E., and Bonczar, T.P. (2010). *Probation and Parole in the United States, 2009.* Washington, DC: BJS, p. 3.

Decisions to Revoke Probation

The decision to grant offenders probation is revocable, because probation is granted under the stipulation that offenders meet all the conditions of their release. Probation status can be revoked at any time if offenders test positive for drugs, are found in possession of a weapon, commit another crime, lose employment, or fail to complete a treatment program. Offenders whose probation status is revoked are returned to prison to serve their entire sentences.

Prior to the Warren Court, probation was considered an "act of grace," and the Court did not recognize that the probationer has any due process rights following revocation of probation. In 1967, however, the Court reversed that opinion and ruled that probationers are entitled to due process hearings to establish that they violated their conditions of probation.[8] Today, the Court has ruled that probationers also are entitled to certain due process rights before their probation is revoked.[9]

Different rules of evidence apply to the probation revocation hearing from those of a trial. For example, probation officers have the right of search and seizure of the probationer and his or her residence without a search warrant, consent, or probable cause.[10] Probation officers do not have to advise probationers of their rights against self-incrimination, and probationers have only limited protection against self-incrimination.[11] Probation officers also can enter and search the probationer's vehicle at any time without permission. Probationers do have the right to counsel at their revocation hearing, and if they cannot afford counsel, they are entitled to a defense counsel paid for by the government.[12]

Technical Violations Imprisonment for violating a condition of probation is called a **technical violation**. Drug use is the most frequent reason that probationers are returned to prison for technical violations. Imprisonment for committing a new crime is not punishment for the new crime but for the crime they committed previously for which they received probation. Offenders are rearrested and tried for the new crime. If they are found guilty, their sentence for the new crime is added to the sentence they must serve for their previous crime. Even if the probationer is not convicted in court of committing the new crime, or if charges are reduced through plea bargaining or dismissed, the court still may revoke probation.

Probationers cannot be returned to prison for technical violation for failure to pay a fine or restitution, if it can be proved that the probationer was not responsible for this failure. For example, probationers might lose their jobs through no fault of their own, incur medical bills that prevent them from making payment, or experience some other financial crisis not under their control. These probationers cannot be returned to prison because they lack the money to fulfill their

Revocation of Parole

Probation officer (PO) decides the probationer has violated his/her conditions of probation (technical violation) or has committed a new crime

The PO may arrest the probationer,

or the PO will direct the police to make the arrest

The PO writes a report detailing the alleged violation or new crime and forwards it to the court and a hearing is held to determine if probable cause exists to revoke probation

Yes probable cause exists

No probable cause exists, return to the community

A **probation revocation hearing** is held. The hearing official renders a decision based on the following:

Is the alleged violation sufficient to revoke probation?

Is the evidence sufficient and trustworthy?

Revoked If probation is revoked, the probationer is returned to court for resentencing

Not Revoked If probation is not revoked, the probationer is returned to the community

technical violation grounds for imprisonment of a probationer or parolee based on his or her violation of a condition of release

conditions of probation. However, personal bankruptcy ultimately does not excuse the probationer from paying court-ordered fines or restitution.[13]

Parole

People often minimize the distinction between probation and parole, but the two are very different practices and have distinct characteristics. Whereas the origins of probation can be directly traced to the early practices of John Augustus, the origins of parole are more diverse. The concept of parole encompasses the practice of conditionally releasing prisoners to the community and the supervision of the released prisoner, or the parolee, in the community. The parolee's early release from prison is conditional, based on compliance with the conditions of release and absence of criminal activity.

CROFTON'S IRISH SYSTEM PROVIDED A CONTINUUM OF CONDITIONS OF SUPERVISION BASED ON THE PRISONER'S BEHAVIOR. THE AMERICAN PAROLE SYSTEM IS BASED ON THIS MODEL.

Parole d'Honneur The historical roots of parole can be traced to practices of the French, English, and Irish. The term *parole* comes from the French phrase ***parole d'honneur***—the practice of releasing a prisoner for good behavior based on his word of honor that he would obey the law upon release.[14]

The Mark System Alexander Maconochie often is credited with developing the **mark system**, a forerunner of the parole system. Maconochie developed this early type of parole system between 1840 and 1844 while he was administrator of Norfolk Island, a prison colony off the coast of Australia. He pioneered the innovative penal strategy of releasing prisoners early on the basis of points, or marks, for good behavior and work performed in prison. The system operated according to a prison token economy in which the prisoner earned marks for good behavior. On imprisonment, each prisoner was assessed a debt in marks to be paid. Additional marks could be assessed against the prisoner for misbehavior or violation of prison rules. At the same time, the prisoner could earn good-credit marks for working, participating in educational programs, and good behavior. Prisoners who earned enough marks to offset the debt of their crime—and any additional debts they incurred while in prison—could buy their freedom. If prisoners had more than enough marks to buy their freedom, the extra marks could be redeemed for cash upon their release.

Maconochie's mark system was based on the premise that prisoners must demonstrate rehabilitation to earn their release from prison. This same basic assumption underlies the use of parole. Parole is based on the idea that prisoners should be released not because they have served a fixed amount of time, but because they have changed their ways. However, unlike modern-day parole, the **ticket of leave** that Maconochie's prisoners purchased with their marks granted them an unconditional release from prison. Released prisoners were not supervised in the community nor subject to any terms of conditional release. Today, on the contrary, parole is always conditional. Parolees can be returned to jail or prison for rule violations or other offenses.

The Irish System Sir Walter Crofton pioneered the practice of conditional release for inmates prior to completing their sentences based on good behavior. In 1854, Crofton was chairman of the board of directors of Irish prisons. He adopted Maconochie's mark system and ticket of leave to solve the problem of prison overcrowding. However, Crofton's **Irish system** provided a continuum of conditions of supervision based on the prisoner's behavior. Initially prisoners were placed in solitary confinement but could work their way to greater freedom. In the final stages of the Irish system, prisoners were assigned to work programs outside the prison and could earn a ticket of leave entitling them to early release under supervision. If they disobeyed the terms of their release or committed a new crime, they could be summarily tried and, if convicted, have their ticket of leave revoked. Crofton's Irish system is the model on which the American parole system is based.

Pros and Cons of Parole

Youthful Offenders Good-time laws were passed as early as 1817 in New York, and they allowed the early release of prisoners with sentences of 5 years or less.[15] However, parole did not emerge as common practice until the end of the 1800s. Even the term *parole* was not used in the United States until 1846.[16] The development of parole came with the use of indeterminate sentencing and efforts to address the correctional needs of youthful offenders. In 1869, Michigan adopted the first indeterminate sentencing law.[17] As explained in Chapter 8, an **indeterminate sentence** bases release on behavior that demonstrates signs of rehabilitation rather than on a fixed prison term. In indeterminate sentencing, the defendant is given a prison term with a minimum and a maximum number of years to serve. Indeterminate prison terms can have a wide range between the minimum and maximum number of years to serve, ranging from 1 year to life in prison.

The indeterminate sentence was extensively used at the Elmira Reformatory for youthful offenders in New York. Prior to the twentieth century and the adoption of the juvenile court system, youthful offenders were not entitled to special treatment in the criminal justice system. Warden Zebulon Brockway instituted the practice of early release at Elmira Reformatory in 1876 as a means to promote rehabilitation of youthful offenders as opposed to punishment. Brockway's use of early conditional release combined with mandatory community

Parole is the practice in which inmates are released early based on good behavior. Advantages of parole are that it bases release on good behavior that demonstrates signs of rehabilitation and addresses the needs of juvenile offenders; disadvantages include the public's desire not to release offenders.

parole d'honneur the origin of parole, based on the concept of releasing prisoners on their honor after serving a portion of their sentences but before the maximum terms are reached

mark system an early form of parole invented by Alexander Maconochie in which prisoners demonstrated their rehabilitation by earning points for good behavior

ticket of leave in the mark system, the unconditional release from prison purchased with marks earned for good behavior

supervision was the first significant use of parole in America.[18] As in the origins of probation, the first parole officers were volunteers.[19]

Promoting of Rehabilitation Although it promoted the rehabilitation of offenders in the community, parole did not become an overnight success. By 1900, 20 states had adopted parole statutes, but it was not until after World War II that every state had a parole system. The first federal parole statute was adopted in 1867, providing for the reduction of sentences of federal prisoners for good conduct. However, the federal parole system was not created until 1910. Even during Maconochie's time, the public was opposed to the concept of early release, as indicated by the fact that Maconochie was removed as prison administrator because of opposition to his mark system.

Public Opposition In the United States, public opposition to parole is still widespread.[20] This disdain for parole is reflected in the abandonment of the practice by the federal court system and many states. By the end of 2001, 16 states had abolished parole board authority for releasing all offenders, and another 4 states had abolished parole board authority for releasing certain violent offenders. The public seems to want criminals sentenced to prison "to get the amount of time they deserve."[21] This belief is based in part on the public's fear that prisoners released early will return to a life of crime. For example, in 1994, when Virginia eliminated parole, Governor George Allen predicted that it would prevent 120,000 felonies over 10 years. Allen said, "Virginia is a safer place because we abolished parole."[22] One reason the public feels safer is because indeed probation (and parole) violators commit a significant number of crimes when released from prison.

Rates of Reoffending Table 10.2 shows that probation and parole violators committed over 13,000 murders. They committed nearly 13,000 rapes and over 50 percent of the victims were under the age of 12. They committed nearly 40,000 robberies, 19,000 assaults, and 40,000 burglaries. Those opposed to early release, especially parole, say that if these offenders had remained in prison, it could be argued that these crimes would not have occurred. They argue that often the cost of the crimes committed by the probation and parole violator is not taken into account when calculating the cost effectiveness of probation and parole.

States That Have Abolished Discretionary Release

Source: Bureau of Justice Statistics. (2009). *Reentry trends in the U.S.* Washington, DC: Author.

Irish system an early form of parole invented by Sir Walter Crofton based on the mark system in which prisoners were released conditionally on good behavior and were supervised in the community

indeterminate sentence a sentence in which the defendant is sentenced to a prison term with a minimum and a maximum number of years to serve

TABLE 10.2 Crimes Committed While on Probation and Parole

Probation Violators	Parole Violators
6,400 murders	6,800 murders
7,400 rapes or sexual assaults (33% of the victims were under the age of 12; 63% under 18)	5,550 rapes or sexual assaults (21% of the victims were under the age of 12; 47% under 18)
17,000 robberies	22,500 robberies
10,400 assaults	8,800 assaults
16,600 burglaries	23,000 burglaries
3,100 motor vehicle thefts	4,800 motor vehicle thefts

Crimes committed by 162,000 state probation violators while under supervision in the community an average of 17 months and 156,000 state parole violators during 13 months in the community.

Source: Bureau of Justice Statistics. (1995, August). *Probation and parole violators in state prison, 1991* (p. 10). Washington, DC: U.S. Department of Justice.

This fear is not entirely groundless, especially for prisoners released on parole. In 2009, only 51 percent of adults successfully completed the conditions of parole, compared to 65 percent of adults who successfully completed probation. Thirty-six percent of adults on parole were returned to incarceration, compared to 17 percent of adults on probation. Ten percent of adults on parole absconded.[23] The failure rate for adults on parole is higher despite the fact that 85 percent of adults on parole are under active supervision, which requires them to report regularly to a parole authority, compared to 71 percent of adults on probation.[24]

51%
percent of adults successfully complete the conditions of parole

65%
percent of adults who successfully completed probation

The public disdain for early release, especially parole, is illustrated by the fact that early release of prisoners on parole has dropped significantly from 1980 to 2003, whereas the percent of prisoners who are released due to expiration of sentence (they served the full mandatory length of their sentence) has increased. Early release on mandatory parole has increased. However, unlike discretionary parole, mandatory parole requires the early release of the inmate. That is to say, in states with mandatory parole, early release is required when a prisoner completes a certain percent of his or her time when specific behavioral conditions have been met (see Figure 10.2).

Public distrust of parole reflects concerns that parolees pose a danger to public safety. This distrust is reinforced by recidivism studies, which indicate that the success rate for nonviolent inmates released from state prisons is dismal (see Table 10.3). The Bureau of Justice Statistics tracked offenders released in 1994 from 15 states with large prison populations for three years after their release. After 3 years 67.5 percent of released inmates had been rearrested, 46.8 percent had been reconvicted, and 25.4 percent had been returned to prison with new sentences. Although nonviolent offenders are more likely to succeed in reentry than violent offenders, the success rate for nonviolent offenders as measured by rearrest suggests offenders are not able to successfully reenter into the community.

Public disdain for early release has a cost. The number of adults incarcerated in jails and prisons continues to increase, so as fewer inmates are released on parole, the demand for bed space in jails and prison increases. Since abolishing parole, Virginia's inmate population has risen 25 percent and the state has had to build new prisons to accommodate over 3,000 prisoners at a cost of over half a billion dollars.[25] Despite this opposition to parole, the number of adults on parole continues to increase due primarily to the increase in the number of persons sentenced to prison.

Parole is advocated as a correctional strategy for many of the same reasons as probation. However, it appears that the public is wary of the ability of the correctional system to accurately predict which prisoners have been successfully rehabilitated. Before going to prison, nearly two-thirds of inmates have been on probation.[26] Thus, to the public, those inmates did not take advantage of the "act of grace" that was offered them, and there is no reason to expect that they would do any better if offered a second chance through parole.

State and Federal Parole Boards

The sentencing judge has the authority to grant probation, but parole is not under the authority of the sentencing judge. The **parole board**, not the judge, is responsible for deciding whether an inmate is to receive early release.

State Parole Boards Each state establishes its own parole board, and no agency has oversight of all the state parole boards. State parole boards are established by state legislation and administered under the authority of the state's executive branch (i.e., the governor). The legislature retains oversight through their powers of law making and budget approval. The governor appoints the director of the parole board and often the members as well. The state supreme courts and the U.S. Supreme Court have oversight powers in that they can declare certain parole practices unconstitutional.

TABLE 10.3 Recidivism Rates of Offenders Released in 1994

Cumulative percent of released nonviolent offenders who were:

Time after Release	Rearrested	Reconvicted	Returned to prison
6 months	29.9%	10.6%	5.0%
1 year	44.1%	21.5%	10.4%
2 years	59.2%	36.4%	18.8%
3 years	67.5%	46.8%	25.4%

Source: Langan, P.A., and Levin, D.J. (2002). *Recidivism of Prisoners Released in 1994.* Washington, DC: Bureau of Justice Statistics, p. 3.

parole board individuals appointed to a body that meets in prisons to make decisions about granting parole release to inmates

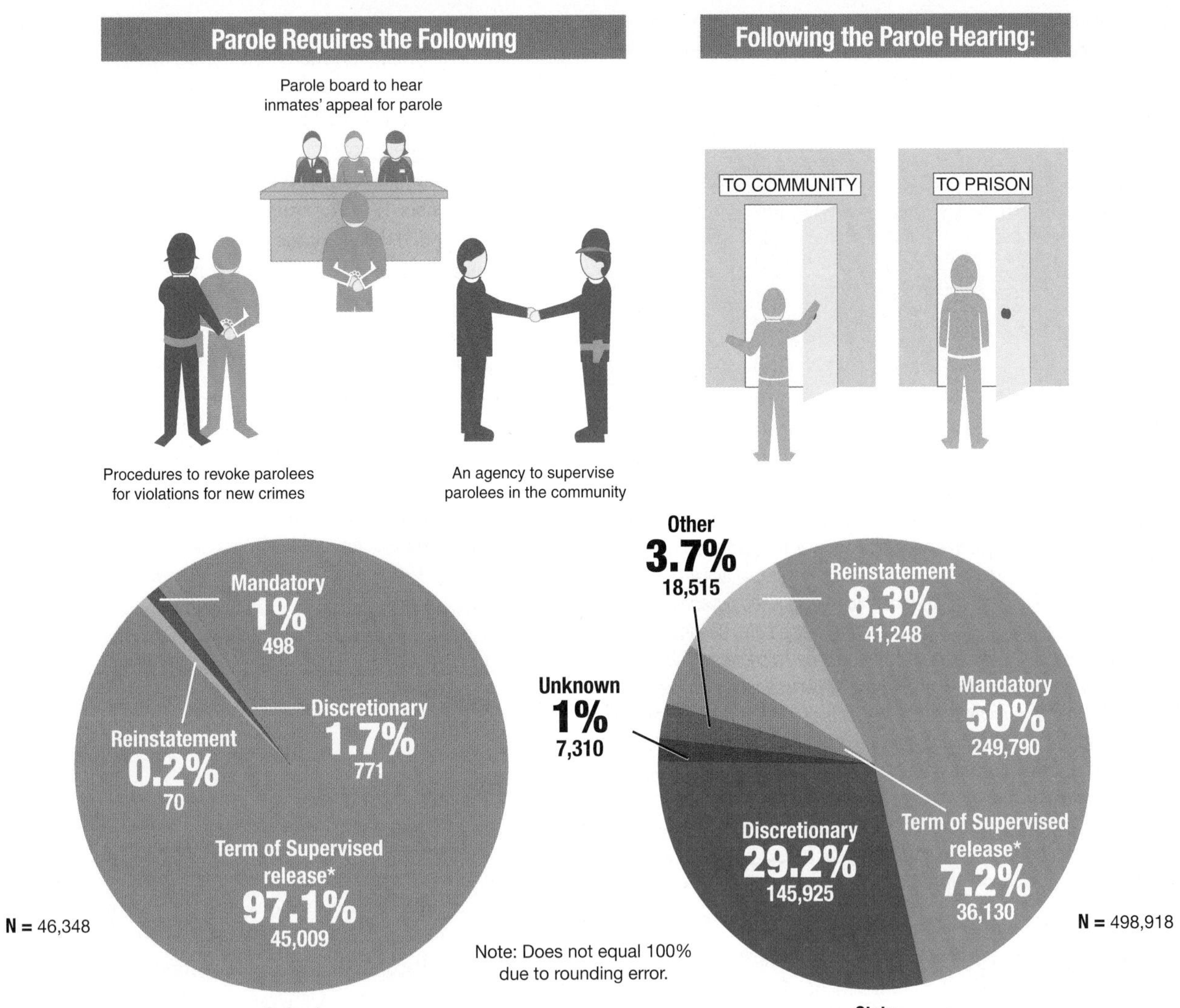

FIGURE 10.2 Number of Adults Entering Parole by Type, 2009

Source: Glaze, L.E., and Bonczar, T.P. (2010). *Probation and Parole in the United States, 2009* (Washington, DC: Bureau of Justice Statistics, p. 34).

Two models for administering state parole boards under the authority of the executive branch of government are the independent model and the consolidated model.[27] In the **independent model**, the parole board is an autonomous administrative unit with the power to make parole release decisions and to supervise all conditionally released inmates. In the **consolidated model**, the parole board is under the authority of the state Department of Corrections as a specialty unit within the department that makes decisions about conditional early releases.

State parole boards usually have fewer than a dozen members who may be full-time or part-time appointees. Final decision-making authority for selecting prisoners to release on parole lies with the parole board, but few states have qualifications for who can serve on the board. State parole board members are not required to have a minimum education, do not obtain their appointment by competitive civil service examination, and need not have any background in criminal justice or a related field such as psychology or sociology. A survey by the American Correctional Association revealed that, in the absence of minimum requirements, some state parole board members lack the educational and vocational experience to equip them to make such decisions.[28]

People who serve on state parole boards receive little pay, and there is little opportunity for advancement because of the small size and specialized nature of the job. Service on state parole boards can be a thankless task. Few appreciate the responsibility and hard work of the board, but everyone is quick to criticize the board if a released parolee commits a crime.

independent model the system in which decision-making about parole is under the authority of an autonomous parole board

consolidated model the system in which decision-making about parole is a function of a state department of corrections

HERE'S SOMETHING TO THINK ABOUT...

Bill Wallshleger, 63, appeared to have a good chance of a favorable recommendation for parole from the Maryland parole board. It was his Sixth hearing and he had an impressive prison record. Convicted of violent sexual assaults the former police officer had undergone treatment for a diagnosed psychosexual disorder, earned four degrees including a doctorate, helped give seminars to other inmates on avoiding violence behind bars, and had a spotless disciplinary record. What changed the outcome was that one of his victims chose to testify at his parole hearing. She appeared before the parole board and gave her account of the brutality of the assault and how the crime had impacted her life.

Notice of parole hearings must be given to victims. Victim testimony has a powerful influence upon parole decisions but it is rare for victims to testify. The Maryland parole board reports that of the 10,000 parole hearings annually, fewer than three rape victims a year typically come to speak. Should victims be encouraged to testify at parole hearings?

Because the governor appoints members, the parole board often reflects the political agenda of the governor. State parole board members are neither correctional officers nor law enforcement officers. They do not have the power to carry concealed firearms, or the powers of arrest, search, and seizure. Their duties are mostly administrative, with a primary responsibility for making decisions about the early release of prisoners. All states have a parole board, even those that have abolished the practice, because states cannot retroactively revoke an inmate's right to parole. Thus, states that have abolished parole must nevertheless maintain the right to early conditional release for inmates sentenced prior to the abolishment of parole.

BECAUSE THE GOVERNOR APPOINTS MEMBERS, THE PAROLE BOARD OFTEN REFLECTS THE POLITICAL AGENDA OF THE GOVERNOR.

Federal Parole Boards The U.S. Congress created the United States Board of Parole in 1930, creating the first federal parole board. In 1976, the Parole Commission and Reorganization Act retitled the agency as the United States Parole Commission. The commission consists of a chairperson and commissioners appointed by the president, and regional offices are staffed by hearing examiners, case analysts, and clerical staff. Despite the increasing numbers of federal inmates, the U.S. Parole Commission is in the process of closing down its operations. The Comprehensive Crime Control Act of 1984 abolished eligibility for parole for federal offenders who committed crimes on or after November 1, 1987. Thus, only federal prisoners who committed crimes prior to that date are eligible for parole. The act provided for the abolition of the Parole Commission on November 1, 1992. However, judicial challenges to the elimination of, or reduction in, parole eligibility for those sentenced prior to November 1, 1997, resulted in the Judicial Improvements Act of 1990 that extended the life of the Parole Commission until November 1, 1997. The Parole Commission Phaseout Act of 1996 again extended the life of the Parole Commission. This act authorized the continuation of the Parole Commission until November 1, 2002. The National Capital Revitalization and Self-Government Improvement Act of 1997 actually gave the Parole Commission significant additional responsibilities, including responsibility for parole within the District of Columbia. Additional responsibilities have been added by other legislation, such as responsibility for making prison-term decisions in foreign transfer treaty cases for offenses committed on or after November 1, 1987, and jurisdiction over all state defendants who are accepted into the U.S. Marshals Service Witness Protection Program. The Twenty-First Century Department of Justice Appropriations Authorization Act of 2002 again extended the life of the Parole Commission until November 1, 2005. Given the fact that the Federal Parole Commission continues to have authority over certain prisoners, the status of the Parole Commission remains unresolved.

The Parole Hearing

Parole boards make decisions through parole hearings. State parole boards have tremendous discretion in deciding which inmates to grant early conditional release, and inmates have little power to appeal these decisions. Parole hearings are not at all like trials, and each state and the federal Parole Commission have different procedures for conducting parole hearings.[29] Generally, parole hearings are brief, private rather than public, and held in the prison where the prisoner is housed. **Parole hearings** are convened by the parole board or by a hearing examiner who acts as the authorized representative of the parole board. The examiner presides over the hearing and makes a recommendation, which is forwarded to the parole board for formal action.

The board has great control over an inmate's eligibility for parole. When an inmate is processed into prison, his or her file is forwarded to the parole board for review to determine a first hearing date. The parole board reviews the circumstances of the crime and information about the offender and sets a date. For most offenders, the first parole hearing is set after serving one-third of their prison time. The parole board may recommend what they expect inmates to do during this time to increase their chances of obtaining parole. Usually, recommendations relate to participation in educational or treatment programs, vocational training sufficient to allow inmates to support themselves if released, and obedience to prison rules.

sex offender registry an open-access online database identifying known sex offenders on parole, maintained to protect communities and potential victims

parole hearing a meeting with an inmate, his or her attorney, and others in which the parole board decides whether to grant, deny, or revoke parole

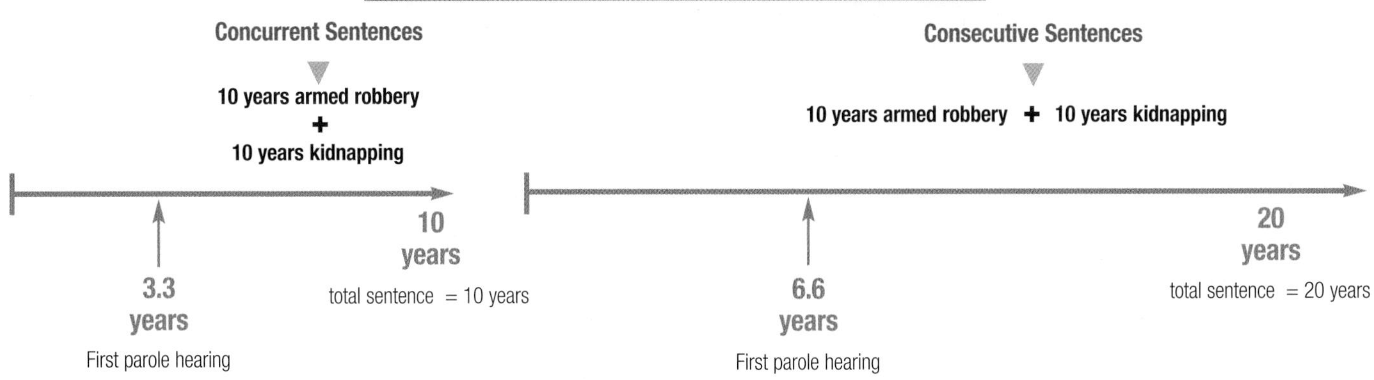

Assuming that an inmate is eligible for his or her first parole hearing after serving one-third of the total sentence, he or she will be eligible for the first parole hearing much sooner under concurrent sentencing.

The power of the parole board to grant early release and the public expectation that the prisoner will serve out the sentence have created considerable public debate. In states using indeterminate sentencing, the sentence handed down by the judge may be quite different from the time actually served. The judge may sentence a defendant who has committed multiple crimes to two sentences of 10 years for each crime to be served consecutively. In this case, the inmate is effectively sentenced to 20 years in prison.

However, in some states, the parole board has the power to decide that the sentence will be served concurrently—the prisoner serves the time for both sentences simultaneously. The difference between these two interpretations has a great impact on calculating when an inmate is eligible for a first parole hearing. Often, the public is critical of parole boards that disregard the judge's instructions and permit concurrent sentences. This lack of truth in sentencing has led many states to adopt new sentencing guidelines that reduce or eliminate parole.

The parole hearing is conducted in a meeting room, not a courtroom. The board reviews the history of the case and all available information about the prisoner, and then the inmate is brought into the room to state his or her case for parole. All inmates are required to submit a parole plan, which contains detailed plans for employment, education, and living arrangements if released. These parole plans also contain statements explaining why inmates think they are ready for parole, what they have done to prepare for release, what they have done to rehabilitate themselves while in prison, and why they are sorry for the crimes they committed. In some states, inmates may request witnesses to appear at the parole hearing to testify in their behalf, but the parole board may deny this request. Inmates are not entitled to an attorney at their parole hearing. In many states, victims of a crime and law enforcement officers must be notified that an inmate is scheduled to receive a parole hearing, and these parties may appear before the board to testify for or against the release of the inmate. Law enforcement officers typically recommend that parole be denied. The prisoner is not entitled to cross-examine any witnesses who testify for or against his or her parole. The entire hearing lasts only a few minutes. Afterward, the parole board notifies the prisoner of the outcome. If parole is denied, the board is required to give written reasons for its decision.[30]

Standards for Granting Parole The parole board's task is difficult, because predicting which prisoners are ready and able to reintegrate into the community is almost an impossible task. Board members often

HERE'S SOMETHING TO THINK ABOUT...

Many factors influence the number of inmates returning to the community. First, 95 percent of inmates return to the community, so record-high prison populations mean record-high numbers of inmates returning to the community. Changes in the Fair Sentencing Act of 2010 will result in shorter sentences for up to 12,000 inmates nationwide. Finally, states are making drastic cuts in their prison populations due to budget shortfalls. Thus, states realize that they must enhance the effectiveness of probation and parole programs. A revolving door policy where prisoners "serve life in prison on the installment plan," one sentence at a time, is not going to work.

Virginia abolished discretionary parole in 1995. Their recidivism rate of 28.3 percent for prisoners 3 years after their release is well below the national average of 43.3 percent. Virginia attributes the better-than-average performance to innovative programs, better assessment of the needs of offenders, keeping offenders out of diversion program who are deemed a recidivism risk, and longer prison sentences which tend to "age-out" offenders. What should states do to improve probation and parole?

rely on feelings, common sense, and a sense of what the community would think. Some states and the U.S. Parole Commission have developed decision-making aids to help them make parole decisions. The probability or risk that a parolee will reoffend or be a danger to the community can be ranked on a scale from 1 to 10. However, in those states that use such an instrument, the parole boards are not bound by these devices and have the authority to deny parole even if the prisoner's score indicates a low risk. The American Law Institute has suggested a model protocol for parole boards based on identifying who should not be paroled rather than who should.

Prison Overcrowding and Parole One of the most difficult decisions that parole boards have to make is who to release when the prison system is ordered to reduce its population due to overcrowding. If the conditions of imprisonment caused by overcrowding violate the Eighth Amendment against cruel and unusual punishment, the state or federal court may order a mandatory reduction in the number of inmates. Overcrowding in itself is not a violation of the Eighth Amendment, but when the overcrowding causes a significant deterioration in the standard of care, prisoners' constitutional rights are violated.

80,000

Number of prisoners that California's prison system was designed to house.

150,000

Actual number of prisoners in California prisons in 2009.

40,000

Number of prisoners that a Federal Judiciary panel ordered that California reduce its prison population by.

In 2009, for example, a federal judicial panel ordered California to reduce its prison population to 110,000 to improve medical and mental treatment services provided to inmates. At the time, California had 150,000 prisoners in facilities that were designed to house 80,000. California appealed the mandatory reduction to the U.S. Supreme Court and in 2011 the Court upheld the lower court's ruling. In a rare decision the Court declared that the number of prisoners and the level of services offered rendered the California prison system in violation of the Eighth Amendment prohibiting cruel and unusual punishment. The Court gave California until 2013 to reduce its prison population to 110,000, meaning a reduction of approximately 30,000 to 40,000 inmates. The Court did not mandate that this many inmates must be released, only that the state's prisons must be reduced by this number. California has several options and most of them involve some form of early release. It can give inmates additional good-time credit, reduce the number of prisoners sent back to prison for technical parole violations, house inmates in private prisons, and increase the number of inmates eligible for various early release programs such as house arrest.

California is not the only state that has found itself under court order either to reduce or to limit its prison population. Many states have found themselves in a similar situation. In these cases, the parole board must meet and decide which inmates can be released immediately, even ahead of their scheduled release dates, to make room for new inmates.

At these "midnight parole hearings," the parole board must meet quickly and release inmates even before they have a parole plan in place. In the late 1990s, the State of Hawaii was under a court order to limit the state prison population to a capped number. To comply with the court order, if the evening prisoner count exceeded the cap, the parole board had to meet during the night to release prisoners before the official morning count. Such parole practices are not sound correctional policy but are political and legal necessities.

Prison overcrowding also has encouraged states to give inmates liberal good-time credit to speed releases. At the height of overcrowding in the Florida state prison system, some inmates were serving only a small percentage of their original sentences.[31] In 1990, states such as Arkansas, California, Indiana, and Louisiana were granting inmates more than 30 days' good-time credit per month![32] The parole board's task of deciding who to release early is complicated by mandatory sentencing laws. These laws prohibit early release for drug offenders, for example. Thus, parole boards are forced to give early release to violent offenders who are not serving mandatory sentences instead of to nonviolent drug offenders.

Conditions of Parole

Parolees are subject to conditions of release very similar to those for probationers. The conditions of release relate to security (will the parolee abide by the conditions of release?) and to plans for treatment and rehabilitation. Each state has different standard conditions of release, but most are similar to those of the U.S. Parole Commission. Federal parolees are required to abide by 14 **standard conditions of release.**[33] These standard conditions require the parolee to report to his or her parole advisor within 3 days of release, restrict where the parolee can live and work, require him or her to abide by all laws, and report contacts with the police to his or her parole officer. The conditions prohibit consumption of alcoholic beverages to excess, the use of illegal drugs, association with criminals, and possession of firearms. Parolees are required to cooperate with their probation officer and to submit to drug tests whenever ordered.

In addition to these standard conditions of release, parolees may, and often do, receive other conditions of release that are applicable to the individual's crime and circumstances. For example, sex offenders may be prohibited from living or being near schools, playgrounds, or other areas where children are present. Persons convicted of domestic violence may be prohibited from contact with their victims. Prisoners with a history of drug or alcohol abuse may be required to attend treatment programs.

standard conditions of release federal and state guidelines with which parolees must comply to meet their conditions of release

UNITED STATES PAROLE COMMISSION STANDARD CONDITIONS OF RELEASE FOR U.S. CODE OFFENDERS

1. You shall go directly to the district shown on this CERTIFICATE OF RELEASE (unless released to the custody of other authorities). Within three days after your arrival, you shall report to your parole advisor if you have one, and the United States Probation Officer whose name appears on this Certificate. If in any emergency you are unable to contact your parole advisor, or your Probation Officer or the United States Probation Office, you shall communicate with the United States Parole Commission, Department of Justice, Chevy Chase, Maryland 20815.
2. If you are released to the custody of other authorities, and after your release from physical custody of such authorities, you are unable to report to the United States Probation Officer to whom you are assigned within three days, you shall report instead to the nearest United States Probation Officer.
3. You shall not leave the limits fixed by this CERTIFICATE OF RELEASE without written permission from your Probation Officer.
4. You shall notify your Probation Officer within 2 days of any change in your place of residence.
5. You shall make a complete and truthful written report (on a form provided for that purpose) to your Probation Officer between the first and third day of each month, and on the final day of parole. You shall also report to your Probation Officer at other times as your Probation Officer directs, providing complete and truthful information.
6. You shall not violate any law. Nor shall you associate with persons engaged in criminal activity. If you are arrested or questioned by a law-enforcement officer, you shall within 2 days report such contact to your Probation Officer or the United States Probation Office.
7. You shall not enter into any agreement to act as an "informer" or special agent for any law-enforcement agency.
8. You shall work regularly unless excused by your Probation Officer, and support your legal dependents, if any, to the best of your ability. You shall report within 2 days to your Probation Officer any changes in employment.
9. You shall not drink alcoholic beverages to excess. You shall not purchase, possess, use or administer marijuana or narcotic or other habit-forming or dangerous drugs, unless prescribed or advised by a physician. You shall not frequent places where such drugs are illegally sold, dispensed, used or given away.
10. You shall not associate with persons who have a criminal record unless you have permission of your Probation Officer.
11. You shall not possess a firearm/ammunition or other dangerous weapons.
12. You shall permit confiscation by your Probation Officer of any materials which your Probation Officer believes may constitute contraband in your possession and which your Probation Officer observes in plain view in your residence, place of business or occupation, vehicle(s) or on your person.
13. You shall make a diligent effort to satisfy any fine, restitution order, court costs or assessment, and/or court ordered child support or alimony payment that has been, or may be, imposed, and shall provide such financial information as may be requested, by your Probation Officer, relevant to the payment of the obligation. If unable to pay the obligation in one sum, you will cooperate with your Probation Officer in establishing an installment payment schedule.
14. You shall submit to a drug test whenever ordered by your Probation Officer.

Source: www.usdoj.gov/uspc/release.htm

Revocation of Parole

Violations of Parole and New Crimes Similar to probation, parole is revocable. Parole can be revoked for violation of a condition of release, a technical violation, or for commission of a new crime. Revocation of parole is common, because less than 33 percent of parolees are successful in maintaining their freedom 3 years after release.[34] Compared to probationers, parolees are more likely to be returned to prison for the commission of a new crime.[35] Prisoners released on parole (and probation) are prohibited from possessing firearms, yet 21 percent reported possessing a firearm while under supervision. Of those arrested for committing a new offense, almost three of every four reported being armed when they committed their offense.[36]

32.5% of parolees are successful in maintaining their freedom 3 years after release.

The U.S. Supreme Court has decided that parolees are entitled to certain due process rights, although these rights are substantially less than those of defendants in a trial. Most rights of parolees were established in the 1972 case of *Morrissey v. Brewer*,[37] which gave parolees some protection against arbitrary and capricious revocation of parole. *Morrissey v. Brewer* secured the right to notice and a revocation hearing.

The supervising parole officer initiates proceedings for parole revocation by filing notice of a technical violation or a charge that the parolee has committed a new crime. As noted earlier, the parole officer can file notice of revocation of parole even if charges against the parolee are dropped. A standard of proof that is not sufficient for conviction in court may nevertheless be sufficient to revoke parole.

Revocation Hearings Revocation hearings most often are held in a prison facility and are conducted by the parole board or hearing officers representing the parole board. The parolee has the right to present evidence on his or her behalf and to cross-examine witnesses but may not have the right to representation by an attorney. The U.S. Supreme Court has ruled that states do not have to provide parolees with appointed legal counsel if they cannot afford one. Normally, it is the inmate's responsibility, not the state's, to arrange for legal representation at revocation hearings.

Parole violators returned to prison are still entitled to additional parole hearings and may be released on parole again at a later date.[38] Only 16 to 36 percent of rereleased parolees successfully complete parole on their second attempts.[39] For most state and federal parolees, at least a portion of their "street time" will be credited toward their original sentences.[40] Usually, the parole time preceding the violation, noncompliance, or commission of a new crime is counted toward completion of the original sentence. For example, an offender with 5 years left on the original sentence who successfully completes 3 years of parole would have to serve only 2 years on return to prison to complete the sentence.

5 **Probation and parole officers supervise inmates released on probation and parole by helping to integrate them back into society; by helping them obtain shelter, jobs, and educational and other opportunities; and by making sure that they comply with all orders of the court and with the law.**

Supervision of Probation and Parole

Social Work and Rehabilitation Skills

The actual supervision of defendants released on probation and inmates released on parole is the work of state and federal probation officers and **parole officers**. As noted earlier, in many states and in the federal system, the same officers supervise both probation and parole and also perform pretrial investigation reports for the court. Probation and parole officers usually are considered law enforcement officers, with the power to carry concealed weapons and the power of arrest. At the same time, probation and parole officers are expected to perform rehabilitation work. This work strongly emphasizes social work and rehabilitation skills as opposed to investigative and police skills. One indicator of the preference for this skill mix is the fact that a federal probation and pretrial services officer must have a bachelor's degree and postgraduate experience in fields such as probation, pretrial services, parole, corrections, criminal investigations, and substance abuse or addiction counseling and treatment. Basic experience as a police officer, a correctional officer, or a security officer does not meet this requirement.[41] Many probation and parole officer applicants have master's degrees.

Parole Officer as Counselor

Parole Officer as Resource Broker

Parole Officer as Rule Enforcer

Here's Something to Think About...

According to the Bureau of Labor Statistics (BLS) there are over 100,000 jobs for probation and parole officers and by 2018 that number will increase by 19 percent. Also, probation and parole has been much more successful in attracting females than police or corrections. The reasons may be related to the lower physical fitness requirements and a work schedule more aligned with the traditional Monday–Friday work week.

Most employers do not require completion of a training academy as employers expect applicants to have obtained the necessary knowledge, skills, and abilities to perform the job from education and previous experience. Criminal justice majors interested in these jobs should be aware that many criminal justice curriculums do not require the prerequisite counseling, human relations, and psychology classes required for the position. Many applicants major in social work, counseling, psychology, or other fields.

Obstacles to employment are that the entry-level education requirement is higher than that of police or correctional officers. Most state positions require a minimum of a bachelor's degree, and a master's degree is required for federal positions. The job has a heavy workload and high stress. Also, the salary is low compared to other positions requiring similar educational level. The BLS reports the middle 50 percent earn between $35,990 and $60,430. Would you find a career as a probation and parole officer appealing? Why?

Measures of Success

The success of probation and parole officers is judged not by the number of clients he or she returns to prison for violating the conditions of their release but by the number of clients who successfully complete probation and parole. To help the offenders succeed, in addition to providing counseling and guidance, the officer helps them obtain entry into drug treatment programs, vocational training, jobs, housing, medical care, rehabilitation services, and other referrals. The probation and parole officer protects the community from any harm that may be done by conditionally released offenders and deters and detects criminal activity on the part of the released offenders. The probation and parole officer also verifies compliance with the terms of release, authenticates the clients' residency and employment, and

parole officer a state or federal professional employee who reports to the courts and supervises defendants released from prison on parole confirms court-ordered payments of fines or restitution and court-ordered attendance at rehabilitation or treatment sessions. Because of their power to initiate revocation proceedings to return clients to prison, probation and parole officers are more influential than social workers in motivating clients toward rehabilitation and treatment.

You Can Lead a Horse to Water, But . . .

It is said that you can lead a horse to water, but you can't make it drink. The criminal justice system invests substantially in keeping offenders out of jails and prisons. Many people may think that the primary purpose of the criminal justice system is to detect law violators, convict them, and punish them. However, through probation and parole, the criminal justice system also tries to rehabilitate offenders and return them to the community.

ALTHOUGH MANY ARE CRITICAL OF PROBATION AND PAROLE THERE SIMPLY ARE TOO MANY OFFENDERS TO HOUSE THEM ALL IN PRISON.

In the beginning, concerned citizens, alarmed by the awful conditions of jails and prisons and the complete lack of emphasis on rehabilitation, looked for ways to move offenders out of jails and prisons and into treatment programs. Those volunteer initiatives became an integral part of the criminal justice system. Unfortunately, many offenders do not take advantage of the "act of grace" offered them. Unlike the successful early reforms of Augustus, Maconochie, and Crofton, many of today's conditional release programs appear to be failing both in rehabilitating the offender and in protecting the community. John Augustus's work was not formally evaluated, but he concluded that "most of his probationers eventually led law abiding lives."[42] Less than 3 percent of the 1,450 inmates discharged from Maconochie's penal colony under the mark system were convicted of new crimes.[43] Between 1856 and 1861, 1,227 tickets of leave were issued by Crofton's Irish system and only 5.6 percent were revoked.[44] Results like these are enviable in light of today's programs, wherein success rates are as low as 14 percent.[45]

Although many are critical of probation and parole, and the federal and state criminal justice systems have been abandoning the use of parole, there simply are too many offenders under correctional supervision to house them all in prison. Furthermore, despite the discouraging statistics, other data suggest that prison is not the most appropriate punishment for many offenders. As you will see in the next chapter, in corrections, the criminal justice system is undergoing major changes to attempt to provide rehabilitation services to offenders, to provide corrections in the community, and to prevent crime.

CHAPTER 10

Probation and Parole

Check It!

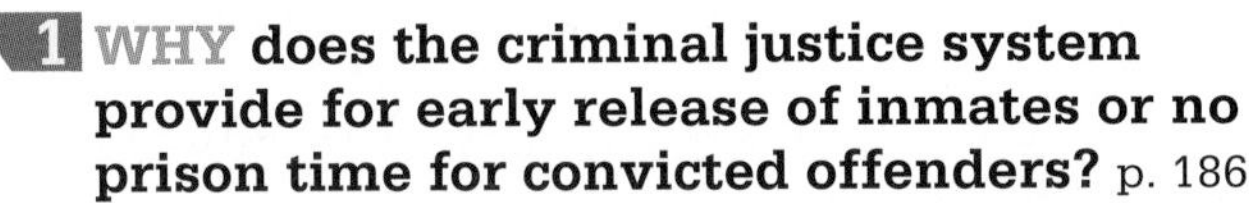

1 WHY does the criminal justice system provide for early release of inmates or no prison time for convicted offenders? p. 186

The costs of prisons are expensive and compete with many other community needs. Also, probation and parole make better use of resources for some nonviolent, nonsexual offenders than does long-term incarceration.

2 WHAT are the differences among diversion, probation, and parole, and among mandatory release, good-time release, and pardon or commutation of sentence? p. 187

- In diversion a defendant is offered an alternative to a trial and possible prison sentence, such as a drug court, boot camp, or a treatment program.
- A suspended sentence is another word for *probation*; convicted offenders must serve their full sentences if they violate the terms of release.
- Parole is the release of an inmate before he or she has served his or her sentence.
- Mandatory release is the requirement that prisoners be released after they serve the entire length of their maximum sentence.
- Good-time credit reduces an inmate's sentence term based on good behavior.
- An executive pardon is an act by a governor or the president that forgives a prisoner and commutes or reduces his or her sentence.

3 WHAT are the origins, reasons for, processes, and advantages of probation? p. 188

In 1841, Boston shoemaker John Augustus started the concept of probation, whereby he oversaw minor offenders being incarcerated. Judges use probation for offenders for whom prison time seems inappropriate and who pose no risk to society. Probation saves the community the costs of incarceration and promotes rehabilitation of offenders by allowing them to function in the community.

4 WHAT are the origins, the pros and cons of parole, the process of granting parole, and the conditions of parole? p. 192

Parole originated with the French, Irish, and Australian systems, in which inmates earned early release for good behavior. Parole promotes rehabilitation, especially for juveniles, and reduces the costs of incarceration; however, there is great distrust of parole by the public, who fear that released prisoners will reoffend, and also the desire to have offenders serve the full amount of their sentence. Parole boards review the history of inmates and hold parole hearings, in which they decide whether or not to grant early release, which is contingent upon a variety of conditions, including checking regularly with a parole officer, restrictions on where the parolee can live and work, and obeying all laws.

5 HOW are probation and parole supervised? p. 199

Probation and parole officers supervise inmates released on probation and parole by

1. helping to integrate them back into society,
2. helping them obtain shelter, jobs, and eduational and treatment opporuntities, and
3. making sure that they comply with all orders of the court and with the law.

Assess Your Understanding

1. Which of the following is a form of early release prior to serving any time in prison for a convicted offense?
  a. parole
  b. mandatory release
  c. probation
  d. pardon

2. Which of the following forms of release is granted by the governor or U.S. president?
  a. parole
  b. mandatory release
  c. probation
  d. pardon

3. Who is credited with being the early founder of probation?
  a. John Augustus
  b. Alexander Maconochie
  c. Walter Crofton
  d. Zebulon Brockway

4. Which of the following can be revoked for cause?
  a. probation
  b. parole
  c. neither probation nor parole
  d. both probation and parole

5. Which of the following has the authority to provide early release through diversion or a suspended sentence?
  a. parole board
  b. governor
  c. appellate court
  d. trial judge

6. What is the standard of proof required to revoke parole in a parole revocation hearing?
  a. There is no standard of proof required and each member of the board uses his or her personal judgment as to whether parole should be revoked.
  b. whether the evidence is sufficient and trustworthy
  c. the same as for a civil trial, the preponderance of the evidence
  d. the same as for a criminal trial, beyond a reasonable doubt

7. Who supervises persons granted early release from prison or a suspended sentence?
  a. the judge
  b. probation and parole officers
  c. the law enforcement agency in which the person resides
  d. the parole board

8. The American system of parole is most similar to which of the following?
  a. Irish system
  b. mark system
  c. *parole d'honneur*
  d. ticket of leave

9. Which of the following is true regarding the rate of reoffending when comparing probationers and parolees?
  a. Persons on probation and parole reoffend at about the same rate.
  b. Persons on probation reoffend at a greater rate than persons on parole.
  c. Persons on parole offend at a greater rate than persons on probation.
  d. The reoffending rate for both persons on probation and parole is less than 10 percent.

10. Which of the following is used to judge the success of probation and parole officers?
  a. the number of clients who successfully complete probation and parole
  b. the number of clients he or she returns to prison for violating the conditions of their release
  c. the number of successful revocation hearings for probation or parole
  d. none of the above

11. Which of the following is required for most state probation/parole entry-level positions?
  a. GED or high school diploma and completion of a 12-week training academy
  b. a minimum education of a high school diploma
  c. a bachelor's degree in a related field
  d. a doctorate degree in counseling or social work

ESSAY

1. Why does the criminal justice system provide for early release of inmates?
2. Describe the different types of early release.
3. Compare and contrast probation and parole.
4. Discuss the evolution of the use of probation.
5. Discuss the evolution of the use of parole.
6. Discuss the supervision of inmates who are released early into the community.
7. Describe the due process rights of a probationer or parolee in regard to the revocation of probation or parole.
8. Describe how members of the parole board are selected, their powers, and duties.

ANSWERS: 1. c, 2. d, 3. a, 4. d, 5. d, 6. b, 7. b, 8. a, 9. c, 10. a, 11. c

Media

Go to the *Chapter 10: Probation and Parole* section in *MyCJLab* to test your understanding of this chapter, access customized study content, engage in interactive simulations, complete critical thinking and research assignments, and view related online videos.

Additional Links

Go to http://www.corrections.ky.gov/KOOL.htm to view the Commonwealth of Kentucky's Offender Online Lookup.

Visit the Federal Bureau of Investigation's national sex offender registry portal at www.fbi.gov/hq/cid/cac/registry.htm to select a state to view the sex offender registry for that state.

Go to www.appa-net.org to view the Web site of the American Probation and Parole Association.

Go to http://bjs.ojp.usdoj.gov/index.cfm?ty=tp&tid=1 to view probation and parole statistics from the Bureau of Justice Statistics.

To view a discussion about the Casey Anthony probation case, go to http://abcnews.go.com/US/casey_anthony_trial/casey-anthony-served-probation-jail-judge-belvin-perry/story?id=14239437

To watch a video discussion about a career in probation, go to www.youtube.com/watch?v=luMshrlKi5Q

To view an inmate's story of how he transitioned from prison to parole, go to www.time.com/time/video/player/0,32068,696072585001_2035840,00.html

To watch the video, "A Day in the Life of a Washington, DC, Probation and Parole Officer" go to www.dailymotion.com/video/xdv819_parole-and-probation-officersya-day_news

To view a Massachusetts parole board member discuss what she considers in making parole decisions, go to http://vimeo.com/25191368

WANTED BY THE FBI

Armed Bank Robbery

RYAN EDWARD DOUGHERTY

Ryan Edward Dougherty | Lee Grace Dougherty | Dylan Dougherty Stanley

Aliases:
Ryan Dougherty, Ryan E. Dougherty

DESCRIPTION

Date(s) of Birth Used:	August 21, 1989	**Hair:**	Brown
Place of Birth:	Florida	**Eyes:**	Brown
Height:	5'10"	**Sex:**	Male
Weight:	170 to 190 pounds	**Race:**	White
NCIC:	W573218866	**Nationality:**	American

Scars and Marks: Ryan Edward Dougherty has tattoos on both of his shoulders and on his back. He has scars on his right shoulder and right wrist.

Remarks: Ryan Edward Dougherty is known to use illegal narcotics. He is thought to be traveling with his two siblings, Dylan and Lee. They may be driving a white, four-door, 2006 Subaru Impreza with New York license tag FBE 5900.

CAUTION

On August 2, 2011, at approximately 12:20 p.m., law enforcement officials responded to an armed robbery at Certus Bank, 460 Norman Drive in Valdosta, Georgia. Three individuals, later identified as siblings Ryan Edward Dougherty, Lee Grace Dougherty, and Dylan Dougherty Stanley, had entered the bank through the front entrance. As the robbers entered the bank, shots were fired towards the ceiling and everyone in the bank was instructed to get down. At least two of the robbers brandished weapons, one described as being an AK-47 type assault rifle and the other appearing to be a machine pistol, while the other robber obtained an undisclosed amount of money. All three robbers then departed the bank and were observed fleeing in an older model white, four-door sedan.

It should be noted that these individuals are also suspects in the attempted murder of a Zephyrhills, Florida, police officer earlier that same day. On August 2, 2011, at 7:00 a.m., a patrol officer for that department was in pursuit of a four-door white vehicle. The suspects in the vehicle began to shoot at the patrol officer and subsequently disabled the patrol vehicle. Multiple calibers were used in that shooting. The suspect vehicle was described as being a 2006 white Subaru Impreza, New York license plate FBE 5900.

On August 4, 2011, the United States Magistrate, Middle District of Georgia, Macon, Georgia, issued warrants for the arrest of Ryan Edward Dougherty, Lee Grace Dougherty, and Dylan Dougherty Stanley for the crime of armed bank robbery.

SHOULD BE CONSIDERED ARMED AND DANGEROUS AND AN ESCAPE RISK

If you have any information concerning this person, please contact your local FBI office or the nearest American Embassy or Consulate.

CORRECTIONS IN THE COMMUNITY

11

MICHELLE ALEXANDER SAYS THAT TO RETURN TO 1970S INCARCERATION RATES, FOUR OUT OF FIVE INMATES WOULD HAVE TO BE RELEASED FROM PRISON.

1 Why are the federal government and states turning to community corrections sanctions?

2 What is the cycle of offending?

3 What opposition is there to community corrections sanctions?

4 What are the various community corrections sanctions used by the criminal justice system, and how are they different from traditional early-release programs?

5 What new strategies are being used to promote reentry into the community for ex-offenders?

6 What programs are being used to promote reentry into the community for drug offenders?

Ryan Dougherty, 21, has an arrest record extending back to age 15 that includes 13 felonies. His sister, Lee Grace Dougherty, 29, has been charged with five felonies and six misdemeanors. The third sibling, Dylan Dougherty Stanley, 26, has only a single drug conviction. In August 2011, all three were on the FBI's "Most Wanted" list and were considered armed and dangerous and described as having an arsenal of weapons. The trio was wanted for allegedly firing over 20 rounds at a Zephyrhills (Florida) police officer and for armed robbery of the Certus Bank in Valdosta, Georgia.

Just a day prior to the crime spree, Ryan registered as a sex offender and was released into the community wearing a monitoring bracelet. He was sentenced to 2 years community control and 10 years probation. The Associated Press reported that he was "unbearably discouraged by the terms of his probation." He cut off his GPS monitoring bracelet and joined his siblings in a crime spree.

There are numerous examples of persons with multiple felony convictions being released early from prison who have endangered public safety. For example, in August 2008, Illinois released Derrick King early from prison. King brutally attacked a couple when they refused to give him a cigarette when he approached them on the street. He was arrested and sent back to prison. Illinois released him again on parole in 2009. Within days King approached a woman who was smoking and asked her for a smoke. When she refused, he told her, "Remember the couple who got beat real bad for not giving a cigarette? That was me." King assaulted the woman but was quickly arrested by two police officers patrolling nearby.

Often early release is motivated by the financial crisis that states are experiencing. States find they cannot support the nearly 40-year record-high incarceration rate. Michelle Alexander, author of *The New Jim Crow: Mass Incarceration in an Age of Colorblindness,* says that to return to 1970s incarceration rates, four out of five inmates would have to be released from prison.

To deal with the crisis, states are turning to traditional early release; but often these early release programs are seen as posing serious risk to public safety. For example, in 2010, Illinois suspended an early release program when the public became concerned that those released were a threat to public safety. Of the 1,754 inmates who were released early, 65 percent were returned to prison within 3 months. The program was suspended and Illinois will have to find $175 million per year to house the inmates who would have been released under the program.

This chapter examines the alternatives to traditional early release programs. These alternative programs attempt to balance the need for cost containment with public safety to achieve the safe reentry of prisoners back into society.

Why Intermediate Sentences?

Three out of four persons released from prison and jail have a substance abuse problem, but only 10 percent in state prisons and 3 percent in local jails will receive formal treatment prior to release. About 41 percent of inmates in the nation's state and federal prisons and local jails have not completed high school or its equivalent, compared to 18 percent of the general population.[1] Nearly half of those in jail earned less than $600 per month just prior to incarceration. More than one out of three jail inmates have some physical or mental disability. Ten thousand parolees will be homeless when released.[2] It is little surprise that two out of three adults released from prisons and jails will be rearrested within 3 years.

adults released from prisons and jails will be rearrested within 3 years

Traditional incarceration, probation, and parole are failing to stem the tide of prisoners returning to prison after their release. Many are calling for new strategies and programs in offender rehabilitation. Despite long prison terms, prison time alone does not change behavior. Experts are recognizing that community-based organizations, not prisons, have the best chance of rehabilitating prisoners.[3] The "get tough on crime" philosophy of the 1980s has proven both costly and ineffective in long-term rehabilitation. Furthermore, given that nearly all of the persons sentenced to prison return to the community, incarceration without rehabilitation does not guarantee community safety.

As a result, the criminal justice system is turning to new sanctions for offenders. These sanctions are known as intermediate sanctions and community-based corrections—sanctions somewhere between prison and traditional probation and parole. These sanctions are carried out in the community rather than in prison. These new sanctions create a challenge: to rehabilitate the offender while ensuring community safety.

This chapter examines why prisoner reentry in the criminal justice system is in a crisis and discusses some of the many new prevention and community corrections programs that are being used to promote successful prisoner reentry into the community.

Incarceration Fails to Prepare Offenders for Reentry

Huge Expense and Number of Prisoners The United States is transforming itself into a nation of ex-convicts. In 2008, more than 7.3 million people were on probation, in jail or prison, or on parole—3.2 percent of all U.S. adult residents, or 1 in every 32 adults. The U.S. imprisons people at 14 times the rate of Japan, 8 times the rate of France, and 6 times the rate of Canada. Thirteen million people, or about 7 percent of the U.S. adult population, have been convicted of a felony and spent some time in prison. That number is more than the population of Sweden, Bolivia, Senegal, Greece, or Somalia.[4]

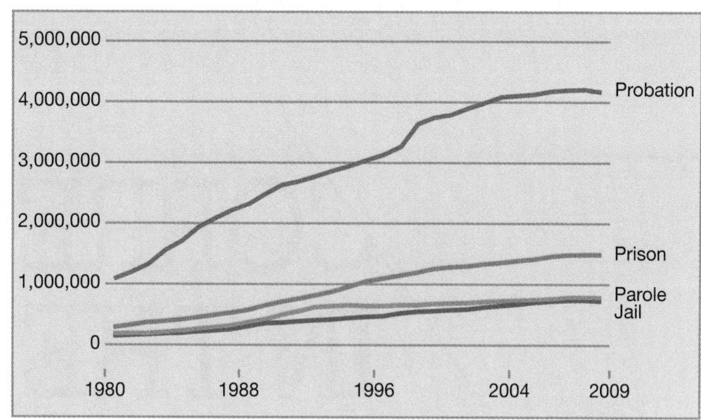

FIGURE 11.1 Adult Correctional Populations, 1980–2009
For many states, corrections is the fastest growing budget item. In 2009, for the first time in nearly 40 years the correctional population growth declined.

Source: Bureau of justice Statistics Correctional Surveys (The Annual Probation Survey, National Prisoner Statistics Program, Annual Survey, of Jails, and Annual Parole Survey) as presented in *Correctional Populations in the United States, 2009, Prisoners in 2009, Probation and Parole in the United Stated, 2009,* and *Jail Inmates at Midyear 2009 - Statistical Tables.*

1 in every 32
adults is on probation, parole, or in jail or prison as of 2009

The United States has the largest, most expensive, and fastest-growing prison system in the world. See Figure 11.1. The United States spends more than $60 billion per year for corrections, compared to just $9 billion a year two decades ago. Corrections is the second-fastest-growing expense in state budgets, after Medicaid.[5] To keep up with the demand for new bed space, the federal government and states have had to build a record number of prisons in the last decade. As a result, prisons and jails have become a mammoth industry with powerful constituencies that favor the status quo. Many rural communities and politicians who represent these communities depend on prisons for their economic viability.[6] As a result, changing sentencing and prison policy is not a simple matter. However, states cannot keep pumping more and more money into prisons.

FOR MANY STATES, CORRECTIONS IS THE FASTEST GROWING BUDGET ITEM

1 **Incarceration, probation, and parole are expensive and fail to stop a large number of ex-prisoners from returning to prison after their release because the criminal justice system traditionally has not prepared inmates to return to society.**

Record Numbers of Released Prisoners Despite the record number of persons sentenced to prison, there is a record number of persons being released from prisons. Nationwide at least 95 percent of all state prisoners will be released from prison at some point. This financial burden has caused 25 states to ease mandatory and long-term sentencing policies and reinstate early-release and treatment programs for drug offenders; this is about 25 percent of the nation's prisoners.[7] At the same time, while concerned about increased costs of corrections, some are concerned about what will be the economic impact when prison populations decline. Those communities that have come to depend on the revenues generated by the prison industry will suffer economic distress.

In effect, the attempt to make communities safe and to prosper from the prison industry is having the opposite effect. Most offenders sentenced to prison return to the community within 2 years. In California in any given year, about 40 percent of its prisoners are released back into the community. Tougher and longer sentencing strategies only result in more and more offenders being released back into the community.[8] Nationwide, nearly 640,000 inmates arrive yearly on the doorsteps of the community,[9] compared to fewer than 170,000 released offenders in 1980.[10]

58%

The number of California paroled felons who reoffend within 36 months

Unsuccessful Reentry into Communities Unfortunately most released offenders do not make a successful reentry back into the community. Nearly 58 percent of California's paroled felons reoffend within 36 months. The failure rate of paroled inmates is so high that 40 percent of all admissions to California state prisons are parole violators".[11] In 1978, parole violators accounted for only 8 percent of the total felons admitted to prison.[12]

Most states require offenders to be returned to the counties where they lived before entering prison. According to Joan Petersilia, a leading researcher in corrections, "Since the vast majority of offenders come from economically disadvantaged, culturally isolated, inner-city neighborhoods, they return there upon release."[13] Once returned to their old neighborhoods, most offenders quickly fall into the lifestyles that led to their arrests. Most will last only 6 months on the street before they are rearrested. Two-thirds of all parolees are rearrested within 3 years.[14]

WHEREAS DETROIT IS HOME TO 44% OF THE COUNTY'S ADULTS, IT ACCOUNTS FOR 75% OF THE COUNTY'S CORRECTIONAL POPULATION.

Lack of Support Services Furthermore, there is an inverse relationship between time in prison and successful reentry. For example, offenders who served 5 years or more in federal prison were more likely to return to federal prison (25 percent) than those who served terms of less than 5 years (15 percent).[15] Upon their release from prison, most inmates are not prepared to successfully reenter the community. Among state prisoners expected to be released, 84 percent report being involved in drugs or alcohol at the time of the offense that led to their incarceration. Nearly 25 percent were alcohol dependent. Twenty-one percent reported they had committed the offense to obtain money for drugs. Fourteen percent were classified as having mental illness upon their release. Most will have nowhere to go, because they do not have family or friends to support them, and 12 percent reported being homeless at the time of their arrest. Those communities to which offenders are returned are not prepared to provide the services that these persons need. For example, in Connecticut, almost half of the prison and jail population is from just a handful of neighborhoods in five cities, which have the most concentrated levels of poverty and nonwhite populations in the state.[16] In Chicago, only 24 percent of identified organizations that provide services to reentering individuals were located in any of the six communities to which the highest numbers of people returned from prison in 2001. No services were located in two of those six neighborhoods.[17] California had 200 shelter beds for more than 10,000 homeless parolees. A 2009 study released by the Pew Center on the States documented that 1 in 25 adults in Detroit, Michigan, is under correctional control. Whereas Detroit is home to 44 percent of the county's adults, it accounts for over 75 percent of the county's correctional population.[18]

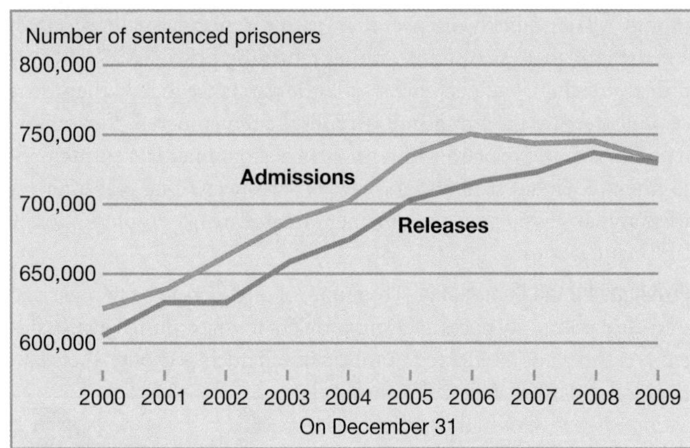

FIGURE 11.2 In 2009, the prison population slowed as the number of admissions was about the same as the number of releases. It is not known if this is the start of a downward trend or just a brief pause.

Source: West, H.C., and Sabol, W.J. (2010). *Prisoners in 2009* (Washington, D.C.: Bureau of Justice Statistics), p. 4.

Ineffectiveness of Parole Offenders released under traditional parole are finding that the shortage of probation and parole officers means they infrequently see their supervising officer. Many parolees see their parole officer for less than two 15-minute, face-to-face contacts per month.[19] They quickly discover that "parole is more a legal status than a systematic process of reintegrating returning prisoners."[20] There is little oversight of their activities and little assistance to help them successfully reenter the community. It must be remembered, "the majority of inmates leave prison with no savings, no immediate entitlement to unemployment benefits, and few job prospects. One year after release as many as 60 percent of former inmates are not employed in the legitimate labor market."[21]

Problems for the Community The failure of offenders to be reintegrated into the community poses a serious problem for the criminal justice system. As these unprecedented numbers of offenders go home, their failure results in other social problems, such as increases in child abuse, family violence, the spread of infectious diseases, homelessness, and community disorganization.[22] Incarceration of adults results in problems for children. Among those born in 1990, 1 in 4 Black children, compared with 1 in 25 White children, had a father in prison by age 14.[23] Adult imprisonment has economic, sociological, and psychological impacts on children that often results in behavioral and psychological problems for the children. Without alternatives to incarceration that separates parents from children the criminal justice system fosters a new generation of potential offenders. The criminal justice system and society in general do not appear to have prepared for this problem. As Petersilia states, "Virtually no systematic, comprehensive attention has been paid by policymakers to dealing with people after release."[24] The rate of failure suggests that the criminal justice system lacks the organizational capacity to manage the integration of released offenders.[25]

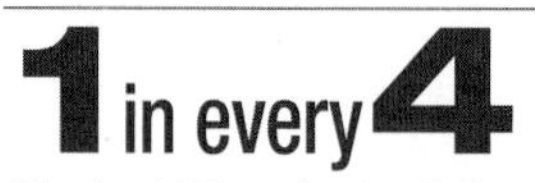

Black children had a father in jail by the age of 14

Thus, as measured by recidivism, traditional incarceration, probation, and parole programs have not been successful. In light of serious threats to community safety, new community-based correctional programs and innovative sanctions are being developed and implemented to promote effective crime prevention, treatment, and offender reentry into the community.

Based on past trends, criminal justice experts predict that two out of every five inmates released this year will be reincarcerated within 3 years. Offenders who routinely enter, leave, and reenter prison are said to be "serving a life sentence on the installment plan." This pattern of repeated incarceration and release is costly in terms of both dollars to the taxpayers and harm to the community.

Concern for Community Safety

Community-based corrections are sanctions that are alternatives to incarceration in jail or prison, such as boot camps, house arrest, community service, electronic monitoring, or supervision in the community after a sentence of incarceration has been served, such as furloughs, work releases, or halfway houses. Citizen opposition to locating community-based programs in their neighborhoods is one of the primary obstacles to community-based corrections. Few politicians are willing to risk the wrath of their constituents who are opposed to locating community-based treatment and prevention programs in their neighborhoods. Community opposition to locating prisons and correctional facilities in their neighborhood is so strong and common that there is even a name for it—NIMBY, or "not in my back yard."

Sometimes public fear is such that a single incident of harm to the community can close down an entire program. The dilemma is that public demand for imprisonment is strong, but those who are imprisoned are returned in a condition not much improved from the one that led to their imprisonment.[26]

Not only are communities opposed to community-based facilities being located in their neighborhoods, but crime victims and the police are opposed to reentry of individual offenders back into the community. Crime victims fear contact with the offender and can be resentful of the memories that the offender's presence in the community can trigger. Police fear that offenders released back into the community will contribute to the crime problem.

CITIZEN OPPOSITION TO LOCATING COMMUNITY-BASED PROGRAMS IN THEIR NEIGHBORHOODS IS ONE OF THE PRIMARY OBSTACLES TO COMMUNITY-BASED CORRECTIONS.

2 **Most prisoners who are released from prison have few support services, often find it difficult to find a job; and are returned to their old, economically disadvantaged inner-city communities, which leads to these ex-prisoners reoffending and returning to prison.**

community-based corrections prevention and treatment programs designed to promote the successful transition of offenders from prison to the community

Cycle of Offending

Newly Convicted Offender

Many criminal justice professionals believe that the use of imprisonment creates a vicious cycle of offending. In the absence of effective community-based treatment and prevention programs and intermediate sanctions, offenders revert to their criminal lifestyles. The failure of offenders to reenter the community without reoffending then causes the public to demand more use of imprisonment.[27]

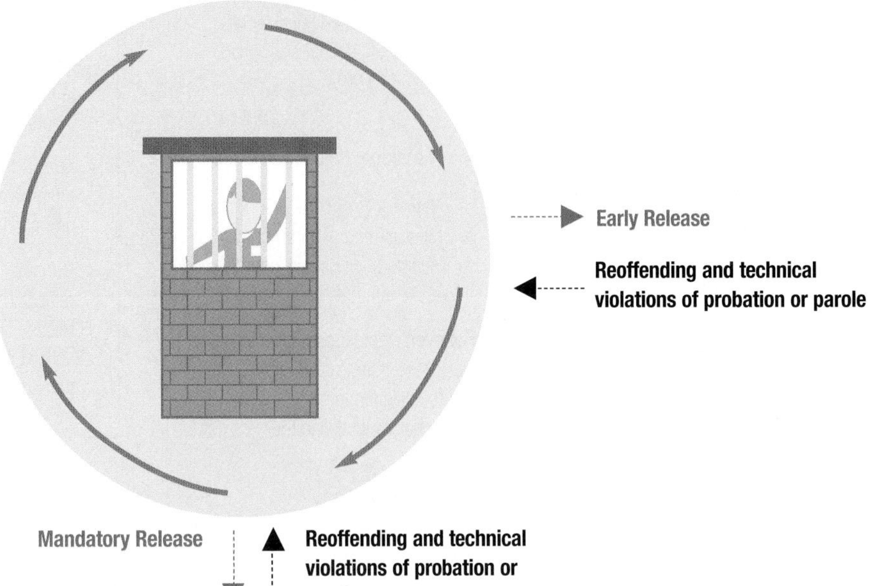

Intermediate Sanctions and Community Corrections

Community-based treatment and prevention programs were virtually unknown before the late 1960s. One of the pioneers of community-based programs was the Vera Institute of Justice in New York,[28] which in the 1980s spearheaded the use of community-based programs to promote the successful transition of offenders from prison to society. These programs were described as intermediate punishments and later as intermediate sanctions.[29] Many early programs addressed pressing concerns of prison overcrowding and skyrocketing costs and were not built on research and experimentation relating to criminological or correctional theory. Instead, early programs grew out of the search for practical and expedient solutions to pressing problems.[30] Thus, there is little surprise that many of the programs have not lived up to expectations. Some have even resulted in substantial harm to the community. According to subsequent research, rehabilitation programs and new forms of supervision in the community have been faulted for not reducing recidivism or providing adequate safeguards for community protection.[31]

Returning prisoners who cannot rejoin the community as law-abiding citizens can have a detrimental impact on the community's quality of life. The impact of this influence is made greater by the fact that prisoners tend to return to certain neighborhoods in a city or state rather than being distributed throughout the state. For example, 11 percent of the city blocks in Brooklyn are home to 50 percent of the people in that borough of New York City who are on parole.[32] Also, approximately 1,800 out of 7,400 adult prisoners released each year in Kansas return to a handful of neighborhoods in Wichita.[33] The failures of the returning prisoners influence what are known as the "tipping points," beyond which communities can no longer favorably influence residents' behavior.[34] Sociologist Elijah Anderson argues that as more and more street-smart young offenders are released back into the community, they exert a strong influence on community disorganization, general demoralization, and higher unemployment. They can weaken the influence of family values and legitimate role models.[35] As the number of offenders in the community increases, their negative influence can reach the point where the community is powerless to exert stable, positive influences over them. The structure of the community changes, disorder and incivilities increase, out-migration follows as desirable residents leave, and crime and violence increase.[36] This flood of returning offenders also increases the influence of gang activity in the community.[37]

Community-based intermediate sanctions are strategies aimed at stopping the revolving door of incarceration. The most commonly used programs are:

- intensive probation supervision programs,
- shock probation and shock incarceration (boot camps),
- home confinement and electronic monitoring,
- work and education release programs, and
- halfway houses and day reporting centers.

3 **Communities are opposed to community-based facilities being located in their neighborhoods, crime victims fear contact with and resent the offender, and police fear that offenders released back into the community will contribute to the crime problem.**

Sentencing Options

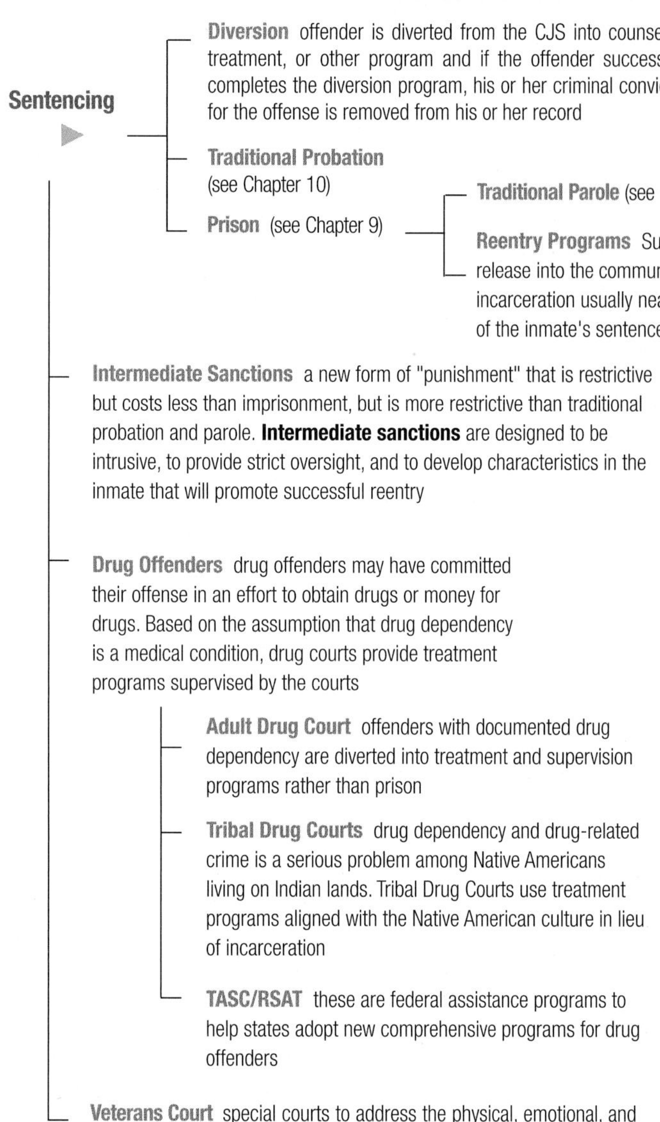

Work Release work release provides inmates with work skills necessary for successful reentry. Inmates may first acquire some skills in prison programs followed by on-the-job training and/or work in the community. Inmates on work release may return to some form of incarceration (prison or halfway house) following work

Education Release similar to work release but allows the inmate to attend a college or vocational school. Inmates may receive academic preparation in prison such as completion of the high school GED

Halfway House in the last months of imprisonment the inmate is relocated to a residential dormitory environment and has supervised release time in the community for education, work, or preparatory actions necessary to enter the community, i.e., looking for a job, getting a social security card, etc.

Day Reporting Center bed space is one of the scarce resources in jails and prisons. Day Reporting Centers require the offender to report to jail or prison in the morning for programs, treatment, and/or supervision but the inmate returns "home" in the evening. Often inmates with jobs are allowed to keep working

Intensive Parole inmates are released from prison early but unlike traditional parole may have to report up to six times a week to the parole officer to submit to frequent random drug tests; to consent to frequent and random searches of person, residence, and automobile; and to demonstrate compliance with his or her terms of release by supplying documentation, i.e., pay receipts, rent receipts, etc.

Split Sentencing/Shock Probation usually for first-time nonviolent offenders this form of intermediate sanction aims to "get the attention" of youthful offenders who have become accustomed, perhaps as juvenile offenders, to warnings and probation rather than prison time

Shock Incarceration or "Boot Camps" used primarily with youthful (under 25) nonviolent offenders. Most offenders have little self-discipline and poor life skills for success in the community. Styled after military boot camps, shock incarceration programs are designed to build self-discipline, character, and life skills

Home Confinement/Electronic Monitoring can be used in lieu of prison or as a reentry program near the end of the inmate's prison term. Through the use of GPS monitoring, the offender is confined within his or her residence except for authorized activities such as work, shopping, medical appointments, etc.

Intensive Probation Supervision

The three roles of the probation and parole officer, discussed in Chapter 9, include law enforcement officer, caseworker, and community resource broker. However, a factor contributing to the offender's failure is a lack of clarity or agreement about the purpose of probation and parole.[38] There also is a certain amount of conflict among these three roles. The probation and parole officer is faced with conflicting goals and objectives as he or she tries to both enforce obedience to the conditions of supervised release and at the same time act as counselor and encourager. Often, the role mix favors caseworker and community resource broker, and as a result, critics have charged that probation and parole officers have not been very good at ensuring that their clients fulfill the conditions of their treatment.[39] Sometimes, probationers or parolees simply abscond, and probation and parole officers are unable to locate them. In 2009, parole agents in California, for example, lost track of about one-fifth of the parolees they were assigned.[40] Nationwide, about 1 in 11 released offenders abscond.

In an effort to improve the effectiveness of probation and parole, to ensure community safety, and to promote greater success in reentry,

intermediate sanctions punishments that restrict offenders' freedom without imprisoning them and that consist of community-based prevention and treatment programs to promote the successful transition of offenders from prison to the community

HERE'S SOMETHING TO THINK ABOUT . . .

About 68 percent of state prison inmates lack a high school diploma. About half of those reported they were drug offenders and 66 percent reported they had learning disabilities. Without a minimum education, prisoners reentering the community have little chance of finding employment that will provide them with a sustainable income. Studies indicate that those inmates who obtain a GED or college degree while in prison are more likely to find employment when released.

Prison educational programs are expensive due to the need to provide state-certified teachers, classrooms, and supplies. In an effort to reduce the cost of prison education program, especially GED programs, some Texas state legislators are suggesting online educational programs to reduce personnel and classroom costs. The Texas prison school system has about 77,500 inmate-students and an annual operating budget of $128 million. In 2011, Texas State Senators Florence Shapiro (R) and John Whitmire (D) suggested that prison education could be better accomplished through online education. They suggested that inmates would be more comfortable with an online environment than the traditional classroom where many of them performed rather poorly.

Online education is commonplace outside the prison environment; however, within prisons it is virtually nonexistent. Correctional-education experts are skeptical that online education would work in prisons. They point to the high number of inmates who report having learning disabilities and the near absolute opposition of prison security officials to allow inmates access to the Internet for education. Do you think online education would work for prisoners? Why?

probation and parole officers have adopted a new form of supervision of offenders, called **intensive probation supervision (IPS)**. In IPS, the probation and parole officer has a smaller caseload and more emphasis is placed on offender compliance with the conditions of supervision.[41] The offender may be supervised by a team of probation and parole officers. Instead of meeting briefly twice a month, the offender may be required to report daily as well as submit to on-site visits by the probation and parole officer. Intensive probation supervision can be used with either probationers or parolees. Its use dates back to the early 1950s when California Probation and Parole began to experiment with different-size probation caseloads.[42] Today, IPS programs have been implemented in every state as well as in the federal system.

PROBATION AND PAROLE ADMINISTRATORS ADMIT THAT TRADITIONAL PROGRAMS MAY HAVE BEEN TOO LENIENT.

On reflection, even some probation and parole administrators admit that traditional programs may have been too lenient in enforcing the conditions of release.[43] Probation and parole officers often believed incorrectly that released offenders would assume responsibility for compliance with the conditions of release. Leniency also stemmed from impossible caseloads and insufficient funding. Despite increases in spending for corrections, few dollars have gone to rehabilitation or probation and parole. Most of the new dollars have gone primarily to building new prisons, maintaining facilities, and paying for the correctional staff to operate institutions.[44] However, only about 5 percent of inmates complete a reentry program prior to release.[45]

Accustomed to being told exactly what to do and how to do it, parolees often expect their supervision officers to relate to them in the same way.[46] They assume that the probation and parole officer will find a job for them, provide them with the guidance they need to find a treatment program, and in general direct their actions to ensure compliance with the conditions of their release.[47] In traditional probation and parole, these expectations are unrealistic, and released offenders often need much more direct supervision than can be given to them.

Strict Supervision Intensive probation supervision was designed to provide that direct supervision. As a result, IPS is more punitive and controlling than regular probation and is much more intrusive into the offenders' lives. Probation and parole officers may awaken them during the night with phone calls to verify that they are at home. Supervisors may visit offenders at work sites and at home and routinely conduct searches for possible evidence that they are not in compliance with the conditions of release. Officers search for drugs, child pornography, excessive alcohol, firearms, or expensive possessions that would not be consistent with the offenders' legitimate incomes.

In 1982, Georgia implemented one of the earliest IPS programs. In the Georgia IPS program, probation and parole officers acted more like law enforcement officers than caseworkers.[48] Offenders were held to strict accountability for compliance with the conditions of probation and parole.

New Jersey has one of the most successful and prominent IPS programs, which is designed to handle about 1,200 offenders at a time. The program provides strict supervision and requires such strict compliance with the terms of release that few offenders have been able to avoid being returned to prison. More than 25 percent of participants have been expelled from the program for violations.[49] However, of offenders who successfully completed the program and have been in the community for **9** years, fewer than **17** percent have committed new, indictable offenses,[50] compared to a nationwide average of about **52** percent.

Many other communities have adopted similar programs that have achieved goals of accountability, public safety, and cost savings.[51] Still, some probation and parole officers complain that IPS programs substantially change the relationship they have with their clients.

intensive probation supervision (IPS) probation supervised by probation and parole officers with smaller caseloads, placing a greater emphasis on compliance with the conditions of supervision

Probation and parole officers who view their primary role as counselor and facilitator find that the role of law enforcement officer often runs counter to many of the characteristics that promote effective counseling. In addition, the effective implementation of IPS requires new working conditions and hours, including nights and weekends. As a result, not all probation and parole officers are comfortable with the call for more IPS programs.

Split Sentencing and Shock Probation

When first-time, nonviolent offenders, especially youthful offenders, are convicted of a crime, they assume that they will receive a suspended sentence. Most of the time, they are correct in this assumption. As a result, these offenders often view their first convictions as minor inconveniences, and their encounters with the criminal justice system do little to deter them from further criminal activities. What can a judge do when faced with a first-time offender who is wise to the ways of the system and is anticipating a suspended sentence? To deal with such an offender, judges have adopted the use of split sentencing and shock probation. Both sentences are similar in their goal of impressing on offenders the possible consequences of their behavior by exposing them to a brief period of imprisonment before probation.

Split Sentencing In **split sentencing**, after a brief period of imprisonment, usually in a jail for as little as 30 days rather than in a long-term confinement facility, the offender is brought back to court. At that time, the judge then offers the option of probation. In split sentencing, the offender does not have to apply for parole, have a parole hearing, or present a parole plan to obtain his or her release from prison. Split sentencing is effective in two ways. First, the offender was not expecting any prison sentence. Thus, even a brief period of imprisonment comes as a shock. Second, the sentence exposes the offender to the realities of institutional confinement, but the offender is removed before he or she has time to adjust to institutionalization. The belief is that this "shock" will have a deterrent effect on future criminal behavior.

Shock Probation The sentence of shock probation is similar to split sentencing, but in **shock probation**, the offender is transferred to the custody of the state's department of corrections rather than the local jail and must apply for parole. Again, the offender serves only a brief period of incarceration before becoming eligible for parole. The major difference between split sentencing and shock probation is that in the former, the judge has control over the release of the offender, whereas in the latter, the offender's fate is in the hands of the Department of Corrections or the parole board. In shock probation, the offender must convince the paroling authorities that he or she should be released from prison. Technically, this is a form of parole because of the very brief period of incarceration, but it is commonly called shock probation rather than shock parole.

New Jersey's shock probation program is typical.[52] Offenders must serve a minimum of 30 days in prison before they can apply for release. They must submit a personal plan describing what they will do when released. This plan has many of the same requirements as a parole plan. It must detail the problems the inmate has that may jeopardize successful completion of parole, such as alcohol or drug abuse, lack of anger management, or lack of legitimate employment. The plan must detail the community resources that the offender can use to help with these problems. The offender also must have a community sponsor and is required to reside with the sponsor on release. If the paroling authority is satisfied with the offender's personal plan, he or she will be granted a 90-day trial release period. If the offender is successful in complying with the conditions of the release plan during this 90-day period, he or she is granted conditional early release, or shock probation.[53]

Shock Incarceration: Boot Camps

Shock incarceration programs are commonly called "boot camps" because they are modeled after military-style, entry-level training programs. Boot camps are designed to provide alternative sentencing for young, nonviolent offenders. Offenders who participate in boot camps are offered a reduced sentence followed by parole if they successfully complete the program.[54] If they do not complete the program, they are returned to the regular prison population. Although Ohio passed the first shock incarceration law in 1965, the practice did not become common until after 1980.[55] The first shock incarceration programs of nationwide significance began operating in 1983 in Oklahoma and Georgia.[56]

SHOCK INCARCERATION PROGRAMS ADAPT MILITARY-STYLE PHYSICAL FITNESS AND DISCIPLINE TRAINING TO THE CORRECTIONAL ENVIRONMENT, AS IN BASIC TRAINING IN MILITARY BOOT CAMPS.

Shock incarceration programs adapt military-style physical fitness and discipline training to the correctional environment, as in basic training in military boot camps. Inmates participate in drill and ceremony, physical training, work (usually hard manual labor), and education. Inmates are organized into platoons of 50 to 60 inmates and may be required to wear military-style clothing. Correctional leaders are called drill sergeants, and inmates are expected to demonstrate unquestioning obedience to their orders. Inmates in boot camps frequently must perform community service work. Inmates of the New York shock incarceration programs, for example, help cut firebreaks, maintain public-use areas, help in the aftermath of emergencies such as forest fires and tornadoes, and assist local municipalities and community groups.[57] Shock incarceration programs are rigorous, and a substantial number of inmates do not complete them and are returned to the regular prison population.[58]

split sentencing after a brief period of imprisonment, the judge brings the offender back to court and offers the option of probation

shock probation a sentence for a first-time, nonviolent offender who was not expecting a sentence, intended to impress on the offender the possible consequences of his or her behavior by exposure to a brief period of imprisonment before probation

shock incarceration programs (boot camps) that adapt military-style physical fitness and discipline training to the correctional environment

HERE'S SOMETHING TO THINK ABOUT . . .

Keith Gruber, 49, arrived at the Sullivan County (NY) Courthouse for his DWI hearing an hour and a half late. The judge may have forgiven his tardiness but he also was drunk and was carrying an open can and four unopened cans of beer as he attempted to walk through the metal detector. Judge Frank LaBuda revoked his bail and sent him to jail. Many believe that offenders are their own worst enemy and it is their fault that they reoffend. What do you think? Why?

Effectiveness of Boot Camps Participation in boot camps is voluntary. The inducement to participate in shock incarceration programs is the opportunity for early parole. Inmates who participate in boot camps serve substantially shorter prison time. A typical boot camp may only be 6 months in length. One of the main purposes of brief, intensive, shock incarceration programs is to reduce the need for prison bedspace by permitting shorter terms of imprisonment. Although boot camps may be more expensive to operate on a per-day, per-inmate basis, they save money in the long run, because inmates serve less time in a boot camp than they would in a regular prison.[59] The return-to-prison rate for offenders successfully completing adult boot camps is comparable to that of parolees who did not participate in or complete the program.[60] Supporters of the program argue that if the return-to-prison rate for offenders is comparable, boot camps pose no increased risk to the community, cost less than prison, and reduce the need to build more prisons, then they are indeed effective alternatives to prison.[61]

In shock incarceration, the inmate is released to the community well before the normal parole date. The underlying premise is that boot camps promote public safety by building character, instilling responsibility, and promoting a positive self-image so that nonviolent offenders can return to society as law-abiding citizens.[62] There is little direct evidence to support this claim, but boot camps remain popular with the public because they are perceived as being tough on crime.[63] Many state departments of corrections recognize the lack of research underlying the use of boot camps and describe their programs as "experiments."[64]

A PREREQUISITE FOR HOME CONFINEMENT IS TO HAVE A PLACE TO LIVE AND A JOB OR OTHER FINANCIAL RESOURCES FOR SELF-SUPPORT.

Home Confinement and Electronic Monitoring

Home Confinement **Home confinement** is a sentence imposed by the court in which offenders are legally ordered to remain confined in their own residences.[65] Similar to parents telling their teenager that he or she is "grounded" as punishment for some misdeed, home confinement severely restricts the offender's mobility. Schedules are worked out that allow the offender to leave his or her home for work, medical appointments and services, court-ordered treatment or community service, grocery shopping, and other necessary responsibilities. Offenders cannot leave home for entertainment, to visit friends or family, to take vacations, or for any other purpose not explicitly authorized by the court. Rehabilitation was not one of the goals of early home confinement programs. Early home confinement programs were an intermediate sanction or punishment adopted primarily to reduce prison populations, reduce costs, and increase control of offenders in the community.[66]

The sentence of home confinement is a kind of probation or suspended sentence that carries greater restrictions on the freedom of the offender in the community. Offenders must live in their own home or that of a sponsor (usually a relative) and must pay all of their housing costs. Thus, a prerequisite for home confinement is to have a place to live and a job or other financial resources for self-support. A difficulty of early home confinement programs was ensuring that the offender abided by the restrictions of his or her release and did not leave the home. Probation officers used a combination of phone calls and random home visits or stakeouts to verify that the offender was at home. These practices were labor intensive, however, and ineffective due to the shortage of probation officers to conduct a sufficient number of random home visits to ensure compliance.

Electronic Monitoring The breakthrough in home confinement programs came with the use of electronic monitoring to ensure the offender's compliance. **Electronic monitoring** uses signaling technology to achieve a greater degree of certainty in compliance and at a fraction of the cost of using probation officers for this purpose. The first formal electronic monitoring program was implemented in 1983 in Albuquerque, New Mexico, when district court judge Jack Love, reputedly inspired by a "Spiderman" comic strip, placed a probation violator on electronic monitoring.[67]

Since 1983, the use of electronic monitoring has expanded rapidly. It has been adopted in all 50 states by local, state, and federal correctional agencies.[68] Florida's Community Control Program has one of the most ambitious home confinement and electronic monitoring programs in the United States.[69] Spurred in part by an explosive rise in the need for prison bedspace, Florida's Correctional Reform Act of 1983 authorized the use of electronically monitored house arrest as a means to reduce the prison population.

home confinement a court-imposed sentence requiring offenders to remain confined in their own residences

electronic monitoring an approach in home confinement programs that ensures compliance through electronic means

Technological Advances in Electronic Monitoring In the past two decades, there have been significant changes in the technology for monitoring offenders sentenced to home confinement.[70] Early systems were passive-programmed contact systems, which used a computer programmed to make random calls to the offender at times when he or she was supposed to be home.

The next generation of electronic monitoring systems used continuous signaling systems. The advantage of continuous signaling systems is that they monitor the offender's movements 100 percent of the time. The older passive-programmed contact systems have loopholes in that offenders willing to risk it could slip out of the house as long as they did not miss one of the programmed contacts.

With both the passive-technology-programmed reporting devices and the continuous signaling technology devices, the probation officer needs to confirm that an actual violation has occurred. When the offender fails to answer the telephone or when there is a break in the continuous signal during times when the offender is supposed to be home, a probation officer must contact the offender to confirm the violation.

The third generation of electronic monitoring devices began to emerge in 1997. They incorporated the advantages of global positioning system (GPS) technology, involving the use of satellites, not only to monitor the offender at home, but to have the ability to track every movement of the offender in real time.[71] This technology allows the system to confirm that the offender not only is at home when he or she is supposed to be but also is not violating restraining orders, visiting places where drugs are known to be sold or used, and frequenting off-limits places such as schools or playgrounds. Another advancement in electronic monitoring is the ability to monitor all communications by the offender on the Internet.[72] This ability is especially useful for monitoring sex offenders to ensure that they do not use the Internet for the purposes of contacting and enticing potential victims.

Evaluation and Critique of Electronic Monitoring Counting the number of people on electronic monitoring as potential prison inmates, there is no doubt that home confinement and electronic monitoring have saved the states money, compared with the costs of incarceration. There are significant start-up costs for the equipment purchases required to use home confinement and electronic monitoring, but even after factoring in these costs, most jurisdictions report that the program saves money over prison confinement.[73] Critics claim that this is a false savings, because offenders selected for release subject to home confinement and electronic monitoring are those who probably would have been given a suspended sentence.[74] Another criticism is that the system discriminates against the homeless and the unemployed. These offenders usually are excluded from home confinement programs because of their lack of a place to live, a telephone, and means of support.

A potentially serious criticism of electronic monitoring is that it may interfere with First Amendment and Fourth Amendment rights of offenders and of others with whom offenders come into contact.[75] New GPS tracking technologies combined with other emerging technologies possibly could identify people the offender contacts or could listen in on conversations. At what point will technological advances overintrude on people's privacy and other constitutional rights?

HERE'S SOMETHING TO THINK ABOUT . . .

Perhaps the public's greatest fear is the return of the sex offender to the community. The public fears that sex offenders are more likely to reoffend than non–sex offenders. The data are inconclusive. A 2003 Bureau of Justice Statistics study reported that sex offenders were four times more likely to be rearrested for a sex crime than non–sex offenders within 3 years of their release. A 2011 study found lower recidivism rates for sex offenders released from Maine prisons than non–sex offenders. What is your opinion?

Reentry Programs: Preparing Offenders to Take Responsibility

In addition to the intermediate sanctions of IPS, shock probation, shock incarceration, home confinement, and electronic monitoring, there is a need for treatment programs that focus on preparing inmates for reentry rather than punishing them.[76] Many states and the federal correctional system have implemented programs for preparing returning inmates through treatment and therapeutic programs such as work release, education release, halfway houses, day reporting centers, and drug treatment programs. For example, Ohio has taken initiative to move corrections "toward a new vision of the offender reentry dialogue,"[77] and Michigan has created the Office of Community Corrections with the specific purpose of improving rehabilitative services and strengthening offender accountability.[78]

The federal system has recognized the importance of reentry programs. U.S. Code Title 18, Section 3624 requires that authorities should "to the extent practicable, assure that a prisoner serving a term of imprisonment spends a reasonable part" of the last 6 months or 10 percent of his or her sentence "under conditions that will afford the prisoner a reasonable opportunity to adjust to and prepare for the prisoner's reentry

4 **Unlike traditional early-release programs, community corrections sanctions are designed to reduce recidivism and protect the community; community corrections sanctions include intensive probation supervision programs, split sentencing, shock probation and shock incarceration (boot camps), and home confinement with electronic monitoring.**

into the community."[79] The Reentry Partnership Initiative is a federal effort to help jurisdictions meet the challenges of offenders returning to the community. The goal is "to improve the risk management of released offenders by enhancing surveillance and monitoring, strengthening individual and community support systems, and repairing the harm done to victims."[80] Other federal legislation recognizes the need for effective community-based reentry programs for adults and juveniles that focus on treatment as well as punishment. Programs organized with the assistance of the Serious and Violent Offender Reentry Initiative divide reentry programs into three phases:

1. Protect and Prepare
2. Control and Restore
3. Sustain and Support[81]

1913

Huber Law initiated first work release program in Wisconsin

In 2004, the Department of Justice announced that it was committing $6.7 million to the Serious and Violent Offender Reentry Initiative in the effort to improve public safety by addressing the successful reintegration of high-risk, serious offenders returning to their communities from imprisonment. Since 2004, the initiative estimates that more than $300 million has been committed to designing and carrying out adult and juvenile reentry strategies. Other government-sponsored reentry initiatives include the Council of State Governments Re-entry, the federal Bureau of Prisons National Institute of Corrections, and the National Re-entry Resource Center.

Faith-Based Programs A new strategy to promote successful reentry has been the use of **faith-based programs**. In his 2004 State of the Union address, President Bush proposed a $300 million initiative for reentry programs to be conducted by religious-based groups. The faith-based rehabilitation movement extends beyond community services and reaches into the prisons. Many prisons are allowing faith-based groups to provide programs such as vocational classes combined with religious instruction inside the prisons in an effort to prepare the offender for release. The American Civil Liberties Union opposes faith-based groups receiving government money for their programs, claiming it is a violation of the separation of church and state. Others criticize faith-based programs because the programs often require inmates to participate in Bible studies and attend church services. To avoid these criticisms, some faith-based programs operate without receiving government funding. It is too soon to evaluate the effect of faith-based programs on successful reentry. One study of the faith-based rehabilitation group InnerChange suggested that offenders who participated in the program were 50 percent less likely to be arrested and 60 percent less likely to be reincarcerated than those who did not participate.[82]

A significant appeal of reentry programs is that they cost much less than imprisonment. Whereas prison costs can average about $25,000 a year, reentry programs cost about $3,000 annually per inmate. Also, in addition to being cheaper, reentry programs allow states and the federal government to focus on removing the obstacles that keep the recidivism rates high. With two out of three adult offenders returning to prison within 3 years, there is a lot of room for improvement. Some legislators have championed reentry programs as significant breakthroughs that would break the cycle of offending. In 2004, Senator Sam Brownback (R-KS) expressed his belief that reentry programs could reduce recidivism to 20 percent.[83]

The most often used reentry programs are work release, education release, halfway houses, day reporting centers, and drug treatment programs.

Work Release

How can state and federal programs help to sustain and support inmates in the community? Former inmates have more difficulty than other people in finding and keeping a job.[84] **Work release** programs were first initiated under Wisconsin's Huber Law in 1913 but did not become commonplace until the latter half of the twentieth century.[85] Wisconsin's Huber Law permitted county correctional facilities to release misdemeanants for paid work in the community. In 1965, the Prisoner Rehabilitation Act of 1965 authorized work release for inmates in federal institutions. By 1975, all 50 states and the federal system had some form of work release operating.[86]

Obstacles to Employment The most serious obstacles facing offenders looking for jobs are as follows:

1. public prejudice against hiring ex-offenders;
2. lack of knowledge of how to find jobs; and
3. lack of the kinds of documentation required by employers.

Public Prejudice Public prejudice against hiring ex-offenders is strong. In one survey, 65 percent of all employers said they would not knowingly hire an ex-offender, regardless of the offense, and 30 to 40 percent said they check for criminal records when they hire employees.[87] Furthermore, ex-offenders are barred from many occupations that require occupational licenses, including law, real estate, medicine, nursing, physical therapy, dentistry, engineering, pharmacy, and education.[88] Often, employers refuse to hire offenders for fear of potential lawsuits through liability for negligent hiring should the offender commit a crime or harm the employers' customers.[89] These fears by employers are not groundless. For example, a family film company that hired inmates as telemarketers was sued by a woman who claimed that a prisoner misused company information by sending her 14-year-old daughter a personal letter.[90] A company that hired a woman who, unknown to them, had been convicted of embezzlement found that after 6 years with the company she allegedly embezzled more than $5 million from the organization.[91]

65%

of employers said they would not knowingly hire an ex-offender.

faith-based programs programs provided by religious-based and church-affiliated groups; their role in rehabilitation is controversial because they receive federal money and may combine religious instruction with rehabilitation

work release a program that allows facilities to release inmates for paid work in the community

Lack of Knowledge Ex-offenders often lack the basic knowledge to conduct a successful job search. Many do not know how to fill out employment applications, how to conduct themselves during interviews, how to dress for job interviews, or how to present the attitude of self-confidence that employers want in their employees. Frequently, offenders have had little experience or success in employment prior to prison. Thus, they do not have basic life skills related to job hunting that are often taken for granted by the general population. Furthermore, offenders need to unlearn passive behavior patterns that work well in prison but are a liability in searching for and retaining a job.[92] In prison, offenders become accustomed to being told what to do, when to do it, and how to do it. Obedience to the rules is one of the most important values in prison. When asked to show initiative, demonstrate decision-making skills, and be innovative, inmates often do not have these abilities.[93]

Lack of Documents A unique problem that offenders have in getting employment is lack of proper identification (ID). Most people leave prison without a driver's license, passport, social security card, birth certificate, or other photo ID. Many are clueless as to how to obtain the identification they need.[94] Offenders find that even if they are successful in obtaining employment, they may lose their jobs because they cannot supply their employers with proof of identification and citizenship, as required by law.[95]

MANY EMPLOYERS COMPLAIN THAT LAWS BANNING THEM FROM CONSIDERING A JOB APPLICANT'S CRIMINAL RECORD IS NOT "BUSINESS-FRIENDLY."

Work Release Strategies Removing the obstacles to employment requires both community-based and in-prison programs. For example, Texas's Project RIO (Re-Integration of Offenders) provides in-prison vocational training programs to prepare inmates for the workforce and helps them obtain the IDs and documentation needed in the outside world, such as their birth certificate, social security identification, and state photo ID. Authorities hold the documentation for the prisoner and then forward it to the employer or agency as needed after the inmate is released.[96] New York provides inmates with a work release furlough for 6 weeks up to 3 months to allow them to find employment.

Limited Protection Against Discrimination Recognizing the difficulty that ex-offenders face in finding employment, several states have laws that limit when and to what extent an employer may consider an applicant's criminal record. These laws make it illegal for an employer to discriminate against an ex-offender unless his or her conviction record is related to the duties of the job. Some states allow ex-offenders to seal or expunge their criminal records. Some states offer certificates of rehabilitation to ex-offenders who either have minimal criminal histories or have remained out of the criminal justice system for specified periods.[97] Title VII of the Federal Civil Rights Act of 1964 offers some protection against job discrimination against ex-offenders. The Equal Employment Opportunity Commission has determined that policies that exclude individuals from employment on the basis of their arrest and conviction records may violate Title VII, because such policies disproportionately exclude minorities.[98]

Many employers complain, however, that laws banning them from considering a job applicant's criminal record is not "business-friendly." They claim that such laws "ignore the liability employers face regarding the actions of their workers. Employers get squeezed in the middle. If you don't hire, you get sued, but if you do hire and something happens to customers or other workers, you get sued."[99] To induce employers to hire ex-offenders, the federal government has made tax credits available to employers who do so and has established insurance programs to reduce the employer's exposure to liability for possible misdeeds by inmates.[100]

Job Fairs Some state correctional agencies are becoming more proactive in helping inmates find jobs after release by sponsoring job fairs. Some job fairs are held within the correctional institutions. Prison officials help the inmates prepare résumés and train them in job interview skills. Ohio's Department of Rehabilitation and Correction has sponsored more than 140 job fairs and even holds teleconferences for companies that cannot send representatives.[101]

Partnerships with Businesses Other correctional agencies have entered into joint ventures with private businesses to offer inmates the chance to work for private companies while in prison and then to transition to civilian employment with the company when they are released from prison.[102] Such partnerships are made possible by changes in federal and state laws that formerly prevented inmates from working in private-sector prison jobs. In 1979, Congress enacted Public Law 96-157 (18 U.S.C. 176(c) and 41 U.S.C. 35), which created the Private Sector/Prison Industry Enhancement Certification Program. This program authorizes correctional agencies to engage in the interstate shipment of prison-made goods for private businesses, providing certain conditions are met.[103] The law allows private companies to operate businesses from within the prison and to use inmate labor. The law requires that inmates must be paid at a rate not less than the rate paid for work of a similar nature in the locality in which the work takes place. Prison officials allow the inmates to send some of the money to support their families and to keep a small portion for themselves, and the rest is retained for them until their release. These partnerships help reduce the burden on the state of supporting the inmates' families, provide a source of labor for the businesses, and help the inmates make successful transitions from prison to work after release.

Education Release

Education is recognized as a factor that can make an important difference in the successful transition of offenders from correctional systems back to their communities.[104] Education can make a tremendous difference for offenders, because many are high school dropouts and the workforce has few positions for high school dropouts that pay a living wage. It costs an estimated minimum of $22,000 to $60,000 per year to incarcerate an offender, which is much more than the average cost for 1 year of college or vocational training.[105] Correctional officials have recognized the importance of education, and while in prison it is usually mandatory that inmates without a high school education be given the opportunity to earn a high school equivalency or general education development (GED) degree.

Some correctional institutions bring educational programs into the institution so inmates can further their education while in prison. Others provide education release opportunities for inmates both while in prison and as part of their parole plan. The typical **education release** program gives inmates the opportunity to attend college or university classes but requires them to return to the institution each day. When educational release is a part of an inmate's parole plan, the inmate is required to attend a vocational training program, community college, or university rather than go to full-time employment. However, inmates must have the means to support themselves and pay for their schooling.

Effectiveness Research has shown that offenders who participate in education programs are less likely to commit new crimes than are inmates who do not participate in such programs.[106] One study tracked 2,305 inmates over three years at the Bedford Hills Correctional Facility, a maximum-security prison for women in New York that has an educational program sponsored by a consortium of private colleges. The study found that only 7.7 percent of the inmates who had taken college courses while incarcerated committed new crimes and were returned to prison after their release, whereas 29.9 percent of the inmates who did not take courses were jailed again.[107]

7.7%
of inmates who had taken college courses while in prison returned to jail after their release, compared to
29.9%
of those who did not take courses

College Discrimination However, despite the demonstrated benefits of education, similar to employers who are prejudiced against hiring released prisoners, colleges can be prejudiced against admitting ex-offenders—even those who have served their time. For example, in 2005, the University of Alaska refused to admit Michael Purcell to its social work program. Purcell served 20 years for killing a convenience-store clerk when he was 16 years old. He was released on parole in September 2004. Upon his release on parole, he entered a halfway house and took classes at the University of Alaska. However, when he applied for admission to the social work degree program he was denied admission. In rejecting Purcell's application, the social work department cited its policy that they considered persons with criminal records unfit for social work practice.[108] The University of Alaska is not the only university that has such policies discriminating against ex-felons.

Halfway Houses

Halfway houses are transition programs that allow inmates to move from prison to the community in steps rather than all at once by simply opening the prison doors and having them enter the community directly. The first halfway houses in the United States were opened in the mid-1800s, but their use did not become commonplace until the 1950s.[109] The use of halfway houses was encouraged because such a program provided what was considered an essential transition, whereby an inmate could gradually adjust to freedom by a short stay, usually about 6 months, in a halfway house at the end of his or her sentence.[110]

Gradual Transition Today, most halfway houses are nonprofit foundations.[111] The state departments of corrections contract with these nonprofit organizations to provide a gradual transition for the offender from an environment that maintains total control to one that permits partial control before the offender is released into the community. The typical halfway house provides services for 6 to 30 inmates in a minimum-security facility, often a residential home that has been converted into a halfway house. Inmates who do not follow the rules or who "walk away" from the halfway house are returned to prison or charged with the felony offense of escape. The combination of nearing the end of their sentence and risking return to prison with possible added time is an effective deterrent for most participants.

Halfway houses have full-time staff members who provide for the custody and treatment of the offenders. Offenders observe strict curfews, participate in treatment programs conducted by the house staff or community-based agencies, and seek employment or enroll in vocational training or college classes. The program allows a transition period from prison to freedom in that the offender is closely supervised but is given limited freedom within the community and is required to take responsibility for preparing for his or her successful reentry into the community. During the offender's stay in the halfway house, he or she does not have to report to a probation officer, because the house staff perform this function. Usually, the offender is released from the halfway house into the community under the supervision of a parole officer. Halfway houses are excellent opportunities for inmates seeking parole who do not have family or sponsors in the community to help them when they leave prison. Without halfway houses, many of these inmates would not be able to prepare an acceptable parole plan.

Community Opposition The most significant obstacle to halfway houses is the strong community opposition to having such a facility located in one's neighborhood. As mentioned previously, even those who support the concept of halfway houses suffer from NIMBY—"not in my back yard." Who wants to live next to a halfway house? Who wants to raise a family, have children play in the yard and neighborhood parks on the same block as a halfway house? Locating communities that are close to employment opportunities and public transportation, essential characteristics for a successful halfway house program, and that are willing to allow halfway houses to operate in the community is a difficult challenge.

education release a program in which inmates are released to attend college or vocational programs

halfway house a transition program that allows inmates to move from prison to the community in steps

Day Reporting Centers

Day reporting centers are relatively new reentry programs dating to the early 1970s.[112] **Day reporting centers** provide for release from prison that is closely supervised by the state's department of corrections. Inmates live at home rather than being imprisoned or housed in a privately managed halfway house. As the name suggests, inmates report to supervisory centers on a daily basis. Inmates may be sentenced to day reporting centers rather than prison or may be released from prison to day reporting centers during the last months of their sentence. Inmates report to and leave from the center during the day to work, to participate in treatment programs, to attend classes or training programs, or to hunt for employment. Day reporting centers maintain daily schedules that must accurately account for inmates' time while in the community. Participants must submit to certain conditions similar to those in a parole plan, such as random drug tests.

51–83%
Number of arrested adult men who were under the influence of drugs

The purpose of the day reporting center is to act as an intermediate sanction for some inmates and to permit a gradual adjustment to reentry for others. Day reporting centers allow departments of corrections to reduce the need for prison bedspace by placing low-security-risk inmates in day reporting centers.[113] For inmates transitioning from prison, day reporting centers allow them the opportunity to reenter the community under closely monitored conditions. Because day reporting centers are not widely used, extensive data are not available to judge their effectiveness. However, data from the Metropolitan Day Reporting Center in Boston, Massachusetts, indicate that inmates who enter the community from the day reporting center rather than directly from jail are less likely to commit new crimes and are more likely to be employed. Furthermore, only about 1 percent of inmates committed a crime while they were in the program.[114]

HERE'S SOMETHING TO THINK ABOUT . . .

Convicted felons lose civil rights in addition to imprisonment and fines. In 14 states felons lose the right to vote for life. Many more states bar felons from voting for a period of time or require them to apply for reinstatement. Felons are prohibited from holding certain public offices. Felons are prohibited from obtaining certain state licensures, which effectively bars them from professions requiring these licenses. Sex offenders may be required to register for the rest of their life. Sex offender registers are public record and many employers do not hire registered sex offenders. The loss of civil rights has both short- and long-term impacts. Short-term loss of civil rights is additional punishment that can result in lifetime alienation from society. Long-term disenfranchisement disproportionately affects minorities. Is it fair to deny felons these civil rights?

Reentry Programs for Drug Offenders

Drug use forecasting (DUF) data collected on defendants in 23 cities indicate that 51 to 83 percent of arrested adult men and 41 percent to 84 percent of arrested adult women were under the influence of at least one illicit drug at the time of arrest.[115] In addition, drug use is a significant factor in property offenses, as 16 percent of adult prisoners indicated that they committed their offenses to get money for drugs.[116] Although drug offenders may be nonviolent, during 1999, 12 percent of convicted federal drug defendants received a sentence enhancement for the use or possession of a firearm or other weapon.[117]

Drug crimes have occupied more and more resources of the criminal justice system. Between 1984 and 1999, the number of defendants charged with a drug offense in the federal courts increased from 11,854 to 29,306.[118] The Bureau of Justice Statistics estimates that two-thirds of federal and state prisoners and probationers could be characterized as drug involved.[119] In response to the increased frequency of drug crimes, the criminal justice system has enhanced drug law enforcement efforts and has adopted a get-tough sentencing policy for drug offenders. This tough federal stance has resulted in 62 percent of convicted federal drug defendants receiving statutory minimum sentences of at least 5 years or more.

However, enhanced enforcement and tough sentencing policies have failed to stem the number of drug offenders. Over 73 percent of state inmates reentering prison have admitted to drug or alcohol involvement while released.[120] Even when sentenced to prison, inmates continue to find ways to obtain drugs. Thus, incarceration in itself does little to break the cycle of illegal drug use and crime. Furthermore, the traditional case disposition process appears to lack the capacity to bring about any significant reduction in drug usage by persons convicted of drug offenses.[121] For a little over a decade, a new strategy to break the cycle of drug use and crime that has led to the

5 **Some new strategies that focus on preparing inmates for reentry rather than punishing them include faith-based programs, work release, education release, halfway houses, and day reporting centers.**

day reporting center an intermediate sanction to provide a gradual adjustment to reentry under closely supervised conditions

The Ten Key Components of Drug Courts

The operations and components of drug courts vary from jurisdiction to jurisdiction, but the following 10 key components identify state adult drug court programs as prescribed by the Drug Courts Program Office:

- Drug courts integrate alcohol and other drug treatment services with justice system case processing.
- Using a nonadversarial approach, prosecution and defense counsel promote public safety while protecting participants' due process rights.
- Eligible participants are identified early and promptly placed in the drug court program.
- Drug courts provide access to a continuum of alcohol, drug, and other related treatment and rehabilitation services.
- Abstinence is monitored by frequent alcohol and other drug testing.
- A coordinated strategy governs drug court responses to participants' compliance.
- Ongoing judicial interaction with each drug court participant is essential.
- Monitoring and evaluation measure the achievement of program goals and gauge effectiveness.
- Continuing interdisciplinary education promotes effective drug court planning, implementation, and operations.
- Forging partnerships among drug courts, public agencies, and community-based organizations generates local support and enhances drug court effectiveness.

Source: Defining Drug Courts: The Key Components (Washington, DC: Office of Justice Programs, Drug Courts Progam Office, January 1997), pp. 1–3.

revolving door syndrome for drug offenders has been the drug court. The **drug court** approach was started in 1989 as an experiment by the Dade County (Florida) Circuit Court. Today, nearly every state uses some form of drug court program to handle drug offenders. Drug courts have proved effective with adult and juvenile offenders and for use in tribal courts.

Adult Drug Courts

In states that have adult drug courts, adult offenders arrested for drug offenses are diverted from traditional case disposition processing as soon as possible. These offenders are offered the opportunity to participate in the drug court program rather than traditional case disposition, which results in incarceration. Drug court programs use intermediate sanctions, community-based treatment, and intensive probation supervision to achieve a twofold purpose:

1. to get offenders clean and sober, and
2. to compel offenders to participate in a comprehensive treatment program while being monitored under strict conditions for drug use.

Almost all drug courts require participants to obtain a GED if they have not finished high school, to maintain or obtain employment, to be current in all financial obligations (including drug court fees and any court-ordered support payments), and to have a sponsor in the community. Some drug programs require offenders to perform community service hours.[122] Figure 11.3 illustrates how offenders are selected for inclusion in the Superior Court Drug Intervention Program.

If offenders accept the offer to enter into the drug court program and are accepted, "they are referred immediately to a multi-phased out-patient treatment program entailing multiple weekly (often daily)

Case Identification for Superior Court Drug Intervention Program

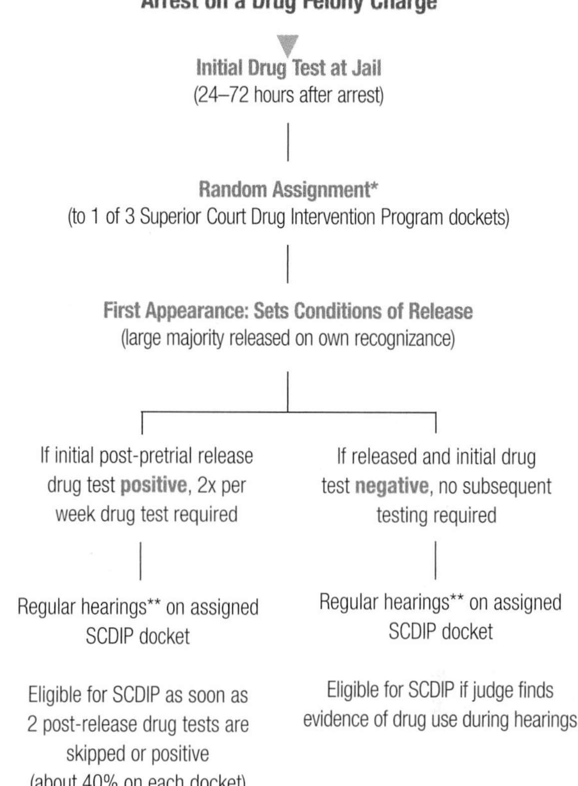

FIGURE 11.3 Admission to drug court requires that defendants must meet strict guidelines and, if admitted to drug court, must follow a program of testing and counseling.

*Defendants were not allowed to transfer to another SCDIP docket.

**Plea offers were made at regular docket hearings and could occur before, after, or at the same time as defendant became eligible for SCDIP, and the program offer was not contingent on acceptance of the plea. However, if the plea was rejected, the defendant transferred out of the SCDIP dockets to a trial docket.

Source: Adele Harrell, Shannon Cavanaugh, and John Roman, *Evaluation of the D.C. Superior Court Drug Intervention Programs* (Washington, DC: U.S. Department of Justice, April 2000), p.3.

drug court an approach that provides drug offenders the opportunity for intermediate sanctions, community treatment, and intensive probation supervision instead of prison time

6 **The rampant use of drugs among offenders and reoffenders has led to a separate system of drug courts and drug rehabilitation programs designed to reduce the cycle of drugs and crime.**

contacts with the treatment provider for counseling, therapy and education; frequent urinalysis (usually at least weekly); frequent status hearings before the drug court judge (biweekly or more often at first); and a rehabilitation program entailing vocational, education, family, medical, and other support services."[123] Figure 11.4 shows the broad variety of treatment programs and support services that are available to participants in drug court programs.

Effectiveness In contrast to the traditional adjudication process in the criminal court, drug court programs are experiencing a significant reduction in recidivism among participants. Whereas about 45 percent of defendants convicted of drug possession will reoffend with a similar offense within 2 to 3 years, only 5 to 28 percent of drug court participants reoffend, and 90 percent have negative urinalysis drug reports.[124] Drug court programs also have been shown to save money. By avoiding the high cost of incarceration, some cities have been able to save up to $2.5 million per year in criminal justice costs.[125] By eliminating the **revolving door syndrome,** drug court programs not only save on the cost of incarcerating repeat offenders but they also save police, prosecutors, and courts the additional costs of processing the offenders through the system. Drug court programs also help save welfare benefits, because offenders who are employed when arrested often are able to maintain their employment and continue to support themselves and their families. By not having drug offenders repeatedly enter and exit the criminal justice system, criminal justice agencies are able to more efficiently allocate their resources to address more pressing needs and crimes.[126] A testament to the effectiveness of drug court programs is that in a poll of 318 police chiefs, almost 60 percent advocated court-supervised treatment programs over other justice system options for drug users.

$2.5 million
amount saved by sending offenders to drug court programs rather than prison

Tribal Drug Courts

Unique problems of crime on Native American reservations include a disproportionately high rate of crime compared to general crime statistics. Alcohol and other substance abuse contributes substantially to the crime problem on Native American lands, because more than 90 percent of the criminal cases in most tribal courts involve alcohol or substance abuse.[127] In addition to alcohol abuse, many Native American communities have substantial problems with toxic inhalants. Drug courts were first adopted by Native American and Alaska Native tribal courts in 1997. Interest is growing, however, because drug court programs are more closely aligned with tribal justice concepts and methods than are traditional criminal justice processes.[128] Nevertheless, there are unique problems associated with adapting the drug court concept to meet the specific needs of Native Americans:[129]

- Tribal courts must address the specific cultural needs of their individual communities, including the challenge of incorporating tribal custom and tradition into the tribal drug court.
- The nature and high volume of alcohol abuse cases in most tribal courts present unique adaptation issues.
- Tribal courts face jurisdictional barriers that complicate their ability to implement an effective drug court process.
- Tribes seeking to establish drug court systems often face a broad range of other issues and challenges, including isolated rural locations, small-community issues, lack of resources and services, and lack of funding.

Tribal drug courts generally are called **Tribal Healing to Wellness Courts**. Some programs have developed individual names, using words from their native languages.[130] Healing to Wellness Courts may use traditional treatment processes involving tribal elders, traditional healing ceremonies, talking circles, peacemaking, sweats and sweat lodges visits with a medicine man or woman, the sun dance, and a vision quest.[131]

Jurisdictional barriers to tribal drug courts include the lack of criminal jurisdiction over non-Native Americans, concurrent state jurisdiction, legal limits in sentencing (to 1 year or a fine of $5,000, or both), and a historically strained relationship with state courts and state agencies.[132] Also, more than 50 percent of the reservation population is under the age of 18,[133] requiring greater demand for juvenile drug court programs than is the case in the traditional criminal justice system. Data for traditional drug court programs are promising, however, and it is hoped that the drug court concept will prove flexible enough to work with traditional Native American justice concepts and methods.[134]

TASC and RSAT

Federal assistance programs such as **Treatment Accountability for Safer Communities (TASC)** and the **Residential Substance Abuse Treatment (RSAT)** for the State Prisoners Formula Grant Program have helped states adopt new comprehensive programs for drug offenders. Federal legislation designed to help states break the addiction-crime cycle of nonviolent, drug-involved offenders include the 1972 Drug Abuse and Treatment Act and the Violent Crime Control and Law Enforcement Act of 1994. Both laws provide federal funds to states to allow them to link the legal sanctions of the criminal justice system with the federally funded therapeutic interventions of drug treatment programs.[135] The major premise of programs funded by the grants is that criminal sanctions can be combined with the reintegration of offenders into the community, and that this can be done through a broad base of support from both the criminal justice system and the treatment community.[136] Combining intermediate sanctions and drug offender

revolving door syndrome the repeated arrest and incarceration of an offender

Tribal Healing to Wellness Courts Native American drug treatment programs that adopt traditional cultural beliefs and practices

Treatment Accountability for Safer Communities (TASC) a federal assistance program that helps states break the addiction-crime cycle

Residential Substance Abuse Treatment (RSAT) a federal assistance program that helps states provide for treatment instead of prison for substance abusers

Treatment and Services Provided by Drug Court Programs

Types of Dedicated and External Treatment Programs

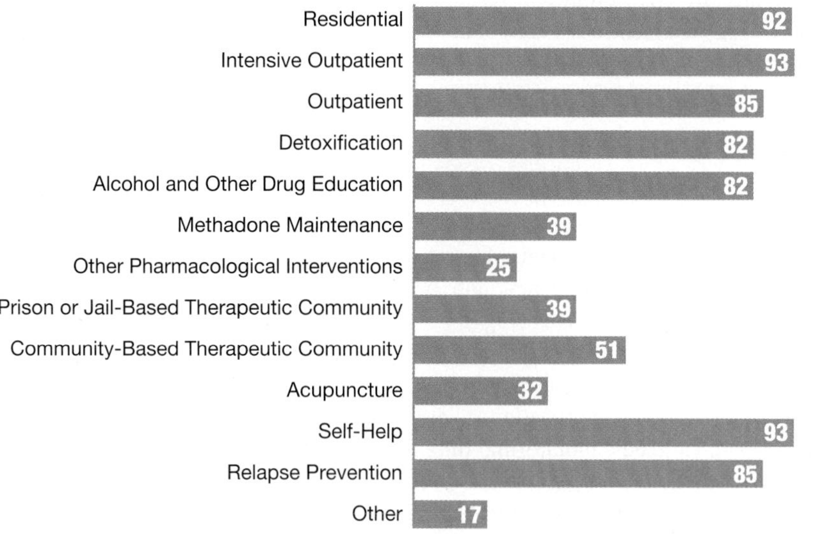

Support Services Available to Program Participants

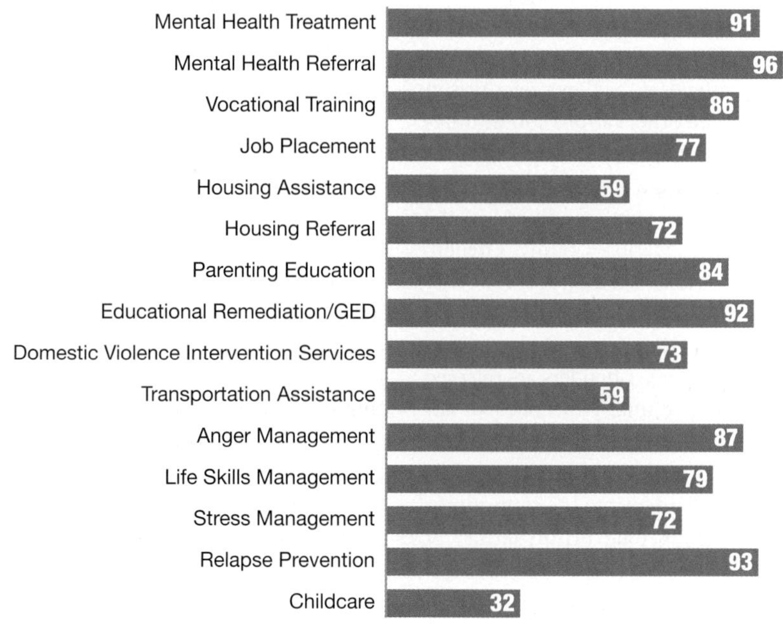

FIGURE 11.4 Offenders directed into drug treatment programs participate in a number of rehabilitation programs. Often referred to as the "medical model," drug courts focus on treating and rehabilitating offenders rather than punishing offenders. The programs include not only breaking the offender's dependence on drugs, but also equipping the offender to become a fully functional member of society.

treatment programs is both effective and cost efficient. To prevent a return to drug use, these programs provide treatment both in prison and after release through postincarceration supervision. The combination of treatment strategies can reduce recidivism by about 50 percent. In addition to reducing recidivism, drug treatment costs are about $6,500 per year per inmate, whereas imprisonment costs are 4 to 10 times higher.[137]

Try, Try Again

The criminal justice system involves a dynamic process that is undergoing constant change, including the corrections component. Many correctional programs, philosophies, and challenges are new and evolving. Jails and prisons used for more than 100 years are being replaced by new structures that are radically different. Probation and parole, which emerged in the early twentieth century, are already being transformed by the new philosophies of intensive probation supervision (IPS) probation and parole and electronic monitoring. In the past 20 to 30 years, new intermediate sanctions have appeared that focus on control and treatment in the community. In the past decade, new programs for addressing the crisis of drug-addicted inmates are winning greater acceptance by the entire criminal justice system and the public.

Ways of looking at corrections are changing as new experiments in control and treatment are being tried. New research indicates that prisoners actually may prefer prison to many of the new intermediate and community-based sanctions. When polled as to their opinion of the harshness of punishments, many offenders say they prefer prison to the intrusiveness and control of IPS and other various community-based programs.[138] Fifteen percent of the participants who apply for early release under the New Jersey IPS program withdraw their application once they understand the restrictions and conditions of the program. When nonviolent offenders in Marion County, Oregon, were offered a choice between a prison term or release under IPS, one-third of the offenders chose prison.[139]

The perfect method to rehabilitate offenders and the perfect method to provide for community safety when offenders are released back into the community have not been found. However, like law enforcement and the judicial system, the correctional system continues to look for new and better ways to protect the community while providing for the successful reentry of offenders into the community. Despite the boisterous rhetoric promoting long prison terms for offenders, the truth of the matter is that most offenders remain under supervision in the community rather than in prison.

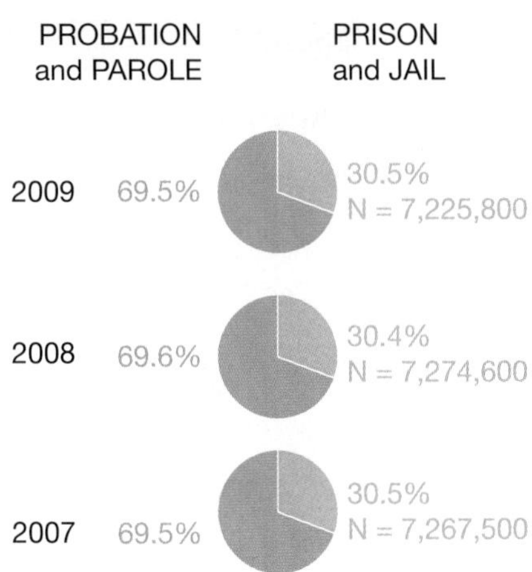

Nearly 70% of persons under correctional supervision are on probation and parole, not in jails or prisons.

Source: Glaze, L.E. (2010). *Correctional Populations in the United States, 2009* (Washington, DC: Bureau of Justice Statistics), p. 2.

IN THE PAST 20 TO 30 YEARS, NEW INTERMEDIATE SANCTIONS HAVE APPEARED THAT FOCUS ON CONTROL AND TREATMENT IN THE COMMUNITY.

Why should you be concerned about the success of reentry programs? In 2004, when Oklahoma prisons started a six-part course on maintaining a healthy marriage, many questioned the expense and resources of inaugurating marriage programs in the prison. The response by prison officials to this challenge was simple and direct. "There are 600,000 Americans leaving prison in the next few years. And those guys are all coming to an apartment complex near you."[140] When inmates leave prison and return to the community, it is much better if they are rehabilitated rather than recidivists.

HERE'S SOMETHING TO THINK ABOUT . . .

The Washington Post *reported that in February 2010, Louis Sawyer, an African American, was released from the Federal Correctional Center at Allenwood, Pennsylvania. He returned to the Washington, D.C., area and checked into a halfway house. He had 4 months to find permanent housing. In May he had not found new housing or a job, but was invited to testify before a House subcommittee concerning the Revitalization Act which addressed court services and offender supervision in Washington, D.C. Sawyer said someone returning from prison needs five things: transportation, clothing, physical and mental health care, employment, and housing. Sawyer found housing, but it took him 6 months to find a job. Many returning prisoners find neither.*

Four of 10 adults will return to prison within 3 years of their release. The criminal justice system may spend millions to convict a defendant and $25,000 or more per year to incarcerate a prisoner, but spends little to provide for reentry despite the fact that 95 percent of inmates will be released back into the community. Reentry programs are often the first to be cut in a budget crisis. For example, starting in 2007, Texas focused on developing alternatives to prison and reentry services. As a result in 2011, there were 7,000 fewer inmates in Texas prisons than the number that had been projected in 2007. In 2010, the number of inmates actually decreased by 1,250 from 2009.

However, when the state suffered an estimated $15 to $27 billion budget shortfall, Texas legislators proposed cutting $162 million from rehabilitation and treatment programs. Under the proposal, for example, the money given to inmates exiting prison, known as gate money, would be reduced from $100 to $50. Supporters of reentry programs urged legislators to find other cuts as proposed cuts would undo the progress made in reducing recidivism and Texas could find itself right back where it was in 2007 looking at the need to build new prisons rather than funding reentry and treatment programs.

How long could you live on $50 gate money—and then what would you do?

Corrections in the Community

Check It!

1 WHY are the federal government and states turning to community corrections sanctions? p. 206

The traditional processes of incarceration, probation, and parole are expensive and fail to stop a large number of ex-prisoners from returning to prison after their release because inmates are not prepared to reenter the community.

2 WHAT is the cycle of offending? p. 208

Most inmates who are released from prison are ill-prepared and unsuccessful in reentering the community. They often return to their old neighborhoods and resume the lifestyle that led to their arrest, are arrested again, and return to prison in a vicious cycle.

3 WHAT opposition is there to community corrections sanctions? p. 209

- The public is opposed to community-based corrections facilities being located in their communities.
- Crime victims fear and resent the offender's presence in the community.
- Police believe that offenders released back into the community will contribute to the crime problem.

4 WHAT are the various community corrections sanctions used by the criminal justice system, and how are they different from traditional early-release programs? p. 214

Unlike traditional early-release programs, community corrections sanctions are designed to reduce recidivism and protect the community. Community correction sanctions include the following:

1. intensive probation supervision programs, which place offenders under very strict conditions;
2. split sentencing, in which the offender serves a brief period of imprisonment and is then offered the option of probation;
3. shock probation, in which a first-time offender expecting probation spends a brief period of imprisonment and then is put on probation;
4. shock incarceration, which is a military-style boot camp designed to promote discipline and self-confidence; and
5. home confinement, whereby offenders are confined to their homes and are electronically monitored.

5 WHAT new strategies are being used to promote reentry into the community for ex-offenders? p. 218

Some new strategies that focus on preparing inmates for reentry rather than punishing them include the following:

1. faith-based programs, which are church-affiliated programs that may include religious teaching;
2. work release, whereby inmates are released for paid work in the community;
3. education release, whereby inmates are released for college or vocational programs;
4. halfway houses, which are homes that transition inmates from prison to the community in steps; and
5. day reporting centers to which inmates allowed to live at home must report regularly.

6 WHAT programs are being used to promote reentry into the community for drug offenders? p. 219

Drug courts provide drug offenders the opportunity for intermediate sanctions, community treatment, and intensive probation supervision instead of prison time.

Treatment Accountability for Safer Communities (TASC), a federal assistance program, helps states break the addiction-crime cycle by providing funds for drug-treatment programs.

Residential Substance Abuse Treatment (RSAT), a federal assistance program, helps states provide for treatment instead of prison for substance abusers.

Assess Your Understanding

1. Which of the following countries has the largest incarceration rate per 100,000 persons?

a. Russia
b. India
c. United States
d. Mexico

2. Which of the following is a significant obstacle for community-based correctional programs?

a. public opposition to locating programs within their neighborhood due to public safety concerns
b. inmates' lack of participation in community-based correctional programs
c. government prohibitions upholding First Amendment separation of church and state which ban the use of churches as faith-based community halfway houses
d. both a and b

3. Shock probation and incarceration programs, commonly called boot camps, are usually designed for which of the following correctional populations?

a. sex offenders
b. violent offenders
c. first-time, youthful offenders
d. all offenders

4. In intensive probation supervision which role of the probation and parole officer is emphasized more than in traditional probation supervision?

a. role as law enforcement officer to ensure compliance with the terms of probation
b. role as caseworker to provide effective counseling for reentry success
c. role as community resource broker to help clients find jobs, housing, and services
d. none of the above

5. House arrest is normally paired with which of the following community corrections sanctions?

a. drug courts
b. GPS monitoring
c. tribal wellness courts
d. both a and c

6. What is an obstacle to employment for persons entering the community from prison?

a. employer prejudice against ex-offenders
b. lack of knowledge of how to find jobs
c. lack of required official documentation and identification
d. all of the above

7. When are prisoners normally released to halfway houses?

a. near the end of their prison sentence
b. at the beginning of their prison sentence, and if they do well they do not have to serve time in prison
c. near the middle of their prison sentence as a test of how well they may do if released early on parole
d. after demonstrating they are ready for early release by successfully completing at least one-third of their parole

8. TASC and RSAT are programs designed to serve which of the following correctional populations?

a. Native Americans
b. youthful, first-time offenders
c. sex offenders
d. drug offenders

9. The "revolving door syndrome" refers to which of the following?

a. the transfer of a prisoner from one prison to another for behavior problems
b. the repeated arrest and incarceration of an offender
c. day reporting centers and the practice of sending inmates home at night rather than housing them in jail facilities
d. faith-based rehabilitation and reentry programs

10. What is the comparison of "boot camp" programs compared to traditional imprisonment?
    a. Boot camp works best with older offenders who have learned to "game the system."
    b. Boot camp and traditional imprisonment have about the same recidivism rate but boot camps are less expensive.
    c. Boot camps have higher recidivism rates than traditional imprisonment and cost more.
    d. Traditional imprisonment costs less and has a lower recidivism rate than boot camps.

ESSAY

1. Why are the federal government and states developing new intermediate sanctions for convicted offenders?
2. Explain the cycle of offending.
3. Compare and contrast the various community correction sanctions used by the criminal justice system.
4. Compare and contrast intensive probation supervision with traditional probation.
5. Discuss the purpose of reentry programs and the needs they fulfill for inmates released from incarceration.
6. What unique services do drug court programs offer to drug offenders?
7. Discuss the major obstacle to the development of new halfway houses in the community for reentering offenders.
8. Discuss what populations are served by tribal drug courts and what are some barriers to the success of these courts.

ANSWERS: 1. c, 2. a, 3. c, 4. a, 5. b, 6. d, 7. a, 8. d, 9. b, 10. b

Media

Go to the *Chapter 11: Corrections in the Community* section in *MyCJLab* to test your understanding of this chapter, access customized study content, engage in interactive simulations, complete critical thinking and research assignments, and view related online videos.

Additional Links

See www.allencountycorrections.com/ to visit the home page of the Allen County Community Corrections—Fort Wayne, Indiana, Web site. Established in 1984 by the Community Corrections Advisory Board, Allen County Community Corrections is one of the more comprehensive community corrections programs in the nation.

Go to www.judiciary.state.nj.us/drugcourt/index.htm to obtain information about the New Jersey Adult Drug Court programs.

To view information about New York's veterans court see www.erie.gov/veterans/veterans_court.asp

The National Reentry Resource Center provides a number of resources and information on reentry at www.nationalreentryresourcecenter.org/

To watch a video on the Newark, New Jersey, Reentry Initiative, go to www.youtube.com/watch?v=V9DjXONghpo

The Voices of Hope film discusses the problems facing inmates upon reentry (New Jersey) at www.youtube.com/watch?v=3HpF286vhkg

To view a video of The Policy and Politics of the Michigan Prisoner ReEntry Initiative, go to www.ustream.tv/recorded/5811856

To view a video regarding the special reentry problems for Native Americans in Wisconsin, go to http://milwaukee.jobing.com/video_details.asp?i=56532&segment=32710

Dr. Garland of the University of Missouri discusses his Prisoner Re-entry Research for small metropolitan communities (Springfield, Missouri), at www.youtube.com/watch?v=5OVtKkKVnk5A

To view a Mock Huikahi Restorative Circle and Interview with Circle Former Participants (Hawaii), go to http://vimeo.com/6673308

To view information about the New Jersey Intensive Probation Supervision program, go to www.judiciary.state.nj.us/probsup/isp_intro.htm

To view information about Georgia's boot camp, go to www.dcor.state.ga.us/Divisions/Corrections/BootCamps.html

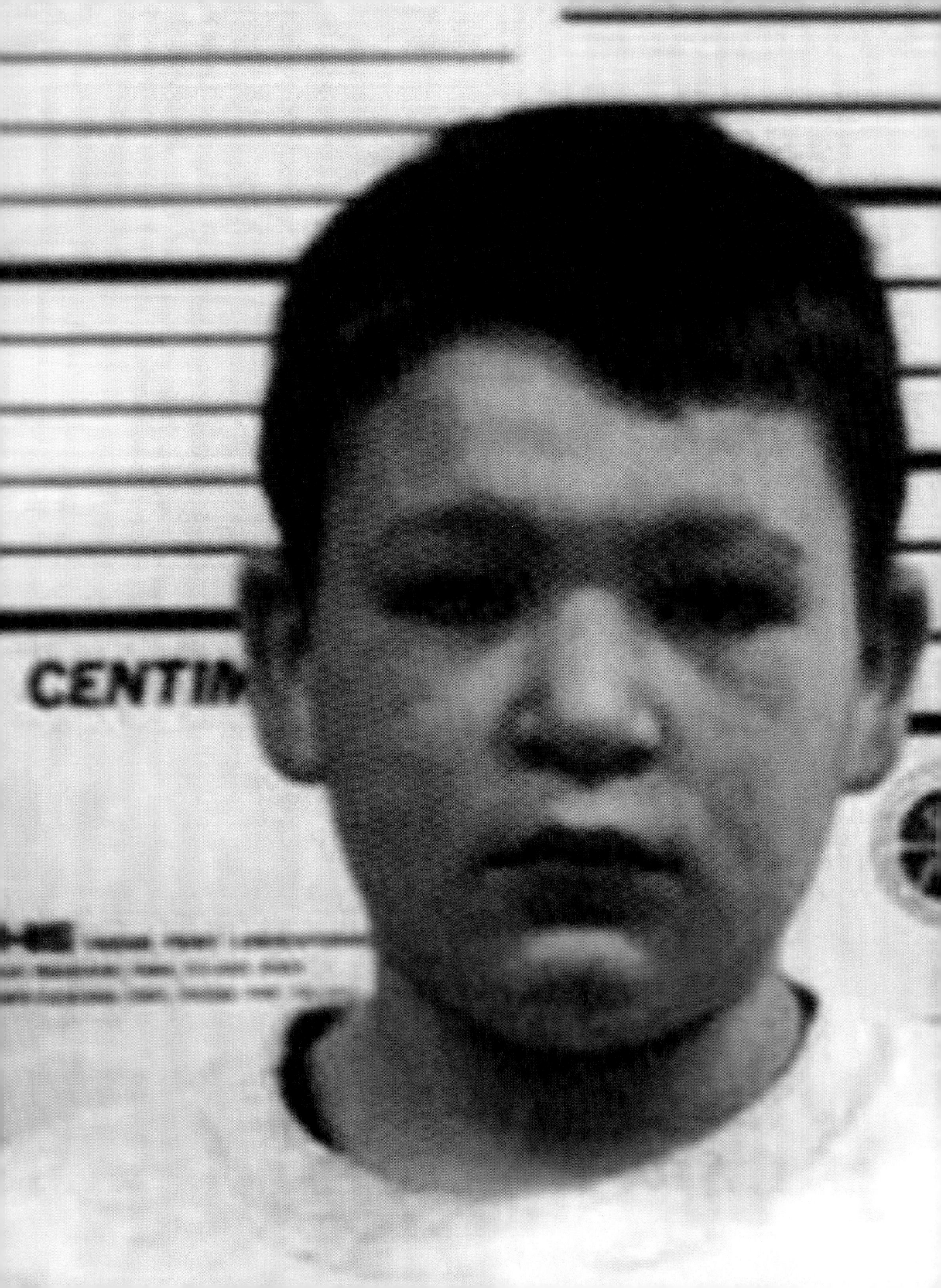

THE JUVENILE JUSTICE SYSTEM

12

1. **What are the goals of the juvenile criminal justice system?**
2. **What were the foundations for the early juvenile criminal justice system?**
3. **How did the establishment of the first juvenile court and following major court cases shape the jurisdiction for and due process rights of juvenile offenders?**
4. **Why and in what ways are states beginning to hold juveniles more accountable for crime?**
5. **How are juveniles processed through the juvenile justice system?**
6. **What are some of the unique problems posed by youthful offenders, such as very young offenders, youth gangs, and substance abuse?**
7. **What strategies are being used to reduce violence in schools?**

The media paints a portrait of violent juveniles preying on society. In one story a 15-year-old girl allegedly shot her mother in the back of the head after having an argument over the girl's relationship with an older boy. After shooting her mother, the girl is accused of inviting the boyfriend over and having sex with him. Another story reported Tyler Hadley, a 17-year-old Florida boy, bludgeoned his parents to death with a hammer and then invited about 60 of his friends to a house party to drink beer and smoke marijuana. In Cleveland, Texas, 18 young men and teenage boys ranging in age from 14 to 27 were accused of repeatedly raping an 11-year-old girl over a period of 3 months. Five suspects were students at Cleveland High School, including two members of the basketball team. Reuters reported that 14-year-old Edgar Jimenez worked for a Mexican drug cartel as a "hit man." Jimenez admitted to killing at least seven people. In 2011, a Mexican court convicted Jimenez of murder, kidnapping, and trafficking cocaine, but because of his age he was sentenced to 3 years in a juvenile prison.

IF CONVICTED AND SENTENCED TO LIFE IN PRISON WITHOUT PAROLE, BROWN WOULD BE THE YOUNGEST IN U.S. HISTORY TO RECEIVE SUCH A SENTENCE.

The public's perception of juvenile violence has resulted in changes to the juvenile justice system. Many states have removed adolescents from the protection of the juvenile court. Pennsylvania is one of the strictest states in holding juveniles accountable in criminal court. Pennsylvania law requires any person charged with homicide to be charged in a criminal court unless a judge decides otherwise.

In August 2011, Pennsylvania Judge Dominick Motto listened to arguments as to whether Jordan Brown should be charged as an adult. In 2009, Brown, then age 11, allegedly shot his father's pregnant fiancée with a 20-gauge shotgun he received as a Christmas gift from his father. Under Pennsylvania law he was charged as an adult and faces a maximum sentence of life in prison without parole. If convicted and sentenced, Brown would be the youngest in U.S. history to receive such a sentence. The United States is only one of two countries in the world that refuses to ratify the United Nations Convention on the Rights of the Child, which would ban life without parole sentences for juveniles—Somalia is the other. Judge Motto will have to decide if it is appropriate to send Brown to a juvenile facility for rehabilitation or to send him to criminal court for trial and punishment.

A Changing View of Young Offenders

The juvenile justice system is based on the premise that young offenders can be rehabilitated and that society would be better served by rehabilitating children rather than punishing them. Juveniles have not always enjoyed the benefits of the juvenile justice system. The separation of juveniles and adults in the criminal justice system is a relatively new practice, dating back only to 1899. However, children may not be as secure in relying on the protection of the juvenile justice system, not because of corrupt judges, but because recent events have caused some to give considerable thought to the functioning of the juvenile justice system.

School shootings, gang violence, depraved killings, rape, and even accusations of juvenile suicide bombers have caused some to call for the examination of the principles on which the juvenile justice system is founded, the criminological theories that focus on young offenders, and the ability of the juvenile justice system to rehabilitate the offenders and protect society from juvenile violence and mayhem.

THE JUVENILE JUSTICE SYSTEM IS BASED ON THE PREMISE THAT YOUNG OFFENDERS CAN BE REHABILITATED.

Despite statistics that show otherwise, there is a public perception of a widespread violent juvenile crime wave that has had substantial influence on the juvenile justice system. Juvenile offenders are seen as a threat to be punished and incarcerated. Those who believe juvenile crime is "out of control" also believe that the juvenile justice system is perceived as an "easy out that gives a meaningless slap on the wrist to violent youth."[1] Thus, there are forces at work that continue to transform the juvenile justice system.

This chapter examines the development of the juvenile justice system, including its goals, agencies, processes, and results. It explores the two-sided problem of juveniles as victims and juveniles as offenders. The examination of juvenile offenders focuses on substance abuse, violent crimes, gangs, and school violence. The examination of juveniles as victims focuses on violence against children, sexual exploitation and child pornography, and missing children.

Development of the Juvenile Justice System

Before There Was a Juvenile Justice System

In his classical theory of crime causation, Cesare Beccaria (1738–1794) made no distinction between adult and juvenile offenders and suggested no special considerations for the punishment of juvenile offenders. Neoclassical criminological theorists such as Jeremy Bentham (1748–1832) carved out an exemption for very young offenders, allowing that young offenders cannot appreciate the criminality of their actions. The legal system of the American colonies allowed this defense based on youth. See Table 12.1.

Juvenile cases were fairly rare in the founding years of the United States. State courts preferred to let parents or local officials handle juvenile offenders. However, as industrialism and immigration gave rise to swelling populations in cities such as New York and Philadelphia, the public began to perceive that there was a problem with the "disorderly conduct" of children that was not being contained by parents. As a result, young offenders found themselves being processed by a criminal justice system that often failed to distinguish whether the young offender's behavior was motivated by criminal intent or poverty and need. Many felt that if

TABLE 12.1 Colonial American Court Treatment of Youthful Offenders

Age	Ability to Form *Mens Rea*	Response of the Justice System
Below age 7	Child does not have the ability to form *mens rea* (guilty intent) and cannot be held accountable for any crime.	Parents of offending children were expected to assume responsibility for the child.
Between ages 7 and 14	The capacity for *mens rea* was a rebuttable defense. Prosecution would have to prove the capacity for *mens rea* and defense could present evidence against the capacity to form *mens rea*.	If the defense was successful the offender would be treated the same as children under age 7. If not, the offender would be tried in adult criminal court and sentenced to adult institutions. Some colonies provided a reduction in sentence for children.
Over age 14	The capacity for *mens rea* was presumed but incapacity for criminal intent could be offered as a defense. Most often this applied to persons with mental retardation.	Without benefit of a defense of youth, the offender would be tried in adult criminal court and sentenced the same as adult offenders, including execution by hanging.

1 **The juvenile justice system is based on the premise that young offenders can be helped and rehabilitated, but current public concern that juvenile violence is widespread and out of control is causing juveniles to be more accountable for violent crimes.**

imprisonment could help the adult criminal, it would surely assist a youth less practiced in crime, and so the courts became more disposed to using the criminal justice system to deal with the problem of juvenile disorderly conduct.[2]

Political, social, and economic practices of the eighteenth and nineteenth centuries tended to provide little distinction among the poor, the mentally ill, and the criminal element of society. In a society that had no "social safety net" to provide for persons in need, institutions of confinement often housed all "offenders" together without regard for separation by offense, age, or gender. Thus, the orphan, runaway child, debtor, or widow without means of support could end up in the same conditions of confinement as the criminal. Needless to say, such penal institutions were appalling places in terms of sanitation, safety, and rehabilitation. They were characterized by disease as well as violence and victimization of the young, females, and helpless by both fellow inmates and their guards.

Reform Movements The modern juvenile justice system has its roots in reform movements to "save" children from such conditions. The foundation of the various reform movements was the acceptance by society of the premise that there are significant and fundamental differences between adults and juveniles. As early as the sixteenth century, various reform movements argued against the traditional wisdom that children were "miniature adults." These reform movements advocated that children had less developed moral and cognitive capacities.[3]

In the 1800s, several reform movements focused on the general well-being of children, which included not only children charged with crimes but also children who had come into the custody of the state due to poverty, abandonment, and vagrancy. Many private reform movements focused on providing care for children and removing them from the criminal justice system. Because the criminal court during the early 1800s did not distinguish among juveniles in the custody of the state for criminal offenses and orphaned, runaway, or abandoned children, the early reform movements often offered services that tried to encompass the entire spectrum of children's needs.

Foundations of the Juvenile Justice System

The New York House of Refuge In the early 1800s, various private reform groups attempted to provide services to divert young offenders from the criminal justice system. The primary focus of these groups was to remove youths from the criminal justice system and place them in group houses, institutions, and other facilities that were designed to provide for the care, education, and rehabilitation of the child. The **New York House of Refuge** was the first of such juvenile reformatories in the nation. The House of Refuge was initiated by the private efforts of a philanthropic association originally called the Society for the Prevention of Pauperism.

The New York House of Refuge juvenile reformatory was established in 1824 and on January 1, 1825, admitted nine children (six boys and three girls) committed for vagrancy and petty crimes.[4] The House of Refuge was privately managed and funded but was endorsed and financially supported by the state of New York. The state passed legislation authorizing courts statewide to commit juveniles convicted of crimes or adjudicated as vagrants to the New York House of Refuge rather than the state's criminal justice system.[5] Like most of the juvenile reformatories of the era that were to follow, supervised labor, education, and discipline were considered the essential elements of rehabilitation for children.[6] In addition, the New York House of Refuge and other early reform movements separated children by gender and took into account the reason or crime for their commitment.

THE CRIMINAL COURT DID NOT DISTINGUISH AMONG JUVENILES IN THE CUSTODY OF THE STATE FOR CRIMINAL OFFENSES AND ORPHANED, RUNAWAY, OR ABANDONED CHILDREN.

The New York House of Refuge had the authority to place those under its charge in private industry through indenture agreements by which employers agreed to supervise the youths in exchange for their labor. Those placed in private industry primarily were sent to work on farms and as domestic laborers, and a few of the boys were indentured to merchant sailing ships.[7] The popularity and the number of wards of the House of Refuge quickly grew. The New York House of Refuge was visited by and received praise from people all over the world, including Alexis de Tocqueville, Frances Trollope, and Charles Dickens. In 1857, it was the largest juvenile reformatory in the United States (with over 1,000 inmates) and was praised as "the greatest reform school in the world."[8]

January 1, 1825

The New York House of Refuge juvenile reformatory admitted nine children (six boys and three girls).

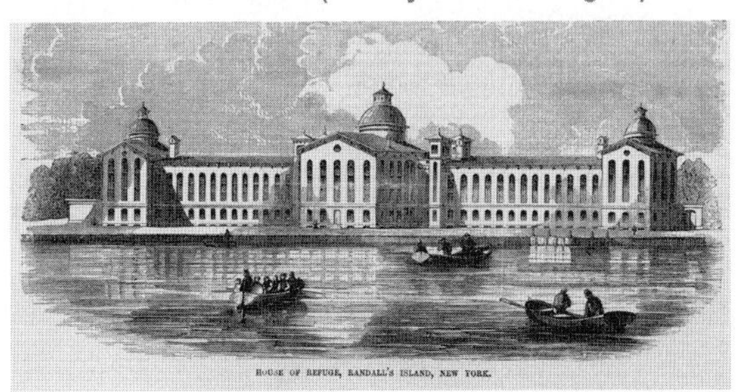

Other Reformatories Followed Other states quickly imitated New York's model and adopted similar alternative institutions for juveniles. Like the New York House of Refuge (some of these institutions were also named "House of Refuge"), they could be characterized as "work houses," "training schools," "reform schools," "schools of industry," or other such names, whose primary purpose was to develop employable skills for youths. In the nineteenth century, children were sent to juvenile reformatories

New York House of Refuge an early juvenile reformatory established by New York state in 1824 that was to become the model for most juvenile reformatories

2 **In the 1880s, reformers established juvenile reformatories that were designed to separate children from adult criminals, as well as to separate young offenders by gender and to take into account whether they were in custody because of poverty, abandonment, or crime.**

for a wide variety of "offenses," including petty crime, vagrancy, and begging. Juveniles could be sent to juvenile reformatories because they were "incorrigible minors" or "disorderly children." In 1865, in New York, any child could be sent to the House of Refuge upon the complaint of a guardian, a magistrate, or a justice of the peace that the child was "disorderly."

These quasi-public juvenile reformatories, despite their emphasis on job training and the subsequent income produced by that endeavor, did not prove to be financially sustainable. Further, because each reformatory was independently established, governed, staffed, and financed, there was little or no oversight over the conditions of confinement, the rights of the children, or the qualifications of the staff. There was no standard of care. Many were criticized as ineffective in their mission, providing substandard care and abusing the rights of children.[9] Many of the reformatories operated on limited funding and could not provide the level of services needed for proper care and reform. As a result, these reform programs failed to rehabilitate the youths and they returned to crime, the streets, or the reformatory.

Crisis in the System By the mid-1800s, private institutions had proliferated in all of the large cities but still did not provide sufficient services to provide alternative incarceration for children. After the Civil War, the growing population and the increase in immigration in America's large cities added to the juvenile problem. By the end of the nineteenth century, it was evident that there was a crisis in the criminal justice system as to how to handle children in the system. For example, in 1849, approximately 8 percent of Maryland penitentiary prisoners were between the ages of 13 and 18. In 1897, 15 percent of the prisoners in the penitentiary were between 12 and 20 years of age, and 21 percent were between 10 and 20 years old. Many states found it necessary to assume control over the various private juvenile reformatories or to provide greater financial support and oversight. States began to see the necessity of providing dedicated court agencies to deal with the problem of young offenders.

ONLY THE JUVENILE JUDGE—NOT THE PROSECUTOR OR THE CRIMINAL COURT JUDGE—HAD THE AUTHORITY TO WAIVE THE JUVENILE TO CRIMINAL COURT.

21% of Maryland penitentiary prisoners in 1897 were between the ages of 10 and 20 years

The Youthful Offender and the Criminal Justice System

Toward the end of the nineteenth century, the concept of ***parens patriae***, or "state as parent and guardian," began to become the predominant theme in structuring state agencies responsible for juveniles. For example, the adoption of legal reforms that granted the state the inherent right to assume custody of children and a codified assemblage of children's laws culminated in the creation of a separate children's court system in 1892.[10] Cook County (Chicago), Illinois, is recognized as the site of the first juvenile court. Established in 1899, the distinguishing characteristic of the Illinois juvenile court was the concept of **original jurisdiction**. Unlike other states that had separate courts for young offenders that were part of the criminal justice system, the Chicago juvenile court had exclusive jurisdiction over juveniles. Juveniles could not be tried, for any offense, by the criminal court unless the juvenile court granted its permission for the accused juvenile to be moved from the authority of the juvenile court. This process was referred to as "waiving" the juvenile to the criminal court.

1899 Cook County, Illinois, establishes the first juvenile court.

Furthermore, only the juvenile judge—not the prosecutor, the police, or the criminal court judge—had the authority to waive the juvenile to criminal court. The juvenile court was self-contained in that it had its own intake process; it did not depend on the prosecutor to bring cases before the court. Also, it had its own probation and parole system and its own correctional system. The juvenile court did share the services of the police in that the court did not have its own law enforcement agents responsible for the detection and apprehension of juvenile offenders.

The beginning of the twentieth century, known as the Progressive Era, was a time of extensive social reform. Social reform movements had been active in campaigning against "social evil" in the latter part of the nineteenth century. Thus, it is not surprising that with the emergence of a juvenile court with original jurisdiction in Cook County, Illinois, other states quickly adopted this model. By 1910, 32 states had established juvenile courts and/or probation services. By 1925, all but two states had established juvenile courts with exclusive original jurisdiction.[11]

In addition to processing youthful offenders for criminal offenses, the Cook County juvenile court assumed total and in a sense "absolute" control over the juvenile. In exercising the right of *parens patriae*, the juvenile court assumed superior authority over the authority of the "natural" parents or guardian. The juvenile court was established not as a criminal court but as a government agency to provide youthful offenders and their victims with a comprehensive and balanced approach to justice.[12] The court operated on the principle of "the best interests of the child."[13] As a result, the court had original exclusive jurisdiction not only of children who had committed crimes but of any child whose welfare and well-being was in question. In a sense, the court had the same interest in the overall welfare and well-being as the child's parent. The philosophy underlying this authority was that "the delinquent child was also seen as in need of the court's benevolent intervention."[14]

3 **In 1899, Cook County, Chicago, Illinois, established the first juvenile court that had sole jurisdiction for juvenile offenders, but not until a number of decisions beginning in the 1960s did the Supreme Court award to juveniles many due process rights that they had been denied based on the previous view that this denial was balanced by the greater concern for juvenile offenders accorded by the state in its role of parent and guardian.**

parens patriae the legal assumption that the state has primary responsibility for the safety and custody of children

original jurisdiction the concept that juvenile court is the only court that has authority over juveniles, so they cannot be tried, for any offense, by a criminal court unless the juvenile court grants its permission for the accused juvenile to be waived to criminal court

The **juvenile court** removed the child from the authority of the criminal court but it also assumed a much greater authority over the child than the criminal court has over accused adults. Not only was the juvenile court "benevolent," it was much more intrusive and had the power to intervene in noncriminal matters. The juvenile court assumed authority over children in three situations:

1. when the welfare of the child was threatened;
2. when the child was a status offender; or
3. when the child was a delinquent.

In court review of welfare cases, the child did not commit a crime but the court's focus was on what is best for the child.

Classification of Juvenile Offenders

Status Offenders Juveniles are classified as **status offenders** or delinquents. Status offenders are children who have committed an act or failed to fulfill a responsibility that if they were adults the court would not have any authority over them. Common status offenses are failure to attend school, running away from parents or guardians, and engaging in behaviors while legal for adults is considered harmful for children.

Delinquents On the other hand, **delinquents** are accused of committing an act that is criminal for both adults and juveniles. The criminal justice system divides crimes into felonies and misdemeanors, but there is no similar division in the juvenile court. Because the focus of the court is on the welfare of the child, there is less concern about serious versus minor offenses, as such concern focuses on the punishment for the offense and not on the welfare of the offender. Further, the authority of the juvenile court is time-limited. Felonies have sentences of 5, 10, 20 years, or even life without parole. The juvenile court has custodial authority of the offender only during his or her youth. This limit has been defined differently by the various states. In some states, the custodial authority of the juvenile court extends until the offender is 18 years old; in other states, the juvenile court may retain custodial authority until the offender is 23 years old. With such limited custodial authority it is not possible for the court to impose lengthy sentences. Thus, the distinction between misdemeanor crimes and felony crimes is not as pivotal in juvenile court as in the criminal justice system. Hence, a juvenile delinquent is a person under the authority of the juvenile court who has committed an offense for which, if he or she were an adult, would be considered criminal. Therefore, the term *juvenile delinquent* fails to clearly identify the nature of the offender's crime. Juvenile delinquents include offenders who have committed petty crimes such as theft, vandalism, and simple assault (or fighting); and also robbery, rape, and murder. However, in 2000, the Office of Juvenile Justice Delinquency and Prevention sought to identify juveniles who had committed serious crimes. They used the term **juvenile superpredators** to identify juvenile delinquents who engage in serious violent crime.

THE CRIMINAL JUSTICE SYSTEM DIVIDES CRIMES INTO FELONIES AND MISDEMEANORS, BUT THERE IS NO SIMILAR DIVISION IN THE JUVENILE COURT.

Due Process for Juveniles

In the beginning, unlike for the criminal justice system, neither state supreme courts nor the United States Supreme Court provided significant review and oversight of juvenile justice courts. The Supreme Court essentially adopted a "hands-off" policy similar to its view of prisoner rights for adults prior to the Warren Court. Juvenile jurisdiction extended well beyond the jurisdiction exercised over adults by the criminal courts. As such, juveniles were effectively denied the rights afforded under the equal protection clause of the Fourteenth Amendment. The justification for this exclusion was that the juvenile received less due process but the court demonstrated a greater concern for the interests of the juvenile. Essentially the view underlying the position of the Court was that operating under the doctrine of *parens patriae* the purpose of the court was not to punish the juvenile but to provide "solicitous care and regenerative treatment."[15]

From the beginning, some were critical of the lack of due process based on the assumption of the benevolent nature of the juvenile court. For example, the state of Maryland's Children's Code Commission of 1922 published a report critical of the lack of due process for juveniles. It cited the case of a 2-year-old child committed to reform school as an incorrigible minor until the age of 21. However, these complaints were ignored because, on balance, juvenile courts appeared to offer compensating benefits to the juvenile that offset the lack of due process rights. Although there were some abuses of due process, many of the juvenile courts did indeed operate with the intent to promote the best interests of the child. The State of Oregon, for example, adopted legislation in the 1930s declaring that juveniles were not responsible for the underlying causes of their delinquency because the children had no control over their environment or heredity, which were identified as the underlying causes of juvenile delinquency.[16] Thus, based on the juvenile court's balance between prevention and treatment goals versus punishment, the Supreme Court did not require juvenile courts to provide due process protection to juveniles.

During the 1960s, the Supreme Court abandoned its "hands-off" doctrine and began to examine the need for due process rights for juveniles. In a series of decisions the Supreme Court radically redefined the due process rights of juveniles. Supreme Court decisions regarding the juvenile death penalty will be discussed in a later section.

Kent v. United States*—Waiver Hearing Rights** The first due process case that the Supreme Court considered was ***Kent v. United States (1966),[17] which marked the departure of the Supreme Court from its

juvenile court a court that handles juvenile welfare cases and cases involving status offenders and delinquents; some juvenile courts may handle additional matters related to the family

status offender a child who has committed an act or failed to fulfill a responsibility for which, if he or she were an adult, the court would not have any authority over him or her

delinquent a juvenile accused of committing an act that is criminal for both adults and juveniles

juvenile superpredator OJJDP term used to describe juveniles who commit violent felony crimes

Kent v. United States a 1961 Supreme Court case that marked the departure of the Supreme Court from its acceptance of the denial of due process rights to juveniles

Comparison of State Juvenile Courts and Criminal Courts

Juvenile Justice System		Criminal Justice System
Rehabilitation Rehabilitation of the juvenile is the primary goal	**versus**	**Sanctions** Sanctions are used against the offender
Prevention Focus on all risk factors including the family and the environment	**versus**	**Prevention** Prevention activities are generalized and aimed at deterrence
Law Enforcement Specialized juvenile units are used and the confidentiality of juvenile identity is ensured	**versus**	**Law Enforcement** Open public access to all information is required
Intake Intake based on social service model; the court is seen as the guardian of the defendant	**versus**	**Prosecution** Advisorial system
Detention Separate detention facilities for juveniles	**versus**	**Jail/lockup**
Adjudication Different rights afforded and no jury trial for juveniles	**versus**	**Conviction** at criminal trial with right to appeal to higher court
Disposition Rehabilitation of the juvenile is the primary goal	**versus**	**Sentencing**

acceptance of the denial of due process rights to juveniles based on the assumption that juveniles received compensating benefits. In 1961, while on probation from an earlier case, Morris Kent, age 16, was charged with rape and robbery. Kent confessed to the offenses as well as to several similar incidents.[18] Because of Kent's age and the fact that he was considered a repeat violent offender, Kent's attorney, believing that the case may be waived to criminal court, filed a motion requesting a hearing on the issue of jurisdiction. The judge denied the hearing and ruled that the case would be transferred to criminal court. The judge stated that the court had made a "full investigation" of the case but refused to disclose the details of the investigation or to provide Kent's attorney with the opportunity to refute the waiver.

At the time, the decision of juvenile judges could not be appealed, so Morris Kent was tried in criminal court. He was found guilty and sentenced to 30 to 90 years in prison. His attorney appealed the conviction to the Supreme Court, arguing that Kent's due process rights were violated when he was waived to criminal court without the opportunity of a hearing. The Supreme Court ruled that Kent was deprived of the "compensating benefit of the solicitous care and regeneration treatment postulated for children" and thus received the "worst of both worlds"—neither the protection accorded to adults nor the benefits promised for juveniles.[19] The Court ruled that Kent was entitled to due process rights under the equal protection clause of the Fourteenth Amendment. Specifically, the Court prescribed juveniles

1. the right to a waiver hearing,
2. the right to counsel at waiver hearings,
3. the right to access any reports and records used by the court in deciding waiver, and
4. the right to a statement issued by the juvenile judge justifying waiver to the criminal court.

In Re Gault*—Due Process Rights** In 1967, one year after the Kent case, the Supreme Court expanded the due process rights of juveniles. In reviewing ***In re Gault (1967),[20] the Supreme Court abandoned the arguments justifying lack of equal protection for juveniles under the Fourteenth Amendment. Gerald Gault, age 15, was on probation in Arizona for a minor property offense when, in 1964, he and a friend made a crank telephone call to an adult neighbor. At the court proceedings Gault did not have an attorney. The victim did not testify and it was not established that Gault was the one who made the "obscene" remarks during the call. However, Gault was committed to a training school until he was 21 years old—a sentence of 6 years. The maximum sentence for the same offense had Gault been an adult in criminal court would have been a $50 fine or 2 months in jail. Under state juvenile proceedings, Gault was not entitled to an appeal of the adjudication.

After the commitment to training school, Gault obtained an attorney who appealed the case to the Supreme Court. The issue presented was that Gault's constitutional rights to notice of charges, counsel, questioning of witnesses, protection against self-incrimination, a transcript of the proceedings, and appellate review were denied.[21] The Supreme Court agreed with the challenge and ruled that in hearings that could result in commitment to an institution, juveniles have the right to due process rights.

In re Gault a case in which the Supreme Court provided due process rights to juveniles, including notice of charges, counsel, right to examine witnesses, and right to remain silent

Supreme Court Decisions Affecting Juvenile Due Process

1966 ***Kent v. United States*** Courts must provide the "essentials of due process" in transferring juveniles to the adult system.

1967 ***In re Gault*** In hearings that could result in commitment to an institution, juveniles have four basic constitutional rights.

1970 ***In re Winship*** In delinquency matters, the State must prove its case beyond a reasonable doubt.

1971 ***McKeiver v. Pennsylvania*** Jury trials are not constitutionally required in juvenile court hearings.

1975 ***Breed v. Jones*** Waiver of a juvenile to criminal court following adjudication in juvenile court constitutes double jeopardy.

1977 ***Oklahoma Publishing Co. v. District Court***
1979 ***Smith v. Daily Mail Publishing Co.***
The press may report juvenile court proceedings under certain circumstances.

1982 ***Eddings v. Oklahoma*** Defendant's youthful age should be considered a mitigating factor in deciding whether to apply the death penalty.

1984 ***Schall v. Martin*** Preventive "pretrial" detention of juveniles is allowable under certain circumstances.

1988 ***Thompson v. Oklahoma***
1989 ***Stanford v. Kentucky***
Minimum age for death penalty is set at 16.

2005 ***Roper v. Simmons*** Minimum age for death penalty is set at 18.

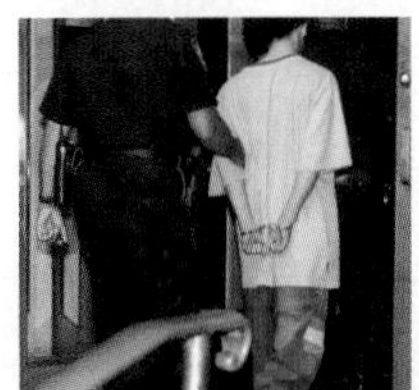

2010 ***Graham v. Florida*** Life without parole for juveneiles can violate the Eighth Amendment

The Supreme Court criticized the "welfare of the child" doctrine of the juvenile court, concluding, "Juvenile court history has again demonstrated that unbridled discretion, however benevolently motivated, is frequently a poor substitute for principle and procedure."[22] The Supreme Court made significant changes to the very nature of the juvenile justice court proceedings, declaring that juveniles have the due process rights of:

1. right to reasonable notice of the charges,
2. right to counsel as well as appointed counsel if indigent,
3. right to confront and cross-examine witnesses, and
4. right against self-incrimination, including the right to remain silent.

In re Winship*—Burden of Proof** Juvenile court proceedings are not criminal trials, so one of the differences between juvenile court proceedings and criminal trials prior to ***In re Winship was the standard of proof required for a judge to adjudicate, which is to hear and judge, an offender. In civil cases the **burden of proof** is "a preponderance of the evidence;" that is, is it more likely that the matter is true or not true? In criminal cases the burden of proof is a much stricter "proof beyond a reasonable doubt." Again, because of the mission of the juvenile court, the Supreme Court was silent on which standard should apply to juvenile court proceedings. State supreme courts were also silent on the issue or operated under the "preponderance of evidence," or the 50 percent rule. Judges based their rulings on whether they believed it was more likely than not likely that the accused juvenile committed the act. *In re Winship* concerned Samuel Winship, age 12, who was charged with stealing $112 from a woman's purse in a store.[23] There were no eyewitnesses who saw Winship steal the money but there was a witness who claimed to have seen Winship running from the scene just before the woman noticed the money missing from her purse. The New York juvenile court, where Winship's case was heard, used the preponderance of evidence rule. The court agreed with Winship's attorney that there was "reasonable doubt" of Winship's guilt but that it was more likely that he committed the act than not.[24]

Again, the state argued before the Supreme Court that because juvenile courts were designed to rehabilitate children rather than to punish them, it was not necessary for the state to use the higher standard of proof. As in the Kent and Gault cases, the Supreme Court rejected the juvenile court's claim to waiver due process protections based on benefits afforded the juvenile. The Supreme Court ruled that the reasonable doubt standard, the same used in criminal trials, should be required in all delinquency adjudications.

***McKeiver v. Pennsylvania*—Right to Jury Trial** In 1966, 1967, and 1970 rulings, the Supreme Court significantly expanded the due process rights of juveniles when accused of acts for which they could be confined, even if that confinement was in a state facility with the stated purpose of "helping" the juvenile. With these expanded due process rights, juvenile hearings adhered to many of the standards used in criminal trials. One of the due process rights denied juveniles was trial by a jury of their peers. A judge presided over the juvenile hearing and rendered the final judgment and disposition. Joseph McKeiver, age 16, was charged with robbery, larceny, and receiving stolen goods. He was accused of being with a gang of other youths who chased three children and took 25 cents from them.

THE SUPREME COURT RULED THE DUE PROCESS CLAUSE OF THE FOURTEENTH AMENDMENT DID NOT REQUIRE JURY TRIALS IN JUVENILE COURTS.

At McKeiver's adjudication hearing, his attorney requested a jury trial. The request was denied and McKeiver was adjudicated and placed on probation. The case was appealed to the Supreme Court. Unlike previous cases that favored the expansion of due process rights, the Supreme Court ruled that the due process clause of the Fourteenth Amendment did not require jury trials in juvenile courts. The decision also noted that judges presided in bench trials in criminal court and there was no evidence to suggest that juries are more accurate than

In re Winship a case in which the Supreme Court ruled that the reasonable doubt standard, the same used in criminal trials, should be required in all delinquency adjudications

burden of proof the standard required for adjudication

judges in the adjudication stage. In ***McKeiver v. Pennsylvania*** the Supreme Court agreed with the state's argument that a jury trial would most likely "destroy the traditional character of juvenile proceedings."

Breed v. Jones*—Double Jeopardy** In 1970, Gary Jones, age 17, was charged with armed robbery. Jones appeared in Los Angeles juvenile court and was adjudicated delinquent on the original charge and two other robberies.[25] The prosecutor sought to try Jones in criminal court for the same actions after his adjudication in juvenile court. Jones's attorney asserted that trial in criminal court on the same charges violated the double jeopardy clause of the Fifth Amendment. The state argued that juvenile adjudication was not a trial, and, therefore, trial in a criminal court did not constitute double jeopardy. The California Court upheld the ruling and the case was appealed to the United States Supreme Court. In ***Breed v. Jones (1975), the United States Supreme Court ruled that juvenile adjudication is equivalent to a trial in criminal court and once a juvenile has been adjudicated by a juvenile court, he or she cannot be waived to criminal court for trial for the same charges.

THE STATE ARGUED THAT PREVENTIVE DETENTION SERVES A LEGITIMATE STATE OBJECTIVE IN PROTECTING BOTH THE JUVENILE AND SOCIETY FROM PRETRIAL CRIME AND IS NOT INTENDED TO PUNISH THE JUVENILE.

Schall v. Martin*—The Right to Bail** Gregory Martin, age 14, was arrested in 1977 and charged with robbery, assault, and possession of a weapon. He and two other youths allegedly hit a boy on the head with a loaded gun and stole his jacket and sneakers.[26] Arguing that there was a serious risk that Martin would commit another crime, the state held Martin in a juvenile facility pending adjudication rather than release him to a parent or guardian.[27] Martin's attorney filed a *habeas corpus* action, arguing that because in most cases an adjudicated child was released back to the custody of his or her parent or guardian, preventive detention was punishment. Martin's attorney argued that his client was being denied the right to bail. The lower appellate courts agreed with Martin's attorney and reversed the juvenile court's detention order. The case was appealed to the Supreme Court, where the state argued that preventive detention serves a legitimate state objective in protecting both the juvenile and society from pretrial crime and is not intended to punish the juvenile. In ***Schall v. Martin (1984), the U.S. Supreme Court upheld the constitutionality of the preventive detention of juveniles. The Supreme Court agreed that the doctrine of *parens patriae* applied to preventive detention of juveniles and accepted that the state was acting in the best interest of the child.[28] The ruling had the effect of allowing the juvenile court to deny the right to bail to juveniles prior to adjudication.

Privacy of Juvenile Court Proceedings

One of the characteristics distinguishing juvenile court proceedings from criminal trials is that juvenile court proceedings are not open to the public. Many courts prohibit news media from publishing the names of juveniles involved in court proceedings. However, in a 1977 case and a 1979 case the Supreme Court granted the news media the right to publish the names of juveniles involved in court proceedings. In *Oklahoma Publishing Company v. District Court* in and for Oklahoma City (1977)[29] and *Smith v. Daily Mail Publishing Company* (1979),[30] the Court refused to uphold the traditional ban on the publication of juvenile's names. In the Oklahoma Publishing Company case, a court order prohibited the press from reporting the name and printing a photograph of a youth involved in a juvenile court preceding, which it had obtained legally from a source outside the court. Likewise, in the *Daily Mail* case, the juvenile court sought to prohibit the publishing of a juvenile's name that had been obtained independently of the court. In both cases the Supreme Court ruled that the First Amendment interests in a free press take precedence over the interests in preserving the anonymity of juvenile defendants. In cases where the media obtains the name or photograph of a juvenile legally and independently of the court record, the media have the right to publish or broadcast the information. The Court's ruling did not open up juvenile court proceedings or juvenile court records to the public or the media.

Juvenile Justice System in the Twenty-First Century

Juvenile Justice and Delinquency Prevention Act

Separation of Juveniles and Adults Today's juvenile justice system is extensively influenced by the federal **Juvenile Justice and Delinquency Prevention Act of 1974** (JJDPA), amended in 2001. The act provides the major source of federal funding to states for the improvement of their juvenile justice systems, services, and facilities. The JJDPA influences state juvenile justice systems by requiring states to maintain the standards set forth in the JJDPA if they receive federal funds. The primary intent of the JJDPA is to ensure that children do not have contact with adults in jails and other institutional settings and that status offenders are not placed in secure detention. Based on research, the JJDPA provides that juveniles may not be detained in adult jails and lock-ups except for limited times before or after a court hearing. Recognizing the difference in the level of resources between urban and rural juvenile courts, juveniles may be detained up to 6 hours before or after a court hearing in urban areas but up to 24 hours plus weekends and holidays in rural juvenile courts. Also, the JJDPA regulates the travel conditions for juveniles. The JJDPA

4 **Although federal law has protected juveniles from contact with adults while in state custody since 1974, public fear that juvenile crime is out of control and that juveniles should be held accountable for violent crimes has led to many state laws that remove such juveniles from the protection of juvenile courts into the adult criminal system.**

McKeiver v. Pennsylvania a case in which the Supreme Court denied juveniles the right to a trial by jury

Breed v. Jones a case in which the Supreme Court ruled that once a juvenile has been adjudicated by a juvenile court, he or she cannot be waived to criminal court to be tried for the same charges

Schall v. Martin a case in which the Supreme Court upheld the right of juvenile courts to deny bail to adjudicated juveniles

Juvenile Justice and Delinquency Prevention Act of 1974 a law that sets federal standards for the treatment and processing of juveniles in the criminal justice system

regulations do not apply to children who are tried or convicted in adult criminal court of a felony-level offense.

When children are placed in an adult jail or lock-up, as provided by the exceptions in the JJDPA, "sight and sound" separation is required between adults and juveniles to keep children safe from verbal or psychological abuse that could occur from being within sight or sound of adult inmates. Children also cannot be housed next to adult cells; share dining halls, recreation areas, or any other common spaces with adults; or be placed in any circumstances that could expose them to threats or abuse from adult offenders.

Community-Based Facilities The JJDPA provides that juvenile status offenders should not be housed in secure facilities while waiting for their juvenile court hearing or waiting for the juvenile intake officer to review their case. Juvenile status offenders are to be housed in community-based facilities, day treatment or residential home treatment facilities, foster homes, or other age-appropriate nonsecure facilities. The JJDPA does allow for juvenile status offenders to be held for up to 24 hours in secure detention or confinement under some circumstances. Also, the JJDPA provides that juvenile status offenders should receive appropriate treatment, counseling, mentoring, alternative education, and job development support while in state custody.

Treatment of Minority Juveniles Finally, a broad mission of the JJDPA is to address the problem of disproportionate minority confinement. Minority children make up approximately one-third of the youth population but two thirds of children in confinement. Further, studies indicate that minority youths receive tougher sentences and are more likely to be incarcerated than nonminority youths for the same offenses. The JJDPA requires states to assess their treatment of minority juveniles to ensure that they are being treated fairly and equitably by the juvenile justice system.

Judicial Waiver: Abandoning the Great Experiment

In the twenty-first century, the juvenile court remains distinct from the criminal court but the state juvenile courts provide juvenile offenders with most of the same rights as adult offenders. The Supreme Court has declared that the rights in the Fifth, Sixth, and Seventh Amendments are not restricted by age or the professed intent of the court to "help" the child. However, public perception of juvenile crime exerted pressure for change. Contrary to statistical data, public perception is that juveniles are more violent and commit more crime than in previous periods. The juvenile crime index reached a historical high in 1994 but then declined 49 percent to a historic low in 2004. The juvenile violent crime index arrest rate then rose by 12 percent over the next 2 years. Since 2006 the juvenile crime rate has continued to decline. The FBI Uniform Crime Report recorded an 8.9 percent drop in juvenile arrests for all offenses in 2009 compared to 2008. The adult rate declined only 1.2 percent.

Comparison of National Crime Victimization Survey data and self-reported data complicates the analysis. Changes in record keeping, in reporting requirements for crimes on school property, and in society suggest that there may be a discrepancy between reported juvenile crime and actual increase or decrease in juvenile crime. For example, prior to the adoption of federally mandated reporting requirements, many schools did not report crimes such as theft, assault, and robbery that occurred on school property. If a child took money by force from another child on school property, the incident was handled by school authorities and the offender was punished by the school without the intervention of the police and the juvenile court system. However, as a result of new reporting requirements, schools must now report these incidents and crimes, which results in a rise in the juvenile crime rate but, in reality, no change in the actual number of crimes.

Despite the inclusive conclusions derived from crime statistics as to whether there is a greater rate of violent juvenile crime in the twenty-first century, the public perception is that violent juvenile crime is a serious problem. Thus, over the past two decades there have been significant changes in the processing of juveniles by the juvenile and criminal justice systems. Spurred by public concern over violent juvenile crimes, states have abandoned the "great experiment" that juveniles were not responsible for the crimes they commit. Many states have adopted a philosophy of accountability for violent crimes and have changed the provisions for transferring juveniles to the criminal court.

Mens Rea and Youthful Violent Offenders

One of the problems with juveniles who commit violent offenses, even murder, is the debate as to whether the youthful offender has sufficient *mens rea* to appreciate the criminality of his or her act. The causes of youth violence have been attributed to neighborhood decay and poverty in U.S. urban centers; unemployment (especially unemployment due to

HERE'S SOMETHING TO THINK ABOUT . . .

The U.S. Supreme Court has consistently ruled that the Constitution gives different rights to children than to adults. In the 2011 session the Supreme Court considered the Miranda rights of juveniles. In J.D.B. v. North Carolina, *the Supreme Court had to determine when a student was "in custody" when questioned in school by school administrators and police resource officers. In* Camreta v. Greene, *the Court was asked to decide when a child had the right to remain silent. In both cases, the Court ruled that a suspect's age must be taken into consideration in deciding whether to issue Miranda warnings. What should trigger when students should be read their Miranda rights?*

lack of minimal education, training, and skills); weak social networks such as those found in impoverished and ethnically diverse neighborhoods; and family and individual risk factors.[31]

Many researchers argue that youthful offenders

1. are not fully responsible for their criminal actions, or
2. do not have the same *mens rea* or criminal intent as adults due to their immaturity.

Often, this belief is reflected in state law. However, as has been previously discussed, state legislatures have become concerned about violent juvenile offenders and have enacted laws to remove violent juvenile offenders from the protection of the juvenile court.

Waiver to Criminal Court At what age a juvenile has the necessary maturity to form criminal intent and be fully accountable for his or her crime has not been resolved by researchers or state law. The minimum age for criminal liability varies by each state. However, beginning in the 1970s, state legislatures have increasingly moved juvenile offenders into criminal court based on age and/or offense seriousness, without the case-specific consideration offered by the discretionary juvenile court judicial waiver process.[32] This movement reduced the exclusive original jurisdiction of juvenile courts over youthful offenders. Each state has its own name for the process of moving the juvenile from the authority of the juvenile court to the adult criminal justice system. Common terms for the process include *judicial* ***waiver***, *certification, remand, bind over for criminal prosecution, transfer,* and *decline* (when waiver is denied). New provisions regulating waiver to criminal court have provided a variety of methods by which the juvenile can be waived to criminal court without the approval or, in some cases, without any intervention by the juvenile court.

Seriousness of the Offense Some states have established waiver criteria based on the offense independent of the age of the accused offender. Often, the criteria involve commission of crimes with firearms or other weapons or capital offenses. The majority of states have lowered the age at which juveniles can be waived to criminal court to below 17 years old. Some states have no minimum age for waiving a juvenile to criminal court for certain offenses. About 15 states have revoked the exclusive original jurisdiction granted to juvenile courts and replaced it with concurrent jurisdiction. In concurrent jurisdiction, the prosecutor has discretion to file certain cases, generally involving juveniles charged with serious offenses, in either criminal court or juvenile court. In states with concurrent jurisdiction, when a case meets certain criteria such as minimum age, crime committed with a weapon, prior criminal record, certain felonies (murder), or special circumstances, the prosecutor has the discretion of filing the case in criminal court. This **statutory exclusion** provision allows for transferring juveniles to criminal court without review and approval of the juvenile court. A majority of the states have adopted statutory exclusion and exclude certain serious offenses from juvenile court jurisdiction. The offenses most often excluded are capital crimes, murders, and other serious offenses against persons.[33] A majority of the states provide that if the juvenile has ever been tried and convicted as an adult, then he or she must be prosecuted in criminal court for any subsequent offenses regardless of the offense or age of the juvenile. In addition, about half the states have **blended sentencing options** to create a middle ground between traditional juvenile sanctions and adult sanctions.

22

States that have no minimum age for some juveniles to be waived to criminal court

HERE'S SOMETHING TO THINK ABOUT . . .

The criminal justice system is charged with protecting the health and safety of children. Many are concerned when they examine the statistics of children in the United States. The cases of child maltreatment has escalated since 1980, and in 2009 child protective services investigated nearly 2 million reports of maltreatment involving 3.6 million children. The most common types of victimization are neglect (62 percent), physical abuse (14 percent), and sexual abuse (8 percent). Over 50 percent of the victims are under 7 years of age. Parents are most often (80.7 percent) the perpetrators of these victimizations. Thirty percent of children live in one-parent or no-parent family arrangements. For about 40 percent of children in the United States, the family is low income to below the poverty level. Only 87 percent of Blacks and 76 percent of Hispanic completed high school in 2009. Explain how these statistics could suggest an increased risk of offending for at-risk adolescents.

Age of Accountability In 1899, when the Cook County (Chicago), Illinois, court system implemented the first separation of juvenile offenders and adult offenders, it was necessary to set an age that divided the two systems. Cook County set the legal end of childhood at age 18, which was actually quite old compared with the life experiences of the time. The average life expectancy at birth for Whites in 1900 was 46.3 for males (most delinquents were male). For Blacks the average life expectancy for males was only 32.5 years. At age 18 the average Black male could be considered "middle aged" in that he had less than 15 years' life expectancy. In 1899, it was not uncommon for 17-year-olds to marry, have gainful employment, and live separately from their parents. There is no evidence that Cook County used any scientific evidence or any criminological theories or studies to set the dividing line between adult and juvenile at 18 years old.

There is no agreement among states as to what constitutes the age of accountability. Although 17 years of age is the norm for state and federal courts, each state has established a lower age at which the juvenile offender can be transferred to the adult court. In recent years, many have questioned at what age an offender should be treated differently by the criminal justice system. Some members of the public believe 17 years of age is too old. They argue that children are more mature today, have

waiver the process of moving a juvenile from the authority of juvenile court to the adult criminal justice system

statutory exclusion provisions that allow for the transfer of juveniles to criminal court without review and approval of a juvenile court for certain crimes

blended sentencing option an option that allows the juvenile court or the criminal court to impose a sentence that can include both confinement in a juvenile facility and/or confinement in an adult prison after the offender is beyond the age of the juvenile court's jurisdiction

access to and use guns in the crimes they commit, and use the protection of the criminal justice system to avoid punishment for serious crimes such as murder, rape, drug trafficking, robbery, gang-related violence, and burglary. From 1985 to the early 1990s, the number of teenagers arrested for murder nearly tripled before declining sharply in the mid- and late 1990s. The fact that the juvenile crime rate dropped appears to be lost on the public. Among other factors causing public fear are media reports of violent attacks by youth gangs. For many, juvenile violence is perceived as "out of control" and more violent than ever before.

Processing the Youthful Offender Through the System

The adult criminal justice system has been shaped and influenced by extensive Supreme Court rulings, legislation, and oversight by the public and media. As a result, a general overview of the adult criminal justice system can fairly accurately reflect the processing of adult offenders among the various states. However, the juvenile justice system is much more diverse. Although Supreme Court decisions have provided more commonality in the due process rights of juveniles, the actual processing, the agencies, and the personnel involved in moving a juvenile from intake to rehabilitation differs from state to state. In a sense, there is no single juvenile justice system but a collection of juvenile justice systems. How juveniles are processed through the system depends a great deal on which state and sometimes which geographical region of the state the juvenile court is located.

Classification of Processing States can be divided into three general models of juvenile justice processing:

1. Centralized states
2. Decentralized states
3. Combination states[34]

The classification is based on how states organize their juvenile system, the delivery of services to juveniles, and who has authority over the juvenile system. The 12 centralized states[35] are characterized by a state executive agency having across-the-board state control of delinquency services, including state-run juvenile probation services, institutional commitments, and aftercare. The 18 states with decentralized juvenile systems are characterized by local control of the various juvenile services, such as juvenile courts, child welfare agencies, and aftercare services (i.e., probation services).[36] There are 21 states classified as having a combination juvenile system. Each of these states has a different juvenile system that is often an evolutionary outcome reflecting the unique problems, geography, and resources of the state. In combination states, the organization of the juvenile system is a mixture of state-controlled and locally operated juvenile services.[37] In these states, the juvenile court may be state controlled but aftercare facilities may be locally controlled. Another option is that the juvenile court

Juvenile Blended Sentencing Options

Blended sentencing options create a "middle ground" between traditional juvenile sanctions and adult sanctions.

Blended Sentencing Option	State
Juvenile-exclusive blend: The juvenile court may impose a sanction involving either the juvenile or adult correctional systems.	New Mexico

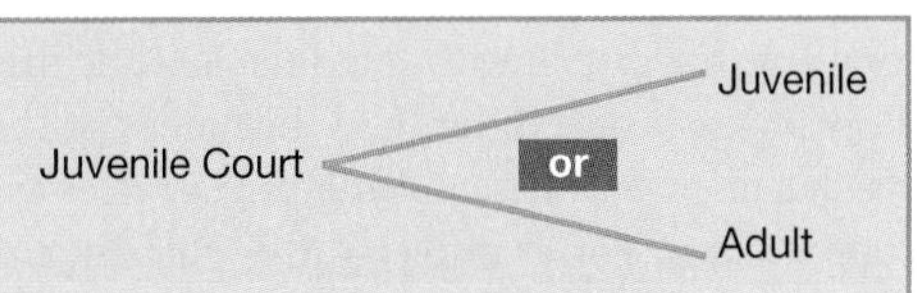

Blended Sentencing Option	State
Juvenile-inclusive blend: The juvenile court may impose both juvenile or adult correctional sanctions. The adult sanction is suspended pending a violation and revocation.	Connecticut Kansas Minnesota Montana

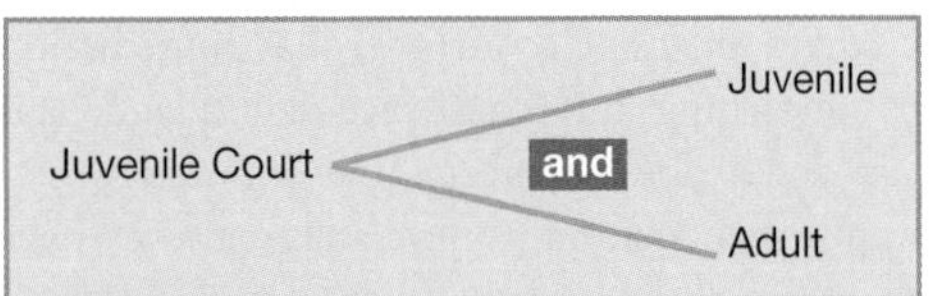

Blended Sentencing Option	State
Juvenile-contiguous blend: The juvenile court may impose a juvenile correctional sanction that may remain in force after the offender is beyond the age of the court's extended jurisdiction, at which point the offender may be transferred to the adult correctional system.	Colorado* Massachusetts Rhode Island South Carolina Texas

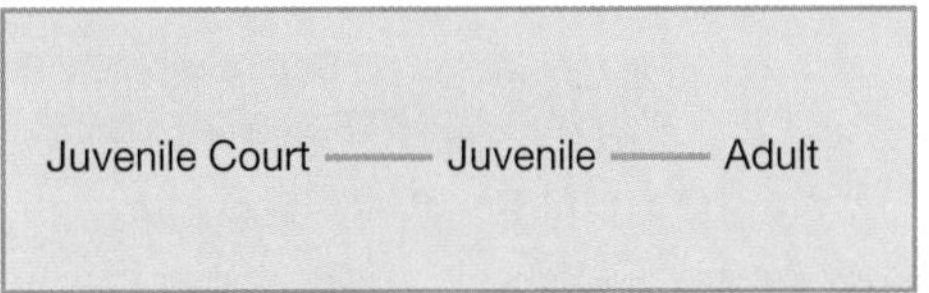

Blended Sentencing Option	State
Juvenile-exclusive blend: The criminal court may impose a sanction involving either the juvenile or adult correctional systems.	California Colorado** Florida Idaho Michigan Oklahoma Virginia West Virginia

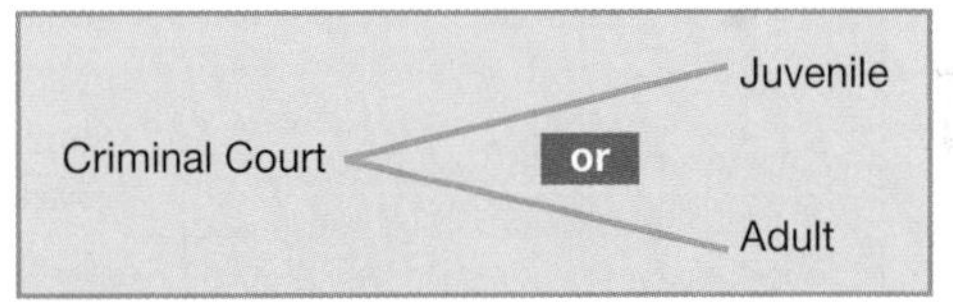

Blended Sentencing Option	State
Criminal-inclusive blend: The criminal court may impose both juvenile and adult correctional sanctions. The adult sanction is suspended, but is reinstated if the terms of the juvenile sanction are violated and revoked.	Arkansas Iowa Missouri Virginia***

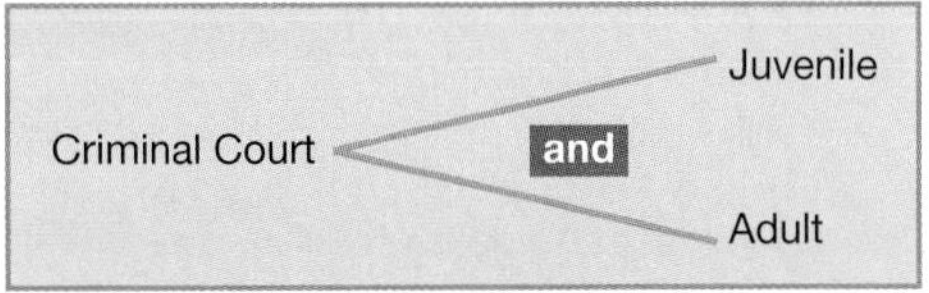

Note: Blends apply to a subset of juveniles specified by state statute.
*Applies to those designated as "aggravated juvenile offenders."
**Applies to those designated as "youthful offenders."
***Applies to those designated as "violent juvenile felony offenders."
Source: *Juvenile Offenders and Victims: 1999 National Report* (Washington DC: Office of Juvenile Justice and Delinquency Prevention, 1999), p. 108.

may be a combination of state-controlled courts for rural areas and locally controlled juvenile courts for major metropolitan areas. The authority responsible for the various juvenile services may be split between the executive and judicial branches. A common example of such a split is juvenile courts controlled by the judicial branch of state government and juvenile lockup facilities controlled by the executive branch of state government.

The unique nature of the juvenile system of each state provides some difficulty in generalizing the case flow through the juvenile justice system. The case flow for each state differs and the names of the various agencies, courts, detention facilities, and aftercare services are not consistent from state to state. For example, in this chapter, the term *juvenile court* has been used to describe the place and agency where juvenile court proceedings occur, but most states do not use this term. Such courts may be called *family court, probate court,* or terms similar to those used to identify the adult court system, such as *district court, superior court,* or *circuit court.* Such courts may have jurisdiction over a number of issues concerning children, such as delinquency, status offense, child welfare due to abuse or neglect, adoption, termination of parental rights, and emancipation. Some courts may even have jurisdiction over adult criminal acts involving the family, such as spouse abuse. For these reasons, the flowchart below, which shows a general diagram of the processing of a case through the juvenile justice system, may not be a good representation of the case flow in each state. However, it does provide a general overview of the processing of juveniles from intake to disposition.

Intake

There is significant difference in terminology in describing the juvenile justice system and the adult justice system, starting with the term to describe how the juvenile is processed into the system. In the adult system, the suspected offender is "arrested." Juveniles are not "arrested." The process whereby a juvenile enters the juvenile justice system is called **intake**. About 85 percent of juvenile intakes are initiated by the police. Larger police departments have special units staffed by police officers who are trained and specialize in handling juvenile offenders. This special training is necessary, as legislation and federal programs encourage and provide for the separation of adults from juveniles in all stages of processing through the system. The other 15 percent of juveniles can enter the system through *referral* by a parent or guardian, school official, social worker, juvenile probation officer, or juvenile court officer.

85% of juvenile intakes are initiated by the police.

15% enter the system through referral by parent or guardian, school official, social worker, juvenile probation officer, or juvenile court officer.

Unlike adults who are suspected and apprehended by the police for criminal activity, juveniles are not booked and generally are not placed in a lockup facility. Most juveniles who are apprehended by

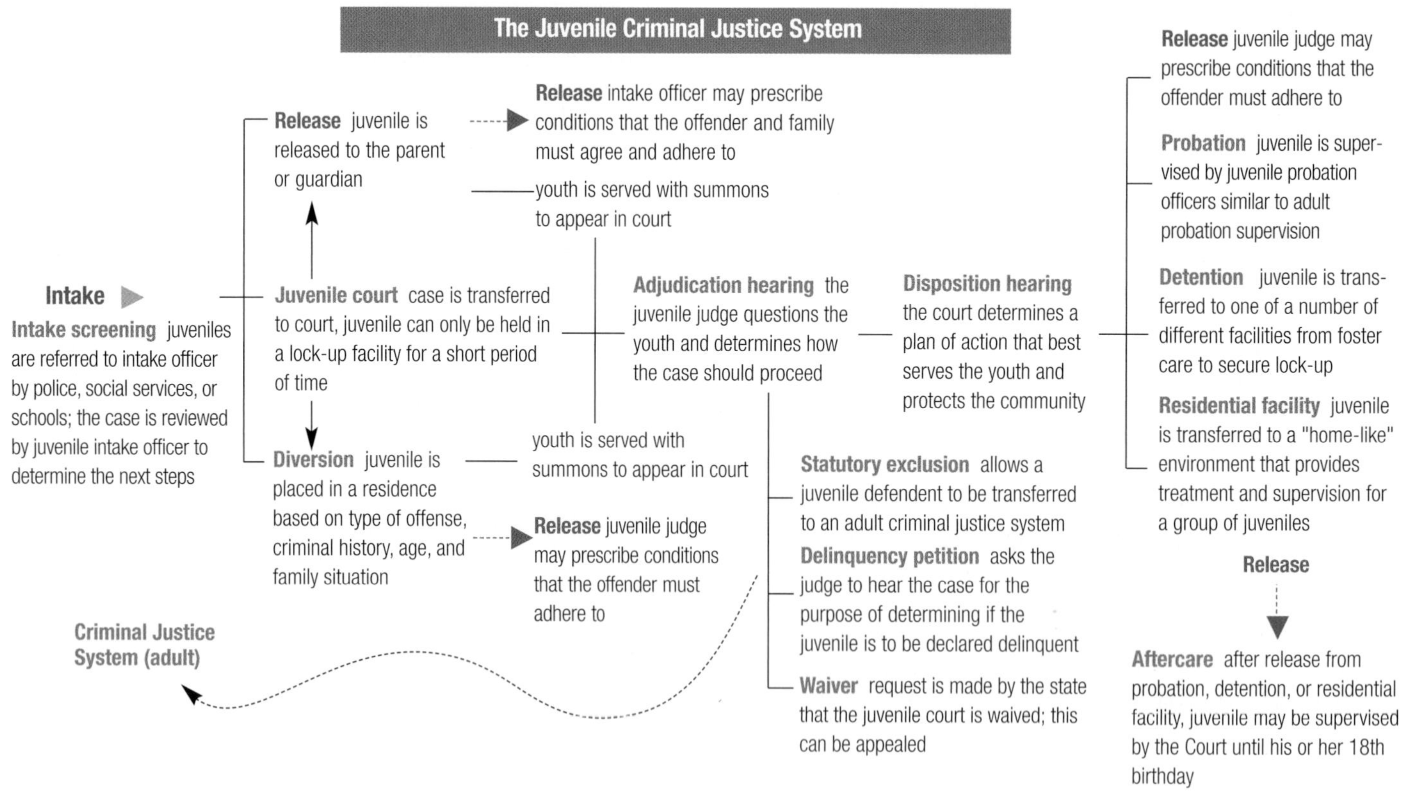

5 **A juvenile intake officer interviews and investigates the juvenile, his or her family, and environment and then decides whether to send the juvenile to juvenile court for formal processing, in which case a judge decides whether the juvenile is delinquent and should be placed in a residential facility or be diverted to more informal rehabilitation.**

intake the process whereby a juvenile enters the juvenile justice system

the police for criminal activity are released to a parent or guardian. In the case of apprehension for serious crimes or where the juvenile is thought to be a danger to himself or herself or to society, the juvenile may be placed in a secure lockup facility. Generally, federal regulations permit the police to detain a juvenile in a lockup facility for only a short period of time (6 hours) for the purpose of contacting the parent, guardian, or juvenile court. Juvenile lockup facilities cannot be within sight or sound of adult inmates.

If the juvenile is not a danger to self or society, the police may simply gather information concerning the alleged incident, return the child to the custody of a parent or guardian, and notify the juvenile court of the contact and forward a copy of the report to the juvenile court. The parent or guardian may be instructed to contact the juvenile court to make an appointment with an intake officer or the juvenile court may contact the parent or guardian when the court receives the police report.

Deciding Between Juvenile and Adult Jurisdiction

As previously mentioned, there are a number of offenses and circumstances in which the prosecutor for the criminal justice system may have concurrent jurisdiction or, in some cases, original jurisdiction. If the state law provides for statutory exclusion, the juvenile is transferred to the adult (criminal justice) system if the criteria for exclusion are satisfied. In cases of concurrent jurisdiction, the prosecuting attorney or district attorney and the juvenile court judge may confer as to whether to transfer the juvenile to the adult system. In some states the prosecuting attorney has the authority to request transfer without the consent of the juvenile court. In cases of certain violent crimes in all states the prosecuting attorney may request waiver of the juvenile to the adult system. In states with a minimum age for waiver, however, the juvenile may not be waived to the adult system if he or she was younger than this age when alleged to have committed the crime. Before the juvenile can be waived to the adult system, he or she is entitled to a waiver hearing in the juvenile court and is guaranteed certain due process rights previously discussed. If it is decided that the juvenile court will retain jurisdiction over the child, he or she is referred to a juvenile court intake officer. If the juvenile is waived to adult criminal court, the prosecuting attorney assumes responsibility for the case.

The Juvenile Intake Officer: Gatekeeper and Counselor

In some states juvenile court intake officers are essentially "probation officers," but unlike the adult system, where probation officers become involved after conviction, **juvenile intake officers** or juvenile probation officers are involved both when the child enters the system and in aftercare. Juvenile court intake officers "screen" cases with the purpose of diverting as many cases as possible from formal processing by the juvenile court judge. Juvenile intake officers have significant latitude in making decisions about how a juvenile case is to be processed. Their mission is to consider what is best for the child and, if possible, provide minimum contact with the juvenile justice system. Juvenile intake officers, unlike police in the adult system, are not bound by rigid prohibitions regarding "interrogation" and Miranda rights. The Supreme Court has provided juveniles with Miranda rights due process protection but generally the juvenile intake officer can extensively question the youth and/or the parents or guardian not only about the specific incident in question but also about the child's home life, behavior at school, past problems, social development, and general health.

In a typical intake interview, the juvenile intake officer interviews both the child and the parent or guardian and takes a "life history" of the child. For example, a child referred by the police for shoplifting may be asked by the juvenile intake officer to complete psychological

HERE'S SOMETHING TO THINK ABOUT . . .

Each state and the federal government has its own separate juvenile justice system and structure. Thus, applying for employment and the minimum requirements differ by state. A juvenile probation officer may be an employee of the district court, the state administrative office of the court, or in some cases a combination of structures. Juvenile probation officers perform many tasks that differ from adult probation officers. In a sense, they act as prosecutors in that they screen which cases are to be referred for formal adjudication and which will be handled by other means. Juvenile probation officers routinely are expected to conduct life histories, investigate home conditions, and provide counseling services. The most common form of counseling that the juvenile probation officer provides is group counseling. The minimum educational requirement for state juvenile probation officers is a bachelor's degree, and a master's degree for federal employment. Often those who apply for these positions have degrees in fields other than criminal justice such as counseling, social work, and psychology. Juvenile probation officers usually are not law enforcement officers and do not carry weapons or have general powers of arrest, search, and seizure. The typical workweek is Monday through Friday and the salary range is $25,271 to $56,049. What are some college classes that would be essential for those considering employment in juvenile probation?

juvenile intake officer a person who is responsible for both processing a juvenile into the juvenile justice system and for aftercare if the juvenile is adjudicated, and has duties similar to a police officer and a probation and parole officer

and social assessment instruments. Rather than focus on the immediate "crime" in question, as is required in the adult system, the juvenile intake officer may attempt to determine if there are other emotional, cognitive, or affective behaviors that should be examined. The juvenile intake officer, in a sense, tries to find the cause of the behavior and assess the overall well-being of the child. He or she wants to know why the child shoplifted: was it due to poor parental supervision, gang involvement, peer pressure, need, or what? Are there other behaviors, such as depression or suicidal thoughts, that should be addressed? Is the child in an abusive environment? Frequently, the same juvenile intake officer who handles children accused of crimes will also handle other referrals, such as child abuse cases, school delinquency, and status offenders. Regardless of the reason for which the child is referred to the juvenile court, the intake process strives to provide for a thorough review of the total conditions in the child's life.

One of the purposes of this review is to determine if the child can be diverted from further processing by the juvenile justice system. If possible, in lieu of further processing, the juvenile intake officer will refer the juvenile and/or parents to mental health care, a welfare agency, a diversion program, a counseling program, a school program, or some similar alternative. The juvenile intake officer may simply "counsel" the juvenile and/or parents or guardian and close the case. About half the cases referred to juvenile court are handled informally.

Likewise, the juvenile intake officer might believe that the case merits further review. Even a referral for a minor offense can result in extensive mandatory psychological examinations and investigations into the well-being and living environment of the child. If it is decided that the living environment of the child is a major contributor to the delinquent behavior and/or is a threat to the welfare of the child, the juvenile intake officer may initiate proceedings to remove the child from the parent or guardian and place him or her in foster or residential care. In such cases, the child is not being punished. The juvenile intake officer makes such recommendations because he or she is concerned about the welfare and best interests of the child.

If a case is handled "informally" by the juvenile intake officer, it is common for him or her to prescribe behaviors and conditions to which the juvenile and/or parents or guardian must agree. These conditions can include regular school attendance, attendance in drug or alcohol programs, attendance in special diversion programs designed to cause a change in the child's behavior, curfew, restitution if there was property damage, counseling, abstaining from gang membership, and so on. The juvenile intake officer will commit these conditions to writing, specify the time frame, and obtain the agreement of the child and/or parents or guardian. These conditions are generally called a *consent decree.*

THE DISCRETION AND POWER OF JUVENILE INTAKE OFFICERS IS QUITE EXTENSIVE AND THERE IS NO EQUIVALENT POSITION IN THE ADULT CRIMINAL JUSTICE SYSTEM.

The discretion and power of juvenile intake officers is quite extensive and there is no equivalent position in the adult criminal justice system. Juvenile intake officers have authority similar to "beat" police officers in that they can decide to handle a referral informally or to process the youth formally. They also have authority similar to prosecuting attorneys in that they act as gatekeepers as to which cases are forwarded to the court and which are handled by diversion.

Formal Processing

If the juvenile intake officer determines that it is appropriate to refer the child to the juvenile court for formal processing, he or she must decide if the child is to remain with the parent or placed in the care of the state while waiting for processing by the juvenile court. Most children remain in the custody of their parent or guardian while waiting for their court appearance before the juvenile judge. Thus, there is no arraignment, grand jury, or preliminary hearing necessary, or even possible, as there is in bringing an adult offender before a criminal court for trial.

Once the case is referred to the juvenile court for formal processing, known as a **juvenile adjudication hearing**, the juvenile judge becomes the central figure in determining how the case is to be processed. The juvenile judge is much more involved in the formal hearing than the judge in a criminal trial and may question the youth and witnesses and be more involved in the inquiry of facts concerning the case. Again, there is a difference in the terminology describing the juvenile justice system and the criminal justice system. Juveniles have hearings or formal court proceedings but not trials. If the juvenile intake officer deems a formal hearing appropriate, a **delinquency petition** or waiver petition is forwarded to the juvenile court judge. A delinquency petition asks a judge to adjudicate, or hear and judge, the case in a formal hearing to determine whether the juvenile is to be declared delinquent. A waiver petition requests that the judge transfer the youth to criminal court.

Unlike adult criminal trials that are rigorously scripted as to form and procedure, there is much more leeway in juvenile adjudication hearings. This apparent informality in court procedure is not surprising, given that until *In re Gault* (1967), attorneys representing the defense were conspicuously absent from the juvenile adjudication hearing. However, as previously mentioned, recent Supreme Court rulings have established that the juvenile be afforded certain due process rights at these court proceedings, and as a result the juvenile hearing has more characteristics of a "trial" than before due process rights were required. The juvenile has the right to cross-examine the witnesses and evidence against him or her and to call witnesses on his or her behalf. However, juvenile hearings are distinct from criminal trials. One of the most obvious differences is that neither juvenile hearings nor a transcript of the trial is available to the public. If the

juvenile adjudication hearing the formal hearing conducted by a juvenile judge to conduct an inquiry of the facts concerning a case and to decide the disposition of the case and any rehabilitation, supervision, or punishment for the juvenile

delinquency petition a request to a judge to hear and judge a juvenile case in a formal hearing for the purpose of determining whether the juvenile is to be declared delinquent

case is referred to the juvenile court for formal processing, one of the options of the court is to deem it appropriate and legally permissible to transfer the juvenile to the adult system. An alternative to formal processing by the juvenile court is for the juvenile to be referred to an alternative court, such as teen court or drug court. These courts handle specialized cases.

Teen Courts Teen courts are usually used for younger juveniles (ages 10 to 15) with no prior arrest record who are charged with less serious law violations, such as shoplifting, vandalism, and disorderly conduct.[38] Teen courts are described by the Office of Juvenile Justice and Delinquency Prevention as different from other juvenile justice programs because young people rather than adults determine the disposition, given a broad array of sentencing options made available by adults overseeing the program.[39] The premise underlying teen courts is that peer pressure is a powerful deterrent to delinquent behavior.

Juvenile Drug Courts Drug use among teenagers is a significant problem, and **juvenile drug courts** are being used instead of traditional adjudication processes to work toward long-term success and rehabilitation of these offenders. According to the Office of Juvenile Justice and Delinquency Prevention, "Juvenile drug courts provide (1) intensive and continuous judicial supervision over delinquency and status offense cases that involve substance-abusing juveniles and (2) coordinated and supervised delivery of an array of support services necessary to address the problems that contribute to juvenile involvement in the justice system."[40] Juvenile drug courts, like adult drug courts, have emerged only since 1989 but are quickly being adopted nationwide.

JUVENILE DRUG COURTS, LIKE ADULT DRUG COURTS, HAVE EMERGED ONLY SINCE 1989 BUT ARE QUICKLY BEING ADOPTED NATIONWIDE.

Juvenile drug courts are designed to respond as quickly as possible to delinquent activity so that offenders are held accountable and intrusive intervention can occur to provide treatment and sanction options.[41] Programs provide for court-supervised substance abuse treatment and core services addressing the needs of the juveniles and their families, including educational needs, behavioral problems, and family therapy. The hallmark of juvenile drug courts is the intensive, continuous judicial monitoring and supervision of participants.[42]

1/2 to 3/4

of youths who enter juvenile drug court programs complete the program.

Juvenile drug court programs recognize the challenge of addressing family issues. The operating premise is that if family issues are not addressed, it is likely that the child will continue to be involved with drugs and delinquent activity. As a result, a number of programs require parent or guardian supervision and utilize the Multi-Systemic Therapy (MST) approach to provide family-based treatment and to teach parenting skills.[43]

Extensive data are not available to evaluate the effectiveness of juvenile drug courts, but "judges anecdotally report that these programs are able to achieve greater accountability and provide a broad array of treatment and other services to youth and their families than traditional juvenile courts."[44] One half to three fourths of youths who enter juvenile drug court programs complete the program.[45] Initial analysis of indicators such as recidivism, drug use, and educational achievement seems to indicate that juvenile drug courts are providing better rehabilitation of youths than are traditional juvenile courts.[46]

Adjudication

The juvenile judge has great latitude in conducting juvenile hearings. There is no constitutional right to a jury trial (although a few states do provide for this option), so the final decision as to the outcome of the case is made by the judge. If the judge concludes that the juvenile committed the offense, the judge does not find the juvenile "guilty" but "delinquent."

If the youth is declared delinquent, similar to the sentencing hearing in the adult criminal justice system, there is a procedure to determine the appropriate course of action. This procedure is called a *disposition hearing* in some states. However, unlike the adult criminal justice system, delinquency does not mean the juvenile is to be punished. Delinquency means the court will develop a plan of action that best benefits the youth and provides for the safety of the community. The juvenile judge has the option of referring the delinquent to a secure lockup facility similar to a prison, mandating counseling, or imposing an informal plan of action. Judges can be quite creative in the action plans they develop. For example, when a 14-year-old Roanoke, Virginia, youth was adjudicated of sending threatening e-mails to federal officials, including a threat to kill President Bush, bomb the White House, and bomb the library, Juvenile and Domestic Relations Court Judge Joseph Bounds ordered the youth to complete a stay at a group home for boys, complete 48 hours of community service, and write a research paper on homeland security without using the Internet.

Similar to the presentence investigation prior to the dispositional hearing, a juvenile probation officer or court officer may be asked to make a dispositional recommendation. The recommendation will be based on data about the juvenile's past criminal and/or gang involvement; background investigations, especially the performance and behavior of the youth in school; interviews and/or psychological evaluations and diagnostic tests; and information gathered from the delinquent's

juvenile drug court an alternative to the traditional adjudication process for juveniles with substance abuse problems that focuses on rehabilitation and eliminating drug abuse

Very young offenders are at high risk of becoming serious, chronic, and violent offenders; youth gangs are often gateways into adult criminal gangs but new hybrid youth gangs are difficult for communities and law enforcement to identify; there is very little research on female gangs; and juvenile drug use appears to be increasing in some areas.

6

parents or guardians. At the dispositional hearing, the court officer prosecuting the case and the juvenile or his or her attorney will have the opportunity to make their own recommendations and to comment on the recommendations of the juvenile probation officer or court official.

Detention and Probation (Aftercare)

Unlike the adult criminal justice system, juveniles are not sentenced to jail or prison. When a juvenile is adjudicated and his or her petition is sustained, the judge then decides whether the delinquent youth should become a ward of the state and be placed in a residential facility or enter a course of rehabilitation, such as drug or alcohol counseling, restitution, or community service. Because the action of the juvenile judge is not a "sentence" and is not prescribed by legislation or sentencing guidelines, juvenile judges have great latitude in setting a course of action for the delinquent. The judge may but does not have to place a specific time for the termination of the court's authority over the adjudicated delinquent. The jurisdiction of the juvenile court is limited by legislation when the juvenile reaches a certain age, usually 21 years old, but notwithstanding this limit, the orders of the court may specify that the delinquent remain under the court's jurisdiction until specific requirements are met or until the delinquent is "cured."

Data from the state of California's Legislative Analyst's Office indicate that few juveniles are processed through the entire juvenile justice system and arrive at this end point. For every 1,000 juveniles in the California system cited by the police, only 25 will be referred for formal hearings and of that 25, only 12 will actually have a formal hearing. Of the 12 formal hearings, 6 juveniles will be referred to formal probation. Only 1 in 1,000 youths will be removed to residential placement.

25 of every **1,000**
juveniles in the California system will be referred for formal hearings

of that **25** only **12** will have a formal hearing

and of that **12** only **6** juveniles will be referred to formal probation

and **1** of the original 1,000 juveniles will be removed to residential placement.

Residential Placement As in the case of adult prisons, juvenile residential placement has levels of security. Residential placement must be able to accommodate not only juveniles who have committed serious violent crimes but also status offenders and juveniles who have been removed from parents or guardians for their own welfare due to neglect or physical or sexual abuse.[47] Thus, residential placement facilities can range from foster care in individual homes, to group homes, to long-term placement residential facilities, to secure lockup facilities that very much resemble adult medium-security prisons. The type of placement will depend on the characteristics of the youth, such as age and mental health, and the crime committed by the youth. Violent offenders who have committed crimes against persons, especially gang-related crimes and crimes involving firearms, will generally be placed in secure lockup facilities, whereas nonviolent and status offenders are more likely to be placed in homelike settings with minimum security. Often, the latter will be placed in a residential facility but will attend a local school. On the other hand, violent juvenile offenders will not be allowed to leave the secure lockup facility in which they are placed and the state must provide for continued opportunities for school within the facility.

Mental Health Concerns One of the major concerns of the juvenile court when a child is placed in a residential facility is the mental health of the child. Surveys indicate that a very high percentage of children under the authority of the juvenile system have psychiatric disorders. One survey by the Office of Justice Programs reported that approximately 67 percent of youths in the juvenile justice system have mental health problems that may have contributed to their criminal behavior and that are likely to interfere with rehabilitation. Also, these children have emotional impairments due to an untreated mental disorder that may contribute to an adverse reaction to confinement.[48] Mental disorders can be divided into two primary groups: those related to alcohol and drug use, and those described as nonsubstance use disorders, such as anxiety disorders, conduct disorders, depression, obsessive-compulsive disorders, posttraumatic stress, and social phobias. Most disorders of youths in the juvenile setting (49.3 percent) are related to substance use. Another concern for the mental health of youths is juvenile suicides. Juvenile suicides are a major cause of death for juveniles older than age 6. For example, the number of youth ages 13 to 14 who commit suicide equals the number who are murdered.[49] Over 9 percent of youths in juvenile settings report thinking about committing suicide in the past month, nearly 12 percent report attempting suicide, and almost 3 percent report attempting suicide within the past month.[50]

67%
of youths in the juvenile system have mental health problems.

49.3%
of youths in the juvenile system have disorders related to substance abuse.

12%
of youths in juvenile settings report that they have attempted suicide.

Juvenile Probation (Aftercare) Juvenile probation or aftercare is similar to the concept of adult probation. In fact, John Augustus, a founder of the probation movement, started the movement by diverting boys from 7 to 15 years of age away from sentencing. Juvenile probation is also called *aftercare*. The goal of probation or aftercare is to provide treatment services that will extinguish the delinquent behavior and prevent the juvenile from reentering either the juvenile justice system or the adult criminal justice system. Probation service agencies and personnel are divided into those that provide for juvenile probation services and those that provide for adult probation services. Similar to the criminal justice system, the juvenile justice system has experimented with various forms of probation services, including intensive probation. However, an evaluation of model juvenile intensive aftercare programs does not suggest that there is any difference between "regular" juvenile aftercare services and intensive aftercare services, as measured by subsequent delinquent/criminal involvement of participants and areas of youth functioning (e.g., substance abuse, family functioning) that are theoretically and empirically linked to recidivism.[51] One of the suggestions of the study was that the no-difference finding may be explained by the fact that unlike "typical" adults on probation, juveniles already receive a relatively high level of probation services, and the intensity of supervision provided by the intensive aftercare programs may not have been significantly different from that of the control group.[52]

THE GOAL IS TO ALTER THE CHARACTER AND VALUES OF THE OFFENDER, AS JUVENILES ARE SEEN AS MORE LIKELY TO CHANGE.

Juvenile Boot Camps A hybrid model of treatment for juveniles that involves elements from both residential placement and probation is **juvenile boot camps**. Juvenile boot camps are popular treatment programs for juvenile delinquents.[53] The goal of treatment is to alter the character and values of the offender, as juveniles are seen as more likely to change than are older offenders.[54] Some authorities are critical of this modality of treatment for juvenile offenders, however. They argue that the military-style strict discipline and group-oriented environment "is a direct opposition to the type of positive interpersonal relationships and supportive atmosphere that are needed for youths' positive development."[55]

Another major criticism of juvenile boot camps is the lack of follow-up after release. Adults released from boot camp usually are released to the supervision of probation and parole. In fact, many adult shock incarceration programs release offenders into intensive probation services programs rather than regular probation and parole supervision. Critics of juvenile boot camps express the concern that if juveniles are released back into the community after these brief periods in boot camps, without community-based supervision and follow-up support, they will "revert to their old ways of surviving in and relating to the community in which they live."[56] Research indicates that youths who participate in boot camps have more positive perceptions of their institutional environment than do juveniles in traditional facilities, but the lack of follow-up data makes it difficult to judge the impact of boot camps on recidivism rates.[57]

Private Boot Camp Programs An interesting development in shock incarceration or boot camp programs is the proliferation of private programs for troubled youths. These private programs occur in a wide variety of settings, including wilderness camps, at-sea camps, and military-style camps. These private camps mimic state-operated camps but charge parents for treatment programs that promise to help them with their delinquent or out-of-control children. Some states allow for juveniles to be diverted from the formal juvenile justice system into these private camps. Although they may appear similar to state-operated programs, many are unregulated businesses and have been criticized for their lack of standards and even the safety of the environment in which the juvenile is placed. One Arizona state senator, critical of the lack of regulation, said of private boot camps in the state of Arizona, "You have to provide more documents to get a fishing license than to run a camp for young boys. We require nothing to demonstrate you have the qualifications to engage in this type of activity."[58]

Nationwide, there are approximately 400 private boot camps for juveniles.[59] Many are not regulated by the state in which they operate, and there have been numerous complaints of child abuse and questionable therapeutic programs and practices. Often, parents who place their children in these facilities have high hopes but little knowledge of the practices and competency of the staff.[60] As a result of the reports of abuse and questionable practices, there is a movement toward bringing proper oversight to private boot camps and strengthening state laws to regulate them to protect the children and youths they are intended to serve.[61]

HERE'S SOMETHING TO THINK ABOUT . . .

According to the Office of Juvenile Justice and Delinquency the number of delinquency cases judicially waived to criminal court grew by 90 percent between 1985 and 1994 and then declined 35 percent through 2008. Crimes against persons cases (50 percent) represent the largest share of waived cases in 2008. What factors do you think account for the changes in the number of delinquency cases waived to criminal court?

juvenile boot camp a military-style group-oriented rehabilitation program designed to alter the character and values of the juvenile offender

HERE'S SOMETHING TO THINK ABOUT . . .

Scared straight programs are aimed at reducing juvenile offending. The program usually involves visits by at-risk youth to adult prisons and interactions with adult offenders who explicitly impress upon them the harsh reality of prison life. In 2011, A&E Television Networks aired the reality show Beyond Scared Straight. *While popular with the public and often used throughout the United States, "scared straight" type programs do not work. Studies have shown that the use of such programs generally increased crime up to 28 percent. The Justice Department has denounced the use of these programs as ineffective and potential violations of the law. Why do you think these programs remain popular with the public?*

Juvenile Death Penalty

The death penalty is not a sanction permitted by the juvenile court. However, juveniles who have been waived to the criminal justice system or who have committed murder in a state where the criminal court has concurrent or original jurisdiction over juveniles have been sentenced to the death penalty. The practice of allowing persons under the age of 18 at the time of their crime to be in jeopardy of capital punishment, even though they have been declared an adult by the court system or state legislation, is highly controversial in the United States.

Thompson v. Oklahoma Nationwide concern over the evolving standards of decency has resulted in scrutiny of the question by the United States Supreme Court. The courts have been actively involved in monitoring the juvenile death penalty as illustrated by the fact that 50 percent of under-age-18 death sentences have been reversed.[62] In early cases, the Supreme Court considered the merits of each case in deciding whether to reverse the death sentence but did not make a general ruling on the constitutionality of the juvenile death penalty. However, in *Thompson v. Oklahoma* (1988), the Supreme Court ruled that national standards of decency did not permit the execution of any offender under age 16 at the time of the crime.[63] The plurality of the Court concluded that "it would offend civilized standards of decency to execute a person who was less than 16 years old at the time of his or her offense." The Court cited the U.S. Anglo-American heritage, the practices of the state, the standards of Western Europe, and the practices of other nations as the criteria for arriving at a standard of decency that prohibited the death penalty for those younger than age 16 at the time they committed their crime. Also, the opinion of the Court was based on its belief that there was lesser culpability for offenders under age 16 and that offenders under 16 years old did not engage in "the kind of cost-benefit analysis that attaches any weight to the possibility of execution," thereby making the death penalty an ineffective deterrent. A year later, the Supreme Court ruled in *Stanford v. Kentucky* that although standards of decency prohibited the execution of juveniles under 16 years old at the time of their crime, the Eighth and Fourteenth Amendments did not prohibit the execution of juvenile offenders over 15 years old but under 18 years old.[64]

Juvenile Death Penalty Revisited In 2005, the Supreme Court again visited the question of the juvenile death penalty. In 1993, at the age of 17, when he was still a junior in high school, Christopher Simmons conspired with two friends, ages 15 and 16, to commit burglary and murder. Simmons, the ringleader, assured his coconspirators that they could "get away with it" because they were minors. The 16-year-old renounced his intention to conspire with the other two to follow through with the crimes on the night of the murder, but the other two carried out their plan, which resulted in the death of the victim, Shirley Crook. Simmons was quickly connected to the crime because of his public statements about killing Crook. He was arrested by the police, advised of his Miranda rights, and after 2 hours of interrogation confessed to the crime. Citing aggravating factors, the State of Missouri was successful in obtaining the death penalty for Simmons in adult court. The prosecutor argued to the jury that the murder "involved depravity of mind and was outrageously and wantonly vile, horrible, and inhuman." Simmons's attorney appealed the death sentence to the Missouri Supreme Court and to the United States Supreme Court but both upheld the death sentence.[65]

Roper, Superintendent, Potosi Correctional Center v. Simmons After Simmons lost his appeal, the Supreme Court held in *Atkins v. Virginia* (2002) that the Eighth and Fourteenth Amendments prohibit the execution of persons with mental retardation,[66] which was held to be subject to the excessive sanctions clause of the Eighth Amendment due to the reduced culpability of offenders with mental retardation. When the Court recognized diminished culpability as a mitigating factor in the death penalty and previous Court cases had already established that juveniles have diminished culpability, Simmons's attorney asked the Court to reconsider the case. In ***Roper, Superintendent, Potosi Correctional Center v. Simmons*** (2005), the Supreme Court held that the Eighth and Fourteenth Amendments forbid imposition of the death penalty on offenders who were under the age of 18 when their crimes were committed. The ruling closes the debate on the juvenile death penalty for now. The ruling also voided the death sentence of approximately 70 juveniles on death row. (The ruling does not void their conviction, but their sentence will be changed from death to life in prison.)

Roper, Superintendent, Potosi Correctional Center v. Simmons a case in which the Supreme Court held that the Eighth and Fourteenth Amendments forbid imposition of the death penalty on offenders who were under the age of 18 when their crimes were committed

Life Imprisonment Without Parole The United States was virtually alone in allowing juveniles who did not commit homicide to be sentenced to life without parole. In *Graham v. Florida* (2010) the Court reconsidered the application of the Eighth Amendment to life sentences for juveniles for nonhomicide crimes. Some states such as Texas had already banned such sentences, but 37 states and the federal government allowed life sentences without parole for juveniles. When the Court heard arguments in the case that such sentences were so harsh as to be unconstitutional, there were 129 juveniles in 11 states who had not committed homicides but were serving sentences of life without parole.

The Court found that "denying juveniles who have not committed homicide a chance to ever rejoin society is counter to national and global consensus and violates the Constitution's ban on cruel and unusual punishment." The ruling does not ban life sentences without parole for homicide.

The Juvenile as Offender

Sociological Explanations

Sociological explanations of criminal behavior were the most popular theories during the twentieth century. In general, sociological studies attempted to identify when children first started offending, what influenced their decision, what reinforced delinquent behavior, and what was the impact of such influences as social norms, school, culture, self-image, and parenting on juvenile behavior. Especially in the mid-twentieth century, the predominant sociological theories explaining criminal behavior identified environmental and social factors as strong determinants of criminal behavior. Theorists hypothesized that adult criminals did not suddenly undergo a transformation in adult life from being a law-abiding citizen to a criminal. They based their theories on the premise that criminal behavior was learned behavior or was behavior that resulted from influences acting over time to shape and determine behavior. Thus, if criminal behavior was learned or developed over time as a result of interaction, the criminologists reasoned that if one could isolate and identify those variables that promoted criminal behavior and those that suppressed criminal behavior, it would be possible to understand the processes that cause a person to become an adult criminal. Sociologists studied populations of children in an effort to identify the onset of delinquency and the earliest determinants that influenced children's behavior and development.

Over time, some of the hypotheses as to the cause of juvenile delinquency and later adult criminality have been discarded or minimized. However, research and criminal justice practitioners have reinforced the hypothesis of other theories. Many of the researchers whose theories have been helpful in the clarification of juvenile delinquency tended to focus their research on delinquency in school-aged children. Recent research has suggested that the origins of serious and violent juvenile criminality (and later adult criminality) may have its origins in risk factors that begin in early childhood.

OJJDP's Study Group on Very Young Offenders

The study of very young children may yield knowledge that can reduce juvenile delinquency and diminish the number of delinquents who continue their criminality into adulthood. In 1998, the Office of Juvenile Justice and Delinquency Prevention (OJJDP) formed a Study Group on Serious and Violent Juvenile Offenders. The group undertook a 2-year analysis of existing data focusing on the preschool and elementary years. The OJJDP described the group as consisting of 16 primary study group members and 23 coauthors who were experts on criminology, child delinquency, psychopathology, and the law. The group reviewed hundreds of studies, undertook many special analyses, and gathered data from a survey of more than 100 practitioners in the field, concentrating on the delinquent behavior of children ages 7 to 12 and on children's persistently disruptive and precociously deviant behavior from the toddler years up to adolescence.[67]

Early Delinquency Leads to Later Delinquency The Study Group on Very Young Offenders reported that child delinquents (juveniles between the ages of 7 and 12) are two to three times more likely to become serious, violent, and chronic offenders than adolescents whose delinquent behavior begins in their teens.[68] "In more than 20 studies they reviewed, the Study Group found a significant relationship between an early onset of delinquency and later crime and delinquency. Child delinquents, compared with a later onset of delinquency, are at greater risk of becoming serious, violent, and chronic offenders and have longer delinquency careers."[69] The Study Group reported that there was a significant relationship between delinquency and persistent disruptive behavior as a

HERE'S SOMETHING TO THINK ABOUT . . .

Status offenses are acts committed by juveniles which are only illegal because of their age. One of the acts of most concern is underage drinking. At one time the legal age for drinking some alcoholic beverages was 18. Now it is 21 in most states. Thus, underage drinking can be a juvenile status offense and an adult criminal offense. Media campaigns such as the 0013 campaign attempt to discourage underage drinking and DWI by youths. One of the problems in stopping underage drinking is the ready and inexpensive availability of high-quality fake identification cards from the Internet. While such IDs are illegal they are difficult to police as many come from suppliers outside the United States. Often those who use fake IDs have little appreciation for the criminality of their actions. Are public media campaigns effective in influencing the illegal behavior of adolescents?

young child (i.e., preschool aged).[70] Further, the data showed that children with persistent disruptive behavior are likely to become child delinquents and, in turn, child delinquents are likely to become serious, violent, or chronic juvenile offenders. The research data showed that the antisocial careers of male juvenile offenders start, on average, at age 7. The conclusion of the Study Group was that the preschool period is critical in setting a foundation for preventing the development of disruptive behavior and, eventually, child delinquency.[71] The group concluded that the majority of child delinquents have a history of disruptive behavior, such as aggressive, inattentive, or sensational-seeking behavior, in the preschool period but the majority of preschoolers with such behavior problems do not go on to become young offenders.[72] Figure 12.1 shows the relationship between child delinquency and serious, violent, or chronic offending as a teen or adult.

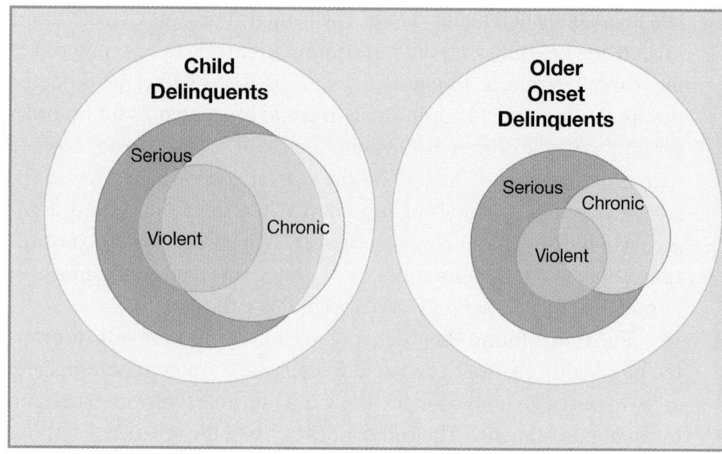

FIGURE 12.1 Very young offenders have a greater percentage of serious, violent, and chronic careers than older onset delinquents.

Source: R. Loeber, D. Farrington, and D. Petechuk. *Child Delinquency: Early Intervention and Prevention.* (Washington, D.C. U.S. Department of Justice Office of Juvenile Justice and Delinquency Prevention), May 2003.

At-Risk Factors The Study Group reported that behavior and influences that place a child at risk for an early career of disruptive behavior and child delinquency can be identified as early as 2 years of age and include many factors that have been identified by the more popular criminological theories of crime causation.[73] The Study Group concluded that no single risk factor explains child delinquency but the greater the number of risk factors, the greater the number of risk-factor domains (family, school, etc.), and the greater the exposure to these risks, the greater the likelihood of early-onset offending.[74]

During the preschool years, the most important risk factors stem from the individual and family. This finding is consistent with theories that genetic factors, personality, and family environment and parenting skills predetermine behavior. As the child matures, later influences include peers, school, and community. The data are especially supportive of Sutherland's differential association theory, Reckless's containment theory, and Hirschi's social bond theory regarding the predicting of delinquent behavior. The data showed a correlation between such factors as delinquent behavior and deviant peers, commitment to school and community, and the presence or lack of supervision or outside forces to prevent or intervene in the event of aggressive, antisocial, or disruptive behaviors. Also, the data supported social disorganization and zone theories of crime causation. The study showed a high correlation between a high level of poverty in a neighborhood and early onset of aggressive, inattentive, or sensation-seeking behavior in the preschool years. The data did not demonstrate a relationship between very young offending and race and gender.[75] Figure 12.2 summarizes the risk factors associated with disruptive and delinquent behavior identified by the Study Group.

THERE SHOULD BE A SHIFT OF FOCUS FROM ADOLESCENT DELINQUENTS TO CHILD DELINQUENTS TO PREVENT HIGH-RISK CHILDREN FROM BECOMING TOMORROW'S INCARCERATED OFFENDERS.

The Study Group concluded that there should be a shift of focus from adolescent delinquents to child delinquents to prevent high-risk children from becoming tomorrow's incarcerated offenders.[76] The group also concluded that current juvenile justice, mental health, and child welfare programs were ineffective in dealing with child delinquents.[77] According to the study, effective preventive intervention required the coordinated delivery of services from numerous agencies but that these agencies were severely fragmented, resulting in ineffective preventive intervention. As a result, the juvenile court has come to serve as a "dumping ground for a wide variety of problem behaviors of children that other institutions (e.g., social, mental health, and child protective services) fail to serve adequately."[78] Finally, the Study Group concluded that policymakers were misguided in focusing on programs for older adolescent delinquents. Early preventive interventions were said to be more effective in terms of both reducing delinquency and cost effectiveness. For example, the Study Group asserted that for every dollar spent on preventive interventions for very young at-risk children, taxpayers and crime victims were saved more than $7.[79]

Youth Gangs

There are various types of gangs—motorcycle gangs, hate or ideology groups, prison gangs, and others. Many researchers are especially interested in youth gangs. The term *youth gangs* is difficult to define. Even the OJJDP depends on local definitions when it conducts its national survey on youth gangs and asks respondents to report data on youth gangs. In the survey, a youth gang is defined as "a group of youths or young adults in your jurisdiction that you or other responsible persons in your agency or community are willing to identify or classify as a 'gang.'"[80] The

Approximate Development Ordering of Risk Factors Associated with Disruptive and Delinquent Behavior

	Risk Factors Emerging During Pregnancy and From Infancy Onward		Risk Factors Emerging from Mid-childhood Onward
Child	Pregnancy and delivery complications	***Child***	Stealing and general delinquency
	Neurological insult		Early onset of other disruptive behaviors
	Exposure to neurotoxins after birth		Early onset of substance use and sexual activity
	Difficult temperament		Depressed mood
	Hyperactivity/impulsivity/attention problems		Withdrawn behavior
	Low intelligence		Positive attitude toward problem behavior
	Male gender		Victimization and exposure to violence
Family	Maternal smoking/alcohol consumption/drug use during pregnancy	***Family***	Poor parental supervision
	Teenage mother	***School***	Poor academic achievement
	High turnover of caretakers		Repeated grade(s)
	Poorly educated parent		Truancy
	Maternal depression		Negative attitude toward school
	Parental substance abuse/antisocial or criminal behavior		Poorly organized and functioning schools
	Poor parent-child communication	***Peer***	Peer rejection
	Poverty/low socioeconomic status		Association with deviant peers/siblings
	Serious marital discord	***Community***	Residence in a disadvantaged neighborhood
	Large family size		Residence in a disorganized neighborhood
			Availability of weapons
	Risk Factors Emerging From Toddler Years Onward		**Risk Factors Emerging From Mid-adolescence Onward**
Child	Aggressive/disruptive behavior	***Child***	Weapon carrying
	Persistent lying		Drug dealing
	Risk taking and sensation seeking		Unemployment
	Lack of guilt, lack of empathy	***School***	School dropout
Family	Harsh and/or erratic discipline practices	***Peer***	Gang membership
	Maltreatment or neglect		
Community	Television violence		

FIGURE 12.2 A 2-year study by the OJJDP suggests that there are identifiable factors that suggest that young children may exhibit serious delinquent behaviors later in life.

Source: R. Loeber, D. Farrington, and D. Petechuk. *Child Delinquency: Early intervention and prevention.* (Washington, D.C. U.S. Department of Justice Office of Juvenile Justice and Delinquency Prevention), May 2003, p. 9.

imprecise definition reflects the lack of knowledge about youth gangs. However, the proliferation of youth gangs starting in the 1980s has resulted in both researchers and the criminal justice system examining the causes, characteristics, and mitigation of youth gang membership.

One of the reasons for the intense concern over the problem of youth gangs is that although gangs have differing characteristics from city to city and gang to gang, many youth gangs are significant sources of criminal activity and violence. Often youth gangs are the gateway into adult criminal gangs, an even greater criminal problem. In an effort to prevent the recruiting of children into criminal gangs, the federal government and the states have adopted legislation making it an offense to attempt to entice a juvenile to join a criminal gang or to prevent a juvenile from leaving a criminal gang.

According to a review of the research data by the OJJDP, historically, gang members have been primarily young adult males from homogeneous lower-class, inner-city, ghetto or barrio neighborhoods. Traditionally, gangs have been racially/ethnically segregated and actively involved in a variety of criminal activities.[81] The typical age for gang members is 15 to 24 years old, and the peak age for joining a gang is 15 years old.[82] About 50 percent of gang members are ages 18 to 24.[83]

Hybrid Youth Gangs One of the interesting discoveries to emerge from research on youth gangs is the evolving nature of these groups. Contemporary youth gangs appear to have different characteristics from pre-1980s gangs. The differences are sufficiently different that post-1990s youth gangs have been given a new name—**hybrid gangs.** A majority of members in gangs that emerged prior to 1981 were Hispanic (58 percent), whereas the majority of gang membership is White (37 to 40 percent) for gangs emerging after 1991.[84] New hybrid gangs have younger members, have more female members, and are less involved in drug trafficking and violent crimes than traditional youth

hybrid gangs a new type of youth gang with distinctive characteristics that differentiate them from traditional gangs; they are frequently school based, less organized, less involved in criminal activity, and less involved in violence than are traditional gangs

HERE'S SOMETHING TO THINK ABOUT . . .

Adolescent children of illegal immigrants who have resided in the United States for most of their life often find their life difficult. They fear the police and cannot get jobs. Educational advancement can be complicated by the lack of scholarships and laws that could result in their deportation if their illegal status is discovered. The "Dream Act" would provide children of illegal immigrants a pathway to legal residence. Should these children be afforded an opportunity for legal residence?

gangs.[85] Hybrid gangs are less territorial, more likely to migrate, frequently begin as school-based gangs, and are more likely to appear outside of large cities.[86]

Hybrid gangs have significantly different patterns of membership and organizational structure than traditional gangs. Hybrid gangs may use the names and gang symbols of traditional gangs, but they are very different in how they operate. Traditional gangs tend to have an age-graded structure of subgroups or cliques, organizational charts, explicit rules of conduct and regulations, concepts of "territory," and coalitions with other gangs often for the purpose of defining "turf."[87] Hybrid youth gangs are less territory based, racially mixed, lacking in formal organizational structure and rules, and are much more transient in membership. In some ways, hybrid gangs are quite unremarkable in their ability to imitate more traditional gangs. Starbuck and colleagues describe hybrid youth gangs as "cut and paste bits of Hollywood's media images and big-city gang lore into new local versions of nationally known gangs with which they may claim affiliation."[88] Fleisher described one such gang as "a haphazardly assembled social unit composed of deviant adolescents who shared social and economic needs and the propensity for resolving those needs in a similar way."[89] Gang expert David Kennedy called such gangs "hyperactive street groups of high-rate offenders."[90]

Starbuck and colleagues provided the following description of hybrid youth gangs:[91]

- Hybrid gangs may borrow symbols, graffiti, and gang colors from different gangs and mix them. For example, gang graffiti may illustrate symbols from the Blood gang in blue, which is the color of the rival Crip gang.
- Local gangs may adopt the symbols of large gangs in more than one city.
- Gang members may change their affiliation from one gang to another.
- Gang members may have multiple affiliations, including membership in rival gangs.
- Existing gangs may change their names or merge with other gangs to form new ones.
- Gangs are not organized along strict race/ethnicity lines.
- When gang members move, they may leave their old gang and align themselves with a new local gang that has no ties to their original gang.
- Members of rival gangs may cooperate in criminal activity.

Although hybrid gangs appear less of a concern because they engage in less violent criminal activities and do not have the high degree of organization and strict membership code of more traditional gangs, they actually pose a very significant problem for society. As mentioned, hybrid youth gangs frequently are school-based gangs. Any activity that could promote school violence is considered a serious problem. Hybrid gangs tend to migrate. Because of the younger age of the gang members, migration can be due to simple reasons such as the child's parents' move to another city. In fact, the most common reason for gang migration "is family relocation to improve the quality of life or to be near relatives and friends."[92] Hybrid youth gangs can be invisible to the community and law enforcement because they often do not behave in such a way as to quickly identify themselves as a "gang" and their membership is small. Some rural youth gangs may depend on only one or two persons to maintain "the gang."[93]

As a result of these characteristics, the most significant problem in addressing hybrid gangs is that programs that have successfully reduced gang membership and activity in large cities have little or no effect on hybrid gangs.[94] Further, because of the unique characteristics of each local gang and the absence of centralized and organized leadership, what succeeds in reducing gang membership and activity in one city may have little effect in another.[95] Community and law enforcement efforts to reduce gang membership and activity must be based on local conditions, culture and knowledge of the community, and the juveniles involved. In fact, some stereotypes about traditional gangs are opposite for hybrid gangs. For example, research has found that traditional gangs flourish in large inner-city environments characterized by declining prosperity and social conditions, but hybrid gangs prosper in cities with populations of less than 50,000 during times of economic prosperity. Also, because members may leave a gang, often with little or no consequences, law enforcement efforts to break up a gang may simply result in gang members

THE MOST COMMON REASON FOR GANG MIGRATION IS FAMILY RELOCATION TO IMPROVE THE QUALITY OF LIFE.

migrating and forming other gangs or joining other gangs. Some experts argue that when the community and law enforcement agencies attempt to respond to hybrid youth "gang problems" using knowledge and experience gained from "traditional" gangs, often the result is that they are "extremely ineffective at both seeing what's right in front of . . . [them], and doing something about it."[96]

Female Gangs Gathering data about youth gangs is difficult. Gangs are secret societies, outsiders are easily identified, and the gang seldom desires to reveal its inner workings to scholars, researchers, or the media. However, as difficult as the problem of researching youth gangs is, these problems pale compared to the problems of obtaining data to describe female gangs. Significant scholarly gang research has emerged only since the 1980s and most of that research has focused exclusively on male gangs. Some researchers have argued that female gangs are not "real gangs" or are only "imitations of male gangs" or "extensions" of male gangs.[97] The lack of research data regarding female gangs results in conflicting descriptions of gang members, activities, and values. Chesney-Lind and colleagues assert that public knowledge of female gangs is based primarily on media-produced stereotypes, which are largely inaccurate.[98]

Despite the reported increase of female membership in hybrid gangs, estimates of the number of female gang members remain low. Nationwide surveys of law enforcement agencies result in various estimates of female gang members, ranging from 3.7 to 11 percent.[99] Data from self-reported studies indicate a higher number of members, ranging from 8 to 38 percent.[100] A review of the research concerning female gangs by the OJJDP indicates that, similar to hybrid gangs, female gangs are more likely to be found in small cities and rural areas than in large cities. Most female gangs are either Black or Latina, with a smaller number of Asians and whites.[101] Latina gangs (Mexican Americans in the Southwest and Puerto Ricans in New York) have been studied more than Black female gangs.[102]

A review of the literature of female gangs by an OJJDP study indicates that female gangs have significantly different and unique characteristics when compared to male gangs.[103] One difference reported in the study is that females tend to leave the gang by the time they have reached their late 20s. Another characteristic the data suggest is that, in general, female gang members commit fewer violent crimes than male gang members. Drug offenses are among the most common offenses committed by female gang members. The data tend to suggest that females join gangs because of victimization at home, especially sexual abuse. For example, in Los Angeles, 29 percent of Mexican American female gang members reported being sexually abused at home, and a study of female gang members in Hawaii found that almost two thirds reported sexual abuse at home.[104]

29%

of Mexican American female gang members reported being sexually abused at home.

The OJJDP's report recommended that additional research is needed to answer basic questions about female gangs, such as:

1. What factors cause the formation of female gangs?
2. Why do females join gangs?
3. What is the role of ethnicity in female gangs?
4. What is the role of gender in female gangs and between male and female gangs?
5. What are the patterns of delinquency and criminality in female gangs? and
6. What are the later-life consequences of female gang membership?[105]

Juvenile Substance Abuse

Drug use and addiction are a serious problem in the United States. Juvenile drug use is also a serious problem and is becoming more serious. There appears to be a link between substance abuse and delinquency, as data indicate that 80 to 90 percent of youths detained for delinquency offenses reported use of an illicit substance in the past 6-months and virtually all had used drugs during their lifetime.[106]

Education Programs The U.S. government and criminal justice system have chosen to take a different approach to juvenile drug use from its War on Drugs approach for adult offenders. The cornerstone of the White House Office of National Drug Control Policy is education.

The history of drug education has not been a stellar example of an effective antidrug strategy. One of the first attempts at drug education was the 1936 pseudodocumentary *Reefer Madness*, which is now viewed as a farce and comedy. Early drug education programs used fear and exaggeration in an attempt to convince the viewer not to use drugs. For example, one popular 1980s media campaign showed an egg sizzling in a frying pan as the narrator announced, "This is your brain on drugs." Rather than dissuade youths not to use drugs, most of these media educational programs seem to convince youth not to believe the propaganda about drugs released by the government.

DARE Other than media advertising, the **Drug Abuse Resistance Education (DARE)** program initiated by the Los Angeles Police Department in 1983 is the most popular antidrug education program. Given that 35 percent of youths who reported using drugs said they first used them at or before age 11, the DARE program targets children in kindergarten through ninth grade. The DARE program is unique in that it is an in-school program and its instructors are local law enforcement officers. Despite its nationwide use by schools (80 percent of U.S. public schools use the DARE program), the program's effectiveness has come under criticism. Data have been inconclusive as to its effectiveness. Studies have not demonstrated that DARE is a research-based and effective antidrug program.[107] DARE dismisses this criticism. Furthermore, the DARE program claims to have "re-invented" itself and "evolved to be more than just about resisting drug abuse."[108] DARE now claims to include programming on "Internet safety, prescription and over-the-counter drug abuse, cyber-bullying, and safety and health."

DARE one of the most popular in-school drug education programs

TABLE 12.2 Percent of Students Reporting Use of Any Illicit Drugs, 2008–2010*

	8th Grade		10th Grade		12th Grade	
	2008	2010	2008	2010	2008	2010
Lifetime	19.6	21.4	34.1	37.0	47.4	48.2
Past Year	14.1	16.4	26.9	30.2	36.6	38.3
Past Month	7.6	9.5	15.8	18.5	22.3	23.8

**Source:* National Institute on Drug Abuse, NIDA InfoFacts: High School and Youth Trends

There are indicators that juvenile drug use is increasing in some niches. Methamphetamine use by students in smaller cities, especially in the West and Midwest appears to be a growing problem.[109] Also, abuse of prescription drugs is becoming a serious problem among juveniles. Teens said the number-one factor for using prescription medications was "ease of access." Most reported they obtained the medications from the medicine cabinet at home or at a friend's home.[110] The Monitoring the Future (MTF) survey by the National Institute on Drug Abuse has measured drug and alcohol use among adolescent students nationwide since 1975. The 2010 survey indicated daily marijuana use was at its highest point among twelfth graders since the early 1980s. In 2010, marijuana use was ahead of cigarette smoking by high school seniors—21.4 percent compared to 19.2 percent.[111] After marijuana, prescription and over-the-counter medications account for most of the top drugs abused by twelfth graders. Abuse of Vicodin decreased from 9.7 to 8 percent and abuse of OxyContin remained unchanged at about 5 percent. After several years of decline, current and past-year use of ecstasy has risen to 3.3 percent for eighth graders, 6.4 percent for tenth graders, and 7.3 percent for twelfth graders.[112]

1 in a million
the chances of a child being killed at school

Schools and Juvenile Violence

In August 1966, a student, Charles Whitman, dragged a foot locker filled with hunting rifles onto the observation deck of the clock tower at the University of Texas (Austin) and opened fire, killing 14 and wounding 31 others. Prior to the Whitman attack, schools were considered one of the safest places in the United States. Today, school violence is a major concern of society. Although a student is more likely to be victimized away from school rather than at school, findings from *Indicators of School Crime and Safety: 2004* show violent victimization at school is still a serious problem, evidenced by the fact that students ages 12 to 18 were victims of about 1.8 million nonfatal crimes of violence or theft at school.

STUDIES OF VIOLENT OFFENDERS HAVE ATTEMPTED TO UNDERSTAND WHAT CAUSES THEM TO KILL.

The Justice Policy Institute, the research arm of the Center on Juvenile and Criminal Justice, has determined that the chances of a child being killed at school are nearly 1 in a million. The National Center for Education Statistics report, Indicators of School Crime and Safety: 2004, reports that youths from ages 5 to 19 were at least 70 times more likely to be murdered away from school than at school.[113] Again, despite these statistics, parents, students, school officials, public officials, and the general public express genuine concern over the problem of school violence. The fear and reaction to school violence may be due in part to the media coverage of such incidents and to the historical expectation of relative safety that has characterized schools.

Further, it is not just large, crowded, inner-city schools that have suffered such attacks. In fact, the most serious attacks have occurred at schools in suburban or rural environments such as Moses Lake, Washington; Pearl, Mississippi; West Paducah, Kentucky; Jonesboro, Arkansas; Springfield, Oregon; Littleton, Colorado; Conyers, Georgia; Edinboro, Pennsylvania; Santee, California; Red Lake, Minnesota; Nickel Mines, Pennsylvania; Dekalb, Illinois; and Blacksburg, Virginia.

Strategies for Safe Schools

The sudden rise of school violence appears to be a mystery. Why does a child with an unremarkable history become a mass murderer who randomly kills teachers and classmates? The reasons given by juvenile murderers are diverse and do not seem adequate to explain the crime. For example, consider the following explanations offered by students who murdered or threatened to murder fellow students and teachers. Victor Cordova Jr., age 13, said he shot a 13-year-old classmate in the head because "other kids were bothering me."[114] A seventh-grader shot and killed his teacher because he had been sent home for throwing water balloons in class.[115] A 12-year-old student pulled a gun in class and threatened to shoot the teacher and classmates because he wanted to join his mother, who was in jail.[116] Two teens accused of killing two Dartmouth College professors did so because they were committed to "an evil-game dare."[117] John Romano, age 16, walked into Columbia High School (New York) on February 9, 2004, and opened fire with a shotgun, hitting a teacher in the leg. In his police statement, Romano's explanation was, "I have had fantasies for about the last year of going into Columbia and shooting up the place."[118] Finally, two second-grade boys and an 11-year-old schoolmate buried a loaded handgun in a playground sandbox and plotted to shoot and stab a third-grade student during recess. The students told authorities they intended to kill the third-grade girl "because she had teased two of them."[119]

Numerous studies of violent offenders have attempted to understand what causes them to kill. Sociological theories point to diverse reasons, such as environmental influence, peer pressure, lack of opportunity for legitimate advancement, and learned behavior. None of these theories alone seems to hold the explanation for the increase in homicides and violent crimes at schools. A study by the Secret Service

7 **Some commonly used strategies to reduce violence in schools include programs to reduce weapons on school property, programs to address the problem of bullying, expelling or arresting disruptive students, and increased presence of police officers on school property.**

National Threat Assessment Center of 40 cases of school violence or shootings over the past 20 years concluded that there is no single profile of a school shooter. However, schools have engaged in a number of strategies in the attempt to prevent school violence. Besides simply expelling or arresting disruptive students, among the more frequently used strategies are programs to reduce weapons on school property, programs to address the problem of bullying, and increased presence of police officers on school property.

Responding to Violence on School Property

There have been a number of significant changes in security and response to school shootings as a result of the 1999 Columbine High School shooting by Eric Harris and Dylan Klebold in Littleton, Colorado. Prior to the Columbine High School shooting, police departments were trained to respond to school shootings in a strategy known as contain-and-wait, which had its origins in the 1966 sniper attack at the University of Texas at Austin in which Charles Whitman killed 14 people. The contain-and-wait strategy emphasized the deployment of SWAT teams, negotiations, and perimeter containment. When applied to the Columbine High School shooting, the result was a disaster. Initially the shooters were unchallenged as police waited for SWAT teams to respond, resulting in continued shooting as Harris and Klebold were not interested in negotiating, only killing. One victim bled to death due to failure of the police to aggressively enter the high school.

When shooters have no desire to negotiate and their only goal is to kill as many as possible, rapid response is absolutely necessary. The new police strategy adopted since Columbine is called "active-shooter" response. This strategy trains police officers to form on-the-spot response teams called "contact teams" rather than wait for SWAT or special response teams and to enter the building and make their way toward the shooter while ignoring all other demands such as wounded victims and persons needing evacuation. The purpose of the "contact team" is to locate and neutralize the shooter. Studies suggest that in a mass shooting a gunman kills a person every 15 seconds. The police cannot delay or wait for SWAT. This strategy has become standard training for police responding to school shootings. Also, states have passed legislation requiring schools, colleges, and universities to engage in active planning and preparation for school shootings and other emergencies.

A STUDY BY THE SECRET SERVICE OF 40 CASES OF SCHOOL VIOLENCE CONCLUDED THAT THERE IS NO SINGLE PROFILE OF A SCHOOL SHOOTER.

Many claim that the availability of firearms, especially handguns, is a major contributing factor in serious violent crime at schools. Proponents of this theory believe that school shootings are possible only because weapons are so easily available to children. They argue that gun control legislation mandating safer guns and penalties against adults who allow children to obtain guns would help promote a safer school environment. Firearms have been brought to school by kindergartners to high school seniors; thus, any strategy that would promote a gun-free environment at schools appears to have merit.

HERE'S SOMETHING TO THINK ABOUT . . .

In 2011, Warren Jeffs was convicted by the states of Arizona, Utah, and Texas of various charges of sexual assault against girls as young as age 12. He was sentenced by the Texas court to life in prison plus 20 years to be served consecutively. Jeffs was President of the Fundamentalist Church of Jesus Christ of Latter Day Saints (FLDS) and his defense was that the practice of sex with underage girls, multiple marriages, and arranged marriages between young girls and much older men was commanded by God in the FLDS religion. The Catholic Church has faced an ongoing crisis of worldwide allegations of cover-up of sexual assaults by priests upon young boys and girls. Many other lesser-known religious groups also have been accused of sexual abuse of boys and girls. Protecting children from sexual assault in the name of religion or aided by the cover-up of religious authorities is a serious concern. What are some unique obstacles that make it difficult to discover and prosecute such sexual abuse?

Unfortunately, such strategies are unlikely to have much impact on school violence, as schools and state legislatures have already recognized that weapons, especially guns, on school property are an inherent risk and have taken measures to make schools a weapon-free environment. In every case in schools where students have used guns in violent crimes on school property, it was illegal to bring guns to school. Rather than focus on new laws or stiffer penalties, schools have focused on screening for weapons and strategies for responding to shooters. Schools, even elementary schools, have adopted the use of metal detector screening and zero-tolerance policies prohibiting any weapon, including sharp scissors, pocket knives, or any object that could be used as a weapon. States have passed laws mandating schools as "gun-free" zones. Often, these laws have mandatory sentences or lengthy prison sentences for those who bring firearms onto school property. Even in states that permit private citizens to carry firearms, often the law does not permit them to carry the weapon on school property.

Despite laws and punishments, students continue to bring weapons and guns onto school property. The 2008 report of the National Center of Education *Indicators of School Crime and Safety: 2008* data indicated that 18 percent of students in grades 9 through 12 reported carrying a weapon such as a gun, knife, or club on school property.

Reducing Bullying

Bullying has been identified as a common factor among school shooters. The Secret Service's National Threat Assessment Center's analysis of school shooters found that two thirds of school shooters saw themselves as bullied. One in 11 students surveyed in 2003 said they had been threatened with or injured by a weapon on school property. About one out of every 20 high school students said they skipped at least one day of school because of fear for their safety. A study conducted by the University of California Los Angeles by Adrienne Nishina in 2005 reported that about half of the students in sixth grade reported being bullied on at least one out of five school days. A larger percentage of students reported witnessing someone else getting bullied. Many of these students stated that teachers appeared to take no action against the bullies.[120] The study reported that children who were bullied, including verbal abuse, or who witnessed others being bullied frequently suffered emotional anxiety and physical symptoms such as feeling sick. The study stated that "the more bullying they [the students] experience, the more they dislike school and want to avoid school." Whereas those bullied suffer emotionally and physically, other studies report that "bullies are often popular and viewed by classmates as the 'coolest' in their classes; they don't show signs of depression or social anxiety, and do not suffer from low self-esteem."[121]

Estimates of the extent of bullying in schools vary and are difficult to validate. One report is that there are an estimated 3.7 million bullies—children who regularly verbally taunt or physically torment others—in sixth to tenth grades. Jim Snyder, a psychologist at Wichita State University, reported that his study of bullying in kindergartners showed that they bully each other once every 6 minutes.[122]

These findings have stimulated many schools to reexamine their reaction to bullies and bullying. Studies have reported that bullies often are the popular kids and are protected not just by students but also by teachers and administrators eager to promote "superstars." These studies suggest that cultural values condone and support "rudeness as a means to get ahead not just on the playground, but into adulthood."[123] As a result, antibullying strategies and programs are being promoted as a means to prevent school violence. These programs teach students mediation and negotiation skills, train teachers and staff in intervention techniques, and stress the importance of intervening. Some state and school districts have adopted formal laws and policies to reduce bullying.

POLICE HAVE USED MACE TO SUBDUE CHILDREN IN SECOND GRADE.

Increasing Police Presence

Other schools have adopted programs that emphasize the use of unarmed and armed law enforcement officers and/or school safety agents to patrol school property. For example, in 2004, New York City schools targeted "problem schools" and assigned extra police officers and safety agents to patrol the schools. The targeted schools adopted the successful "broken windows" model that has been credited for reducing crime in New York City as a strategy to reduce school crime. The schools adopted zero-tolerance policies on violation of school rules and emphasized paying attention to details such as a clean environment and no tolerance of graffiti. The schools use police officers and school safety agents to enforce these rules. These officers issue citations for criminal and noncriminal incidents, screen students with metal detectors, patrol hallways, and strictly enforce security rules. For example, at one school there were 115 arrests, summonses, and juvenile reports for the period from January 5 to March 22, 2004.[124]

New York schools using the police strategy to reduce school violence reported a 48 percent decrease in major crime, but one of the problems of the programs that use on-campus law enforcement officers to reduce school violence is the conflict between school administrators and teachers and the law enforcement officers. Often, school administrators and teachers are opposed to the presence of armed law enforcement officers on school property and feel that such a strategy is only treating the symptoms and not the cause of the problems of violence. School administrators, teachers, and staff may be critical of police policies such as arresting and handcuffing students for apparently minor violations. In some cases, law enforcement officers have been criticized for arresting and handcuffing students as young as 5 years old.

The presence of police officers in the school has raised serious questions, such as "What is the relationship between the police and the principal?"[125] Also, there is debate as to what is the appropriate level of force for police to use upon school children in response to violent behavior or aggression. In some cases police have used mace to subdue children in second grade. Also, there are cases where police have used stun guns to subdue juveniles in school and the child has suffered cardiac arrest and died. A 2011 Supreme Court case considered whether it was required to advise children questioned in the presence of the police or by police of their Miranda rights.

Some School Safety Programs Create New Problems

A plethora of programs have been adopted by schools and communities to reduce school violence, which has declined since 2000. However, the role of the various preventive programs to reduce school violence is not clear. Although the data suggest that specific categories of interventions or arrangements in schools can reduce or prevent delinquent behavior, drug use, and school disorder, the data do not suggest that schools have adopted the more effective programs or have implemented good programs that have been adopted.[126] "A national

HERE'S SOMETHING TO THINK ABOUT . . .

Should parents go to jail for the delinquent acts of their children? When flash mobs of juveniles in Philadelphia became a problem in the summer of 2011, parents were warned they would be held legally accountable if their children violated curfew. In 2010, Wayne County Prosecutor Kym Worthy (Michigan) proposed that parents who miss scheduled parent–teacher conferences should be jailed for 3 days. What should be the legal responsibility of parents for the delinquent acts of their children?

study completed in 2000 found that despite the increase in knowledge about 'what works' in school delinquency prevention, most of the Nation's schools use prevention practices that are either unproven or known to be ineffective."[127] Poor implementation, even of good programs, results in poor quality and ineffective programs. Only 10 percent of the nation's schools that adopt "best practices" programs report using the minimally adequate activities and instructional and behavioral programs to plausibly expect the program to have a measurable effect on reducing problem behavior or increasing safety.[128]

Bans on Cell Phones Some school strategies have met with conflict from parents. For example, while some schools have banned cell phones, parents have protested such bans. Parents ignore the problems that can result from abuse of cell phones by students in the classroom and focus on the cell phone as an essential means of communication with their children, especially in the event of an emergency, such as a school shooting. Whereas school administrators see the problems associated with abuse of cell phones, parents see cell phones as "security." Such conflicts only make it more difficult for schools and communities in their effort to promote safe schools.

Transfer to Juvenile Court Some programs to enhance school safety seem to create as many problems as they solve. For example, two popular strategies to promote safe schools are (1) to transfer "troublemakers" to the juvenile court and (2) to expel disruptive or violent students. Many states have passed legislation that allows schools to refer students who commit school-based offenses to juvenile court. In these schools, misdemeanor charges can be filed against a student for anything from disrupting a class to assaulting a teacher. Violators are taken into custody by the police and charges are filed in juvenile court rather than the school handling the disciplinary problem. As school administrators encounter more disruptions, they rely more and more on arrests and referral to the juvenile court. In some school districts, referrals to the juvenile court for school-based offenses has increased 300 percent in the last 10 years. Schools are referring offenders to juvenile court for turning off the lights in the girls' bathroom, not listening in class, not going to class, violating school dress codes, and disrupting the learning process.[129] The problem with such a strategy is that juvenile court intake officers become overwhelmed with school-related cases. Ohio, Virginia, Kentucky, and Florida juvenile court judges have complained that their courtrooms are at risk of being overwhelmed by student misconduct cases that should be handled in the schools.[130]

300%

amount of increase in the last 10 years of school-based incidents referred to juvenile courts

Expulsion Another frequently used strategy to promote school safety that produces serious side effects is the expulsion of disruptive or violent students. Many schools have adopted a "get tough" approach to disruptive students, especially those cases involving firearms or violence. Students who are found to have violated the school's prohibition against firearms or who are violent are not being allowed to attend their regular school. However, most states require young children below a certain age to remain in school. Thus, while they are expelled from attending "regular school," the state must provide them with an educational experience. Some school districts have created "alternative" schools or "second opportunity schools" for such disruptive students. Such schools are the student's last chance before being placed in a secure facility. This solution places all of the most disruptive students into a single environment. Often, such schools lack the resources to provide the students with the counseling and individual attention necessary to rehabilitate them and extinguish their disruptive behavior. Teachers are unable to provide quality educational experiences because an entire class of disruptive students proves impossible to teach. Principals of such schools have problems with very high truancy rates, violent-prone students who assault each other and teachers, and overwhelmed teachers.[131]

The operation of such schools is expensive. These schools have high failure rates and few of the students complete their high school education or GED. Nearly all of the students perform below their grade level or lack basic skills necessary for academic success. Frequently, students in these schools are court supervised due to their delinquency; therefore, multiple agencies, such as the Department of Education, the Juvenile Court, and state child welfare agencies, are involved in monitoring the students. Also, juvenile delinquents who have been in the custody of the state for violent offenses or delinquency but are released from a secure facility while they are still required to attend school are frequently placed in these alternative schools rather than regular schools. The integration of these new court-involved students, often at various times in the school year, creates significant challenges for the school. Such students have a high risk for failure in school.[132]

The Juvenile as Victim

The juvenile justice system is concerned not only about juvenile offenders, but also about children who are victims of crime. Under the doctrine "the state as parent and guardian," the state takes an active role in promoting the health and welfare of juveniles through direct intervention and programs for juvenile victims, as well as through legislation and police, who work to reduce offenses committed by adults against juveniles. Three major concerns of the criminal justice system and the public are violence against children, sexual exploitation of children and child pornography, and missing children.

One of the components of the juvenile justice system is child protective services, or CPS, which provides services to children who are abused, neglected, victimized, or in need of care. Child protective services has the legal responsibility to conduct assessments or investigations of reports of child abuse and neglect and to offer rehabilitative services to families where maltreatment has occurred or is likely to occur.[133] It also has the authority to remove a child from his or her parent or guardian or living environment and place the child under the care of the state if CPS deems there is a serious threat to the health or welfare of the child. The juvenile justice system is concerned about abused and victimized children not only for their own well-being and safety, but also because the data show that there is an increased risk for delinquency for children who are abused and victimized.[134]

HERE'S SOMETHING TO THINK ABOUT . . .

Cyber-bullying has become a national concern as several adolescent deaths have been attributed to it. Often the law on cyber-bullying is vague or nonexistent. As the use of the Internet and smartphones is near universal by adolescents, cyber-bullying can quickly escalate and be near impossible to escape. Should more be done in schools to discourage cyber-bullying?

Innocence Lost?

It has been just a little over 100 years since the first juvenile court assumed jurisdiction over children. However, in the century that has passed, the juvenile justice system has undergone significant changes.

TODAY, JUVENILE COURTS ARE FINDING THAT THEY MUST YIELD SOME OF THE EXCLUSIVE JURISDICTION THEY EXERCISED OVER YOUNG OFFENDERS BACK TO THE CRIMINAL JUSTICE SYSTEM.

Today, juvenile courts are finding that they must yield some of the exclusive jurisdiction they exercised over young offenders back to the criminal justice system. As a result, some young violent offenders find themselves right back where they were in the 1800s, as they are charged as adults and sentenced as adults. The United States Supreme Court has banned the use of the death penalty for juveniles tried as adults, but such offenders can find that they are sentenced to long prison terms, including life without parole, for their crime.

The public has become more willing to accept that juvenile delinquents, especially violent offenders, are fully culpable for their actions. The public has lost faith that, with treatment, a change of environment, discipline, education, and training, juvenile delinquents can be "saved." At the same time, the public continues to recognize that the state has an important role in overseeing the health and welfare of juveniles. Thus, even as more and more juveniles are being diverted from the juvenile justice system to the criminal justice system, the state is pumping more resources into prevention programs and child welfare programs.

One of the challenges of legislating a juvenile criminal justice system that provides the proper balance between the competing goals of public safety and age-appropriate response is the changing environment, social norms, and values. Today's society is far removed from society at the turn of the twentieth century. New influences such as mobility, media, availability of firearms, and changing social norms provide a different environment in which children grow up from the environment they experienced in 1899. Even the attitude of parents concerning their role in child rearing has changed.

The public seems less willing to recognize the "innocence" and "immaturity" of juveniles and more willing to accept that due to changes in environment and values, children are more "adultlike" at a younger age. Thus, the "get tough" policy characteristic of dealing with adult offenders appears to be migrating to juvenile offenders and is resulting in changes to the juvenile justice system. However, the juvenile justice system is an incredibly complex legal and social institution and is not well served by simplistic views of its functions. The proper functioning of the juvenile justice system is extremely important. Historically, the juvenile court has often been a place where theories of delinquency can be tested with the hope that if they are valid, they will enable the juvenile court to respond in such a manner so as to prevent the juvenile offender from becoming an adult offender. However, example after example has often proven that the response of the juvenile court has not been correct in extinguishing criminal behavior in juveniles. Some segments of the public appear willing to some degree to return to pre-1899 treatment of juvenile offenders by transferring them to the criminal justice system.

The financial crisis experienced by many states has resulted in a review of the services the state can offer to juvenile offenders. Many states in response to record budget deficits had to cut juvenile counseling, vocational, treatment, and diversion programs. Often these programs cost little and appear promising in keeping juveniles out of the criminal justice system. However, as states had to make deep cuts in their budgets even the most promising and cheapest programs are being cut.

Parents no longer feel that childhood is a time of innocence. They fear their children will be abducted and molested by child sex offenders. They fear the influences of gangs on their children and the danger posed by gangs to their children. They fear their children will abuse drugs. They fear their children will be murdered at school. In the midst of all this fear, it is important for the public to realize that despite the well-publicized failures of the juvenile justice system and the dangers parents fear will befall their children, the juvenile justice system has been remarkably successful and the public should not be so quick to abandon or radically change it. Children are still safer at school than they are at home, and an overburdened and underfunded juvenile justice system has been remarkably successful in providing for the welfare of children and diverting the majority of children from a career of crime.

HERE'S SOMETHING TO THINK ABOUT . . .

Frequently sensational crimes result in the introduction of new laws. Crimes against children provide several examples of how well-known laws have resulted from these tragedies. One of the earliest crimes to result in a new law was the 1932 kidnapping of the 18-month-old son of Charles Lindbergh. As a result of the kidnapping, the federal government passed the Federal Kidnapping Act, better known as the Lindbergh law, which made it a federal crime to transport a kidnap victim across state lines.

The 1994 death and sexual assault of Megan Kanka, age 7, resulted in the passage of the 1996 federal sex offender registry. Today all sex offenders are required to register with law enforcement and the information is available to the public. The public can easily and freely obtain information about sex offenders in their neighborhood through the Internet.

The 1996 abduction and death of Amber Hagerman, age 9, resulted in the development and nationwide use of the Amber Alert system. The Amber Alert system enables law enforcement to broadcast timely alerts of missing or abducted children by use of multimedia such as radio, television, Twitter, and smartphones. The 2003 death and kidnapping of Polly Klass, age 12, resulted in legislation requiring enhanced sentencing for repeat offenders. These sentences became known as the "three-strikes" law aimed at keeping violent repeat offenders off the street. The movement continues.

The death of Caylee Anthony, age 2, and the subsequent trial of Casey Anthony for her murder, has resulted in a movement to pass legislation that would make it a crime to fail to report a missing child in a timely manner. Caylee's disappearance was not reported to law enforcement for 31 days. However, in many states there is no law requiring that parents report missing children to law enforcement. As a result of the attention that resulted from the Casey Anthony trial there is a movement to pass legislation that would make it a crime to fail to report a missing child in a timely manner. Several states have already passed such legislation. What can be some problems in new laws based upon highly emotional reaction of the public to sensational crimes?

CHAPTER 12

The Juvenile Justice System

Check It!

1 WHAT are the goals of the juvenile criminal justice system? p. 228

The juvenile justice system is designed to help and rehabilitate young offenders, but there are public perceptions that juvenile violence is out of control and that juvenile offenders must be punished more harshly and incarcerated.

 WHAT were the foundations for the early juvenile criminal justice system? p. 229

In the early 1800s, reformers established juvenile reformatories that were designed to save children from facilities that were unsanitary, unsafe, had no type of rehabilitation, and did not separate inmates by age, gender, or whether they were in custody because of poverty, abandonment, or crime. These reformatories intended to reform children through supervised labor, education, and discipline.

3 HOW did the establishment of the first juvenile court and following major court cases shape the jurisdiction for and due process rights of juvenile offenders? p. 230

The first juvenile court took exclusive jurisdiction over juveniles and prevented them from being tried for any offense in criminal court without the authority of the juvenile court but also denied juveniles due process rights. The following Supreme Court cases had significant impacts on due process rights of juveniles:

1. *Kent v. United States* granted juveniles the rights to a waiver hearing, counsel at this hearing, access to court records, and a judge's statement of waiver.
2. *In re Gault* granted juveniles the rights to notice of charges, counsel, examination of witnesses, and the right to remain silent.
3. *In re Winship* required the reasonable doubt standard to be used in all delinquency adjudications.
4. *McKeiver v. Pennsylvania* denied juveniles the right to a trial by jury.
5. *Breed v. Jones* ruled that double jeopardy applies to juveniles.
6. *Schall v. Martin* upheld the right of juvenile courts to deny bail to juveniles.

4 WHY and in what ways are states beginning to hold juveniles more accountable for crime? p. 234

Public perception that juvenile crime is out of control and the belief that violent juvenile offenders should be held accountable have led many states to adopt laws that remove such juveniles from the protection of juvenile courts by lowering the age at which juveniles can be waived to criminal court and waiving juveniles to criminal court for very serious violent offenses.

5 HOW are juveniles processed through the juvenile justice system? p. 238

The following are steps in the processing of juveniles:

1. Intake, which is similar to arrest for adults.
2. The decision between juvenile or adult jurisdiction is made.
3. An interview with and investigation by a juvenile intake officer.
4. Either a delinquency petition asking for a hearing or a waiver asking for transfer to criminal court is forwarded to a juvenile court judge.
5. A dispositional hearing is held by a judge.
6. The result might be detention, residential placement, alternative courses of treatment, or probation.

6 WHAT are some of the unique problems posed by youthful offenders, such as very young offenders, youth gangs, and substance abuse? p. 241

1. Very young offenders are at great risk of becoming serious, violent, chronic offenders.
2. Youth gangs often are a source of crime and violence and the gateway to adult gangs, little is known about female gangs, and hybrid gangs can be hard to identify.
3. Delinquency is associated with juvenile drug use, which appears to be rising despite antidrug programs.

7 WHAT strategies are being used to reduce violence in schools? p. 250

Some strategies that are being used to reduce school violence include programs to reduce weapons on school property, programs that address bullying, expelling or arresting disruptive students, and increased police presence on school property.

Assess Your Understanding

1. Why was a separate system created for juvenile offenders?

a. to create more jobs in the criminal justice system
b. because of the assumption that youthful offenders did not have the same capacity for *mens rea* as adult offenders
c. it was an experiment funded by a federal grant
d. as a means to reduce overcrowding in adult prisons

2. What is *parens patriae*?

a. the legal assumption that parents are responsible for damages caused by their children
b. the assumption that children under age 7 do not have the capacity to form *mens rea*
c. the legal assumption that the state has primary responsibility for the safety and custody of children
d. the law limiting the control of youthful offenders to a maximum age of 21

3. Juvenile offenses are classified as which of the following?

a. delinquent and status offenses
b. misdemeanor and felony offenses
c. minor and serious offenses
d. regular and super-delinquent offenses

4. What is the standard of proof required to adjudicate an accused offender in juvenile court?

a. preponderance of the evidence
b. clear and convincing evidence
c. the judge believes it was more likely than not likely that the accused juvenile committed the act
d. proof beyond a reasonable doubt

5. What issue was decided in *McKeiver v. Pennsylvania* (1971)?

a. whether juveniles were entitled to the due process right of a trial by jury
b. whether juveniles were entitled to the due process right to confront their accusers
c. whether juveniles were entitled to the right to an attorney
d. whether states could deny juveniles pretrial release

6. Which of the following occurs in the juvenile justice system?

a. Juvenile offenders are booked at which time the police establish their identity and file charges against the accused.
b. Juveniles are convicted of their offense at a court trial and the judge decides the sentence to be served.
c. Juveniles are arrested by the police and the prosecutor files charges by use of a preliminary hearing or grand jury.
d. During the intake process the juvenile may be asked questions about his or her life history.

7. What is the minimum age at the time of the offense that a convicted offender can be sentenced to death for a capital crime?
   a. 14 c. 18
   b. 16 d. 21

8. What is the relationship between the age at the onset of offending and the seriousness of adolescent offending?
   a. There is no relationship between the age at the onset of offending and the seriousness of adolescent offending.
   b. The younger the age at the onset of offending the more serious is the adolescent offending.
   c. The offender who starts offending at an early age usually offends as a teenager.
   d. the later the age at onset of offending the more serious will be the offending as an adolescent.

9. Which of the following is usually true when comparing traditional criminal gangs and hybrid youth gangs?
   a. Members can exit hybrid youth gangs with little consequences.
   b. Both are organized around territory and racial identification.
   c. Hybrid youth gangs are not allowed to adopt the gang colors and symbols of traditional gangs.
   d. Hybrid youth gangs have more structured leadership and clarity of mission than traditional gangs.

10. Which of the following correctly states the problem of school violence?
    a. A student is eight times more likely to be killed at school or near school than at home.
    b. A student is just as likely to be killed at school or near school than at home.
    c. School violence is a major concern but a student is more likely to be victimized away from school.
    d. School violence is a problem only for urban, inner-city schools.

11. What is the purpose of child protective service (CPS) agencies?
    a. CPS agencies act similar to police and apprehend serious violent juvenile offenders.
    b. CPS agencies are concerned with the welfare and health of children.
    c. CPS agencies supervise juveniles adjudicated by the juvenile court and placed on probation.
    d. CPS agencies monitor the due process rights of youthful offenders and work with the ACLU to promote justice for juveniles.

12. At what age can a juvenile offender be waived to criminal court?
    a. 14
    b. 14 for murder and 16 for other serious violent felonies
    c. 16 for federal court and 15 for state courts
    d. the age depends upon the state law and the offense

ESSAY

1. Why are there separate criminal justice systems for adults and juveniles?
2. Prior to the adoption of a juvenile justice system by the United States, how did the criminal justice system handle youthful offenders?
3. Explain the significance of the juvenile justice court having original jurisdiction. How does this affect juvenile offenders?
4. Why was there a movement away from giving original and near exclusive jurisdiction to juvenile courts and providing more waivers and joint jurisdiction with the criminal courts for juvenile offenders?
5. What are some of the major differences between the juvenile justice system and the adult criminal justice system?
6. Do juvenile offenders have the same due process rights in the juvenile justice system as adult offenders have in criminal court? If not, describe the differences.
7. What is the role of the juvenile intake officer in the juvenile justice system?
8. Describe some of the major strategies that are being used to reduce violence in schools.

ANSWERS: 1. b, 2. c, 3. a, 4. d, 5. a, 6. d, 7. c, 8. d, 9. a, 10. c, 11. b, 12. d

Media

Go to the *Chapter 12: The Juvenile Justice System* section in *MyCJLab* to test your understanding of this chapter, access customized study content, engage in interactive simulations, complete critical thinking and research assignments, and view related online videos.

Additional Links

To find the complete text of U.S. Supreme Court decisions such as Winship, Gault, and Kent, go to www.findlaw.com/casecode/supreme.html

Information about the national drug policy of the White House can be viewed at www.whitehousedrugpolicy.gov

The FBI provides a portal for access to the various state sex offender registry Web sites at www.fbi.gov/hq/cid/cac/registry.htm

To view a video of Judge Andrew Valdez addressing high school students on how to stay out of gangs, go to www.ksl.com/index.php?sid=8021454

To view a video showing juveniles in lockup facilities, go to www.youtube.com/watch?v=tMjqND0_viA

The Office of Juvenile Justice and Delinquency Prevention provides many resources on juvenile justice. To view OJJDP's homepage, go to www.ojjdp.gov/

You can view the complete text of the Juvenile Justice and Delinquency Prevention Act at www.ojjdp.gov/about/jjdpa2002titlev.pdf

To view the Los Angeles Police Department Boot Camp for delinquents, go to www.youtube.com/watch?v=1MNPmfjqn7s

HOMELAND SECURITY

13

September 11, 2011, was the tenth anniversary of the attack on the World Trade Center and the Pentagon which marked the beginning of the "War on Terrorism." In the 10 years since the attacks there has been a transformation of society and in particular of the criminal justice system. In the twenty-first century, American policing is terror-focused and has assumed new responsibilities, missions, and powers. The international nature of terrorism has thrust federal law enforcement agencies into a new role of prominence and leadership. Local and state law enforcement, referred to as first responders, have a new relationship with federal agencies. Billions of dollars fund homeland security initiatives. The creations of the Department of Homeland Security and the USA Patriot Act have transformed the criminal justice landscape.

Following the September 11 attacks, Osama bin Laden, the accused mastermind of the attacks, became the most wanted person in the world. On May 1, 2011, in a dramatic Sunday late-night news briefing, President Obama announced that an elite Navy Seal team had killed bin Laden, captured persons residing in the compound, and taken numerous documents. Without prior notice to the Pakistani government, the military raid clandestinely entered Pakistan to conduct the operation. Following the raid bin Laden was buried at sea and the Pakistani government issued official protests of the U.S. actions.

During his public statement President Obama said, "The death of bin Laden marks the most significant achievement to date in our nation's effort to defeat al Qaeda. But his death does not mark the end of our effort. There's no doubt that al Qaeda will continue to pursue attacks against us. We must and we will remain vigilant at home and abroad."

THE DEATH OF BIN LADEN MARKS THE MOST SIGNIFICANT ACHIEVEMENT TO DATE IN OUR NATION'S EFFORT TO DEFEAT AL QAEDA.

1. **WHAT is terrorism, and how has it affected the criminal justice system?**
2. **HOW has the United States reorganized law enforcement agencies to respond to terrorism?**
3. **HOW has the new emphasis on homeland security impacted the relationship among federal, state, and local police agencies?**
4. **HOW has fear of terrorist attacks influenced legislation, homeland security strategies, and search and seizure?**
5. **HOW is concern about possible terrorist attacks affecting policing?**
6. **WHAT concerns regarding border security have been raised by threats to homeland security?**
7. **WHAT are the concerns about the impact of homeland security legislation and law enforcement powers on basic constitutional rights?**

This chapter discusses U.S. efforts to ensure homeland security. It discusses the difficult problem of defining terrorism, the development of the Department of Homeland Security, and how American policing and the criminal justice system have changed as a result of the War on Terrorism. It closes with a discussion of issues raised by concerns over border security, cyberterrorism, and threats of civil liberties.

What Is Terrorism?

Although the United States has long endured domestic terrorism, it has not impacted the criminal justice system in the same way that the threat of international terrorism has since September 11, 2001. For the most part, the criminal justice system effectively responded to the threats of domestic terrorism. However, effective counterterrorism actions against international groups using terrorism require resources that far exceed local police budgets and require international intelligence-gathering powers that are possessed only by federal and military agencies. Although local and state police have a vital role as first responders in homeland security, their traditional relationship with federal and military agencies has been significantly changed.

WHETHER ONE IS VIEWED AS A TERRORIST OR FREEDOM FIGHTER DEPENDS TO A GREAT DEGREE ON WHETHER ONE AGREES OR DISAGREES WITH THE POLITICAL IDEOLOGY.

A strategy of terrorism is to convince the citizens of a legitimate government that their government has rendered them powerless and that they are oppressed. Terrorists want citizens to believe that they are victims of social injustice and that their only recourse is violence against the government.

One of the factors that has suppressed widespread terrorism in the United States is the fact that the criminal justice system reflects changing social values. During the course of U.S. history, laws and the criminal justice system have from time to time discriminated against classes of people, have been unjust in their protection of civil and constitutional rights for all people, or have turned a blind eye toward justice for some. However, often these offenses are corrected without violence or overthrow of the government. Such corrections can be seen in U.S. Supreme Court rulings that have offered greater protections to citizens, such as requiring states to provide indigent defendants with free legal counsel, rulings that have restricted the power of the police in interrogating suspects, and civil rights decisions requiring equality for all citizens.

Terrorist Tactics Generally, terrorists use tactics such as random attacks on noncombatants, symbolic buildings and landmarks, and the infrastructure of a society to achieve their goal of causing general disruption and widespread fear. They typically do not expect this destructiveness to topple the legitimate government, however. On the contrary, terrorists achieve their goals through the response of the government to their acts. They count on overreaction of the government and the media. The ability to create widespread fear does not depend on military strength but on the ability of the mass media to magnify terrorist actions and to broadcast this image internationally. Terrorists can count on the media to make their actions widely known. As early as 1976, the National Advisory Commission on Criminal Justice Standards and Goals' Report of the Task Force on Disorder and Terrorism concluded, "The spectacular nature of terrorist activities assures comprehensive news coverage; modern communications make each incident an international event."[1]

Terrorist or Freedom Fighter? It is said that "one man's terrorist is another man's freedom fighter." Whether one is viewed as a terrorist or freedom fighter depends to a great degree on whether one agrees or disagrees with the political ideology and goals of those engaged in violence. The American Revolution against England, the Russian Revolution against the Czar, the Hungarian revolt against the Soviet Union, Castro's overthrow of the government of Cuba, the Iranian revolution against the Shah, the Solidarity union movement of Poland, the Irish Republican Army's rejection of British rule, and the Palestine struggle for a homeland are examples of situations in which political leaders used violence to achieve the political and social change they desired.

HERE'S SOMETHING TO THINK ABOUT . . .

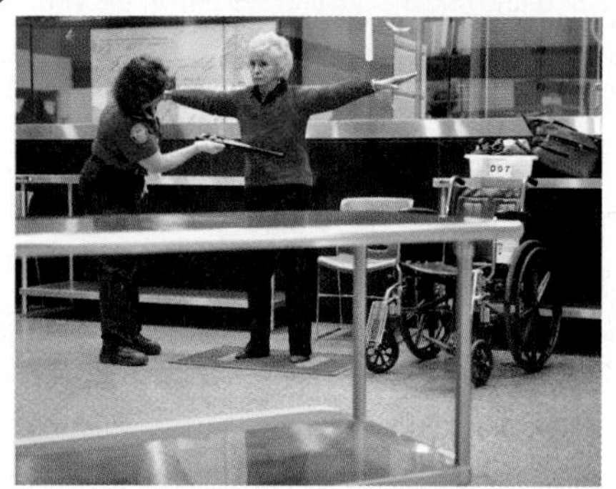

Airport security is technology-focused. Also, the TSA adopts screening procedures based on past attacks. Thus, passengers must surrender sharp objects, take off their shoes, discard liquids past security checkpoints, and submit to body scans. The TSA has spent billions of dollars on technology that did not work and had to be abandoned. TSA security has been described as "trial and error." It depends on the checkpoint screen of every passenger. Critics call this "security theater" as persistent flaws have resulted in ineffective security screening and excessive costs. A 2009 Government Accountability Office report criticized the TSA for not conducting a risk assessment, cost-benefit analysis, or established quantifiable performance measures. Despite spending nearly $60 billion since 2001, TSA screening has not caught a single terrorist. Recent would-be aviation attacks have been averted by the actions of passengers, intelligence, or the incompetence of the perpetrators. The Israeli model focuses on identifying persons who are threats rather than on screening for weapons. Many consider the Israeli model more effective and efficient than the U.S. model. The problem is that the Israeli model includes ethnical and national profiling which is illegal in the United States. Should profiling be allowed in TSA security screening?

1 **Terrorism is a strategy of using random, violent attacks on noncombatants, symbolic buildings and landmarks, and the infrastructure of a society to cause general disruption and widespread fear and threats; terrorist attacks and threats within the United States have transformed criminal and judicial problems into national security threats.**

What Is Terrorism?

What is terrorism? Terrorism is a strategy, not a person, group, or nation. Terrorism can be used both by governments and persons and groups opposed to government.

What is the origin of the term? Although the use of terrorism as a tactic and strategy can be traced back to ancient times the terms *terror, terrorism,* and *terrorist* originated in the Reign of Terror of the French Revolution (1793–1794). Maximilien Robespierre, one of the leaders of the revolution, used violence as the primary strategy to overthrow the existing monarchy and install a new democratic government for France.

What is terrorism? Title 22 of the United States Code Section 264f(d)–**terrorism** is the premeditated, politically motivated violence perpetrated against noncombatant targets by subnational groups or clandestine agents, usually intended to influence an audience. The term **international terrorism** means terrorism involving citizens or the territory of more than one country. The term terrorist group means any group that practices, or has significant sub-groups that practice, international terrorism. For the purposes of this definition, the term *noncombatant* in addition to civilians includes military personnel who at the time of the incident are unarmed and/or not on duty. It also includes acts of terrorism on military installations or on armed military personnel when a state of military hostilities does not exist at the site.

What are some actions used by terrorists? Attacks on civilians, indiscriminate bombings, assasinations, destruction of buildings, symbolic targets, or infrastructure targets such as bridges, airports, transportation facilities, energy and communication networks, and attacks using weapons of mass destruction. Terrorists attack their target in stealth and then blend back into the civilian population.

What is the international definition of terrorism? None. Terrorism is a value-laden term and what one nation considers terrorism another nation or people consider freedom fighting, liberation movement, or overthrowing of an oppressive government, or occupying army.

What is the appeal of terrorist groups? Groups using terrorism for political influence emphasize the social injustice of the existing government or military occupation.

What are the goals of groups/nations that use terrorism? Nations use terrorism to keep populations under state control. Groups opposed to existing governments use terrorism to generate widespread fear, to get government to overreact, and to gain media attention. Terrorists do not engage in "military battle" for geopolitical territory. They use "hit and run" tactics to win by gradual surrender due to a lack of will to continue the "fight" rather than military superiority.

Domestic and International Terrorism

To a large degree, U.S. criminal justice agencies abstain from the political and ethical debates regarding the justification for the use of political violence. The criminal justice system focuses on the criminal nature of terrorism, regardless of the motivation or political ideology, and pursues the goals of protecting the public, apprehending perpetrators of such violence, and determining the guilt and punishment of those accused of terrorism.

However, law enforcement agencies do distinguish between terrorist acts committed by domestic perpetrators of terrorism and foreign perpetrators of terrorism. According to the Federal Bureau of Investigation's Office of Domestic Terrorism and Counterterrorism Planning, perpetrators of **domestic terrorism** include lone offenders and extremist elements of groups. Lone offenders often are seeking revenge for individual grievances, carrying out vendettas against other citizens, or protesting against government policies or laws. Many are mentally unstable or belong to countercultures that believe in the violent overthrow of government. Some acts of domestic terrorism are pranks or frauds designed to spread panic or force the government into an emergency response. Such actions also include false bomb threats and mailing threatening letters containing substances that the person claims to be or appears to be a biological agent.

The three most common acts of domestic terrorism are:

1. acts of violence committed by militias and extremist groups or individuals in protest against government policies, laws, or authority,
2. violence by single-issue extremist groups such as antiabortion groups, and
3. ecoterrorism.

terrorism premeditated, politically motivated violence perpetrated against noncombatant targets by subnational groups or clandestine agents, usually intended to influence an audience

international terrorism terrorism perpetrated by state-sponsored groups, international terrorist organizations, and loosely affiliated international extremists' groups

domestic terrorism acts of terrorism committed in the United States by individuals or groups that do not have ties with or sponsorship from foreign states or organizations

September 11, 2001: The Tipping Point

The founding fathers of the United States drafted a constitution that reflected a distrust of a strong centralized government. The Constitution defined a government consisting of three independent branches of government (executive, legislative, and judicial) with checks and balances to prevent any one branch from becoming too powerful. It set up a federal court system and gave power to the states to set up court systems as they deemed appropriate. Law enforcement was primarily a local or state responsibility, because there were only two federal law enforcement agencies (the U.S. Marshal's Office and the Office of Postal Inspector) and few federal crimes defined by law. However, the new focus on homeland security is resulting in an increase in federal law enforcement powers and a shift from local to federal law enforcement.

AS EARLY AS 1998, SOME AUTHORITIES QUESTIONED WHETHER THE U.S. WAS FACING A NEW UPSURGE OF TERRORISM.

As a result, new federal law enforcement powers, new federal agencies, new federal legislation, and a changing national political ideology have had a great impact on the criminal justice system. In defending the homeland, there has been a shift from local law enforcement to federal law enforcement. Federal agencies and federal legislation have assumed greater importance than local agencies and state laws.

Capacity of State and Local Criminal Justice Systems Questioned

As early as 1998, some authorities questioned whether the United States was facing a new upsurge of terrorism,[2] and whether the U.S. law enforcement system, with its thousands of semiautonomous local law enforcement agencies, would prove effective in fighting international terrorism.[3] The escalation of terrorist attacks resulted in greater reliance on the federal government and the use of the military.

Shift to Reliance on the Federal Government The tipping point whereby there was a significant shift to reliance on the federal government was the September 11, 2001, attacks on the World Trade Center and the Pentagon. On September 12, 2001, in response to these attacks, President Bush declared war on terrorism and began pursuing a two-prong strategy of

1. aggressive use of military force overseas, and
2. greater reliance on federal agencies in responding to terrorism on U.S. soil.

Following the September 11, 2001, attacks, the Federal Bureau of Investigation made counterterrorism its highest priority, but the Bush administration claimed that this was not sufficient in fighting terrorism. The criminal justice system as it existed was considered inadequate in its ability to prevent terrorism by foreign perpetrators. Thus, the Bush administration requested new powers for federal agencies, the formation of new federal agencies, and the suspension of certain civil rights of accused terrorists, known as enemy combatants. These rights are considered by some to be fundamental to a democratic government.

Others concurred with the assessment that the criminal justice system as structured prior to 2001 had inherent organizational and legal obstacles that precluded it from preventing future attacks by international terrorists.[4] The report of the Strategies for Local Law Enforcement Series concluded that one of the critical obstacles in responding to terrorism in the United States was that law enforcement does not have the necessary infrastructure and powers to respond to international terrorism. The report declared that September 11, 2001, was a turning point for U.S. law enforcement as immediately following the attacks, local, state, and federal law enforcement agencies faced service demands, problems, and issues that they had never seen before. The report concluded that in examining the collective response and capacity of the various government agencies prior to the September 11 attacks, U.S. law enforcement simply was not prepared for major attacks by international terrorists. Furthermore, the report concluded that there was no simple fix, no quick solution to equipping law enforcement agencies with the ability to prevent and respond to terrorism. The report called for significant and long-term changes, asserting,

> For more than 125 years, American law enforcement has been organized around the principles of independence and decentralization. Some 18,000 local, state and federal agencies operate as autonomous entities, often unconnected to those in neighboring jurisdictions or at different levels of government. The threat of terrorism in America's cities and towns, however, has revealed the critical need to develop a formidable strategy to counter future acts of terrorism.[5]

Thus, the September 11, 2001, terrorism attacks were considered the tipping point for U.S. law enforcement.[6]

The New Federalism for Counterterrorism

The criminal justice system in the United States lacks the resources, training, intelligence-gathering capacity, and coordinated programs necessary to counter international terrorism. Prior to the September 11, 2001, terrorist attacks, the federal government's role in responding to major disasters was defined by the Stafford Act,[7] which makes most federal assistance contingent on a finding that the disaster is so severe as to be beyond the capacity of state and local governments to respond effectively.[8] Prior to the 9/11 terrorist attacks, few police departments trained and prepared to respond to a major terrorist attack. State and local law enforcement agencies are best prepared to respond to crime,

2 **New federal law enforcement powers, federal legislation, and federal agencies, and a changing national political ideology have had a great impact on the criminal justice system by causing a shift from local law enforcement to federal law enforcement.**

Domestic Terrorism			
Planned, funded, and executed by person or persons living within the United States without any assistance from a foreign group or state.			
	Ideology	**Examples**	**Actions**
Militias and Extremist Groups	Includes right-wing and left-wing extremist groups. Right-wing terrorist groups often are race-based, antigovernment. Left-wing groups profess a revolutionary socialist doctrine, which is anti-capitalism and anti-imperialism	Ku Klux Klan, World Church of the Creator, Aryan Nations, Southeastern States Alliance, Armed Forces for Puerto Rican National Liberation (FALN), Workers' World Party, Reclaim the Streets, and Carnival Against Capitalism	FALN carried out bombings in NYC, race-based hate crimes, assaults on judicial personnel. Many groups engage in public rhetoric and protests, which encourage race-based or anti-government violence but which may be protected by the First Amendment
Single-Issue Extremist	Focus on special interests that are considered foundational to the values of the group. Groups have different special interests and seldom do these groups work with other special interest groups	Army of God, Black Liberation Army, Symbionese Liberation Army, Weathermen and other anti-gay rights groups, pro-life groups, anti-immigration groups, anti-war groups, and anti-nuclear groups	Ted Kaczynski Unabomber attacks, 1978–1995; Timothy McVeigh and Terry Nichols Oklahoma City Federal Building bombing, 1996; Centennial Olympic Park bombing by Eric Robert Rudolph, 2001; anthrax attacks on Congress and media; 2009 Holocaust Memorial Museum shooting
Ecoterrorist Groups	Similar to single-issue groups but their focus is on environmental issues or animal rights	Animal Liberation Front (ALF), Earth Liberation Front (ELF)	Arson fires in Vail, Colorado, 1998; destruction of laboratory research facilities and the "liberation" of animals used in testing; attacks on car dealers selling SUVs
International Terrorism			
Planned, funded, and executed in part or whole by a foreign state, subnational group, or an extremist group. The violent acts of the group are intended to intimidate or coerce a civilian population, influence the policies of a government, or affect the conduct of a government.			
	Ideology	**Examples**	**Actions**
Loosely Affiliated Extremists	Motivated by political or religious beliefs. Often the goal of the group is to achieve power to force adoption of radicalized religious ideologies	Al Qaeda, Sunni Islamic extremists, various religious-based jihad movements	August 1998 bombings of U.S. Embassies in East Africa, the planning and carrying out of large-scale, high-profile, high-casualty terrorist attacks against U.S. interests and citizens
Formal Terrorist Organizations	Transnational organizations have their own infrastructures, personnel, financial arrangements, and training facilities	Hizballah, Palestinian Hamas, Irish Republican Army, the Egyptian Al-Gama Al-Islamiyya, and the Lebanese Hizballah	Hizballah is responsible for the 1983 truck bombings of the U.S. Embassy and the U.S. Marine Corps barracks in Lebanon, the 1984 bombing of the U.S. Embassy Annex in Beirut, and the 1985 hijacking of TWA Flight 847
State-Sponsored Terrorism	Countries that view terrorism as a tool of foreign policy	Iran, Sudan, Libya, Syria, Cuba, and North Korea	Targets dissidents living outside the country, supports anti-Western acts of terrorism by others, engages in cyber attacks against the United States. North Korea is of particular concern due to its pursuit of nuclear weapons and long-range rockets

*Adapted from Freeh, L. J. (2001, May 10). *Threat of terrorism to the United States: Congressional Testimony Before the United States Senate, Committees on Appropriations, Armed Services, and select Committee on Intelligence.*

to provide crime prevention services, and to provide and maintain order. Despite the call for counterterrorism strategies and capacities, local law enforcement agencies are grossly unprepared to respond to terrorism or to mount an effective counterterrorism campaign. As a result, federal agencies have been tasked with the primary responsibility for fighting terrorism and the powers of these agencies have been greatly enhanced by the USA Patriot Act, which gives federal law enforcement agencies expanded powers to detect, detain, and prosecute terrorists. Other federal legislation and presidential executive orders have also expanded the powers of federal law enforcement.

Department of Homeland Security: Building a Better Defense

The overlapping system of federal, state, and local governance in the United States results in more than 87,000 different jurisdictions. Prior to the September 11, 2001, terrorist attacks, lack of coordination of the mission, resources, and programs of these thousands of agencies to create a unified defense against and response to terrorism was a key weakness in the War on Terrorism. In an effort to increase homeland security following the September 11 terrorist attacks on the United States, President Bush sought to organize for a secure homeland by issuing the National Strategy for Homeland Security in July 2002 and signed legislation creating the Department of Homeland Security (DHS) in November 2002 and the cabinet-level Department of Homeland Security was implemented in March 2003.[9] Homeland security is defined as "a concerted national effort to prevent terrorist attacks within the United States, reduce America's vulnerability to terrorism, and minimize the damage and recover from attacks that do occur."[10] Many other federal, state, and local agencies are involved in homeland security but the DHS has the dominant role as it is the lead federal agency in most homeland security initiatives and it has the dominant share of homeland security funding.[11]

Creating the Department of Homeland Security The **Department of Homeland Security** is described as "a historic moment of almost unprecedented action by the federal government to fundamentally transform how the nation protects itself from terrorism."[12] The creation of the DHS is the most significant reorganization of the United States government since 1947. The DHS consolidates 22 federal agencies and 180,000 employees to create a single agency whose primary mission is to protect the homeland of the United States. In all, the DHS has responsibility for homeland security responsibilities that were dispersed among more than 100 different government organizations.[13] The changes brought about by the creation of the DHS, enabling legislation and changing political ideology, have had a significant impact on the criminal justice system.

22

federal agencies were combined to create the Department of Homeland Security

180,000

people are employed by the DHS

One of the important new missions of the DHS is to increase the domestic intelligence capacity of federal and local agencies. The DHS works with the CIA, the FBI, the Defense Intelligence Agency (DIA), and the National Security Agency (NSA) to analyze intelligence and information and to disseminate that intelligence to agencies that need it to counter terrorism. It should be noted that despite the many responsibilities of the DHS for homeland security, the FBI is the primary law enforcement federal agency responsible for the investigation of crimes of terrorism and the apprehension of suspected terrorists.

The 22 federal agencies that became part of the DHS include such diverse agencies as:

- U.S. Department of Treasury (U.S. Customs Service and Federal Law Enforcement Training Center)
- Department of Justice (some functions of Immigration and Naturalization Service, Office for Domestic Preparedness, and Domestic Emergency Support Teams)
- Department of Defense (National BW Defense Analysis Center and National Communications System)
- Federal Bureau of Investigation (National Domestic Preparedness Office and National Infrastructure Protection Center)
- Department of Energy (Nuclear Incident Response Team, CBRN Countermeasures Programs, and Energy Security and Assurance Program)
- Federal Emergency Management Agency
- Federal Protective Service

HERE'S SOMETHING TO THINK ABOUT . . .

The enhanced powers the law allows for investigations of terrorism can be attractive to those pursuing other criminals. In 2011, Representative Michael McCaul (R-TX) introduced a bill to designate top Mexican cartels as "foreign terrorist organizations." This would allow the United States to freeze money tied to the organizations and enhance the criminal penalties for those aiding the cartels. Some oppose the bill claiming it is unnecessary and others fear Mexico would object. One argument is that Mexican drug cartels are criminal organizations and are not ideologically motivated. Defenders of civil liberties fear that it could lead to a slippery slope and one type of criminal activity after another would be designated as terrorism. What do you think?

Department of Homeland Security (DHS) a newly created federal agency responsible for a wide range of security measures to protect against terrorist attacks

- Department of Agriculture (some functions of the Animal and Plant Health Inspection Service and Plum Island Animal Disease Center)
- Department of Health and Human Services (Strategic National Stockpile and the National Disaster Medical System)

Mission and Organization of the Department of Homeland Security

It appears that the DHS has not achieved the results promised in the rhetoric justifying the creation of this new federal agency. An April 2005 report by the Government Accountability Office (GAO) reported that in an earlier review of DHS in 2003, the GAO designated DHS's transformation as high risk due to the enormous challenges in implementing an effective transformation process, developing partnerships, and building management capacity.[14] The 2005 report credited DHS with making "some progress in its management integration efforts" but cited the need for continued improvements. In July 2005, then-DHS Secretary Michael Chertoff announced his plans to reorganize the DHS and promised to address many of the deficiencies pointed out by the GAO. Chertoff said that the DHS did not have the resources to protect against every threat and that the DHS must reorganize and "identify the most catastrophic possible terrorist attacks and do what it can to prevent them."[15] The goal of the DHS is to prevent the most nightmarish attacks and the most consequential threats.[16]

Transportation Security Administration With the exception of the **Transportation Security Administration (TSA)** most of the 180,000 staff of the DHS consisted of existing personnel from existing federal agencies. The DHS reorganized federal agencies to move those agencies with homeland security responsibilities under the DHS, as opposed to creating completely new federal agencies and hiring new personnel. The TSA is the exception in that prior to its formation, airport security and passenger screening were the shared responsibility of the government and the private airlines. After the September 11, 2001, attacks, this responsibility was transferred exclusively to the federal government. The Aviation and Transportation Security Act of November 2001 (Public Law 107-71) created the TSA to oversee security in all modes of travel.

The DHS assumed responsibility for the TSA on March 1, 2002, with the passage of the Homeland Security Act of 2002. The primary goals of the newly formed TSA were to increase the effectiveness and efficiency of (1) identifying passengers who were potential threats and (2) screening passengers and luggage for potential weapons and explosives. Shortly after assuming responsibility for aviation security, the TSA hired and deployed over 55,000 federal passenger screeners, hired and deployed more than 20,000 baggage screeners, implemented 100 percent screening of all checked baggage, and implemented screening of all cargo carried aboard commercial passenger aircraft. The creation of the TSA was the largest increase in federal employees in recent history.

55,000
number of new passenger screeners the TSA hired in 2002

20,000
number of new baggage screeners the TSA hired in 2002

Assessing the New TSA Responsibility for airport security and passenger screening was transferred to the DHS because it was believed that the previous partnership between the Federal Aviation Agency (FAA) and the airlines had failed to provide adequate security for the traveling public. Prior to 2001, the FAA issued several reports critical of the ability of airline employee screeners to prevent passengers from boarding with potential weapons and explosives.[17] Unfortunately, transferring responsibility to a federal agency did not seem to achieve the anticipated increase in effectiveness and efficiency of identifying passengers who were potential threats and screening passengers and luggage for potential weapons and explosives. Evaluations by the GAO in September 2002 and February 2004 of the performance of TSA personnel concluded that the new federal agency performed no better than the system it replaced, and the TSA continued to face the same challenges in hiring, deploying, and training its screener workforce as before.[18]

Multiple Agency Coordination

One of the premises underlying the prevention of and response to terrorist attacks, especially attacks involving weapons of mass destruction, is that no single agency has the capacity to prevent and to respond to a terrorist attack. Prevention of catastrophic terrorism is dependent on a unity of effort not only by federal agencies but also between federal and local agencies and among the various local and state agencies at both the operational and tactical levels.[19] Although the DHS provides overall guidance and coordination for the 22 agencies under its control, there is still the need to provide guidance and coordination for numerous other federal, state, and local agencies.

United States Government Interagency Domestic Terrorism Concept of Operations Plan

To promote a coordinated response by federal agencies, the federal government developed the **United States Government Interagency Domestic Terrorism Concept of Operations Plan (CONPLAN).** The CONPLAN was developed through the efforts of the primary departments and agencies with responsibilities for preventing and responding to terrorist attacks.[20] The purpose of the CONPLAN is to outline an organized and unified capability for a timely, coordinated response by federal agencies to a terrorist threat or act. It establishes conceptual guidance for assessing and monitoring a developing threat, notifying appropriate federal, state, and local

Transportation Security Administration (TSA) a newly created agency under the Department of Homeland Security that is responsible for airport security and passenger screening

United States Government Interagency Domestic Terrorism Concept of Operations Plan (CONPLAN) federal guidelines that designate which federal agency is the lead agency responsible for command and control in the event of a terrorist incident involving multiple federal agencies

3 **The prevention of terrorism depends on increased intelligence and on a new unified effort not only by federal agencies but also among the various federal, state, and local agencies at both the operational and tactical levels.**

History: Who Became Part of the Department?

The following agencies became part of the Department of Homeland Security in 2003.

Original Agency (Department)	**Current Agency/Office**
The U.S. Customs Service (Treasury)	U.S. Customs and Border Protection – inspection, border and ports of entry responsibilities U.S. Immigration and Customs Enforcement – customs law enforcement responsibilities
The Immigration and Naturalization Service (Justice)	U.S. Customs and Border Protection – inspection functions and the U.S. Border Patrol U.S. Immigration and Customs Enforcement – immigration law enforcement: detention and removal, intelligence, and investigations U.S. Citizenship and Immigration Services – adjudication and benefits programs
The Federal Protective Service	U.S. Immigration and Customs Enforcement
The Transportation Security Administration (Transportation)	Transportation Security Administration
Federal Law Enforcement Training Center (Treasury)	Federal Law Enforcement Training Center
Animal and Plant Health Inspection Service (part)(Agriculture)	U.S. Customs and Border Protection – agricultural imports and entry inspections
Office for Domestic Preparedness (Justice)	Responsibilities distributed within FEMA
The Federal Emergency Management Agency (FEMA)	Federal Emergency Management Agency
Strategic National Stockpile and the National Disaster Medical System (HHS)	Returned to Health and Human Services, July, 2004
Nuclear Incident Response Team (Energy)	Responsibilities distributed within FEMA
Domestic Emergency Support Teams (Justice)	Responsibilities distributed within FEMA
National Domestic Preparedness Office (FBI)	Responsibilities distributed within FEMA
CBRN Countermeasures Programs (Energy)	Science & Technology Directorate
Environmental Measurements Laboratory (Energy)	Science & Technology Directorate
National BW Defense Analysis Center (Defense)	Science & Technology Directorate
Plum Island Animal Disease Center (Agriculture)	Science & Technology Directorate
Federal Computer Incident Response Center (GSA)	US-CERT, Office of Cybersecurity and Communications in the National Programs and Preparedness Directorate
National Communications System (Defense)	Office of Cybersecurity and Communications in the National Programs and Preparedness Directorate
National Infrastructure Protection Center (FBI)	Dispersed throughout the department, including Office of Operations Coordination and Office of Infrastructure Protection
Energy Security and Assurance Program (Energy)	Integrated into the Office of Infrastructure Protection
U.S. Coast Guard	U.S. Coast Guard
U.S. Secret Service	U.S. Secret Service

The following three directorates, created by the Homeland Security Act of 2002 were abolished by a July 2005 reorganization and their responsibilities transferred to other departmental components:

- Border and Transportation Security
- Emergency Preparedness and Response
- Information Analysis and Infrastructure Protection

Source: Department of Homeland Security, www.dhs.gov/xabout/history/editorial_0133.shtm

agencies of the nature of the threat, and deploying the requisite advisory and technical resources to assist the lead federal agency (LFA) in facilitating inter-departmental coordination of crisis and consequence management activities.[21]

The CONPLAN establishes the **lead federal agencies (LFA)**. The LFA is responsible for providing leadership, crisis management, and consequence management actions in the event of a catastrophic terrorist attack. The CONPLAN identifies the LFA that has been established by policy and legislation for various aspects related to a terrorist attack. The purpose of the CONPLAN is to ensure the implementation of a coordinated response by federal agencies.

Responsiblities of Federal Agencies

The CONPLAN defines the following lead federal agencies and their responsibilities:

THE LFA IS RESPONSIBLE FOR PROVIDING LEADERSHIP, CRISIS MANAGEMENT, AND CONSEQUENCE MANAGEMENT ACTIONS IN THE EVENT OF A CATASTROPHIC TERRORIST ATTACK.

- The **attorney general,** the head of the U.S. Justice Department, is responsible for ensuring the development and implementation of policies directed at preventing terrorist attacks domestically, and will undertake the criminal prosecution of acts of terrorism that violate U.S. law. The Department of Justice has charged the FBI with execution of its lead federal agencies (LFA) responsibilities for the management of a federal response to terrorist incidents. As the lead agency for crisis management, the FBI will implement a federal crisis management response. As an LFA, the FBI is responsible for designating a federal on-scene commander to ensure appropriate coordination of the overall U.S. government response with federal, state, and local authorities until such time as the attorney general transfers the lead federal agency role to the Federal Emergency Management Agency.
- The **Federal Emergency Management Agency** (FEMA) is the LFA responsible for implementing the Federal Response Plan to manage and coordinate the federal consequence management response in support of state and local authorities.
- The **Department of Defense** is responsible for providing military assistance to the LFA and/or the CONPLAN primary agencies during all aspects of a terrorist incident upon request by the appropriate authority and approval by the secretary of defense.
- The **Department of Energy** is responsible for providing scientific-technical personnel and equipment in support of the LFA during all aspects of a terrorist attack involving a nuclear or radiological weapon of mass destruction.
- The **Environmental Protection Agency** (EPA) is responsible for providing technical personnel and supporting equipment to the LFA during all aspects of a terrorist incident involving a weapon of mass destruction. The EPA assistance and advice includes threat assessment; consultation; agent identification; hazard detection and reduction; environmental monitoring; sample and forensic evidence collection/analysis; identification of contaminants; feasibility assessment and cleanup; and on-site safety, protection, prevention, decontamination, and restorative activities.
- The **Department of Health and Human Services** (HHS) serves as a support agency to the FBI for technical operations and a support agency to FEMA for consequence management. The HHS provides technical personnel and supporting equipment to the LFA during all aspects of a terrorist incident. Technical assistance to the FBI may include identification of agents and medical management planning. Operational support to FEMA may include mass immunization, mass prophylaxis, mass fatality management, pharmaceutical support operations, contingency medical records, patient tracking, and patient evaluation and definitive medical care provided through the National Disaster Medical System.

First Responders

Historical Lack of Coordination of First Responders In responding to terrorist attacks, it is essential that there is cooperation between the federal government and local or state agencies known as **first responder** agencies and among the various first responder agencies themselves.[22] The most

HERE'S SOMETHING TO THINK ABOUT . . .

The federal government provides financial assistance to help first responders be prepared to respond to terrorist attacks. Government grants help buy equipment, fund training, and conduct multiagency training exercises. As a result of the demand for federal spending cuts in 2011, there are fewer grants available to local and state first responders. Do you think first responders should receive priority funding to ensure homeland security?

lead federal agency (LFA) the agency that is designated as being primarily in charge of an incident and has the power to direct the actions of other agencies and to call for the use of their resources, even though the lead agency may not have direct authority over these other agencies

first responders law enforcement, firefighters, and medical personnel who are the first to respond to a crisis or incident

important first responders at the operational/tactical level are police departments, fire departments, and local and state health providers. However, historically, the semiautonomous status of the thousands of first responder agencies has not promoted cooperation between federal agencies and first responders or interagency cooperation among first responders. Instead of cooperation, the various agencies have sought to control each other and "to be in charge" at the scene of the crisis.

The negative impact of this lack of interagency cooperation was clearly demonstrated during the response to the attacks on the World Trade Center Twin Towers. Lacking a culture of cooperation among the first responder agencies, police, fire, and health agencies "neglected to perform the critical task of information sharing."[23] Even if the police and the fire departments had wanted to share critical information during the crisis, it would not have been possible because the two departments did not have compatible emergency communications equipment. Further, the lack of compatible emergency communications capabilities and interoperable systems is not unique to New York City's police and fire departments. It is more common than not that state and local government first responders lack interoperable communications systems.[24]

Improving Coordination Since 2001, the federal government and first responders have taken actions to improve response capacity, communication, cooperation, and interoperable communication systems.

Mutual aid agreements provide for neighboring jurisdictions to assist in providing personnel and resources to their impacted counterparts. There are three types of mutual aid agreements:

1. mutual aid agreements with adjacent jurisdictions;
2. mutual aid agreements between states or between agencies of different states; and
3. mutual aid agreements that allow states and local governments to leverage existing and new assets to the maximum extent possible. Typically, they address such things as the mutual sharing of personnel resources and equipment, communications interoperability, and training.

Radio Codes One of the changes made to improve interagency communication has been inexpensive but has received universal notice among the public and police. This change is that first responder agencies no longer use "radio 10-codes" in radio communication. These codes, such as "10-4" meaning "acknowledge," have been ubiquitous in radio and personal communication, especially for police. However, there is no uniformity among departments as to the meanings of the various radio codes. The federal government and other studies of crisis response found that these codes have the potential to cause confusion and could even result in inappropriate or dangerous responses if codes were misunderstood among the various departments responding to a common crisis. Therefore, based on its power to regulate by controlling the purse strings, the federal government mandated that first responder departments that receive federal grants and funding (all police and fire departments receive federal funding) will use "plain English" rather than radio 10-codes.

Conflict Between Police and Fire Departments Police departments and fire departments are considered the most important first responders in responding to a terrorist attack but the autonomous relationship between the two departments has created serious debates regarding crisis management command and control. Fire departments and police departments often have conflict when responding to an incident as to who is in charge. In some extreme incidents, police officers have even arrested firefighters on obstruction charges as police and fire personnel disagree over who has the final authority to give orders and make decisions at the scene.

Most cities have favored placing the fire department in charge of hazardous materials incidents. Some cities have devised compromise plans to provide for public safety and coordinate the efforts of the fire department and police department. However, for some cities the question has generated significant debate. The conflict between NYPD and NYFD serves as a powerful example. In New York City, the fire department has been given exclusive command at hazardous materials incidents until it determines if a crime or terrorist act has taken place.

Intelligence and Homeland Security

In a large city there are an infinite number of targets that terrorists could choose to attack: buildings, bridges, tunnels, the electrical grid, the water supply, shopping malls, subways, buses, and more. No police department has the resources to provide security for every potential target. Thus, it is necessary to pick and choose which targets are to be protected. Accurate and timely intelligence that provides advance warning of possible terrorist attacks is critical if local and state police are to engage in preventive actions to minimize the threat of a terrorist attack.

Historic Separation of FBI and CIA The FBI is responsible for domestic intelligence and the Central Intelligence Agency (CIA) is responsible for foreign intelligence. Prior to September 11, 2001, the FBI and CIA did not share intelligence. Intelligence gathered by the CIA was fed primarily to the president, various federal government agencies, and the Pentagon and various military units. Local and state law enforcement agencies were critical of their dependency on the FBI for intelligence and they complained that the information flow between federal and local agencies is one-way: Local agencies give more to the federal agencies than they get in return.[25]

The 9/11 Commission criticized the lack of intelligence sharing among agencies as one of the reasons that the United States failed to "connect the dots" and piece together the intelligence information that would have enabled action to prevent the September 11 terrorist attacks. For example, there are claims that a secret military intelligence unit called "Able Danger" identified Mohammed Atta and three other of the 9/11 hijackers as likely members of a cell of al Qaeda operating in the United States but did not share this information with the FBI.[26] Other criticisms include charges of the failure of the FBI to integrate intelligence gathered from its own field offices to be able to connect the dots that could have alerted them to the fact that international terror suspects were taking flight training lessons.

Post–September 11, 2001, Intelligence Reforms

Following the September 11, 2001, attacks, intelligence gathering and sharing has been reengineered and a greater emphasis has been placed on intelligence sharing between federal and local law enforcement. New legislation, including the Patriot Act, allows the FBI and CIA to share terror-related intelligence. The FBI and the DHS have been charged with gathering and disseminating intelligence to local and state law enforcement agencies. New counterintelligence strategies call for coordination among the different agencies responsible for terror-related intelligence and the ability to take preemptive action before a terrorist attack occurs.

One of the reforms was to remove "the wall" established by the Foreign Intelligence Surveillance Act that prevented criminal investigators from using intelligence gathered in national security cases in criminal cases such as terrorist attacks. Prior to the Patriot Act, the Justice Department did not use intelligence gathered in national security cases to obtain search warrants when subjects were suspected of criminal activity. Under the provisions of the Foreign Intelligence Surveillance Act, search warrants and wiretaps could be obtained by showing that "there was probable cause that the subject was the agent of a foreign power." However, under the Fourth Amendment, search warrants require that the law enforcement agency establish that there is probable cause to believe a crime has occurred.

There have been several reorganizations of the intelligence community in an attempt to promote coordination and cooperation among the CIA, the FBI, and the DHS.[27] The DHS has its own intelligence directive agency, the Information Analysis and Infrastructure Protection (IAIP) directorate. The responsibilities of the IAIP are to coordinate the gathering of intelligence from all possible sources, both public and covert; to assess the scope of terrorist threats to the homeland from the intelligence gathered; and to respond appropriately by disseminating this information to those agencies that are responsible for providing security against terrorist attacks. In addition to the IAIP, another newly created agency to promote sharing of intelligence is the **Terrorist Threat Integration Center (TTIC)**. The mission of the TTIC is to "merge and analyze terrorist-related information collected domestically and abroad in order to form the most comprehensive possible threat picture."[28] The TTIC will have "unfettered access to all terrorist threat intelligence information, from raw reports to finished analytic assessment, available to the U.S. government."[29]

Joint Local–Federal Counterterrorism Task Forces

Some large police departments have turned to joint local–federal counterterrorism task forces to counter the threat of terrorist attacks. **Joint local–federal counterterrorism task forces (JTTFs)** are used to provide additional personnel to focus on counterterrorism activities and as a way to funnel intelligence from federal agencies to local agencies. However, many local departments are critical of JTTFs and do not believe JTTFs are a viable long-term solution.[30] The primary argument is that federal agencies often "do not draw on the full capabilities" of local law enforcement, and local law enforcement agencies "often get little back from their investment" in the JTTF.[31]

ONE OF THE REFORMS WAS TO REMOVE "THE WALL."

joint local–federal counterterrorism task force (JTTF) a working group of FBI and state and or local law enforcement officers that focuses on preventing terrorism by their joint cooperation and intelligence sharing

HERE'S SOMETHING TO THINK ABOUT . . .

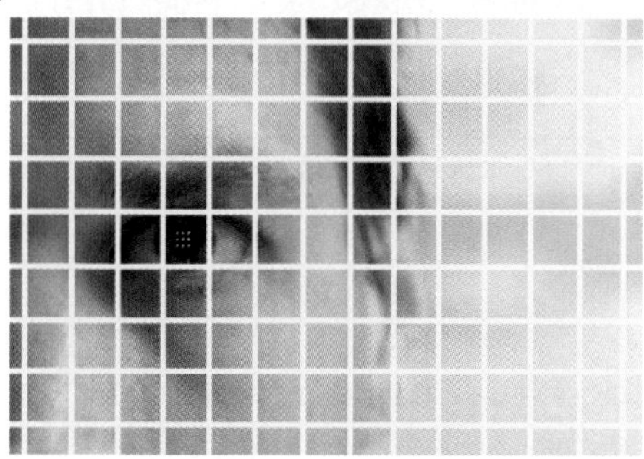

In the twenty-first century, law enforcement is using the Internet and social media to gather intelligence. The adoption of "face recognition" by Facebook enables law enforcement personnel to scan the social media and identify persons of interest. It also enables them to upload surveillance photographs and use face recognition software to identify persons in the photos. Does face recognition technology violate privacy rights?

Informal Intelligence Networks

Frustrated by the "slow and sometimes grudging way that federal officials share information about terrorist incidents," police chiefs are creating their own informal networks for the exchange of intelligence.[32] Local law enforcement officials say they are still not getting all the information they need from the federal government and what they are getting does not come in a timely fashion.[33] For example, William J. Bratton, former Los Angeles police chief, said joint terrorism task forces and the DHS are not geared "to providing real-time intelligence to local police" and as a result he often has to rely on cable news networks for information rather than the DHS or other federal agencies.[34] Charles H. Ramsey, former chief of the Washington Metropolitan Police, said, "Terrorism always starts as a local event. We're the first responders."[35] He emphasized that local police need real-time raw intelligence immediately, as opposed to the threat advisories and terror analysis issued by the DHS and the FBI. Local police executives stress that they must often make decisions immediately as to how to respond to a possible terrorist attack and that even waiting a day for information passed through federal intelligence networks could be too late.[36]

Fusion Centers

To overcome the deficiencies of JTTFs and the delay in obtaining intelligence from federal sources, local and state law enforcement agencies have established Fusion Centers. Fusion Centers, usually set up by states or major urban areas and run by state or local authorities, are intelligence

TABLE 13.1	Difference Between Fusion Centers and Joint Terrorist Task Forces (JTTFs)
Fusion Centers	**Joint Terrorism Task Forces**
Run by state and local authorities	Sponsored by the FBI
Are state/local-centric	Regionally and nationally focused
Deal with terrorism, criminal, and public safety matters	Deal exclusively with terrorism matters
Produce actionable intelligence for dissemination to appropriate law enforcement agencies but do not generally conduct investigations	Conduct investigations Local and state law enforcement personnel are "loaned" to JTTFs to promote federal-local cooperation
Financed and staffed by state and local funds but also may be supported by the FBI	

Source: Adapted from Federal Bureau of Investigation, "Fusion Centers," March 12, 2009.

networks designed to collect, to analyze, and to disseminate information critical to state and local law enforcement operations related both to homeland security and crime fighting. Fusion Centers are more than depositories for information already gathered. Fusion Center personnel integrate, evaluate, and analyze data to generate data that will assist police departments in responding to homeland security threats and crime.[37]

Expanding Federal Power to Fight Terrorism

One of the most significant changes in the criminal justice system has been the shifting balance of power between federal and state and local law enforcement agencies. The federal government has sought and received new powers to fight terrorism. In fact, during times of national security crises often the federal government has been given new powers as a means to defend the United States.

Thus, it is not surprising that in the focus on homeland security the federal government has asked for new powers to promote national security and to fight terrorism. Many of these early efforts to promote national security were through classified presidential **national security decision directives (NSDDs)**. Prior to 2001, the most significant antiterrorism legislation was the Anti-Terrorism and Effective Death Penalty Act of 1996. After 2001, the cornerstone legislation in the War on Terrorism became President Bush's **Enemy Combatant Executive Order** and the USA Patriot Act.

Enemy Combatant Executive Order

President Bush authorized a military invasion of Afghanistan, claiming that Afghanistan was the base for al Qaeda and state-sponsored terrorist attacks on the United States, particularly the September 11, 2001, terrorist attacks. On November 13, 2001, President Bush issued an executive order concerning how certain prisoners who were captured in Afghanistan would be detained and treated. The executive order declared such persons unlawful combatants as opposed to classifying them as prisoners of war. As unlawful combatants, their status is similar to that of enemy spies or saboteurs who are captured behind enemy lines without uniform. The executive order also provided that the captured persons would be detained in a military prison, without charges, without access to an attorney, without access to the civilian courts, and without protection of constitutional rights.

The Bush administration declared that such persons were not entitled to the rights accorded to prisoners of war under the Geneva Convention. The Geneva Convention Prisoner-of-War Pact proscribes that prisoners will not be questioned and do not have to reveal information other than their name, rank, and serial number. It provides for humane treatment in regard to housing and food. It guarantees prisoners' fair treatment and protection against criminal charges or the soldier's battlefield participation except in certain circumstances wherein the captured solder is charged with war crimes. The pact also provides that in the event of charges against a prisoner, the prisoner has the right to a civilian attorney of his or her choice and has the right to a trial in a civilian court. The provisions of the Geneva Convention provide for the right of prisoners to communicate and to receive communication. It also provides the right of inspection of the imprisonment of prisoners by international humanitarian organizations such as the Red Cross.

680
approximate number of enemy combatants captured in Afghanistan

The approximately 680 enemy combatants captured in Afghanistan, including several juveniles, were deemed to be terrorists and were given neither the rights accorded by the Geneva Convention or U.S. civilian law. They were transported to a military prison camp at Guantanamo Bay, Cuba. There, they were interrogated using tactics that some, including the International Red Cross and

HERE'S SOMETHING TO THINK ABOUT . . .

In 2011, the FBI issued a new Domestic Investigations and Operations guide to its 14,000 agents. The manual gives agents more latitude in their investigations. It enhances the ability of agents to look into people and organizations proactively without probable cause for suspected criminal or terrorist activity. It requires a lower standard of suspicion to search databases or people's trash. It allows agents surreptitiously to attend up to five meetings of a group to gather information. The ACLU fears these more lenient rules will lead to abuse. Do you agree?

4 **After the September 11 attacks, under the Bush administration, the federal government received new powers allowing it to hold persons deemed to be terrorists, including U.S. citizens, without rights accorded by the Geneva Conventions or U.S. civilian law and to loosen judicial review of federal law enforcement agencies using wire taps, intelligence gathering, and search and seizures.**

national security decision directives (NSDDs) directives issued by the president that are binding on federal agencies under executive command; NSDDs may proscribe actions to be taken by the agency or may direct the agency to take certain actions

Enemy Combatant Executive Order was issued by President Bush, providing for the detention of terrorists without access to due process rights

Amnesty International, have characterized as torture. The Bush administration claimed to have the right to hold these prisoners indefinitely without charge or access to the civilian courts.

Military Tribunals The Bush administration provided that these prisoners would be tried by special military tribunals.[38] These tribunals are unlike civilian courts or traditional military court martial courts. Unlike a military court martial governed by the Uniform Code of Military Justice, these military tribunals consist of three to seven judges, all of whom must be commissioned military officers. The accused does not have the right to confront witnesses or to challenge evidence that in the opinion of the tribunal would reveal national security information. The prisoner does not have the right of ***habeas corpus***—that is, the right to challenge the lawfulness of his imprisonment. Attorneys who represent accused terrorists in military tribunals must sign a list of promises and agree to certain conditions regarding disclosure of information and are prohibited from consulting civilian lawyers.[39] The military tribunal can sentence the prisoner to incarceration or impose the death penalty.[40]

U.S. Citizens as Military Combatants The Bush administration exercised this authority to apprehend U.S. citizens as enemy combatants. For example, Jose Padilla, an American citizen, was taken into military custody at Chicago O'Hare Airport in May 2002. Padilla was a former Chicago gang member with a long criminal record who converted to Islam. The government arrested him after he returned from a trip to Pakistan. Government officials claimed that he was associated with al Qaeda, met officials of the group in Afghanistan, and received training in explosives in Pakistan. In June 2003, President Bush declared Padilla an enemy combatant and he was moved from a federal jail in Lower Manhattan to a Navy brig in Charleston, South Carolina.[41] The legality of denying U.S. citizens access to the courts and to constitutional rights has been an ongoing dispute in the courts. The circumvention of the criminal court system to prosecute and punish persons accused of terrorism has alarmed many constitutional scholars.

Criticisms Public opinion regarding whether "terrorists" should be tried in civilian criminal courts or military tribunals is sharply divided. When Attorney General Eric Holder proposed trying accused terrorists Khalid Sheikh Mohammed and others for the 2001 terrorist attacks in civilian criminal courts in New York City, Senators John McCain (R-AZ) and Joseph Lieberman (I-Conn) proposed legislation to ban the use of civilian courts in prosecutions of terrorists. Supporters of military tribunals argue evidentiary rules should reflect battlefield conditions, but critics argue constitutional rights are the foundation of a democratic government.

Criminal Justice System Ill-Equipped to Try Terrorists Those opposed to civil trials argue if accused terrorists were granted traditional constitutional rights it would jeopardize national security, create unnecessary risk, create a significant financial burden for the city, and give the accused a forum for propaganda.

For example, in a civilian criminal trial defendants would have the right of discovery (the right to examine all the evidence of the prosecutor) and the right to confront witnesses. These rights would mean that evidence gathered by intelligence agencies and operatives would have to be revealed to the defendant. It is argued the defendant could pass this information along to terrorist networks.

Also, it is feared that civilian criminal trials would expose civilian jurors, prosecutors, and judges to potential violence and retaliation. The necessary actions to ensure courtroom and public safety would impose an extreme financial burden upon the city and state. New York officials estimated it would have cost $200 million for additional security to try Khalid Sheikh Mohammed in New York.

Finally, those opposed to granting civilian criminal trials to accused international terrorists claim that the defendant would only use the public forum of the trial as a means to promote radical ideologies and propaganda and defame the image of the United States.

Civil Rights Concerns Proponents of civil criminal trials for accused terrorists acknowledge the problems such trials propose but they argue denying civil rights to accused terrorists is dangerous. Attorney General Holder argued denying accused terrorists, including international terrorists, constitutional rights traditionally granted to the accused in criminal trials would harm—not promote—our national security. He said to deprive the accused of important constitutional rights would change the principle of the rule of law upon which the American criminal justice system is based.[42] The rule of law guarantees that all persons accused of wrongdoing before the courts will be judged by a

HERE'S SOMETHING TO THINK ABOUT . . .

U.S. law prohibits any aid to nations identified as sponsors of terrorism, including humanitarian aid. These laws have hampered the delivery of urgently needed aid to famine-stricken parts of Somali. U.S. laws prohibit any relief aid which may assist al-Shabab, an Islamic extremist group linked to al Qaeda, which controls parts of southern Somalia. The State Department says it is working to allow humanitarian groups to deliver aid but is concerned that aid may be diverted and al-Shabab could be strengthened by the aid or by claiming credit for the aid. An estimated 2.2 million are affected by the famine. Humanitarian groups argue all restrictions should be lifted. Do you think restrictions should be completely lifted even if it helps al-Shabab?

habeas corpus a writ or request to the court to review whether a person is imprisoned lawfully and that alleges that a person is detained or imprisoned illegally

single standard of justice which does not depend upon who they are but whether they violated the legal codes of the land. Supporters of civilian criminal trials argue that public trials are the best way to show the world that the United States respects the rights of all persons.

Furthermore, it is feared is that if certain civil rights can be denied to accused terrorists based upon arguments of national security, public safety, and costs, these same arguments could be used to strip other accused persons of their civil rights.

The USA Patriot Act

Following the September 11, 2001, terrorist attacks, Congress quickly enacted legislation to enhance national security. In October 2001, the **USA Patriot Act** (commonly called the Patriot Act) was quickly passed by Congress by an overwhelming majority and signed into law by the president. In the words of then-Attorney General John Ashcroft, the Patriot Act provided new powers to federal law enforcement agencies "to close gaping holes in our ability to investigate terrorists."[43]

Despite the broad new powers granted to federal law enforcement by the Patriot Act, there was little consideration and debate by the public or Congress as to the impact of these new powers on basic principles of due process on which the criminal justice system is based. In the post–September 11 environment, while the Justice Department continues to uphold the necessity and effectiveness of the Patriot Act, there is extensive criticism that the Patriot Act infringes on constitutional rights and has given federal law enforcement too much unchecked power. The extent of this opposition is evident by the fact that over 150 local governments and several states have passed resolutions objecting to the legislation.[44]

Section 213
of the Patriot Act authorizes expanded search powers.

The Patriot Act provides federal law enforcement greater surveillance powers, it expands federal jurisdiction of terror-related crimes, and it removes some civil liberties protections for those accused or detained under the provisions of the Patriot Act. The Patriot Act provides less judicial review of federal law enforcement agencies in regard to wire taps, intelligence gathering, and search and seizures.

Summary of the key provisions of the USA Patriot Act:

- Expands the range of crimes trackable by electronic surveillance.
- Allows police to use roving wiretaps to track any phone a terrorist suspect might use.
- Permits law enforcement to conduct searches with delayed notifications—the so-called sneak-and-peek provision.
- Allows FBI agents, with secret court orders, to search personal records (business, medical, library, etc.) without probable cause in a national-security case.
- Lowers legal barriers in information sharing between criminal investigators and intelligence officials.
- Provides new tools for fighting international money laundering.
- Makes it a crime to harbor terrorists.
- Increases penalties for conspiracy, such as plotting arson, killing in federal facilities, attacking communications systems, supporting terrorists, or interfering with flight crews.
- Makes it easier for law enforcement agents to obtain search warrants any place where "terrorist-related" activities occur; allows nationwide search warrants (including the monitoring of Internet use, e-mail, and computer bills) in terrorism investigations.
- Allows the attorney general to detain foreign terrorism suspects—but charges, deportation proceedings, or release must come within a week.
- Sends more federal agents to patrol the United States–Canada border.
- Ends surveillance and wiretap measures in 2005 (renewed).

Expanded Search Powers One of the most significant effects on the criminal justice system is that the authority of federal law enforcement agents to execute searches has been greatly expanded under the Patriot Act. Prior to the Patriot Act, law enforcement could conduct searches without a search warrant issued by the court only under a number of limited circumstances, such as incident to arrest, plain view searches, and emergency situations. Other than these circumstances, it was necessary for law enforcement agents to present evidence to the court that there was probable cause to conduct the search to obtain permission to perform the search. Further, the court search warrant limited the scope of the search.

The Patriot Act authorized expanded search power, required less judicial oversight of these search powers, and in some cases provided for secrecy concerning the search. A controversial provision of the Patriot Act is Section 213, the so-called sneak-and-peek provision. The sneak-and-peek provision gives federal law enforcement agents the authority to conduct a search with limited judicial review and authorization and provides for delayed notification of the search. Thus, federal agents could enter a house or business and execute a search in secret. If authorities did not find any incriminating evidence, they would not have to inform anyone of the search at that time. If the authorities did find incriminating evidence, they can use the evidence they found to obtain a search warrant by the court. The Patriot Act does not limit the use of this authority only to terrorist-related cases. In addition to the increased power to search under the Patriot Act, federal authorities can use the Foreign Intelligence Surveillance Act to perform similar searches as authorized by Section 213 of the Patriot Act. However, unlike the Patriot Act that provides for delayed notification, the Foreign Intelligence Surveillance Act provides that the subject may never be told about the search at all. The FBI first publicly acknowledged the use of this expanded authority granted by the Patriot Act and the Foreign Intelligence Surveillance Act in the search

USA Patriot Act legislation that gives federal law enforcement agencies expanded powers to detect, detain, and prosecute suspected terrorists

THE FBI CAN DEMAND THAT LIBRARY PERSONNEL PROVIDE THEM WITH ANY INFORMATION THEY HAVE ABOUT A PATRON AND CAN REQUEST INFORMATION ABOUT DOCUMENTS A PATRON HAS CHECKED OUT.

of the home of Brandon Mayfield, a Portland, Oregon, lawyer who was wrongly arrested and jailed in 2004 in connection with the March 2004 train bombings in Madrid, Spain.[45]

Another controversial section of the Patriot Act is Section 215. Under the authority of Section 215, the FBI has the authority to demand access to certain records without a warrant or demonstrating probable cause to the court. Under this provision any third party—such as a doctor, library, bookstore, university, bank, or Internet service provider—must turn over records requested by the FBI. Furthermore, they are forbidden by law to inform the subject or the public of this release of information.[46]

One of the most controversial debates related to Section 215 is the right of the FBI to use a national security provision to demand records of the reading habits of library patrons. Under this provision the FBI can demand that library personnel provide them with any information they have about a patron and the FBI can request information about documents a patron has checked out of the library. Further, the library personnel cannot tell the patron that they have released this information to the FBI and they cannot make any public comment about the release of the information. The Justice Department argues that if it was revealed that the FBI was seeking information from a certain library or about an individual, the revelation of that information could jeopardize an FBI counterterrorism investigation.

Criticisms of the Patriot Act Calls by the public and congressional members for repeal of some of the more controversial provisions of the Patriot Act were mounting until the July 2005 terrorist attacks on the London transit system. Following these attacks there was renewed belief by Congress in the necessity for a strong defense against terrorism and so the movement to repeal some of the provisions of the Patriot Act that were set to expire at the end of 2005 lost momentum.[47] However, revelations in December 2005 just prior to the expiration of some of the provisions of the Patriot Act that the Bush administration had engaged in extensive spying on U.S. citizens, secretly searched mosques for radioactive material, and conducted thousands of searches without court authorization resulted in a backlash of opposition against the Patriot Act. In last-minute negotiations the controversial provisions of the Patriot Act were extended and the renewal of the Patriot Act was approved in early 2006.

The Justice Department defends the use of the powers granted by the Patriot Act by pointing to the over 5,000 foreign nationals that have been detained since the September 11, 2001, attacks. However, of these thousands of detentions very few were ever charged with any crime.[48] Also, there have been over one thousand complaints of Patriot Act-related abuse of civil rights or civil liberties.[49]

In some cases, local police have not been in complete agreement regarding the constitutionality of the powers given to federal law enforcement by post–September 11 legislation. As a result, at times there have been conflicts between local and federal agencies as to the "legality" of certain law enforcement actions. One of the most prominent conflicts was when the Portland (Oregon) Police Department refused to interview foreign students as requested by the FBI. The police department refused to conduct the interviews because it claimed that the FBI did not offer any specific information about any crimes with which the individuals might be involved. Furthermore, the Portland Police Department said it believed that the questions that the FBI wanted the department to ask the students were not appropriate questions, as they asked about noncriminal matters such as religious beliefs and other questions not specifically related to criminal activity or knowledge.[50]

Fortress Urbanism: Terror-Focused Policing

Federal, state, and local law enforcement agencies have been diligent since the September 11, 2001, terrorist attacks in trying to detect perpetrators planning another terrorist attack on the United States. Since the September 11 attacks there has been constant warning of possible, sometimes imminent, terrorist plots. The Department of Homeland Security threat advisories have warned of terrorist plots to attack the New York financial district, commuter trains, symbolic landmarks such as the Brooklyn Bridge and the Golden Gate Bridge, and other targets.

Fear of a terrorist attack is transforming cities into **urban fortresses** as citizens and authorities fearing such attacks have reshaped the cityscape, increased security, blocked off streets, established security screening checkpoints, and imposed random searches of baggage and backpacks of subway passengers. Although federal authorities have assumed much of the responsibility for preventing another major 9/11 aviation-type terrorist attack, the responsibility and costs of providing everyday security to the average citizen as he or she goes about his or her business in the city has fallen primarily on local police.

Homeland Defense: Straining Police Resources

Cities that are considered likely to be targeted by terrorists are being transformed by roadblocks, checkpoints, and barriers. Parking lots near buildings thought to be at risk are being closed. Even sidewalks

urban fortresses cities that have adopted extensive and visible physical security measures and barriers in response to the threat of terrorist attack

5 **Fear of terrorist attacks is transforming cities into urban fortresses as citizens and authorities have established terrorist advisories, reshaped cityscapes, increased security, established security screening checkpoints, and imposed random searches of baggage and backpacks of subway passengers, all of which are putting strains on police forces.**

are being closed or transformed with security precautions. Concrete barriers, called Jersey barriers, are popping up as authorities take security measures to protect buildings and people. In cities such as New York and Washington, DC, public officials and citizens are complaining that physical security measures are becoming intrusive, backing up traffic, and making the city look uninviting for tourists and residents.[51] Washington, DC, officials complain that the proliferation of concrete barricades and checkpoints is making "this place feel like Fortress Washington."[52] One of the primary reasons for this increased security is fear of terrorists exploding a car or truck bomb, as in the 1993 World Trade Center and the bombing of the Murrah Federal Building in Oklahoma City, or a terrorist suicide bomber.

DURING THE 2004 REPUBLICAN NATIONAL CONVENTION, ALL HEARINGS AND TRIALS WERE SUSPENDED IN NEW YORK CITY COURTS.

Such threats are difficult to prevent. It is costing police departments millions of dollars in overtime costs, training, and equipment to fulfill this responsibility. During the heightened public transit alert in New York City following the July 2005 London subway bombings, New York police spent nearly $800,000 a day in additional costs to provide for subway security.[53]

When the terrorist alert level is raised, it is the local police who are expected to provide the increased security. Additional security duties during times of high alert have strained some local resources to the point that during terrorist alerts they can no longer provide routine services. Even large police departments such as New York City can reach this point. For example, during the 2004 Republican National Convention, all hearings and trials were suspended in New York City courts because police officers had to devote their time to convention security.

Also, as first responders, police officers need the training and equipment to respond effectively and to protect themselves against potential hazards such as toxic substances, chemicals, and radioactivity. Few departments have the budget to purchase such equipment or to provide officers with the necessary training to properly respond to a biological, chemical, or nuclear terrorist attack.

HERE'S SOMETHING TO THINK ABOUT . . .

The federal government has exclusive constitutional authority to regulate immigration. However, several states including Alabama, Arizona, Georgia, and Utah have protested that the federal government has failed to stem the violence, drugs, and illegal immigrants flowing across the southern border and have taken their own actions. Arizona passed controversial legislation in 2010, parts of which were ruled unconstitutional. In 2011, Arizona is seeking private donations to build a border wall. Is the federal government failing to secure the borders?

Terrorist Threat Advisories

Following the 9/11 attacks the federal government wanted to provide the law enforcement community and the public with timely warnings of potential terrorist attacks. These warnings were to flow from the intelligence gathered by federal agencies such as the CIA, FBI, and DHS. In 2002, the DHS implemented the Homeland Security Advisory System (HSAS) as the means to disseminate this information. The HSAS was a color-coded system using green, blue, yellow, orange, and red to indicate the level of threat.

$800,000

additional amount spent on security per day in New York City following the 2005 London subway bombings

The HSAS was not well received by the public nor the law enforcement community. The Government Accountability Office confirmed the public's skepticism of the effectiveness of the HSAS when its report concluded that warnings were often "vague and inadequate, and had hindered their ability to determine whether they were at risk and what protective measures to take in response."[54] The law enforcement community found the HSAS warning expensive to respond to, as a warning of high risk frequently resulted in overtime expenses and additional security-related costs. Furthermore, the heightened diligence of the law enforcement community was never rewarded with the apprehension of a terrorist as the warning did not specify the source or nature of the possible attack. Even worse, sometimes the statements issued by the FBI and the DHS provided conflicting advisory warnings.[55] As a result of strong pressure from both the public and the law enforcement community the DHS eliminated the HSAS and replaced it with a new threat advisory system in April 2011.[56]

Terror Alerts and Crime One interesting question regarding the HSAS has been the effect of terror alerts on crime. The Kansas City Preventive Patrol experiment suggested that routine preventive patrol did not have an impact on crime rates. That is to say, when routine preventive patrol was increased, crime rates did not decrease and vice versa.

Homeland Security Advisory System (HSAS)
a daily color-coded threat advisory to government agencies, police, and the public that recommends appropriate actions in response to the forecasted risk of terrorists attack

DATE & TIME ISSUED: XXXX

SUMMARY

The Secretary of Homeland Security informs the public and relevant government and private sector partners about a potential or actual threat with this alert, indicating whether there is an "imminent" or "elevated" threat.

DURATION

An individual threat alert is issued for a specific time period and then automatically expires. It may be extended if new information becomes available or the threat evolves.

DETAILS

- This section provides more detail about the threat and what the public and sectors need to know.
- It may include specific information, if available, about the nature and credibility of the threat, including the critical infrastructure sector(s) or location(s) that may be affected.
- It includes as much information as can be released publicly about actions being taken or planned by authorities to ensure public safety, such as increased protective actions and what the public may expect to see.

AFFECTED AREAS

- This section includes visual depictions (such as maps or other graphics) showing the affected location(s), sector(s), or other illustrative detail about the threat itself.

HOW YOU CAN HELP

- This section provides information on ways the public can help authorities (e.g. camera phone pictures taken at the site of an explosion), and reinforces the importance of reporting suspicious activity.
- It may ask the public or certain sectors to be alert for a particular item, situation, person, activity or developing trend.

STAY PREPARED

- This section emphasizes the importance of the public planning and preparing for emergencies before they happen, including specific steps individuals, families and businesses can take to ready themselves and their communities.
- It provides additional preparedness information that may be relevant based on this threat.

STAY INFORMED

- This section notifies the public about where to get more information.
- It encourages citizens to stay informed about updates from local public safety and community leaders.
- It includes a link to the DHS NTAS website http://www.dhs.gov/alerts and http://twitter.com/NTASAlerts

If You See Something, Say Something™. Report suspicious activity to local law enforcement or call 911.

The National Terrorism Advisory System provides Americans with alert information on homeland security threats. It is distributed by the Department of Homeland Security. More information is available at: www.dhs.gov/alerts. To receive mobile updates: www.twitter.com/NTASAlerts

If You See Something Say Something™ used with permission of the NY Metropolitan Transportation Authority.

The new Terrorism Advisory System (NTAS) is designed to address the shortcomings of the HSAS. It has eliminated the color-coded alerts. The NTAS has only two alert levels: elevated and imminent. "Elevated" means the DHS has no specific information about the timing or location of the threat. "Imminent" means the threat is impending or very soon. NTAS alerts are not issued unless there is a specific threat. The NTAS alerts will be disseminated to the press and will also be distributed using DHS's social media channels, including Twitter, Facebook, and RSS feeds. NTAS advisors carry an expiration date. The NTAS advisors provide a concise summary of the potential threat, information about actions being taken to ensure public safety, and recommended steps for the public and governments to take in response to the threat.

Source: Department of Homeland Security www.dhs.gov/files/publications/ntas-public-guide.shtm.

However, preliminary statistical studies on the effect of changes in the terror alert level and crime rates have suggested that contrary to previous studies there is a relationship between crime rates and increased police presence. One study indicated that on high-alert days total crimes in Washington, DC, decreased by 6.6 percent and some crimes decreased even more. For example, burglary declined by 15 percent.[57] The study estimated that if there is a 10 percent increase in police presence, crime decreases by about 4 percent.[58] If other studies examining the relationship between high terror alerts yield similar results, conclusions drawn from previous studies such as the Kansas City Preventive Patrol experiment may be revised.

Closing the Borders to Terrorists

Fear that international terrorists could slip into the United States or could enter under false pretenses such as a student visa or tourist visa has resulted in a transformation of federal agencies and legislation concerning border security.

However, border security is a complex issue and raises questions of how to handle illegal immigrants, amnesty for the estimated 12 million illegal immigrants residing in the United States, and designing fair immigrant policies and laws. These problems are compounded by demographic shifts in the U.S. population as an increasing number of U.S. residents are nonwhite. Studies find that nonwhites and the younger generation see immigration policy through a different set of values. These groups are more receptive to amnesty programs and open borders.

Sealing the Borders

Border security and immigration control have been long-standing concerns. Prior to September 11, 2001, the primary concern was the U.S.–Mexican border. In the post–September 11 environment the concern is that if "ordinary" persons simply seeking employment can so easily enter the United States illegally, then international terrorists intent on committing acts of violence can just as easily enter the country. Also of concern is the fear that terrorists could smuggle a nuclear weapon into the United States. Auditors from the GAO and scientists testifying before a House committee warned that "the federal government's efforts to prevent terrorists from smuggling a nuclear weapon into the United States are so poorly managed and reliant on ineffective equipment that the nation remains extremely vulnerable to a catastrophic attack."[59]

Also, the DHS is concerned that terrorists could enter the United States as illegal immigrants and obtain jobs in risk-sensitive facilities that would enable them to carry out a terrorist attack against the United States. The DHS is concerned that illegal immigrants could obtain jobs as airline mechanics, at nuclear facilities, or at other critical

6 **Fear of terrorism has increased existing concerns about immigration control, and radical changes are being proposed in U.S. immigration policies and enforcement that most likely otherwise would not have been supported by the majority of the public.**

infrastructure facilities.[60] To prevent this possibility, legislation makes employers responsible for verifying that their workers are legally entitled to work in the United States. Despite the DHS's warning that hiring undocumented workers poses a serious homeland security threat, illegal immigrants do find employment in such industries.

The DHS fears that even if these illegal immigrants are not terrorists, their illegal status could make them vulnerable to potential exploitation by terrorists and other criminals who could threaten to expose their illegal status to authorities. Thus, in addition to border security, the DHS **Immigration and Customs Enforcement (ICE)** agency conducts investigations to determine if illegal immigrants are employed in such facilities. Past sweeps have found illegal immigrants working in facilities considered to be critical infrastructure sites. One raid by ICE in May 2005 resulted in the arrest of 60 illegal immigrants in sensitive jobs in six states, including seven petrochemical refineries, three electric power plants, and a pipeline facility.[61]

THE UNITED STATES PLANS TO CONSTRUCT A PHYSICAL OR VIRTUAL FENCE ALONG THE ENTIRE U.S.–MEXICAN BORDER.

Immigration Control and Enforcement

Since 2001, one of the goals of the federal government has been to prevent international terrorists from entering the United States. There are several ways terrorists can enter the country. They can use false immigration papers, they can enter under the pretext of being legal tourists and then not leave when their tourist visa expires, they can enter using student visas, and they can enter illegally and undetected at some point in the 8,000 miles of the Canadian and Mexican borders plus the Atlantic and Pacific coastlines.

The power to regulate immigration is an exclusive power given to the federal government; therefore, the DHS is primarily responsible for immigration control and border security. In an attempt to seal the borders against terrorists the DHS has initiated a number of changes, including better tracking of foreign visitors, airline passenger screening, smart passports, and stricter accountability for foreign students and scholars.

United States Visitor and Immigrant Status Indicator Technology The cornerstone of the DHS's efforts to track foreign nationals entering and exiting the United States is the **United States Visitor and Immigrant Status Indicator Technology** program. Known as US-VISIT, the program requires most foreign visitors to be fingerprinted and photographed when entering the United States. At first, the program applied only to those visitors arriving at airports from countries for which entry visas were required. Today, the program has expanded to include most foreign travelers and continues to expand to include seaports and land border crossings.

Smart Passports In addition to passenger screening and enhanced airport security, the federal government has initiated the adoption of "smart" passports. **Smart passports** contain microchips and a radio frequency identification system. The microchips contain about 64 kilobytes of data such as the name, birth date, issuing office, and biometric identifier information such as a photograph, iris scans, and digital fingerprints of the traveler. The wireless technology allows travelers to pass through a checkpoint with their passport and have their data confirmed electronically. In August 2005, the first use of radio frequency identification system passports was tested at a Canadian border crossing. Similar to radio frequency identification systems used to collect highway tolls, the radio-tagged passports can be read by electronic equipment from 30 feet as a person passes through the border checkpoint. A DHS spokesperson said the new electronic passports could "help relieve congestion at border crossings, while also helping authorities weed out potential terrorists, drug dealers and other criminals."[62]

Despite attempts to improve passport security a 2009 study by the GAO reported fraudulent passports continue to be a concern. One point noted in the report was that DHS offices are evaluated on the number of passports they issue, not on the quality of the screening to prevent persons from obtaining passports with fraudulent documents. The GAO report recommended that the DHS focus on ensuring that the documents used to obtain passports are valid.

Student and Exchange Visitor Information System (SEVIS) Several of the hijackers involved in the September 11, 2001, terrorist attacks entered the United States on student visas. Under the system in place prior to September 11, 2001, the Immigration and Naturalization Service (INS) had limited capacity to verify if students actually enrolled and attended the college or program they indicated on their student visa applications.

To close this vulnerability a new tracking system for international students was implemented. The new system converted what was a manual procedure into an automated process and provided stricter monitoring of the attendance of international students. The new system, called the **Student and Exchange Visitor Information System (SEVIS)**, is a Web-based system for maintaining information on international students and exchange visitors in the United States. It is administered by U.S. Immigration and Customs Enforcement (ICE) and U.S. Customs and Border Protection (CBP). The cost of the SEVIS program is paid for by fees collected from those applying for student, exchange visitor, or scholar visas.

The Fence The United States shares a vast land border with Canada to the north and Mexico to the south. As a strategy of the Secure Border Initiative begun in 2003, the United States plans to construct a physical or virtual fence along the entire U.S.–Mexican border and to significantly enhance security of the U.S.–Canadian border. Hundreds of miles of the physical and virtual border fence between the United States and Mexico have been constructed. The physical fence aims to

Immigration and Customs Enforcement (ICE) a new federal agency under the DHS responsible for enforcement of immigration laws

United States Visitor and Immigrant Status Indicator Technology (US-VISIT) a new system of registering the entry of foreign visitors to the United States and tracking when and where they exit the United States

smart passports new passports that contain machine-readable data about travelers

Student and Exchange Visitor Information System (SEVIS) a Web-based information database containing information on international students studying in the United States

prevent illegal crossings into the United States. The virtual fence is a network of towers equipped with cameras, sensors, and communications equipment. In 2011, the Department of Homeland Security (DHS) cancelled the billion-dollar virtual fence project citing technical problems, cost overruns, and delays. DHS plans to use other technologies to perform border surveillance.

The fence has been praised and condemned. Those who praise the fence cite its ability to stem the flow of illegal immigrants, drug traffickers, human smugglers, and terrorists into the United States. Those who oppose the fence cite its marginal effectiveness, detrimental impact upon the environment, and negative impact upon good-neighbor relations with Mexico and Canada.

Criticisms of Border Security

Many of the efforts of the DHS to seal the borders have been controversial. The program to identify "special interest" immigrants was criticized as **racial profiling**. The US-VISIT program has been criticized as ineffective. Air travelers have claimed that their names have been included on the **no-fly list** for no reason and they have been unable to appeal the inclusion of their names on the list due to the secrecy that surrounds the making of the list.

In an effort to detect and deport illegal immigrants who have managed to enter the United States, the DHS has adopted an aggressive policy of immigration enforcement. This policy includes checking the names of persons sentenced to jails and prisons to determine if any of the inmates are immigrants that can be deported due to their arrest. It also includes enforcement of immigration laws requiring employers to obtain documentation that the employees they hire are legal immigrants.

Some policies of the DHS have been criticized as "overly aggressive" and creating public safety concerns, as the DHS has used various deceptions to detect illegal workers. One example was the DHS's stepped-up efforts to crack down on illegal immigrants working at chemical plants, nuclear plants, and other sensitive facilities.[63] In order to discover if any illegal immigrants were working at these facilities, the DHS conducted a sting operation. The DHS posted notices announcing that employees were required to attend mandatory safety training by the Occupational Safety and Health Administration (OSHA) to keep their jobs. When the workers showed up for the "training session," immigration officials identified illegal immigrants and arrested them. Many OSHA officials protested the subterfuge, claiming that the use of OSHA's name in the ruse could have serious consequences in getting workers to attend legitimate safety training.[64]

The 9/11 Commission concluded that immigration policies initiated by DHS have been "ineffective, producing little, if any, information leading to the identification or apprehension of terrorists."[65] The 9/11 Commission criticized the immigration polices as neither preventing potential terrorists from entering the country nor clearly distinguishing potential terrorists who should be removed from the country. For example, after assuming control over visas, the new DHS-supervised departments issued visas to 105 foreign men who should have been prevented from entering the United States because their names appeared on government lists of suspected terrorists.[66]

State and Local Actions to Curtail Illegal Immigration

Although immigration is officially the responsibility of the federal government, many state and city governments are greatly concerned and impacted by illegal immigration. State and local governments have expressed concern over public safety issues caused by illegal immigration. Illegal immigration posed such a threat that in August 2005, the governors of Arizona and New Mexico issued a state of emergency declaration in response to what they described as a public safety concern caused by illegal immigration.[67]

State and local governments cite public safety concerns related to illegal immigrants who commit acts of violence, including murder, drug trafficking, human smuggling, and property damage. New Mexico governor Bill Richardson declared that as a result of the illegal border crossings, citizens of New Mexico were "devastated by the ravages and terror of human smuggling, drug smuggling, kidnapping, murder, destruction of property and death of livestock."[68] The extent of the problem is illustrated by the fact that at one point on the New Mexico border the Border Patrol estimated there were an average of 175 persons per day caught trying to enter the United States illegally.[69]

The concern for public safety extends beyond border towns, as once in the United States some illegal immigrants engage in violent gang criminality.[70] Violent criminal gangs composed primarily of illegal immigrants can be found in major cities throughout the United States. One of the most serious concerns among law enforcement is the criminal activity of the gang known as MS-13 or Mara Salvatrucha, which has committed numerous violent attacks in major cities throughout the United States. In 2005 and 2006, in a sweep of suspected immigrant gang members called Operation Community Shield, ICE arrested over 1,000 alleged gang members representing 80 gangs in 25 states.[71] ICE officials said more than 900 of those arrested are eligible for deportation. Antigang ICE officials claim there are thousands of suspected gang members who are in the United States illegally or who have committed serious crimes that make them eligible for deportation. The extent of the criminality of illegal immigrants is seen in that each year ICE deports approximately 80,000 illegal immigrants for criminal activity.[72]

1,000
number of alleged gang members arrested by ICE in 2005 and 2006

900
number of those alleged gang members who were eligible for deportation

In April 2010, claiming that "decades of federal inaction and misguided policy have created an unacceptable situation,"

racial profiling allegations that police search and seizures, traffic stops, field interrogations, and arrests are made on nonbehavioral factors related to race and/or ethnicity rather than suspicious behavior or probable cause

no-fly list a secret list maintained by the Department of Homeland Security that lists the names of persons who are prohibited from flying on a commercial airplane under any circumstances; it also contains the names of persons who should receive additional screening prior to being allowed to board an aircraft

HERE'S SOMETHING TO THINK ABOUT . . .

The Department of Homeland Security (DHS) was created by combining 22 federal agencies under one cabinet-level administration. However, the oversight of each of these agencies was not consolidated. Thus, the DHS answers to 108 congressional committees, subcommittees, and caucuses. DHS officials reported that in 2009 they spent about 66 work years responding to questions from Congress, answered 11,680 letters, gave 2,058 briefings, and sent 232 witnesses to 166 hearings. The cost to the taxpayers was about $10 million. Calls to Congress for streamlining have been ignored due to the desire to preserve turf. Should congressional oversight of DHS be revamped?

Arizona Governor Jan Brewer signed into law a bill making Arizona the first state to criminalize illegal immigration.

$100 to $700 million

The cost of states to conform to the requirements of the Real ID Act

Homeland Security Janet Napolitano, former governor of Arizona, claims the Arizona law is a serious threat to public safety and may promote racial profiling by the police. Hispanic groups have demonstrated across the country against the law. A federal court ruled key provisions of the law unconstitutional but Arizona has appealed the court's verdict to the U.S. Supreme Court. Until the Court rules on the law, Arizona is prohibited from enforcing those provisions ruled unconstitutional. Despite the public protests other states have passed laws against illegal immigration.

Enforcement of immigration laws has become a political and constitutional "hot button" issue. The controversy arises in some interesting circumstances. For example, in *Padilla v. Kentucky* (2010), the U.S. Supreme Court ruled that lawyers must advise their immigrant clients facing criminal charges that pleading guilty could lead to deportation. In another example, in May 2010, during a televised visit to an elementary school, a second-grader confessed to First Lady Michelle Obama that she was concerned about U.S. immigration policy because her mother "did not have papers."

National Identification Card

To enhance national security the DHS has advocated a national identification card. There is controversy over the merits of a national identification card and the potential threat to civil liberties if such a program was adopted. Although not embracing the idea of a national identification card, Congress has been favorable toward adopting uniform standards for state driver's licenses.

Real ID Act The adoption of a standardized state driver's license as required by the **Real ID Act** will create a national database, because it requires states to share driver's license information. Critics of the Real ID Act argue that it will create a national identification card and database.

Estimates suggest that the Real ID Act would require approximately $100 to $700 million for states to conform to the requirements of the act.[73] States would have to pick up most of these costs. Governors have argued that if the provisions of the Real ID Act are implemented, "this is going to drive the cost of driver's licenses for ordinary folks through the roof."[74]

Proponents of the legislation believe that the Real ID Act will eliminate the ability of illegal immigrants to obtain driver's licenses. Presently, many states issue driver's licenses to illegal immigrants because the state does not require that a person prove he or she is a legal resident in order to obtain a driver's license. It is estimated that the Real ID Act would prevent tens of thousands of undocumented persons from obtaining a driver's license.[75] Critics of the act argue that it would create a public safety danger because undocumented immigrants would continue to drive without the benefit of being examined to determine if they have the necessary knowledge and ability to operate a motor vehicle. Those who support the act argue that denying illegal immigrants the right to drive is not "punishment," as they are not entitled to be in the United States in the first place.[76]

IN *PADILLA V. KENTUCKY*, THE COURT RULED LAWYERS MUST ADVISE THEIR IMMIGRANT CLIENTS FACING CRIMINAL CHARGES THAT PLEADING GUILTY COULD LEAD TO DEPORTATION.

Cyberterrorism and Homeland Security

On January 24, 2000, nearly half of the computing power in the world went dead. The top-secret NSA's massive array of supercomputers—which crunch information from America's spy satellites and global eavesdropping network—mysteriously shut down for 3 days. Government officials immediately feared that hackers might have caused the shutdown.[77] In the end, the shutdown was attributed to human and computer error, but the fear that it was deliberate is justified. Previously,

Real ID Act proposed legislation that would require all state driver's licenses to conform to uniform standards set by the Department of Homeland Security

hackers had been successful in shutting down 911 emergency service, severing NASA uplinks to the Atlantis shuttle,[78] shutting down state governments' Web pages,[79] infiltrating and defacing the Senate's main Web site,[80] defacing the U.S. Army's main Web site,[81] and penetrating Defense Department national defense databases and stealing sensitive information.[82]

Responding to cyberterrorism is difficult, as cyber attacks can be executed from anywhere in the world and it is difficult to establish the source of attacks. Cyber attacks can emanate from remotely controlled computers whose owners are not even aware that control of their computers has been hijacked and are being used for attacks. It was this strategy that was used in the summer of 2009 when United States and South Korean computers were attacked. In the United States the computers of the DHS, the FAA, and the Federal Trade Commission were attacked. News released by the United States and South Korea suggested the cyber attacks were connected to the North Korean government.[83] Shortly following these attacks Defense Secretary Robert M. Gates issued an order establishing a command that will defend military networks against computer attacks and develop offensive cyber weapons. The new cyber command will be under the NSA, not the DHS, and will also provide assistance to civilian systems.

EXTREMIST GROUPS USE THE INTERNET TO RECRUIT NEW MEMBERS, TO PROVIDE ONLINE TRAINING FOR JIHADISTS PLOTTING VIOLENT ATTACKS, AND TO DISSEMINATE THEIR MESSAGE WORLDWIDE.

In addition to using the Internet to launch cyber attacks, extremist groups use the Internet to recruit new members, to provide online training for jihadists plotting violent attacks, and to disseminate their message worldwide. In an unusual finding, the federal government has discovered that the relatively low expense and high quality of United States servers seems to attract jihadists, and many of the Taliban Web sites use Internet Provider Services (IPS) located within the United States but run from the Middle East. Usually the IPS has no idea of the content or purpose of these Web sites. Shutting them down can be complicated by the fact that detection of the Web sites and shutting them down may come close to the line regarding constitutional rights of free speech and privacy.

Civil Rights and Homeland Security

The U.S. criminal justice system is based on the principle that persons are entitled to certain inalienable rights provided by the Constitution and Bill of Rights. People are guaranteed such rights as the right of freedom from unreasonable search, the right to confront witnesses, the right to a public trial, the right to know the charges against them, the right to an attorney, and the right of free speech and association. These rights have served as the cornerstone of the U.S. criminal justice system. However, public opinion polls indicate that most Americans believe that some civil rights will have to be sacrificed in the War on Terrorism. The challenge is to balance the loss of civil rights with appropriate national security concerns.

Fewer Liberties, Greater Security?

In the post–September 11, 2001, environment, some acts and behaviors have been prohibited in the effort to promote national security. In the pursuit to discover terrorists who may be in the United States, Congress has provided law enforcement officials with new powers that diminish Fourth Amendment (search and seizure) rights. Often, these new powers provide federal law enforcement with the authority to perform acts that prior to September 11, 2001, would not have been approved by the public or would have been considered unconstitutional. The justification for the curtailing of these rights is that these new powers and laws promote national security and enhance the ability of law enforcement to detect terrorist cells within the United States and secret plots by terrorists before they can launch a terrorist attack. Terrorist cells in the United States are organized into small groups of terrorists (usually four to six individuals) who have entered the country and have "blended in" as they plot or await orders that would enable them to launch a terrorist attack.

Related efforts to promote national security by discovering these terrorist cells have impacted many citizens. For example, in an effort to make it harder for terrorists to avoid detection, policies and practices have been adopted to prevent terrorists from obtaining employment. The purpose of these policies and laws is to make it more difficult for terrorists to remain in the United States or to obtain jobs where they could use their employment to carry out a terrorist attack. However, as a result of such practices, thousands of airline workers who are not terrorists lost their jobs when U.S. citizenship became a job requirement for these jobs. Also, fearing that terrorists may recruit converts from the criminal population, legislation was passed that prohibited persons with felony convictions from obtaining certain employment, such as truck drivers who could transport hazardous materials, or from obtaining jobs on military bases. Because there is no time limit on when one was convicted, some workers with long-past felony convictions have found that they are denied employment or lost their job because of this provision.

In the name of national security, citizens have fewer expectations of privacy rights. Increased domestic intelligence action by the Justice Department has resulted in government access to bank accounts, credit histories, medical records, academic records, travel plans, Internet communications, and cell phone communications. In the effort to ensure national security, the FBI has engaged in extensive spying on Americans, secret searches of mosques, and scrutiny of hundreds of social action groups such as the American Civil Liberties Union.

7 **In the pursuit to discover terrorists in the United States, Congress has provided law enforcement officials with new powers that diminish constitutional rights, such as freedom of speech, due process rights, and rights to privacy, in ways that were unconstitutional before the September 11 attacks.**

HERE'S SOMETHING TO THINK ABOUT . . .

In 2011, U.S. Representative Peter King (R-NY), chair of the House Homeland Security Committee, held a hearing on the threat of Islamic radicalization in the United States. King claims more than 40 Americans have been recruited by Islamic radical groups to join al-Shabab in Somalia. King says 15 have been killed in fighting. King also claims radicalized Islamic groups are recruiting American youths to travel overseas for "programming" and then they are returning to carry out attacks against the United States. Melvin Bledsoe testified that his son Carlos converted to Islam and as a result of overseas "programming" returned to carry out an attack on a military recruiting center in Little Rock, Arkansas. King asserts that mosques in America are "sitting around doing nothing about radical extremists" and discourage members from cooperating with law enforcement. Critics accuse King of inflaming Islamophobia and McCarthyism. What do you think?

Calls for independent bipartisan panels to monitor the possible abuse of civil rights have not overcome the belief by the majority that loss of a certain number of civil rights may be necessary to prevent future terrorist attacks.

Free Speech and Protest Versus Terrorism

As federal law enforcement agencies have gained new powers to conduct domestic intelligence, critics are concerned about possible abuses of these powers. These concerns were heightened when a 2008 Justice Department report concluded that the FBI had abused its intelligence-gathering powers made possible by noncourt-approved search warrants called "national security letters."[84]

A 2008 JUSTICE DEPARTMENT REPORT CONCLUDED THAT THE FBI HAD ABUSED ITS INTELLIGENCE-GATHERING POWERS.

Some antiterrorism laws are vague and may prohibit legitimate activities. For example, federal law prohibits providing material support to groups that the State Department has deemed to be terrorist organizations. Any form of aid to a "terrorist organization" including health, social welfare, or legal assistance is illegal. Solicitor General Elena Kagan defended the law saying, "It was impossible to separate support of any terrorist group's peaceful activities from its violent goals." Critics argue such vague material support laws hinder international efforts to promote human rights and peace through nonviolent means.[85]

Denial of Due Process

Critics accuse the Justice Department of denying due process to many persons accused of or suspected of terrorism. For example, a report by Human Rights Watch accuses the federal government of indiscriminate and arbitrary arrests of males from predominately Muslim countries without sufficient probable cause or even reasonable suspicion.[86]

Also, Human Rights Watch and the American Civil Liberties Union accuse the Justice Department of abusing the **material witness law** to detain terror suspects. The material witness law, enacted in 1984, allows federal authorities to hold a person indefinitely without charging him or her with a crime if they suspect that the person has information about a crime and might flee or be unwilling to cooperate with law enforcement officials.[87] Human Rights Watch and the ACLU charge that the Justice Department has used the material witness law to detain 70 persons, about one-third of them U.S. citizens, on suspicion of terrorism where questionable evidence exists for such detentions. The Justice Department has apologized to at least 13 persons for wrongly detaining them under the material witness law.[88] One of the more publicized abuses of the material witness law was the detention of Portland, Oregon, lawyer Brandon Mayfield, whom the FBI wrongly accused of being connected to the Madrid train bombings of 2004.

Of great concern to those who fear that the loss of due process is eroding due process rights is the Justice Department's denial of access to the civilian courts for those accused or suspected of terrorism. The use of the Enemy Combatant Executive Order to detain alleged terrorists and al Qaeda members has seriously alarmed proponents of constitutional rights. The use of this executive order, combined with the use of military tribunals instead of civilian court trials, denies accused enemy combatants access to the civilian courts. This process of determining guilt denies them the due process rights to an attorney, to confront the witnesses against them, to know of the evidence the government has against them, and the right to a public trial by their peers.

The federal courts have responded to this concern. In 2008, the U.S. Supreme Court ruled that terrorist suspects held at the Guantanamo Bay naval base in Cuba have constitutional rights to challenge their detention in United States courts. In a 2009 ruling the U.S. Supreme Court ruled that enemy combatants held in military prisons on United States soil have the right to sue in civil courts regarding their imprisonment and interrogation. The

material witness law a law that allows for the detention of a person who has not committed a crime but is alleged to have information about a crime that has been committed

decision resulted in the federal government removing Jose Padilla, an accused enemy combatant, from solitary confinement in the Charleston, South Carolina, military brig where he was being held without charges and filing charges against him in federal criminal court. (Padilla was convicted and sentenced to 17 years in prison.)

Racial Profiling Over the years much progress has been made in addressing the problem of racial profiling by law enforcement. Public opinion polls have indicated that most people disapprove of racial profiling by the police. Prior to 9/11, racial profiling was seen as a problem directed primarily against blacks and Latinos. However, since September 11, 2001, racial profiling has become a concern particularly for Middle-Eastern–looking males, as public opinion and legislators seem less opposed to racial profiling of these persons, especially at airports and on public transportation. Since September 11, 2001, some have been so bold as to publicly voice that they favor profiling young Middle Eastern or Islamic men at airports and other high-risk security venues.[89]

The DHS and the Justice Department have denied that any of their policies related to immigration enforcement, screening, or investigation are based on racial profiling. In 2003, the Justice Department issued a policy statement regarding guidelines on racial profiling. The guidelines govern the conduct of 70 federal law enforcement agencies. However, the guidelines do not ban racial profiling. They do bar federal agents from using race or ethnicity in their routine investigations, but the guidelines allow for clear exemptions for investigations involving terrorism and national security matters.

Muslims in the United States point out that hate crimes against Muslims have increased since September 11, 2001, and rose again after the 2005 London transit bombings. They also point out that in some cities with large Muslim populations, the number of Middle Easterners citied for offenses by law enforcement has been significantly higher than all others charged with offenses.[90] Many Muslims report that they fear that "the motives behind some of the post-9/11 security efforts seem aimed at Muslims."[91] As a result, they report that they "keep as low a profile as they can" because they believe that Americans "feel the next terrorist attack will be from a Muslim."[92]

Rendition and Torture One of the most serious concerns of denial of due process is allegations of torture and the practice of rendition. As a result of the revelation of the torture of the prisoners of Abu Ghraib prison in Iraq and the report of alleged torture of prisoners at Guantanamo Bay, Cuba, by the International Committee of the Red Cross, some have alleged that there is evidence to suggest that the United States has chosen to systematically engage in or to permit the torture of terror suspects. They argue that the fear that another 9/11-type terrorist incident would occur caused the U.S. government to be willing "to consider doing almost anything—including actions previously thought morally suspect—to prevent another such catastrophe."[93]

The emergence of "torture memos" exchanged between the Justice Department and President Bush seem to suggest that the Bush administration operated on the premise that in a time of necessity, the president and the military could disregard torture conventions, international treaties, and the law of the land.[94] In legal memorandums by the Justice Department and the Defense Department, President Bush was advised that the Geneva Convention and other antitorture covenants do not apply to suspected terrorist detainees.[95]

Another serious charge by critics regarding the denial of due process related to torture is that the federal government has engaged in a practice called **rendition**. Rendition is when the U.S. government arranges for the transfer of a suspected terrorist from the United States or another country to a country such as Pakistan or Egypt where the suspect can be interrogated by the use of torture by local authorities. Rendition often involves the clandestine kidnapping of the "terror suspect" and the clandestine transportation of the suspect to such a country. The Bush administration is accused of using this extreme denial of due process rights to those suspected of terrorism both in the United States and in other countries such as Germany and Italy.

The Obama administration has renounced the use of what it calls "harsh treatment" of detainees, primarily the use of "waterboarding."

HERE'S SOMETHING TO THINK ABOUT . . .

Concerned that Iran would use its nuclear program to produce nuclear weapons rather than electricity, the United States engaged in a number of diplomatic and economic strategies to deter Iran from achieving this objective. In a demonstration of the importance of "cyber attacks," Iran's nuclear program was slowed not by economic and diplomatic gambits but by a malicious cyber attack upon the computers that controlled the speed of the centrifuges spinning to enrich uranium. The worm, called Stuxnet, causes the centrifuge motors to spin faster and faster until it destroys the centrifuges. Just before destroying the centrifuge the program returns all operating systems to normal, thus concealing the reason for the failure. Analysis of the Stuxnet worm suggests that due to its complexity it must be a state-sponsored cyber attack. The United States and Israel are both high on the list of possible suspect nations. Many think that cyber attacks, including those originated by terrorists groups, will be the new wave of terrorism. Do you agree?

rendition the illegal transportation of a person to a foreign country for the purpose of having officials of that country interrogate the person using torture or practices not permitted in the United States

Waterboarding was used under the Bush administration in the interrogation of al Qaeda leaders in an effort to obtain information from them. There is sharp debate between the Obama administration and proponents of "harsh treatment" as to whether valuable information was obtained from the detainees and terrorist plots were foiled.

Although the Obama administration has declared that it will not use Executive Orders to imprison enemy combatants without habeas corpus rights, it also has said that terrorist suspects could be held in "prolonged detention" without trial. This practice has been referred to as "preventive detention." Many legal scholars argue that there is no constitutional foundation for "preventive detention" and any person detained on United States soil is entitled to due process rights and access to the civil courts to appeal their detention.[96]

Turning the Criminal Justice System Upside Down

Homeland security concerns have had a significant impact on the police and the criminal justice system. Doubtful that the criminal justice system is up to the challenge of responding to terrorism, the federal government has assumed considerable new powers and at the same time has curtailed civil rights that have been considered foundational to the U.S. criminal justice system, such as the right to an attorney, the right of a defendant to know the charges against him or her, the right to remain silent, and the right to a public trial.

The DHS and the FBI have assumed major responsibilities in homeland security. In their new roles, the traditional relationships between federal and local law enforcement have changed and federal agencies have assumed the lead role in investigating terrorist incidents. The role of police as first responders and the need for coordinated multiagency response to terrorist attacks have exposed critical shortcomings in infrastructure, training, and equipment. The powers of federal agencies have been bolstered by new legislation. However, many of these new powers have been challenged as serious and needless infringement on civil rights.

In summary, the criminal justice system has been turned upside down. Whereas traditionally the focus of the criminal justice system was the local government, the new focus today is the federal government. The War on Terrorism has resulted in a reexamination of some of the most basic practices underlying the criminal justice system.

Finally, the focus on homeland security poses a unique challenge for criminal justice scholars and programs. Criminal justice scholars have spent considerable effort and research during the past half century describing and understanding the U.S. criminal justice system. The focus on homeland security is fundamentally changing the criminal justice system, and scholars will need to examine and explain to what extent the focus on homeland security is altering the criminal justice system. Also, there is the need for research to understand what motivates one to engage in terrorism. As hundreds of years of criminology research has produced extensive knowledge of criminals and victims, now there is the need for research to increase our understanding of terrorism. We need to know the answer to such questions as: Why do some people choose terrorism? Why do some choose to be suicide bombers? What is the impact of terrorism on victims? and What are the best practices for responding to terrorism? The more information that scholars can bring to focus on the understanding of terrorism and terrorists, the more likely it is that the government and the criminal justice system will respond with effective actions that diminish terrorism and preserve civil liberties.

HERE'S SOMETHING TO THINK ABOUT . . .

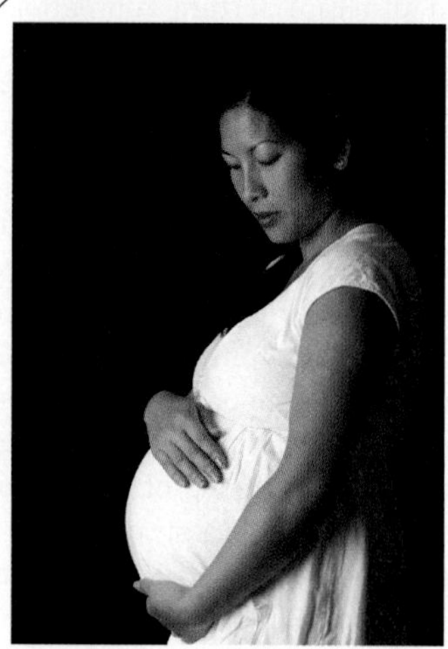

The Fourteenth Amendment adopted in 1868 provides that all persons born or naturalized in the United States are citizens of the Country. Babies born in the United States automatically qualify for U.S. citizenship regardless of the nationality and immigration status of their parents. When these persons, called "anchor babies," turn 21 they may petition the U.S. government to grant their parents permanent residence status.

Although normally associated with births of children to poor illegal immigrants, evidence is emerging to suggest that an underground business of "maternity tourism" is emerging. Relatively wealthy women on legal tourist visas are coming to America for the specific purpose of giving birth to their child on U.S. soil. Maternity tourism violates no federal laws. Also, a tourist visa cannot be denied to a woman simply because she is pregnant. To date the evidence suggests that most of these women are coming from China, Mexico, and South Korea. Businesses in these countries offer complete "maternity tourism packages" for pregnant women including doctors, insurance, and postpartum care. These packages may cost tens of thousands of dollars. Although it is difficult to gather precise and contemporary data, the best available data indicate that of the 4.3 million births in 2008, only 7,462 births were by foreign residents in the United States.

Some are alarmed by anchor babies for two reasons: (1) They see the babies as a way for illegal immigrants to remain in or to return to the United States if deported; and (2) a more ominous fear is that terrorists may use anchor babies as a long-term strategy to infiltrate sleeper agents into the United States.

In 2010, Arizona Senator Russell Pearce (R) introduced a bill that would have denied birth certificates to children of illegal immigrants born in Arizona. Others have advocated for a revision of the Fourteenth Amendment that would deny citizenship to babies of foreign visitors—legal and illegal—born in the United States. They argue the United States is one of the few countries to provide such a path to citizenship and residence, and anchor babies pose a risk to homeland security. Do you favor a change in the Fourteenth Amendment to deny citizenship to babies of foreign women born in the United States?

CHAPTER 13

Homeland Security

Check It!

1 WHAT is terrorism, and how has it affected the criminal justice system? p. 260

Homeland security resulting from terrorist attacks in the United States has become a central focus of the criminal justice system, especially the FBI. Terrorism, including international terrorism, is a strategy of premeditated, politically motivated violence targeted against civilian and military members unarmed and not on duty by subnational groups or clandestine agents, usually intended to create fear and influence an audience.

2 HOW has the United States reorganized law enforcement agencies to respond to terrorism? p. 262

A number of law enforcement agencies have been created and reorganized to combat terrorism:

- The FBI's primary priority and jurisdiction is now counter-terrorism.
- The Department of Homeland Security (DHS) is the most significant reorganization of the United States government since 1947 and consolidates 22 federal agencies, including the Transportation Security Administration, to create a single agency whose primary mission is to protect the homeland of the United States.

3 HOW has the new emphasis on homeland security impacted the relationship among federal, state, and local police agencies? p. 265

No single agency can prevent and respond to a terrorist attack. Guidance and coordination with numerous federal, state, and local agencies are required.

- The United States Government Interagency Domestic Terrorism Concept of Operations Plan is responsible for preventing and responding to terrorist attacks and designating lead federal agencies to do so.
- First responder agencies respond to terrorist attacks, based on cooperation between the federal government and local or state agencies, although there is conflict between police and fire responders about who is in charge of such threats.
- There is greater coordination and cooperation among the CIA and the FBI, than previously existed as well as with the DHS.
- Joint local–federal counterterrorism task forces provide additional personnel to focus on counterterrorism activities and to funnel intelligence from federal agencies to local agencies.
- Frustrated by the lack of federal sharing of terrorist incidents, police chiefs are creating their own informal networks to exchange intelligence.

4 HOW has fear of terrorist attacks influenced legislation, homeland security strategies, and search and seizure? p. 270

After the September 11 attacks, the federal government received new powers to promote homeland security, including:

1. The Enemy Combat Executive Order, by which the United States
   - entered into the war with Afghanistan
   - treated those captured as "enemy combatants" not entitled to the rights of prisoners under the Geneva Conventions
   - established military tribunals, under which prisoners have no right to habeas corpus or other rights
   - expanded the battlefield beyond Afghanistan in the pursuit of al Qaeda
2. The USA Patriot Act, which gives federal law enforcement agencies
   - expanded powers of surveillance and search and seizure
   - expanded federal jurisdiction of terror-related crimes
   - authority to extend some civil liberties of those detained or abused under the act

5 HOW is concern about possible terrorist attacks affecting policing? p. 273

Fear of terrorist attacks is transforming cities into urban fortresses. Although the federal government has authority for preventing major terrorist attacks, much of the responsibility for carrying out additional physical security measures for the safety of ordinary citizens falls on local police agencies, including in cases in which terror threat advisories are issued in specific areas.

6 WHAT concerns regarding border security have been raised by threats to homeland security? p. 275

Fear of terrorism has increased existing concerns about immigration control. Some changes being implemented and proposed for tightening U.S. immigration policies include the following:

- sealing the borders and conducting searches to find illegal immigrants working in sensitive jobs, such as in the airline industry, power plants, and infrastructure
- using United States Visitor and Immigrant Status Indicator Technology (US-VISIT), a system of registering the entry of foreign visitors and tracking when and where they exit
- tightening airline security and maintaining a no-fly list, secretly maintained by the DHS, that lists persons prohibited from flying on a commercial airplane under any circumstances and persons who should receive additional screening prior to being allowed to board an aircraft

- using smart passports that will contain machine-readable data about travelers
- using Student and Exchange Visitor Information System (SEVIS), a Web-based information database containing information on international students studying in the United States
- enforcing the Real ID Act, which requires that all state driver's licenses conform to uniform standards set by the DHS
- using the National Security Control's new cyber command to prevent cyberterrorism

7 WHAT are the concerns about the impact of homeland security legislation and law enforcement powers on basic constitutional rights? p. 279

In the effort to discover terrorists who may be in the United States, Congress has provided law enforcement officials with new powers that diminish Fourth Amendment search and seizure rights and privacy rights, including privacy of financial, medical, credit, and travel information. Actions of law enforcement justified under the pretense of homeland security can significantly affect First Amendment rights to free speech, free association, and civil protests, as well as rights of due process, especially for those targeted by racial profiling.

Assess Your Understanding

1. What are the expectations of groups that use terrorist attacks upon legitimate governments?

a. The attacks will topple the government.
b. The attacks will result in the seizure and control of geographical territory.
c. The attacks will generate public fear and lack of confidence in the government.
d. The attacks will result in the overthrow of the military.

2. For many people in the world what determines whether a group or person is seen as a "terrorist" or a "freedom fighter"?

a. the United States Criminal Code
b. the United Nations Convention on Terrorism
c. the World Court's definition of terrorism
d. whether one agrees or disagrees with the political ideology and goals of those engaged in violence

3. The Ku Klux Klan is an example of what type of domestic terrorism group?

a. extremist group
b. single-issue extremist
c. formal terrorist organization
d. ecoterrorist group

4. Which of the following has the dominant role as the lead federal agency in most homeland security initiatives?

a. FBI
b. DHS
c. CBP
d. CIA

5. Aviation security is the responsibility of which of the following agencies?

a. FBI
b. TSA
c. ICE
d. a partnership between the airlines and the government

6. What is the purpose of the Domestic Terrorism Concept of Operations Plan (CONPLAN)?

a. to identify lead federal agencies and the responsibilities they have in the event of a catastrophic event or terrorist attack
b. to define the various classifications of terrorist groups
c. to enhance the ability of the FBI to respond to threats of terrorism through expanded search and seizure powers
d. to transfer the responsibility for aviation security to the DHS

7. What is the responsibility of the Federal Emergency Management Agency under CONPLAN?

a. to ensure the development and implementation of policies directed at preventing terrorist attacks
b. to provide scientific-technical personnel and equipment in the event an attack involves nuclear or radiological weapons
c. to manage and coordinate the federal consequence management response in support of state and local authorities
d. to serve as a support agency to the FBI for technical operations

8. Which agency is responsible for domestic intelligence?

a. CIA
b. DHS
c. White House
d. FBI

9. What is the difference between a joint local–federal counterterrorism task force and a fusion center?

a. Fusion centers are run by state and local authorities.
b. Fusion centers are sponsored by the FBI.
c. Fusion centers are financed exclusively by the federal government.
d. Fusion centers provide for the fusion of intelligence produced by the FBI and the CIA.

10. What civil rights are denied to enemy combatants under the Enemy Combatant Executive Order?

a. the prohibition against holding a person without criminal charges
b. the right to an attorney
c. the right to a trial by jury in a criminal court
d. all of the above

11. The USA Patriot Act provides which of the following powers to law enforcement agencies?

a. It allows local and state police to stop and question anyone who appears to be an illegal immigrant.
b. It gives the FBI extended powers of search and seizure without a court order.
c. It allows persons suspected of terrorism to be held for 72 hours without charges or the benefit of an attorney.
d. It provides for the death penalty for anyone convicted of aiding and abetting a terrorist group registered with the U.S. Department of State.

12. Which program provides for stricter oversight of foreign students and visiting foreign scholars entering the United States for educational purposes?
    a. US-VISIT
    b. ICE
    c. SEVIS
    d. Foreign Educational Regulation and Oversight Act of 2009
13. How do terrorist groups use the Internet?
    a. They make little use of the Internet due to their limited technical abilities and knowledge.
    b. They use the Internet for recruiting, training, and issuing propaganda.
    c. They use the Internet primarily for issuing propaganda.
    d. U.S. and international laws have effectively stopped terrorist groups from having access to the Internet.
14. What is rendition?
    a. searches performed without a court warrant
    b. racial profiling
    c. a form of cyber attack
    d. the illegal transportation of a terrorist suspect to a foreign country for interrogation

ESSAY

1. What is the U.S. legal definition of terrorism?
2. Does the United Nations have a universally accepted definition of terrorism by member nations? Why or why not?
3. How has the United States reorganized federal law enforcement agencies to better respond to threats to homeland security?
4. What is the mission of the Department of Homeland Security?
5. How has the new federal emphasis upon homeland security affected the relationship between local/state law enforcement agencies and federal agencies?
6. How has homeland security affected state and local law enforcement agencies?
7. Why is border security a major concern in regard to better homeland security?
8. Why is intelligence gathering an important strategy for effective homeland security?
9. Why is the CONPLAN important for federal agencies in responding to terrorist attacks?
10. What role has the Internet played in terrorism and counter-terrorism?

ANSWERS: 1. c, 2. d, 3. a, 4. b, 5. b, 6. a, 7. c, 8. d, 9. a, 10 d, 11. b, 12. c, 13. b, 14. d

Media

Go to the *Chapter 13: Homeland Security* section in *MyCJLab* to test your understanding of this chapter, access customized study content, engage in interactive simulations, complete critical thinking and research assignments, and view related online videos.

Additional Links

To view the homepage of the Department of Homeland Security, go to www.dhs.gov

The homepage of the Whitehouse provides homeland security information at www.whitehouse.gov

Go to www.ready.gov for information to help citizens prepare for emergencies.

Visit the homepage of the U.S. House of Representatives Committee on Homeland Security at http://hsc.house.gov/

To examine the focus of the Department of Transportation Security Administration, which is aviation security, go to www.tsa.gov

Visit the homepage of the U.S. Immigration and Customs Enforcement Agency at www.ice.gov

Go to www.cbp.gov, the homepage of the U.S. Customs and Border Protection, to find travel information for those going overseas.

Visit www.fema.gov, the homepage of the Federal Emergency Management Agency. FEMA is responsible for responding to major disasters including terrorist attacks.

Go to www.cbp.gov, the homepage of the U.S. Customs and Border Protection Agency, to see how it secures the homeland by preventing the illegal entry of people and goods.

The Web site www.state.gov contains information about travel warnings, crisis awareness, and preparedness, as well as information about countries and regions.

Most states have state-level homeland security agencies. Each state has a different name for its agency. You can use Google to find the state of your choice. Here are three examples: Arizona Department of Homeland Security at www.azdohs.gov; the Texas Homeland Security Department at www.texashomelandsecurity.com; and Pennsylvania's Emergency Management Agency at www.homelandsecurity.state.pa.us/

The electronic portal for applying for positions with the Department of Homeland Security (and other government positions) is http://jobsearch.usajobs.opm.gov/dhscareers/

For information about homeland security issues and RSS feeds see one of the following:

The homepage of George Washington University's Homeland Security Institute, at www.gwumc.edu/hspi/

The homepage of the Homeland Security Studies & Analysis Institute, at www.homelandsecurity.org

To watch Homeland Security Secretary Janet Napolitano talk about national security following the killing of Osama bin Laden, and 10 years after the September 11, 2001, attacks, go to www.c-spanvideo.org/program/JanetNap

ENDNOTES

Chapter 1 CRIMINAL JUSTICE

1. James Q. Wilson, *Thinking about Crime* (New York: Basic Books, 1975), p. 65.
2. Robert Fogelson, "Reform at a Standstill," in Carl Klockars and Stephen Mastrofski (eds.), *Thinking about Police* (New York: McGraw-Hill, 1991), p. 117.
3. Fogelson, "Reform at a Standstill," p. 119.
4. Aristotle, *Politics,* translated by Benjamin Jowett (Cambridge, MA: MIT Press, 1994–2000), p. 1118.
5. Ron Fournier, "Americans Face World of Sudden Terror," *Pocono Record,* October 8, 2001, p. A1.
6. Peter McWilliams, *Ain't Nobody's Business If You Do* (Los Angeles: Prelude Press, 1993), p. 43.
7. James Davidson and John Batchelor, *The American Nation* (Englewood Cliffs, NJ: Prentice-Hall, 1991), p. 799.
8. McWilliams, *Ain't Nobody's Business,* p. 2.

Chapter 2 CRIME: WHY AND HOW MUCH

1. "Son, is Your Name Trouble?: *Chicago Tribune,* January 30, 2009, Section 1, p. 3.
2. "Is Crime Drop Out of the Blue?" *Chicago Tribune,* December 19, 2008, Section 1, p. 55.
3. Norimitsu Onishi, "Sinatra Song Often Strikes Deadly Chord," *New York Times Online,* February 7, 2010.
4. Cesare Bonesana and Marchese Beccaria, *Of Crimes and Punishments* (Philadelphia: Philip H. Nicklin, 1819).
5. Jeremy Bentham, "An Introduction to the Principles of Morals and Legislation," in J. E. Jacoby (ed.), *Classics of Criminology* (Oak Park, IL: Moore, 1979).
6. Richard Louis Dugdale, *The Jukes: A Study in Crime, Pauperism, Disease and Heredity,* 3rd ed. (New York: G.P. Putnam's Sons 1985).
7. Henry Herbert Goddard, *The Kallikak Family: A Study in the Heredity of Feeblemindedness* (New York: Macmillan, 1912).
8. Lombroso, *Crime.*
9. Ibid.
10. Karl Christiansen, "A Preliminary Study of Criminality among Twins," in Sarnoff Mednick and Karl O. Christiansen (eds.), *Biosocial Bases of Criminal Behavior* (New York: Simon and Schuster, 1985).
11. Sigmund Freud, *A General Introduction to Psychoanalysis* (New York: Boni and Liveright, 1920); Sigmund Freud, *An Outline of Psychoanalysis* (New York: Norton Press, 1963).
12. Trine Tsouderos, "Exploring Links Between Genes, Violence, Environment: As Science Looks at Possible Links and Treatments, Critics Warn of Overzealous Intervention," *Chicago Tribune,* February 25, 2010.
13. Adrian Raine, *The Psychopathology of Crime: Criminal Behavior as a Clinical Disorder* (Orlando: Academic Press, 1993).
14. Ian Urbina, "Animal Abuse as Clue to Additional Cruelties," *New York Times Online,* March 17, 2010.
15. Robert E. Park and Ernest Burgess, *Introduction to the Science of Sociology,* 2nd ed. (Chicago: University of Chicago Press, 1942).
16. Robert E. Park (ed.), *The City* (Chicago: University of Chicago Press, 1925).
17. Clifford R. Shaw, *Juvenile Delinquency in Urban Areas* (Chicago: University of Chicago Press, 1942).
18. Clifford R. Shaw and Henry D. McKay, "Social Factors in Juvenile Delinquency," in Volume II of the Report of the Causes of Crime, National Commission on Law Observance and Enforcement. Report no. 13 (Washington, DC: U.S. Government Printing Office, 1931).
19. Mark H. Moore, Robert C. Trojanowicz, and George L. Kelling, *Crime and Policing* (Washington, DC: U.S. Department of Justice, June 1988).
20. Edwin H. Sutherland, *Principles of Criminology,* 6th ed. (Philadelphia: Lippincott, 1966).
21. Francis T. Cullen, *Rethinking Crime and Deviance Theory* (Totowa, NJ: Rowman and Allenheld, 1969).
22. Cullen, *Rethinking Crime,* pp. 137–142.
23. Gresham Sykes and David Matza, "Techniques of Neutralization: A Theory of Delinquency," *American Sociological Review,* 22 (1957): 664–670.
24. Robert Merton, "Social Structure and Anomie," *American Sociological Review,* 3 (1938): 672–682.
25. Robert Merton, *Social Theory and Social Structure* (New York: Free Press, 1968).
26. Albert K. Cohen, *Delinquent Boys: The Culture of the Gang* (Glencoe, IL: Free Press, 1958).
27. Associated Press, "Group Urges More Polygamy Prosecutions," *New York Times Online,* www.nytimes.com, June 16, 2005.
28. Gary Becker, "Crime and Punishment: An Economic Approach," *Journal of Political Economy,* 76 (1968): 169–217.
29. Michael J. Lynch and W. Byron Graves, *A Primer in Radical Criminology,* 2nd ed. (Albany, NY: Harrow and Heston, 1989).
30. Richard Quinney, *The Social Reality of Crime* (Boston: Little, Brown, 1970).
31. Ivan Taylor, Paul Walton, and Jock Young, *The New Criminology* (New York: Harper and Row, 1973).
32. Richard Quinney, *The Crime Problem* (New York: Dodd, Mead, 1970).
33. Austin Turk, *Criminality and the Legal Order* (Chicago: Rand McNally, 1969).
34. Freda Adler, *Sisters in Crime: The Rise of the New Female Criminal* (New York: McGraw-Hill, 1975).
35. Daly and Chesney-Lind, *Feminism and Criminology.*
36. Sally S. Simpson, "Feminist Theory, Crime and Justice," *Criminology,* 27 (1989).
37. Gwynn Nettler, *Explaining Crime,* 2nd ed. (New York: McGraw-Hill, 1978).
38. William J. Chambliss, "Toward a Radical Criminology," in D. Kairys (ed.), *The Politics of Law: A Progressive Critique* (New York: Pantheon Books, 1982).
39. Candace Kruttschnitt with Rosemary Gartner and Kathleen Ferraro, "Women's Involvement in Serious Interpersonal Violence," *Aggression and Violent Behavior, 7* (2002): 529–565.
40. R. B. Felson and S. F. Messner, "Disentangling the Effects of Gender and Intimacy on Victim Precipitation in Homicide," *Criminology, 36,* no. 2 (1998): 414.
41. Macmillian and Kruttschnitt, "Patterns of Violence against Women," p. 419.
42. Steven W. Perry, *American Indians and Crime: A BJS Statistical Profile, 1992–2002* (Washington, DC: U.S. Department of Justice, Office of Justice Programs), NCJ Document No. 203097, December 2004.
43. Patrik Jonsson, "Small Cities Cope with Crime Surge," *Christian Science Monitor,* July 6, 2004, p. 1.
44. M. E. Wolfgang and S. L. Singer, "Victim Categories of Crime," *Journal of Criminal Law and Criminology, 69,* no. 3 (1978): 379–394.

45. Ibid.

46. L. E. Cohen and M. Felson, "Social Change and Crime Rate Trends: A Routine Activity Approach," *American Sociological Review, 44,* no. 4 (1979): 588–608.

47. Cohen and Felson, "Social Change and Crime Rate Trends," p. 589.

48. M. Maguire, "The Needs and Rights of Victims of Crime," in M. Tonry and N. Morris (eds.), *Crime and Justice: An Annual Review of Research* (Chicago: University of Chicago Press, 1991), pp. 363–433.

49. F. Carrington and G. Nicholson, "Victims' Rights: An Idea Whose Time Has Come—Five Years Later: The Maturing of an Idea," *Pepperdine Law Review, 18* (1989): 1–18.

50. Edwin Schur, *Crimes without Victims: Deviant Behavior and Public Policy: Abortion, Homosexuality, Drug Addiction* (Upper Saddle River, NJ: Prentice Hall, 1965); Edwin M. Schur, *Victimless Crimes: Two Sides of a Controversy* (Upper Saddle River, NJ: Prentice Hall, 1974).

51. Richard C. McCorkle, *Gambling and Crime among Arrestees: Exploring the Link,* (Washington, DC: U.S. Department of Justice, National Institute of Justice), NCJ Document No. 203197, July 2004, p. 1.

52. Mireya Navarro, "Long Silent, Oldest Profession Gets Vocal and Organized," *New York Times Online,* www.nytimes.com, December 18, 2004.

53. Ibid.

54. Ibid.

55. U.S. Department of Justice, Office of Justice Programs, Office for Victims of Crime, *Legal Remedies for Crime Victims* (Washington, DC: U.S. Department of Justice, 1999).

56. D. Rosenweig, "Simpson Seeks to Overturn Judgment," *Los Angeles Times,* April 27, 2002, p. 3.

57. U.S. Department of Justice, Office of Justice Programs, Office for Victims of Crime, *Legal Remedies for Crime Victims;* U.S. Department of Justice, Office of Justice Programs, Office for Victims of Crime, *New Directions from the Field.*

58. The Cleveland Foundation Survey of the Administration of Justice in Cleveland, Ohio, *Criminal Justice in Cleveland* (Cleveland: Cleveland Foundation, 1922).

59. Illinois Association for Criminal Justice, *The Illinois Crime Survey,* (Chicago: Illinois Association for Criminal Justice, 1929).

60. Robert Tannehill, "The History of American Law Enforcement," in Dae Change and James Fagin (eds.), *Introduction to Criminal Justice: Theory and Application,* 2nd ed. (Lake Geneva, WI: Paladin House of the Farley Court of Publishers, 1985), p. 159.

61. The URC also reports data for "all other offenses" and "suspicion." All other offenses include all violations of state or local laws except those listed in Part I and Part II and traffic offenses. Suspicion includes all offenses in which suspects are released without formal charges being filed against them.

62. C. Kindermann, J. Lynch, and D. Cantor, *Effects of the Redesign on Victimization Estimates* (Washington, DC: Bureau of Justice Statistics, 1997), p. 1.

63. U.S. Department of Justice, Office of Justice Programs, Bureau of Justice Statistics, *NCVS Resource Guide,* October 2004, www.icpsr.umich.edu/NACJD/NCVS/index.html.

Chapter 3 CRIMINAL LAW CONTROL VS. LIBERTY

1. Joel Samaha, *Criminal Law* (Belmont, CA: West/Wadsworth, 1999), p. 3.

2. American Law Institute, *Model Penal Code and Commentaries.* vol. 1 (Philadelphia: American Law Institute, 1985), pp. 1–30.

3. U.S. Constitution, Article X, Section 10. Based on the seventeenth-century philosophy expressed by Lord Edward Coke, "No Crime without Law; No Punishment without Law." Jerome Hall, *General Principle of Criminal Law,* 2nd ed. (Indianapolis: Bobbs-Merril, 1960).

4. *Lonzetta v. New Jersey,* 306 U.S. 451, 453 (1939).

5. *Weems v. United States,* 217 U.S. 349, 30 S.Ct. 544, 54 L.Ed. 793 (1910).

6. *Harmelin v. Michigan,* 50 1 U.S. 957, 111 S.Ct. 2680, 115 L.Ed. 2d 836 (1991); *Robinson v. California,* 370 U.S. 660, 82 S.Ct. 1417, 8 L.Ed. 2d 758 (1962).

7. *People v. Lauria,* 251 Cal.App.2d 471, 59 Cal.Rptr. 628 (1967).

8. *Young v. State,* Md. 298, 493 A. 2d 352 (1985).

9. *Le Barron v. State,* 32 Wis.2d 294, 145 N.W.2d 79 (1966).

10. "The Roush-Sex Defense," *Time,* May 23, 1988, p. 55.

11. *People v. Alderson and Others,* 144 Misc. 2d 133, 540 N.Y. S. 2d 948 (N.Y. 1989).

12. *People v. Goetz,* 68 N.Y. 2d 96, 506 N.Y. S. 2d 18, 497 N.E. 2d 41 (1986).

13. Alan Dershowitz, *The Abuse Excuse and Other Cop-Outs, Sob Stories and Evasions of Responsibility* (Boston: Little, Brown, 1994).

14. *State v. Mitcheson,* 560 P. 2d 1120 (1977).

15. *State v. Valentine,* 935 P. 2d 1294 (Wash. 1977).

16. Thomas A. Johnson, *Introduction to the Juvenile Justice System* (St. Paul, MN: West, 1975), pp. 1, 3.

17. Samaha, *Criminal Law,* p. 317.

18. M'Naghten's Case, 8 Eng. Rep. 718 (1843).

19. American Law Institute, *Model Penal Code and Commentaries,* Section 221.1.

20. Samaha, *Criminal Law,* p. 358.

Chapter 4 ROLES AND FUNCTIONS OF THE POLICE

1. David Ascoli, *The Queen's Peace: The Origins and Development of the Metropolitan Police 1829–1979* (London: Hamish Hamilton, 1979), pp. 16–17.

2. Carrie Johnson, "Justice Dept. Focusing on Indian Country Crime," *Washington Post,* June 15, 2009.

3. C. Reith, *A Short History of the Police* (Oxford: Oxford University Press, 1948).

4. Thomas A. Reppetto, *The Blue Parade* (New York: Free Press, 1978), p. 17.

5. Samuel Walker, *Popular Justice: A History of American Criminal Justice* (New York: Oxford University Press, 1980), p. 191.

6. Ibid.

7. Don Van Natta Jr. and David Johnson, "Wary of Risk, Slow to Adapt, F.B.I. Stumbles in Terror War," *New York Times Online,* www.nytimes.com, June 2, 2002.

8. See www.dea.gov.

9. Bureau of Justice Statistics, *Local Police Departments, 1999.*

10. Ibid.

11. Charles R. Swanson, Leonard Territo, and Robert W. Taylor, *Police Administration: Structures, Processes, and Behavior* (Upper Saddle River, NJ: Prentice-Hall, 1998), pp. 160–161.

12. For a description of campus police and their responsibilities, see Bureau of Justice Statistics, *Campus Law Enforcement Agencies, 1995* (Washington, DC: U.S. Department of Justice, December 1996).

13. Kenneth J. Peak, *Policing America* (Upper Saddle River, NJ: Prentice-Hall, 1997), pp. 64–65.

14. Swanson, Territo, and Taylor, *Police Administration,* pp. 290–293.

15. James Fagin, "Authority," in Jay M. Shafritz (ed.), *International Encyclopedia of Public Policy and Administration* (Boulder, CO: Westview Press, 1998), p. 163.

16. Bureau of Justice Statistics, *Law Enforcement Management and Administrative Statistics, 1997,* pp. 91–120.

17. Title VII of the Civil Rights Act of 1964 as amended in 1972 required that employment screening be based on bona fide occupational requirements (BFOQ). This requirement was further defined in *Griggs* v. *Duke Power Company* (1971), 401 U.S. 424; *Albemark Paper Company* v. *Moody* (1975), 422 U.S. 405; and *Washington* v. *Davis* (1979), 426 U.S. 299.

18. Brian A. Reaves and Andrew L. Goldberg, *Law Enforcement Management and Administrative Statistics, 1997: Data for Individual State and Local Agencies with 100 or More Officers* (Washington, DC: U.S. Department of Justice, April 1999), pp. 31–40.

19. Herman Goldstein, *Policing a Free Society* (Cambridge, MA: Ballinger, 1977), pp. 283–284.

20. Robert E. Worden, "A Badge and a Baccalaureate: Policies, Hypotheses and Further Evidence," *Justice Quarterly,* 7 (September 1990): 565–592.

21. Reaves and Goldberg, *Law Enforcement Management,* pp. 41–50.

22. National Advisory Commission on Criminal Justice Standards and Goals, *Police* (Washington, DC: Government Printing Office, 1973), p. 369.

23. As of June 1997, local and state law enforcement agencies required the following minimum level of education to apply for a position as a police agent: 78% require a minimum of a high school diploma, 13% require some college, 7% require a 2-year college degree, and 2% require a 4-year college degree. See Reaves and Goldberg, *Law Enforcement Management,* p. xiv.
24. Peak, *Policing America*, p. 86.
25. Matthew J. Hickman and Brian A. Reaves, *Local Police Departments, 1999* (Washington, DC: U.S. Department of Justice, May 2001), pp. 17–18.
26. Reaves and Goldberg, *Law Enforcement Management.* pp. 41–50.
27. Peak, *Policing America,* pp. 78–84.
28. Reaves and Goldberg, *Law Enforcement Management,* pp. 41–50.
29. Peak, *Policing America,* pp. 84–85.
30. Egon Bittner, "Popular Conceptions about the Character of Police Work," in Carl B. Klockars and Stephen D. Mastrofski (eds.), *Thinking about Police: Contemporary Readings* (New York: McGraw-Hill, 1991), pp. 35–51.
31. Robert M. Fogelson, "Reform at a Standstill," in Carl B. Klockars and Stephen D. Mastrofski (eds), *Thinking about Police: Contemporary Reading* (New York: McGraw-Hill, 1992), pp. 117–119.
32. Mark H. Moore and Robert C. Trojanowicz, "Corporate Strategies for Policing," *Perspectives on Policing, No. 6* (Washington, DC: National Institute of Justice, November 1988).
33. George Kelling, "Police and Communities: The Quiet Revolution," *Perspectives on Policing, No. 1* (Washington, DC: National Institute of Justice and Harvard University, June 1988).
34. Swanson et al., *Police Administration,* p. 13.
35. Herman Goldstein, *The New Policing: Confronting Complexity* (Washington, DC: National Institute of Justice, December 1993), p. 1.
36. George Kelling and Mark H. Moore, "The Evolving Strategy of Policing," *Perspectives on Policing,* No. 4 (Washington, DC: National Institute of Justice and Harvard University, November 1988), p. 1.
37. George L. Kelling and William J. Bratton, "Implementing Community Policing: The Administrative Problem," *Perspectives on Policing, No. 17* (Washington, DC: National Institute of Justice and Harvard University, July 1993), p. 2.
38. Herman Goldstein, *The New Policing*: Confronting Complexity (Washington, DC: National Institute of Justice, December 1993), p. 4.
39. Lee P. Brown, "Community Policing: A Practical Guide for Police Officials," *Perspectives on Policing, No. 12* (Washington, DC: National Institute of Justice and Harvard University, September 1989).
40. Kelling and Bratton, "Implementing Community Policing," p. 2.
41. "Jaywalking Ban," *Honolulu Advertiser,* August 8, 1998, p. E1.
42. Edwin Meese III, "Community Policing and the Police Officer," *Perspectives on Policing, No. 15* (Washington, DC: National Institute of Justice and Harvard University, January 1993).
43. Ibid., p. 2.
44. William Spelman and John E. Eck, *Problem-Oriented Policing* (Washington, DC: National Institute of Justice, January 1987), p. 2.
45. Ibid., p. 3.
46. Ibid., p. 4.
47. James Hernandez, *The Custer Syndrome (Salem, WI: Sheffield, 1989),* p. 184.
48. Meese, "Community Policing and the Police Officer," p. 5.
49. Hubert William and Patrick V. Murphy, "The Evolving Strategy of Police: A Minority View," *Perspectives on Policing, No. 13* (Washington, DC: National Institute of Justice and Harvard University, January 1990), pp. 2, 12.
50. George L. Kelling, *What Works—Research and the Public* (Washington, DC: National Institute of Justice, 1988), p. 2.

Chapter 5 POLICE OFFICERS AND THE LAW

1. *Weeks v. United States,* 232 U.S. 383 (1914).
2. *Mapp v. Ohio,* 367 U.S. 643 (1961).
3. *Silverthorne Lumber Co. v. United States,* 251 U.S. 385 (1920).
4. *Wolf v. Colorado,* 338 U.S. 25 (1949).
5. *Mapp v. Ohio* (1961).
6. *Chimel v. California,* 395 U.S. 752 (1969).
7. *Harris v. United States,* 390 U.S. 234 (1968).
8. *Horton v. California,* 110 S.Ct. 2301 47 CrL. 2135 (1990).
9. *Arizona v. Hicks,* 107 S.Ct. 1149 (1987).
10. *Horten v. California,* (1990).
11. *Florida v. Jimeno,* 111 S.Ct.1801 (1991).
12. *Carroll v. United States,* 267 U.S. 132 (1925).
13. *Ormelas v. United States,* 116 S.Ct. 1657 L.Ed. 2d 911 (1996).
14. *Colorado v. Bertive,* 479 U.S. 367, 107 S.Ct. 741 (1987).
15. *Terry v. Ohio,* 3129 U.S. 1 (1968).
16. *Minnesota v. Dickerson,* 113 S.Ct. 2130, 124 L.Ed. 2d 334 (1993).
17. *Hiibel v. Sixth Judicial District Court of Nevada,* No. 03-5554 (2004).
18. Although a search warrant is required to conduct such a search, the court has ruled that a suspect may be x-rayed and detained until the subject passes the swallowed objects. See *United States v. Montoya de Hernandez,* 473 U.S. 531, 105 S.Ct. 3304 (1985).
19. *New York v. Quarles,* 104 S.Ct. 2626, 81 L.Ed. 2d 550 (1984).
20. *Florida v. Bostick,* 111 S.Ct. 2382 (1991).
21. *United States v. Martinez-Fuerte,* 428 U.S. 543 (1976).
22. *Safford Unified School District v. Redding,* No. 08-479 2009.
23. *Illinois v. Gates,* 416 U.S. 318 (1982).
24. *United States v. Leon,* 468 U.S. 897, 104 S.Ct. 3405, 82 L.Ed. 2d 677, 52 U.S.L.W. 5515 (1984); *Massachusetts v. Sheppard,* 104 S.Ct. 3424 (1984).
25. *Olmstead v. United States,* 277 U.S. 438 (1928).
26. *Katz v. United States,* 389 U.S. 347 (1967).
27. *Tennessee v. Garner,* 471 U.S. 1 (1985).
28. Terry R. Sparher and David J. Goacopassi, "Memphis Revisited: A Reexamination of Police Shootings after the *Garner* Decision," *Justice Quarterly,* 9 (1992): 211–225.
29. *Graham v. Connor,* 490 U.S. 386, 396–397 (1989).
30. Shankar Vedantam, "Confessions Not Always Clad in Iron," *Washington Post,* October 1, 2007, p. A03.
31. *Gideon v. Wainwright,* 372 U.S. 335 (1963).
32. *Argersinger v. Hamlin,* 407 U.S. 25 (1972).
33. *In re Gault,* 387 U.S. 1 (1967).
34. *Escobedo v. Illinois,* 378 U.S. 478 (1964).
35. Kevin Johnson and Gary Fields, "Jewell Investigation Unmasks FBI 'Tricks'," *USA Today,* April 9, 1997, p. 13A.
36. *Leyra v. Denno,* 347 U.S. 556 (1954).
37. *Miranda v. Arizona,* 384 U.S. 436 (1966).
38. *United States v. Karo,* 468 U.S. 705 (1984).
39. *United States v. Dionisio,* 410 U.S. 1 (1973).
40. *United States v. Wade,* 388 U.S. 218 (1067); *Kirby v. Illinois,* 406 U.S. 682 (1972); *Foster v. California,* 394 U.S. 1 (1973).
41. *Jacobsen v. United States,* 112 S.Ct. 1535 (1992).
42. Michael Kinsley, "When Is Racial Profiling Okay?" *Law Enforcement News,* October 15, 2001, p. 9.
43. Human Rights Watch, *Presumption of Guilt: Human Rights Abuses of Post-September 11 Detainee* (New York: Human Rights Watch, 2002), pp. 3, 6, 46, 55.
44. Eric Lichtblau, "Two Groups Charge Abuse of Witness Law," *New York Times Online,* www.nytimes.com, June 27, 2005.
45. Human Rights Watch, *Presumption of Guilt,* p. 5.

Chapter 6 THE COURT SYSTEM

1. *Sourcebook of Criminal Justice Statistics Online,* www.albany.edu/sourcebook/1995/pdf/t573.pdf, Table 5.76, U.S. Supreme Court Cases Argued and Decided on Merits, 1982–1999.

Chapter 7 COURTROOM PARTICIPANTS AND THE TRIAL

1. Bail is not required in a civil trial, as the court has no jurisdiction to incarcerate either party of a civil suit prior to trial.
2. *Hudson v. Parker,* 156 U.S. 277 (1895).
3. *McKane v. Durston,* 153 U.S. 684 (1894).
4. *Stack v. Boyle,* 342 U.S. 1 (1951).
5. *Carlson v. Landon,* 342 U.S. 524 (1952); *U.S. v. Salerno,* 55 U.S.L.W. 4663 (1987).
6. *Bail Reform Act of 1984,* 18 U.S.C. 4142(e).
7. *U.S. v. Hazzard,* 35 CrL. 2217 (1984); *U.S. v. Motamedi,* 37 CrL. 2394, CA 9 (1985).
8. Wayne R. LaFave and Jerald H. Israel, *Criminal Procedure* (St. Paul, MN: West, 1984), p. 626.
9. *United States v. Werker,* 535 F.2d 198 (2d Cir. 1976), certiorari denied 429 U.S. 926.
10. *Klopfer v. North Carolina,* 386 U.S. 213 (1967).
11. *Beavers v. Haubert,* 1998 U.S. 77 (1905).
12. *Klopfer v. North Carolina,* 386 U.S. 213 (1967).
13. *Barker v. Wingo,* 407 U.S. 514 (1972).
14. A 30-day extension is granted for indictment if the grand jury is not in session, and a 110-day extension can be granted between indictment and trial in cases in which the delay is due to problems associated with calling witnesses.
15. One of the strategies used against organized crime figures is to grant them immunity so that they cannot take the Fifth Amendment, and then ask them questions regarding their organized crime activities and partners. If they refuse to answer, they can be held in prison for contempt of court.
16. Bureau of Justice Statistics, *Indigent Defendants* (Washington, DC: Bureau of Justice Statistics, February 1996).
17. Bureau of Justice Statistics, *Indigent Defense Services in Large Counties, 1999* (Washington, DC: Bureau of Justice Statistics, November 2000), p. 1.
18. Ann Fagan Ginger, *Minimizing Racism in Jury Trials* (Berkeley, CA: National Lawyers Guild, 1969).
19. *Taylor v. Louisiana,* 419 U.S. 522 (1975).
20. Bureau of Justice Statistics, *Report to the Nation on Crime and Justice* (Washington, DC: U.S. Department of Justice, 1988), p. 86.

Chapter 8 SENTENCING

1. Associated Press, "Teen Who Threw Up on Teacher Sentenced," *New York Times Online*, www.nytimes.com, July 27, 2005.
2. Associated Press, "Man Jailed for Not Licensing Cat in N.D.," *New York Times Online*, www.nytimes.com, November 5, 2005.
3. Joyce Purnick, "Can Bench Set Rules for Bedroom?" *New York Times Online*, www.nytimes.com, May 13, 2004.
4. Associated Press, "Convicted Rapist Tells Judge He's Rude," *New York Times Online*, www.nytimes.com, November 11, 2005.
5. Catrin Einhorn, "4 Decades after Shooting, Effort to Make Punishment Fit the Crime," *New York Times Online*, February 23, 2008.
6. Ibid.
7. Associated Press, "Conn. Police Fine Students for Cursing," *New York Times Online*, www.nytimes.com, December 1, 2005.
8. "Britain Toughens Punishment Laws," *Honolulu Advertiser,* January 19, 2000, p. A3.
9. Associated Press, "Woman Sentenced to 100 Lashes for Extramarital Sex," *Pocono Record,* August 13, 2001, p. A5.
10. Associated Press, "Fourteen Men Lashed in Public in Iran for Drinking," *Pocono Record,* August 15, 2001, p. A5.
11. Associated Press, "Mayor: Sever Thumbs of Graffiti Artists," *New York Times Online*, www.nytimes.com, November 5, 2005.
12. Los Angeles Times, "Sweden Pays 200 Who Were Forcibly Sterilized," *Honolulu Advertiser,* November 14, 1999, p. A17.
13. Associated Press, "Japanese Sterilized in Eugenics Program Demand Apology, Money," *Honolulu Advertiser,* December 21, 1997, p. G12.
14. Ira J. Silverman and Manuel Vega, *Corrections: A Comprehensive View* (Minneapolis: West, 1996), p. 63.
15. Associated Press, "That Man Needs to Be Dragged Himself," *Honolulu Advertiser,* February 24, 2000, p. A6.
16. Associated Press, "Woman Gets House Arrest in Fla. Hit-and-Run," *New York Times Online*, www.nytimes.com, November 5, 2005.
17. Paul J. Weber, "Police: Mother Says Devil Made Her Decapitate Infant Son," *Pantagraph,* July 28, 2009.
18. Joel Samaha, *Criminal Law* (Belmont, CA: West/Wadsworth, 1999), p. 317.
19. 18 U.S.C. Section 17.
20. *United States v. Cameron,* 907 F.2d 1051, 1065 (11th Cir., 1990).
21. Ira Mickenberg, "A Pleasant Surprise: The Guilty but Mentally Ill Verdict Has Both Succeeded in Its Own Right and Successfully Preserved the Traditional Role of the Insanity Defense," *University of Cincinnati Law Review, 55* (1987): 943, 987–991.
22. Samaha, *Criminal Law,* p. 315.
23. Ibid.
24. Carrie Johnson, "Parity in Cocaine Sentences Gains Momentum," *Washington Post,* July 25, 2009.
25. Adam Liptak, "Rendering Justice, with One Eye on Re-election," *New York Times,* May 25, 2008.
26. Ashley Surdin, "Radio Hosts Gleefully Try to Taint Jurors," *Washington Post,* May 17, 2008, p. A2.
27. Matthew R. Durose and Patrick A. Langan, *Felony Sentences in State Courts, 2002* (Washington, DC: Bureau of Justice Statistics, 2004), p. 9.
28. Even the U.S. Supreme Court has argued both sides of the argument on the constitutionality of victim impact statements. In *Booth v. Maryland,* 197 S.Ct. 2529 (1987), the U.S. Supreme Court ruled that victim impact statements in capital murder cases could lead to the risk that the death penalty might be imposed in an arbitrary and capricious manner. In *Payne v. Tennessee,* 501 U.S. 808 (1991), the U.S. Supreme Court reversed itself and ruled that, in imposing sentence, victim impact statements were a legitimate method of presenting the harm done by the defendant.
29. G. Kleck, "Racial Discrimination in Criminal Sentencing: A Critical Evaluation of the Evidence with Additional Evidence on the Death Penalty," *American Sociological Review, 46* (1981): 783–805.
30. National Council on Crime and Delinquency, *National Assessment of Structured Sentencing* (Washington, DC: Bureau of Justice Administration, 1996).
31. Associated Press, "Courts Concentrate on Domestic Violence," *Honolulu Advertiser,* November 23, 1997, p. A16.
32. Alexandra Marks, "Prisons Review Results from 'Get-Tough' Era," *Christian Science Monitor,* May 12, 2004, p. 2.
33. Dean E. Murphy, "California Rethinking '3-Strikes' Sentencing," *New York Times Online*, www.nytimes.com, October 24, 2004.
34. Associated Press, "ABA: End Mandatory Minimum Prison Terms," *New York Times Online*, www.nytimes.com, June 23, 2004.
35. Ibid.
36. Ibid.
37. U.S. Sentencing Commission, *Federal Sentencing Guidelines Manual* (Washington, DC: Government Printing Office, 1987).
38. *Mistretta v. United States,* 488 U.S. 361 (1989).
39. *Melendez v. United States,* 117 S.Ct. 383, 136 L.Ed. 2d 301 (1996).
40. Charles Lane, "Justices Order Review of 400-Plus Sentences," *Washington Post,* January 25, 2005, p. 7.
41. Linda Greenhouse, "Supreme Court Transforms Use of Sentence Guidelines," *New York Times Online*, www.nytimes.com, January 13, 2005.
42. Carl Hulse and Adam Liptak, "New Fight over Controlling Punishments Is Widely Seen," *New York Times Online*, www.nytimes.com, January 13, 2005.
43. Harry Elmer Barnes, *The Repression of Crime* (New York: George H. Doran, 1926), p. 220.
44. "Pakistan Criminal to Be Strangled," *Honolulu Advertiser,* March 17, 2000, p. A2.
45. Bureau of Justice Statistics, *Capital Punishment 2000* (Washington, DC: U.S. Department of Justice, December 2001).

46. Peter Slevin, "More in U.S. Expressing Doubts about Death Penalty," *Washington Post,* December 2, 2005.
47. Plato, "Crito," in Benjamin Jowett, trans., *The Apology, Phædo and Crito of Plato* (New York: P. F. Collier & Son, 1937), p. 40.
48. Richard Cohen, "Despite Data, Politicians Continue to Support Death Penalty," *Pocono Record,* October 1, 2000, p. A7.
49. Southern Center for Human Rights, www.schr.org, January 1, 2002.
50. *Witherspoon v. Illinois,* 391 U.S. 510 (1968).
51. *Wilkerson v. Utah,* 99 U.S. 130 (1878).
52. *In re Kemmler,* 136 U.S. 436 (1890).
53. *Louisiana ex. Rel. Francis v. Resweber,* 329 U.S. 459 (1947).
54. *Baze et al. v. Rees, Commissioner, Kentucky Department of Corrections, et al.* No. 07-539, decided April 16, 2008.
55. *Furman v. Georgia,* 408 U.S. 238 (1972).
56. *Woodson v. North Carolina,* 428 U.S. 280 (1976).
57. *Coker v. Georgia,* 433 U.S. 584 (1977).
58. *Gregg v. Georgia,* 428 U.S. 153 (1976).
59. Used in Arizona, Idaho, Montana, and Nebraska.
60. Used in Alabama, Delaware, Florida, and Indiana.
61. Associated Press, "Several States Reconsider Death Penalty Laws," *Honolulu Advertiser,* February 13, 2000, p. A10.
62. Associated Press "Several States Reconsider Death Penalty Laws," *Honolulu Advertiser,* February 13, 2000, p. A10.
63. "Georgia's Electric Chair Found Cruel and Unusual," Southern Center for Human Rights, www.schr.org, December 28, 2001; Associated Press, "Judge Clears Florida to Use Injection for Execution," *Honolulu Advertiser,* February 13, 2000, p. A10; "Gory Death on Florida Electric Chair Creates Furor," *Honolulu Advertiser,* July 9, 1989, p. A9.
64. "Texas Passes Ban on Executing Mentally Retarded Murderers," *Pocono Record,* May 27, 2001; Charles Lane, "High Court to Review Executing Retarded," *Washington Post,* March 27, 2001, p. 1; Charles Lane, "Court Hears Death Penalty Case: Justices to Rule if Jury Got Proper Instruction on Retardation," *Washington Post,* March 28, 2001, p. A8.
65. Reuters, "Court Finds Death Penalty Is Misused in Kansas," *New York Times Online,* www.nytimes.com, December 30, 2001.
66. "An Irrevocable Error," *Washington Post,* August 23, 2005, p. A14.
67. Associated Press, "Executed Woman to Get Pardon in Georgia," *New York Times Online,* www.nytimes.com, August 16, 2005.
68. Michael L. Radelet and Hugo Adam Bedau, "Fallibility and Finality: Type II Errors and Capital Punishment," in Kenneth C. Hass and James A. Inciardi (eds.), *Challenging Capital Punishment: Legal and Social Science Approaches* (Newbury Park, CA: Sage, 1988), pp. 91–112.
69. Adam Liptak, "Study Suspects Thousands of False Convictions," *New York Times Online,* www.nytimes.com, April 19, 2004.
70. Deborah Hastings, "Police Say Evidence That Led to Execution Doesn't Actually Exist," *Pocono Record,* August, 30, 2001, p. A5; "Reasonable Doubts: Work under the Microscope," *Law Enforcement News,* May 31, 2001.
71. "Condemned Man Exonerated," *Honolulu Advertiser,* May 19, 1999, p. 3.
72. Associated Press, "Prosecutors on Trial in False Charge of Murder," *Honolulu Advertiser,* March 21, 1999, p. A10.
73. Todd S. Purdum, "Los Angeles Police Officer Sets Off Corruption Scandal," *New York Times Online,* www.nytimes.com, September 18, 1999.
74. Associated Press, "30 Freed from Death Row Support Reform," *Honolulu Advertiser,* November 8, 1998, p. A10.
75. "Center Director Presents Wrongfully Convicted Client to U.S. Senate Judiciary Committee in Calling for Competent Counsel," Southern Center for Human Rights, www.schr.org, January 2, 2002.
76. Associated Press, "Judge Overturns Murder Conviction," *New York Times Online,* www.nytimes.com, December 28, 2001.
77. Larry McShane, "62,000 Letters and 13 Years Later, Innocent Man Goes Free," *Pocono Record,* September 23, 2001, p. A4.
78. Associated Press, "Charges Dismissed for 17-Year Death Row Inmate," *Honolulu Advertiser,* March 12, 1999, p. A11.
79. Isidore Zimmerman, *Punishment without Crime* (New York: Manor, 1973).
80. "Justice System Abuses Minorities at All Levels, Study Finds," *Honolulu Advertiser,* May 4, 2000, p. A3.
81. C. Spear, *Essays on the Punishment of Death* (London: John Green, 1844), pp. 227–232.
82. David A. Jones, *The Law of Criminal Procedure* (Boston: Little, Brown, 1981), p. 543.
83. President's Commission on Law Enforcement and Administration of Justice, *The Courts* (Washington, DC: U.S. Government Printing Office, 1967), p. 28.
84. Marvin E. Wolfgang and Marc Riedel, "Race Judicial Discretion, and the Death Penalty," *Annals of the American Academy of Political and Social Science,* 407 (May 1973): 129.
85. Thomas J. Keil and Gennaro F. Vito, "Race and the Death Penalty in Kentucky Murder Trials: 1976–1991," *American Journal of Criminal Justice,* 20 (1995): 17–36.
86. "Judge Overturns Death Sentence for Abu-Jamal," *Pocono Record,* December 19, 2001, p. A8.
87. "Judge Asks Prosecutors to Address Race Question in Death Penalty Case," *Pocono Record,* December 6, 2001, p. A4.
88. *McCleskey v. Kemp,* 41 CrL 4107 (1987).
89. Ibid.
90. "Justice System Abuses Minorities at All Levels, Study Finds."
91. Ibid.
92. "DNA Tests Clear 3,000 Suspects," *Honolulu Advertiser,* November 30, 1997, p. G2.
93. Associated Press, "Two Inmates Freed after New DNA Tests," *Honolulu Advertiser,* December 7, 1997, p. G10; Associated Press, "DNA Testing Frees Two Inmates Imprisoned 12 Years for Murder," *Honolulu Advertiser,* April 16, 1999, p. A6; Associated Press, "DNA Test Frees 60-Year-Old Inmate," *Honolulu Advertiser,* September 2, 1999, p. 3A; Helen O'Neil, "False Conviction," *Pocono Record,* October 1, 2000, p. A5; Associated Press, "Convicted Killer Freed on New DNA Evidence," *Pocono Record,* March 16, 2001, p. B6; Associated Press, "Convicted Murderer Finally Acquitted," *Pocono Record,* April 5, 2001, p. A4; Associated Press, "DNA Clears Man Jailed for 13 Years for Rape," *Pocono Record,* October 19, 2001, p. C10.
94. R. H. Melton, "Gilmore Sets Limit on DNA Evidence: Window Would Close 3 Years after Trial," *Washington Post,* March 28, 2001, p. 1.
95. Brooke A. Masters, "New DNA Testing Urged in Case of Executed Man," *Washington Post,* March 28, 2001, p. B1.
96. F. Carter Smith and Corbis Sygma, "A Life or Death Gamble," *Newsweek,* May 29, 2000, pp. 22–27.
97. Liptak, "Study Suspects Thousands of False Convictions."
98. Smith and Sygma, "A Life or Death Gamble."
99. Ibid.
100. Shaila Dewan, "Prosecutors Block Access to DNA Testing for Inmates," *New York Times,* May 17, 2009.
101. National Institute of Justice, *Effects of Judges' Sentencing Decisions on Criminal Careers* (Washington, DC: U.S. Department of Justice, November 1999).
102. Ibid.
103. Ibid.

Chapter 9 JAILS AND PRISONS

1. Law Enforcement Assistance Administration (LEAA), *Two Hundred Years of American Criminal Justice: An LEAA Bicentennial Study* (Washington, DC: U.S. Department of Justice, 1976), p. 46.
2. Harry B. Weiss and Grace M. Weiss, *An Introduction to Crime and Punishment in Colonial New Jersey* (Trenton, NJ: Past Times Press, 1960), pp. 17–18.
3. Ibid., p. 18.
4. Ibid., p. 64.
5. Ibid., p. 10.

6. Ibid., p. 47.
7. Ibid.
8. Norman Johnston, *The Human Cage: a Brief History of Prison Architecture* (New York: Walker and Company, 1973), pp. 13–14.
9. The society still operates under the name of the Philadelphia Prison Society.
10. Joseph M. Hawes, "Prisons in Early Nineteenth-Century America: The Process of Convict Reformation," in Joseph M. Hawes (ed.), *Law and Order in American History* (Port Washington, NY: National University Publications, 1979), p. 39.
11. LEAA, *Two Hundred Years,* p. 47.
12. Hawes, "Prisons in Early Nineteenth-Century America."
13. Ibid., p. 40.
14. Ibid., p. 39.
15. LEAA, *Two Hundred Years,* p. 49.
16. O. L. Lewis, *The Development of American Prisons and Prison Customs, 1776–1845* (Montclair, NJ: Patterson Smith, 1996/1922).
17. D. J. Rothman, *The Discovery of the Asylum: Social Order and Disorder in the New Republic* (Boston: Little, Brown, 1971), p. 106.
18. Ira J. Silverman and Manuel Vega, *Corrections: A Comprehensive View* (Minneapolis/St. Paul: West, 1996), p. 78.
19. Ibid.
20. LEAA, *Two Hundred Years,* p. 49.
21. Lewis, *The Development of American Prisons.*
22. John W. Fountain, "Time Winds Down at a Storied Prison," *New York Times Online,* www.nytimes.com, December 26, 2001.
23. E. Ayers, *Vengeance and Justice: Crime and Punishment in the 19th-Century American South* (New York: Oxford University Press, 1984).
24. M. C. Moos, *State Penal Administration in Alabama* (Tuscaloosa, AL: Bureau of Public Administration, University of Alabama, 1942), p. 18.
25. B. McKelvey, *American Prisons: A History of Good Intentions* (Montclair, NJ: Patterson Smith, 1977).
26. Thomas Murton and J. Hyams, *Accomplices to the Crime: The Arkansas Prison Scandal* (New York: Grove Press, 1969).
27. Holt v. Sarver, 300 F. Supp. 825 (1969); Holt v. Sarver, 309 F. Supp. 362 (E.D. Ark. 1970); Jackson v. Bishop, 404 F. 2d 571 (8th Cir., 1968).
28. *Holt v. Sarver,* 309 F. Supp. 362 (E.D. Ark. 1970).
29. Adam Liptak, "Inmate Count in U.S. Dwarfs Other Nations," *New York Times,* April 23, 2009.
30. Ibid.
31. Sandhya Somashekhar, "Webb Sets His Sights on Prison Reform," *Washington Post,* December 29, 2008, p. B01.
32. Adam Liptak, "Inmate Count."
33. N.C. Aizenman, "New High in U.S. Prison Numbers: Growth Attributed to More Stringent Sentencing Laws," *Washington Post,* February 29, 2008, p. A01.
34. David Jones, *History of Criminology: A Philosophical Perspective* (New York: Greenwood Press, 1986), p. 123: Bureau of Justice Statistics, *Census of Jails, 1999* (Washington, DC: U.S. Department of Justice, August 2001), pp. 1, 7.
35. American Correctional Association, *The American Prison from the Beginning* (Lanham, MD: American Correctional Association, 1983), p. 220.
36. Ibid.
37. Bureau of Justice Statistics, *Census of Jails,* p. 3.
38. Shaila K. Dewan, "Sheriff Accepts Takeover of a Troubled Jail," *New York Times Online,* www.nytimes.com, July 12, 2004.
39. Ibid.
40. Bureau of Justice Statistics, *Law Enforcement Management and Administrative Statistics, Sheriffs' Offices, 1999* (Washington, DC: U.S. Department of Justice, May 2001), p. 7.
41. Ibid., p. 3.
42. Bureau of Justice Statistics, *Census of Jails,* p. 4.
43. Associated Press, "Arizona: Halt to a Detention Practice," *New York Times,* May 30, 2009.
44. Harrison and Beck, *Prisoners in 2004,* p. 1.
45. Samantha Henry, "Prison Consultants Help Inmates Get Good Digs," *Pantagraph,* July 28, 2009.
46. American Correctional Association, *The American Prison,* p. 172.
47. Samantha Henry, "Prison Consultants Help Inmates Get Good Digs," *Pantagraph,* July 28, 2009.
48. Kevin Johnson, "Inmate Swap Worked—Until Impostor Fled," *USA Today,* October 25, 2000, p. 2.
49. Ibid.
50. Gary Marx, "Illinois Prisons: Low-level is Killed by Cellmate with Violent Past when Illinois Prison Officials OKd Housing Them Together," *Chicago Tribune,* May 5, 2009.
51. American Correctional Association, *The American Prison,* p. 172.
52. Harrison and Beck, *Prisoners in 2004,* p. 4.
53. Allen Beck and Jennifer Karberg, *Prison and Jail Inmates at Midyear 2000* (Washington, DC: U.S. Department of Justice, March 2001), p. 5.
54. John Scalia, *Federal Drug Offenders, 1999, with Trends 1984–99* (Washington, DC: U.S. Department of Justice, August 2001), p. 6.
55. Anne L. Stahl, *Drug Offense Cases in Juvenile Courts, 1989–1998* (Washington, DC: U.S. Department of Justice, September 2001), p. 1.
56. Chen, "Number of Women."
57. Ibid.
58. Laura Maruschak, *HIV in Prisons and Jails, 1999* (Washington, DC: U.S. Department of Justice, July 2001), p. 4.
59. Chen, "Number of Women."
60. Caroline Wolf Harlow, *Prior Abuse Reported by Inmates and Probationers* (Washington, DC: U.S. Department of Justice, April 1999), p. 2.
61. Lennie Magida, "Doing Hard Time," *Honolulu Weekly,* July 14, 1993, p. 4.
62. Joan Petersilia, *When Prisoners Return to the Community* (Washington, DC: U.S. Department of Justice, November 2000), p. 4.
63. Marilyn C. Moses, *Keeping Incarcerated Mothers and Their Daughters Together: Girl Scouts beyond Bars* (Washington, DC: U.S. Department of Justice, October 1995), p. 1.
64. Petersilia, *When Prisoners Return.*
65. Chen, "Number of Women."
66. Moses, *Keeping Incarcerated Mothers.*
67. Bureau of Justice Statistics, *Capital Punishment 2000* (Washington, DC: U.S. Department of Justice, December 2001), p. 7.
68. Victor L. Streib, "Death Penalty for Female Offenders January 1, 1973, to December 31, 2000." See www.law.onu.edu/faculty/steib/femdeath.htm, February 14, 2002.
69. Thomas Bonczar and Allen Beck, *Lifetime Likelihood of Going to State or Federal Prison* (Washington, DC: U.S. Department of Justice, March 1997), p. 1.
70. Ibid.
71. Gannett News Service, "13% of U.S. Black Men Barred from Voting," *Honolulu Advertiser,* October 23, 1998, p. A3.
72. Ibid.
73. Ibid.
74. Nearly all jails, state prisons, and federal prisons have abandoned the use of the term *guard* to describe security personnel. In the federal prisons, these employees are called *correctional officers.* Correctional institutions do not consider the job title "guard" as appropriately describing the duties of the employee, and use of the term is considered rather derogatory and demeaning of the professionalism required for the position.
75. Associated Press, "Private Prisons Said to Do Little for Communities," *Pocono Record,* October 22, 2001, p. A5.
76. Ibid.

77. Associated Press, "Private Prisons Said to Do Little for Communities," *Pocono Record,* October 22, 2001, p. A5.
78. Ibid.
79. *Richardson et al. v. McKnight,* No. 96-318.
80. Bureau of Justice Statistics, *Challenging the Conditions of Prisons and Jails: A Report on Section 1983 Litigation* (Washington, DC: U.S. Department of Justice, December 1994).
81. Solomon Moore, "Texas: Inmate's Family Wins 2.5 Million Judgment," *New York Times,* April 10, 2009.
82. Adam Liptak, "Inmate Was Considered 'Property' of Gang, Witness Tells Jury in Prison Rape Lawsuit," *New York Times Online,* www.nytimes.com, September 25, 2005.
83. Ibid.
84. Human Rights Watch, *No Escape: Male Rape in U.S. Prisons,* www.hrw.org, 2004.
85. Allen J. Beck and Timothy A. Hughes, *Sexual Violence Reported by Correctional Authorities, 2004* (Washington, DC: Bureau of Justice Statistics, 2005), p. 1.
86. Allen Beck and Paige Harrison, *Sexual Victimization in Local Jails Reported by Inmates,* 2007 (Washington, D.C.: Bureau of Justice Statistics), June 2008.
87. Allen Beck and Paige Harrison, *Sexual Victimization in State and Federal Prisons Reported by Inmates, 2007* (Washington, D.C.: Bureau of Justice Statistics), December 2007.
88. Carrie Johnson, "Panel Sets Guidelines for Fighting Prison Rape," *Washington Post,* June 23, 2009.
89. Joan Petersilia, *When Prisoners Return to the Community: Political, Economic, and Social Consequences* (Washington, DC: U.S. Department of Justice, November 2000), p. 4.
90. William J. Fraser, "Getting the Drop on Street Gangs and Terrorists," *Law Enforcement News,* November 30, 2001, p. 11.
91. Silverman and Vega, *Corrections,* p. 208.
92. Kevin Dayton, "Release Foreseen for Comatose Halawa Inmate," *Star-Bulletin & Advertiser,* December 8, 1991, p. A3.
93. Petersilia, *When Prisoners Return to the Community,* p. 4.
94. Maruschak and Beck, *Medical Problems of Inmates,* p. 1.
95. "Unintended Consequences of Sentencing Policy: The Creation of Long-Term Healthcare Obligations," in *Research in Review* (Washington, DC: U.S. Department of Justice, November 2001), p. 1.
96. Bureau of Justice Statistics, *Challenging the Conditions of Prisons and Jails: A Report on Section 1983 Litigation* (Washington, DC: U.S. Department of Justice, December 1994), p. 8.
97. Tammerlin Drummond, "Cellblock Seniors," *Time,* June 21, 1999, p. 60.
98. Ibid.
99. Adam Nossiter, "As His Inmates Grew Thinner, a Sheriff's Wallet Grew Fatter," *New York Times,* January 9, 2009.
100. Rebecca Widom and Theodore M. Hammett, *HIV/AIDS and STDs in Juvenile Facilities* (Washington, DC: U.S. Department of Justice, April 1996), p. 1.
101. Laura M. Maruschak, *HIV in Prisons and Jails, 1999* (Washington, DC: U.S. Department of Justice, July 2001), p. 1.
102. Ibid.
103. Ibid.
104. Ibid.
105. Ibid.
106. Lawrence K. Altman, "Much More AIDS in Prisons Than in General Populations," *New York Times Online,* www.nytimes.com, September 2, 1999.
107. Ibid.
108. Karen Wilcock, Theodore M. Hammett, Rebecca Widom, and Joel Epstein, *Tuberculosis in Correctional Facilities, 1994–1995* (Washington, DC: U.S. Department of Justice, July 1996), p. 1.
109. Ibid.
110. Doris James and Lauren Glaze, *Mental Health Problems of Prison and Jail Inmates* (Washington, D.C.: Bureau fo Justice Statistics, September 2006), p. 1.
111. Fox Butterfield, "Experts Say Study Confirms Prison's New Role as Mental Hospital," *New York Times Online,* www.nytimes.com, July 12, 1999.
112. Ibid.
113. Ibid.
114. ACLU Newswire, "Jails No Place for the Mentally Ill, ACLU of Mississippi Says," www.aclu.org/news, January 16, 2002.
115. Paula M. Ditton, *Mental Health and Treatment of Inmates and Probationers* (Washington, DC: U.S. Department of Justice, July 1999), p. 1.
116. Petersilia, *When Prisoners Return to the Community,* p. 2.
117. ACLU News Wire, "Jails No Place."
118. Butterfield, "Experts Say Study Confirms."
119. Erving Goffman, *Asylums: Essays on the Social Situation of Mental Patients and Other Inmates* (Garden City, NY: Anchor Books, 1961).
120. Ditton, *Mental Health and Treatment,* p. 9.
121. Linda A. Teplin, *Assessing Alcohol, Drug, and Mental Disorders in Juvenile Detainees* (Washington, DC: U.S. Department of Justice, January 2000), p. 1.
122. Debbie Cenziper and James Hohmann, "Some Guards at Md. Jail Have Arrest Records," *Washington Post,* July 25, 2008, p. A01.
123. John Eligon, "Correction Officers Accused of Letting Inmates Run Rikers Island Jail," *New York Times,* January 23, 2009.
124. David T. Johnson and Meda Chesney-Lind, "Does Hawaii Really Need Another Prison?" *Honolulu Advertiser,* March 29, 1998, p. B1.
125. William D. Nueske, "Four Prisoners Who Killed Themselves Did Us a Favor," *Honolulu Star-Bulletin,* January 13, 1992.
126. Associated Press, "Official Resists Plan of Computers for Jail," *Pocono Record,* January 17, 2002, p. A4.
127. Ibid.

Chapter 10 PROBATION AND PAROLE

1. Ian Urbina, "Virginia Governor Sets Free 3 Sailors Convicted in Rape and Murder," *New York Times,* August 7, 2009.
2. Ibid.
3. Ibid.
4. Ira Silverman and Manuel Vega, *Corrections: A Comprehensive View* (Minneapolis/Saint Paul: West, 1996), p. 495.
5. Lauren E. Glaze and Seri Palla, *Probation and Parole in the United States, 2004* (Washington, DC: Bureau of Justice Statistics, 2005), p. 1.
6. Ibid.
7. James M. Byrne, *Probation: A National Institute of Justice Crime File Series Study Guide* (Washington, DC: U.S. Department of Justice, 1988), p. 1.
8. In *Escoe v. Zerbst,* 295 U.S. 490 (135), the Court ruled that probation was an act of grace, and thus the probationer was without due process rights. In *Mempa v. Rhay,* 389 U.S. 128 (1967), the Court reversed the ruling of *Escoe v. Zerbst* and ruled that probationers were entitled to due process rights.
9. *Gagnon v. Scarpelli,* 411 U.S. 778 (1973).
10. *Griffin v. Wisconsin,* 483 U.S. 868, 107 S.Ct. 3164 (1987).
11. *Minnesota v. Murphy,* 465 U.S. 420, 104 S.Ct. 1136, 79 L. Ed. 2d 409 (1984).
12. *Gagon v. Scarpelli* (1973); *Mempa v. Rhay* (1967).
13. *Kelly v. Robinson,* 479 U.S. 36, 107 S.Ct. 353, 93 L. Ed. 2d 216 (1986).
14. *Silverman and Vega, Corrections,* p. 501.
15. H. Burns, *Corrections Organization and Administration* (St. Paul, MN: West, 1975).
16. G. I. Giardini, *The Parole Process* (Springfield, IL: Charles C. Thomas, 1959), p. 9.
17. David Dresser, *Practice and Theory of Probation and Parole* (New York: Columbia University Press, 1969), pp. 56–76.
18. Marjorie Bell (ed.), *Parole in Principle and Practice* (New York: National Probation and Parole Association, 1957).
19. A. W. Pisciotta, "Scientific Reform: The 'New Penology' at Elmira, 1876–1900," *Crime and Delinquency, 29* (1983): 613–630.

20. Bureau of Justice Statistics, *Probation and Parole Statistics.*

21. Chris L. Jenkins, "Ten Years after It Eliminated Parole, VA Considers Costs," *Washington Post,* December 25, 2004, p. B1.

22. Ibid.

23. Glaze and Palla, *Probation and Parole in the United States,* p. 9.

24. L. E. Glaze and T. P. Bonczar, *Probation and Parole in the United States.* (Washington, D.C. Bureau of Justice Statistics, 2009) pp. 39–40.

25. Jenkins, "Ten Years," p. B1.

26. Bureau of Justice Statistics, *Likelihood of Going to State or Federal Prison* (Washington, DC: U.S. Department of Justice, March 1997). p. 5.

27. Task Force on Corrections, *Task Force Report: Corrections* (Washington, DC: President's Commission on Law Enforcement and the Administration of Justice, U.S. Government Printing Office, 1967).

28. William Parker, *Parole: Origins, Development, Current Practices and Statutes* (College Park, MD: American Correctional Association, 1975).

29. *Menechino v. Oswald,* 430 F. 2d 403 (2d Cir., 1970); *Greenholtz v. Inmates of Nebraska Penal and Correctional Complex,* 422 U.S. 1 (1979).

30. *Johnson, U.S. ex. Rel. v. Chairman, New York State Board of Parole,* 363 F. Supp. 416, aff'd, 500 F. 2d 925 (2d Cir., 1971).

31. James Austin, "The Consequences of Escalating the Use of Imprisonment," *Corrections Compendium,* September 1991, pp. 1, 4–8.

32. Ibid.

33. See www.usdoj.gov/uspc/release.htm, February 4, 2002.

34. Glaze and Palla, *Probation and Parole in the United States,* p. 9.

35. Ibid.

36. Bureau of Justice Statistics, *Probation and Parole Violators in State Prison, 1991* (Washington, DC: U.S. Department of Justice, August 1995), p. 1.

37. *Morrissey v. Brewer,* 408 U.S. 471 (1972).

38. See www.usdoj.gov/uspc/questions.htm, February 4, 2002.

39. Bureau of Justice Statistics, *Trends in State Parole,* p. 11.

40. See www.usdoj.gov/uspc/questions.htm, February 4, 2002.

41. See www.usdoj.gov/uspc, February 4, 2002.

42. Silverman and Vega, *Corrections,* p. 495.

43. J. V. Barry, *Alexander Maconochie of Norfolk Island: A Study of Prison Reform* (London: Oxford University Press, 1958).

44. E. E. Dooley, "Sir Walter Crofton and the Irish or Intermediate System of Prison Discipline," *New England Journal on Prison Law, 72,* Winter 1981.

45. Bureau of Justice Statistics, *Probation and Parole Violators in State Prison.*

Chapter 11 CORRECTIONS IN THE COMMUNITY

1. Caroline Wolf Harlow, *Education and Correctional Populations* (Washington, DC: Bureau of Justice Statistics, 2003), p. 1.

2. Jeremy Travis, Amy L. Solomon, and Michelle Waul, *From Prison to Home: The Dimensions and Consequences of Prisoner Reentry* (Washington, DC: The Urban Institute, April 2003).

3. Sara B. Miller, "A Shift to Easing Life after Prison," *Christian Science Monitor,* February 23, 2005, p. 1.

4. Jennifer Gonnerman, *Life on the Outside* (New York: Farrar, Straus & Giroux, 2004).

5. "New Strategies for Curbing Recidivism," *New York Times Online,* www.nytimes.com, January 21, 2005.

6. Brent Staples, "Why Some Politicians Need Their Prisons to Stay Full," *New York Times Online,* www.nytimes.com, December 27, 2004.

7. "Creating the Next Crime Wave," *New York Times Online,* www.nytimes.com, March 13, 2004.

8. Joan Petersilia, "Challenges of Prisoner Reentry and Parole in California," California Policy Research Brief Series, June 2000, www.ucop.educ/cprc/parole.html.

9. Joan Petersilia, *When Prisoners Return to the Community: Political, Economic, and Social Consequences* (Washington, DC: U.S. Department of Justice, November 2000), p. 1.

10. Jeremy Travis, *But They All Come Back: Rethinking Prisoner Reentry* (Washington, DC: U.S. Department of Justice, May 2000), p. 1.

11. "Pew Center on the States." *State of Recidivism: The Revolving Door of America's Prisons* (Washington, D.C.: The Pew Charitable Trusts, April 2011), pp. 10, 14.

12. Ibid.

13. Petersilia, *When Prisoners Return,* p. 3.

14. Ibid., p. 3.

15. William J. Sabol, William P. Adams, Barbara Parthasarathy, and Yan Yaun, *Offenders Returning to Federal Prison, 1986–1997* (Washington, DC: Bureau of Justice Statistics), 2000, p. 1.

16. Council of State Governments, "Building Bridges: From Conviction to Employment, A Proposal to Reinvest Corrections Savings in an Employment Initiative," January 2003, www.csgeast.org/crimpub.asp.

17. Nancy LaVigne, Cynthia A. Mamallian, Jeremy Travis, and Christy Visher, *A Portrait of Prisoner Reentry in Illinois* (Washington, DC: The Urban Institute, 2003).

18. Pew Center on the States, *One in 31: The Long Reach of American Corrections* (Washington, D.C.: The Pew Charitable Trusts, March 2009), p. 8.

19. Petersilia, *When Prisoners Return,* p. 3.

20. Travis, *But They All Come Back,* p. 1.

21. Sara Rimer, "At Last, the Windows Have No Bars," *New York Times Online,* www.nytimes.com, April 29, 2004.

22. Petersilia, *When Prisoners Return,* p. 3.

23. Kirk Eckholm, "In Prisoners' Wake, a Tide of Troubled Kids," *New York Times,* July 5, 2009.

24. Petersilia, *When Prisoners Return,* p. 3.

25. Travis, *But They All Come Back,* p. 3.

26. *New York Times,* April 6, 1994f, p. A16.

27. Travis, *But They All Come Back,* p. 3.

28. Mark S. Umbreit, "Community Service Sentencing: Last Alternative or Added Sanction?" *Federal Probation, 45,* 1981, pp. 3–14.

29. Ira J. Silverman and Manuel Vega, *Corrections: A Comprehensive View* (St. Paul, MN: West, 1996), p. 515.

30. Ibid., p. 516.

31. Travis, *But They All Come Back,* p. 3.

32. Analysis by Eric Cadora and Charles Swartz for the Community Justice Project at the Center for Alternative Sentencing and Employment Services (CASE), 1999, cited in Travis, Solomon, and Waul, *From Prison to Home.*

33. "Report of the Re-Entry Policy Council: Report Preview: Charting the Safe and Successful Return of Prisoners to the Community," www.reentrypolicy.org.

34. Petersilia, *When Prisoners Return,* p. 3.

35. Elijah Anderson, *Streetwise: Race, Class, and Change in an Urban Community* (Chicago: University of Chicago Press, 1990), p. 4.

36. Joan Petersilia, "Challenges of Prisoner Reentry and Parole in California," California Policy Research Brief Series, June 2000, www.ucop.educ/cprc/parole.html.

37. Joan Moore, "Bearing the Burden: How Incarceration Weakens Inner-City Communities." Paper read at the Unintended Consequences of Incarceration Conference at the Vera Institute of Justice, New York City, 1996.

38. Office of Justice Programs, *Rethinking Probation: Community Supervision, Community Safety* (Washington, DC: U.S. Department of Justice, December 1998), p. 1.

39. Ibid.

40. Petersilia, *When Prisoners Return,* p. 3.

41. T. Clear and P. Hardyman, "The New Intensive Supervision Movement," *Crime and Delinquency, 35,* 1990, pp. 42–60.

42. R. Carter and L. Wilkins, "Caseloads: Some Conceptual Models," in R. Carter and L. Wilkins (eds.), *Probation, Parole and Community Corrections* (New York: John Wiley and Sons, 1976).

43. Office of Justice Programs, *Rethinking Probation,* p. 2.

44. Petersilia, "Challenges of Prisoner Reentry," p. 2.

45. Ibid.

46. Marta Nelson and Jennifer Trone, *Why Planning for Release Matters* (New York: Vera Institute of Justice, 2000), p. 2.
47. Ibid.
48. James P. Levine et al., *Criminal Justice in America: Law in Action* (New York: John Wiley, 1986), p. 549.
49. Administrative Office of the Courts, "New Jersey Intensive Supervision Program, Progress Report 12, No. 1" (Trenton, NJ: State of New Jersey, 1995), p. 3.
50. New Jersey Intensive Probation Supervision Program Statistical Highlights, December 31, 2010. http://www.judiciary.state.nj.us/probsup/isp_stat_highlights.pdf.
51. "Going Home: Serious and Violent Offender Reentry Initiative." See "Communities in Action," www.ojp.usdoj.gov/reentry/communities.htm, February 16, 2002.
52. Joan Petersilia, *Expanding Options for Criminal Sentencing* (Santa Monica, CA: The Rand Corporation, 1987).
53. Ibid.
54. Cherie L. Clark, David W. Aziz, and Doris L. MacKenzie, *Shock Incarceration in New York: Focus on Treatment* (Washington, DC: U.S. Department of Justice, August 1994), p. 2.
55. Silverman and Vega, *Corrections,* p. 529.
56. Doris Layton MacKenzie and Deanna Bellew Ballow, "Shock Incarceration Programs in State Correctional Jurisdictions—An Update," *NIJ Report: Shock Incarceration,* May/June 1989, pp. 9–10; D. G. Parent, *Shock Incarceration: An Overview of Existing Programs* (Washington, DC: U.S. Department of Justice, 1989).
57. Clark, Aziz, and Mackenzie, *Shock Incarceration in New York,* p. 5.
58. Ibid., p. 4.
59. Ibid., p. 3.
60. Ibid., p. 9.
61. Ibid., p. 10.
62. Ibid., p. 6.
63. Doris MacKenzie and Claire Souryal, *Multisite Evaluation of Shock Incarceration* (Washington, DC: National Institute of Justice, September 1994), p. 1.
64. Clark, Aziz, and Mackenzie, *Shock Incarceration in New York,* p. 4.
65. Joan Petersilia, "House Arrest," *National Institute of Justice, Crime File Study Guide* (Washington, DC: U.S. Department of Justice, 1988), p. 1.
66. Silverman and Vega, *Corrections,* p. 523.
67. Ibid., p. 524.
68. M. Renzema and D. Skelton, *Final Report: The Use of Electronic Monitoring by Criminal Justice Agencies* (Washington, DC: U.S. Department of Justice, 1990), pp. 1–3.
69. Petersilia, "House Arrest," p. 1.
70. David C. Anderson, *Sensible Justice: Alternatives to Prison* (New York: The New Press, 1998), p. 44.
71. Ibid.
72. John Schwartz, "Internet Leash Can Monitor Sex Offenders," *New York Times Online,* www.nytimes.com, December 31, 2001.
73. Christopher Baird and Dennis Wagner, *Evaluation of the Florida Community Control Program* (Madison, WI: National Council on Crime and Delinquency, 1990).
74. J. Muncie, "A Prisoner in My Home: The Politics and Practice of Electronic Monitoring," *Probation Journal, 37,* 1990, pp. 72–77.
75. *Federal Government Information Technology, Electronic Surveillance and Civil Liberties* (Washington, DC: Congress of the United States, Office of Technology Assessment, 1985); R. Ball, R. C. Huff, and J. P. Lilly, *House Arrest and Correctional Policy: Doing Time at Home* (Newbury Park, CA: Sage, 1988).
76. Reginald A. Wilkinson, "Offender Reentry: A Storm Overdue," www.drc.state.oh.us/Articles/article66.htm, January 16, 2002.
77. Ibid.
78. "History of the Office of Community Corrections," www.michigan.gov, February 16, 2002.
79. National Criminal Justice Reference Service, "Prisoner Reentry Resources—Legislation," www.ncjrs.org/reentry/legislation.htm, February 17, 2002.
80. Ibid.
81. Serious and Violent Offender Reentry Initiative, "See Communities in Action," www.ojp.usdoj.gov/reentry/communities.htm, February 18, 2002.
82. Jacqui Goddard, "Florida's New Approach to Inmate Reform: A 'Faith-Based' Prison," *Christian Science Monitor,* December 24, 2003, p. 1.
83. Fox Butterfield, "Repaving the Long Road Out of Prison," *New York Times Online,* www.nytimes.com, May 4, 2004.
84. Marta Nelson and Jennifer Trone, *Why Planning for Release Matters* (New York: Vera Institute of Justice, 2000), p. 2.
85. Elmer H. Johnson and Kenneth E. Kotch, "Two Factors in Development of Work Release: Size and Location of Prisons," *Journal of Criminal Justice, 1* (March 1973): 44–45.
86. Silverman and Vega, *Corrections,* p. 520.
87. Harry Holzer, *What Employers Want: Job Prospects for Less-Educated Workers* (New York: Russell Sage, 1996).
88. Petersilia, *When Prisoners Return,* p. 4.
89. U.S. Department of Labor, *From Hard Time to Full Time: Strategies to Move Ex-Offenders from Welfare to Work* (Washington, DC: U.S. Department of Labor, June 2001), p. 7.
90. "Woman Files Lawsuit against Company for Using Inmate Telemarketers," *Pocono Record,* November 15, 2001, p. A5.
91. Cheryl Dahle, "What's That Felony on Your Resume," *New York Times Online,* www.nytimes.com, October 17, 2004.
92. Nelson and Trone, *Why Planning for Release Matters,* pp. 4–5.
93. Ibid.
94. Ibid., p. 3.
95. Rhonda Cook, "State Prison-to-Work Program Falls Short," *Atlanta Journal-Constitution,* June 1, 2000.
96. Nelson and Trone, *Why Planning for Release Matters,* p. 2.
97. U.S. Department of Labor, *From Hard Time to Full Time: Strategies to Help Move Ex-Offenders from Welfare to Work* (U.S. Department of Labor, Washington, DC: June 2001), p. 10.
98. Ibid., p. 11.
99. Susan Kreifels, "New Rules Add Teeth to Convict-Hiring Law," *Honolulu Star-Bulletin,* January 9, 1998, pp. A1, A8.
100. U.S. Department of Labor, *From Hard Time to Full Time,* pp. 9–10.
101. David Koeppel, "Job Fairs Give Ex-Convicts Hope in Down Market," *New York Times Online,* www.nytimes.com, December 26, 2001.
102. George E. Sexton, *Work in American Prisons: Joint Ventures with the Private Sector* (Washington, DC: U.S. Department of Justice, November 1995), pp. 2, 10.
103. Ibid., p. 3.
104. Ronald D. Stephens and June Lane Arnette, *From the Courthouse to the Schoolhouse: Making Successful Transitions* (Washington, DC: U.S. Department of Justice, February 2000), p. 1.
105. Ibid., p. 3.
106. Thomas Barlett, "Prime Numbers," *Chronicle of Higher Education,* January 19, 2002, p. A7.
107. Ibid.
108. Peter Monaghan, "U. of Alaska Declines to Admit a Killer to Its Social-Work Program, Raising Questions—and a Lawsuit," *Chronicle of Higher Education,* July 13, 2005.
109. O. I. Keller and B. S. Alper, *Halfway Houses: Community-Centered Correction and Treatment* (Lexington, MA: Heath Lexington Books, 1970).
110. Task Force on Corrections, *Task Force Report: Corrections* (Washington, DC: President's Commission on Law Enforcement and the Administration of Justice, U.S. Government Printing Office, 1967); Task Force on Corrections, *Task Force Report: Corrections* (Washington, DC: National Advisory Commission on Criminal Justice Standards and Goals, 1973).
111. Office of Justice Programs, *Rethinking Probation,* pp. 19–21.
112. Dale G. Parent, *Day Reporting Centers for Criminal Offenders: A Descriptive Analysis of Existing Programs* (Washington, DC: U.S. Department of Justice, 1990), p. 1.

113. Dale G. Parent, "Day Reporting Centers," in Michael Tonry and Kate Hamilton (eds.), *Intermediate Sanctions in Overcrowded Times* (Boston: Northeastern University Press, 1995), p. 15.

114. *Criminal Justice Abstracts* (Monsey, NY: Willow Tree Press, 1998), pp. 105–106.

115. Drug Court Clearinghouse and Technical Assistance Project, "Looking at a Decade of Drug Courts," www.ojp.usdoj.gov/, November 16, 2001.

116. Adele Harrell, Shannon Cavanagh, and John Roman, *Evaluation of the D.C. Superior Court Drug Intervention Programs* (Washington, DC: National Institute of Justice, April 2000), pp. 1–2.

117. John Scalia, *Federal Drug Offenders, 1999 with Trends 1984–1999* (Washington, DC: U.S. Department of Justice, August 2001), p. 10.

118. Ibid., p. 1.

119. Elizabeth A. Peyton and Robert Gossweiler, *Treatment Services in Adult Drug Courts: Report on the 1999 National Drug Court Treatment Survey Executive Summary* (Washington, DC: U.S. Department of Justice, May 2001), p. 5.

120. Allen J. Beck, "State and Federal Prisoners Returning to the Community: Finding from the Bureau of Justice Statistics." Paper presented at the First Reentry Courts Initiative Cluster Meeting, Washington, DC, April 13, 2000.

121. Drug Court Clearinghouse and Technical Assistance Project, "Looking at a Decade."

122. Ibid.

123. Ibid.

124. Ibid.

125. Adele Harrell, Shannon Cavanagh, and John Roman, *Evaluation of the D.C. Superior Court Drug Intervention Programs* (Washington, DC: U.S. Department of Justice, April 2000), p. 2.

126. Ibid.

127. Tribal Law and Policy Institute, *Healing to Wellness Courts: A Preliminary Overview of Tribal Drug Courts* (Washington DC: U.S. Department of Justice, July 1999), p. 14.

128. Ibid., p. 9.

129. Ibid., p. 2.

130. Ibid., p. 4.

131. Ibid., pp. 9–10.

132. Ibid., p. 12.

133. Ibid., p. 13.

134. Ibid., p. 14.

135. National Institute of Justice, *Reducing Offender Drug Use,* p. 21; Bureau of Justice Assistance, *Treatment Accountability for Safer Communities* (Washington, DC: U.S. Department of Justice, November 1995), pp. 1–2.

136. Bureau of Justice Assistance, *Treatment Accountability for Safer Communities* (Washington, DC: U.S. Department of Justice, November 1995), p. 1.

137. National Institute of Justice, *Reducing Offender Drug Use,* p. 21.

138. Joan Petersilia and Elizabeth Piper Deschenes, "What Punishes? Inmates Rank the Severity of Prison versus Intermediate Sanctions," in Joan Petersilia (ed.), *Community Corrections: Probation, Parole and Intermediate Sanctions* (New York: Oxford University Press, 1998), pp. 149–159.

139. Joan Petersilia, "When Probation Becomes More Dreaded Than Prison," *Federal Probation, 54,* 1990, pp. 23–27.

140. Rick Lyman, "Marriage Programs Try to Instill Bliss and Stability Behind Bars," *New York Times Online*, www.nytimes.com, April 16, 2005.

Chapter 12 THE JUVENILE SYSTEM

1. *Juvenile Justice: A Century of Change* (Washington, DC: Office of Juvenile Justice and Delinquency Prevention, December 1999), p. 1. NCJ No. 178995.

2. "Juvenile Detention in New York—Then and Now," New York City Department of Juvenile Justice, www.correctionhistory.org/html/chronicl/djj/djj20yrs3.htm, April 28, 2005.

3. *Juvenile Justice: A Century of Change,* p. 2.

4. "A Brief History," New York House of Refuge, www.archives.nysed.gov/a/researchroom/rr_ed_reform_intro.shtml.

5. Ibid.

6. Ibid.

7. Ibid.

8. Ibid.

9. "Department of Juvenile Services: Origin," Maryland Department of Juvenile Services, www.djs.state.md.us/history.html.

10. "Juvenile Delinquency: A Rising Concern: 1861–1916," www.archives.nysed.gov/a/researchroom/rr_ed_reform_intro.shtml.

11. *Juvenile Justice: A Century of Change,* p. 2.

12. Ibid., p. 1.

13. Ibid., p. 3.

14. Howard N. Snyder and Melissa Sickmund, *Juvenile Offenders and Victims: 1999 National Report* (Washington, DC: Office of Juvenile Justice and Delinquency Prevention, September 1999), p. 86. NCJ Document No. 178257.

15. *Juvenile Justice: A Century of Change,* p. 6.

16. "History of Juvenile Justice in Oregon," Oregon Youth Authority, www.oregon.gov/OYA/history.shtml.

17. *Kent v. United States* 383 U.S. 541, 86 S.Ct. 1045 (1966).

18. Snyder and Sickmund, *Juvenile Offenders and Victims,* p. 90.

19. Ibid.

20. *Re Gault* 387 U.S. 1, 87 S.Ct. 1428 (1967).

21. Snyder and Sickmund, *Juvenile Offenders and Victims,* p. 90.

22. Ibid., pp. 90–91.

23. *In re Winship* 397 U.S. 358, 90 S.Ct. 1068 (1970).

24. Snyder and Sickmund, *Juvenile Offenders and Victims,* pp. 90–91.

25. Ibid., p. 92.

26. Ibid.

27. Ibid.

28. *Schall v. Martin* 467 U.S. 253, 104 S. Ct. 2403 (1984).

29. *Oklahoma Publishing Company v. District Court* in and for Oklahoma City 480 U.S. 208, 97 S. Ct. 1045 (1977).

30. *Smith v. Daily Mail Publishing Company* 443 U.S. 97, 99 S.Ct. 2667 (1979).

31. Wendy S. McClanahan, *Alive at 25: Reducing Youth Violence through Monitoring and Support* (Philadelphia, PA: Public/Private Ventures, 2004), p. 1.

32. Snyder and Sickmund, *Juvenile Offenders and Victims,* p. 103.

33. Ibid., p. 106.

34. Patrick Griffin and Melanie Bozynski, "National Overviews." *State Juvenile Justice Profiles* (Pittsburgh, PA: National Center for Juvenile Justice, May 1, 2005), www.ncjj.org/statgeprofiles/.

35. Ibid.

36. Ibid.

37. Ibid.

38. Jeffrey A. Butts and Janeen Buck, *Teen Courts: A Focus on Research* (Washington, DC: Office of Juvenile Justice and Delinquency Prevention, October 2000). NCJ Document No. 183472.

39. Ibid., p. 1.

40. Caroline S. Cooper, *Juvenile Drug Court Programs* (Washington DC: U.S. Department of Justice, May 2001), p. 1.

41. Ibid., p. 3.

42. Ibid., p. 6.

43. Ibid., p. 9.

44. Ibid., p. 13.

45. Ibid., p. 11.

46. Ibid., p. 13.

47. Melissa Sickmund, *Juveniles in Correction* (Washington, DC: Office of Juvenile Justice and Delinquency Prevention, June 2004). NCJ Document No. 202885.

48. Gail A. Wasserman, Susan J. Ko, and Larkin S. McReynolds, *Assessing the Mental Health Status of Youth in Juvenile Justice Settings* (Washington, DC: Office of Juvenile Justice and Delinquency Prevention, August 2004), pp. 3–4. NCJ Document No. 202713.

49. Howard N. Snyder and Monica Swahn, *Juvenile Suicides, 1981–1998* (Washington, DC: Office of Juvenile Justice and Delinquency Prevention, March 2004), pp. 1–2. NCJ Document No. 196978.

50. Wasserman, Ko, and McReynolds, "Assessing the Mental Health Status."

51. Richard G. Wiebush, Dennis Wagner, et al. *Implementation and Outcome Evaluation of the Intensive Aftercare Program: Final Report* (Washington, DC: Office of Juvenile Justice and Delinquency Prevention, March 2005). NCJ Document No. 206177.

52. Ibid., pp. 82–83.

53. Doris MacKenzie, Angela Gover, Gaylene Armstrong, and Ojmarr Mitchell, *A National Study Comparing the Environment of Boot Camps with Traditional Facilities for Juvenile Offenders* (Washington, DC: U.S. Department of Justice, August 2001), p. 1.

54. Ibid., pp. 3–4.

55. Ibid., pp. 1–2.

56. Ibid., p. 2.

57. Ibid., p. 11.

58. Michael Janofsky, "States Pressed as 3 Boys Die at Boot Camps," *New York Times Online*, www.nytimes.com, September 7, 2001.

59. Ibid.

60. Michael Janofsky, "Boot Camp Proponent Becomes Focus of Critics," *New York Times Online*, www.nytimes.com, August 9, 2001.

61. James Sterngold, "Head of Camp in Arizona Is Arrested in Boy's Death," *New York Times Online*, www.nytimes.com, February 16, 2002.

62. Snyder and Sickmund, *Juvenile Offenders and Victims,* p. 211.

63. *Thompson v. Oklahoma,* 487 U.S. 815, 818–838 (1988).

64. *Stanford v. Kentucky,* 492 U.S. 361 (1989).

65. *State v. Simmons,* 944 S. W. 2d 165 (en banc), cert. denied, 522 U.S. 953_(1997); *Simmons v. Bowersox,* 235 F. 3d 1124, 1127 (CA8), cert. denied, 534 U.S. 924 (2001).

66. *Atkins v. Virginia,* 536 U.S. 304 (2002).

67. Rolf Loeber, David P. Farringtron, and David Petechuk, *Child Delinquency: Early Intervention and Prevention* (Washington, DC: Office of Juvenile Justice and Delinquency Prevention, May 2003), p. 3. NCJ No. 186162.

68. Ibid., p. 1.

69. Ibid., p. 4.

70. Ibid.

71. Ibid.

72. Ibid., p. 5.

73. Ibid.

74. Ibid., p. 6.

75. Ibid., p. 8.

76. Ibid., p. 14.

77. Ibid., p. 10.

78. Ibid., p. 11.

79. Ibid., p. 13.

80. Arlen Egley, Jr., and Aline K. Major, *Highlights of the 2002 National Youth Gang Survey* (Washington, DC: Office of Juvenile Justice and Delinquency Prevention, April 2004), p. 1.

81. James C. Howell, Arlen Egley, Jr., and Debra K. Gleason, *Modern-Day Youth Gangs* (Washington, DC: Office of Juvenile Justice and Delinquency Prevention, June 2002), p. 1. NCJ No. 191524.

82. Karl G. Hill, Christina Lui, and J. David Hawkins, *Early Precursors of Gang Membership: A Study of Seattle Youth* (Washington, DC: Office of Juvenile Justice and Delinquency Prevention, December 2001), p. 4. NCJ No. 190106.

83. Arlen Egley, Jr. *Highlights of the 1999 National Youth Gang Survey* (Washington, DC: Office of Juvenile Justice and Delinquency Prevention, November 2000), p. 1.

84. Howell, Egley, Jr., and Gleason, *Modern-Day Youth Gangs,* p. 3.

85. David Starbuck, James C. Howell, and Donna J. Lindquist, *Hybrid and Other Modern Gangs* (Washington, DC: Office of Juvenile Justice and Delinquency Prevention, December 2001). NCJ No. 189916; Howell, Egley, Jr., and Gleason, *Modern-Day Youth Gangs.*

86. Starbuck, Howell, and Lindquist, *Hybrid and Other Modern Gangs.*

87. Ibid.

88. Ibid., p. 5.

89. M. S. Fleisher, *Dead End Kids: Gang Girls and the Boys They Know* (Madison, WI: University of Wisconsin Press, 1998), p. 264; Starbuck, Howell, and Lindquist, *Hybrid and Other Modern Gangs.*

90. "Sending Gangs the Message: Change, or Else," *Law Enforcement News, xxxi,* No. 620, March 2005, p. 4.

91. Starbuck, Howell, and Lindquist, *Hybrid and Other Modern Gangs,* p. 5.

92. Ibid., p. 4.

93. Ralph A. Weisheit and L. Edward Wells, "Youth Gangs in Rural America," *National Institute of Justice Journal, 251,* July 2004, p. 4.

94. Starbuck, Howell, and Lindquist, *Hybrid and Other Modern Gangs,* p. 6.

95. Howell, Egley, Jr., and Gleason, *Modern-Day Youth Gangs,* p. 8.

96. "Sending Gangs the Message: Change, or Else," p. 4.

97. John Moore and John Hagedorn, *Female Gangs: A Focus on Research* (Washington, DC: Office of Juvenile Justice and Delinquency Prevention, March 2001), pp. 1–2. NCJ No. 186159.

98. M. Chesney-Lind, R. Shelden, and K. Joe, *Girls, Delinquency, and Gang Membership,* in *Gangs in America,* 2nd ed., edited by C. R. Huff (Newbury Park, CA: Sage Publications, 1996).

99. Moore and Hagedorn, *Female Gangs,* p. 2.

100. Ibid.

101. Ibid., p. 6.

102. Ibid.

103. Ibid.

104. Ibid., p. 3.

105. Moore and Hagedorn, *Female Gangs.*

106. Gary M. McClelland, Linda A. Teplin, and Karen M. Abram, *Detection and Prevalence of Substance Use among Juvenile Detainees* (Washington, DC: Office of Juvenile Justice and Delinquency Prevention, June 2004). NCJ No. 203934.

107. "Has the DARE Curriculum Gone to Pot?" *Law Enforcement News,* December 15/31, 2001, p. 6.

108. Elizabeth Armstrong, "Leave Them Alone," *Christian Science Monitor,* September 23, 2003, p. 12.

109. Associated Press, "States Grapple with Growing Teen Meth Use," *New York Times Online*, www.nytimes.com, April 10, 2005.

110. Associated Press, "AP: 1 in 5 Teens Abused Prescription Drugs," *New York Times Online*, www.nytimes.com, April 21, 2005.

111. "NIDA InfoFacts: High School and Youth Trends," Washington, DC: National Institute on Drug Abuse, March 2011, p. 1.

112. "NIDA InfoFacts: High School and Youth Trends," Washington, DC: National Institute on Drug Abuse, March 2011, p. 2.

113. Jill F. DeVoe, Katharin Peter, Amanda Miller, Thomas D. Snyder, and Katrina Baum, *Indicators of School Crime and Safety: 2004* (Washington, DC: National Center for Education Statistics, November 2004), p. 1. NCJ No. 205290.

114. Associated Press, "Schoolmate Held in Shooting Death of Girl, 13," *Honolulu Advertiser,* November 21, 1999, p. A22.

115. Jon Nordheimer, "Seventh-Grade Boy Held in Killing of Teacher," *New York Times Online*, www.nytimes.com, May 26, 2000.

116. Associated Press, "12-Year-Old Pulls Gun on Classmates," *Honolulu Advertiser,* March 24, 2000, p. A5.

117. Associated Press, "Expert: Suspects Spurred by Dares," *New York Times Online*, www.nytimes.com, February 24, 2002.

118. Associated Press, "Student Guilty in Albany School Shooting," *New York Times Online*, www.nytimes.com, November 23, 2004.

119. Associated Press, "Neb. Teen Charged in school Murder Plot," *New York Times Online*, www.nytimes.com, March 19, 2004.

120. "Bullying among Sixth Graders a Daily Occurrence, UCLA Study Finds," *UCLA News,* March 28, 2005. http://newsroom.ucla.edu/page.asp?RelNum=6006. Viewed April 5, 2005.

121. Ibid.

122. Patrik Jonsson, "Schoolyard Bullies and Their Victims: The Picture Fills Out," *Christian Science Monitor,* May 12, 2004, p. 1.

123. Ibid.

124. Elissa Gootman, "Crime Falls as Citations Surge in Schools With Extra Officers," *New York Times Online*, www.nytimes.com, March 25, 2004.

125. Elissa Gootman, "Case Dismissed for Principal in Bronx Clash," *New York Times Online*, www.nytimes.com, April 13, 2005.

126. Gary D. Gottfredson, Denise C. Gottfredson, Ellen R. Czeh, David Cantor, Scott B. Crosse, and Irene Hantman, *Toward Safe and Orderly Schools—The National Study of Delinquency Prevention in Schools* (Washington, DC: National Institute of Justice, November 2004), p. 2. NCJ No. 205005.

127. Ibid., p. 1.

128. Ibid., p. 4.

129. Sara Rimer, "Unruly Students Facing Arrest, Not Detention," *New York Times Online*, www.nytimes.com, January 4, 2004.

130. Ibid.

131. Sara Rimer, "Last Chance High," *New York Times Online*, www.nytimes.com, July 25, 2004.

132. Cora Roy-Stevens, *Overcoming Barriers to School Reentry* (Washington, DC: Office of Justice Programs, October 2004).

133. Snyder and Sickmund, *Children as Victims*, p. 17.

134. Ibid., p. 1.

Chapter 13 HOMELAND SECURITY

1. National Advisory Commission on Criminal Justice Standards and Goals, *Report of the Task Force on Disorder and Terrorism* (Washington, DC: U.S. Government Printing Office, 1976).

2. Jonathan S. Landay, "As Radicalism Declines, Terrorism Surges," *The Christian Science Monitor,* August 20, 1998, pp. 1, 10.

3. Peter Grier and James N. Thurman, "Age of Anonymous Terrorism," *The Christian Science Monitor,* August 20, 1998, p. 10; Evan Thomas et al., "The Road to September 11," *Newsweek,* October 1, 2001, p. 40.

4. Gerald R. Murphy and Martha R. Plotkin, *Protecting Your Community from Terrorism: Strategies for Local Law Enforcement, Volume I: Local-Federal Partnerships* (Washington, DC: U.S. Department of Justice, 2003), p. 61.

5. Ibid., p. 1.

6. Ibid., p. 11.

7. Robert T. Stafford Disaster Relief and Emergency Assistance Act (42 U.S.C. § 121 et seq.)

8. Patricia A. Dalton, *Effective Intergovernmental Coordination Is Key to Success* (Washington, DC: General Accounting Office, GAO-02-1011T, August 2002), p. 3.

9. Homeland Security Act of 2002, Pub. L. No. 107–296 (Nov. 25, 2002); Normal J. Rabkin, *Homeland Security: Overview of Department of Homeland Security Management Challenges* (Washington, DC: Government Accountability Office, April 2005), p. 3.

10. *National Strategy for Homeland Security* (Washington, DC: Office of Homeland Security, July 2002), p. 2.

11. Rabkin, *Homeland Security,* p. 3.

12. Ibid., p. 5.

13. *National Strategy for Homeland Security,* p. 13.

14. Ibid., p. 2.

15. Eric Lipton, "Homeland Security Chief Announces Overhaul," *New York Times Online*, www.nytimes.com, July 14, 2005.

16. Eric Lipton, "For New Chief, A New Approach to Homeland Security," *New York Times Online*, www.nytimes.com, July 18, 2005.

17. Gerald L. Dillingham, *Transportation Security: Post-September 11th Initiatives and Long-Term Challenges* (Washington, DC: United States General Accounting Office GAO-03-616T, April 1, 2003), p. 3.

18. *Aviation Security: Screener Training and Performance Measurement Strengthened, But More Work Remains* (Washington DC: Government Accountability Office GAO-05-457 May 2005).

19. *National Strategy for Combating Terrorism: February 2003* (Washington, DC: Department of State, Publication 11038, April 2003), p. 27.

20. *CONPLAN: United States Government Interagency Domestic Terrorism Concept of Operations Plan* (Washington, DC: Government Printing Office, 2001).

21. Ibid., p. iii.

22. Dalton, "Effective Intergovernmental Coordination," p. 10.

23. McIntire and O'Donnell, "Fire Chief Challenges New York Emergency Plan."

24. Dalton, "Effective Intergovernmental Coordination," p. 14.

25. Gerald R. Murphy and Martha R. Plotkin, *Protecting Your Community from Terrorism,* p. 53.

26. Douglas Jehl, "Four in 9/11 Plot are Called Tied to Qaeda in '00," *New York Times Online*, www.nytimes.com, August 9, 2005; Douglas Jehl and Philip Shenon, "9/11 Commission's Staff Rejected Report on Early Identification of Chief Hijacker," *New York Times Online*, www.nytimes.com, August 11, 2005; Dan Eggen, "Sept. 11 Panel Explores Allegations about Atta," *Washington Post,* August 12, 2005, p. A9.

27. Dan Eggen and Walter Pincus, "Bush Approves Spy Agency Changes," *Washington Post,* June 30, 2005, p. A1.

28. George W. Bush, "Fact Sheet: Strengthening Intelligence to Better Protect America," www.whitehouse.gov/news/release/2003/01/print/20030128l2.html, January 28, 2003.

29. Associated Press, "Details of Counterterror Center Unveiled," *New York Times Online*, www.nytimes.com, February 14, 2003.

30. Murphy and Plotkin, *Protecting Your Community from Terrorism,* p. 31.

31. Ibid., p. 32.

32. John M. Broder, "Police Chiefs Moving to Share Terror Data," *New York Times Online*, www.nytimes.com, July 19, 2005.

33. Eric Lichtblau and William K. Rashbaum, "U.S. Steps Down Threat Level for Mass Transit Systems by a Notch," *New York Times Online*, www.nytimes.com, August 12, 2005.

34. Broder, "Police Chiefs Moving to Share Terror Data."

35. Ibid.

36. Ibid.

37. Federal Bureau of Investigation, "Headline Archives—Fusion Centers: Unifying Intelligence to Protect Americans," March 12, 2009.

38. Associated Press, "Feds Outline Plan on Enemy Combatants," *New York Times Online*, www.nytimes.com, December 17, 2003.

39. Associated Press, "ABA Panel Wants Tribunal Rules Changed," *New York Times Online*, www.nytimes.com, August 12, 2003.

40. Neil A. Lewis, "Rules on Tribunal Require Unanimity on Death Penalty," *New York Times Online*, www.nytimes.com, December 28, 2001.

41. William Glaberson, "Judges Question Detention of American," *New York Times Online*, www.nytimes.com, November 18, 2003.

42. Spencer S. Hus, "Holder prefers keeping option of civilian courts for terrorism suspects," *Washington Post,* April 16, 2010, p. A11.

43. Dante Chinni, "Ashcroft on Tour and Unplugged," *Christian Science Monitor,* August 26, 2003, www.csmonitor.com.

44. Brian Knowlton, "Ashcroft Pushes Defense of Terror Law," *New York Times Online*, www.nytimes.com, August 19, 2003.

45. Dan Eggen, "Flawed FBI Probe of Bombing Used a Secret Warrant," *Washington Post*, April 7, 2005, p. A3.

46. Jeffrey R. Young, "FBI Seeks Library Data from Connecticut Institution Under Patriot Act, Curt Records Show," *Chronicle of Higher Education*, August 29, 2005.

47. Dan Eggen, "Renewed Patriot Act Gets Boost in House, Senate Panel," *Washington Post*, July 22, 2005, p. A12.

48. Warren Richey and Linda Feldmann, "Has Post-9/11 Dragnet Gone Too Far?" *Christian Science Monitor*, September 12, 2003, www.csmonitor.com.

49. Philip Shenon, "Report on USA Patriot Act Alleges Civil Rights Violations," *New York Times Online*, www.nytimes.com, July 21, 2003; Paul von Zielbauer, "Detainees' Abuse Is Detailed," *New York Times Online*, www.nytimes.com, December 19, 2003.

50. Jennifer Nislow, "Portland Just Says 'No' to FBI," *Law Enforcement News*, November 30, 2001, pp. 1, 9.

51. David W. Dunlap, "Financial District Security Getting New Look," *New York Times Online*, www.nytimes.com, November 27, 2003.

52. Rachel L. Swarns, "Is Anti-Terrorist Anti-Tourist? *New York Times Online*, www .nytimes.com, October 31, 2004.

53. Thomas J. Lueck, "Convention to Delay Some Cases in City Courts," *New York Times Online*, www.nytimes.com, July 21, 2004.

54. Eric Lichtblau, "Report Questions the Value of Color-Coded Warnings," *New York Times Online*, www.nytimes.com, July 13, 2004.

55. Eric Lichtblau, "F.B.I. Issues and Retracts Urgent Terrorism Bulletin," *New York Times Online*, www.nytimes.com, May 29, 2004.

56. Stephen E. Flynn, "Color Me Scared," *New York Times Online*, www.nytimes.com, May 25, 2005; John Mintz, "DHS Considers Alternatives to Color-Coded Warnings," *Washington Post*, May 10, 2005, p. A6.

57. Jonathan Klick and Alexander Tabarrok, "Using Terror Alert Levels to Estimate the Effect of Police on Crime," *Journal of Law and Economics, 48,* no. 1 (February 16, 2005), http://mason.gmu.edu/~atabarro/TabarrokPublishedPapers.html.

58. Virginia Postrel, "One Possible Cure for the Common Criminal," *New York Times Online*, www.nytimes.com, June 16, 2005.

59. Eric Lipton, "U.S. Borders Vulnerable, Witnesses Say," *New York Times Online*, www.nytimes.com, June 22, 2005.

60. Associated Press, "Illegal Workers Raise Security Concerns," *New York Times Online*, www.nytimes.com, April 13, 2005.

61. John Mintz, "DHS Arrests 60 Illegals in Sensitive Jobs," *Washington Post*, May 21, 2006, p. A3.

62. Associated Press, "Officials Test Radio Tags at Canada Border," *New York Times Online*, www.nytimes.com, August 9, 2005.

63. Steven Greenhouse, "Immigration Sting Puts 2 U.S. Agencies at Odds," *New York Times Online*, www.nytimes.com, July 16, 2005.

64. Ibid.

65. Michael Janoesky, "9/11 Panel Calls Policies on Immigration Ineffective," *New York Times Online*, www.nytimes.com, April 17, 2004.

66. Associated Press, "United States Issued Visas to 105 Men on Anti-Terror List," *Pocono Record*, November 27, 2002, p. A5.

67. Ralph Blumenthal, "Citing Violence, 2 Border States Declare a Crisis," *New York Times Online*, www.nytimes.com, August 17, 2005.

68. Ralph Blumenthal, "For One Family, Front Row Seats to Border Crisis," *New York Times Online*, www.nytimes.com, August 23, 2005.

69. Ibid.

70. Timothy Egan, "A Battle against Illegal Workers, With an Unlikely Driving Force." *New York Times Online*, www.nytimes.com, May 30, 2005.

71. Dan Eggen, "Customs Jails 1,000 Suspected Gang Members," *Washington Post*, August 2, 2005, p. A2.

72. Ibid.

73. Dibya Sarkar, "Fight Over Driver's License Standards." *Federal Computer Week*, June 23, 2005, www.fcw.com.

74. Associated Press, "Governors: Drivers License Costs to Soar," *New York Times Online*, www.nytimes.com, July 18, 2005.

75. T. R. Reid and Darryl Fears, "Driver's License Curtailed as Identification," *Washington Post*, April 17, 2005, p. A3.

76. Daniel B. Wood, "Driver IDs for Illegals Raise Security Concerns," *Christian Science Monitor*, July 12, 2004, p. 3.

77. Stephen E. Flynn, "Color Me Scared," *New York Times Online*, www.nytimes.com, May 25, 2005; John Mintz, "DHS Considers Alternatives to Color-Coded Warnings," *Washington Post*, May 10, 2005, p. A6.

78. Jonathan Klick and Alexander Tabarrok, "Using Terror Alert Levels to Estimate the Effect of Police on Crime," *Journal of Law and Economics, 48,* no. 1 (February 16, 2005), http://mason.gmu.edu/~atabarro/TabarrokPublishedPapers.html.

79. Virginia Postrel, "One Possible Cure for the Common Criminal," *New York Times Online*, www.nytimes.com, June 16, 2005.

80. Eric Lipton, "U.S. Borders Vulnerable, Witnesses Say," *New York Times Online*, www.nytimes.com, June 22, 2005.

81. Associated Press, "Illegal Workers Raise Security Concerns," *New York Times Online*, www.nytimes.com, April 13, 2005.

82. John Mintz, "DHS Arrests 60 Illegals in Sensitive Jobs," *Washington Post*, May 21, 2006, p. A3.

83. Ellen Nakashima, Brian Krebs, and Blaine Harden, "U.S., South Korea targeted in swarm of internet attacks," Washington Post, July 9, 2009.

84. Federal Bureau of Investigation, Press Release "Response to DOJ Inspector General's Review of FBI's Use of National Security Letters & Corrective Actions," March 13, 2009.

85. Robert Barnes, "Supreme Court weighs free speech against aid to terrorists," *Washington Post*, February 24, 2010, p. A3.

86. Human Rights Watch, *Presumption of Guilt: Human Rights Abuses of Post-September 11 Detainee* (New York: Human Rights Watch, 2002), pp. 3, 6, 46, 55.

87. Eric Lichtblau, "Two Groups Charge Abuse of Witness Law," *New York Times Online*, www.nytimes.com, June 27, 2005.

88. Human Rights Watch, *Presumption of Guilt*, p. 5.

89. Tracey Maclin, "'Voluntary' Interviews and Airport Searches of Middle Eastern Men: The Fourth Amendment in a Time of Terror" *Mississippi Law Journal* (January 21, 2005), p. 521.

90. Associated Press, "Dearborn, Mich., Arabs Cited More Often," *New York Times Online*, www.nytimes.com, November 20, 2003.

91. Laurie Nadel, "For Island's Muslims, a Time to Be Wary," *New York Times Online*, www.nytimes.com, September 4, 2005.

92. Ibid.

93. Peter Grier, "Bush Team and the Limits on Torture," *Christian Science Monitor*, June 10, 2004, p. 1.

94. Peter Grier, "Bush Team and the Limits on Torture," *Christian Science Monitor*, June 10, 2004, p. 1."

95. Ibid.

96. William Glaberson, "President's Detention Plan Tests American Legal Tradition," *New York Times*, May 23, 2009.

GLOSSARY

abolitionists people opposed to the death penalty

actus reus an element of crime in which people are punished for their actions; thus, the law does not prosecute persons for actions that are not voluntary or that are accidental and do not involve recklessness or negligence

appellate courts state or federal have the authority to review the proceedings and verdicts of general trial courts for judicial errors and other significant issues

arraignment a short hearing before the judge in which the charges against the defendant are announced

arrest restricting the freedom of a person by taking him or her into police custody

arson the malicious burning of a structure

Article 3, Section 2 the part of the U.S. Constitution that defines the jurisdiction of the federal courts

assault the crime of willfully inflicting injury on another

atavistic stigmata the study of the physical traits of criminals, a method used by Lombroso

attempt an incomplete criminal act; the closest act to the completion of a crime

bail a promise, sometimes backed by a monetary guarantee, that the accused will return for further proceedings

bail bondsagent an agent of a private commercial business that has contracted with the court to act as a guarantor of a defendant's return to court

bailiff a county deputy sheriff or U.S. deputy marshal responsible for providing security and maintaining order in a courtroom

banishment the removal of an offender from the community

Barker v. Wingo the court ruled that the defendant's failure to request a speedy trial does not negate the defendant's right to a speedy trial

bench trial a trial in which the judge rather than a jury makes the determination of guilty

bifurcated trial a two-part trial structure in which the jury first determines guilt or innocence and then considers new evidence relating to the appropriate punishment

Bill of Rights delineates certain guaranteed freedoms of citizens, such as trial by jury and freedom of speech

biocriminology the study of the roles of genetic and neurophysiological variables as they relate to criminal behavior

blended sentencing option an option that allows the juvenile court or the criminal court to impose a sentence that can include both confinement in a juvenile facility and/or confinement in an adult prison after the offender is beyond the age of the juvenile court's jurisdiction

booking police activity that establishes the identification of an arrested person and formally charges that person with a crime

Breed v. Jones a case in which the Supreme Court ruled that once a juvenile has been adjudicated by a juvenile court, he or she cannot be waived to criminal court to be tried for the same charges

brief a written statement submitted by an appellant's attorneys that states the substantial constitutional or legal issue that they believe the court should address

broken window theory the belief that ignoring public order violations and disruptive behavior leads to community neglect, which fosters further disorder and crime

burden of proof the standard required for a legal verdict

Bureau of Alcohol, Tobacco, Firearms, and Explosives the federal agency responsible for regulating alcohol, tobacco, firearms, explosives, and arson

Bureau of Justice Statistics a federal agency that gathers and disseminates data about almost all aspects of the criminal justice system

burglary a combination of trespass and the intent to commit a crime

capital punishment the sentence of death

Carroll doctrine terms allowing admissibility of evidence obtained by police in a warrantless search of an automobile when the police have probable cause that a crime has occurred and delaying a search could result in losing evidence

certiorari power the authority of the Supreme Court, based on agreement by four of its members that a case might raise significant constitutional or federal issues, to select a case for review

chain gang in the Southern penal system, a group of convicts chained together during outside labor

charge to the jury written instructions about the application of the law to a case that the judge gives to the jury to help them reach a verdict

chief law enforcement officer the highest-ranking law enforcement official within a system; the sheriff is the chief law enforcement officer of a county; the attorney general is the chief law enforcement officer of a state; and the U.S. attorney general is the chief law enforcement officer of the United States

chief of police the chief administrative officer of a municipal police agency

circuit court the geographical jurisdiction of a federal appeals court

circumstantial evidence evidence that implies that the defendant is connected to the crime but does not prove it

civil commitment process a determination of whether the defendant should be released or confined to an institution for persons with mental illness

civil death the legal philosophy that barred any prison inmate from bringing a lawsuit in a civil court related to their treatment while incarcerated or conditions of incarceration

civil law also called private law, the body of law concerned with the definition, regulation, and enforcement of rights in noncriminal cases in which both the person who has the right and the person who has the obligation are private individuals

civil remedies processes in civil courts that enable victims to recover from the psychological, financial, emotional, and physical damages of crime

Civil Rights Act of 1964 declares that it is illegal for businesses, hotels, restaurants, and public transportation to deny citizens service based on their race

classical school theories the school of thought that individuals have free will to choose whether or not to commit crimes and that criminals should have rights in the criminal justice system

clear and present danger a condition relating to public safety that may justify police use of deadly force against a fleeing suspect

clearance rate the percentage of crimes solved versus those that are unsolved

clearing cases refers to the status of a criminal offense. When the police or prosecutor assert that the perpetrator of the crime is known the case is "cleared"

clerk of court a government employee who works directly with the trial judge and is responsible for court paperwork and records before and during a trial

common law unwritten, simply stated laws from the English common laws, based on traditions and common understandings in a time when most people were illiterate

community-based corrections prevention and treatment programs designed to promote the successful transition of offenders from prison to the community

community policing decentralized policing programs that focus on crime prevention, quality of life in a community, public order, and alternatives to arrest

commutation of sentence a reduction in the severity or length of an inmate's sentence issued by a state governor or the president of the United States

competent to stand trial the concept that a defendant comprehends the charges against him or her and is able to assist his or her attorney with the defense

conditional release a bail alternative in which the defendant is released from custody if he or she agrees to court-ordered terms and restrictions

conflict theories theories based on the idea that the most politically and socially powerful individuals and organizations use the legal system to exploit less-powerful individuals and to retain their power and privileges

congregate work system the practice of moving inmates from sleeping cells to other areas of the prison for work and meals

consolidated model the system in which the organization of decision-making about parole is a function of a state department of corrections

conspiracy the planning by two or more people to commit a crime

constructive intent criminal intent in which a person does not intend to harm anyone but should have known that his or her actions created the risk of harm

constructive possession a person being in control of contraband but not having actual possession of it

contempt of court a charge against any violator of the judge's courtroom rules, authorizing the judge to impose a fine or term of imprisonment

contraband illegal goods, such as drugs, cigarettes, money, and pornography

convict lease system a practice of some Southern penal systems of leasing prisoners to private contractors as laborers

corporal punishment the administration of bodily pain as punishment for a crime

correctional officer a uniformed jail or prison employee whose primary job is the security and movement of inmates

county department of corrections when the sheriff does not supervise the county jail, it is administered by an independent county department

court docket the calendar on which court cases are scheduled for trial

court of last resort a state court of final appeals that reviews lower court decisions and whose decisions can be appealed to the U.S. Supreme Court

court recorder (court reporter) a stenographer who transcribes every word spoken by the judge, attorneys, and witnesses during a trial

courts of limited jurisdiction state courts of original jurisdiction that are not courts of record (e.g., traffic courts, municipal courts, or county courts)

courts of record courts in which trial proceedings are transcribed

Crime Clock a method used by the FBI to report how often crimes occur

crime control model a model of the criminal justice system in which emphasis is placed on fighting crime and protecting potential victims

crime prevention through environmental design (CPTED) government-sponsored programs that are based on the theory that crime can be prevented through environmental design, especially housing design

Crime Victims' Rights Act enacted in 2004, a law that guarantees crime victims a number of rights, including the right to be involved in various stages of the criminal justice system and the rights to protection and restitution

criminal justice system the enforcement, by the police, the courts, and correctional institutions, of obedience to laws

criminology theories attempts to generalize principles that can explain factors which influence offending, victimization, and rehabilitation

cultural deviance theories theories based on the idea that the values of deviant subcultural groups within society, such as organized-crime families, juvenile gangs, and hate groups, have great power over individuals' behavior

day reporting center an intermediate sanction to provide a gradual adjustment to reentry under closely supervised conditions

deadly force the power of police to incapacitate or kill in the line of duty

defense attorney the defendant will have an attorney appointed by the court or a private attorney paid for by the defendant to represent him or her in the trial

defense of duress a legal claim by a defendant that he or she acted involuntarily under the threat of immediate and serious harm by another

defenses justifications or excuses defined by law by which a defendant may be released from prosecution or punishment for a crime

deinstitutionalization the movement of mentally ill offenders from long-term hospitalization to community-based care

delinquency petition a request to a judge to hear and judge a juvenile case in a formal hearing for the purpose of determining whether the juvenile is to be declared delinquent

delinquent a juvenile accused of committing an act that is criminal for both adults and juveniles

Department of Homeland Security (DHS) a newly created federal agency responsible for a wide range of security measures to protect against terrorist attacks

deputy chief the second in command of a police department usually selected by the chief of police

determinate sentencing a model of sentencing in which the offender is sentenced to a fixed term of incarceration

deterrence the philosophy and practices that emphasize making criminal behavior less appealing

differential association the concept that those who associate with people engaged in criminal activities are at risk of being victimized

differential association theory the concept that criminal and delinquent behaviors are learned entirely through group interactions, with peers reinforcing and rewarding these behaviors

differential opportunities the chances of individuals being victimized based on the structure of their everyday lives

diplomatic immunity the granting of immunity, or protection from any kind of criminal prosecution, to foreign diplomats

direct evidence evidence that connects the defendant with the crime

disproportionate confinement refers to the non-random distribution of persons by race in correctional institutions. If the prison population reflected the same demographic as the general population, confinement would not reflect racial bias

diversion a defendant is offered an alternative to criminal trial and a prison sentence, such as drug courts, boot camps, and treatment programs

domestic terrorism acts of terrorism committed in the United States by individuals or groups that do not have ties with or sponsorship from foreign states or organizations

double jeopardy the rule that a defendant can be charged only once and punished only once for a crime; if tried and found innocent, the defendant cannot be retried even if new evidence of his or her guilt is discovered

Drug Abuse Resistance Education (DARE) one of the most popular in-school drug education programs

drug court an approach that provides drug offenders the opportunity for intermediate sanctions, community treatment, and intensive probation supervision instead of prison time

Drug Enforcement Administration (DEA) the federal agency that enforces U.S. laws and regulations regarding controlled substances and that supports nonenforcement programs intended to reduce the availability of illicit controlled substances domestically and internationally

dual court system the political division of jurisdiction into two separate systems of courts: federal and state; in this system, federal courts have limited jurisdiction over state courts

due process rules and procedures for protecting individuals accused of crimes from arbitrary and excessive abuse of power by the government

education release a program in which inmates are released to attend college or vocational programs

electronic monitoring an approach in home confinement programs that ensures compliance through electronic means

elements of a crime the required motive and actions necessary to establish that a person has committed a crime

Eleventh Amendment a provision that prohibits a citizen from one state from suing the government of another state in federal court

entrapment the illegal arrest of a person based on criminal behavior for which the police provided both the motivation and the means, tested in *Jacobsen v. United States* (1992)

Enemy Combatant Executive Order Executive Order issued by President George W. Bush that allowed for the apprehension and detention of persons accused of terrorism without due process rights or access to the courts, including *habeas corpus*

***ex post facto* laws** laws providing that citizens cannot be punished for actions committed before laws against the actions were passed and that the government cannot increase the penalty for a specific crime after the crime was committed

excessive bail Eighth Amendment prohibits bail which is excessive but there is no uniform standard as what "excessive" is

exclusionary rule a rule that prohibits the use of evidence or testimony obtained in violation of due process rights afforded by the U.S. Constitution, established in *Weeks v. United States* (1914) and extended to all state courts in *Mapp v. Ohio* (1961)

executive pardon an act by a governor or the president that forgives a prisoner and rescinds his or her sentence

expert witness gives testimony based on his or her expert knowledge and can make inferences beyond the facts

failure to act an exception to *actus reus* in which a person fails to act when there is a legal duty to act

faith-based programs programs provided by religious-based and church-affiliated groups; their role in rehabilitation is controversial because they receive federal money and may combine religious instruction with rehabilitation

Federal Bureau of Investigation (FBI) the federal agency responsible for protecting the U.S. from terrorist attacks, foreign intelligence and espionage, cyber-based attacks, and high-technology crimes, and for combating public corruption at all levels

federal law enforcement agencies agencies that enforce only federal laws and are under the control of the executive branch of the federal government

felony serious criminal conduct punishable by incarceration for more than one year

feminist criminology the proposal that female criminal behavior is caused by the political, economic, and social inequality of men and women

field-training program a probationary period during which police academy graduates train in the community under the direct supervision of experienced officers

Fifth Amendment provides several important due process rights regarding the rights of the defendant

first responders law enforcement, firefighters, and medical personnel who are the first to respond to a crisis or incident

fleeing-felon doctrine the police practice of using deadly force against a fleeing suspect, made illegal in *Tennessee v. Garner* (1985), except when there is clear and present danger to the public

formal sanctions social norms enforced through the laws of the criminal justice system

fruit of the poisoned tree doctrine a rule of evidence that extends the exclusionary rule to secondary evidence obtained indirectly in an unconstitutional search, established in *Silverthorne Lumber Co. v. United States* (1918) and in *Wolf v. Colorado* (1949)

gag order a judge's order to participants and observers at a trial that the evidence and proceedings of the court may not be published, broadcasted, or discussed publicly

general deterrence the concept based on the logic that people who witness the pain suffered by those who commit crimes will desire to avoid that pain and will refrain from criminal activity

general intent criminal intent in which a person has common sense understanding that the results of his or her actions might cause harm

general prison population is the non-restricted population of prison inmates who have access to prison services, programs, and recreations

general trial courts state courts of original jurisdiction that hear all kinds of criminal cases

good faith exception an exception to the requirement that police must have a valid search warrant or probable cause when they act in good faith on the belief that the search was legal

good-time credit a strategy of crediting inmates with extra days served toward early release in an effort to encourage them to obey rules and participate in programs

grand jury a panel of citizens that decides whether there is probable cause to indict a defendant on the alleged charges

guilty but mentally ill a new type of verdict in which the jury finds a defendant mentally ill but sufficiently aware to be morally responsible for his or her criminal acts

habeas corpus a writ or request to the court to review whether a person is imprisoned lawfully and alleges that a person is detained or imprisoned illegally

habitual offender laws tough sentencing laws to punish repeat offenders more harshly

halfway house a transition program that allows inmates to move from prison to the community in steps

hearsay evidence information about a crime obtained secondhand from another rather than directly observed

hierarchy rule an old police method of counting only the most serious crime in a single incident involving multiple crimes

highway patrol state law enforcement agencies that focus on traffic enforcement

HIV/AIDS Acquired Immune Deficiency Syndrome (AIDS) is caused by a virus called Human Immuno-deficiency Virus (HIV). The disease is a deficiency of the body's immune system. A person can be HIV positive but not have AIDS

home confinement a court-imposed sentence requiring offenders to remain confined in their own residences

Homeland Security Advisory System (HSAS) a daily color-coded threat advisory to government agencies, police, and the public that recommends appropriate actions in response to the forecasted risk of terrorist attack

homicide the killing of one human being by another

hybrid gangs a new type of youth gang with distinctive characteristics that differentiate them from traditional gangs; they are frequently school based, less organized, less involved in criminal activity, and less involved in violence than are traditional gangs

Immigration and Customs Enforcement (ICE) federal agency created after the 9/11 attacks and charged with the responsibilities of border security and enforcement of immigration laws and processes. ICE replaced the Immigration and Naturalization Services (INS).

In re Gault a case in which the Supreme Court provided due process rights to juveniles, including notice of charges, counsel, right to examine witnesses, and right to remain silent

In re Winship a case in which the Supreme Court ruled that the reasonable doubt standard, the same used in criminal trials, should be required in all delinquency adjudications

incapacitation deterrence based on the premise that the only way to prevent criminals from reoffending is to remove them from society

incarceration the bodily confinement of a person in a jail or prison

inchoate offense an action that goes beyond mere thought but does not result in a completed crime

independent model the system in which decision making about parole is under the authority of an autonomous parole board

indeterminate sentence a sentence in which the defendant is sentenced to a prison term with a minimum and a maximum number of years to serve

indeterminate sentencing a model of sentencing in which judges have nearly complete discretion in sentencing an offender

indictment the legal process of formally charging a person with the specific crime(s) for which he or she will be tried in court and the opportunity for the defendant to enter a plea

indigent defense the right to have an attorney provided free of charge by the state if a defendant cannot afford one, established in *Gideon v. Wainwright* (1963)

informal sanctions social norms that are enforced through the social forces of the family, school, government, and religion

initial appearance the Court determines the charges against the defendant are legitimate, advises the defendant of his or her rights, sets bail, and assesses the need for legal representation for the defendant

initial placement the first institution and security level of the convicted defendant

insanity a legal claim by a defendant that he or she was suffering from a disease or mental defect and that the defect caused the defendant not to understand the difference between right and wrong

inside cell block prison construction in which individual cells are stacked back to back in tiers in the center of a secure building

intake the process whereby a juvenile enters the juvenile justice system

intensive probation supervision (IPS) probation supervised by probation and parole officers with smaller caseloads, placing a greater emphasis on compliance with the conditions of supervision

intermediate sanctions punishments that restrict offenders' freedom without imprisoning them and that consist of community-based prevention and treatment programs to promote the successful transition of offenders from prison to the community

international terrorism terrorism perpetrated by state-sponsored groups, international terrorist organizations, and loosely affiliated international extremist groups

Irish system an early form of parole invented by Sir Walter Crofton based on the mark system in which prisoners were released conditionally on good behavior and were supervised in the community

jails short-term, multipurpose holding facilities that serve as the gateway into the criminal justice system

Joint Local–Federal Counterterrorism Task Force (JTTF) a working group of FBI and state and or local law enforcement officers that focuses on preventing terrorism by their joint cooperation and intelligence sharing

judicial review the power of the U.S. Supreme Court to review legislation for the purpose of deciding the constitutionality of the law

jurisdiction the geographical limits of responsibility and legitimate duties of law enforcement officers

jurisprudence a philosophy or body of written law used to settle disputes

jury trial the jury determines the guilt of the defendant

juvenile adjudication hearing the formal hearing conducted by a juvenile judge to conduct an inquiry of the facts concerning a case and to decide the disposition of the case and any rehabilitation, supervision, or punishment for the juvenile

juvenile boot camp a military-style group-oriented rehabilitation program designed to alter the character and values of the juvenile offender

juvenile court a court that handles juvenile welfare cases and cases involving status offenders and delinquents; some juvenile courts may handle additional matters related to the family

juvenile drug court an alternative to the traditional adjudication process for juveniles with substance abuse problems that focuses on rehabilitation and eliminating drug abuse

juvenile intake officer a person who is responsible for both processing a juvenile into the juvenile justice system and for aftercare if the juvenile is adjudicated, and has duties similar to a police officer and a probation and parole officer

Juvenile Justice and Delinquency Prevention Act of 1974 a law that sets federal standards for the treatment and processing of juveniles in the criminal justice system

juvenile superpredator OJJDP term used to describe juveniles who commit a violent felony charge

Kent v. United States a 1961 Supreme Court case that marked the departure of the Supreme Court from its acceptance of the denial of due process rights to juveniles

knowing possession a person actually being in possession of an item and knowing that it is contraband

landmark cases U.S. Supreme Court cases that mark significant changes in the interpretation of the Constitution

larceny the wrongful taking of another's property with the intent to permanently deprive its owner of its possession

Law Enforcement Educational Program (LEEP) is created, the goal of which is to promote education among criminal justice personnel

lay witness a citizen who testifies only to what he or she heard, saw, felt, smelled, or otherwise directly experienced

lead federal agency (LFA) the agency that is designated as being primarily in charge of an incident and has the power to direct the actions of other agencies and to call for the use of their resources, even though the lead agency may not have direct authority over these other agencies

legal standards of evidence standards requiring that evidence and the testimony of witnesses must be competent, material, and relevant

legislative immunity the protection of senators and representatives of Congress from arrest only while the legislature is in session, except for felonies and treason

Lombroso-based correctional philosophies divided persons into two distinct types: criminal and non-criminal. Non-criminals were biologically determined and therefore not amenable to rehabilitation or reform

mala in se acts that are crimes because they are inherently evil or harmful to society

mala prohibita acts that are prohibited because they are defined as crimes by law

mandatory release the release of prisoners required by law after they have served the entire length of their maximum sentence

mandatory sentencing the strict application of full sentences in the determinate sentencing model

manslaughter the killing of another without the specific intent to kill

mark system an early form of parole invented by Alexander Maconochie in which prisoners demonstrated their rehabilitation by earning points for good behavior

material witness law a law that allows for the detention of a person who has not committed a crime but is suspected of having information about a crime and might flee or refuse to cooperate with law enforcement officials

McKeiver v. Pennsylvania a case in which the Supreme Court denied juveniles the right to a trial by jury

mens rea an element of crime in which a person must have criminal intent, or a "guilty mind," for his or her actions to be criminal

mere possession a person actually being in possession of an item but not knowing that it is contraband

metro police local police agency that serves several geographic locations, such as a large city or county

military police police who are members of the military and provide law enforcement services on military bases, on certain federal lands, and in cases involving military personnel

Miranda rights rights that provide protection from self-incrimination and confer the right to an attorney, of which citizens must be informed before police arrest and interrogation, established in *Miranda v. Arizona* (1966)

misdemeanor less serious criminal conduct punishable by incarceration for less than a year

mistake or ignorance of fact an affirmative legal defense in which the defendant made a mistake that does not meet the requirement for *mens rea*

Model Penal Code guidelines for U.S. criminal codes published in 1962 by the American Law Institute that classify and define crimes into categories

municipal jail city-administered jails for the incarceration of offenders who are convicted of violating city ordinance in a municipal court

murder all intentional killings and deaths that occur in the course of aggravated felonies

National Commission on Criminal Justice Standards and Goals formulates specific standards and goals for police, courts, corrections, and crime prevention

National Crime Victimization Survey (NCVS) a survey that gathers detailed information about crimes from victims using a representative sample of U.S. households

National Incident-Based Reporting System (NIBRS) a database that includes specific data about reported crimes, including the place of occurrence, weapon used, type and value of property damaged or stolen, and personal characteristics of any relationship between the offender and the victim

National Organization for Victim Assistance (NOVA) an organization that helped to pass the 1984 Victims of Crime Act and the 1982 Victim and Witness Protection Act, both of which provide counseling, information, and assistance to crime victims

National Security Decision Directives (NSDDs) directives issued by the president that are binding on federal agencies under executive command; NSDDs may proscribe actions to be taken by the agency or may direct the agency to take certain actions

Native American jails are short-term incarceration facilities on Native American land which are under the sovereign control of the Native American tribe

necessity an affirmative legal defense claiming that the defendant committed an act out of need, and not *mens rea*

neoclassical school theories a school of thought that is similar to classical school theories, except for the beliefs that there are mitigating circumstances for criminal acts, such as the age or mental capacity of the offender, and that punishment should fit the crime

neutralization theory the concept that most people commit some type of criminal act in their lives and that many people are prevented from doing so again because of a sense of guilt, while criminals neutralize feelings of guilt through rationalization, denial, or an appeal to higher loyalties

New York House of Refuge an early juvenile reformatory established by New York state in 1824 that was to become the model for most juvenile reformatories

no-fly list a secret list maintained by the Department of Homeland Security that lists the names of persons who are prohibited from flying on a commercial airplane under any circumstances; it also contains the names of persons who should receive additional screening prior to being allowed to board an aircraft

not guilty by reason of insanity a verdict by which the jury finds that a defendant committed the crime but was insane

officer of the court a law enforcement officer who serves the court by serving papers, providing courtroom security, and transporting incarcerated defendants

Omnibus Crime Control and Safe Streets Act of 1968 creates the Law Enforcement Assistance Administration (LEAA) to act as a conduit for the transfer of federal funds to state and local law enforcement agencies

order maintenance noncrime-fighting services performed by police, such as mediation, providing for the welfare of vulnerable persons, and crime control

original jurisdiction the concept that juvenile court is the only court that has authority over juveniles, so they cannot be tried, for any offense, by a criminal court unless the juvenile court grants its permission for the accused juvenile to be waived to criminal court

parens patriae the legal assumption that the state has primary responsibility for the safety and custody of children

parole early release from prison before the maximum sentence is served, based on evidence of rehabilitation and the good behavior of the inmate

parole board individuals appointed to a body that meets in prisons to make decisions about granting parole release to inmates

parole d'honneur the origin of parole, based on the concept of releasing prisoners on their honor after serving a portion of their sentences but before the maximum terms are reached

parole hearing a meeting with an inmate, his or her attorney, and others in which the parole board decides whether to grant, deny, or revoke parole

parole officer a state or federal professional employee who reports to the courts and supervises defendants released from prison on parole

pat-down doctrine the right of the police to search a person for a concealed weapon without a search warrant or reasonable suspicion to ensure the personal safety of the police officer established in *Terry v. Ohio* (1968)

penitentiary a correctional institution based on the concept that inmates could change their criminality through reflection and penitence

per curiam opinion a case that is disposed of by the U.S. Supreme Court without a full written opinion

picket fence model model of the criminal justice system, with the local, state, and federal criminal justice systems depicted as three horizontal levels connected vertically by the roles, functions, and activities of the agencies that comprise them

plain-view search the right of the police to gather without a warrant evidence that is clearly visible

plaintiff the party who files a civil lawsuit against the party who is alleged to have done harm (the defendant)

plea bargaining the negotiation between defendant and prosecutor for a plea of guilty for which in return the defendant will receive some benefit such as reduction of charges or dismissal of some charges

police academy a facility or program for the education and training of police officers

police lineup an opportunity for victims to identify a criminal from among a number of suspects

positive school modern theories of crime, primarily based on sociology and psychology, that people commit crimes because of uncontrollable internal or external factors, which can be observed and measured

possession an element of the crime in which the *actus reus* is satisfied by demonstrating exclusive control and knowledge of possession of prohibited items or illegal property

predatory crime crime involving direct physical contact between the offender and his or her target, which may be a person or an object, that the offender intends to damage or take

preliminary hearing a hearing before a magistrate judge in which the prosecution presents evidence to convince the judge that there is probable cause to bring the defendant to trial

presentence investigator a person who works for the court and has the responsibility of investigating the background of the convicted offender and the circumstances surrounding the offense

President's Commission on Law Enforcement and Administration of Justice a series of Presidential Commissions charged with in-depth investigation of the criminal justice system in response to public perception that the system was failing

presumption of innocence most important principle of the due process model, requiring that all accused persons are treated as innocent until proven guilty in a court of law

presumptive sentencing a structured sentencing model that attempts to balance sentencing guidelines with mandatory sentencing and at the same time provide discretion to the judge

pretrial motions are requests by the prosecutor or defense made in advance of the trial

principle of legality the principle that citizens cannot be punished for conduct for which no law against it exists

prison code is the informal rules and expected behavior established by inmates. Often the prison code is contrary to the official rules and policies of the prison. Violation of the prison code can be punished by use of violence or even death

prison consultants private persons, who provide convicted defendants advice and counsel on how best to present themselves during classification and how to behave in prison

prison economy refers to the exchange of goods, services, and contraband by prisoners in the place of money

prison farm system in the Southern penal systems, the use of inmate labor to maintain large, profit-making prison farms or plantations

Prison Rape Elimination Act of 2003 required the Bureau of Justice statistics to survey jails and prisons, to determine the prevalance of sexual violence within correctional facilities

prisoner classification the reception and diagnosis of an inmate to decide the appropriate security level in which to place the prisoner and the services of placement

prisonization socialization into a distinct prison subculture with its own values, morals, norms, and sanctions

privatization a trend toward jails and prisons being run by for-profit, private companies

privilege a type of defense in which the defendant claims immunity from punishment for an admitted violation of the law because it was related to his or her official duties

probable cause the likelihood that there is a direct link between a suspect and a crime

probation a disposition in which a convicted defendant is offered an opportunity to avoid serving any time in prison by agreeing to fulfill conditions set forth by the court

probation officer a state or federal professional employee who reports to the courts and supervises defendants released on probation

problem-oriented policing a proactive type of community policing that focuses on solving the underlying problems of delinquency and crime

procedural law the body of laws governing how things should be done at each stage of the criminal justice process

prosecutorial discretion the power of a prosecutor to decide whether or not to charge a defendant and what the charge(s) will be, as well as to gather the evidence necessary to prosecute the defendant in a court of law

psychoanalytic theory the concept that behavior is not a matter of free will but is controlled by subconscious desires, which includes the idea that criminal behavior is a result of unresolved internal conflict and guilt

public safety exception the right of the police to search without probable cause when not to do so could pose a threat of harm to the public

racial profiling allegations that police search and seizures, traffic stops, field interrogations, and arrests are made on nonbehavioral factors related to race and/or ethnicity rather than suspicious behavior or probable cause

rape (sexual assault) nonconsensual sexual acts

reaction formation a term that Cohen used to describe the rejection of middle-class values by lower-class youths, who believe that they cannot attain these values and therefore create unique countercultures

real evidence physical evidence, such as a gun, a fingerprint, a photograph, or DNA matching

Real ID Act proposed legislation that would require all state driver's licenses to conform to uniform standards set by the Department of Homeland Security

rehabilitation deterrence based on the premise that criminals can be "cured" of their problems and criminality and can be returned to society

release on recognizance (ROR) provides for the pretrial release of the accused, based merely on the defendant's unsecured promise to appear at trial

remanded after the U.S. Supreme Court's reversal of a decision of a lower court, the return of the case to the court of original jurisdiction with instructions to correct the judicial error

rendition the illegal transportation of a person to a foreign country for the purpose of having officials of that country interrogate the person using torture or practices not permitted in the United States

Residential Substance Abuse Treatment (RSAT) a federal assistance program that helps states provide for treatment instead of prison for substance abusers

restorative justice a model of deterrence that uses restitution programs, community work programs, victim-offender mediation, and other strategies to not only rehabilitate the offender but also to address the damage done to the community and the victim

retribution deterrence based on the premise that criminals should be punished because they deserve it

revolving door syndrome the repeated arrest and incarceration of an offender

right to privacy the principle that laws that violate personal privacy cannot be upheld

robbery the taking away of property from a person by force or the immediate threat of force

Roper, Superintendent, Potosi Correctional Center v. Simmons a case in which the Supreme Court held that the Eighth and Fourteenth Amendments forbid imposition of the death penalty on offenders who were under the age of 18 when their crimes were committed

routine activities theory an analysis of changes in levels of crime over time that recognizes people's everyday actions as components of victimization

rule of law the principle that standards of behavior and privilege are established by laws and not by monarchs or religious leaders

rules of evidence administrative court rules governing the admissibility of evidence in a trial

Schall v. Martin a case in which the Supreme Court upheld the right of juvenile courts to deny bail to adjudicated juveniles

search incident to lawful arrest the right of police to search a person who has been arrested without a warrant

search warrant legal permission, signed by a judge, for police to conduct a search

Section 1983 lawsuits are civil lawsuits filed in federal court alleging that the government has violated a constitutional right of the citizen

security-risk groups groups that raise special threats, such as prison gangs

self-defense an affirmative legal defense in which a defendant claims that he or she acted to protect himself or herself or another person against a deadly attack or invasion of his or her home

self-incrimination statements made by a person that might lead to criminal prosecution

sentence the punishment determined by a judge for a defendant convicted of a crime

sentence bargaining the defendant negotiates with the prosecutor for a reduction in length of sentence, reduction from capital murder to imprisonment, probation rather than incarceration, or institution where the sentence is to be served in return for a guilty plea

sentencing guidelines a sentencing model in which crimes are classified according to their seriousness and a range of time to be served is mandatory for crimes within each category

sex offender registry an open-access online database identifying known sex offenders on parole, maintained to protect communities and potential victims

shock incarceration programs (boot camps) that adapt military-style physical fitness and discipline training to the correctional environment

shock probation a sentence for a first-time, nonviolent offender who was not expecting a sentence, intended to impress on the offender the possible consequences of his or her behavior by exposure to a brief period of imprisonment before probation

signature bond the release of a defendant based on his or her signature on a promise to appear in court, usually for minor offenses such as traffic violations

silent system the correctional practice of prohibiting inmates from talking to other inmates

Sixth Amendment provides the defendant constitutionally protected rights related to the trial, witnesses, and right to counsel

smart passports new passports that contain machine-readable data about travelers

social control theory the focus on the social and cultural values that exert control over and reinforce the behavior of individuals

social determinism the idea that social forces and social groups are the cause of criminal behavior

social disorganization theory the idea proposed and researched by Park and his colleagues that supports the notion that criminal behavior is dependent on disruptive social forces, not on individual characteristics

social norms the expected normative behavior in a society

solicitation the requesting or commanding of another to commit a crime

solitary confinement the practice of confining an inmate such that there is no contact with other people

special police police with limited jurisdiction. Special police have very narrowly defined duties and sometimes extremely limited geographical jurisdiction

specific deterrence a concept based on the premise that a person is best deterred from committing future crimes by the specific nature of the punishment

specific intent criminal intent in which a person knowingly takes action to commit a crime

split sentencing after a brief period of imprisonment, the judge brings the offender back to court and offers the option of probation

standard conditions of release federal and state rules with which parolees must comply to meet their conditions of release

stare decisis the U.S. system of developing and applying case law in the basis of precedents established in previous cases

state prisons correctional facilities for prisoners convicted of state crimes

status offender a child who has committed an act or failed to fulfill a responsibility for which, if he or she were an adult, the court would not have any authority over him or her

statute of limitations legal limits regarding the length of time between the discovery of a crime and the arrest of the defendant

statutory exclusion provisions that allow for the transfer of juveniles to criminal court without review and approval of a juvenile court for certain crimes

strain theory the assumption that individuals resort to crime out of frustration from being unable to attain economic comfort or success

strict liability crimes actions that are considered criminal without the need for criminal intent

structured sentencing a sentencing model (including determinate sentencing, sentencing guidelines, and presumptive sentencing) that defines punishments rather than allowing indeterminate sentencing

Student and Exchange Visitor Information System (SEVIS) a Web-based information database containing information on international students studying in the United States

supermax prison is the highest security level of prison operated by the U.S. Bureau of Prisons. Supermax prisons are considered "escape-proof" regardless of the resources of the inmate

suspended sentence another term for *probation*, based on the fact that convicted offenders must serve their full sentence if they violate the terms of release

system of social control a social system designed to maintain order and regulate interactions

target hardening crime-prevention measures such as Neighborhood Watch groups, anti-theft devices, and increased street lighting

Taylor v. Louisiana ruled the exclusion of women from jury duty created an imbalance in the jury pool

team policing a decentralizing development during the 1960s and 1970s in which small units of police personnel took responsibility for a particular geographical area

technical violation grounds for imprisonment of a probationer or parolee based on his or her violation of a condition of release

Tenth Amendment a provision that powers not specifically delegated to the federal government are reserved for the states

terrorism premeditated, politically motivated violence perpetrated against noncombatant targets by subnational groups or clandestine agents, usually intended to influence an audience

testimonial evidence the testimony of a witness

theory of personal victimization the theory that a person's lifestyle contributes to the predictability of high-risk situations

three-strikes law the application of mandatory sentencing to give repeat offenders longer prison terms

ticket of leave in the mark system, the unconditional release from prison purchased with marks earned for good behavior

tort a private wrong that causes physical harm to another

total institutions institutions that meet all of the inmate's basic needs, discourage individuality, punish dissent, and segregate those who do not follow the rules

transferred intent criminal intent in which a person intends to harm a person but instead harms a different person

transportation the eighteenth-century practice by Great Britain of sending offenders to the American colonies and, later, to Australia

Transportation Security Administration (TSA) a newly created agency under the Department of Homeland Security that is responsible for airport security and passenger screening

Treatment Accountability for Safer Communities (TASC) a federal assistance program that helps states break the addiction-crime cycle

Tribal Healing to Wellness Courts Native American drug treatment programs that adapt traditional cultural beliefs and practices

tribal police police that provide law enforcement services on Native American reservations, where local and state police have no jurisdiction, and federal police have only limited jurisdiction

truth in sentencing in the application of presumptive sentencing in states that cannot eliminate parole, the legal requirement that courts disclose the actual prison time that the offender is likely to serve

tuberculosis (TB) is a contagious infectious disease caused by a bacterial infection that primarily affects the lungs

urban fortresses a term to describe emotional and physical reaction of citizens to extensive security measures instituted in metropolitan areas in response to the threat of terrorist attacks

U.S. courts of appeals the third tier of the federal court system where decisions of lower courts can be appealed for review for significant judicial error which may have affected the verdict

U.S. district courts trial courts of the federal system

U.S. magistrate courts federal lower courts with powers limited to trying lesser misdemeanors, setting bail, and assisting district courts in various legal matters

U.S. Marshals Service the federal agency that provides security for federal courts, is responsible for the movement, custody, and capture of federal prisoners, and provides protection of witnesses in federal cases

U.S. Postal Inspection Service the federal agency responsible for the security of U.S. mail and mail carriers and for investigation of mail fraud

U.S. Secret Service the federal agency that protects the president, the vice president, members of their families, major candidates for president and vice president, and visiting heads of foreign governments

U.S. Supreme Court the highest court in the U.S. judiciary system, whose rulings on the constitutionality of laws, due process rights, and rules of evidence are binding on all federal and state courts

Uniform Crime Report (UCR) a database of information about reported crimes collected by the FBI over time

United States Government Interagency Domestic Terrorism Concept of Operations Plan (CONPLAN) federal guidelines that designate which federal agency is the lead agency responsible for command and control in the event of a terrorist incident involving multiple federal agencies

United States Visitor and Immigrant Status Indicator Technology (US-VISIT) a new system of registering the entry of foreign visitors to the United States and tracking when and where they exit the United States

unsecured bond releases the defendant based on his or her signing a promissory note agreeing to pay the court an amount similar to a cash bail bond if he or she fails to fulfill the promise to appear at trial

USA Patriot Act legislation that gives federal law enforcement agencies expanded powers to detect, detain, and prosecute suspected terrorists

victim contribution the idea that victims' actions or lack of action creates the likelihood of their being victimized

victim impact statements testimony by victims at a convicted offender's sentencing hearing

victimology the study of victims and the patterns of how they are victimized

victim-precipitation theories theories based on the concept that victims in some way contribute to or provoke crimes committed against them

victim proneness the idea that certain victims are likely to be targeted as victims because of some individual or group quality that they have

victim provocation the idea that a victim is the main cause of his or her victimization

victims' rights movement a movement that emerged from public concern about civil rights, women's rights, gay rights, students' rights, inmates' rights, and from government initiatives for increased victim awareness and financial compensation

void for overbreadth the principle that laws go too far in that they criminalize legally protected behavior in an attempt to make some other behavior illegal cannot be upheld

void for vagueness the principle that laws that do not use clear and specific language to define prohibited behaviors cannot be upheld

voir dire the process through which a jury is selected from the members of the jury pool who have been determined to be eligible for service

waiver the process of moving a juvenile from the authority of juvenile court to the adult criminal justice system

War on Crime was declared by President Lyndon Johnson to counter crime and social disorder

War on Terrorism is declared by President George W. Bush in response to the attacks of September 11, 2001. The new cabinet position of Secretary of the Office of Homeland Security is created

Warren Court the U.S. Supreme Court years (1953–1969) during which Chief Justice Earl Warren issued many landmark decisions greatly expanding the constitutional right of inmates and defendants

wiretapping a form of search and seizure of evidence involving communication by telephone

witness immunity a situation in which a defendant admits to committing a crime but is granted immunity from prosecution in exchange for cooperation with a government investigation

work release a program that allows facilities to release inmates for paid work in the community

writ of certiorari an order to a lower court to forward the record of a case to the U.S. Supreme Court for review

XYY chromosome theory the idea that violent behavior in males can in part be attributed to the presence of an extra Y chromosome in male offenders

zero-tolerance strategy strict enforcement of the laws, even for minor violations

zone theory a concept developed by Park and his Chicago School colleague Burgess that juvenile delinquency is caused by zones of social environments based on status differences, including poverty, illiteracy, lack of schooling, unemployment, and illegitimacy—but not ethnicity

PHOTO CREDITS

Chapter 1 CRIMINAL JUSTICE

p. 2 Dennis Brack/Newscom

p. 4 top left: © Bettmann/CORBIS

p. 4 middle right: John Filo/Getty Images

p. 4 middle left: Tyrone Dukes/The New York Times/Redux Pictures

p. 4 bottom left: © Sean Adair/Reuters/CORBIS

p. 6 Corbis

p. 8 Ethan boisvert/Shutterstock.com

p. 9 trekandshoot/Shutterstock.com

p. 10 Lisa F. Young/Shutterstock.com

p. 13 James Fagin

Chapter 2 CRIME: WHY AND HOW MUCH

p. 16 z03/ZUMA Press/Newscom

p. 18 Matteson, Tompkins Harrison/The Bridgeman Art Library International

p. 21 Tristan Scholze/Shutterstock.com

p. 23 James Fagin

p. 25 pistolseven/Shutterstock.com

p. 27 James Fagin

p. 29 Edw/Shutterstock.com

p. 31 Photosani/Shutterstock.com

p. 32 James Fagin

p. 36 michaeljung/Shutterstock.com

Chapter 3 CRIMINAL LAW CONTROL VERSUS LIBERTY

p. 40 stocklight/Shutterstock.com

p. 43 Andre Blais/Shutterstock.com

p. 46 James Fagin

p. 47 James Fagin

p. 51 Kim Seidl/Shutterstock.com

Chapter 4 ROLES AND FUNCTIONS OF THE POLICE

p. 54 COUGHLIN/SIPA/Newscom

p. 56 left: The Image Works

p. 56 right: Library of Congress, National Photo Company Collection, LC-DIG-npcc-00622

p. 57 U.S. Immigration and Customs

p. 58 left: UPI/Bettmann/Corbis

p. 58 right: AP Images

p. 59 left: Drug Enforcement Agency

p. 59 right: FBI

p. 60 left: Charlotte Mecklenburg, NC Police Department

p. 60 right: Bureau of Alcohol, Tobacco, Firearms and Explosives

p. 61 SuperStock

p. 62 Maricopa County Sheriff's Office

p. 63 © Mikael Karlsson/Alamy

p. 66 FBI

p. 69 Boston Police Department

Chapter 5 POLICE OFFICERS AND THE LAW

p. 74 emin kuliyev/Shutterstock.com

p. 78 Malyshev Maksim/Shutterstock.com

p. 83 Monkey Business Images/Shutterstock.com

p. 84 Monika Wisniewska/Shutterstock.com

p. 88 Nick Stubbs/Shutterstock.com

p. 89 Natalia Bratslavsky/Shutterstock.com

Chapter 6 THE COURT SYSTEM

p. 92 TFoxFoto/Shutterstock.com

p. 99 zimmytws/Shutterstock.com

p. 100 Steve Mitchell/AP Images

p. 103 John Barrett/Newscom

Chapter 7 COURTROOM PARTICIPANTS AND THE TRIAL

p. 106 POOL/Reuters

p. 113 Derek Shook / Splash News/Newscom

p. 115 trekandshoot/Shutterstock.com

p. 117 REUTERS/Lucas Jackson

p. 121 Sashkin/Shutterstock.com

p. 122 Orange Line Media/Shutterstock

p. 123 Darren Mower/iStockphoto.com

Chapter 8 SENTENCING

p. 128 Jon-Are Berg-Jacobsen/AP Images

p. 131 Linda Bucklin/Shutterstock.com

p. 132 akg-images/Newscom

p. 134 AP Images

p. 136 ARIF ALI/AFP/Getty Images/Newscom

p. 138 photopixel/Shutterstock.com

p. 140 http://webb.senate.gov/photos/images/official1.jpg

p. 143 Tammy Allen/Shutterstock.com

p. 144 Robert J. Daveant/Shutterstock.com

p. 148 James Fagin

p. 149 ZUMA Press/Newscom

Chapter 9 JAILS AND PRISONS

p. 154 James Fagin

p. 157 James Fagin

p. 158 James Fagin

p. 161 James Fagin

p. 170 James Fagin

p. 171 top: REUTERS/Lucy Nicholson

p. 171 bottom: Dorling Kindersley Media Library

p. 174 Galyna Andrushko/Shutterstock.com

p. 175 Dan Bannister/Shutterstock.com

p. 179 AURELIA VENTURA/LA OPINION/Newscom

p. 180 U. S. Department of Defense

Chapter 10 PROBATION AND PAROLE

p. 184 HO/AFP/Getty Images/Newscom

p. 188 Lou Oates/Shutterstock.com

p. 196 Picsfive/Shutterstock.com

p. 197 sommthink/Shutterstock.com

p. 199 © Janine Wiedel Photolibrary/Alamy

Chapter 11 CORRECTIONS IN THE COMMUNITY

p. 204 FBI

p. 211 Roxanne McMillen/Shutterstock.com

p. 213 pixelman/Shutterstock.com

p. 214 Steven Frame/Shutterstock.com

p. 218 Frontpage/Shutterstock.com

p. 223 Jon Le-bon/Shutterstock.com

Chapter 12 THE JUVENILE JUSTICE SYSTEM

p. 226 HO/AFP/Getty Images/Newscom

p. 229 Corbis

p. 233 Chet Gordon/The Image Works

p. 235 Brenda Carson/Dreamstime

p. 236 Olga Yarovenko/Shutterstock.com

p. 239 Lisa F. Young/Shutterstock.com

p. 241 Yellowj/Shutterstock.com

p. 243 ene/Shutterstock.com

p. 244 Thinkstock Images

p. 245 Monkey Business Images/Shutterstock.com

p. 248 Ryan Rodrick Beiler/Shutterstock.com

p. 251 REUTERS/Steve Marcus

p. 253 ejwhite/Shutterstock.com

p. 254 Yuri Arcurs/Shutterstock.com

p. 255 © Spencer Grant/Alamy

Chapter 13 HOMELAND SECURITY

p. 258 AUSAF NEWS PAPER/AFP/Newscom

p. 260 Carolina K. Smith, M.D./Shutterstock.com

p. 261 Paul Fleet/Shutterstock.com

p. 264 United States Drug Enforcement Administration

p. 267 Patricia Marks/Shutterstock.com

p. 269 zimmytws/Shutterstock.com

p. 270 FBI

p. 271 U.S. Department of State

p. 274 Department of Homeland Security

p. 278 US Customs and Border Protection

p. 280 US Customs and Border Protection

p. 281 Balefire/Shutterstock.com

p. 282 Erika Cross/Shutterstock.com

NAME INDEX

INDEX

R

S

T